VOLUME 115 • NUMBER 1 • FEBRUARY 2010

The American Historical Review

AMERICAN HISTORICAL ASSOCIATION

Contents VOLUME 115 • NUMBER 1 • FEBRUARY 2010

VOLUME 115 • NUMBER 1 • FEBRUARY 2010

The American Historical Review

AMERICAN HISTORICAL ASSOCIATION
Founded in 1884. Chartered by Congress in 1889.

Cover Illustration: It was not until the early 1960s that the mass killings we now refer to as "the Holocaust" became a subject for historical consideration. Yet even before there was a name for what was happening in Europe, visual representations of the atrocities were being shared with the rest of the world. In this issue's *AHR* Forum, four historians look at how the Holocaust was represented in photographs, monuments, and film. *None Shall Escape* (1944) was part of the first wave of American "Holocaust" cinema, idealizing the role of the United States in hunting and trying Nazi war criminals, and helping to raise public awareness of the human toll that Hitler's policies had taken. Paramount Pictures/Photofest.

The American Historical Review is the official publication of the American Historical Association and appears in February, April, June, October, and December of each year. The journal is published by The University of Chicago Press, 1427 E. 60th Street, Chicago, IL 60637 on behalf of the American Historical Association, 400 A St. SE, Washington, DC 20003 (phone 202-544-2422). Our editorial offices are located at Indiana University, where our mailing address is 914 E. Atwater Ave., Bloomington, IN 47401. Phone: 812-855-7609; fax: 812-855-5827; e-mail: ahr@indiana.edu. Our web address is www.americanhistoricalreview.org. The *AHR* is sent to members of the American Historical Association and to institutions holding subscriptions.

Membership dues: Contributing Member, $225 annually; for incomes over $70,000, $150; over $55,000, $124; over $45,000, $111; over $40,000, $94; over $25,000, $82; under $25,000, $45; for early career members (first three years after student member), $50; for students, $39; for teachers of K–12 (AHA/SHE) without the *AHR*, $68; for K–12 with the *AHR*, $98; for joint members or spouse/partners, $45; for emeritus and retired historians, $55; for associate members (nonhistorians), $55. A life membership is $2,600. Non-U.S. members add $20 for postage. The proportion of dues allocated to the *AHR* is $17. Members also receive *Perspectives* and the program of the annual meeting.

Further information on membership is available at http://www.historians.org/, or at the back of the journal on page 1(a), immediately preceding the advertisements.

Institutional subscription rates: The basic print + electronic subscription rate for institutions is $328. Additional taxes and/or postage for non-U.S. subscriptions may apply. For additional tiered subscription rates, including those for print only and electronic only, please visit http://www.journals.uchicago.edu/subs.html. Single copies of the *AHR* are available through The University of Chicago Press for issues in volume 111 (2006) through volume 115 (2010) at $45 for individuals and $79 for institutions. Issues published prior to 2006 can be purchased from Periodical Services Company, 11 Main St., Germantown, NY 12526. Institutional subscribers now have full access to the online version of the *American Historical Review*. Access is made available through the University of Chicago Press and is enabled through the use of institutional IP numbers. To activate access for your institution, please visit http://www.journals.uchicago.edu/AHR/order.html.

Manuscript submissions: For basic information on the submission and publication of manuscripts, see p. 1(a) at the back of the journal, immediately preceding the advertisements. Full guidelines and policies can be found at http://www.americanhistoricalreview.org or will be sent upon request. **Unsolicited book reviews are not accepted.**

For permission to reprint: Contact Permissions Coordinator, Journals Division, University of Chicago Press, 1427 E. 60th Street, Chicago, IL 60637 USA. Fax: 773-834-3489; e-mail: journalpermissions@press.uchicago.edu.

For inquires about advertising: Contact Cheryl Jones, Journals Advertising, University of Chicago Press, 1427 E. 60th Street, Chicago, IL 60637. Phone: 773-702-7361; fax: 773-702-0172; e-mail: j-advertising@press.uchicago.edu.

Periodicals postage paid at Chicago, IL, and at additional mailing offices.

Postmaster: Please send notification (Form 3579) regarding undelivered journals to: American Historical Association, 400 A St. SE, Washington, DC 20003. Publication identification number: *American Historical Review* (ISSN 0002–8762).

 The paper used in this publication meets the minimum requirements of the American National Standard for Information Sciences—Permanence of Paper for Printed Library Materials, ANSI Z39.48–1984.

Featured Reviews

Reviews of Books

Contents, continued

Contents, continued

CARIBBEAN AND LATIN AMERICA

viii   *Contents, continued*

MIDDLE EAST AND NORTHERN AFRICA

SUB-SAHARAN AFRICA

Collected Essays

Topical Table of Contents

In This Issue

The February issue contains the AHA Presidential Address, an *AHR* Forum on "Representing the Holocaust," and an *AHR* Exchange on "The Question of 'Black Rice.'" There are also five featured reviews, followed by our usual extensive book review section. One distinctive feature of this issue is its visual richness: it includes more than sixty illustrations.

Presidential Address

The Presidential Address, "An American Album, 1857," by **Laurel Thatcher Ulrich**, is a meditation on the history and meaning of one particular quilt made in the Territory of Utah by a group of female members of the Church of Latter-day Saints. The quilt survives today, and Ulrich is able to use it as an artifact of history in order to examine, among other things, conflicts over marriage in the United States in the nineteenth century. While providing a micro-history of the provenance of the quilt, including information on some of the sixty-seven women who stitched their names into its fabric, her story takes us deep into the history of frontier life; the struggles between Mormons and the federal government; marriage, sexuality, gender roles, and religion; Indian-Mormon relationships; immigration; and, ultimately, the "aspirations and contradictions embedded in the history of the American republic."

AHR Forum

The *AHR* Forum, "Representing the Holocaust," comprises three articles plus a comment. The articles look at three different forms of representation in the years after, and in the first case during, the period of the destruction of European Jewry. A series of photographs taken by Russian Jewish photojournalists in 1942 is the focus of "Picturing Grief: Soviet Holocaust Photography at the Intersection of History and Memory," by **David Shneer**, who uses these illustrations to analyze the Soviet Union's contradictory and often fraught treatment of the mass murder of the Jews. **Harold Marcuse** turns to the aesthetic and political meanings of monuments in "Holocaust Memorials: The Emergence of a Genre." Analyzing a whole series of these physical commemorations of the Judeocide, dating from the immediate aftermath of the liberation of the death and concentration camps to more recent decades, he argues that the evolution of the aesthetics of these displays reveals important changes in our appreciation of the Holocaust and its various meanings. The third essay, "The First Wave of American 'Holocaust' Films, 1945–1959," by **Lawrence Baron**, focuses on early movies that, sometimes obliquely, sometimes more directly, evoked the Holocaust while largely leaving the Jewish identity of its victims unacknowledged. **Sarah Farmer**'s comment on the three essays, "Going Visual: Holocaust Representation and Historical Method," not only offers some critical suggestions about their findings and approaches but also reflects on how we should asses and use visual evidence in our historical accounts.

AHR Exchange

History thrives through controversy, and in the *AHR* Exchange, we open our pages to three critiques of an article that we published in the 2007 issue. "Agency and Diaspora in Atlantic History: Reassessing the African Contribution to Rice Cultivation in the Americas," by **David Eltis**, **Philip Morgan**, and **David Richardson**, has clearly challenged some established views on the subject of "black rice." The three comments—"Beyond 'Black Rice': Reconstructing Material and Cultural Contexts for Early Plantation Agriculture," by **S. Max Edelson**; "Africa and Africans in the African Diaspora: The Uses of Relational Databases," by **Gwendolyn Midlo Hall**; and "From 'Black Rice' to 'Brown': Rethinking the History of Risiculture in the Seventeenth- and Eighteenth-Century Atlantic," by **Walter Hawthorne**—not only criticize the original article but also offer analytical and methodological alternatives. In their response, Eltis, Morgan, and Richardson defend their findings against these critiques and conclude that despite their skepticism regarding the African origin of risiculture in the Americas, this is not meant to deny the role of African agency in this historical context.

The April issue will include an article by Lyndal Roper titled "Martin Luther's Body," and an *AHR* Forum on "East Meets West in South Asia."

In Back Issues

In the hope of encouraging readers to dip into the long history of scholarship contained in the pages of the *American Historical Review* (now in the 115th year of its publishing history), and to take advantage of the digital availability of this archive to most readers, the *AHR* editors offer a look back at issues from one hundred, seventy-five, and fifty years ago. What follows is not a comprehensive survey of the contents of those issues, but rather a glance at some of the articles and other features that might be of interest, or even of use, today.

Volume 15, Number 2 (January 1910)

The first issue of 1910 contains four articles, as well as a 56-page document, "Papers Relating to Bourbon County, Georgia, 1785–1786." The book review section includes a separate section devoted to textbooks. The issue's last article might strike today's readers as particularly interesting, in part because it is by a female scholar, in part because it treats a subject that still has not received much attention. "The Indians in the Civil War," by Annie Heloise Abel, is a careful account of the reaction of a range of Indian tribes to the move toward secession of the Southern states. Some tribes, or rather factions within the tribes, remained pro-Union or neutral in the conflict, but those in the Central and Southern superintendencies tended to ally themselves with the Confederacy. Indeed, Abel shows that Indians were quite aware of the emerging crisis. The legislature of the Chickasaw Nation, for example, began deliberations toward convening an intertribal conference "to secure co-operative activity of some sort on the part of the Five Civilized Tribes should a political separation occur between the North and the South" on the very day a caucus of Southern senators made their decisive move toward secession, January 5, 1861. The next month, the General Council of the Choctaw Nation voted to ally with their "neighbors and brethren of the Southern States," largely, suggests Abel, because they were slaveholders themselves. While many tribes followed suit, there was rarely a consensus. Abel's analysis, following a logic that is as problematic as it is tendentious, is that "half-breeds, who were naturally the more intelligent body in an Indian community," tended to embrace the Confederacy, while "full-blooded" Native Americans remained neutral or sided with the North. In the Cherokee Nation, this division was embodied in rival secret societies, with the secessionist members joining a "Knights of the Golden Circle," and their tribal rivals organized in a society of

"Pins"—referring, apparently, to the fact that "the meetings were held among the hills, where the members tried to hide their real object by connecting serious business with bowling." In any case, in the course of the war, these alliances shifted and often foundered. Ultimately, the Indians paid dearly for casting their lot with the South, losing even more of their rights and protections. Abel concludes: "it was a sad picture of charred dwellings, broken fences, unstocked homesteads, and woe-begone people that presented itself to the white squatters who thronged into the Indian Territory during the Reconstruction Period."

Volume 40, Number 2 (January 1935)

Lest we conclude that transnational history is merely a contemporary fad, and that historical scholarship in the past was confined to the category of the nation-state, the three articles in the January 1935 issue serve as an interesting correction. The Presidential Address by William E. Dodd, "The Emergence of the First Social Order in the United States," which offers an interpretation of American political culture from colonial times to the end of the Civil War, emphasizes both the importance of the social profile and character of the legions of settlers who came from Stuart England and the profound effects of the Restoration in 1661 in altering life in the colonies across the Atlantic. Dodd, by the way, like Theodore Roosevelt and Woodrow Wilson before him, was one of several presidents of the AHA to serve as statesmen: in 1939, President Franklin Roosevelt appointed him ambassador to Nazi Germany. In the second article, "The Influence of Irish Monks on Merovingian Diocesan Organization," Helen Robbins Bittermann examines the question of whether these migrating monastic agents ("Their foreheads shaven back to the middle of the skull, with long, stringing locks and painted eyelids," in her vivid description) were responsible for the dissolution of the Merovingian diocesan organization in Gaul and lands farther to the east. Finally, "Fur Trade Strategy and the American Left Flank in the War of 1812," by Julius W. Pratt, offers a now-familiar scene of American, British, and Indian forces locked in a complex struggle along the northern frontier of that early-nineteenth-century conflict.

Volume 65, Number 2 (January 1960)

It was not only presidents of the AHA who sometimes were prominent figures outside the profession; at times, the authors of articles in the *AHR* also had a high public profile. This was certainly the case with George F. Kennan, the well-known diplomat and foreign policy critic, whose "Soviet Historiography and America's Role in the Intervention" was published in the "Notes and Suggestions" section of the journal in January 1960. By then, Kennan had already had a long career in the foreign policy establishment, serving at one point as ambassador to the Soviet Union; he was also an academic, with a position in the School of Historical Studies at the Institute for Advanced Study in Princeton, New Jersey, to which he was appointed in 1956. His "Note" is, in fact, a twenty-page, point-by-point critique of the claims made by the

Soviet historian S. F. Naida in "Concerning the Role of the Imperialists of the USA in Carrying Out the Intervention in the USSR in the Years 1917–1920," a chapter from the first volume of his *Concerning Certain Questions of the History of the Civil War in the USSR*. It is interesting to speculate about Kennan's purpose in publishing this piece. What sort of readership did he have in mind? He surely did not think that American historians needed convincing that an official Soviet history on this subject was ideologically driven, highly partisan, and lacking in conformity to generally held notions of historical argumentation. Indeed, he calls Naida to task for relying throughout his text on terms such as "American imperialists," "the American re- actionaries," "the American capitalists," "imperialist circles of the USA," "American bourgeois politicians," "the interventionists," "aggressive imperialist circles," "the American millionaires," and "American leading circles," commenting wryly that "these expressions are not sufficiently precise to serve a serious historical purpose." Despite his clear abhorrence of Naida's approach, Kennan does take his claims quite seriously, as is evident in the painstaking, rigorously empirical manner in which he first cites and then refutes ten assertions found in the chapter in question regarding the nature, scope, and motivation of U.S. intervention in Russia, primarily in 1917– 1918. If we can assume that Kennan was not targeting primarily an American read- ership, then it is plausible to conclude that he wanted to appeal to Naida and other Soviet historians as professional colleagues and not ideological apparatchiks who, despite their distorted writings, might still harbor an allegiance to "a common stan- dard in the treatment and use of historical evidence, and in particular a common willingness to respect not only the individual fact but the preponderant and obvious weight of available factual evidence as the supreme arbiter of historical controversy." In any case, his relentlessly empirical, sober-minded, and respectful article serves as an instructive foil to Naida's rather more inflammatory and ideologically colored history. Kennan's article is clearly a Cold War document. Perhaps it can be seen as well as an invitation to his Soviet counterparts to step out of this conflict, with all its intellectual constraints and ideological imperatives, and into the world of schol- arly exchange and academic comity.

LAUREL THATCHER ULRICH

Presidential Address
An American Album, 1857

LAUREL THATCHER ULRICH

SOMETIMES THE BEST WAY to approach a big topic is to focus on a small one. I would like to address a very large topic—conflict over marriage in the nineteenth-century United States—by considering a single object, a quilt made in the Territory of Utah in 1857.

The quilt survives today in two parts. According to family tradition, a twelve-year-old boy won it in a raffle in Salt Lake City in 1857, then years later, when his own children were grown, cut it in two for his oldest daughters. In 1996, Carol and Dan Nielson of Salt Lake City inherited one half. Carol was determined to find the other. Through savvy research and a bit of luck, she did. Then she set about identifying the sixty-three women whose signatures—in thread and in ink—are clearly visible on the squares. In 2004 she published the results of her research in *The Salt Lake City 14th Ward Album Quilt*.[1] Her objective was to tell stories meaningful to the descendants of the quilters and to others interested in local and family history.

My objectives are different. Building on Carol's work, I would like to convince my fellow historians that focusing on a single artifact can yield unexpected insights. Like other forms of micro-history, an object-centered inquiry enlarges details, allowing us to see connections that might otherwise be invisible. The year 1857 was an important one in history. Specialists might point to the Dred Scott decision in the United States, the Great Mutiny against British rule in India, filibustering in Nicaragua, the Divorce and Matrimonial Causes Act in England, apocalyptic cattle-killing in South Africa, or the publication in France of Gustave Flaubert's novel of adultery, *Madame Bovary*. The quilt focuses attention on a different mix of race, imperialism, insurrection, religion, sex, and the law in a raging public controversy over the practice of polygamy by the Latter-day Saint (Mormon) inhabitants of the territory of Utah.

To their antagonists, the Latter-day Saints were not just sexual deviants. They were aliens. In the words of Representative Justin S. Morrill of Vermont, "Under the guise of religion this people has established and seek to maintain and perpetuate,

I would like to thank Nancy Cott, Jill Lepore, and Sarah Pearsall for comments on an earlier draft of this essay; Brittany Chapman, David Whittaker, and Ronald Walker for assistance in locating documents; and Carol Nielson for showing me the quilt and answering my many queries about it.

[1] Carol Holindrake Nielson, *The Salt Lake City 14th Ward Album Quilt, 1857: Stories of the Relief Society Women and Their Quilt* (Salt Lake City, 2004), 7–11, 203, 206. Shirley Mumford, who owns the missing segment, is also a descendant of Richard Henry Horne, the boy who won the raffle.

FIGURE 1: Fourteenth Ward Album Quilt. Salt Lake City, Utah, 1857. Courtesy of Dan and Carol Nielson and Shirley Mumford. Photographs by Dan Nielson. (The figures can be viewed in color in the online version of the article at http://www.journals.uchicago.edu/ahr.)

a Mohammedan barbarism revolting to the civilized world."[2] Novelists and the new illustrated weeklies took up the chorus, linking Utahns with Turks, Africans, and Indians on both sides of the world.[3] Utah leaders responded in kind. Characterizing

[2] Justin S. Morrill, "Utah Territory and Its Laws—Polygamy and Its License," February 23, 1857, U.S. Congress, House, *Appendix to the Congressional Globe*, 34th Cong., 2nd Sess., 284–290, quoted in William P. MacKinnon, ed., *At Sword's Point, Part I: A Documentary History of the Utah War to 1858* (Norman, Okla., 2008), 87.

[3] Compare, for example, "The Outbreak in India," *Harper's Illustrated Weekly*, August 1, 1857, 493–494, with "Scenes in an American Harem," *Harper's Illustrated Weekly*, October 10, 1857, 648–650. See

federal appointees as "dogs and skunks," they vowed to resist those who trampled on their constitutional rights. In New York, St. Louis, and San Francisco, Mormon editors and their opponents exchanged charges and countercharges, multiplying claims of oppression on one side and sedition on the other. The conflict escalated until in 1857, President James Buchanan dispatched one-sixth of the U.S. Army to Utah to put down a supposed rebellion.[4]

Events played out in seemingly random ways. In May, near a rural courthouse in Arkansas, an aggrieved husband gunned down a Mormon apostle who he claimed had seduced his wife. In September, at Mountain Meadows, a lush grazing spot on the Old Spanish Trail through southern Utah, a group of Mormon settlers and their Paiute allies ambushed an emigrant wagon train bound for California and slaughtered most of its members. In early October, far to the north in Salt Lake City, sixty-three members of the Fourteenth Ward Female Relief Society won a prize for their "Album Quilt."

At first glance, the quilt appears unrelated to the tumult. In fact, there are both direct and indirect links to public events of that year. Among the quilters were three wives of Parley P. Pratt, the apostle murdered in Arkansas. A more tenuous link runs through the origins of the Female Relief Society to the fateful alliance between Southern Paiutes and Latter-day Saints in the massacre at Mountain Meadows. More significant is the interplay between the seemingly innocuous imagery of the quilt and the coming of the federal army. The quilt does more than connect a particular group of women to a set of sensational events. It takes us beneath the headlines to unresolved issues about family, faith, marriage, and public authority, issues that mattered in 1857 and that matter today. It helps us to see that on both sides of the conflict, the issue was what it meant to be an American.

There are obvious differences between the fight over polygamy in the nineteenth century and the fight over same-sex marriage today. But there are also some striking similarities. Both conflicts involved a struggle between local and national authority and between minority rights and majority rule. In 1857, as today, people argued over what was innate and what was chosen, grounding their arguments both in science and in scripture. And in both cases, a stigmatized but assertive minority became the locus for extravagant fears over the survival of the nation.

TODAY THE CHURCH of Jesus Christ of Latter-day Saints dissociates itself from polygamy, which officially ended in 1890.[5] But for more than half a century, it fought

---

also Nancy F. Cott, *Public Vows: A History of Marriage and the Nation* (Cambridge, Mass., 2000), 72–76, 111–131; Sarah Barringer Gordon, *The Mormon Question: Polygamy and Constitutional Conflict in Nineteenth-Century America* (Chapel Hill, N.C., 2002), 29–54.

[4] Important works relating to the Utah War include, in addition to the documentary edition by MacKinnon cited above, Norman F. Furniss, *The Mormon Conflict, 1850–1859* (New Haven, Conn., 1960); Kenneth M. Stampp, *America in 1857: A Nation on the Brink* (New York, 1990); Juanita Brooks, *The Mountain Meadows Massacre* (1950; repr., Norman, Okla., 1961); Ronald W. Walker, Richard E. Turley, Jr., and Glen M. Leonard, *Massacre at Mountain Meadows* (New York, 2008); Will Bagley, *Blood of the Prophets: Brigham Young and the Massacre at Mountain Meadows* (Norman, Okla., 2002); Matthew J. Grow, *"Liberty to the Downtrodden": Thomas L. Kane, Romantic Reformer* (New Haven, Conn., 2009).

[5] For official statements on this issue, see the many entries under "Polygamy" on the official church website, http://newsroom.lds.org/ldsnewsroom/eng/.

the U.S. government's attempts to squelch the practice. Although rumors of po- lygamy contributed to the murder of Joseph Smith in Illinois in 1844, the church did not publicly endorse "plural marriage" until 1852, five years after the arrival in Utah. The announcement came in a sermon preached at Brigham Young's behest by Orson Pratt, a member of the Quorum of Twelve Apostles.

Pratt began with a seemingly conventional point, that God instituted marriage in the Garden of Eden and that he commanded Adam and Eve to "multiply and replenish the earth." But he took that idea of multiplying to unimagined heights, arguing that even in the next life, a man's posterity would "constitute his glory, his kingdom, and dominion." He estimated that less than one-fifth of the nations of the earth embraced monogamy, and suggested that those who did showed themselves to be contracted in spirit and in mind. By accepting the new order of marriage, righteous men could inherit the promise God gave to Abraham, that his posterity would be as numberless as the stars in the heavens or the sands of the sea. Righteous women could also achieve exaltation by preparing bodies for preexistent spirits that were clamoring to come to earth.[6]

To the astonishment of the nation, Mormons not only admitted to this strange new practice, they gloried in it, publishing tracts and engaging in public debate. As a consequence, polygamy became the focus of anti-Mormon writing. In the two years before the Utah War, four anti-polygamy novels and dozens of periodical pieces appeared. Building on a handful of known facts and a great deal of fantasy, writers defined Brigham Young as an oriental despot, Mormon men as lechers, and Mormon women as victims or dupes.[7]

Benjamin G. Ferris, a federal official who served six months in the Territory of Utah in 1852–1853, laid down the essential argument: polygamy was incompatible with American civilization. Although God had allowed it to exist among the ancient Jews because of the "hardness of their hearts," no modern civilized nation had adopted such a system. "It belongs now to the indolent and opium-eating Turks and Asiatics, the miserable Africans, the North American savages, and the Latter-day Saints. It is the offspring of lust, and its legitimate results are soon manifest in the rapid degeneracy of races." The only solution was the "ultimate disorganization of the Mormon community."[8]

Francis Lieber, soon to be elevated to the first chair in history and political sci- ence at Columbia University, built upon Ferris's narrative in an article addressing

[6] "A Revelation on Celestial Marriage," *Deseret News Extra*, September 24, 1852, in B. Carmon Hardy, ed., *Doing the Works of Abraham: Mormon Polygamy—Its Origin, Practice, and Demise* (Norman, Okla., 2007), 76–79.

[7] Gary L. Bunker and Davis Bitton, "Illustrated Periodical Images of Mormons, 1850–1860," *Di- alogue: A Journal of Mormon Thought* 10, no. 3 (Spring 1977): 82–94. For overviews that assume a consistency in this literature from the 1830s to the end of the century, see Terryl L. Givens, *The Viper on the Hearth: Mormons, Myths, and the Construction of Heresy* (New York, 1997); and Megan Sanborn Jones, *Performing American Identity in Anti-Mormon Melodrama* (New York, 2009). Important recent essays include Nancy Bentley, "Marriage as Treason: Polygamy, Nation, and the Novel," in Donald E. Pease and Robyn Wiegman, eds., *The Futures of American Studies* (Durham, N.C., 2002), 341–370; and Bruce Burgett, "On the Mormon Question: Race, Sex, and Polygamy in the 1850s and the 1990s," *Amer- ican Quarterly* 57 (March 2005): 75–102.

[8] Benjamin G. Ferris, *Utah and the Mormons: The History, Government, Doctrines, Customs, and Prospects of the Latter-day Saints, from Personal Observations during a Six Months' Residence at Great Salt Lake City* (New York, 1854), 246, 249, 253, 257, 258.

Utah's petition for statehood. The real question for Congress, he argued, was whether granting such a request would infuse "a foreign and disturbing element" into the American system. It was not an issue of religious freedom, he continued. Mormons were free to believe anything they wished. It was a question of whether they should be allowed to undermine monogamy, which in his view was "one of the elementary distinctions—historical and actual—between European and Asiatic humanity." Unless Congress stood firm, the foundation of the nation might collapse. Another state or territory might adopt French communism or "become so filled with Chinese that the whites were absorbed," or worse yet, "become *bona fide* Africanized."[9]

The anti-polygamy crusade played into what Amy Kaplan has called "manifest domesticity," a discourse of imperialism that linked the security of the Christian home with the suppression of all things foreign. Popular writers not only patrolled the boundaries between civilized and savage nations, they attempted to eradicate "traces of the savage within."[10] It didn't help that Mormons showed some sympathy for American Indians, whom they identified with a people described in the Book of Mormon as "Lamanites," descendants of ancient Israelites who had migrated to the Americas before the fall of Jerusalem. Although God had cursed the Lamanites with dark skin for their sinfulness, he would eventually fulfill the promise made to their fathers that they would prepare the earth for the second coming of Jesus. Anti-Mormon writers picked up on this theme. An anonymous letter in the *American Journal* in the spring of 1857 even claimed that 100,000 Mormons allied with 200,000 spies and 300,000 Indians were prepared to fight the U.S. Army.[11]

Ironically, Mormons did not differ a great deal from other Americans in their racial assumptions. In his discourse on polygamy, Pratt assumed that in distributing preexistent spirits, God favored the mostly Caucasian converts to Mormonism over "the Hottentots, the African negroes, the idolatrous Hindoos, or any other of the fallen nations that dwell upon the face of this earth."[12] But to its detractors, Mormonism represented virtually anything and everything that appeared "un-American"—Islamic and Hindu religion, African and ancient Jewish religious practice, slavery in the American South, savagery on the American frontier, and heterodox ideas that to all appearances emanated from civilized countries. One of the characters in Metta Victor's novel *Mormon Wives*, which sold more than 40,000 copies in the 1850s, admitted that it was easy for her to accept Mormonism after she had "tainted the sweetness of womanhood, by yielding a belief to the philosophy of Socialism."[13] A character in Maria Ward's novel *Female Life among the Mormons*

[9] Francis Lieber, "The Mormons: Shall Utah Be Admitted to the Union?" *Putnam's Monthly* 5, no. 27 (March 1855): 225–236. On the continuing use of racial tropes in attacking polygamy, see Cott, *Public Vows*, 73–76, 88–89, 92.

[10] Amy Kaplan, "Manifest Domesticity," in Pease and Wiegman, *The Futures of American Studies*, 129.

[11] Givens, *The Viper on the Hearth*, 57; Walker, Turley, and Leonard, *Massacre at Mountain Meadows*, 28. See also MacKinnon, *At Sword's Point*, 41–52. On Mormon relations with Utah Indians, see Ned Blackhawk, *Violence over the Land: Indians and Empires in the Early American West* (Cambridge, Mass., 2006), chap. 7; Jared Farmer, *On Zion's Mount: Mormons, Indians, and the American Landscape* (Cambridge, Mass., 2008), chap. 2; and Martha C. Knack, *Boundaries Between: The Southern Paiutes, 1775–1995* (Lincoln, Neb., 2001), 48–94.

[12] "A Revelation on Celestial Marriage," 79.

[13] Metta Victoria Fuller, *Mormon Wives: A Narrative of Facts Stranger Than Fiction* (New York, 1856), 313; Burgett, "On the Mormon Question," 87–90.

blamed her acceptance of polygamy on the "mystical magical influence" of the Mormon prophet, who had learned the art of mesmerism from a German peddler.[14]

A writer in *Harper's Illustrated* in the spring of 1857 raised an even more alarming possibility—that in addition to the dangers of mesmerism, socialism, and mental magnetism, Mormon women may have been tainted by what later generations would call feminism. Describing a purported visit to Utah, he said that among Brigham Young's wives were homely creatures "dressed in a kind of Bloomer costume, with pantaloons like those of the men, dresses made like a man's over-coat, tall straw hats with broad ribbons." In Utah, he concluded, strong-minded women actually helped their husbands get more wives. "What a lesson for Miss Lucy Stone!" he exclaimed.[15]

With anti-polygamy arguments echoing through the nation, Buchanan felt safe in sending federal troops to Utah. The problem was getting them there. It took months to assemble and supply them, and even longer to move them across the plains to an uncertain welcome in the Rockies. As rumors flew back and forth across the mountains, the women of the Fourteenth Ward assembled their quilt. The quilt helps us to see the many ways in which they were like their fellow Americans. They, too, believed in the civilizing power of marriage, in the sanctity of motherhood, and in the necessity of monitoring and suppressing the savage within. Like women in the East, they contributed to their communities not only as wives and mothers but also through productive labor and their work in charitable societies. And like women elsewhere, they struggled with contradictions between the ideals they embraced and the realities they lived. In the face of their own private troubles and a federal assault on their homes and families, they created an American album.

ALBUM QUILTS WERE all the rage in the United States in the 1840s and 1850s. Like the paper albums popular among middle-class Americans, they brought together signatures, mottoes, and images contributed by many persons. Quilts of this sort are a treasure trove for historians. Signatures reveal local networks. Mottoes and images connect the quilters to a repertoire of national values, while place names and dates situate them in a specific setting. The Fourteenth Ward quilt is a model of the form. Every technique and most of the images used in it can be found in other quilts made in the United States in the same period.[16] Its historical significance comes from the interplay of these images with the lives of particular women in a moment of crisis.

Significantly, twenty-five of the seventy squares portray some sort of flower. The square made by Mary Isabella Horne, one of the officers of the Female Relief Society

[14] Maria Ward, *Female Life among the Mormons: A Narrative of Many Years' Personal Experience* (London, 1855), 38, 9, 230, quoted in Givens, *The Viper on the Hearth*, 139, 140.

[15] "Scenes in an American Harem."

[16] Sandi Fox, *For Purpose and Pleasure: Quilting Together in Nineteenth-Century America* (Nashville, Tenn., 1995), 34–42 (chintz cut-outs); 45–47, 86, 87, 134, 138 (geometric); 26–28, 50–67 (red and green); 148, 152 (mixed); and the many examples of mixed motifs and techniques in Patricia Cox Crews, ed., *A Flowering of Quilts* (Lincoln, Neb., 2001), 32–39, 46–49. The one unusual addition is three squares worked in worsted yarn. Although embroidered woolen coverlets were common in the Northeast, wool and cotton did not usually appear together. Perhaps Phebe Woodruff's sister, who was a native of Maine, brought a bit of unused worsted with her. The motifs that she used are very similar to those appearing on all-wool coverlets from the same period. See Carleton L. Safford and Robert Bishop, *America's Quilts and Coverlets* (New York, 1980), 64–72; Laurel Thatcher Ulrich, *The Age of Homespun: Objects and Stories in the Creation of an American Myth* (New York, 2001), 323–339.

FIGURE 2: M. Isabella Horne, detail, Fourteenth Ward Album Quilt.

and the mother of the twelve-year-old boy who won the raffle, exemplifies nine-teenth-century floral needlework, from the serrated edges on the leaves to the fil-igree overlay on the pot. Although scarcity forced her to use two different kinds of fabric for the leaves, she compensated by cutting carefully so that the pattern on the now-blue and probably once-green print suggested veins in the leaves. She finished her flat roses with graceful loops representing the flowers' pistils and stamens. One scholar has argued that nineteenth-century floral quilts reflected principles of land-scape gardening in which each plant was meant to be unique yet contribute to an overall harmony.[17] The Fourteenth Ward quilt fits that description. Working with a limited repertoire of materials, the quilters created remarkable variety. Each square is unique. Where a pattern is repeated, different fabric is used; where common fab-rics are used, different designs are employed. Blue strips, like gardens paths, si-multaneously separate and unify the squares.

[17] Susan Curtis, "Blessed Be God for Flowers: Nineteenth-Century Quilt Design," in Crews, *A Flow-ering of Quilts*, 11–23.

Given their decade-long struggle to overcome drought and insect infestation, the emphasis on flowers is significant. In the early years of the settlement, many of the quilters had lived in dugouts, wagon beds, and temporary adobe shelters, eking out scarce harvests by gathering sego lily roots and wild berries. Utahns still feared drought and famine, yet in February 1857, the territory's Agricultural and Manufacturing Society announced that prizes would be given in the fall not only for field crops, vegetables, and fruits, but also for ornamental plants such as roses, dahlias, and asters.[18] For Latter-day Saints, the ability to grow flowers in the sagebrush-covered valley of the Great Salt Lake was a fulfillment of biblical prophecy: "The wilderness and the solitary place shall be glad for them; and the desert shall rejoice and blossom as the rose" (Isaiah 35:1). In an inscription, now almost too faint to read, one quilter captured the essence of that prophecy: "The desert shall blossom as a rose."[19] In their mountain fastness, Latter-day Saints were also bent on achieving respectability. This was no small feat. All the materials in the quilt, with the possible exception of bits of carded wool in the filling, had traveled more than a thousand miles by wagon train. One square, an intricately pieced patchwork, even displays sewing machine stitches around the borders of the central patch, announcing to the world that even though the woman who made it lived in the middle of nowhere, she had access to the latest technology.[20]

The quilters, too, had traveled. Elizabeth Cain, the owner of the sewing machine, was one of the twenty quilters who had been born in England. Five came from Scotland, and one each from Wales, Canada, and Switzerland. Of those born in the United States, thirteen were born in New England, nine in the Mid-Atlantic, seven in the Midwest, and five in the South.[21] But a simple identification of birthplace can be misleading. Almost all had moved several times, even before joining the Latter-day Saints. The quilter from Switzerland had spent time in Russia. A seamstress from New York City had accompanied her missionary husband to Chile, where in Valparaiso she gave birth to her second child.[22] Another was born in Georgia, moved with her family to Texas, then, after marrying a former Texas Ranger, moved to Kansas before migrating to Utah in 1855.[23]

There is little evidence of these diverse origins in the quilt. The one self-consciously ethnic square was made by Jane Ballantyne Taylor, the Scots-born wife of Apostle John Taylor, who created a thistle and a butterfly with plaid wings.[24] The

[18] *Deseret News*, February 25, 1857, 408.

[19] Nielson, *The Salt Lake City 14th Ward Album Quilt*, 93. Because Catherine Church's square is stained, the inscription on the pot is too faded to show up well in a photograph.

[20] Mrs. J. Cain square, in Nielson, *The Salt Lake City 14th Ward Album Quilt*, 85.

[21] I computed these numbers from the biographical sketches in Nielson's book. For a broader picture of Mormon immigration, see Dean May, "A Demographic Portrait of the Mormons, 1830–1980," in D. Michael Quinn, ed., *The New Mormon History: Revisionist Essays on the Past* (Salt Lake City, 1992), 126. According to the 1860 census, 13.7 percent of the inhabitants of the United States in that year were foreign-born. The figure for Utah is 31.7 percent. Campbell J. Gibson and Emily Lennon, "Historical Census Statistics on the Foreign-Born Population of the United States, 1850–1990," U.S. Bureau of the Census, Population Division Working Paper No. 29 (February 1999), http://www.census.gov/population/www/documentation/twps0029/twps0029.html (accessed October 7, 2009).

[22] Nielson, *The Salt Lake City 14th Ward Album Quilt*, 156–158. The published edition of Pratt's biography acknowledges his wife's presence on this mission but gives few details; *Autobiography of Parley P. Pratt*, edited by Parley P. Pratt, Jr., 5th ed. (Salt Lake City, 1961), 386–393.

[23] Nielson, *The Salt Lake City 14th Ward Album Quilt*, 98–100.

[24] Ibid., 182–183.

emphasis was not on national or regional identity but on creativity. These were women interested in making the desert blossom.

As Donald Worster has observed, the writings of the world's great religions are filled with images of "gardens and oases that have been wrested from barren deserts by concerted, righteous human labor." In the western part of the United States—the Great American Desert—Latter-day Saints attempted to make that dream real, believing that if nature could be made productive, "then humanity too would be restored to its original innocence and peace."[25] This was a vision not just of earthly abundance, but of equality. In the words of a Mormon hymn written in Missouri but still sung today, "This earth was once a garden place, with all her glories common."[26]

That dream received new expression in the so-called Mormon Reformation of 1856–1857. Worried that the rigors of pioneering and an influx of immigrants were weakening spiritual commitment, Brigham Young and other church leaders urged the bishops who presided over individual parishes or wards to re-baptize their members and invite them to consecrate their worldly goods through token deeds of gift to the church. They also urged male members, especially those who held church positions, to take additional wives.[27] Every woman, they said, should have the opportunity to have a righteous husband and to become a mother. It is hardly surprising, then, that of the fifty-nine married women who contributed to the Album Quilt, forty-nine were involved in what Mormons called "plural marriage." The numbers reflect the religious commitment of the quilters as well as the status of their husbands.[28]

Equality meant cooperation, not sameness. Unlike some nineteenth-century utopian groups or twentieth-century polygamous sects, nineteenth-century Mormons did not dress alike or cultivate common fields. They were bound by their acceptance of a new religious vision and the opprobrium it brought.

PHEBE WOODRUFF'S SQUARE, now sadly split, was once at the center of the quilt. She probably modeled her old-fashioned bee skep on one portrayed in the emblem of the Deseret Agricultural and Manufacturing Society.[29] Although the beehive was a common symbol in the early United States, Latter-day Saint scripture gave it additional meaning. The original name for the Territory of Utah was Deseret, a term derived from an obscure passage in the Book of Mormon describing an ancient migration to the Americas in which voyagers carried, in addition to seeds of all kinds,

[25] Donald Worster, "The Kingdom, the Power, and the Water," in Thomas G. Alexander, ed., *Great Basin Kingdom Revisited: Contemporary Perspectives* (Logan, Utah, 1991), 35, 36.

[26] *Hymns of the Church of Jesus Christ of Latter-day Saints* (Salt Lake City, 1985), 49; Karen Lynn Davidson, *Our Latter-day Hymns: The Stories and the Messages* (Salt Lake City, 1988), 78, 79.

[27] Stanley S. Ivins, "Notes on Mormon Polygamy," in Quinn, *The New Mormon History*, 171, found 65 percent more plural marriages in 1856 and 1857 than in any other period in his tabulation. His essay was first published in *Western Humanities Review* 10, no. 3 (Summer 1956): 229–239.

[28] This is a much higher proportion (84 percent) than in Salt Lake City as a whole, where 56 percent of married women were polygamists. Marie Cornwall, Camela Courtright, and Laga Van Beek, "How Common the Principle? Women as Plural Wives in 1860," *Dialogue: A Journal of Mormon Thought* 26, no. 2 (Summer 1993): 139–153.

[29] The Utah certificate was similar to those used in other states. See Hal Cannon, ed., *Utah Folk Art: A Catalog of Material Culture* (Provo, 1980), 87; and Tammy Horn, *Bees in America: How the Honey Bee Shaped a Nation* (Lexington, Ky., 2005), 56–57.

FIGURE 3: Phebe W. Woodruff, detail, Fourteenth Ward Album Quilt.

"*deseret*, which, by interpretation, is a honey bee."[30] Although there was not much honey raised in this period in Utah, bees flourished as a symbol.[31] The Fourteenth Ward quilters embellished their squares with everything but the buzz. They were no

[30] Book of Mormon, Ether 2:3. On the transformation of the beehive from a monarchial to a republican symbol, see Ann Fairfax Withington, "Republican Bees: The Political Economy of the Beehive in Eighteenth-Century America," *Studies in Eighteenth-Century Culture* 18 (January 1988): 39–77.

[31] When the bees they brought to Utah did not thrive, settlers turned to raising sorghum. See Jill Mulvay Derr, "'I Have Eaten Nearly Everything Imaginable': Pioneer Diet," in Ronald W. Walker and Doris R. Dant, eds., *Nearly Everything Imaginable: The Everyday Life of Utah's Mormon Pioneers* (Provo, 1999), 230–232; Leonard J. Arrington, *Great Basin Kingdom: An Economic History of the Latter-day Saints, 1830–1900*, New Edition (Urbana, Ill., 2005), 116–120; Arrington, *Brigham Young: American Moses* (New York, 1985), 184–185; "A New Sugar Culture," *Deseret News*, September 24, 1856, 3; "A New Plant," *Deseret News*, February 4, 1857, 8; "Message from the Governor," *Deseret News*, December 23, 1857.

FIGURE 4: Deseret Agricultural and Manufacturing Society Diploma. Courtesy LDS Church History Library and Archives.

doubt imitating Brigham Young, who even planted a carved hive on the cupola of his house.[32] For Joseph Cain, whose wife Elizabeth was one of the quilters, bees symbolized the wanderings of the Latter-day Saints. In Utah, he believed, the saints had at last found a hive. If their enemies dared to follow them there, they would discover that like "the bees who work and sing, / The Saints of God can also sting."[33]

Phebe had also been a wanderer. Born in Scarborough, Maine, in 1807, she joined the Latter-day Saints in Kirtland, Ohio, in 1834. There she met and married Wilford Woodruff, a charismatic preacher whose expansive diaries tell us just enough about her to make us want to know more. In the next fifteen years, Phebe gave birth to nine children and lost five. One child died shortly after the Saints were driven from Missouri. Six years later, while huddled in Indian territory after fleeing her home in Nauvoo, Phebe lost a two-year-old son and a newborn baby. In July 1848, while she and Wilford were en route to Boston, where he would preside over the New England mission, their nine-month-old daughter Shuah died. "Mrs. Woodruff expressed her

[32] Rickey Lynn Hendricks, "Landmark Architecture for a Polygamous Family: The Brigham Young Domicile, Salt Lake City, Utah," *The Public Historian* 11 (Winter 1989): 25–47; Colleen Whitley, ed., *Brigham Young's Homes* (Logan, Utah, 2002), 100, 124. See also Hal Cannon, *The Grand Beehive* (Salt Lake City, 1980); Marilyn Conover Barker, *The Legacy of Mormon Furniture: The Mormon Material Culture, Undergirded by Faith, Commitment, and Craftsmanship* (Salt Lake City, 1995), 58, 59; Grow, "Liberty to the Downtrodden," 68.

[33] Joseph Cain, "The Bee," *Deseret News*, January 25, 1851, 1; Michael Hicks, *Mormonism and Music: A History* (Urbana, Ill., 1989), 59–60, 65.

feelings concerning the loss of her Children & refused to be comforted," Wilford wrote. Three years later in Utah, she gave birth to a daughter, who lived, and then two years later to a son, her ninth child, who did not.[34] For her, the Mormon epic of persecution was a lived reality.

The motto on her square—"By industry we thrive"—reflects her investment in her family's survival. Although Wilford did not report on her ordinary labors, he did notice when something unusual happened, as in the fall of 1856, when the territory faced famine after grasshoppers devastated their crops. One day Phebe took her daughters into the field to glean wheat, sleeping over and coming home wet after it rained. Things were more promising in 1857. In the first two weeks of March, Wilford sowed gooseberry, currant, and cherry seeds, set out grapevines, transplanted almond, peach, apricot, and plum seedlings, and began grafting apples and pears. On April 23, he enumerated twenty-three varieties of apples in his orchard. The appliquéd fruit on Phebe's square acknowledges those labors.[35]

In the triangular space below the beehive on her square, Phebe claimed the honor of being "President of the 14th Ward Female Relief Society." This was not her first experience with such an organization. She was in Nauvoo in 1842 when Joseph Smith spoke to the first Relief Society, telling them that the "organization of the Church of Christ was never perfect until the women were organized." He promised them power and knowledge from on high and defended them against those who thought it was a sin for women to lay hands on the sick for healing. He urged them to do good works, to care for the poor, and to sustain and support their husbands. Although the minutes of the Relief Society do not reveal it, he also told them that part of their responsibility in the new dispensation was to accept plural marriage. In an interpretation that many of them carried with them into old age, this meant they would receive a holy endowment that would make them queens and priestesses in heaven. The sisters selected Emma Smith, the prophet's wife, as president.[36]

After Smith's death, conflict between Brigham Young and Emma, who did not go west, as well as the trials of relocation to Utah, ended formal meetings. Young reportedly told a group of church leaders, "When I want Sisters or the Wives of the members of the church to get up Relief Society I will summon them to my aid but until that time let them stay at home & if you see Females huddling together veto the concern."[37] Although Phebe and others continued to meet informally, especially during the difficult period after the expulsion from Nauvoo, there was no longer a church-sanctioned organization.[38]

In 1853, a shift in policy toward Utah Indians provided a new opportunity for the

[34] *Wilford Woodruff's Journal*, edited by Scott G. Kenney, 9 vols. (Midvale, Utah, 1983), 1: 272, 348, 349, 426, 484, 485, 537; 2: 157, 264; 3: 95, 97, 358, 359, 361; Augusta Joyce Crocheron, *Representative Women of Deseret: A Book of Biographical Sketches, to Accompany the Picture Bearing the Same Title* (Salt Lake City, 1884), 33–39; Thomas G. Alexander, *Things in Heaven and Earth: The Life and Times of Wilford Woodruff, a Mormon Prophet* (Salt Lake City, 1991), 51–53, 76, 99–100, 168.

[35] *Wilford Woodruff's Journal*, 5: 29, 31, 32, 47, 67; 4: 436.

[36] Jill Mulvay Derr, Janath Russell Cannon, and Maureen Ursenbach Beecher, *Women of Covenant: The Story of Relief Society* (Salt Lake City, 1992), 43–58.

[37] "Seventies Record," March 9, 1845, LDS Archives, quoted in Linda King Newell and Valeen Tippetts Avery, *Mormon Enigma: Emma Hale Smith, Prophet's Wife, "Elect Lady," Polygamy's Foe, 1804–1879* (Garden City, N.Y., 1984), 352 n. 27.

[38] Maureen Ursenbach Beecher, *Eliza and Her Sisters* (Salt Lake City, 1991), 93–95.

women to exercise their organizational power.[39] Responding to the call to "redeem the Lamanites," a group of Salt Lake City women met under the leadership of Matilda Dudley, who had been a member of the Nauvoo Relief Society, to form a society for Indian relief. They met weekly, elected officers, organized fundraising projects, and took in contributions in cash and in kind.[40] Their initiative reminded Brigham Young that women could be not only troublesome, but useful. Impressed with their efforts but perhaps just as concerned about their independence, he urged bishops to organize societies in each ward.[41]

By 1854, the bishops had called women to preside over at least twenty-four Indian Relief Societies. Within a few months, they had contributed nearly nine hundred items of clothing, valued at over $1,500. At the peak of activity, women in one ward contributed an average of almost one day per week to the work.[42] Soon they had produced more clothing than the Indian mission could use. Brigham asked them to produce rag carpeting for the Salt Lake Tabernacle, a public meeting hall. Next he gave them responsibility for relieving the poor, including immigrants pouring into the valley.[43] Wilford Woodruff mentioned the society three times in his diary in 1857, the last time on June 17, when he addressed a meeting at his house where about fifty women were "knitting, sewing carpet rags, making quilts, etc." He pronounced it a "laudable undertaking," noting that the women met each Wednesday afternoon. "I wish all to go and do likewise," he said.[44] Sharing their small cache of scraps, the Fourteenth Ward quilters demonstrated their charitable instincts, their artistic sensibilities, and their collective identity as heirs to the promises made in Nauvoo.

SARAH ANN CHURCH WAS probably not thinking of human reproduction when she appliquéd a cucumber vine on her square. She nevertheless portrayed all the stages of vegetable gestation, from the bright yellow and orange blossoms on the vine, to the tiny green bulges emerging from them as the fruit began to form. Her green cucumbers have prickles, and her ripe one has yellow flecks on its bright orange skin, just as real cucumbers would have had. If the maturing of the plants in her garden reminded her of the stages of pregnancy or of the seasons in a woman's life, it would not be surprising. She gave birth to her fourth child on July 8, 1857. A few years later, she herself became a midwife. "The tree is known by its fruit," she wrote across the top of her square.[45]

In the winter of 1857, Apostle Orson Hyde told a mixed audience of Saints in

---

[39] Nielson, *The Salt Lake City 14th Ward Album Quilt*, 19; Richard L. Jensen, "Forgotten Relief Societies, 1844–67," *Dialogue: A Journal of Mormon Thought* 16, no. 1 (Spring 1983): 105–125; Derr, Cannon, and Beecher, *Women of Covenant*, 75–82.

[40] Jensen, "Forgotten Relief Societies," 110; Derr, Cannon, and Beecher, *Women of Covenant*, 75; Record of the Female Relief Society Organized on the 9th of Feby in the City of Great Salt Lake 1854, Louisa R. Taylor Papers, Special Collections, Harold B. Lee Library, Brigham Young University.

[41] Matilda Dudley became president of the new church-sanctioned society in her own ward; Phebe Woodruff was called in hers. Record of the Female Relief Society, n.p. It is not clear whether Phebe was involved with Dudley. She was later active in encouraging women to organize. Nielson, *The Salt Lake City 14th Ward Album Quilt*, 19–20; *Wilford Woodruff's Journal*, 4: 281.

[42] Jensen, "Forgotten Relief Societies," 113–115.

[43] Ibid., 118.

[44] *Wilford Woodruff's Journal*, 5: 26, 59, 60.

[45] For Church's biography, see Nielson, *The Salt Lake City 14th Ward Album Quilt*, 91–93. Her hus-

Figure 5: Sarah Ann Church, detail, Fourteenth Ward Album Quilt.

Springville, Utah, that human propagation was much like gardening. "You wouldn't plant even a squash seed in the *Fall*," he said. In like manner, there were times and seasons for sexual intercourse.[46] He said that husbands should leave their wives alone during pregnancy and lactation. "It is true that goats it is said will have sexual intercourse within fifteen minutes of the moment when the kid is born. Monkeys also, as some writers affirm are as debased in their practices, but most of the lower animals, may give us a lesson." At stake was not just the health of the mother and the safety of the child, but the spiritual authority of the father. "I say suppose a family,

band's second wife was a woman much older than she who had no children of her own but helped raise Sarah Ann's.

[46] Orson Hyde, in Luke William Gallup, Reminiscences and Diary, February 11, 1857, LDS Archives, 193–195, in Hardy, *Doing the Works of Abraham*, 133–135.

where there is no intercourse of this kind, only with the prospect of having children born,—*That family can be governed.*"[47]

In a letter originally written to her sister in New Hampshire, Belinda Pratt, Parley P. Pratt's sixth wife, explained that nature had prepared males and females for different purposes. "The strength of the female constitution is . . . to nourish and sustain the embryo, to bring it forth, and to nurse it on her bosom." A man had no such demand on his energies. "If God shall count him worthy of an hundred fold in this life, of wives and children, and houses and lands and kindreds, he may even aspire to patriarchal sovereignty, to empire; to be the prince or head of a tribe, or tribes; and like Abraham of old, be able to send forth for the defence of his country, hundreds and thousands of his own warriors, born in his own house."[48]

Mormons meant it when they described their marriage system as a "patriarchal order." But achieving Abrahamic command was not easy. In a sermon preached in February 1857, Apostle Lorenzo Snow warned those who thought that acquiring wives was an easy path to heaven. "Almost any fool can go & preach the gospel but it requires a very wise man to be a patriarch & save his own household," he said.[49] Wilford Woodruff understood that only too well. He had baptized hundreds, perhaps thousands, into the faith, but for years he had struggled with polygamy. In the spring of 1857, he was in divorce negotiations with one wife while in the process of marrying another. Over his lifetime, half of his ten plural marriages ended in divorce.[50]

But you would not know that from the quilt. Each of Woodruff's four wives at the time and all three of his daughters contributed squares, their shared fabric suggesting a harmony that may or may not have existed.[51] Sarah Brown Woodruff, who gave birth to her second son in January 1857, pictured two birds tending a nest. Fifteen-year-old Phebe Jr. and her father's nineteen-year-old wife Emma cut their flowers from the same printed fabric. Fourteen-year-old Susan and the newest bride, Sarah Delight Woodruff, each stitched bright-breasted birds. Since neither Emma nor Sarah Delight yet had a child, they may have related to the Woodruff girls more like sisters than wives. Six-year-old Bulah Woodruff, Phebe's youngest child, completed the portrait of family harmony by offering a spotted cat sitting contentedly on a tasseled cushion.[52]

A quite different pair of squares issued from the family of sixty-year-old Abraham Hoagland, bishop of the Fourteenth Ward. Although his own diary is silent on the

---

[47] Hyde, in Gallup, *Reminiscences and Diary.*

[48] [Belinda Pratt], *Defence of Polygamy, by a Lady of Utah* (1854), in Hardy, *Doing the Works of Abraham,* 96–97.

[49] *Wilford Woodruff's Journal,* 5: 14, 15.

[50] Alexander, *Things in Heaven and Earth,* xiv, 168. See also Nielson, *The Salt Lake City 14th Ward Album Quilt,* 56–58, which has excerpts on Sarah Delight Stocking Woodruff from unpublished family histories. Todd Compton, "The Wives of Wilford Woodruff," http://www.geocities.com/Athens/Oracle/7207/WWfamilies.htm, lists eleven women presumably sealed to Woodruff during his lifetime.

[51] Alexander, *Things in Heaven and Earth,* 161–189; Nielson, *The Salt Lake City 14th Ward Album Quilt,* 39–58.

[52] I have drawn birth and marriage dates from familysearch.org. See also Nielson, *The Salt Lake City 14th Ward Album Quilt,* 39–58; and Alexander, *Things in Heaven and Earth,* 167–168. Alexander surmises that even though Woodruff married teenagers, he refrained from sexual relations until they became older. At the age of nineteen, Emma Brown had her first child.

topic, other sources tell us there was trouble in the family.[53] On January 22, 1857, Woodruff preached a sermon in the Fourteenth Ward, telling the people to "sustain their Bishop" and reminding them that "a mans family was his throne & kingdom & no man had a right to interfere with him." But he was not really talking about interference from *men*. His real complaint was with women, who "would spin street yarn & go from house to House & try to turn away women from their Husbands & stir up strife in families."[54]

The issue would not go away. On March 23, Woodruff attended a "council with the Presidency & Twelve & others on the Case of Bishop Hoagland & his wife Agnes. She brought a Complaint against him that He did not pay attention enough to her & provide well enough for her."[55] Converted to Mormonism around the same time as her brother, Apostle John Taylor, Agnes Taylor Rich joined Hoagland's family as a plural wife in 1847, after leaving her first husband, a non-Mormon who reportedly had tried to put her in jail to keep her from going west. Taking her three children with her, she gave birth to five more by Hoagland. In 1857 she had six living children, ranging in age from seventeen to one. She was clearly overwhelmed.[56] Brigham had little sympathy. He was weary from counseling disgruntled couples, who lined up at his doors at all hours of the day. Among them were women asking for a "bill of divorce," a document legal only in Utah.[57]

Historians now know that informal and extralegal separations and remarriage were far more common in the nineteenth century than either legal records or prescriptive literature would imply. Marriages broke up because wives as well as husbands ran away, and because increased mobility and multiple jurisdictions allowed them to do so.[58] The Mormon system brought such practices within a system of church law. During his administration, Brigham Young authorized 1,645 divorces, three-fourths of those before 1866. One scholar estimates that divorces among women married in polygamy were three times as common as among those in monogamous marriages. Divorce was perhaps a safety valve that made polygamy work.[59]

But in this case, Brigham resisted Agnes Hoagland's plea. "There is many women

[53] "History and Journal of Abraham Hoagland," 3, available as a PDF file on the George Q. Cannon Family History website, http://www.georgeqcannon.com/GQC_Docs.htm.

[54] *Wilford Woodruff's Journal*, 5: 11.

[55] Ibid., 5: 42, 43.

[56] Nielson, *The Salt Lake City 14th Ward Album Quilt*, 187–193. See also "Abraham Lucas Hoagland 1" at http://www.georgeqcannon.com/ (accessed August 3, 2009); Catherine Rich South Spencer, "Elizabeth Taylor Rich South," November 1937, http://allenhackworth.com/South/elizabethsouthbio.htm (accessed October 3, 2009); and Abraham Hoagland and Samuel Taylor Rich files on familysearch.org. The 1850 census lists "Agnes Taylor" in the Hoagland household along with children John, age 10; Elisabeth, 8; Samuel, 7; Abraham, 5; and Agnes, 1. The first three are presumably her children by her first husband, John Rich.

[57] *Wilford Woodruff's Journal*, 5: 7.

[58] Hendrik Hartog, *Man and Wife in America: A History* (Cambridge, Mass., 2000); Beverly Schwartzberg, "'Lots of Them Did That': Desertion, Bigamy, and Marital Fluidity in Late-Nineteenth-Century America," *Journal of Social History* 37, no. 3 (Spring 2004): 573–600; Schwartzberg, "Grass Widows, Barbarians, and Bigamists: Fluid Marriage in Late Nineteenth-Century America" (Ph.D. diss., University of California, Santa Barbara, 2002).

[59] Jessie L. Embry, *Mormon Polygamous Families: Life in the Principle* (Salt Lake City, 1987), 176, 177. See also Richard S. Van Wagoner, *Mormon Polygamy: A History*, 2nd ed. (Salt Lake City, 1989), 92, 93; Eugene E. Campbell and Bruce L. Campbell, "Divorce among Mormon Polygamists: Extent and Explanations," in Quinn, *The New Mormon History*, 181–200. On divorce as a theme in anti-Mormon critiques, see Cott, *Public Vows*, 110–111.

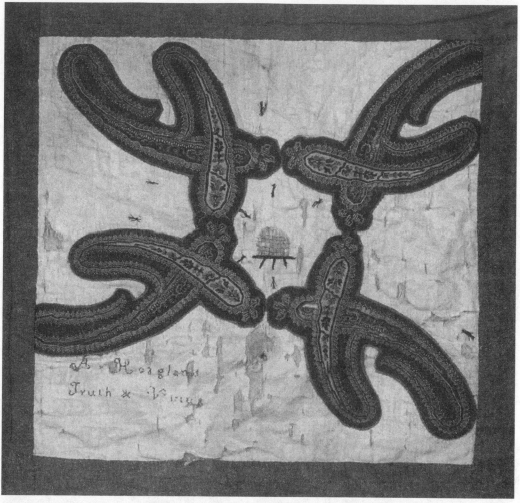

Figure 6: A. Hoagland, detail, Fourteenth Ward Album Quilt.

that care more about their Husband sleeping with them than they do about God or his kingdom," he said, adding, "if a man was to submit to such women he would not be worth shucks in building up the kingdom of God." From all appearances, Bishop Hoagland was a good bishop. If Agnes would follow his counsel, she would be saved. Her problem was that she wanted "pillow council instead of ward council." He told her that if she never again got "pillow council," she should simply "go home & do right." Then he told Hoagland to "Baptize her if she wishes to be."[60] That very day, Bishop Hoagland began to re-baptize members of his ward. Whether Agnes was among them, we do not know.

A square inscribed "A. Hoagland" is without question the least accomplished piece on the quilt. Cut-outs from a paisley print extend ominously from a womblike center where elongated black bees appear to be attacking a miniature hive. In halting letters just below the name are the words "Truth & Virtue." Perhaps Agnes made the square in haste or despair. Or maybe, in an attempt to keep up with Bulah

[60] *Wilford Woodruff's Journal*, 5: 42, 43.

Figure 7: E. A. Hoagland, detail, Fourteenth Ward Album Quilt.

Woodruff, her seven-year-old daughter, also named Agnes, did the work. Whatever its origins, it contrasts with the perfectly pieced Mariner's Compass made by the bishop's childless third wife, Ester Ann. Ester pieced forty-eight perfect points, then added eight-pointed stars and delicate buds in the four corners. In the center, she embroidered the comforting words "Father is at the helm. All is right." She surely meant God the Father, not any earthly man, though in Mormon theology there was a blurring of the two.

ALTHOUGH THERE IS no way of knowing when the quilters began to work on their squares, the nine squares that give a month or day indicate a flurry of activity in July and August.[61] That was, of course, precisely the time when the threat of war became

[61] This dating of the quilt is reinforced by the presence of a square by Sarah Delight Woodruff, who

evident. Word of Parley Pratt's murder reached Salt Lake City on June 23. "We learn that all Hell is boiling over against the saints in Utah," Woodruff wrote. "The papers of the United States are filled with bitter revileings against us. The devil is exceeding mad."[62]

Papers from New York to San Francisco published details of the murder. In most accounts, Pratt appeared as a classic seducer, a man who, in the judgment of the *New York Herald*, "had great ability, which he perverted to the worst purposes." While living in San Francisco, he supposedly had enticed a respectable woman named Eleanor McLean to desert her children and become his ninth "concubine." When her husband, Hector McLean, sent his children to their grandparents in New Orleans, she followed them there, kidnapped them, and sped to a rendezvous with Pratt in Arkansas. McLean tracked them down and had Pratt arrested. When an Arkansas court dismissed the case, McLean had no choice but to kill Pratt.[63] "Thus did the hoary old villain meet a just retribution at the hands of a man whom he had most outrageously injured!" declared the writer for the San Francisco *Daily Evening Bulletin*.[64] The *Fort Smith Herald* admitted, "We are pleased to see that such men—not men, demons—pursuing such a course cannot, with impunity, come into our midst, in Arkansas."[65]

It must have surprised readers to find a few days later a rejoinder from Eleanor McLean. Where the press portrayed Pratt as a seducer, she lauded him as an apostle of light. Where they pictured Hector McLean as an aggrieved husband, she condemned him as a drunken brute. Where they described her as a fallen woman, she insisted on her honesty and virtue. "I am free to declare, before angels and men, that Parley P. Pratt was innocent of the charges made against him."[66]

By August 1, Eleanor was back in Utah. At some point—perhaps shortly after her return, perhaps later—she completed a sixty-two-page handwritten account that in its intensity and detail reads like a pro-polygamy novel that never got published. In it, she sketched out a personal struggle carried out in a world of duplicity and danger. At one point, she described "officers, merchants, & clergymen" pushing into the room where she was being held awaiting trial. "The gentlemen apologized for crowding to see me, by saying they had never seen a Lady from Utah . . . I told them I was aware a living Mormon woman who had been so fortunate as to escape from Salt Lake City was a great curiosity, but they must not take me as a fair specimen

---

was married on July 28 and therefore could not have signed as a "Woodruff" before then. *Wilford Woodruff's Journal*, 5: 70, July 28, 1857.

[62] Ibid., 5: 61.

[63] "Obituary," *New York Herald*, May 27, 1857, 4; "Another Startling Tragedy," *New York Herald*, May 28, 1857, 8. Reports of the story appeared in many newspapers, including the *Daily Chronicle & Sentinel* (Augusta, Ga.), May 29, 1857; *Frank Leslie's Illustrated Newspaper* (New York), June 6, 1857, 3; and the *Daily Evening Bulletin* (San Francisco), July 1, 1857, col. A. The most detailed secondary account is Steven Pratt, "Eleanor McLean and the Murder of Parley P. Pratt," *BYU Studies* 15 (Winter 1975): 1–27. I also thank Patrick G. Mason for allowing me to read his unpublished paper "Honor, the Unwritten Law, and Extralegal Violence: Contextualizing Parley Pratt's Murder" (given at the Mormon History Association Conference, Springfield, Ill., May 21–24, 2009), and Terryl Givens and Matthew Grow for sharing a chapter from *Parley P. Pratt: The Paul of Mormonism* (forthcoming from Oxford University Press).

[64] San Francisco *Daily Evening Bulletin*, July 1, 1857, col A.

[65] *Fort Smith Herald*, May 16, 1857, reprinted in the *New York Herald*, May 28, 1857, 8, col. E.

[66] *New York Herald*, June 9, 1857, 2, col. A.

for they had so nearly killed me that I could not be like myself."[67] Her sarcasm betrayed both her anger and her awareness of the self-righteousness of those who claimed to be protecting Latter-day Saint women by assaulting their choices.

To the judge who asked if Pratt had lured her away from her family, she responded that long before she heard of Mormonism, McLean had driven "happiness from our home by imbibing that spirit that comes in bottles . . . Who but a wife knows bedroom scenes. It is true if I had gone for my neighbours and brought them to see him lying with his head hanging nearly off the bed, one coat sleeve off, and the other on, one boot off and the other on, and the vomit over his boots and all richly perfumed with old bourbon, (or some other well known beverage that adorns the shelves of the fashionable saloon) then I might have hundreds of witnesses to what I now state." But she was ever a faithful wife, keeping her husband's failings to herself, cleaning up after him, and providing clean clothing and a warm breakfast before he left for the day. And if he chose to preach a temperance sermon to his fellow lodge members at night, no one would know his secret.[68] When challenged with the assertion that polygamy was unjust by giving one man sixty wives and leaving fifty-nine others without, she had a quick response: What virtuous woman would not prefer one-sixtieth of a man like Pratt to all of a husband like McLean?[69]

Eleanor did not contribute to the quilt, but Kezia Pratt, the sister wife who was closest to her, contributed one of the two American eagles on the quilt. Kezia cut her dignified bird from pre-printed fabric, then stitched it onto a plain background with hundreds of invisible stitches. The thirteen stars and the motto *e pluribus unum* proclaim her allegiance to the United States, even though she had been born in England. The print she used was probably a decade or two older than the quilt, suggesting that it had been saved for years in someone's scrap bag for just such an important project.[70] Aura Annette Cummings, who made the second eagle, used plain bright cottons to construct a jaunty bird with flamboyant striped legs. Designs like these, based on the spread eagle in the Great Seal of the United States, were common in American folk art from the 1830s to the end of the century.[71] For Latter-day Saints, however, eagles had complex meanings. As early as 1839, a Mormon poet described the country's treatment of Mormons as a "foul stain on the Eagle's crest."

[67] Eleanor J. McComb [McLean Pratt], Account of the Death of Parley P. Pratt, ca. 1857, MS 525, LDS Church History Library and Archives, Salt Lake City, Utah, 7–9.

[68] Ibid., 12–15.

[69] Ibid., 17, 18.

[70] Born in Chestershire, England, in 1812, she was baptized by Parley P. Pratt in 1842, then married him shortly after arriving in Salt Lake City. The fabric she used, which came in different colorways, may have been manufactured in England for the American market. Linda Eaton, *Quilts in a Material World: Selections from the Winterthur Collection* (New York, 2007), 160, 161; and e-mail communication from Linda Eaton, July 23, 2009. On other uses of the American eagle, see Eaton, *Quilts in a Material World*, 93, 109; on politics in quilts, see chap. 6. For sales of artifacts made from the same fabric, see "Garth's Auction" in the database of past auction prices at http://www.prices4antiques.com/; and "Auction Fall 2006" at http://www.cowanauctions.com/past_sales_view_item.asp?itemid=36136 (accessed July 18, 2009).

[71] Nielson, *The Salt Lake City 14th Ward Album Quilt*, 95–97. On eagle designs, see Celia Y. Oliver, *55 Famous Quilts from the Shelburne Museum in Full Color* (New York, 1990), 46; Amelia Peck, *American Quilts and Coverlets in the Metropolitan Museum of Art* (New York, 1990), 48–49; Pat Ferrero, Elaine Hedges, and Julie Silber, *Hearts and Hands: The Influence of Quilts on American Society* (San Francisco, 1987), 20. See also variants in the eagle motif from the 1830s to the present by searching the Quilt Index, http://www.quiltindex.org/.

FIGURE 8: Kezia Pratt, detail, Fourteenth Ward Album Quilt.

Others insisted that Latter-day Saints were the true custodians of liberty, and that with them the American eagle had "fled to the mountains."[72] No piece of needlework constructed in Utah in 1857 could have avoided that meaning.

On August 16, a day Woodruff considered "one of the most important days that the Church & kingdom of God has seen in this dispensation," Brigham Young addressed the assembled saints, telling them that the "United States had turned mob & were breaking the Constitution of the United States & we would now have to go forth & defend it & also the kingdom of God." He asked if they were willing to give up all they had accomplished in the past ten years, lay waste to their own homes and farms, and flee into the mountains. In Woodruff's words, "The shout of Yes rent the air of the assembled thousands."[73] One female member of the congregation wrote

[72] "Oh Liberty! O Sound Once Delightful," in Eliza R. Snow, *The Complete Poetry*, ed. Jill Mulvay Derr and Karen Lynn Davidson (Provo, 2009), 85; *Deseret News*, August 3, 1850, 3, 5. Snow used the same image again in "The Fourth of July 1861" and "National Anthem, for the Opening of the Theater in Great Salt Lake City," in *The Complete Poetry*, 674, 631.
[73] *Wilford Woodruff's Journal*, 5: 69, 74, 75–80.

FIGURE 9: A. A. Cummings, detail, Fourteenth Ward Album Quilt.

her fiancé in California, "I have never saw such unity in all my life."[74] Unity was also a theme for the quilters. "United we Stand Divided We Fall," Elizabeth Johnson wrote on her square. "United we Stand City of Brigham," Hannah Morley wrote, making clear which leader she was prepared to follow.

On August 30, Apostle John Taylor gave a powerful sermon on the relationship of the Latter-day Saints to the American tradition of natural rights. The first part of his narrative could have come from any Fourth of July oration in the country, but he moved on to recount the innocence of the Latter-day Saints in their current struggle. "We have turned this desert into a flourishing field, and the desert has blossomed as the rose, and God has blessed our labours. And whom have we interfered with? Have we gone over to the States and interfered with them?" Yet just as monarchs had abused the rights of their subjects and Americans had cheated and oppressed their Indian neighbors, government officials were now denying Mormons their rights.

[74] Harriet Ann Thatcher to William B. Preston, August 5, 1857; MacKinnon, *At Sword's Point*, 236, 237. Either the letter is misdated or there were several meetings at which Young asked the congregation whether they would support him in abandoning their homes.

FIGURE 10: Leonora Taylor, detail, Fourteenth Ward Album Quilt.

"What are we going to do, then?" he asked. "We are going to establish the kingdom of God upon the earth."[75] In the square she contributed to the quilt, Taylor's wife Leonora made the same point more succinctly. She built the first five letters of her motto from eighty-nine pieces of cloth, the smallest only one-quarter inch square, then finished the sentence in crewel embroidery: "In God Is Our Trust."[76]

Through the month of September, someone in the Fourteenth Ward Female Relief Society must have been busy stitching all the squares together with bright blue sashing. By the end of the month, it was ready for display. Then on September 29, shocking news arrived from the southern part of the territory. Wilford Woodruff reported that John D. Lee had come into the city with "an awful tale of Blood." Over

[75] John Taylor, "The Rights of Mormonism . . . Delivered in the Bowery, Great Salt Lake City, August 30, 1857," *Journal of Discourses* 5 (1858): 182–192.
[76] Nielson, *The Salt Lake City 14th Ward Album Quilt*, 33.

a hundred California emigrants had been slaughtered at Mountain Meadows. Only a few very young children had survived. Lee blamed the slaughter on the Paiutes, who were supposedly enraged by the immigrants' having poisoned a spring and fed them tainted beef. But he betrayed his own feelings when he connected the immigrants with the persecution of the Saints. Some of them "belonged to the mob in Missouri & Illinois," he claimed. He went so far as to say that "He did not think their was a drop of innocent Blood in their Camp for he had too [two] of their Children in his house & he Could not get but one to kneel down in prayer time & the other would laugh at her for doing it & they would sware like pirates." Years later, Lee would hang for his role in the massacre, but at this point, people in Salt Lake apparently believed him. To the quilters, it must have seemed a terrifying sequel to their own work in making clothing for the Paiutes. For his part, Woodruff believed that the slaughter was the beginning of the terrible struggle predicted in the Book of Revelations before the second coming of Christ. "The scene of Blood has Commenced & Joseph said we should see so much of it that it would make our hearts sick."[77]

The next day he went to the Agricultural Fair to judge the fruits and flowers. Although his diary does not mention it, the newspaper tells us that the Fourteenth Ward album quilt won a first prize "for design."[78]

THE FEDERAL ARMY did not make it to Utah that fall, having been stopped by snow and the harassment of Utah troops, but in the spring the inhabitants of Salt Lake City did leave their homes, just as Brigham Young had asked, filling them with straw and leaving behind someone to ignite them should the army attempt to touch their property. In one of the strangest occupations in history, the federal troops marched straight through the silent city and camped in another part of the valley. Within a few weeks, the citizens returned to take up their lives and their long struggle with the U.S. government over whose God, whose economy, whose community, whose families mattered. Although the Relief Society once again disbanded, the quilt survived.

The Fourteenth Ward quilt is an American album. It is American not only because it was made in a territory of the United States from materials and patterns common in other parts of the country, nor because it was displayed at an agricultural fair like those in other states, but because it portrays aspirations and contradictions embedded in the history of the American republic. The quilters stitched mottoes so familiar as to be virtually invisible: In God We Trust. By Industry We Thrive. United We Stand. The Tree Is Known by Its Fruit. But through their lives, they exemplified the fraught meanings of those words. Like other Americans, Latter-day Saints believed that righteous families were the bulwark of the nation. That their homes and families were under attack only reinforced their sense of mission.

The Fourteenth Ward quilt is American in its melding of piety and gentility, domesticity and patriotism. It is also American in its portrayal of a world without

[77] *Wilford Woodruff's Journal*, 5: 102–103, September 29, 1857.
[78] *Deseret News*, October 21, 1857, 8.

Indians, an oasis of potted plants and beehives in the midst of an American desert. Like other Americans, Latter-day Saints appropriated Indian land, established Indian missions, adopted Indian children, enlisted Indian men in their own conflicts with their enemies, and forgot Indians when they could. The quilt is American as well in its origins in a female voluntary society that in supporting the dominant values of its own community found itself at odds both with its male leaders and with a larger American public. Latter-day Saint women supported their church, sustained the local economy, gave generously of their time and talents for the public good, and sometimes found themselves without voice or power either within the United States or in their own towns and territory.

But they used the resources that they had. In 1861, Agnes Hoagland succeeded in divorcing her husband. The next year, at the age of forty-one, she married a twenty-four-year-old German immigrant named Wilhelm Schwartz, and gave birth to three more children. She did not leave Utah or her church.[79] Her story is unusual, but not unique. Eight of the fifty-nine married quilters (14 percent), including Agnes's sister wife Ester Ann, were eventually divorced or separated from their husbands.[80] In this too they were American.

The quilters were American in another way as well. Like generations of the downtrodden before them, they used their own history of oppression to claim their rights as Americans. In 1870, Phebe Woodruff and other members of a newly constituted Female Relief Society participated in an Indignation Meeting to protest a renewed federal assault on plural marriage. In the process, they proved themselves "strong-minded women" by asking for and receiving the vote from the Territorial Legislature. As Willmirth East, one of their fellow quilters, explained, she had always wanted "a voice in the politics of the nation."[81]

[79] Nielson, *The Salt Lake City 14th Ward Album Quilt*, 188.

[80] The women were Ann Carrigan (Nielson, *The Salt Lake City 14th Ward Album Quilt*, 89), Mary Emma Hill (ibid., 104–105), Agnes Hoagland (ibid., 187–189), E. A. Hoagland (ibid., 193), Elizabeth Horne (ibid., 115), Matilda Rhoads (ibid., 163), Josephine Richards (ibid., 60), and Hannah Winder (ibid., 143–144). The Utah Gravestones website has a photograph of a gravestone marked Esther A. Hoagland, Dec. 5, 1826–Sept. 19, 1910, http://www.utahgravestones.org/view.php?id=14275 (accessed August 3, 2009).

[81] Lola Van Wagenen, *Sister-Wives and Suffragists: Polygamy and the Politics of Woman Suffrage, 1870–1896* (Provo, 2003), 7.

Laurel Thatcher Ulrich served as President of the American Historical Association in 2009. She is 300th Anniversary University Professor at Harvard University and formerly Professor of History at the University of New Hampshire. The author of many books and articles on early American history, women's history, and material culture, she is currently writing a book on nineteenth-century Mormon diaries.

It is widely assumed that recognition of "the Holocaust," by both historians and the public, was very late in coming—that it was only in the early 1960s, and especially in the wake of the Eichmann trial in 1961, that the mass killings we now call the Holocaust became a subject of historical consideration and public awareness. Since then, of course, the Holocaust has not lacked for treatment. It might even be said that in our day, the attempted annihilation of European Jewry at the hands of the German Third Reich and its partisans suffers from a surfeit of attention, especially in the realm of popular culture and the media. In this *AHR* Forum, consisting of three articles plus a comment, we turn to the prehistory of what is now commonly known as "the Holocaust," indeed to the period before the term itself was invented. We focus on how the Holocaust was "represented" in three different media: photographs, monuments, and film. Interestingly, all three of the articles demonstrate that these representations were not a delayed reaction to the Jewish genocide; they emerged soon afterward, and even as the killings were taking place, thus suggesting that we should alter our assessment of the historicity of "Holocaust consciousness."

In "Picturing Grief: Soviet Holocaust Photography at the Intersection of History and Memory," David Shneer asks why the Soviet Union's experience has been so marginalized in the general history of the Holocaust, and why historians have left the interpretation of war and Holocaust imagery to cultural theorists, art historians, and other non-historians. He traces the history of several photographs of the mass murder of Jews and others in Kerch and southern Russia in 1942, and examines the Soviet press's use of these images from the first days of the war with Nazi Germany. Shneer shows how state authorities fostered multiple overlapping narratives of the war, both within a single newspaper and in wartime newspapers in different languages, each with its own way of making sense of the events. Most importantly, he traces how photographs that were important documents during the war became central images in war and Holocaust memory long after the Allied victory.

In "Holocaust Memorials: The Emergence of a Genre," Harold Marcuse turns to another form of representation, examining the process by which a new memorial genre emerged in the 1950s. Marcuse pays particular attention to the chronology of the construction of memorials and argues that the earliest, although rooted in the tradition of war and funerary monuments, already showed some unique features. Catalyzed by several international competitions in the 1950s, a new commemorative aesthetic emerged, addressed to an international audience, which explicitly evoked multiple meanings, and employed a new repertoire of forms, symbols, and materials specifically designed to represent those meanings. Since the 1960s, most Holocaust memorials have created complex experiential spaces with significant didactic features, ranging from collections of inscriptions to museums and even research institutions, and their forms tend to be abstract and avant-garde. In any case, Marcuse adds to our appreciation that monumental commemoration of the Holocaust began at a very early date, in some cases even during the war itself.

The medium of film is explored by Lawrence Baron in "The First Wave of American 'Holocaust' Films, 1945–1959." He shows that American filmmakers actually introduced the Holocaust into their works soon after World War II in plotlines that idealized the role of the United States in hunting and trying Nazi war criminals, rehabilitating and resettling Displaced Persons, and thwarting neo-Nazi conspiracies. These cinematic depictions adhered to the Motion Picture Production Code's rules for portraying violence, reflected wartime guidelines for exposing the multinational scope of the Third Reich's ruthless policies, and stressed the ecumenical lessons of succumbing to any form of prejudice. Only in later films, such as *Me and the Colonel*, *The Young Lions*, and *The Diary of Anne Frank*, did Jewish characters emerge as central, which represented, he argues, an incremental rather than sudden shift in American consciousness of antisemitic attitudes in general and the genocidal ideology that motivated the Final Solution.

Finally, Sarah Farmer's comment, "Going Visual: Holocaust Representation and Historical Method," begins by noting what the three articles abundantly document: that "the 'Holocaust' has never not been 'represented.'" She proceeds by assessing the essays on both methodological and interpretive grounds, suggesting some questions the authors fail to pursue and, in the case of Baron's piece, calling into question the appropriateness of the term "Holocaust," which was invented to refer specifically to the annihilation of the Jews, for films that are less pointed in their identification of the victims. Farmer concludes her essay by urging scholars, especially those influenced by the "visual turn," to "explore the relationship between the visual, the spoken word, and the text," a comment that echoes some of the discussion in the *AHR* Conversation on "Historians and the Study of Material Culture" in the December 2009 issue.

AHR Forum
Picturing Grief: Soviet Holocaust Photography at the Intersection of History and Memory

DAVID SHNEER

DESPITE THE EXTENSIVE BOOKSHELF of historical works about World War II and the Holocaust, the scholarly study of war and Holocaust photography has generally been carried out not by historians, but by journalists or cultural theorists. Scholars generally use these "photographs of trauma," to quote Ulrich Baer, to explore the nature and meaning of photography. The late critic Susan Sontag did much to raise awareness of the power of photography, and her 2004 book *Regarding the Pain of Others* reflects in depth on the function that war photography plays (or doesn't play) in politics and national memory.[1]

Historians have rarely touched the field of Holocaust photography. This is a major gap, especially since photography and film were the primary means of representing the war visually to the public worldwide, and because they have become primary means of memorializing the Holocaust. It is also surprising given the deep interest in questions of Holocaust history and memory that historians such as Saul Friedlander, Charles Maier, and Jeffrey Herf have wrestled with since the 1980s. In fact, one could argue that it was the attempt to historicize the Holocaust that forced historians to engage in theoretical questions about history and memory, as a result

Thanks to the following archives for allowing me to work, scan, and photocopy: the Dmitrii Baltermants Archive and the Georgii Zelma Archive, both located in Scarsdale, New York; the Evgenii Khaldei and Arkadii Shaykhet Archives at Fotosoyuz in Moscow; the United States Holocaust Memorial Museum; the Library of Congress; the Yad Vashem Archives; the Russian State Archive of Literature and Art; the Russian State Archive for Political and Social Research; and the State Archive of the Russian Federation. I would like to thank Paul and Teresa Harbaugh, Michael Mattis, Yelena Sitnina, Andrei Baskakov, Valerii Stigneev, Tatiana Baltermants, Anna Khaldei, and Maria Zhotikova. For advice on this particular essay, thanks to Harriet Murav, Oren Stier, Gregg Drinkwater, Vanessa Schwartz, Shannen Hill, Dmitrii Belkin, Stuart Liebman, Joan Neuberger, Alice Nakhimovsky, Amir Weiner, Judy Cohen, Vladimir Sumovsky, Michael Lee, and the anonymous readers. Finally, thanks to the University of Denver, the University of Colorado, the Center for Advanced Holocaust Studies at the United States Holocaust Memorial Museum, the Social Science Research Council, and the National Council for East European and Eurasian Research for supporting my work.

[1] See cultural theorists such as Ulrich Baer, *Spectral Evidence: The Photography of Trauma* (Cambridge, Mass., 2002); Andrea Liss, *Trespassing through Shadows: Memory, Photography, and the Holocaust* (Minneapolis, 1998); Brett Ashley Kaplan, *Unwanted Beauty: Aesthetic Pleasure in Holocaust Representation* (Urbana, Ill., 2006). Journalists and photographers who have written critically about Holocaust photography include Barbie Zelizer, *Remembering to Forget: Holocaust Memory through the Camera's Eye* (Chicago, 2000); and Janina Struk, *Photographing the Holocaust: Interpretations of the Evidence* (London, 2004). See also Susan Sontag, *Regarding the Pain of Others* (New York, 2004).

of which the journal *History & Memory* was launched in the 1980s. In some ways, photographs are historical artifacts that sit at the nexus of history and memory.[2]

If Holocaust photography in general has been well treated by cultural theorists, neither historians, theorists, nor journalists have explored Soviet war photography. Nor have they studied the photographers who took the immensely important pictures that fostered a wartime narrative and historical memory quite different from the history and memory of the Holocaust propagated in the United States, Western Europe, and Israel. Why has there been such a lack of awareness of or interest in the photographs and photographers from the "other ally"? First, public memory of the Holocaust in the West usually centers on the experience of extermination camps such as Auschwitz as understood through the voices of survivors. Only in the past fifteen years has the Holocaust experience in the Soviet Union been widely told, through the voices of Soviet Holocaust survivors, or understood, let alone incorporated into the dominant historical narratives. Because of this, Soviet wartime photographs have not generally been included in the canon of Holocaust imagery that illustrates museums and memorials around the world. Second, Cold War politics made it difficult for those in the West to understand the Soviet Union as one of the primary victims of Nazi atrocities. In the eyes of the West, immediately after the war, the USSR became a perpetrator of crimes against the people of Eastern Europe and elsewhere, and the history of the Soviet, primarily Jewish, experience of genocide during World War II disappeared from the war narrative. In addition, Soviet archives relating to World War II were inaccessible to Western scholars until the fall of the USSR in 1991. Before that time, few scholars in the West had studied the Holocaust in the Soviet Union, or how Soviet citizens, particularly Soviet Jews, related to the event.[3]

[2] Saul Friedlander, *Memory, History, and the Extermination of the Jews of Europe* (Bloomington, Ind., 1993); Charles S. Maier, *The Unmasterable Past: History, Holocaust, and German National Identity* (Cambridge, Mass., 1988); Jeffrey Herf, *Divided Memory: The Nazi Past in the Two Germanys* (Cambridge, Mass., 1999).

[3] Much has been written about Soviet film and photography in the period 1917–1939, in other words, the period in which Soviet visual culture influenced the rest of the world's understanding of visual arts. But very little has been written on Soviet visual culture during World War II. On the earlier period, see Erika Wolf, "Belomorstroi: The Visual Economy of Forced Labor," in Valerie A. Kivelson and Joan Neuberger, eds., *Picturing Russia: Explorations in Visual Culture* (New Haven, Conn., 2008); and Wolf, "*SSSR na stroike*: The Magazine and Its Reader," in Egor Larichev, ed., *USSR in Construction: A Magazine of a New Type* (in Russian) (Moscow, 2006), 11–25; Denise J. Youngblood, *Movies for the Masses: Popular Cinema and Soviet Society in the 1920s* (Cambridge, 1992); Youngblood, *Soviet Cinema in the Silent Era, 1918–1935* (Austin, Tex., 1991); Peter Kenez, *Cinema and Soviet Society: From the Revolution to the Death of Stalin* (London, 2001). On Soviet visual culture during the war, see Richard Stites, ed., *Culture and Entertainment in Wartime Russia* (Bloomington, Ind., 1995); and Denise J. Youngblood, *Russian War Films: On the Cinema Front, 1914–2005* (Lawrence, Kans., 2006). On the history of twentieth-century Russian photography, see Valerii Stigneev, *Vek fotografii: Ocherki istorii otechestvennoi fotografii*, 2nd ed. (Moscow, 2007). Key texts on the Holocaust in the Soviet Union include Zvi Gitelman, ed., *Bitter Legacy: Confronting the Holocaust in the USSR* (Bloomington, Ind., 1997); Il'ia Al'tman, *Zhertvy nenavisti: Kholokost v SSSR, 1941–1945 gg.* (Moscow, 2002); and more recently Frank Grüner, Urs Heftrich, and Heinz-Dietrich Löwe, eds., *"Zerstörer des Schweigens": Formen künstlerischer Erinnerung an die nationalsozialistische Rassen- und Vernichtungspolitik in Osteuropa* (Cologne, 2006). See also Karel C. Berkhoff's important article " 'Total Annihilation of the Jewish Population': The Holocaust in the Soviet Media, 1941–45," *Kritika: Explorations in Russian and Eurasian History* 10, no. 1 (Winter 2009): 61–105, which shows how the Soviet press talked about the Holocaust. As evidence that the Soviet Union is moving to the center of Holocaust research, in 2007 the United States Holocaust Memorial Museum and the Sorbonne sponsored a seminar on the Holocaust in Ukraine, the University of Maryland held a symposium on Holocaust memory in the Soviet Union, and the Association for Jewish Studies spon-

Finally, in contrast to much of the West, where the Holocaust has been widely studied and memorialized since the 1960s, the Holocaust in the Soviet Union became a subject of study only in post-Soviet Russia and other successor states. Ideologically and politically, the Soviet Union did not officially memorialize the Holocaust, meaning that it did not foster a particular memory of the special persecution of the Jews by Nazi Germany and its allies. Historian Amir Weiner has shown that there were very specific political and ideological policy shifts that erased particular Jewish suffering during and shortly after the war. Political scientist Zvi Gitelman has argued that the Soviet Union had a harder time recognizing a specifically Jewish tragedy during the war precisely because Nazi atrocities and mass destruction took place extensively in the Nazi-occupied Soviet Union. The murder of 1.5 to 2 million Jews on Soviet soil could easily be absorbed into the staggering 25 to 30 million Soviet deaths overall. Historian Yehoshua Gilboa has told the story of the Soviet Union's suppression of the Holocaust narrative as part of more general policies of late Stalinist antisemitism, another reason that the Holocaust in the USSR, including the study of its visual representation through photography, has not been at the forefront of the scholarly agenda.[4]

But the Soviet visual record of the war and the Holocaust tells us much about narrative, history, and memory. Because Jews in the USSR were murdered in town after town from the first year of occupation in 1941–1942, Soviet photographers were among the first people in the world to photograph the Nazis' actions from the perspective of the liberator. This also means that Soviet newspapers were the first press outlets to discuss in great detail and to show in very graphic ways Nazi atrocities against Jews *as they were taking place*. Unlike the U.S. press, which tended to put such stories on the inside of the paper, and only rarely at that, the Soviet press gave them extensive first-page coverage as soon as the war began. Only recently have scholars started studying the ways in which Nazi atrocities were represented to the Soviet reading public, or the international Communist readership of Soviet newspapers, as these events were taking place. Studying these early photographs enables us to see how the war was reported visually at the time as news.[5]

---

sored a panel dedicated to Holocaust representation in the Soviet Union. Nearly all theorists who write about liberation photography write about the American liberation photography from Ohrdruf, Buchenwald, and Dachau, and Sontag marks the moment of bearing witness to these photographs as a turning point in her life. On the way in which images have become Holocaust icons, see Oren Stier, "Different Trains: Holocaust Artifacts and the Ideologies of Remembrance," *Holocaust and Genocide Studies* 19, no. 1 (Spring 2006): 81–106.

[4] See Amir Weiner, *Making Sense of War: The Second World War and the Fate of the Bolshevik Revolution* (Princeton, N.J., 2002); Zvi Gitelman, "Politics and the Historiography of the Holocaust in the Soviet Union," in Gitelman, *Bitter Legacy*, 14–42. As for the repression of Jewish culture and discussion of the Holocaust in the postwar period, the suppression of the *Black Book* is the most famous and most concrete example of an emerging Holocaust narrative being suppressed. Assembled by Soviet Jewish journalists Ilya Ehrenburg and Vasilii Grossman, the *Black Book* was a compilation of Holocaust survivors' testimonies and other evidence documenting the Nazi mass murder of Jews on Soviet soil. See Yehoshua A. Gilboa, *The Black Years of Soviet Jewry, 1939–1953*, trans. Yosef Shachter and Dov Ben-Abba (New York, 1971).

[5] Many historians, in fact, date the beginning of the Holocaust to June 1941, when Nazi Germany began its campaign of mass murder in the Soviet Union. But historian Jochen Böhler has shown that the German army was already carrying out major shooting campaigns in Poland in the period 1939–1941, complicating the timeline of the Holocaust. See Böhler, *Auftakt zum Vernichtungskrieg: Die Wehrmacht in Polen 1939* (Frankfurt, 2006). On the *New York Times* coverage of the Holocaust, see Laurel Leff,

In addition to being the first liberation photographs, Soviet war and Holocaust images—taken primarily by Jewish photographers, who made up about 50 percent of the overall Soviet press corps during the war—force us to confront questions of overlapping narratives of the war. What happens when the state gives power to a very visible minority to create the visual record of a nation's war? Although Jews such as Robert Capa, Joe Rosenthal, and Alfred Eisenstaedt were among the most important photographers documenting the war worldwide, the state did not place them in these key positions. Moreover, photographers such as Capa, Rosenthal, and Eisenstaedt were not bearing witness to the unfolding of Nazi atrocities as their Soviet Jewish counterparts were doing. Capa, for example, did not discover his entire family shot and thrown into a mineshaft as the twenty-seven-year-old Soviet Jewish photographer Evgenii Khaldei did when he photographed liberated Donetsk (then called Stalino) in eastern Ukraine in 1943. How did Soviet Jewish photographers navigate the very dicey terrain of overlapping narratives—their personal tragedies of bearing witness to their murdered families and friends, the particular perspective of Jewish suffering, and the general story of the Nazi war against the Soviet Union?[6]

Wartime narratives are always multiple, as much recent scholarship has shown. The story and meaning of the war in the United States and England varied greatly depending on whether one was African American, Latino, Japanese, Jewish, or Anglo, or whether one was a woman. But the state-sponsored Soviet wartime press created explicit multiple narratives of the war by publishing newspapers in Russian (the lingua franca of the Soviet Union) as well as in the national languages of individual Soviet ethnic groups, including Yiddish, the official state language of Soviet Jewry. The Russian- and Yiddish-language Soviet press created different frameworks through which to understand Nazi atrocities. In the Russian-language press, photo and print journalists, as well as their editors, many of whom were also Jewish, generally framed the Nazis' actions as crimes against the Soviet people. Soviet Yiddish newspapers made explicit the Jewishness of the Nazi war against the USSR. Soviet Jewish photographers operated at the intersection of multiple narratives, seeing themselves as Soviet and Jewish simultaneously, and they and their images thus helped incorporate the story of the Holocaust on Soviet soil into the evolving narrative of the Nazi war against the Soviet Union.[7]

Buried by the Times: The Holocaust and America's Most Important Newspaper (New York, 2005). See also Henry L. Feingold, *Bearing Witness: How America and Its Jews Responded to the Holocaust* (Syracuse, N.Y., 1995). On American and other national responses to the Holocaust more generally, see David S. Wyman and Charles H. Rosenzveig, eds., *The World Reacts to the Holocaust* (Baltimore, 1996); and Hasia R. Diner, *We Remember with Reverence and Love: American Jews and the Myth of Silence after the Holocaust, 1945–1962* (New York, 2009).

[6] The story of Khaldei's discovery of his family's murder in the city of Donetsk was recounted to me by his daughter Anna. Interview with Anna Khaldei, September 24, 2007.

[7] On overlapping narratives in the wartime American press, see, for example, Ronald Takaki, *Double Victory: A Multicultural History of America in World War II* (Boston, 2000); Maggie Rivas-Rodriguez, ed., *Mexican Americans and World War II* (Austin, Tex., 2005); Carina A. del Rosario, Ken Mochizuki, and Dean Wong, eds., *A Different Battle: Stories of Asian Pacific American Veterans* (Seattle, 2000). On British national identity, citizenship, and belonging during the war, see Sonya O. Rose, *Which People's War? National Identity and Citizenship in Britain, 1939–1945* (Oxford, 2003). Debates about overlapping American war narratives became part of the national conversation in 2007 over the launching of Ken Burns's documentary on World War II, *The War*, which some Latino organizations thought downplayed Latino contributions to the American war effort. On how Yiddish functioned as an official marker of Soviet

Finally, by studying the history of specific images, we can better understand how news photographs meant to document events at the time were later transformed into both objects of art and emblems of memory. Photography is not simply illustration of historical narrative. We must examine how captions used in wartime photojournalism became titles of exhibition photographs, how the placement and context of an image changed over time, and, most important, how the actual image changed as its role changed from documenting a moment in time to fostering reflection of the past. By doing this, we can trace how overlapping narratives of the war that informed one another at the time became competing memories of the past.

THE GERMAN ARMY INVADED the Soviet Union on June 22, 1941, breaking the Nazi-Soviet Non-Aggression Pact that had shaped Soviet policy for the previous two years. In both print and photojournalism, the Soviet press made Nazi atrocities a primary means of representing the German war against the USSR to Soviet readers. From the first days of the war, the Main Political Administration of the Red Army, which oversaw the military press during the war, sent regular memoranda reminding newspaper and magazine editors of the need to publish both stories and photographs of Nazi atrocities. This material would function as visual evidence of Nazi crimes and as propaganda to rile up the anger of the population. *Ogonek*, the Soviet Union's leading illustrated magazine, published its first atrocity photo on June 25, 1941, the first edition following the invasion. According to the magazine, the photograph was taken by a German soldier who had carried a camera with him on the front lines to document his work for family and friends back home. Dead German soldiers' cameras were left on their bodies to be picked up by Soviet troops and then delivered to the relevant Soviet authorities. Since this particular photograph was published so quickly after the German invasion, and therefore was not likely picked up by Soviet troops, it is clear that the Main Political Administration was already gathering evidence of Nazi atrocities from others who had access to these so-called perpetrator photographs before war broke out. Most major Soviet press outlets published photographs such as "Punishment in Poland," usually called "trophy photos," depicting not only the "bestiality" of the enemy, but also the very fact that these soldiers enjoyed documenting their crimes. In this particular photograph, on the right, the Nazi

Jewish culture, see David Shneer, *Yiddish and the Creation of Soviet Jewish Culture, 1918–1930* (New York, 2004). According to N. P. Popov and N. A. Gorokhov, about 20 percent of the editors of military newspapers during the war were Jewish, including David Ortenberg, who edited *Red Star* (*Krasnaia zvezda*), the most important military newspaper in the Soviet Union, through July 1943. This statistic does not include party and state newspapers such as *Pravda* and *Izvestiia*, which also had many Jews sitting on their editorial boards. See Popov and Gorokhov, *Sovetskaia voennaia pechat' v gody velikoi otechestvennoi voiny, 1941–1945* (Moscow, 1981), 263–264. For a broader discussion of the presence of Jews in the Soviet intelligentsia, see Yuri Slezkine, *The Jewish Century* (Princeton, N.J., 2004). Zvi Gitelman, "Internationalism, Patriotism, and Disillusion: Soviet Jewish Veterans Remember World War II and the Holocaust," in United States Holocaust Memorial Museum, Center for Advanced Holocaust Studies, *Holocaust in the Soviet Union: Symposium Presentations* (Washington, D.C., 2005), 95–126. This was the same rationale that the publisher of the *New York Times*, Arthur Sulzberger, used to explain why stories of the Holocaust were always inside the paper and why Jewish particularity was downplayed. Jews were human beings, and atrocities committed against Jews were a human tragedy, not just a Jewish tragedy. See Leff, *Buried by the Times*.

FIGURE 1: "Punishment in Poland: Those sentenced are forced to dig their own graves." *Ogonek*, June 25, 1941.

soldier-photographer has captured two Jewish victims digging the grave for the pile of corpses in the center of the frame.[8] (See Figure 1.) Throughout 1941, nearly all of the photographs of Nazi atrocities that appeared in the Soviet press were taken by German soldiers themselves.

Soviet photographers did not witness scenes of Nazi destruction with their own eyes until late 1941, when the Red Army began re-conquering cities near Moscow that had been under Nazi occupation for a brief time. Most of what these image-makers saw were gruesome scenes of corpses in the streets, public hangings, looting, and burning. These photographs had everything to do with the Nazis' violent occupation politics in the Soviet Union, but little to do with the Nazi war against the

[8] On the unfolding of the Holocaust in print journalism, see Ilya Altman and Claudio Ingerflom, "Le Kremlin et L'Holocauste, 1933–2001," in Vassili Petrenko, *Avant et après Auschwitz*, as cited in Harvey Asher, "The Soviet Union, the Holocaust and Auschwitz," *Kritika: Explorations in Russian and Eurasian History* 4, no. 4 (2003): 886–912. This image was published in *Ogonek*, no. 18 (June 25, 1941). On orders to editors about Nazi atrocities, see, for example, *Direktiva Glavpu RKKA voennym sovetam i nachal'nikam politicheskikh upravlenii frontov o prisylke v Glavpu RKKA fotodokumentov*, August 1, 1941, Tsentral'nyi arkhiv Ministerstva oborony (TsAMO), f. 32, op. 920265, d. 3, l. 157, as printed in V. A. Zolotarev, ed., *Velikaia Otechestvennaia* (Moscow, 1996), 55.

Jews. No Soviet photographer had witnessed the mass murders of Jews that were going on throughout the occupied Soviet Union in 1941.[9]

The first photographs taken of such scenes by liberators were from the city of Kerch, located on a small peninsula that juts into the Sea of Azov in southern Russia. The Germans had occupied the city in mid-November 1941, but held it for only six weeks. The Gestapo, the German State Secret Police, registered 7,500 Jews who were in Kerch after the arrival of German forces (some had evacuated in advance of German occupation); in the first week of December, they were ordered to Sennaia Square, from which they were deported to an anti-tank ditch in Bagerov, on the outskirts of town, and shot. On December 31, the city was one of the first places with a significant prewar Jewish population to be liberated from Nazi occupation, which meant that it was one of the first places where Soviet soldiers, journalists, and photographers saw what we now call the Holocaust with their own eyes.[10]

The first Kerch photographs, by Mark Redkin, appeared in *Ogonek* on February 4, 1942. A landscape photograph shows bodies strewn along an anti-tank ditch at the center of the composition. Two Soviet soldiers standing on the right investigate the scene as the white of the sky and the white of the snow in the ditch blend together at top left. The photo beneath the landscape image shows a close-up of the dead, in this case a mother surrounded by children. This was the first time that Soviet readers had the chance to see images taken by a Soviet photographer bearing witness to the mass murder of thousands that had to date been visually documented only by the Germans' own cameras.

Redkin, a Soviet Jewish photographer, worked for the Telegraph Agency of the Soviet Union (TASS), the Soviet wire service. The caption beneath the photographs suggests how he and the *Ogonek* editors placed them into an evolving narrative of

[9] The Baltermants Archive in Scarsdale holds many of Baltermants's photographs from November and December 1941 of liberated villages in the Moscow region that had been under Nazi occupation. See the section of the archive labeled "War Photography, 1941." In addition, the Semyon Fridlyand Archive at the University of Denver, which houses the images of a special war correspondent for *Ogonek*, shows similar photographs from late 1941. The two biggest stories about early Nazi atrocities broke after the liberation of Volokolamsk, eighty miles northwest of Moscow, and Rostov, in southern Russia. About the Germans' eight-day occupation of Rostov, journalists and photographers wrote of mass shootings on the streets. See, for example, "Ne zabudem, ne prostim: Fotodokumenty o krovavykh zverstvakh fashistskikh merzavtsev v Rostove-na-donu," *Krasnaia zvezda*, December 11, 1941. The newspaper published stills from a newsreel by the filmmaker G. Popov. About Volokolamsk, journalists and photographers wrote about the gruesome public hangings of eight presumed partisans, whose bodies were left dangling in the town square for days in order to terrorize the population. All Soviet press outlets ran stories on Volokolamsk and how it revealed the depravity of the enemy.

[10] Andrej Angrick's work on Einsatzgruppen D, which carried out the murders in Kerch, is based on German archives and trial testimony taken in the 1960s. His report says that only 2,500 Jews were murdered in that first week of December. The remainder were murdered in the second occupation of the city in June 1942. See Angrick, *Besatzungspolitik und Massenmord: Die Einsatzgruppe D in der südlichen Sowjetunion, 1941–1943* (Hamburg, 2003). Soviet sources, based on survivor testimony, put the number at 7,000 to 7,500. See Leonid Melkov, *Kerch': Povest'-khronika v dokumentakh, vospominaniiakh i pismakh uchastnikov geroicheskoi zashchity i osvobozhdeniia goroda v 1941–1944 godakh* (Moscow, 1981). I base my claim about Jewish demographics and liberation on the dates the Red Army liberated certain cities, comparing them with the Jewish populations of various regions. The cities to be liberated before Kerch were primarily in the Moscow region (Klin and Volokolamsk) and did not have large Jewish populations, as well as Rostov, which was occupied for too short a time for mass executions. For a list with dates of cities liberated by the Red Army, see http://militera.lib.ru. For the demographics of prewar Soviet Jewry, see Mordechai Altshuler, *Soviet Jewry on the Eve of the Holocaust: A Social and Demographic Profile* (Jerusalem, 1998).

the war: "Hitler ordered his bandits to annihilate the peaceful Soviet population. Wherever the Germans found themselves, they murdered thousands of women and children. The bodies of the murdered were dumped in a pit (see top photograph). Among the murdered were many women and children (see bottom photograph). The Hitlerite thugs showed no one any mercy." The caption obscures the perpetrators of the crimes. In one sentence they are followers of Hitler; in another, Germans. And no mention is made of the fact that most of the dead women and children so grotesquely splashed across the pages of the magazine were Jewish women and children.[11]

One month later, *Ogonek* followed up its earlier Kerch images with a two-page layout of photographs by Dmitrii Baltermants and Israel Ozerskii and an article by the journalist I. Antselovich, all three of whom were Jewish. The headline reads: "These photographs were taken after the German occupiers drove [the people] out to this place. 7,500 residents, from the very elderly to breastfeeding babies, were shot from just a single city. They were killed in cold blood in a premeditated fashion. They were killed indiscriminately—Russians and Tatars, Ukrainians and Jews. The Hitlerites have also murdered the Soviet population indiscriminately in many other cities, villages, and in the countryside." (See Figure 2.) It is clear from the caption that by the 1940s, Soviet citizens, including victims of Nazi atrocities, were being divided first and foremost by ethnicity, rather than class as one might expect in a socialist narrative universe. And Jews were included among the Soviet ethnicities. But the captions of the Redkin and Baltermants photographs obscure the fact that the Nazis targeted Jews.

Retrospectively, Baltermants claimed to have understood that the German occupiers did not kill Kerch residents "indiscriminately," as the caption states, but singled out Jews and other politically suspect people. In an interview, he recounted how he took the Kerch photographs: "In fall 1941 the Germans drove 7,000 residents—partisans, Communists, and Jews—to the trench. They drove out whole families—women, the elderly, children. They drove all of them to an anti-tank ditch and shot them." The *Ogonek* editor back in Moscow who captioned the picture only hints at the Jewishness of the story. Antselovich, too, insinuates that the Nazis were not killing indiscriminately when he writes that the first to be shot, on orders from Berlin, were "Soviet citizens of one particular nationality." Some readers, Jews among them, would have understood which nationality the writer was alluding to; others would not have picked up on the reference. According to Gitelman's study of 221 Soviet Jewish war veterans, "Most said they knew about [atrocities against Jews] from newspapers and lectures at the front." However, making the photograph too much about specifically Jewish suffering as opposed to national Soviet suffering ran the risk that general readers would not see themselves in it.[12]

[11] *Ogonek*, February 4, 1942, 4. For biographical information about Mark Redkin, see http://www.sem40.ru, a website that commissions articles about famous Russian Jewish cultural figures. The original photograph can be found in the Yad Vashem Archives, photograph 4331_16. According to one survivor of the Kerch massacres, Jews were rounded up over the course of two weeks and trucked out to the Bagerov trench to be shot. Sinti/Roma (Gypsies) were then rounded up and brought to the same site to be shot. See "Testimony of Neysha Kemilev," Yad Vashem Archives, Group M33, File 88, 102. Angrick suggests that the roundup and mass murder of the city's remaining Jewish population took place over three days, December 3–5, 1941. See Angrick, *Besatzungspolitik und Massenmord*, 356.

[12] Gitelman, "Internationalism, Patriotism, and Disillusion," 116–117. On the story of Baltermants's

FIGURE 2: "Hitlerite Atrocities in Kerch." *Ogonek*, March 2, 1942.

In his 1943 book *Russia at War*, the Soviet Jewish journalist Ilya Ehrenburg, one of the best-known wartime Soviet writers, described the German atrocities at Kerch: "They came to Russia drunk with the blood of Poles, Frenchmen and Serbs, with the blood of old people, girls and infants in arms. And death came with them to our country. I don't mean the death of soldiers, for no war is without its victims. I refer to the gallows from which the bodies of Russian girls are dangling, and the terrible pit near Kerch in which the children of Russians, Tatars and Jews are buried . . . The memory of what we have experienced cannot be wiped out." In 1943, long before the discovery of Auschwitz and other concentration or extermination camps, Kerch symbolized the depths of Nazi atrocities against Russia.[13]

The images in the top left suggest how photographers and editors began telling the story of the Holocaust as it was unfolding. (See Figure 3.) The caption reads: "Residents of Kerch Search for Their Relatives. In the photo: V. S. Tereshchenko digs under bodies for her husband. On the right: the body of 67-year-old I. Kh. Kogan." By placing this photograph alongside one of a corpse named Kogan—one

---

photographs of Kerch, see "Interview with Dmitrii Baltermants," in V. A. Nikitin, *Rasskazy o fotografakh i fotografiiakh* (Leningrad, 1991), 153, 175–176. See also Lev Borodulin, "Lev Borodulin o Dmitrii Baltermantse," http://sem40.ru. In addition to consulting the Baltermants Archive, I interviewed Baltermants's daughter Tatiana on two occasions.

[13] Ilya Ehrenburg, *Russia at War* (London, 1943), 130–131. On Ehrenburg, see Joshua Rubenstein, *Tangled Loyalties: The Life and Times of Ilya Ehrenburg* (Montgomery, Ala., 1999).

FIGURE 3: Dmitrii Baltermants, variant of "Residents of Kerch Search for Their Relatives. In the photo: V. S. Tereshchenko digs under bodies for her husband." *Ogonek*, March 2, 1942. Courtesy of Michael Mattis.

of the mourner, the other of the one she is presumably mourning—the editors suggest that the very Jewish-sounding Kogan (Russian for Cohen) is, in fact, the husband that the very Ukrainian-sounding Tereshchenko was searching for. Although this multiethnic marriage reflected the Soviets' idealized notion that their diverse empire was a happy, integrated "brotherhood of nations," the fact could not have been lost on the reader that after the Nazis left town, the Ukrainian Tereshchenko was alive, and the Jewish Kogan was dead. As with the use of the phrase "Soviet citizens of a particular nationality" in the article text, the Jewishness of the war was implied by the photo editor's placement of the photographs. Thus we see how overlapping narratives began appearing in the Russian-language press, through both text and images, from the earliest discovery of the Holocaust.

One particular image in the series would have a long publication history—the image on the left page, in the lower right-hand corner—which is captioned here "Kerch resident P. I. Ivanova found her husband, who was tortured by the fascist executioners." In this picture, there is no suggestion that Ivanova's husband was Jewish, although he most likely was. The editors chose to publish the fourth image in the strip of negatives, with Ivanova crying and blowing her nose. Seeing the full series of Baltermants's photographs shows how the photographer worked to capture the best image of her grief. (See Figure 4.)

Only a few of Baltermants's Kerch photographs were published in newspapers or magazines at the time. But his images circulated in other ways during the war. Immediately after the city's liberation, Kerch administrators put up posters produced by TASS, known as TASS Windows, in several places around the city, giving visually graphic evidence of what the Nazis had done—as if it was not obvious to the

FIGURE 4: Dmitrii Baltermants, four versions of P. I. Ivanova. The *Ogonek* editors chose to publish the last one. Courtesy of Michael Mattis.

city's residents, who had lived through six weeks of Nazi terror. The posters were intended to shock viewers and encourage them to fight harder to prevent the German army from re-conquering the city, which it would unfortunately do several months later. One poster, titled "Death to the German Occupiers," displayed a montage of twenty Baltermants images taken at the killing fields on the outskirts of town. (See Figure 5.) "7,000 murdered, and they didn't spare old people, women, or children," the banner proclaimed to a traumatized city. This new number, 7,000, would become the accepted number of dead at Kerch, even though the first account had put the number at 7,500.[14]

Photographs of Nazi atrocities were published throughout the war, but after the Soviet victory at Stalingrad in February 1943, their frequency diminished, and those that did appear tended to fall into two categories—images used in Soviet war crimes trials, which began in 1943, and photographs taken at the liberation of concentration camps, especially at Majdanek in July 1944. By May 9, 1945, the day the war officially ended for the Soviet Union, there was little discussion of the Nazis' crimes, since the former "Hitlerites" and "bestial Germans" were now "liberated German people," who would eventually be rehabilitated as the new East Germany. When there was mention of these atrocities in war crimes trials at places such as Krasnodar or Kharkov in 1943 or in connection with the postwar Nuremburg Trials, the Soviet press presented the victims of the crimes as peaceful Soviet citizens or as humanity in general. Jews were included in both of these rubrics, of course, but only implicitly.[15]

---

[14] Rossiiskii gosudarstvennyi arkhiv kino-fotodokumentov (RGAKFD), oborona Kercha 0-276238. TASS Windows was a highly successful propaganda operation that put out posters demonizing the enemy. It used some of the most recognizable figures in the world of illustration, cartoons, and drawing.

[15] *The People's Verdict: A Full Report of the Proceedings at the Krasnodar and Kharkov German Atrocity Trials* (London, 1943).

FIGURE 5: Evgenii Khaldei, "Residents of Kerch Read TASS Windows Poster." USHMM Archives. Courtesy of Anna Khaldei and Agency Fotosoyuz, Moscow. The Russian State Archive for Film and Photography mistakenly credits the photo to I. Antselovich, the print journalist who wrote the article accompanying the Kerch photographs.

IN THE YIDDISH-LANGUAGE PRESS, a different but equally Soviet story unfolded during the war. In the 1940s, there were two regularly published Yiddish newspapers in the Soviet Union, a far cry from the dozens that had circulated in the early 1930s, but a reminder that, during the war, Jews were still visibly marked as one of dozens of Soviet ethnicities, each with its own language and culture. One was the *Birobidzhan Star* (*Birobidzhaner shtern*), from the Jewish Autonomous Region in the Soviet Far East. The other was *Unity* (*Eynikayt*), the weekly newspaper of the Jewish Anti-Fascist Committee (JAFC). The JAFC was established in the summer of 1941, along with four other "special interest" committees organized to foster international support for the Soviet war effort. Despite calls from Yiddish writers to reestablish a Yiddish newspaper in Moscow in 1941, it took nearly a year before *Unity* began appearing from Kuibyshev (contemporary Samara), where many government agencies had been evacuated when the German army was on the outskirts of Moscow.[16]

From the first weeks of its publication, in June 1942, *Unity* "judaized" the war for both its domestic and international Yiddish reading audiences. In late June, for

[16] There were also anti-fascist committees for Slavs, women, scientists, and youth. See Joshua Rubenstein and V. P. Naumov, eds., *Stalin's Secret Pogrom: The Postwar Inquisition of the Jewish Anti-Fascist Committee* (New Haven, Conn., 2001), 7. *Unity*'s editor-in-chief was Shakhne Epshteyn, a long-time Yiddish Communist in both the U.S. and the Soviet Union, who had been one of the early editors of the Soviet Yiddish paper *The Truth* (*Emes*), and the editorial board and list of contributing writers was a who's who of Soviet Yiddish culture, including David Bergelson, Perets Markish, and Itsik Fefer. Ilya Ehrenburg also published in *Unity*, although in translation from Russian.

example, Ehrenburg published an article in *Unity* titled "Why Do the Fascists Hate the Jews So Much?" The Russian-language original, published in May in the Soviet army newspaper *Red Star*, was titled simply "About Hatred," and there was no mention of Jews. All of the well-known Soviet Yiddish writers, among them Perets Markish, Itsik Fefer, and David Bergelson, wrote for the newspaper, and it served as the primary outlet for Soviet Yiddish literary creativity during the war. *Unity* published special columns on Jewish war heroes, including Bergelson's 1944 article on the Soviet Jewish general Yankev Kreyzer; it contained notices about Jewish men and women on the front, and frequently included their portraits.[17]

Throughout 1942, the newspaper published graphic photographs of German atrocities against Jews, but unlike the Russian-language press, whose purpose was to create a nationally unifying narrative of the war, *Unity*, whose political job was to build support for the Soviet Union by creating connections among Jews *across* national borders, marked the victims unambiguously as Jews. There were photographs of Jewish burial sites and the Warsaw ghetto, and other images whose captions clearly noted that the people in the pictures were Jews. On December 27, 1942, for the one-year anniversary of the liberation of Kerch, *Unity* republished Redkin's photograph of the dead women and children. Although the caption spoke about the victims in a universal sense, the well-known Soviet Yiddish writer Itsik Fefer's poem "I Am a Jew" was published on the preceding page. Associating the photograph with Fefer's poem rendered the scene Jewish. If, from the beginning of the war, Russian-language print and photojournalists, including the Jews who wrote and took photographs, stressed a national Soviet experience, subtly incorporating the Jewish side of the war into it, it was precisely the point of *Unity* to develop a specifically Jewish narrative of the Soviet war.[18]

On March 3, 1945, almost exactly three years after the first appearance of the Kerch photographs of Nazi atrocities, *Unity* published a grim layout of five photographs from the Budapest ghetto. The unidentified photographer, Evgenii Khaldei, who had found his family murdered in 1943, photographed the war from its first days, including working alongside Baltermants and Redkin at Kerch in early 1942. Working for TASS, he accompanied the Red Army on its path of liberation in 1944 through southern Russia and the Balkans and found himself in Budapest, Hungary, in January 1945. During the battle to take the city, the Red Army liberated two ghettos— the small international one and the larger Hungarian Jewish one—on January 16 and 18. Khaldei made an unusual trip to these ghettos, established in 1944 to separate the Jewish population of Budapest from the non-Jews, to photograph the specific tragedy of European Jewry.[19]

Since the Soviet press did not simply tell the news but always also interpreted it,

---

[17] Ehrenburg's two articles were Il'ia Erenburg, "O nenavisti," *Krasnaia zvezda*, May 5, 1942; and Ilie Erenburg, "Farvos hasn azoi di fashistn di yidn?" *Eynikayt*, June 28, 1942. On wartime Soviet Yiddish journalism, see David Shneer, "From Mourning to Vengeance: Bergelson's Holocaust Journalism (1941–1945)," in Joseph Sherman and Gennady Estraikh, eds., *David Bergelson: From Modernism to Socialist Realism* (London, 2007), 248–268. These images appeared in the first issue of *Eynikayt*, June 7, 1942.

[18] "Der shlakhtman fun a farnikhtung-batalion," photograph, *Eynikayt*, June 17, 1942, 2. For Redkin's photograph, see *Eynikayt*, December 27, 1942, 3. Fefer was arrested in late 1948 during the anti-cosmopolitan campaign. In his trials, his "nationalistic" poetry written during the war, including "I Am a Jew," was used as evidence against him. See Rubinstein, *Stalin's Secret Pogrom*.

[19] See Tim Cole, *Holocaust City: The Making of a Jewish Ghetto* (New York, 2003).

the caption for the individual photographs had to both describe the awful scene and help readers understand it:

Jews in Budapest. Hitlerites drove tens of thousands of Jews from all over Hungary into the Budapest ghetto region. [Pictured here are] the first building that served as the beginning of the ghetto, and the store in this house, which the fascists transformed into a torture room in which they used to inflict all kinds of things on Jews, shoot them, and then toss their bodies onto the square. Thanks to the hate-driven attack of the Red Army, thanks to the fact that Soviet forces quickly encircled the city, a significant part of Hungarian Jewry was saved from murder.

In the pictures (from right to left): 1. Budapest is liberated. Jews go in every direction back to their places of permanent residence. 2. A mother and daughter whom the fascists dragged out from their cellar, beat in the middle of the street, and then shot. Next to them sits their husband and father. 3. Jews with yellow Stars of David. The fascists forced them to wear these on their chests. 4. A store in which Jews were shot. 5. Slaughtered Jews whom the Germans and fascists murdered before retreating from the city.

Just as a single photograph—of Ivanova, the mourning woman at Kerch—was the one from Baltermants's series to have a long life, the third one in Khaldei's Budapest series would become one of his signature images. Its caption describes the act of visually marking people with a Jewish symbol that the Nazis had turned into a grotesque marker that flattened individual identity. This text, along with the captions to the individual photographs, told readers that by 1945, the Soviets were liberators of Jews from Nazi atrocities, not victims themselves. In addition, *Unity*'s editors chose to express a Jewish and Soviet story in one. Through the use of active verbs such as "murdered," "forced," and "dragged," rather than the passive constructions that would have been more common in both Yiddish and Russian, the caption articulated a clear perpetrator: the fascists/Hitlerites/Germans, and a victim: Jews. In *Unity*, the Soviets' role was as heroic liberators who saved Jews, not "peaceful Hungarian citizens," from murder and destruction.[20]

NOT LONG AFTER VICTORY, the Soviet press stopped talking about war in general and Nazi atrocities in particular. During high Stalinism in the late 1940s and early 1950s, war memory moved out of the public sphere and into the private. The realities of a war that killed between 25 and 30 million Soviets reflected poorly on the USSR's wartime leadership, and the high losses were a permanent scar on the rebuilding process. In 1947, Stalin demoted May 9, Victory Day, from a state holiday to a regular working day. Very few photographs from the war were republished until the early 1960s, and Victory Day was not reinstated as a holiday until 1965, when Leonid Brezhnev officially put war memory at the center of Soviet identity.[21]

Ideological space for war commemoration expanded under Nikita Khrushchev, who ushered in the era known as the "Thaw" of the late 1950s and early 1960s. In

[20] On the Soviet press, see Jeffrey Brooks, *Thank You, Comrade Stalin! Soviet Public Culture from Revolution to the Cold War* (Princeton, N.J., 2001); or Matthew Lenoe, *Closer to the Masses: Stalinist Culture, Social Revolution, and Soviet Newspapers* (Cambridge, Mass., 2004). The photograph appeared in "Yidn in budapesht," *Eynikayt*, March 3, 1945, 1.

[21] Nina Tumarkin, *The Living and the Dead: The Rise and Fall of the Cult of World War II in Russia* (New York, 1995), 98–104.

film, the war came back with a vengeance with such important works as *The Cranes Are Flying* and *Ballad of a Soldier*. These internationally acclaimed films broke through the public silence about the war in Soviet culture. In the mid-1960s, under Brezhnev, war commemoration became a monumental state operation, in the literal sense of the word. Monuments and memorials went up in every part of the country, culminating with a giant motherland statue in Volgograd (formerly Stalingrad), whose construction began under Khrushchev in 1959 and which was unveiled in 1967. If before World War II the Bolshevik Revolution had been the primary event through which Soviet citizens derived a Soviet identity, by the late 1950s and 1960s it had become the war, including for Soviet Jews. As the celebration of wartime heroism opened up before the Soviet public, so too did the tragic loss of the war. *Ballad of a Soldier* features an amputee as the friend of the lead soldier, and in 1961 Baltermants printed a 1943 photograph of injured war veterans in the Kremlin that had not been published during the war. And although the Jewish tragedy had been circulating in Yiddish during and after the war and in Russian war literature subtly since the last years of the war, Yevgeny Yevtushenko, in his poem "Babi Yar," highlighted the mass murder of Soviet Jews in places such as Kiev's Babi Yar and the fact that the story of the Holocaust had been not just universalized, as it was during the war, but explicitly suppressed in the immediate postwar period.[22]

In this context, some of the Nazi atrocity photos that had aroused the anger of the Soviet population during the war reappeared in the Soviet and Communist world press and were shown for the first time in exhibitions as art photographs. These images were no longer documenting crimes but were now part of the process of creating war memory. In January 1965, to commemorate the twentieth anniversary of the end of the war, *Ogonek* published "We Will Not Forget." (See Figure 6.) The editors created a two-page layout of a single, blown-up Baltermants photograph of the weeping woman in Kerch, the third one in the series in Figure 4, whom readers from 1942 would remember to be P. I. Ivanova. The wartime photographer's career had skyrocketed in the postwar period, and in 1961 he became the photo editor of *Ogonek*. In this role, he had the power to shape the visual memory of the war, and was likely the one who created the layout.[23]

Although it was a slightly different photo from the one originally published during the war, this was the first time that any of Baltermants's Kerch images had been published in the Soviet Union since wartime. It appeared at the same time that Baltermants exhibited the photograph in Germany with a newly added title (as opposed to caption), "Grief." The photograph got its name in the early 1960s from the Italian artist Caio Garruba, who first saw it when he was in Moscow looking for images for a sweeping exhibition he was putting together on war. "Grief" made its

---

[22] Weiner, *Making Sense of War*, 18–20. On the subtle incorporation of the Holocaust into literature about the war, see, for example, Ehrenburg's *The Storm* (originally published as *Buria*). Thank you to Harriet Murav for the reference. On how post-Soviet Jews still see their identities through the prism of the war, see Anna Shternshis, "Between the Red and Yellow Stars: Ethnic and Religious Identity of Soviet Jewish World War II Veterans in New York, Toronto, and Berlin," *Journal of Jewish Identities*, forthcoming.

[23] Ol'ga Sviblova, "Biography of Baltermants," in *Dmitri Baltermants* (Moscow, 2005), 4–5. Tatiana Baltermants relates the story in more detail in my interview with her, June 2004.

FIGURE 6: Dmitrii Baltermants, "Grief." Published in *Ogonek*, January 1965, with the title "We Will Not Forget." Courtesy of Michael Mattis.

first appearance in print in 1963 in the Czech illustrated publication *Praha-Moskva*, which published a series of Baltermants photographs in its January edition.[24]

After more than twenty years, the publication of Ivanova's grief now served different purposes. When it was news, the photograph was about the mass murder of Soviet citizens at the hands of the Germans. It was about bearing witness to very specific war crimes against the national enemy. Twenty years later, as an art photograph, it literally pictured grief very differently: no longer focused explicitly on what the Germans did during the war, it was now about the nature of evil and about fostering a new national memory of the war.

Note how Baltermants darkened the sky in the exhibition photograph. In an interview, he explained, "I filled in the sky. But I didn't do this for aesthetic effect, but simply because of specks from the glue." While he was developing the film near Kerch, it apparently got stuck to some contact paper. When he pulled them apart, he noticed that there were specks left on one exposure—the exposure he liked the best, of course, the one that would become his most famous photograph. As one can see from the strip of four images, the wartime image, printed off a different negative, had the flat gray sky over Kerch, not the haunting darkened sky of the 1965 version.[25]

[24] Dmitrij Baltermanc, "Hore," *Praha-Moskva* 1 (1963): 45.
[25] "Interview with Dmitrii Baltermants," 153.

Although Baltermants claims to have altered this particular image because of damage, it was common for Soviet photographers to compose their photographs at every stage of the process, from selecting a scene before taking the picture to manually altering the negatives and creating composite prints of two negatives. News photos were altered at every step of the production process to make them more aesthetically interesting, visually powerful, and politically and ideologically appropriate. Most famously, photographs of Soviet leaders were altered as different people fell out of favor during the height of the Stalinist purges of the 1930s. Some were removed entirely; others were placed closer to or farther away from Stalin. Today's hero could become tomorrow's enemy, and photographs—those seemingly permanent documentary records of the past—needed to be altered to reflect the new changed reality. These photographers worked in an environment in which their images were politically sensitive and carried much ideological weight.[26]

They also worked within different aesthetic and ideological conventions than their colleagues in the West. The boundaries between news journalism and art photography were not nearly as well defined as they were becoming in the West by World War II. This meant that it was acceptable—and often encouraged—to stage scenes, lighten or darken negatives, crop images, and add or subtract details to make a photograph more compelling or more politically "appropriate," even if it meant altering key information. During the war, adding smoke was one of the most frequent manipulations. Baltermants's 1945 photograph "Crossing the Oder" depicts Soviet soldiers pushing heavy artillery through the river enshrouded in thickening smoke from explosions that seem to be right on top of them. He added the smoke to create a more powerful image, one that emphasized imminent danger and Soviet heroism. (See Figure 7.) When he fixed up the damaged Kerch negative for exhibition and publication, he made sure to put out the best possible image of "Grief," one that better reflected the photograph's new function as a universal meditation on loss.

In the 1942 image, the focus is on a single woman, and the discovery of her husband. The image is cropped, so there is less background. The sky is incidental, gray and lifeless. More important, the 1942 image is embedded in a broad narrative about the crimes discovered at Kerch, and her image is just one of many. The darkened sky in the 1965 "Grief" image, whether done for practical or aesthetic purposes, changes the mood and aestheticizes the violence. It becomes more ominous, more threatening, and ironically more heavenly. The sky itself becomes a subject, and the woman is figured as a representative of grief, one of many mourners as the image leads off into infinity on the left side. The 1965 image suggests an endless landscape of grief, while the 1942 image localizes it. Beyond the immediate scene is emptiness, while the 1965 image shows bodies laid out into the distance.

As significant as the differences in the two images was how they were presented. The 1942 photograph was part of a news story about Nazi/German atrocities directed against Ukrainians, Russians, Tatars, and especially Jews, and was one image among many illustrating the event, including the image of the multiethnic marriage of Tereshchenko and Kogan. We might assume that Ivanova was in a similar relationship. The 1965 photograph was no longer documenting a specific crime, but was

[26] The best-known book about photographic manipulation in the Soviet Union is David King, *The Commissar Vanishes: The Falsification of Photographs and Art in Stalin's Russia* (New York, 1997).

FIGURE 7: Dmitrii Baltermants, "Crossing the Oder," 1945. Courtesy of Michael Mattis.

memorializing human tragedy. According to Baltermants, "the photograph expressed not the personal grief of that individual woman, or even a single nationality or country, but it represents the grief of humanity in general," a statement that became true as the image moved from documenting news in a Russian magazine to aestheticizing war memory on the walls of a German exhibition or on the pages of a 1960s Czech journal. Kogan's Jewish corpse does not appear juxtaposed with the crying women. And the surrounding text very clearly marked this reappearance of grief as a *memorial* practice. "We Will Never Forget" trumpeted the sidebar that accompanied the photograph. During the war, those words were an oft-heard call for vengeance against the Nazi enemy; in 1965, they were now cause for reflection and memory.[27]

The caption on the 1965 photograph reads: "January 1942, Kerch. As they were withdrawing, fascist troops shot thousands of peaceful Soviet citizens, tossing their corpses into a nearby anti-tank trench." There is no mention of Germans or Hitler, but merely "fascist troops." Nor is there mention of Jews. By 1965, Germans were liberated friends, not barbaric enemies, and the Great Patriotic War, as World War II was called in the Soviet Union, was figured as a battle of ideologies, not peoples, of Soviets against fascists, not Germans against Jews, Russians, and others. The photo editor, most likely Baltermants himself, also added a comment from the future Nobel Prize–winning German writer Heinrich Böll, who apparently saw the photograph at the German exhibition and said, "Women on the field of battle searching among the dead for their loved ones. Their cry is no longer their own. It has become the cry of humanity." Baltermants made a German writer the one responsible for universalizing the woman's personal grief to his Soviet readership, and an Italian writer gave the photograph its name. The former fascist enemies became partners

[27] Interview with Arnold Drapkin, June 2, 1988; transcript provided by Arnold Drapkin.

with Baltermants in refiguring the atrocity photograph from a record of the news to a memorial device.[28]

Baltermants has been asked to recount the story of the famous "Grief" photograph many times: "During the war I photographed and printed a lot, but here is what's surprising. Fifteen photographs that I'm proud of and that gave me a name as a photographer—'Attack,' 'Tchaikovsky,' 'Battle for the Village,' and finally my most important photograph, 'Grief,' *were never published during the war*. Other photographs appeared in the newspapers ... But these photographs ... that really showed what it was like, and that today have artistic value, found life only after victory." In a 1980s interview with *Time* magazine photo editor Arnold Drapkin, he said, "The [Kerch] pictures were never published during the war, because the editors thought they were too gruesome."[29]

We know that Baltermants's photos from Kerch were published during the war, and that the images circulated widely in TASS Windows posters. But today, when asked "When were Baltermants's Kerch photographs first published?" curators, collectors, and even family members will say "The 1960s," basing their understanding on Baltermants's own story of the photos. Reviews of his exhibitions invariably mention that "Grief," in the words of *New York Times* art critic Charles Hagen, "was censored by the Soviet government for many years." Neither reviewers nor family members seem to know that the Kerch photos were some of the first, if not the very first, published Holocaust liberation images in history. Why would Baltermants claim that his Kerch photographs were censored during the war?

By downplaying the wartime history of the news photograph, the specific story of the mass murder of Kerch's Jews and others murdered by the Nazis, Baltermants could more easily make this photo function as a visual icon in the Soviet war memory that emerged in the 1960s. The story of the wartime censorship of his more gruesome images also helped him craft an identity as a photographer who had been oppressed by Stalin. In the Thaw and the early Brezhnev years, when the photograph made its comeback, all things associated with Stalin (including his namesake city, Stalingrad, whose name was changed to Volgograd in 1961, and his burial spot in Lenin's tomb on Red Square, from which he was removed in the same year) were politically problematic. A changed reality demanded a changed history. With the appearance of "Grief" in the 1960s as an art photograph dedicated to memory, without the complicated and overlapping narratives of Soviet and Jewish loss, it became embedded in a story of universal tragedy, and Baltermants, the photo editor of *Ogonek* in the 1960s, who likely wrote the caption for his own photograph, followed the trend toward universalizing the story of the Holocaust and toward highlighting his own oppression under Stalin.[30]

MANY OF KHALDEI'S WAR PHOTOGRAPHS, especially his famous photo of the Red Flag being raised over the Reichstag, were republished in books, journals, and newspapers and were exhibited throughout the Eastern Bloc in the 1960s, 1970s, and 1980s. (See

[28] "Nikogda ne zabudem," *Ogonek*, January 1965, photo layout.
[29] "Interview with Dmitrii Baltermants," 153, my emphasis; interview with Drapkin.
[30] Interview with Tatiana Baltermants, June 2004.

FIGURE 8: Evgenii Khaldei, "Raising the Red Flag over the Reichstag," May 1945. Scanned from the original negative. Courtesy of Anna Khaldei and Agency Fotosoyuz, Moscow.

Figure 8.) But his photographs of the Budapest ghetto did not make a second appearance in the same way that Baltermants's Kerch photograph did until the fall of the Soviet Union. Although it worked as news in 1945, the two Jews of Budapest were too Jewish for postwar public Russian-language Soviet war memory. The Soviet Yiddish journal *Soviet Homeland* (*Sovetish Heymland*), which began appearing in 1961 and fostered a Soviet Jewish war memory, did not publish many photographs, and Khaldei's Budapest did not appear there, either. But after the fall of the Soviet Union, his "Jews with Yellow Stars on Their Chests" made a fierce return as "Jewish Couple." (See Figure 9.)

In the six years between the end of the Soviet Union and Khaldei's death in 1997, he gave many interviews about his life as a Soviet Jewish photographer and about what was quickly becoming one of his most famous photographs. In one of them he said:

I saw them walking down the street. I was in a black leather coat, and at first they were afraid—they thought I was from the SS. I walked over and tore off their stars, first the woman's, then the man's. She got even more frightened. She said, "No, no, you can't do that, we have to wear them!" I told them that the Russians were here. I told them, "ikh bin oykh a yid. Sholem Aleichem. [I'm Jewish too. Hello.]" Then she cried.[31]

[31] Alice Nakhimovsky and Alexander Nakhimovsky, eds., *Witness to History: The Photographs of Yevgeny Khaldei* (New York, 1997).

Figure 9: Evgenii Khaldei, "Jewish Couple," January 1945. From the original negative. Courtesy of Agency Fotosoyuz, Moscow.

If, in fact, the scene happened as Khaldei describes it, with the symbolic tearing off of the yellow star—a symbol of liberation from both Nazi and Hungarian fascist violence and also from an externally imposed Jewish identity—then the photograph would have been taken *before* he symbolically liberated the couple, because they are shown still wearing their stars. Or Khaldei could have torn off the stars with a penknife to symbolically liberate the couple, and then prepared to photograph them, only to realize that it was the stars, those graphic simplifications of identity, that made a photograph of two people on a street a symbol of Nazi atrocities and Jewish tragedy. (It is not that easy to sew a star back on, nor would the couple have likely agreed to this, so one must presume that he photographed them before their symbolic liberation.) (See Figure 10.) Even if Khaldei's story of the photograph does not reflect the reality of the January 1945 encounter, when he crafted his post-Soviet self for Western audiences, he emphasized his role in the couple's liberation, as the one tearing off their stars and building community between Jews on the streets of Budapest.

"Jewish Couple" has adorned the walls of art galleries and Jewish museums around the world, but it is different from the version that was published in *Unity* during the war. First, the faded photojournalistic image in *Unity* had a descriptive caption rather than a pithy title like "Jewish Couple." If the emphasis during the war was on the violent act of fixing identities—marking Jews with yellow stars—then in the 1990s, the story was about the Jews themselves. The composition of the photographs is also different. In the 1945 photo, the stars are at the center of the frame.

FIGURE 10: Evgenii Khaldei, Survivors in the Budapest Ghetto, one of whose stars has been torn off, 1945. Courtesy of Evgenii Khaldei and Agency Fotosoyuz.

The woman looks away from the camera, suggesting disengagement from the photographer. The image is cropped close in on their bodies, so the viewer sees little of the buildings and streets of grand, but ruined, Budapest. In the exhibition photograph of the 1990s, our gaze is directed into their faces and into the endless street behind them, which suggests the long journey they have travailed and traveled. The exhibition photograph—the better, more compelling of the two—tells a more intimate and more profound story about the Jewish couple. "Jewish Couple" made the people, and not the wartime antisemitic laws about wearing yellow stars, the center of the story.

Although for post-Soviet Western audiences Khaldei emphasized that he was a Jewish photographer and exhibited his work in Jewish venues, including the Jewish Museums in New York and San Francisco and Tel Aviv's Museum of the Diaspora, immediately after the war his national identity proved to be a liability. The superstar photographer of the Red Flag photograph was named the official Soviet photographer of the Nuremberg Trials and the Paris Peace Conference. But unlike Baltermants, whose career soared after the war, Khaldei fell on hard times as the Cold War with the United States heated up and everything smacking of the foreign was deemed suspicious. The anti-cosmopolitan campaign of the late 1940s and early 1950s claimed to target those with too many foreign connections. In fact, it drove out Soviet Jewish doctors, dentists, attorneys, writers, artists, photographers, and others from their positions in the cultural elite. Khaldei lost his job with TASS in

1948, and had difficulty finding stable employment for ten years. Many Jewish photographers lost their staff positions in 1948–1949, although none experienced the
horrible fate suffered by several Yiddish writers, including Fefer, Markish, and Bergelson, who faced arrest and eventually murder in 1952. Khaldei, along with several
other underemployed but well-known Jewish photographers, worked for the magazine *Art Hobby* (*Khudozhestvennaia samodeiatel'nost'*) in the second half of the
1950s, and *Pravda* finally hired him as a staff photographer in 1957.[32]

Khaldei's story about photographing the couple shows just how invested he was
in the Jewishness of his work as he presented it late in life to American and often
Jewish audiences. He always began his life story with his birth in 1917 in Yuzovka
(which would become Stalino in 1924, and then Donetsk in the early 1960s), just
before the outbreak of anti-Jewish pogroms during the Russian Civil War. We learn
of the death of his mother during one of those pogroms and of the murder of many
family members during World War II when the Nazis occupied Stalino in 1941. His
1997 *New York Times* obituary talked in detail about his being raised in an "Orthodox
Jewish family." The word "Soviet" disappears from his own, and from others', description of the photograph, and the focus of Budapest turns to the Jewishness of
the encounter. Just as the subtle Jewishness of the Kerch news photographs drops
out of Baltermants's photograph as it becomes part of Soviet memory, the 1990s
reincarnation of Khaldei's Budapest photograph moves in the opposite direction and
loses the Soviet wartime liberation story as it becomes a Jewish icon of Holocaust
memory.[33]

However, Khaldei's post-Soviet legacy in Russia is quite different from his legacy
in the West. As the war narrative became official Soviet and then post-Soviet war
memory, with Jews the ever-present absence, Khaldei rarely presented himself, or
his story of the Budapest ghetto, as a Jewish story. Rather, he presented himself and
the photo as part of Soviet war memory. This is how he recounted the story of the
Budapest photograph to a Russian journalist in the 1990s:

I was walking along a side street and I ran into these two. Although people knew that Soviet
troops had entered the city, the woman stopped and looked distressed. I began to explain to
them in German that I was Russian, Soviet. The woman began to cry. I photographed them,
and then they immediately began to rip off their stars that had been sewn onto their coats.

The journalist ended the interview by saying that the photograph was left unpublished for years until it came out in the 1990s, a mythic story that had become
so ingrained, like the story of the suppression of Baltermants's "Grief," that it had
become fact. In this interview, Khaldei does not use the word "Jew," instead saying
that he described himself to the couple as "Russian, Soviet." He does not claim to
have spoken Yiddish or Hebrew to them, as he suggests in his other interviews, but
says that he spoke German. Perhaps most important, he says that the couple tore

[32] Ibid., 12–13. On the arrests and murders of Yiddish writers, see Rubenstein, *Stalin's Secret Pogroms.* Khaldei's archives contain documentation about his firing, or as his boss called it, "downsizing
of the staff," including a petition from Khaldei to get his job back on the basis of his outstanding war
photography and the fact that he had never received any kind of political or ideological reprimands. See
"Spravka, fotokhronika TASS," October 25, 1948, as found in the Archive of Evgenii Khaldei, housed
at Agency Fotosoyuz, Moscow.
[33] "Yevgeny Khaldei, 80, War Photographer, Dies," *New York Times*, October 9, 1997.

off their own stars, rather than his doing the symbolic liberating. If in 1945 Khaldei's Budapest photography could be published in a Soviet Yiddish newspaper read by Jews in Moscow, Kiev, New York, or London, in the 1990s Khaldei presented different selves and different frameworks for his photograph to audiences that fifty years later had very different memories of the war.[34]

"Grief" and "Jewish Couple" first appeared as news photographs embedded in a complicated wartime story. At the time, the Soviet story of the war was also the Soviet Jewish story of the war, and the Jewish story of the war in the Soviet Union was the Soviet story. When the photographs reappeared—"Grief" in the 1960s with the emergence of official Soviet war memory, and "Jewish Couple" with the 1990s emergence of the story of the Holocaust (the war against the Jews) on Soviet soil— they became individual icons of seemingly separate memories of World War II and the Holocaust.

IN THE 2000s, TWO EXHIBITIONS attempted to return the photographs to their original context in time and place. In 2005, the European House of Photography in Paris held a solo exhibition for Baltermants and, for the first time since the war, contextualized "Grief" by exhibiting it with other photographs he had taken at Kerch. The photographs were hung together as a series, titled "From the Series 'That's How It Was [*Tak eto bylo*].'" The curators attempted to return the iconic "Grief" photograph back to its historical context, although neither Ivanova, Tereshchenko, nor Kogan was named, and no mention was made of the fact that most of the bodies in the Bagerov trench were Jewish. Contemporary curators continue to see the story of Kerch as a Soviet one, as Baltermants would have wanted.[35]

Also in 2005, at the Russian State Historical Museum on Red Square in Moscow, the late Khaldei and his son Leonid, a budding photographer in his own right, had an exhibition titled "Budapest through the Eyes of Two Generations." It was the first major showing of a wide range of Khaldei's Budapest photographs and included several taken in the Budapest ghetto. Leonid went to Budapest in 2005 to take photographs for the exhibition, nicely contrasting the elder Khaldei's historic photojournalism of violence and destruction with contemporary documentary images of the newly bourgeois capital of a European Union country. Following Khaldei's self-presentation to Russian audiences as a Soviet photographer, the online catalog for the exhibition makes no mention of the fact that both photographers are Jewish, and

[34] See http://cityscan.ru/catalog.php?view=687. The original Russian reads: "Ia idu po ulochke, a eti dvoe mne navstrechu. Khotia v obshchem-to znali, chto sovetskie voiska voshli, zhenshchina ostanovilas', i kakoe-to napriazhenie pochuvstvovalos'. Ia nachal po-nemetski im ob'iasnit', chto ia russkii, sovetskii. Zhenshchina rasplakalas'. Ia ikh sfotografiroval, a potom oni priamo u menia na glazakh stali sryvat' zvezdy, kotorye u nikh byli nashity na pal'to." In my September 2007 interview with Khaldei's daughter, she insisted again that the photograph had never been published in the Soviet Union. I then showed her scanned images of the Yiddish newspaper from March 1945, which are not of high enough quality to reproduce here.

[35] The title of the series came from an unpublished maquette that Baltermants assembled in the 1970s called "That's How It Was." The book included most of his Kerch photographs. Much to Baltermants's dismay, no Soviet publishing house picked up the project, and the book still sits in the Baltermants Archive unpublished. The Paris exhibition was the first time the photographs had been presented together as Baltermants envisioned them in the book. There are two extant copies of the maquette, both of which were consulted for this article.

in the biographical description of the elder Khaldei, it mentions nothing about pogroms, and says that he was fired in 1948 not because he was Jewish, but "because of what was written under 'nationality' in his passport." As befits the Soviet and post-Soviet memory of the war, the word "Jew" never appears.[36]

The fact that these news photographs became icons of distinct war memories makes it difficult to get back to the overlapping narratives that did not divide Jew from Soviet as neatly as contemporary Holocaust and war memory often do. In Russia, the war is still a more powerful memory than is the Holocaust, even for post-Soviet Jews, and especially for World War II veterans, who generally see themselves as Soviet war heroes. According to Gitelman's study of the Soviet Jewish war generation, most elderly Russian Jews understand the importance of the Holocaust to Jewish identity, but when asked about the Holocaust's role during the war, Soviet Jewish veterans told Gitelman that "they did not fight in the war as Jews but as Soviet citizens." The relatively new Holocaust museum located on the grounds of Russia's enormous national war memorial complex in Moscow is hardly utilized, and a good percentage of its visitors are foreign tourists. It does not function as a national pilgrimage site, as the United States Holocaust Memorial Museum does for both American Jews and Americans in general.[37]

Returning iconic photographs to their original news context shows how photographs function in the creation of narratives and memories. Soviet Jews, Baltermants and Khaldei among them, saw the war as many tragedies in one—personal, family, communal, and national. And when these two Soviet Jewish photographers, empowered by the state to create the national war narrative, shot their respective photographs, they were taking news photos of particular aspects of this Soviet and Jewish war. Their employer, the Soviet press, was the first institution to publicly develop a narrative of and an interpretive framework through which to understand Nazi atrocities, in both Russian and Yiddish. When we see these photographs in all of their historic complexity, the distance between Soviet and Jewish, the war and the Holocaust, and Baltermants and Khaldei collapses.

[36] The State Historical Museum's online record of the exhibition, *Budapesht glazami dvukh pokolenii*, is at http://www.shm.ru/ev3884078.html.
[37] Gitelman, "Internationalism, Patriotism, and Disillusion."

David Shneer is Associate Professor of History and Director of the Program in Jewish Studies at the University of Colorado at Boulder. He is the author of *Yiddish and the Creation of Soviet Jewish Culture, 1918–1930* (Cambridge University Press, 2004), *New Jews: The End of the Jewish Diaspora* (New York University Press, 2006), and the forthcoming *Through Soviet Jewish Eyes: Photography, War, and the Holocaust* (Rutgers University Press).

Holocaust Memorials: The Emergence of a Genre

HAROLD MARCUSE

THE EVENT WE NOW KNOW as the Holocaust has been widely represented in a variety of media, from autobiographical and scholarly books; to literature, photography, and film; to art, music, and museums.[1] There has even been an extensive discussion about whether it can be represented at all: Saul Friedlander has described it as being "at the limits of representation."[2] Even before the event itself was defined, however, it was being commemorated in monuments and memorials. Today there are many thousands of memorials marking sites of Nazi persecution and mass murder, and dozens more in cities around the world, with additional monuments being erected each year.[3]

In order to investigate how the Holocaust has been memorialized, we must first delimit what we mean by the term. Not until the 1970s did "Holocaust" become the most widely used word to denote the Nazi program to systematically exterminate all Jews; since the 1990s, it has expanded to include Nazi programs to decimate or eradicate other groups as well.[4] In fact, an awareness of Nazi genocide as a program

---

[1] The works of Lawrence Langer on Holocaust literature and testimony are standard-setting: Langer, *The Holocaust and the Literary Imagination* (New Haven, Conn., 1975); Langer, *Holocaust Testimonies: The Ruins of Memory* (New Haven, Conn., 1991). See also James E. Young, *Writing and Rewriting the Holocaust: Narrative and the Consequences of Interpretation* (Bloomington, Ind., 1988). For art, music, and museums, see, for example, Philip Rosen and Nina Apfelbaum, *Bearing Witness: A Resource Guide to Literature, Poetry, Art, Music, and Videos by Holocaust Survivors* (Westport, Conn., 2002).

[2] Saul Friedlander, ed., *Probing the Limits of Representation: Nazism and the "Final Solution"* (Cambridge, Mass., 1992), 3. Holocaust survivor Elie Wiesel has been one of the most outspoken proponents of the view that the Holocaust cannot be adequately portrayed.

[3] See Ulrike Puvogel, *Gedenkstätten für die Opfer des Nationalsozialismus: Eine Dokumentation*, 2 vols. (Bonn, 1995). Puvogel's location indexes list more than 3,000 sites for Germany alone. The equivalent publication for Poland, Council for the Preservation of Monuments to Resistance and Martyrdom, *Scenes of Fighting and Martyrdom Guide: War Years in Poland, 1939–1945* (Warsaw, 1966), lists more than 1,200 sites. Similar books have been compiled for Austria and the Netherlands: Erich Fein, *Die Steine Reden: Gedenkstätten des österreichischen Freiheitskampfes, Mahnmale für die Opfer des Faschismus, eine Dokumentation* (Vienna, 1975); Wim Ramaker, *Sta een Ogenblik Stil . . . : Monumentenboek, 1940–1945* (Kampen, 1980). A front-page *New York Times* article from January 29, 2008, "Germany Confronts Holocaust Legacy Anew," lists seven major projects in progress for Germany alone.

I do not distinguish rigidly between "monuments" and "memorials," although the choice of terms can be used to reflect objects that may be more heroic versus those that are more contemplative, as in the Washington Monument versus the Lincoln Memorial in Washington, D.C.

[4] See Jon Petrie, "The Secular Word 'Holocaust': Scholarly Myths, History, and 20th Century Meanings," *Journal of Genocide Research* 2, no. 1 (2000): 31–63. See also David Engel, "What Is The Holocaust?" in Gordon Martel, ed., *A Companion to Europe, 1900–1945* (Malden, Mass., 2006), 472–486. Peter Novick discusses the emergence of an awareness of the Holocaust in the United States in *The Holocaust in American Life* (Boston, 1999), 133–134.

distinct from atrocities committed during World War II developed only during the
1960s. Barbie Zelizer, in *Visual Culture and the Holocaust*, her groundbreaking 1998
study of early photographs taken at Holocaust sites and the evolution of their uses,
notes that at the time and during the 1950s, they were called "World War II 'atrocity
photos.' "[5] Raul Hilberg's seminal work, beginning with his 1950 M.A. thesis and
including his 1955 dissertation, published in 1961, used the term "destruction of the
European Jews." That work, along with such events as the trial of Adolf Eichmann
in Jerusalem in 1961–1962, marks a watershed in the recognition of "the Holocaust"
as a discrete event.[6]

From the earliest attempts to represent aspects of the Holocaust at the sites
where it took place, we can derive some principles that have come to characterize
Holocaust memorials as a new genre of commemorative art distinct from older
forms: they are addressed to transnational audiences; they often explicitly represent
multiple meanings; and they use a new repertoire of symbols, forms, and materials
to represent those meanings. By the time they emerged as a distinct genre around
1960, Holocaust memorials tended to be complex experiential spaces, usually going
beyond mere documentary markers to include significant didactic accoutrements.

Since the late 1960s, scholars have attempted to catalogue Holocaust memorials,
presenting us with a rich array of forms, but usually limiting themselves to typological
categorizations with isolated formal interpretations.[7] More recent works offer in-
depth historical portrayals of individual memorials but are organized along national
lines, interpreting the memorials as artifacts of specific national cultures.[8] James E.
Young's seminal 1993 monograph *The Texture of Memory: Holocaust Memorials and
Meaning* constitutes the pinnacle of this approach. Young focuses first on selected
sites in Germany, Austria, and Poland, the primary countries where the Holocaust
was carried out, and then on memorials in Israel and the United States. He does not
treat some of the earliest representations of what we now call the Holocaust, planned
for Warsaw and New York during the war, until chapters 6 and 11, respectively.

[5] Barbie Zelizer, *Visual Culture and the Holocaust* (New Brunswick, N.J., 2001), 1. See also the
excellent study by Cornelia Brink, *Ikonen der Vernichtung: Öffentlicher Gebrauch von Fotografien aus
nationalsozialistischen Konzentrationslagern nach 1945* (Berlin, 1998).

[6] Raul Hilberg, "The Role of the German Civil Service in the Destruction of the Jews" (M.A. thesis,
Columbia University, 1950); Hilberg, "Prologue to Annihilation: A Study of the Identification, Impov-
erishment, and Isolation of the Jewish Victims of Nazi Policy" (Ph.D. diss., Columbia University, 1955);
Hilberg, *The Destruction of the European Jews* (Chicago, 1961). For a cogent argument that the Holocaust
and World War II are actually inseparably linked, see Arno Mayer, *Why Did the Heavens Not Darken?
The "Final Solution" in History* (New York, 1988).

[7] For a typological approach, see Adolf Rieth, *Monuments to the Victims of Tyranny* (New York,
1969); and American Jewish Congress, *In Everlasting Remembrance: A Guide to Memorials and Monuments Honoring the Six Million* (New York, 1969). An excellent annotated bibliography of the literature
can be found in Sybil Milton and Ira Nowinski, *In Fitting Memory: The Art and Politics of Holocaust
Memorials* (Detroit, 1991), 297–315. Many more titles can be found in the "Holocaust: Commemoration
and Memorials" section of *Holocaust Remembrance: A Selected Bibliography*, prepared in 2000 by the
Vidal Sassoon International Center for the Study of Antisemitism at the Hebrew University in Jerusalem, available at http://sicsa.huji.ac.il/remembrance.html (accessed September 2007).

[8] See James Edward Young, *The Texture of Memory: Holocaust Memorials and Meaning* (New Haven,
Conn., 1993); also Judith Miller, *One, by One, by One: Facing the Holocaust* (New York, 1990); Harold
Marcuse, Frank Schimmelfennig, and Jochen Spielmann, *Steine des Anstosses: Nationalsozialismus und
Zweiter Weltkrieg in Denkmalen, 1945–1985* (Hamburg, 1985). For a more comprehensive survey of Ho-
locaust memorialization in eleven European countries, see my essay "Memories of World War II and
the Holocaust in Europe," in Martel, *A Companion to Europe*, 487–503.

In contrast to such geographic analyses, a synchronic approach can show that knowledge about the scope and nature of the Holocaust spread only gradually to a wider public, which then struggled to find proper expressions of its understandings of the events. It allows us to discern how crucial the agents behind Holocaust memorials and their intended audiences were to the forms those projects ultimately attained. It may seem obvious upon reflection, but it was not so much the events themselves that gave shape to the memorials (although the events did give rise to a specific iconography), but the intentions of those who established them. In fact, some of the core event-sites of the Holocaust, including Babi Yar, Belzec, Chełmno, Sobibor, and Treblinka, were not memorialized at all until the 1960s, when agents and audiences emerged who took an interest in transmitting their memory.

THE INITIAL STAGE of Holocaust memorialization is represented by three monuments: one created in the Majdanek concentration camp in 1943; one conceived for the Warsaw Ghetto Uprising in 1943, even as the rebellion was happening, and subsequently implemented in 1948; and one proposed for New York City in 1944 but not realized until the 1990s. While the first two were intended to be or to represent acts of resistance, the third was an attempt by concerned witnesses to commemorate the enormous suffering and sacrifice of the victims. The next stage in the memorialization of Holocaust events is marked by monuments created in or proposed for concentration camps at or shortly after their liberation. Departing survivors of Buchenwald and Flossenbürg wanted to leave behind some marker of their murdered comrades, while Allied army authorities in Belsen and Dachau felt a need to publicize the colossal desecration of humanity they encountered. Slightly later, states that had fallen victim to Nazi aggression set about preserving the remains of sites of repression as memorials: Poland at Auschwitz, Belgium at Breendonk, and Czechoslovakia at Theresienstadt. Sites of Nazi atrocities that were not preserved during this first phase faced the same problem as non-Holocaust sites such as New York: the physical structures were deteriorating, or were unofficially or officially being dismantled and reused, creating a need to represent what was no longer there. This lack of existing forms forced the memorializers to confront more explicitly the question of what meanings they wished to convey.

The memorial at Dachau, delayed until the early 1950s, illustrates the transition to a new phase in which survivors and states worked together, using international artistic competitions, to work out those meanings and find forms that would convey them. A 1952 competition for Buchenwald, then international competitions in 1953 in London and in 1957 for Auschwitz-Birkenau, completed the transition to a specific iconography of the Holocaust, at the time the term itself and its conception as an event *sui generis* was emerging.[9] The Buchenwald project, although envisioned as an international memorial by the camp survivors, was implemented for a national audience by the East German state as a National Site of Admonition and Commemoration (*Nationale Mahn- und Gedenkstätte*) to represent the "anti-fascist" basis of

[9] Petrie, "The Secular Word 'Holocaust,'" gives examples of the use of "Holocaust" as the French and English translation of the Hebrew *sho'uh* in Yad Vashem publications beginning in 1955.

its own legitimacy. However, even its socialist realist design reveals the emerging internationalist trend, which became more pronounced by the end of the decade in Ravensbrück and Sachsenhausen, which are also in East Germany. An explicitly internationalist avant-garde tradition emerged from the London and Birkenau competitions, which shaped most subsequent major Holocaust memorials.

WHAT MAY BE CONSIDERED the first Holocaust memorial was created in May 1943 by prisoners in the Majdanek concentration camp just outside the city limits of Lublin in eastern Poland.[10] An imprisoned Catholic Polish artist persuaded an SS administrator to permit the "beautification" of his section of the camp with sculptures. Albin Boniecki used concrete to create "Three Eagles"—a group of interlinked birds taking flight—which he set atop a column approximately 2 meters tall, into the base of which prisoners secretly placed a small container of human ash. The camp administrators accepted the monument because they saw the eagles as a Nazi symbol. However, the eagle is also a Polish national symbol, and to the prisoners, the three birds taking to the air symbolized the ultimate freedom of the three imprisoned groups: men, women, and children. Boniecki also created a tortoise, to symbolize resistance through work slowdowns, and a lizard baring its teeth in the direction of the guards at the entrance gate. This first memorial contains two features that would prove to be typical of the genre: the use of symbolic materials, and the creation of new symbols that would be appropriately understood by their target audience. A symbolic language of Holocaust memorials, which distinguishes them from earlier memorial traditions of war-related mass death, emerged gradually over the next two decades.

Symbolic materials include stone from concentration camp quarries, such as the granite in the Mauthausen memorial in the Père Lachaise Cemetery in Paris (1958), and also the marble used in the Jewish memorial in Dachau (1967), which is from the city of Peki'in in Israel, believed to have had continuous Jewish settlement since biblical times. Numerous Holocaust memorials incorporate containers of human ash or "blood-soaked" soil from Nazi camps and sites of mass murder.[11] Religious sym-

[10] See Józef Marszałek, *Majdanek: Konzentrationslager Lublin* (Warsaw, 1984), 153, with unnumbered illustration. On the artist Albin Boniecki, see Rosen and Apfelbaum, *Bearing Witness*, 128. According to http://polish-online.com/polen/staedte/lublin-museum-majdanek.php (accessed November 2, 2007), after liberation the sculpture was destroyed by the local populace, who saw it as a symbol of Nazism. If that is true, the present sculpture would be a re-creation, of which I could find no indication in the published literature. See, for example, Detlef Hoffmann, ed., *Das Gedächtnis der Dinge: KZ-Relikte und KZ-Denkmäler, 1945–1995* (Frankfurt, 1997), 10–11, http://books.google.com/books?id=XWRer88ZksUC.

Note: Not all early Holocaust memorial projects are discussed here. For example, too little is known about a 1944 memorial vision for Auschwitz and Birkenau that is mentioned in Isabelle Engelhardt, *A Topography of Memory: Representations of the Holocaust at Dachau and Buchenwald in Comparison with Auschwitz, Yad Vashem and Washington, DC* (Brussels, 2002), 160–161. Also, the 1959 Ravensbrück memorial discussed below is based on a 1941 design for a monument commemorating the shooting of Soviet commissars. See Susanne Lanwerd, "Skulpturales Gedenken: Die 'Tragende' des Bildhauers Will Lammert," in Insa Eschebach, Sigrid Jacobeit, and Susanne Lanwerd, *Die Sprache des Gedenkens: Zur Geschichte der Gedenkstätte Ravensbrück, 1945–1995* (Berlin, 1999), 42–43.

[11] Survivors leaving Buchenwald for their home countries in the spring of 1945 took eighteen urns of human ash with them to create memorials around the world. Some of these urns are in the Central Cemetery in Vienna, the Île de la Cité deportation memorial in Paris, and the Church of the Holy Spirit

bolism, even the use of Jewish symbols, was not common in concentration camp memorials until the 1960s, when the specifically Jewish dimension of the Nazi genocide began to emerge in the public sphere.[12] Instead, the first symbols used at sites of persecution and genocide were taken from iconic features of the Nazi camps: barbed wire and fence posts, smokestacks, and the colored triangle badges that were used to categorize prisoners. Later, more specifically Holocaust-related icons of deportation, such as railroad cars and tracks, and even the sounds of trains, were added to the repertoire of camp memorials.[13] Symbols of victim groups, such as the six-pointed Star of David, a menorah, or the five-pointed communist red star, and, less often, symbols of the perpetrators, including the swastika (usually deformed or broken), help to give Holocaust memorials specificity. More generic symbols of bondage and death, such as chains and urns, are common. Finally, numeric symbolism is frequently employed in Holocaust memorials. The number 6 for the approximately 6 million Jewish victims is most

FIGURE 1: Albin Boniecki, "Three Eagles," on a column erected by prisoners in Majdanek, May 1943; height ca. 2 meters. The original base was said to hide a secret container of human ash. Photo by Ute Wrocklage.

common, but numbers of places (countries) of origin (usually 15–30) or of victims, often with tens or hundreds of thousands of individual elements (as tiles in Paris and Yad Vashem, or names in Prague), can also be found.[14]

Human forms in positions of mourning, solidarity, or resistance are common.

---

in Copenhagen. With 105 urns and twenty-five additional relics in a crypt, the 1949 Hamburg-Ohlsdorf memorial discussed below has the largest collection. See Harold Marcuse, "Das Gedenken an die Verfolgten des Nationalsozialismus, exemplarisch analysiert anhand des Hamburger 'Denkmals für die Opfer nationalsozialistischer Verfolgung und des Widerstandskampfes'" (M.A. thesis, University of Hamburg, 1985), 59 (citing *Hamburger Volkszeitung*, May 3, 1949), 96–98; available at http://www.history.ucsb.edu/faculty/marcuse/publications/ma/marcuse1985.pdf.

[12] For a discussion of the emergence of international awareness of the Jewish dimension of Nazi mass murder, with references to pertinent literature, see Harold Marcuse, *Legacies of Dachau: The Uses and Abuses of a Concentration Camp, 1933–2001* (Cambridge, 2001), 210–214, 266–267. See also Petrie, "The Secular Word 'Holocaust,'" 46–48; and Novick, *The Holocaust in American Life*, pt. 3.

[13] A 1958 design for Birkenau, discussed below, featured a cattle car motif; the 1970 memorial in Dutch Westerbork is a reconstructed section of track; the 1974 Ravensbrück memorial in Amsterdam has a constantly running railway soundtrack. See J. Kruizinga, *Op de Bres voor de Vrijheid: Oorlogs-, Verzets- en Bevrijdingsmonumenten in Amsterdam* (Amsterdam, 1980), 40.

[14] The Paris deportation memorial is discussed below. The memorial in the Pinkas synagogue in Prague (1954–1959) lists the names and vital dates of 77,297 Czech Jews murdered in the Holocaust.

They are universally understandable, and are able to trigger empathy and positive feelings while connoting negative events. Skeletal human forms, widely associated with the camps since the Allied media blitz that accompanied their liberation in the spring of 1945, are less frequently employed, presumably because they do not foster feelings of identification among viewers. Disembodied hands, less graphic but more focused expressions of human emotion, are often found in Holocaust memorials as well.[15]

The need for symbolic representations, however, is predicated on the absence of that which is symbolized. In the early postwar years at many locations, the remnants of the camps themselves were deemed sufficient to represent what had taken place there. Majdanek is again an early example. In July 1944, Majdanek was the first Nazi concentration camp to fall into Allied hands; the following November, the provisional Polish government declared it to be a "memorial site of the martyrdom of the peoples of Poland and other nations." One reason no additional artistic memorial was erected there until 1970 was the existence of the physical remains. In fact, at most of the former camps, the deterioration (or the intentional destruction) of the structures went hand in hand with initiatives to create a symbolic memorial. At Gross Rosen near Łódź, for example, where much of the camp is still largely intact today, there is no sculptural memorial; instead, only a squat, obelisk-like mausoleum was constructed.[16] Similarly, at Theresienstadt, thirty-five miles northeast of Prague, and in Breendonk, between Brussels and Antwerp, the remains of massive pre-Nazi fortresses serve as the primary memorials.[17]

See "Pinkas Synagogue: Memorial to the 80,000 Jewish Victims of the Holocaust from Bohemia and Moravia," http://www.jewishmuseum.cz/en/a-ex-pinkas.htm (accessed November 18, 2007).

[15] Ramaker, *Sta een Ogenblik Stil*, has a chapter devoted to Dutch Holocaust memorials using hands as symbols.

[16] The Gross Rosen mausoleum contains a large volume of human ash discovered in the camp, which was liberated on February 14, 1945, with 30,000 unevacuated survivors. It is barely mentioned in the extant literature. For two cursory references, see Council for the Preservation of Monuments to Resistance and Martyrdom, *Scenes of Fighting and Martyrdom Guide*, 324 and ill. 276; and Reinhard Matz, *Die unsichtbaren Lager: Das Verschwinden der Vergangenheit im Gedenken* (Reinbek bei Hamburg, 1993), 175. In 2007–2008, the Gross Rosen museum's website offered a more detailed postwar history of the memorial site, but it has since been removed. The current homepage is http://www.gross-rosen.pl/gb/main.htm.

[17] On May 6, 1947, the Czech government declared that the "small fortress" section of the Theresienstadt camp, an eighteenth-century fortress, would be preserved as a "memorial site of national suffering." However, the part of the site associated with the Holocaust, the larger section of the fortress across the river Ohře, where approximately 140,000 Jews had been held and about 33,000 died, was not included in the decree. Today that part of the former Theresienstadt "ghetto" is a residential neighborhood. The imposing architecture of the small fortress, where primarily non-Jewish Czech political prisoners were held, serves as a museum and memorial for the entire complex, and has never been complemented by a central artistic memorial. See Vojtěch Blodig, "Die Gedenkstätte Theresienstadt gestern und heute," *Dachauer Hefte* 11 (1995): 102–108; also http://de.wikipedia.org/wiki/Interni erungslager_Theresienstadt_(1945-1948) (accessed October 19, 2007 and December 28, 2009), referencing articles in Czech in the *Theresienstädter Blätter* in 1990 and 1996 (the reference to the 1990 issue was removed when the Theresienstadt_1945-1948 page was renamed in September 2009). Some small memorials and sculptures can be found in the small fortress, including one containing earth from the concentration camps to which the prisoners of the small fortress were transferred. I could not find more specific information about the origins of these memorials. They were likely added after the 1970s, when major improvements to the site were made.

In August 1947, the Belgian parliament passed a bill stipulating that the former SS and SD detention center in the early-twentieth-century fortress at Breendonk, twelve miles south of Antwerp and approximately equidistant from Brussels, would be preserved as a memorial museum. See http://www

FIGURE 2: Nathan Rapoport, Monument to the Heroes of the Warsaw Ghetto, 1948; height 23 meters. The heroic socialist realist style reached its peak in the Eastern Bloc with the Buchenwald memorial of 1958. Photo by Aaron Marcuse-Kubitza.

BY FAR THE MOST ELABORATE and important Holocaust memorial conceived during the war was Nathan Rapoport's monument for the Warsaw Ghetto Uprising. It has been comprehensively researched by James Young.[18] Rapoport, a Jewish refugee from Nazi-occupied Poland, had found sanctuary in the Soviet Union, and was working as a state sculptor in Novosibirsk when he heard news of the uprising in April 1943. He had previously sketched a monument to the destruction of Polish and Russian Jewry, a huddled family watching a girl being led away by armed Germans. A year later, he traveled to Moscow to present his first model for a Warsaw Ghetto monument to the Arts Committee, which rejected it as "too narrow in conception, too nationalistic," meaning that it did not conform to the heroic-universalist Stalinist style. (Young writes that the committee considered it "too Jewish.") Unfortunately, we do not know what that monument looked like, but we do know that memorial designs were often rejected in those early years because they were too specific or too graphic—in other words, because their meanings were not acceptable to those in power. When Rapoport was repatriated to Warsaw in early 1946, he presented a revised maquette to the Warsaw Jewish Committee, which, he learned, had already rejected a proposal from a local artist that was described as looking like "two Ha-

---

.breendonk.be/EN/fort.html (accessed October 19, 2007). A sculptural memorial may have been erected there: a bronze figure of a powerful man, kneeling with his thighs splayed and looking upward, set atop a high brick pedestal, is depicted in Ludo van Eck, *Le livre des camps* (Leuven, 1979), 32. I have been unable to find out more about this sculpture. On the reception of the memorial site, see also http://www.breendonk.be/EN/memorial.html (accessed October 19, 2007).

[18] Young, *The Texture of Memory*, 155–184, esp. 159, 164–170. On p. 166, Young writes that Rapoport returned to Novosibirsk in "mid-1943," but from the context he probably means mid-1944. This detailed and richly illustrated chapter was previously published as James E. Young, "The Biography of a Memorial Icon: Nathan Rapoport's Warsaw Ghetto Monument," *Representations* 26 (Spring 1989): 69–106.

sidim hoeing potatoes." Rapoport's new idea was for a large framing monument, approximately 23 meters high and 27 meters wide, with an 11-meter-tall bronze figure of Mordecai Anielewicz, the head of the Jewish Fighting Organization, at the center. The committee immediately accepted the new design, which was approved a year later by the Warsaw Arts Committee as well, under the provision that it be completed for dedication on April 19, 1948, the fifth anniversary of the uprising and less than a year away.

Rapoport went to Paris to cast the figurative parts of the memorial in bronze. Realizing that his socialist realist style was becoming anachronistic, he isolated himself from the contemporary art scene and found Jewish settlers from Palestine to be his models. He located stone for the framing monument in a quarry in Sweden, where large blocks of granite lay ready for delivery. In an ironic twist of history, they had been ordered by Hitler's favorite sculptor, Arno Breker, for use in a planned victory monument in the Nazi capital, Berlin. The core material beneath the granite inadvertently became symbolic as well. The architect commissioned with building the base had first wanted to clear the rubble of the destroyed ghetto from the site. When this proved impracticable, he poured concrete over the ruins, then encased that core with Breker's granite slabs. Although in this case unplanned, the incorporation of relics draws on a longstanding memorial tradition that reached a qualitatively new level in Holocaust memorials. The practice had underpinned the legitimacy of Christian reliquaries since medieval times. In addition, spoils or remains of war had historically been taken for use in victory monuments, such as Napoleon's looting of the Berlin quadriga in 1806, or the incorporation of cannons and munitions in war memorials at least since the U.S. Civil War.[19] Human remains have been incorporated into the tombs of unknown soldiers since World War I.[20] This practice has become a hallmark of Holocaust memorials, which commemorate an occurrence that was both anonymous and spread over a huge geographic area. In Poland, where a once-vibrant Jewish culture had been all but eradicated, monuments crafted from broken Jewish tombstones are common, for example, in Łódź, Łuków, Sandomierz, and Siedlce.[21]

ANOTHER FEATURE TYPICAL of Holocaust memorials for at least the first decade after the war is that they were initiated by Holocaust and concentration camp survivors, or by refugees such as Rapoport who had narrowly escaped the Nazis' genocidal dragnet. However, they were realized only when they were supported either by the local community or by the governmental authority responsible for the site. The effort

[19] For more examples, see Hans-Rudolf Meier, "Vom Siegeszeichen zum Lüftungsschacht: Spolien als Erinnerungsträger in der Architektur," in Hans-Rudolf Meier and Marion Wohlleben, eds., *Bauten und Orte als Träger von Erinnerung: Die Erinnerungsdebatte und die Denkmalpflege* (Zurich, 2000), 87–98; Annette Schäfer, "Spolien: Untersuchungen zur Übertragung von Bauteilen und ihr politischer Symbolgehalt am Beispiel von St-Denis, Aachen und Magdeburg" (M.A. thesis, Bamberg, 1999).
[20] Ken Inglis, "Grabmäler für unbekannte Soldaten," in Deutsches Historisches Museum et al., *Die letzten Tage der Menschheit: Bilder des Ersten Weltkrieges* (Berlin, 1994), 402–422. See also Linda Granfield, *The Unknown Soldier* (Toronto, 2008).
[21] Young, *The Texture of Memory*, 194–196. These are mentioned but not depicted in Council for the Preservation of Monuments to Resistance and Martyrdom, *Scenes of Fighting and Martyrdom Guide*, 211, 200, 168, 307.

FIGURE 3: A plaque covering soil from concentration camps marks the site of a Holocaust memorial planned for New York City's Riverside Park since 1947. The memorial project was finally realized in 1997, but as a museum in a much more frequented location in Battery Park. Photo by Irene Marcuse, 2008.

to establish a memorial in New York City offers a revealing case study.[22] Since July 1942, a number of public events involving hundreds of thousands of people had been held in New York and other cities around the U.S. to draw attention to the ongoing genocide of Jews in Europe.[23] They culminated in a mass rally on the steps of City Hall on April 19, 1944, the first anniversary of the Warsaw Ghetto Uprising, at which Mayor Fiorello La Guardia spoke. At the same time, the refugee poet Julian Tuwim published his call for a "monument to the ignominy of our foes and to the glory of our tortured heroes."[24] In January 1946, the U.S. National Organization of Polish Jews proposed that an eternal flame be established, dedicated to the "Heroes of the Warsaw Ghetto and the Six Million Jews Slain by the Nazis." It found wide support both from the city administration and from Jews around the world. On October 19, 1947, an inscribed cornerstone was dedicated before a crowd of tens of thousands in Riverside Park near 84th Street. That stone plaque, beneath which a box of soil from concentration camps was interred, bears the text "This is the site for the American memorial to the heroes of the Warsaw ghetto battle April–May 1943 and to the six million Jews of Europe martyred in the cause of human liberty."

Since the New York project did not receive enough support to be initiated until the 1980s, the designs submitted for it in 1948, 1949, and 1950 indicate that spe-

[22] See Young, *The Texture of Memory*, 287–291. Rochelle Saidel, *Never Too Late to Remember: The Politics behind New York City's Holocaust Museum* (New York, 1996), 44–55, offers additional details.

[23] See David S. Wyman, *The Abandonment of the Jews: America and the Holocaust, 1941–1945* (New York, 1985), 24–26, 71, 88, 169–170; also Lucia Ruedenberg, " 'Remember 6,000,000': Civic Commemoration of the Holocaust in New York City" (Ph.D. diss., New York University, 1994), 22–40.

[24] Young, *The Texture of Memory*, 164.

cifically Jewish symbols were problematic in the early memorial iconography of the Holocaust. The 1948 design was a figure by famed New York sculptor Jo Davidson, depicting a muscular, bare-handed fighter with his arms swept back and his chest thrust forward, towering over four figures: a beseeching rabbinical figure, a fighter aiding an injured comrade, and a corpse slumped against the step-like blocks of the pedestal.[25] After it was rejected without comment by the Arts Commission, Columbia University architecture professor Percival Goodman proposed in 1949 that a wall be erected, to measure 36 meters long and 7.6 meters tall, crowned by a menorah on a pedestal nearly 14 meters tall. This design, too, was rejected, ostensibly for its large size, which allegedly would have distracted drivers on the adjacent parkway. We can only speculate that its overt Jewish symbolism played a role in its rejection, as well as in the failure of its biblically themed successor.

In 1951, ground was broken for a design by famed German émigré architect Erich Mendelsohn and renowned Croatian sculptor Ivan Meštrović. Two black granite tablets, 24.4 meters tall and inscribed with the Ten Commandments, were to be set atop an 8-meter-high wall bearing a central inscription. A perpendicular wall 30 meters in length ran along the side of the plaza, at the front end of which was a giant sculpture of Moses urging "struggling humanity," depicted as a procession of figures in bas-relief, to fulfill the Ten Commandments. When fundraising efforts stalled after Mendelsohn's death in 1953, that project, too, was abandoned. Rochelle Saidel suggests that this was because of a lack of support among Jewish organizations in New York, which were wary of antisemitism during that Cold War period.[26]

The subsequent fate of Holocaust memorialization in New York City illustrates how difficult overtly Jewish symbolism remained around the world (with the exception of Israel) until the 1980s. In 1964, two different Jewish groups independently proposed separate designs by Nathan Rapoport, which were again rejected on grounds of "public sensitivity." One, "Scroll of Fire," took the form of Torah scrolls 8 meters high that were carved with bas-relief scenes from the Holocaust. It was erected in Israel in 1971.[27] The other depicted Artur Zygelboim immolating himself in London in 1943 to draw attention to the Nazi genocide of the Jews.[28] The Arts Commission described it as "a bronze figure engulfed in thorns and flames, sharply leaning to the front as if about to fall; emerging from the inferno are heads and hands calling to humanity for rescue."[29] A design for a new location at the tip of Manhattan in Battery Park, commissioned from architect Louis Kahn in 1968, was never realized

[25] Ibid., 290; Saidel, *Never Too Late to Remember*, 49, 253 n. 15.
[26] Saidel, *Never Too Late to Remember*, 51–55; see also Novick, *The Holocaust in American Life*, 123.
[27] See Saidel, *Never Too Late to Remember*, 57–61; Young, *The Texture of Memory*, 200–225. The second scroll of the version erected near Kesalon, Israel, carries scenes depicting the Israeli war of independence.
[28] On Zygelboim, see Wyman, *The Abandonment of the Jews*, 123; and David Roskies, *The Jewish Search for a Usable Past* (Bloomington, Ind., 1999), 138–139. Roskies calls Zygelboim's grave in the Workmen's Circle Plot of the Old Mount Carmel Cemetery in Queens, New York, "the first memorial to the Holocaust on American soil." Saidel, however, gives 1972 as the dedication date of the current monument, a trapezoidal granite tower surmounted by a horizontal disk with a pear-shaped sculptural flame emerging from it; *Never Too Late to Remember*, 61. The Hebrew and English inscription quotes from Zygelboim's suicide note.
[29] See *New York Times*, June 11, 1965, 1, cited in Wayne Jebian, "The Missing Monument," *Columbia Journal of American Studies* 1, no. 1 (1995), http://www.columbia.edu/acis/textarchive/cjas/11/14.html (accessed November 9, 2007).

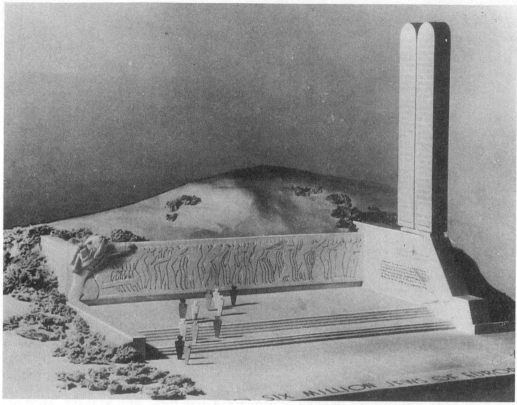

FIGURE 4: Erich Mendelsohn and Ivan Meštrović, design for a Holocaust memorial in Riverside Park, New York City, 1951; planned height ca. 24.4 meters. Prominent Jewish symbolism helped to thwart the realization of this project. Photo from the archives of the YIVO Institute for Jewish Research, New York.

because of a lack of funding. Consisting of six glass cubes approximately 5 meters high arranged around a seventh cube with an entrance archway, it was to have cost $1.5 million. Ultimately a six-sided Museum of Jewish Heritage was built at that location. Begun in 1986, it was dedicated in 1997, with a substantial portion of its exhibition devoted to the Holocaust.

THE FIRST POSTWAR ATTEMPTS at memorialization in Europe were initiated by survivors in the camps that had been liberated before the Germans could evacuate them. These early efforts often went on for years before lasting memorials were erected, both because they were hampered by material conditions and because once the survivors dispersed, no other group lobbied for the creation of a memorial: state agencies had not yet found meanings in Nazi atrocities that they wished to represent.

On April 19, 1945, in Buchenwald, just four days after liberation, a wooden obelisk built by survivors in the camp workshops was erected on the roll-call square.[30] Some 7 to 8 meters tall and culminating in a wooden "fire basin," it carried the inscription "K.L.B." (the official Nazi abbreviation of *Konzentrationslager* Buchen-

[30] See Volkhard Knigge, "Buchenwald," in Hottmann, *Das Gedächtnis der Dinge*, 95–96.

FIGURE 5: A provisional memorial erected on the Buchenwald roll-call square on April 19, 1945. Classical forms such as pyramids and obelisks were typical of the earliest Holocaust memorials. Photo by Sgt. John T. Poulos, courtesy of the Poulos Family.

wald) and the approximate number of people killed in the camp: 51,000.[31] The convergence of a lobby of Buchenwald survivors and the East German state's interest in using the camp to bolster its legitimacy would lead in 1958 to the creation of one of the largest Holocaust memorial ensembles ever built.[32]

In Bergen-Belsen, liberated four days before Buchenwald, catastrophic health conditions and the need to care for thousands of displaced Jews whose repatriation posed problems delayed the realization of a first memorial for a year.[33] Still, the British army quickly decided to designate the camp as a memorial. A sign was erected in English, with a second sign offering a clumsy German translation—an indication that the British also intended to address a German audience. It read:

This is the site of the infamous Belsen concentration camp, liberated by the British on 15th April 1945. 10,000 unburied dead were found here, another 13,000 have since died. All of them victims of the German New Order in Europe and an example of Nazi Kultur.[34]

[31] Of the 34,375 officially registered dead, approximately 11,000 were Jewish. Including executed prisoners and Soviet prisoners of war, as well as those who were dead upon arrival at the camp and those who died on evacuation marches, the death toll is now estimated to be 65,000 or more. Ironically, this obelisk form was identical to a temporary Nazi memorial created in Graz, Austria, in July 1938 to celebrate that city's naming as "City of the People's Uprising." The city's central statue of the Virgin Mary was covered in an obelisk framework draped in red cloth and crowned by a basin. See Hans Haacke, "Und ihr habt doch gesiegt, 1988," in James Young, ed., *The Art of Memory: Holocaust Memorials in History* (New York, 1994), 77–81.

[32] Yad Vashem in Jerusalem, where memorials were begun in the 1960s, and the Berlin Memorial to the Murdered Jews of Europe, dedicated in 2005, are also among the largest.

[33] According to http://www.ag-bergen-belsen.de/guided_tour.html (accessed January 12, 2008), a birchwood "timber cross" erected by (non-Jewish) Polish women after liberation was the first memorial.

[34] A photograph of the sign can be found at http://isurvived.org/Bergen-Belsen_liberation.html

In April 1946, some Jewish survivors who were still living in former German army barracks near the site dedicated a square column approximately 2 meters tall, crowned by a block engraved with a small Star of David, which was in turn surmounted by a small stone sphere. On the side of the memorial facing arriving visitors, which is inscribed in Hebrew, an abstract relief depicts a forest of cut-down trees. The traditional form of the memorial indicates that the survivors had not yet derived a specific meaning from the experience that they wished to represent, as the admonition, translated into English on the back of the memorial, indicates—the words "shall remember" are painted red:

FIGURE 6: Jewish memorial erected by survivors in Belsen, 1946; height ca. 2 meters. Like many of the earliest Holocaust memorials, this monument has a very traditional form, but its inscription is unusually specific, naming its creators as well as the victims and perpetrators, and combining them with an emotional appeal. Photo courtesy of Glenn Austerfield.

Israel and the world shall remember / thirty thousand Jews / exterminated in the concentration camp / of Bergen-Belsen / at the hands of the murderous Nazis
EARTH CONCEAL NOT THE BLOOD / SHED ON THEE!
First anniversary of Liberation / 15th April 1946 / 14th Nissan 5706
Central Jewish Committee / British Zone.[35]

Later that year or in 1947, the British occupiers had German POWs erect a larger memorial, an obelisk 20 meters tall with a wall 40 meters long. It had to be rebuilt in 1958 because of weather damage.[36] That structure, the closest thing West Germany had to a national Holocaust memorial until the completion of the Dachau memorial site in 1968, was dedicated by West German president Theodor Heuss in April 1952.[37] Now 25 meters tall, the re-created obelisk is accompanied by a 50-meter-long stone wall bearing inscriptions from fourteen of the forty countries whose

(accessed October 19, 2007). The German version of the sign is depicted at http://www.bbc.co.uk/ww2peopleswar/stories/50/a8378850.shtml. The sign was erected prior to the 1946 publication of its photograph in Derrick Sington, *Belsen Uncovered* (London, 1946).

[35] For details about the monument's creation, see Marcuse, *Legacies of Dachau*, 264, references in 512 n. 10.

[36] The most detailed postwar chronology of the memorial that I have seen is in *Stuttgarter Zeitung*, February 3, 1960.

[37] A translation of Heuss's speech is printed in Roderick Stackelberg and Sally Anne Winkle, *The Nazi Germany Sourcebook: An Anthology of Texts* (London, 2002), 401–402. The German origi-

FIGURE 7: Dedicated in Bergen-Belsen in 1952, this stone obelisk is 25 meters tall and stands in front of a 50-meter-long wall with inscriptions from fourteen countries; a Sinti inscription was added in 1982. Memorials at Holocaust sites often name the countries of origin of the victims. Photo by Bonnie M. Harris.

citizens died in the Belsen camp.[38] This may be the first example of what has become a hallmark of Holocaust memorials: individual representations of some or all of the countries whose citizens were killed at the site. Other pre-1960 examples can be found in Flossenbürg, Buchenwald, Auschwitz, Ravensbrück, and Sachsenhausen. Mauthausen is perhaps the most noteworthy site exhibiting the national principle; since 1948, twenty national memorials have been erected there on a field outside the former camp walls.[39]

As Buchenwald and Belsen indicate, it took some time after the war for an iconography of symbolic and figurative representation specific to the Holocaust to evolve. Classical forms, such as an obelisk or tall pylon, were used to mark a site as meaningful, but without specifying that meaning. At Belsen, each of the fourteen countries had the opportunity to express its own meaning in an inscription.[40] Other memorials erected in the late 1940s use tall forms that convey no specific meaning— for example, the triangular obelisk 8 to 10 meters tall encircled by three large red stars that was erected by Red Army survivors at the Stukenbrock POW/death camp

nal is available at http://www.derhistoriker.de/deutsch/05+Rede_BP_Heuss_Einweihung_KZ-Gedenk staette_Bergen-Belsen_1952.pdf (accessed October 19, 2007).

[38] Friedrich Bischoff, *Das Lager Bergen-Belsen: Dokumente und Bilder mit erläuternden Texten, im Auftrage des Niedersächsischen Ministers des Innern* (Hannover, 1966), 32.

[39] See Bertrand Perz, *Die KZ-Gedenkstätte Mauthausen: 1945 bis zur Gegenwart* (Innsbruck, 2006). The website of the Mauthausen committee of Austria gives some information about the history of the memorial site: http://www.mkoe.at/gedenkstaette.asp. Yad Vashem in Jerusalem exhibits a variation on this theme: on an adjacent field, it displays scaled replicas of memorials from many sites of the Holocaust, including Warsaw and Dachau.

[40] The inscriptions are listed in "Zur Geschichte des Lagers Bergen-Belsen," http://www.bergen belsen.de/pdf/zurgeschichte.pdf, 6–8 (accessed October 10, 2008); an older html version is still available at the Internet Archive, for example at http://web.archive.org/web/20071018004923/www.bergenbelsen .de/de/zurgeschichte.htm.

FIGURE 9: The first memorial in Neuengamme, 1953, was erected by the city government to appease demands by survivors for a memorial; height ca. 7.5 meters. Photo by the Buchenwald Collective, from the Stiftung Brandenburgische Gedenkstätten/ Archiv Sachsenhausen.

FIGURE 8: This 16-meter-tall memorial in Hamburg-Ohlsdorf, dedicated in 1949, contains 105 urns with ash and soil from Holocaust sites across Europe. Memorials at non-Holocaust sites often contain collections of relics from Holocaust sites to establish their legitimacy and represent the transnational scope of the Holocaust. Photo by Harold Marcuse.

near Bielefeld in April 1945, or the "needle" constructed by French survivors at the Neue Bremm camp in Saarbrücken, dedicated in 1947, which was later interpreted as resembling a French bayonet.[41]

A revealing example of an early "tall form" used to represent the Holocaust at a site not connected to its implementation was dedicated in the Ohlsdorf Cemetery in Hamburg in 1949. A rectangular reinforced concrete pylon 16 meters tall, it holds 105 red stone urns containing ashes and soil from sites of "National Socialist repression and the resistance struggle" across Europe.[42] This memorial, originally planned for the center of the city by the Association of the Persecutees of National Socialism (Vereinigung der Verfolgten des Nationalsozialismus, or VVN), the largest group of survivors of Nazi persecution, might be considered the first all-encompassing "Holocaust" memorial, since it unites relics from Holocaust sites from Aarhus to Zwickau, including not only core sites such as Auschwitz-Birkenau and

[41] The memorial for 45,000–50,000 dead at the Stukenbrock camp was dedicated on May 2, 1945. See Volker Pieper, *Die Vergessenen von Stukenbrock: Die Geschichte des Lagers in Stukenbrock-Senne von 1941 bis zur Gegenwart* (Bielefeld, 1988), 44–46, 132–136; also Carsten Seichter, *Nach der Befreiung: Die Nachkriegs- und Rezeptionsgeschichte des Kriegsgefangenen-Mannschafts-Stammlagers "Stalag 326 VI K" Stukenbrock* (Cologne, 2006). On Saarbrücken, see Puvogel, *Gedenkstätten für die Opfer des Nationalsozialismus*, 1: 706–707.
[42] See Marcuse, *Das Gedenken an die Verfolgten des Nationalsozialismus*, 41–47.

FIGURE 10: Survivors' proposal for an experiential Neuengamme memorial, 1960. The chimney-like tower was to be 18–20 meters tall, the pyramidal pylons 3 meters tall, representing different countries. By the late 1950s, Holocaust memorials were becoming experiential spaces. Photo by Harold Marcuse from print in Hans Schwarz Papers, Forschungsstelle für die Geschichte des Nationalsozialismus, Hamburg.

Treblinka, but also sites in Czechoslovakia, Hungary, Lithuania, and Romania—a remarkable achievement given the material and political situation at that time. Collecting soil from multiple Holocaust sites and/or listing their names as a way to signify the entire event is common in Holocaust memorials not situated at historic locations.[43] It effectively reverses the national principle of enumerating the victims' countries of origin, which is found in the memorials at Holocaust sites themselves.

A few years later, the relatively meaning-neutral tall pylon form of Belsen and Hamburg-Ohlsdorf was adapted once again for the first memorial erected in the Neuengamme concentration camp near Hamburg. Dedicated in 1953, it was styled as a tapered cylinder approximately 7.5 meters tall. It is sometimes described as resembling a crematorium smokestack, although all main concentration camp crematoria had rectangular chimneys.[44] The inscription read simply "To the Victims 1938–1945." After much lobbying by the international association of Neuengamme survivors, which had proposed a much more elaborate experiential memorial in 1960, this small column was replaced by a considerably taller (27 meters) rectangular pylon marked only by two vertical grooves and three triangular pegs—the shape of the camp badges—on which wreaths could be hung.[45] To appease the survivors, who wanted some

[43] In addition to the collection of soil in New York (1947) mentioned above, Hamburg-Ohlsdorf lists 25 sites; further early examples can be found in Dortmund (1959, with 52 site names), Frankfurt (1964, with 53 site names), and Paris (1956 and 1962, with 13 and 15 site names; see below).

[44] See Ute Wrocklage, "Neuengamme," in Hoffmann, *Das Gedächtnis der Dinge*, 174–205, 188–191. I have estimated the height from the 1956 Buchenwald Collective photograph with a man standing next to it in Günter Morsch, ed., *Von der Erinnerung zum Monument: Die Entstehungsgeschichte der Nationalen Mahn- und Gedenkstätte Sachsenhausen* (Berlin, 1996), 178.

[45] Their proposed design, the result of a limited competition, was a triangular chimney 18 to 20 meters high surmounting a descending triangular ramp. The ramp was flanked by obelisk-like pylons 3 meters

representation of human suffering, the Hamburg buildings authority allowed them to add an abstract bronze sculpture, larger than life-size (1.85 meters), depicting a fallen, emaciated "deportee" resting only on its knees and shorn head.

The first memorials in the former Flossenbürg concentration camp, near Nuremberg in southern West Germany, also used classical memorial forms as well as symbolic materials and the symbolic incorporation of human remains.[46] After liberation, the camp served briefly as an internment camp, then from fall 1945 to 1948 as a United Nations Relief and Rehabilitation Administration (UNRRA) displaced persons camp for Catholic Poles who did not want to return to Soviet-dominated Poland. In June 1946, a Committee for Erecting the Monument and Chappel [*sic*] in Concentration Camp Flossenbürg was constituted, including representatives of the refugees in the UNRRA camp, local mayors, and town administrators and businessmen.[47] Although the committee was never able to attain official recognition from the military government or the UN (it unsuccessfully tried to place the site under UN protection), it did succeed in creating

FIGURE 11: The present-day Neuengamme memorial and sculpture, 1965; height 27 meters, with sculpture by Françoise Salmon, 1.85 meters. The city of Hamburg again realized a minimalist design to appease the survivors, who were allowed to contribute the sculpture. Photo from Wikimedia.

several memorials. Several watchtowers were dismantled, with their bricks then used to build a chapel named "Jesus in Prison" attached to a remaining watchtower. The local newspaper reported that the chapel design was the result of a competition, although no records of other designs have been found. In the "valley of death" leading away from the chapel, human ash from the camp was piled into a large pyramid and planted over with sod. An adjacent "square of nations" was marked by stone plaques bearing the insignia of the nations whose citizens had died in Flossenbürg.[48]

---

tall that were to bear national inscriptions. Belsen was explicitly referenced as a model for the inscriptions.

[46] See Peter Heigl, *Konzentrationslager Flossenbürg in Geschichte und Gegenwart* (Regensburg, 1989), 85–100.

[47] "Chappel" was the spelling used in the group's printed letterhead.

[48] An excellent collection of historical and present-day photographs can be found at http://www.thirdreichruins.com/flossenburg.htm. The ash may have come from corpses found in the camp at liberation and cremated before May 1, when that program was stopped. See Heigl, *Konzentrationslager Flossenbürg in Geschichte und Gegenwart*, 63, 67.

FIGURE 12: Memorial inscription on the chimney of the Flossenbürg crematorium, ca. 1946. This is one of the earliest cases where the countries of origin of the victims were listed at a Holocaust site. Photo courtesy of the Dachau Memorial Site.

FIGURE 13: The memorial in the town of Flossenbürg, dedicated October 27, 1946; height 10–12 meters. As with the Jewish memorial in Belsen, its form is very traditional. Photo by the Buchenwald Collective, from the Stiftung Brandenburgische Gedenkstätten/Archiv Sachsenhausen.

On the rectangular brick chimney of the crematorium, under the inscription in Polish and English "1938–1945 / Have been murdered in concentration camp at Flossenbürg," was a list of eighteen nations (including "Jewish") followed by the number of deaths for each of those nations as determined by the memorial committee. They were listed in decreasing order, from 26,430 Russians to 2 Americans (soldiers who died during liberation), with the total given at the bottom: 73,296. Again we see the features typical of this early period: an experiential memorial terrain, incorporation of symbolic materials, multinational representation, and classical symbolic forms that signify generic but not specific meaning.

By the summer of 1946, the Flossenbürg memorial committee had also erected a traditional memorial in a cemetery created in the center of Flossenbürg village, where the 141 inmates who died after liberation were buried by order of the U.S. Army. Standing some 10 to 12 meters high and made from local granite, it consists of six block-like "stories" of decreasing size stacked atop each other, the uppermost bearing a cross and crowned by a symbolic urn. Criticized in September 1946 by the Bavarian Ministry of the Interior and the local county governor as "bordering on the unbearable" and "not satisfying the appropriate cultural and aesthetic standards," this memorial indicates that even right after the war, traditional memorial forms

FIGURE 14: Proposal for a 35-meter-tall memorial on the Leiten gravesite near Dachau, November 1945. This massive memorial, to be built from rubble salvaged from Munich, was deemed inappropriate and was never built. Photo by Harold Marcuse from Landratsamt Dachau.

FIGURE 15: The final Leiten memorial, chosen from a competition in 1950, is 10.5 meters high. Inside it are plaques representing 33 countries whose citizens died in Dachau. This dramatically scaled-down version of the original memorial hall idea is enshrouded by trees today. Photo from *Der Baumeister*, 1954.

were already considered inadequate to commemorate the Holocaust.[49] In Flossenbürg camp and village, with human and material remains lending them legitimacy and a remote location away from national and international attention, these traditional memorial forms have persisted unchanged until today.

In Dachau, as in Buchenwald, a provisional memorial was erected shortly after liberation on the roll-call square, where it stood at least until 1946. Catholic Polish survivors, at 9,082 (including more than 1,000 priests) the largest national group in the camp when it was liberated, constructed a wooden altar with a wooden cross approximately 10 meters tall to celebrate their national holiday on May 3.[50] As in Belsen, the occupying military subsequently ordered local civilians to create a more permanent memorial. On June 14, 1945, the Associated Press reported that German civilians under orders from the Allied Military Government would erect two 15-meter-tall columns topped respectively by a cross and a Star of David at the nearby Leiten Hill mass grave.[51] The columns were to be made of stone from the Nazi Party's rally grounds in Nuremberg (a discordant symbolic material perhaps intended to signify the outcome of Nazi hubris), and they were to be completed by August. This plan was dropped in July, however, when it became known that the German designer had been affiliated with the Nazi Party. Another proposal was presented to the public in November, when the model for a gigantic "monument of liberation" was displayed in Dachau's city hall. A pylon crowned by a gold mosaic sun 6 meters in diameter

[49] See Heigl, *Konzentrationslager Flossenbürg in Geschichte und Gegenwart*, 90–91.

[50] See Detlef Hoffmann, "Dachau," in Hoffmann, *Das Gedächtnis der Dinge*, 51; see also Kathrin Hoffmann-Curtius, "Memorials for the Dachau Concentration Camps," *Oxford Art Journal* 21, no. 2 (1998): 21–44, 32. The survivor statistics at liberation are taken from William W. Quinn, *Dachau* (1945), 65, available at http://digital.library.wisc.edu/1711.dl/History.Dachau. The Polish group was followed by 4,258 Russians, 3,918 French, and 2,539 Jews, many of whom were Polish.

[51] For this and the following memorials, see Marcuse, *Legacies of Dachau*, 189–194. On the Koelle sculptures, see also Hoffmann, "Dachau," 58–62.

rising above a semicircular base 20 meters tall and 35 meters wide, it was to be constructed from bricks salvaged from the ruins of Munich—a symbolic material that would have linked the civilian suffering to the horrors in the camp. This project came under fire because it was deemed too grandiose. Instead, a memorial competition was conducted from April to September 1946. Twenty-one designs were submitted, but none of them were deemed acceptable.

After those maquettes burned and were lost in a fire at the Ministry of Culture, the project was subsequently "forgotten" (neglected) by local authorities until September 1949, when the accidental excavation of several skeletons near the gravesite provoked international outrage. A hastily conducted design competition in the spring of 1950 yielded 175 submissions, from which a proposal for an octagonal hall 10.5 meters high and 9 meters in diameter was selected. The seals of thirty-three countries whose citizens died in Dachau adorn the inside of the almost windowless basalt building, which was completed in 1952, but which so quickly slipped from the public spotlight that it was never formally dedicated. A journalist's satirical description of the 175 models from which this one was chosen indicates that grandiose, especially architectonic memorials were generally not considered appropriate representations of the mass murder that at the time was synonymous with the Holocaust. They included, he wrote, "modified churches of every age, Roman forts, Gothic citadels and neo-Germanic colonial forts, . . . shows of strength in *Heimat* style and transparent industrial halls, and even idyllic Biedermeier garden pavilions, constructions reminiscent of the Leipzig Battle of Nations monument, as well as neoclassical theaters and halls of fame."[52]

If such traditional architectonic memorial halls were seen as inappropriate for Holocaust memorials, realistic figurative memorials presented problems as well. One of the earliest such projects was realized in 1949–1950 in Dachau. This early sculpture was based on a 1946 statuette of two inmates by a German socialist sculptor who had been briefly imprisoned by the Gestapo. Fritz Koelle's "Inferno," depicting a clothed inmate supporting and pointing to a naked, emaciated comrade, was published on invitations to a September 1949 commemorative event, with a call for donations so that it could be erected as a memorial. That design, selected by survivor Philipp Auerbach, who headed the Bavarian state authority responsible for Holocaust survivors (then called "racial, religious, and political persecutees"), was intended to stand in front of the Dachau crematorium. It was immediately criticized by other survivors and the military government as being too graphic and accusatory— meanings they did not wish to represent. One Dachau survivor wrote to his French comrades that the sculpture was "universally condemned" because it "immortalized the horrors." Memories of the Nazi camps were still very vivid at the time, especially amid the plentiful physical remnants, and the sensibilities of survivors and the relatives of the victims had to be considered as well. Soon another design by the same artist was chosen instead: a depiction of a single forlorn-looking inmate, slightly smaller than life-size. It was dedicated in 1950, when the redesign of the Dachau crematorium enclave as a peacefully landscaped park was completed.

A comparison of the two Koelle sculptures reveals some of the formal considerations that still typify Holocaust memorials. The reduction from two figures to one

[52] Marcuse, *Legacies of Dachau*, 195, after *Münchner Merkur/Dachauer Nachrichten*, May 4, 1950.

FIGURE 16: Fritz Koelle, "Inferno" (1946). This statue was proposed for Dachau in 1948, but was withdrawn because it was too graphic. Photo courtesy of the Dachau Memorial Site.

FIGURE 17: Fritz Koelle's 1949 statue of an "Unknown Concentration Camp Inmate," near the Dachau crematorium; height of figure ca. 1.5 meters. Photo by Harold Marcuse.

is typical of memorials in Western Europe, where the anonymity and isolation of individuals caught in the machinery of mass murder tends to be emphasized. The memorials in Western Europe are also far more likely to be abstract than figurative, while in the socialist countries of the Eastern Bloc (with the limited exceptions of Poland and Yugoslavia), most memorials are figurative in the style of socialist realism, and they often depict groups of people so as to express solidarity and symbolize anti-fascist resistance as a movement. In the final Dachau design, the graphic skeletal nudity of the original figures is covered by a baggy overcoat and trousers; the accusatory right hand is concealed in a coat pocket. The forwardly thrust head is drawn back and tilted at a slight angle, giving the figure a contemplative cast. The inscription on the pedestal still melds contemplation with accusation, however: "To honor the dead, to admonish the living."

As the political situation in postwar Europe stabilized and economic conditions improved, the search for memorial forms that would express desired meanings took on much larger dimensions. Memorial competitions held in 1952 for Buchenwald, in 1953 in London for "the unknown political prisoner," and in 1957 for Auschwitz-Birkenau mark a trend away from realistic, figurative memorials toward abstract figures and forms. The first of these competitions, which resulted in one of the largest figurative sculptural Holocaust memorials ever completed, was announced by East Germany for Buchenwald in December 1951.

Because so many politically active survivors remained nearby, and because the state took a strong interest in the project, the Buchenwald memorial is the most complex, best-documented, and most thoroughly researched of all the Holocaust memorials erected prior to the 1990s.[53] We do not know how long the wooden obelisk on the roll-call square remained standing, because the Soviet occupation forces that took over the camp on June 4, 1945, kept it off limits while using it as an internment camp for Nazi suspects (and later socialist opponents of the ruling communists as well). Until the Soviets closed their "Special Camp No. 2" in 1950, the focus of memorialization efforts shifted to the other side of the hill, where the Buchenwald SS had created mass graves in natural depressions, but also where a post-liberation cemetery had been laid out near a 43-meter-tall Bismarck tower monument from 1901.[54] The very first memorial proposal, however, was for a "hall of [inter]national community" to be built in the center of the city of Weimar, five miles away.[55] Soil from thirty-six nations was to be buried in front of the windowless black south facade, where a fountain consisting of thirty-six jets merging into one would symbolize the unity of the thirty-six nations whose citizens had been imprisoned in Buchenwald.[56] Although politics and a lack of funding forced abandonment of the plan, this project is an early embodiment of an important feature of Holocaust remembrance in East Germany: the focus was not commemoration of the victims, but a celebration of anti-fascist resistance and international solidarity.

In spite of that setback, Buchenwald survivors continued to lobby for a memorial at the site. In 1949, plans were made to create a memorial grove around the various gravesites near the camp, and to replace the Bismarck tower with a new memorial. When the tower was demolished in May 1949, its proposed replacement was an inverted triangular pyramid 20 meters tall made of concrete.[57] Derived from the triangular badges worn by camp inmates, it bore the inscription "In memory of the dead victims of fascism, as a warning for us and the world." Its realization was de-layed first by material shortages, then by the sudden availability of the camp itself in February 1950, as well as by political differences between the survivors and the East German government. The survivors wanted to preserve more of the camp and emphasize what state representatives called the "funeral aspect" (*Bestattungsge-danke*), as opposed to the "commemorative aspect" (*Erinnerungsgedanke*)—a con-

[53] My portrayal follows Knigge, "Buchenwald." See also Volkhard Knigge, Jürgen Maria Pietsch, and Thomas A. Seidel, *Versteinertes Gedenken: Das Buchenwalder Mahnmal von 1958*, 2 vols. (Delitsch, 1997). For a shorter summary including more recent developments, see Puvogel, *Gedenkstätten für die Opfer des Nationalsozialismus*, 2: 896–901. Young, *The Texture of Memory*, 72–79, has a brief summary that is inaccurate in some details. Other well-researched Holocaust memorials include the Warsaw Ghetto monument (by James Young) and the memorials at Auschwitz (by Jochen Spielmann and several authors in Hoffmann, *Das Gedächtnis der Dinge*) and Dachau (by this author). Only the Berlin memorial to the murdered Jews of Europe is better documented and researched, with several weighty monographs already published prior to its completion in 2005.

[54] See "Gedenkstätte statt Bismarckturm: Der Bismarckturm in Weimar," updated January 30, 2006, at http://www.bismarcktuerme.de/website/ebene4/thue/weimar.html (accessed October 26, 2007).

[55] The incorrect and presumably inadvertent use of the Nazi term *Volksgemeinschaft* (national community) instead of *Völkergemeinschaft* (community of nations) indicates the difficulty in breaking away from Nazi jargon and traditions, as did the form of the first Buchenwald obelisk.

[56] Knigge, "Buchenwald," 101–102, 104–105.

[57] Ibid., 106–108.

FIGURE 18: Aerial view of the 1958 Buchenwald memorial ensemble, one of the largest Holocaust memorials. Photo courtesy of Gedenkstätte Buchenwald.

flict that would also afflict the Birkenau project a decade later.[58] Even after the international competition had been scaled down to an East German competition in December 1951, the state—including Prime Minister Otto Grotewohl personally—continued to work with Fritz Cremer, one of the prizewinners selected in March 1952, until he produced a satisfactorily heroic group of figures.[59] By 1955, the final design had been worked out. It was by far the largest and most elaborate Holocaust-related memorial created at the time, and remained so for decades.

From a parking lot at the top of the hill, a wide, sloping path descends past seven large bas-reliefs, depicting scenes typical of each year in the seven-year history of the camp, to a funnel-shaped ring grave. Then a wide "avenue of nations," flanked on the right by eighteen massive pylons, each bearing the name of a country and crowned by a large fire basin on a trivet, extends leftward to another funnel-shaped grave. Finally, an ascending broad "stairway of freedom" leads up to Cremer's monumental sculpture in front of a 55-meter-tall bell tower.[60] The bronze sculpture, representing the motto "Through death and battle to victory," is composed of eleven archetypal figures approximately 3 meters tall, including "child," "flag bearer," "fighter," "oath taker," "faller," "fighter in blanket," "caller," "doubter," and "negativist." Dedicated in September 1958, it was the first of three major concentration camp memorials erected by East Germany.

[58] Ibid., 108, 112, 115–117.
[59] Ibid., 124–125.
[60] This height is from Milton and Nowinski, *In Fitting Memory*, 190; Young, *The Texture of Memory*, 77, gives the tower's height as 49 meters (160 feet).

FIGURE 19: The main Buchenwald memorial, 1958, with a tower by the Buchenwald Collective (height 55 meters) and sculpture by Fritz Cremer (height 4 meters). Photo by Eva Wendebourg.

As in Buchenwald, early postwar memorialization attempts at Ravensbrück and Sachsenhausen led only to provisional solutions. Not until 1955, when the East German government decided that there was to be an ensemble of three national memorial sites and created a "curatorium" to oversee nationwide fundraising efforts, did concerted efforts to find permanent memorial designs begin. The first to be completed was at Ravensbrück, a concentration camp specifically for female inmates about 60 kilometers northwest of Berlin. In 1948, 1952, and 1954, temporary monuments had already been erected there for commemorative ceremonies: on a base four steps above the ground, a rectangular block approximately 2.5 meters high was crowned by a stone fire basin.[61] The permanent memorial, dedicated in September 1959, was designed by German sculptor Will Lammert, who had lived in Soviet exile from 1934 to 1951.

The main Ravensbrück memorial, which Lammert worked on from 1954 until his death in 1957, is similar to a monument he designed in exile in 1941, in which a female

[61] On the temporary memorials, see Insa Eschebach, "Zur Formensprache der Totenehrung: Ravensbrück in der frühen Nachkriegszeit," in Eschebach, Jacobeit, and Lanwerd, *Die Sprache des Gedenkens*, 13–39, esp. 25–28. On the 1959 memorial, see Susanne Lanwerd, "Skulpturales Gedenken," ibid., 39–54, and the memorial site's page, http://www.ravensbrueck.de/mgr/english/memorial/1959bis1992.htm (accessed November 2, 2007). See also Puvogel, *Gedenkstätten für die Opfer des Nationalsozialismus*, 2: 272; and Milton and Nowinski, *In Fitting Memory*, 158–161.

allegorical figure, "Constitution," is attached to the front of a high pylon crowned by a fire basin.[62] The memorial, titled "Carrier," depicts a female prisoner holding the limp body of a dead comrade. The sculpture stands 4.2 meters high and is set atop a rectangular pylon approximately 7 meters tall on a stone platform extending into Schwedt Lake, above the spot where ash from the crematorium was rumored to have been dumped. Two additional sculptural groups, by Lammert and Cremer, were placed at other locations in the memorial site. One consists of two individual women looking out over a communal gravesite planted as a rose garden; the other is a "group of mothers": three women holding a cloth with an infant on it.[63]

Sachsenhausen, in Oranienburg on the northern outskirts of Berlin, played a key role in the Nazi concentration camp system. Created in 1936 on undeveloped land with a symbolic triangular prisoners' compound, from 1938 on it housed the central administration of the concentration camp system. After the Soviets turned the camp over to East German authorities in 1950, East German state police were stationed in the SS part of the camp, while the prisoners' compound fell into disrepair. For a commemoration ceremony in May 1954, most of the former prison barracks were demolished, and police trainees used bricks from the former camp prison to construct a provisional memorial on the roll-call square.[64] In the formal tradition of war me-

FIGURE 20: Will Lammert, Ravensbrück memorial "Carrier," 1959. This sculpture is 4.2 meters tall and sits atop a 7-meter pedestal. By the late 1950s, the heroic socialist realist style was becoming more abstract. Photo by Harold Marcuse.

morials, it was composed of a central block approximately 2.7 meters tall, flanked by two blocks around 1.5 meters tall. The central block was adorned by a relief of a Soviet soldier carrying an inmate in his arms, and crowned by a flat triangle standing on its point, bearing the letters VVN, the abbreviation for the German Association of the Persecutees of National Socialism.

[62] Described in Lanwerd, "Skulpturales Gedenken," 42 n. 8.

[63] The Ravensbrück memorials raise the question of the role of gender in Holocaust memorialization. Ravensbrück, the Nazi concentration camp designated for the imprisonment of women, is one of the few Holocaust memorials outside of Israel to use figures of women. On this question, see Judith Tydor Baumel, " 'Rachel Laments Her Children': Representations of Women in Israeli Holocaust Memorials," *Israel Studies* 1, no. 1 (1996): 100–126; Insa Eschebach, Sigrid Jacobeit, and Silke Wenk, eds., *Gedächtnis und Geschlecht: Deutungsmuster in Darstellungen des nationalsozialistischen Genozids* (Frankfurt, 2002).

[64] See Susanne zur Nieden, "Erste Initiativen für Mahnmale in Oranienburg und Sachsenhausen," in Morsch, *Von der Erinnerung zum Monument*, 125–132, esp. 128–130, with photographs.

FIGURE 21: Provisional memorial in Sachsenhausen, 1954. This memorial, ca. 2.7 meters tall, was built from bricks from the camp prison, which had been demolished by state authorities against the wishes of the survivors. Photo from the Stiftung Brandenburgische Gedenkstätten/Archiv Sachsenhausen.

FIGURE 22: Sachsenhausen memorial tower; height 35–40 meters, with sculpture by René Graetz, 4–5 meters tall, 1961. The triangular prisoner's badge is the dominant symbol on this triangular pylon with slightly concave sides. Photo by Bonnie M. Harris.

Since most of the barracks had been razed without their knowledge or approval, the Sachsenhausen survivors were forced to come up with a new plan for the entire site.[65] As in Buchenwald, their wish to preserve and rebuild parts of the camp so as to present the daily persecution of the inmates came into conflict with the vision of state planners, who wanted a more heroic memorialization.[66] After the survivors secured approval from the Central Committee of the ruling Socialist Unity Party for the remaining structures to be preserved and integrated into the memorial site, in the summer of 1956 a group of East German architects who had previously submitted designs for Buchenwald toured Holocaust sites in Europe. The documentation they presented in December of that year offers a photographic record of the major Holocaust memorials at that time: Dachau, Flossenbürg, Auschwitz I and Birkenau, Majdanek, Neuengamme, Belsen, Hamburg, and Warsaw.[67]

[65] My portrayal follows Ulrike Köpp, "Die Studien des Buchenwald-Kollektivs für die Gestaltung der Gedenkstätte Sachsenhausen 1956," ibid., 158–163.

[66] The plan favored by the survivors was sketched by Reinhold Linger, a landscape architect who, with Bertolt Brecht and Fritz Cremer, had already submitted a design in the Buchenwald competition. See Ulrike Köpp, "Der Entwurf Reinhold Lingers für die Gedenkstätte Sachsenhausen," ibid., 148–157.

[67] The Buchenwald collective's report is reprinted ibid., 164–216. It includes two memorials not discussed in this essay (they are not Holocaust memorials in the narrower sense), namely the 1952 memorial by Gerhard Marcks for the 38,000 victims of the 1943 aerial bombing of Hamburg and the monument at the execution site in the Warsaw Citadel.

Although the collective's suggestions contained most of the features of the design that was finally implemented, the demolition of structures on the site continued, much to the dismay of the survivors.[68] As Volkhard Knigge, director of the Buchenwald Memorial site since the 1990s, has written, "The minimization of remains is a prerequisite for the maximization of possibilities for creating new meanings."[69] The memorial site, dedicated in April 1961, turned the entire prisoners' compound into an aesthetic ensemble. A semicircular wall punctured by a network of cruciform holes around bas-reliefs of the end walls of the barracks that formerly bordered that space closed off the former roll-call square opposite the entrance gate. A wide opening in the central axis of the triangular camp allows entering visitors to see the reinforced concrete tower standing 35 to 40 meters high near the apex of the triangle at the opposite corner of the camp perimeter. Triangular in cross-section with slightly concave sides, it is adorned by eighteen red triangular plaques in six rows of three on the top

FIGURE 23: Waldemar Grzimek, sculpture in the ruins of the Sachsenhausen crematorium, 1961; height ca. 2.2 meters. These more abstract figures contrast with the heroic group on the main Sachsenhausen memorial. Photo courtesy of Scrapbookpages.com.

third of each side. In front of the tower on a large block is "Liberation," a sculpture by René Graetz. Standing 4 to 5 meters tall, it depicts a Soviet soldier with his arms draped over the shoulders of two strong inmates standing slightly in front of him. The towering bronze figures are cast in a heroically idealized but realistic style reminiscent of the memorials in Warsaw and Buchenwald. A second memorial sculpture, by Waldemar Grzimek, the sculptor of the bell in the Buchenwald tower, stands among the ruins of the crematorium and execution site at the nearby edge of the prisoners' compound. Only moderately larger than life-size in the more restrained figurative style of the Ravensbrück and Dachau statues, it depicts two inmates, one standing and one bent over, holding a cloth that supports the corpse of a comrade.

---

[68] See Ulrike Köpp, "Die Projektierung der Gedenkstätte Sachsenhausen und die Diskussionen im Wissenschaftlich-Künstlerischen Beirat beim Ministerium für Kultur," ibid., 217–231.

[69] Volkhard Knigge, "Vom Reden und Schweigen der Steine," in Sigrid Weigel and Birgit Erdle, eds., *Fünfzig Jahre danach: Zur Nachgeschichte des Nationalsozialismus* (Zurich, 1996), 193–235, 207.

MOST OF THE EARLY Holocaust memorials were derived from either classical monuments (obelisks and towers) or traditional war memorials. Beginning with the Warsaw Ghetto Memorial and continuing with the three great memorial projects in East Germany, socialist countries were developing a heroic, socialist realist style for their Holocaust monuments. (The Soviet war memorial erected in Berlin-Treptow from 1946 to 1949, which depicts a caped soldier standing on a broken swastika, holding a child in one hand and a bare sword in the other, is another classic example of this tradition.)[70] As can be seen in the Ravensbrück sculptures, however, a more abstract figurative tradition was emerging by the late 1950s, and a modernist architectonic tradition was developing as well. It had roots in the internationalist style of the World War I era, embodied, for example, in Vladimir Tatlin's 1920 constructivist proposal for a monument to the Third International, which was never built but sparked much discussion in art circles.[71] Picasso's famed monumental painting *Guernica*, created for the 1937 International Exposition in Paris and inspired by the Nazi aerial bombardment of the Basque capital city, is an example of the use of abstract forms to represent a barbaric massacre of civilians that can be considered a precursor to the Holocaust.[72]

An international sculptural competition for a "monument to the unknown political prisoner," held in London in 1953, can be seen as setting the stage for a new generation of Holocaust memorials in an abstract, avant-garde style. Unprecedented in scope, it comprised a series of national competitions, from which 3,500 submissions from 57 countries were whittled down to 140 that were judged in London. Joan Marter and Robert Burstow have convincingly argued that Cold War considerations played a crucial role in the competition, in that it was intended to establish an artistic style for the capitalist West that was superior to the socialist realism of the Eastern Bloc.[73] Thus, essentially all of the winning designs—none of them from socialist countries, which were not even invited to participate—were highly abstract. None of them were ever implemented (probably in part because of the taint of the competition's implicit anti-totalitarian thrust), but given the magnitude of the artistic event, it is safe to assume that most of the artists who took part in the next major Holocaust memorial competition were aesthetically influenced by those designs.

[70] The English and German Wikipedia pages offer photographs and accurate information about this 12-meter-tall statue. See http://en.wikipedia.org/wiki/Soviet_War_Memorial_(Treptower_Park) (accessed November 2, 2007).

[71] The Wikipedia page on Tatlin's monument has basic information, illustrations, and references: http://en.wikipedia.org/wiki/Tatlin's_Tower (accessed November 2, 2007). Two other seminal memorials in this tradition are Walter Gropius's 1922 memorial to those killed in the March 1919 putsch in Weimar, and Ludwig Mies van der Rohe's 1926 memorial for Rosa Luxemburg and Karl Liebknecht in Berlin-Lichtenberg. Both were destroyed by the Nazis. See Rieth, *Monuments to the Victims of Tyranny*, 15, plates 22 and 23.

[72] For basic background, see "Guernica: Testimony of War," in the PBS "Treasures of the World" Series, http://www.pbs.org/treasuresoftheworld/a_nav/guernica_nav/main_guerfrm.html (accessed November 2, 2007); or Russell Martin, *Picasso's War: The Destruction of Guernica and the Masterpiece That Changed the World* (New York, 2002). Ossip Zadkine's monument "The Destroyed City" (Rotterdam, 1953) belongs in this tradition. See Johannes Langner, *Ossip Zadkine: Mahnmal für Rotterdam, eine Einführung* (Stuttgart, 1963).

[73] Joan Marter, "The Ascendancy of Abstraction for Public Art: The Monument to the Unknown Political Prisoner Competition," *Art Journal* 53, no. 4 (Winter 1994): 28–36; and Robert Burstow, "The Limits of Modernist Art as a 'Weapon of the Cold War': Reassessing the Unknown Patron of the Monument to the Unknown Political Prisoner," *Oxford Art Journal* 20, no. 1 (1997): 68–80. See also Rieth, *Monuments to the Victims of Tyranny*, 16–17, plates 46–49.

In Auschwitz, memorial efforts began before the end of the war, but the extant structures in its huge component camps Auschwitz I, Birkenau, and Monowitz were themselves so impressive that the need for symbolic representation was not pressing. In fact, in contrast to East Germany, where most of the concentration camp buildings had been torn down, in Auschwitz the preservation of the remnants was given priority over other memorial schemes from the very beginning. On May 1, 1945, even before Germany's surrender, Poland's provisional government placed "those parts of the concentration camp in Oświęcim that were connected to the immediate destruction of millions of people" under the administration of the Ministry of Culture and Art, which was

FIGURE 24: For the tenth anniversary of liberation in 1955, this traditional so-called urn memorial was erected in Auschwitz-Birkenau; height ca. 3 meters. It contained ashes from other concentration camps. Photo by the Buchenwald Collective, from the Stiftung Brandenburgische Gedenkstätten/Archiv Sachsenhausen.

also charged with developing a concept for a museum.[74] The ministry approved a formal proposal in February 1946, and by April, camp survivors were working to create a museum, which officially opened in June 1947.[75] In July 1947, the Polish parliament passed a law stipulating that all remaining structures must be preserved. Around 1950, a small memorial wall resembling a Jewish gravestone was erected by private initiative near Birkenau's crematorium II. With no figurative representations, its three-column inscription read in Polish, Yiddish, and Hebrew: "In memory of the millions of Jewish martyrs and fighters exterminated in the camp Auschwitz-Birkenau by the National Socialist race murderers, 1940–1945."[76]

The wall was removed when the first official memorial was erected in Birkenau for the tenth anniversary of liberation in 1955. Approximately 3 meters tall, it was a nearly cubical trapezoidal "urn" on a three-tiered plinth, set just beyond the end of the so-called ramp: the flat area between two train tracks where deported Jews had disembarked and were sorted for either immediate murder in the gas chambers or the slower "extermination through work." Little is known about this memorial, except that it contained ashes from other extermination camps.[77] Photographs show a block-like sandstone monument with the outline of a triangle badge engraved into the side facing the back of the camp, and a bas-relief inscription around its base that included the Polish name for Auschwitz: Oświęcim. Although that memorial offered a focal point for commemorative activities, the newly created international orga-

[74] Jonathan Huener, *Auschwitz, Poland, and the Politics of Commemoration, 1945–1979* (Athens, Ohio, 2003), 60; unless otherwise noted, the following paragraph is based on 62, 69, 112–114.

[75] On the Auschwitz exhibitions, see Engelhardt, *A Topography of Memory*, 161–165. The dates are conveniently summarized on the Auschwitz museum website: http://en.auschwitz.org.pl/m/index .php?option=com_content&task=view&id=226&Itemid=13 (accessed January 3, 2010).

[76] See Ute Wrocklage, "Auschwitz-Birkenau—Die Rampe," in Hoffmann, *Das Gedächtnis der Dinge*, 278–309; and the illustration in Council for the Preservation of Monuments to Resistance and Martyrdom, *Scenes of Fighting and Martyrdom Guide*, ill. 143.

[77] On the 1955 "urn," see Wrocklage, "Auschwitz-Birkenau," 291 n. 46; and Hoffmann, "Introduction," in Hoffmann, *Das Gedächtnis der Dinge*, 25.

FIGURE 25: Julio Lafuente, Pietro Cascella, and Andrea Cascella, proposal from the first round of the competition for a memorial in Auschwitz-Birkenau, 1958. The railroad symbolism was deemed not comprehensive enough to represent what had taken place in Birkenau. Photo by Jochen Spielmann.

nization of Auschwitz survivors wanted something that would better reflect the camp's meanings to them, of which they may only have had an inchoate idea at that time.

The survivors' association worked out guidelines for a design competition, which were published in 1957. They stipulated that the memorial would stand near the end of the "ramp" where the urn now stood, and that, in accordance with the 1946 law, what was left of the camp could not be altered. British sculptor Henry Moore, a pioneer of abstract modernist sculpture, agreed to chair the selection committee, which met in April 1958 to judge 426 designs submitted by artists from thirty-one countries.[78] Eight finalists were invited to visit the site and refine their designs, which were then judged in Paris in November. The jury did not find any of the designs completely convincing, but they selected the three projects they found most promising and asked those design teams—from Poland, Spain, and Italy—to work together to submit a final proposal. The selection of those three designs, all to varying degrees conceptual and abstract, indicates the difficulty of using human forms to

[78] The most detailed examination of the Auschwitz competition is Jochen Spielmann, "Entwürfe zur Sinngebung des Sinnlosen: Zu einer Theorie des Denkmals als Manifestation des 'kulturellen Gedächtnisses': Der Wettbewerb für ein Denkmal für Auschwitz" (Ph.D. diss., Free University of Berlin, 1990). Spielmann's analysis is summarized by Hoffmann, "Introduction," in *Das Gedächtnis der Dinge*, 25–30. See also Rieth, *Monuments to the Victims of Tyranny*, 17–18, plates 68–71; Katarzyna Murawska-Muthesius, "Oskar Hansen and the Auschwitz 'Countermemorial,' 1958–59," *ARTMargins* e-journal, May 20, 2002, http://www.artmargins.com/index.php/archive/311-oskar-hansen-and-the-auschwitz-qcountermemorialq-1958-59 (accessed January 3, 2010); and Young, *The Texture of Memory*, 133–143. The Auschwitz state museum offers a timeline of the memorial site at http://en.auschwitz.org.pl/m/index.php?option=com_content&task=view&id=226&Itemid=13 (accessed January 3, 2010).

FIGURE 26: The final Birkenau memorial, erected in 1967. It was the result of several rounds of compromises and reductions. Ultimately, the extensive remnants of the camps have remained the true memorial. Photo by Harold. Marcuse.

represent the Holocaust, especially when they would have to compete with extensive architectural remains.

The Polish group proposed a street, 70 meters in width, to be paved with black stones that would symbolically "cancel" the Birkenau camp by obliterating a wide diagonal swath across it, with some features, such as fences and the ruins of the crematoria, remaining to pierce through it. The Italian design carved out a ramp descending from the original unloading "ramp" to an excavated square between the ruins of crematoria II and III, with trench-like corridors extending outward around the perimeters of the two semi-subterranean buildings. This design included groups of sculpted figures at various locations in the camp. Both designs were inadmissible, however, because they altered the remnants of the camp. The Spanish team's design located twenty-three stylized stone railway cars (one for each of the countries of origin of the victims) on the tracks alongside the ramp, with a massive, irregular stone barrier set across the tracks, symbolically blocking the route to the crematoria farther on. It ultimately was rejected because freight cars did not represent the full range of experiences in the camp.

The three teams agreed to work together to form a synthesis of their ideas, which the jury approved in May 1959 with some modifications. Two years later, the group was asked to reduce their synthesis once more, because it was too costly and still required too many modifications to the camp. The symbolic barring of the camp entry arch and the dug-out passage encircling the crematoria were removed. What remained was a modified version of the irregular block-like barrier, now located directly between the two crematoria. It was flattened into a wide row of abstract "sarcophagi" with a low tower near one end, vaguely reminiscent of a crematorium oven

FIGURE 27: This English-language Birkenau inscription plaque from 1967 is one of 20 plaques in different languages. Typical of the time, it lacks specificity in naming the victims. It also contains an estimated number of deaths that later proved incorrect. Photo by Jochen Spielmann.

FIGURE 28: The revised Birkenau plaques from 1995 are more graphic and specific in naming the audience, perpetrators, and victims. The reduced contrast of the all-bronze plaques, however, makes the inscriptions more difficult to read. Photo by Harold Marcuse.

with a stretcher and chimney, with three highly abstract cubic figures, perhaps evoking a man, woman, and child, standing next to the stretcher. The facade of the tower is topped by four rectangular blocks of smooth black marble forming a square slab with a small red triangle badge cut into its center.[79] A row of twenty plaques in front of the sarcophagi bore an inscription in twenty languages: "Four million people suffered and died here at the hands of the Nazi murderers between the years 1940 and 1945." In 1995, after consensus was reached that the figure of 4 million was incorrect, these were replaced with new plaques reading:

For ever let this place be a cry of despair and a warning to humanity, where the Nazis murdered about one and a half million men, women, and children, mainly Jews from various countries of Europe. Auschwitz-Birkenau, 1940–1945.

The restatement goes from a minimalist statement of presumed fact (4 million was the accepted number of deaths at Auschwitz at that time, based on the testimony of its last commandant) to an emotional admonition that definitively names the perpetrator and victim groups. The shift to explicit appeals and specific information evidenced by these inscriptions would come to typify the development of the genre of Holocaust memorials in the 1990s.

After the Auschwitz competition in 1958, Holocaust memorialization began to diverge sharply from the traditional forms of war memorials (stelae, towers, realistic statuary) to larger, more expansive, abstract, avant-garde forms.[80] The six prize-

[79] Young, *The Texture of Memory*, 139–141, notes that last-minute changes were made only days before the unveiling in 1967: the group of abstract figures was moved from near the top of the tower to the ground in front of it, with the tower now culminating in the polished black marble slab. No explanation has been found for the change.

[80] Rieth, *Monuments to the Victims of Tyranny*, contains additional examples of more traditional figurative sculptural memorials from the 1950s at Holocaust-related sites, for example at the Ardeatine Caves near Rome (1950, plate 28), Dortmund (1959, plate 29), and Frankfurt (1964, plate 37). Two of

FIGURE 29: Nandor Glid, international memorial at Dachau, proposed in 1959 and dedicated in 1968; height 6.2 meters. This highly abstract sculpture of skeletal shapes forming a barbed-wire fence is set above a descending ramp on its front side, typical of the experiential spaces used in Holocaust memorials since the early 1960s. Photo by Harold Marcuse.

winning entries in a competition held by the international Dachau survivors' organization from January to November 1959 were highly abstract.[81] The survivors' newsletter described them as a tall, winged iron sculpture; a pyramid with 238,000 pipes, symbolizing the number of inmates who had passed through the camp; a massive, crypt-like "descent into hell"; a "very expressive" skeletal humanoid form over a ramp-like base; a crystalline "cathedral" 15 to 18 meters tall; and a slender lattice-work tower of "thorns" standing 35 meters high, with two angular prisms rising to a height of perhaps 10 meters behind it. The design that was ultimately realized in 1968, by Yugoslavian sculptor Nandor Glid, was a modification of his "very expressive" humanoid form: measuring 6 by 16 meters, it was a tangled mass of highly abstract emaciated bodies with angular barbed hands, supported by two fence posts with fragments of stylized barbed wire to suggest human beings entangled in the fencing that surrounded the concentration camps.

---

the national memorials erected in Mauthausen in 1958, by Italy and Yugoslavia, illustrate the transition with their combination of traditional stelae and abstract sculptures (plates 74–75). For examples of traditional towers, see plates 80–82.

[81] Marcuse, *Legacies of Dachau*, 258–260, figs. 58–62.

FIGURE 30: Bertrand Monnet and Lucien Fenaux, memorial in Natzweiler-Struthof, France, 1960; height 40.5 meters. Typical of the emerging genre of Holocaust memorials, this tower is experiential and abstract, with the Holocaust-specific symbolism of a human form going up a smokestack. Photo by Harold Marcuse.

FIGURE 31: G. H. Pingusson, National Memorial for the Martyrs of the Deportation, Île de la Cité, Paris, 1962; view into the crypt lined with 200,000 lighted translucent pebbles. This experiential space in the symbolic heart of France lists the Holocaust sites to which French citizens were deported. Photo by Harold Marcuse.

Memorials erected in France and Poland in the 1960s culminate this trend toward abstract, avant-garde forms.[82] After a relatively traditional Memorial to the Unknown Jewish Martyr was completed in 1956 in Paris—an aboveground cylinder bearing the names of thirteen Holocaust sites, with a marble Star of David in a subterranean room—a national memorial site in the former Natzweiler-Struthof camp in the Alsace was opened in 1960. Its central memorial is an open stone cylinder, 40.5 meters tall, rising in a graceful curve to a point, with a huge sunken relief of a waif-like human form floating on the inside, like smoke rising up a chimney. France's central Mémorial des Martyrs de La Déportation was dedicated on the tip of the Île de la Cité behind Notre Dame Cathedral in 1962. A narrow stairway descends to a small courtyard with a jaggedly barred opening onto the Seine on one side, and a narrow entry into a geometrically shaped crypt lined with 200,000 backlit quartz pebbles, representing the 200,000 deportees who were French citizens, on the other.[83] Fifteen triangles bearing the names of the primary sites throughout Nazi-

[82] The following memorials are illustrated and described in Rieth, *Monuments to the Victims of Tyranny*, plates 88, 100–102; and Milton and Nowinski, *In Fitting Memory*, 202–210.

[83] For a collection of images of the Paris deportation memorial, see Anthony McNeill and Leigh Kempner, "Occupied France: Commemorating the Deportation," http://new.filter.ac.uk/database/getinsight.php?id=51&seq=211 (accessed September 26, 2008). The memorial's official website is http://www.defense.gouv.fr/sga/enjeux_defense/histoire_et_patrimoine/memoire/monuments/memoriaux/memorial_des_martyrs_de_la_deportation (accessed September 26, 2008).

FIGURE 32: Adam Haupt and Franciszek Duszenko, memorial at Treblinka, 1959/1964. This tower (height ca. 7 meters), set in a symbolic cemetery with more than 17,000 jagged stones, displays overt Jewish symbolism. Photo by Harold Marcuse.

controlled Europe where French citizens were persecuted adorn one of the interior walls, illustrating the "Holocaust principle" of enumerating multiple locations to signify the entire event.

Memorials at the former extermination centers in Poland also illustrate the shift to new forms after the Auschwitz competition. Designed in 1960 and completed in 1964, the memorial for Treblinka consists of a massive 7-meter-tall tower of large granite blocks, cleft down the middle and capped by a rounded, mushroom-like block carved with abstract reliefs and Jewish symbols.[84] It is surrounded by 17,000 loosely spaced jagged stones, evoking a Jewish cemetery, many of which are inscribed with the names of Jewish villages wiped out in the Holocaust. A separate set of larger stones, arranged in a row, bear the names of the countries of origin of the victims of Treblinka, again illustrating the national principle. The other main Polish Holocaust memorial erected in the 1960s was dedicated at Majdanek in September 1969, based on a design by Wiktor Tolkin selected from 130 entries in a competition held in 1967–1968.[85] A huge carved stone block, approximately 15 meters tall, 40

[84] See Young, *The Texture of Memory*, 186–192; Rieth, *Monuments to the Victims of Tyranny*, plates 2–3, 64–65; and Milton and Nowinski, *In Fitting Memory*, 136–147.

[85] See Young, *The Texture of Memory*, 124–126; Milton and Nowinski, *In Fitting Memory*, 148–152. Chełmno, Stutthof, Sobibor, and Belzec are more remote and less well known. The 4-meter-tall memorial at Chełmno, concrete slabs with bas-reliefs balanced on pyramidal supports, was completed in 1964; see Rieth, *Monuments to the Victims of Tyranny*, plate 63. Tolkin had previously designed the memorial for Stutthof (about thirty miles east of Gdansk), dedicated in May 1968. See http://www.in yourpocket.com/poland/gdansk/sightseeing/category/58897-Stutthof.html (accessed February 8, 2008). The tall sculptural memorial in Sobibor was erected in the 1990s. The Belzec memorial was dedicated in 2004; see http://www.chgs.umn.edu/museum/memorials/belzec/index.html (accessed January 18, 2008).

FIGURE 33: Wiktor Tolkin, memorial in Majdanek, 1969; height ca. 15 meters. As one of the last main Holocaust sites to be memorialized, this sculpture combines the abstract and experiential elements typical of Holocaust memorials by the early 1960s. Photo by Harold Marcuse.

meters wide, and perhaps 5 meters deep, is set upon two supports standing almost 4 meters tall, allowing visitors to pass under it on their way toward a domed open-air mausoleum over a huge mound of human ash at the back of the camp. As in the international memorial in Dachau, a ramp-like path descends to the base of the Majdanek memorial, enabling visitors to experience the massive weight of the sculpture from below. Beginning with the Buchenwald memorial and numerous designs for the Birkenau competition, and continuing with the Île de la Cité in Paris, Treblinka, and Yad Vashem near Jerusalem, such experiential spaces have become a hallmark of major Holocaust memorials, including most recently the Memorial to the Murdered Jews of Europe in Berlin, dedicated in 2005.[86]

THE FIRST HOLOCAUST MEMORIALS stood firmly in the tradition of funerary monuments and war memorials: towers and stelae in classical geometric forms. For figurative sculptures, two traditions emerged: first, expressionistic, heroic realism, especially in the Soviet-influenced Eastern Bloc; and slightly later, a more abstract, avant-garde tradition throughout Europe. One might call the former a Rodin-in-

[86] See the online exhibition "Yad Vashem, 1953–2003," at http://www1.yadvashem.org/about_yad/jubilee/history_Brief.html, especially the menu item "Commemoration" on that page (accessed January 11, 2008). The core memorial, the 75-meter-square concrete "Hall of Remembrance" (1961), contains an eternal flame, the names of twenty-one Nazi killing sites engraved in the black basalt floor, and a crypt with ashes of victims. See also Young, *The Texture of Memory*, 249–261; and Rieth, *Monuments to the Victims of Tyranny*, 27, plate 98. For the Berlin memorial, see http://www.holocaust-mahnmal.de/en, especially http://www.holocaust-mahnmal.de/en/thememorial/history/chronology (accessed December 9, 2009). The "Garden of Exile" created by Daniel Libeskind in 1999 at the Jewish Museum in Berlin is another experiential space using closely spaced stelae to disorient visitors. See http://www.juedisches-museum-berlin.de/site/EN/05-About-The-Museum/03-Libeskind-Building/05-Garden-of-Exile/garden-of-exile.php (accessed September 19, 2008).

spired line, with the latter tradition following sculptors such as Ernst Barlach and Käthe Kollwitz. Especially in the early memorials at Holocaust sites, collections of heraldry, inscriptions, or separate monuments contributed by various countries were employed to represent the transnational scope of the Holocaust. Conversely, memorials at non-Holocaust locations often list Holocaust sites or collect soil or relics from those sites with the same intent. The international competition for a memorial for Auschwitz-Birkenau in the late 1950s marks a transition to a wholly new genre of memorial: expansive, complex, avant-garde sculptures that create or incorporate experiential spaces with multiple symbolic elements. Although "the Holocaust" in its specifically Jewish meaning was not a prominent event of public commemoration in the 1950s, the iconography and aesthetic traditions of its later representation did emerge during that decade. In spite of the Cold War–influenced 1953 competition for a "monument to the unknown political prisoner," we find that the emergence of a new memorial tradition for commemorating the Holocaust transcended the political division of the East-West conflict. Examples in France, Poland, and elsewhere in the 1960s show that the new genre had gained currency around the world by that time.[87]

[87] Additional examples of the emerging new genre of Holocaust memorials not discussed here include the West Park Cemetery in Johannesburg, South Africa (1959; photograph at http://www.allatsea.co.za/cems/westparkmemorial.htm), and Philadelphia (1964 by Nathan Rapoport; see http://www.chgs.umn.edu/museum/memorials/philadelphiaMem/). See also the memorials in Pristina and Jasenovac, Yugoslavia (1960 and 1963, respectively), depicted in Rieth, *Monuments to the Victims of Tyranny*, plates 60–61.

Harold Marcuse is Associate Professor of German History at the University of California, Santa Barbara. His works include an exhibition of Holocaust and World War II memorials, published as *Steine des Anstosses: Nationalsozialismus und Zweiter Weltkrieg in Denkmalen, 1945–1985* (Museum für Hamburgische Geschichte, 1985); a monographic history of the post-1945 history of the Dachau concentration camp, *Legacies of Dachau: The Uses and Abuses of a Concentration Camp, 1933–2001* (Cambridge University Press, 2001); and numerous articles about how Germany and other countries have dealt with legacies of the Nazi era.

The First Wave of American "Holocaust" Films, 1945–1959

LAWRENCE BARON

COMMENTING ON MAX WEINREICH'S BOOK *Hitler's Professors* for the *American Historical Review* in 1946, Roland Usher declared, "It is hardly necessary today to prove terrorism and the intentional extermination of the Jews. Murder camps, mass murder, and mass executions have already been extensively described."[1] In retrospect, Usher's confidence in the state of knowledge about Nazi genocidal policies can be attributed to his expertise in German history and the flow of films, news, and photographs showing the liberation of German concentration camps by Allied troops and the first Nuremberg Trial.

Most Holocaust scholars would dismiss Usher's claim as a momentary aberration and trace American public awareness of the Jewish ordeal to the late 1950s, when the term "Holocaust" became synonymous with Hitler's eradication of the Jews.[2] They concur that American consciousness of the subject dissipated quickly after 1946, for a variety of reasons: a failure to comprehend the Nazi assault on European Jewry, the outbreak of the Cold War, the Soviet Union's replacement of Germany as the archenemy of the United States, the pursuit of peacetime normalcy, the rehabilitation of West Germany as a strategic ally, and the tendency to subsume the Nazi onslaught against the Jews under the rubric of war crimes and crimes against humanity. In this standard interpretation, the subsequent popularization of the Holocaust as a distinctly Jewish tragedy emerged as a response to the trial of Adolf Eichmann, the fear that Israel had been on the brink of obliteration before the Six Day War in 1967, the ensuing admiration of its rapid victory in that conflict, perceived parallels to the Vietnam War, the growth of multiculturalism, and the rise of identity politics among disadvantaged minorities who documented their past and present victimization.[3]

I want to thank the following for their useful feedback on earlier drafts of this article: Steven Carr, David Cesarani, Henry Greenspan, Marnie Hughes-Warrington, Joel Rosenberg, and Robert Rosenstone.

[1] Roland G. Usher, review of Max Weinreich, *Hitler's Professors: The Part of Scholarship in Germany's Crimes against the Jewish People*, *American Historical Review* 52, no. 1 (October 1946): 120.

[2] Zev Garber and Bruce Zuckerman, "Why Do We Call the Holocaust 'the Holocaust'? An Inquiry into the Psychology of Labels," *Modern Judaism* 9, no. 2 (1989): 197–211; Gerd Korman, "The Holocaust in American Historical Writing," *Societas* 2, no. 3 (1972): 250–262; Jon Petrie, "The Secular Word Holocaust: Scholarly Myths, History, and 20th Century Meanings," *Journal of Genocide Research* 2, no. 1 (2000): 31–63.

[3] Tim Cole, *Selling the Holocaust: From Auschwitz to Schindler—How History Is Bought, Packaged, and Sold* (New York, 1999), 23–40; Lucy S. Dawidowicz, *The Holocaust and the Historians* (Cambridge, Mass., 1981), 4–19; Norman G. Finkelstein, *The Holocaust Industry: Reflections on the Exploitation of*

The pioneering surveys of Holocaust cinema by Ilan Avisar, Judith Doneson, and Annette Insdorf employ the same periodization for the entry of the Holocaust into American films, citing *The Young Lions* (1958) and *The Diary of Anne Frank* (1959) as the first Hollywood dramatizations of the topic.[4] Avisar distrusted American attempts to depict Nazi genocide on geographical grounds: "Unlike the personal drives of west and east European filmmakers, who deal with the Holocaust in order to explore and express their own national traumas, the American interest in the subject is motivated by other considerations which are not necessarily rooted in a genuine concern with the disturbing truth of the historical tragedy."[5] Insdorf opined that Hollywood exploited the Holocaust "to evoke instant terror or tears" and suspected that the movie industry's commercialism tended "to pre-empt the possibilities of truthful representation."[6]

Doneson, the only historian among the three, contended that the House Committee on Un-American Activities investigation into communist infiltration of Hollywood deterred the Jewish owners of major studios from producing films that dwelled on Jewish suffering. Such special pleading might draw attention to their immigrant origins and alleged unpatriotic priorities. Accordingly, Hollywood's initial response to the Holocaust was limited to exposés of domestic antisemitism, around which the plots of *Crossfire* (1947) and *Gentleman's Agreement* (1947) revolved. Both portrayed their primary Jewish character as a veteran of World War II and discredited antisemitism as one of a myriad of ethnic and religious prejudices that undermined the American ideal of equality. Thus, fighting antisemitism in the United States was synonymous with defending democracy.[7]

The enormous human toll taken by the war did obscure the genocide inflicted on the Jews. The Jewish catastrophe appeared alongside stories about other civilian atrocities and war crimes committed by Hitler's regime. In not singling out the ordeal of the Jews, the films continued to adhere to the wartime government and industry guidelines for how American movies should depict Nazi Germany and its wrongdoing. From its inception in 1930, the film industry's internal censorship board, the Production Code Administration (PCA), stipulated that filmmakers should portray different nations and religions fairly. Joseph Breen, who headed the PCA after 1934,

---

Jewish Suffering (New York, 2000), 11–30; Deborah Lipstadt, "America and the Memory of the Holocaust, 1950–1965," *Modern Judaism* 16, no. 3 (1996): 198–208; Alan Mintz, *Popular Culture and the Shaping of Holocaust Memory in America* (Seattle, 2001), 3–15; Peter Novick, *The Holocaust in American Life* (Boston, 1999).

[4] Ilan Avisar, *Screening the Holocaust: Cinema's Images of the Unimaginable* (Bloomington, Ind., 1988), 90–133; Judith E. Doneson, *The Holocaust in American Film* (Philadelphia, 1987), 59–107; Annette Insdorf, *Indelible Shadows: Film and the Holocaust* (New York, 1983), 1–21.

[5] Avisar, *Screening the Holocaust*, 132–133.

[6] Insdorf, *Indelible Shadows*, 21–28, 42–44. Insdorf qualified her stance by classifying any formulaic movie as a Hollywood film and considering less conventional American productions such as *The Pawnbroker* to be valid representations of the Holocaust.

[7] Doneson, *The Holocaust in American Film*, 50–65. For a similar interpretation of these two postwar films and the forces that influenced their approach to antisemitism, see Omer Bartov, *The "Jew" in Cinema: From "The Golem" to "Don't Touch My Holocaust"* (Bloomington, Ind., 2005), 37–45. The unitary theory of racism typified the social scientific approach to prejudice in the late 1940s. See Michelle Brattain, "Race, Racism, and Antiracism: UNESCO and the Politics of Presenting Science to the Postwar Public," *American Historical Review* 112, no. 5 (December 2007): 1386–1413; Stuart Svonkin, *Jews against Prejudice: American Jews and the Fight for Civil Liberties* (New York, 1997), 23–40.

worried that presenting antisemitic actions and attitudes onscreen would incite rather than inhibit hatred of Jews.[8] He opposed excessively graphic depictions of violence even in war movies documenting the barbarism of the Third Reich. The federal Office of Censorship and Office of War Information warned against emphasizing that Jews were a target of Hitler's wrath, anticipating that German propagandists would cite such movies as symptomatic of the pro-Jewish bias that Hollywood had purportedly cultivated to drag the United States into the war.[9] The Office of War Information directed the media to publicize smaller and verifiable atrocities such as the Lidice massacre of 1942 rather than "rumors" about the unimaginable transgressions that Germany purportedly was perpetrating against the Jews.[10]

The widespread dissemination of footage and photographs of the liberation of concentration camps and death camps in newspapers, newsreels, and magazines in 1944 and 1945 exposed the American public to far more gruesome images.[11] Allied prosecutors compiled a film titled *Nazi Concentration Camps* for the Nuremberg Trials as proof of the crimes they accused the defendants of committing. It consisted of scenes of corpses stacked like firewood and piled in mass graves, crematoria full of ashes and charred bones, emaciated survivors wearing striped uniforms, electrified barbed wire fences, empty canisters of cyanide pellets, gas chambers disguised as shower rooms, red boxcars used to transport Jews, Star of David badges, tattooed numbers on arms, and warehouses overflowing with the personal effects and hair of those who perished.[12]

The revelations about the carnage in Europe seeped into the consciousness of most Americans, even though its Jewish component was lumped together with other German outrages. This ecumenical perspective was evident in public opinion polls conducted in 1945. Following the height of press coverage about the grim discoveries that Allied troops had made when liberating the camps, those queried were asked if they believed that the "Germans have killed many people in concentration camps or let them starve to death." Eighty-four percent of the respondents answered yes; another 9 percent agreed but felt the extent of mass murder had been exaggerated. The question typically skirted the issue of the identity of the victims.[13] The Western Allies liberated concentration and labor camps whose inmates were not primarily Jews. Consequently, the footage and photographs of the death camps that the Soviets

[8] Thomas Doherty, *Hollywood's Censor: Joseph I. Breen and the Production Code Administration* (New York, 2007), 152–171, 199–224.

[9] Thomas Doherty, *Projections of War: Hollywood, American Culture, and World War II* (New York, 1993), 36–59, 122–133; Steven Alan Carr, "Hollywood, the Holocaust, and World War II," *Studies in Jewish Civilization* 17 (2006): 44–48; K. R. M. Short, "Hollywood Fights Anti-Semitism, 1940–1945," in Short, ed., *Film and Radio Propaganda in World War II* (Knoxville, Tenn., 1983), 146–169.

[10] Steven Casey, *Cautious Crusade: Franklin D. Roosevelt, American Public Opinion, and the War against Nazi Germany* (New York, 2001), 56–72.

[11] Barbie Zelizer, *Remembering to Forget: Holocaust Memory through the Camera's Eye* (Chicago, 1998), 49–140.

[12] Lawrence Douglas, *The Memory of Judgment: Making Law and History in the Trials of the Holocaust* (New Haven, Conn., 2001), 11–37; Jeffrey Shandler, *While America Watches: Televising the Holocaust* (New York, 1999), 5–22.

[13] "Enemy Treatment of Prisoners," *Public Opinion Quarterly* 9, no. 1 (1945): 246. During the Nuremberg Trials, another poll characteristically probed whether German and Japanese civilians had known about "atrocities in prison camps while the war was still going on." Once again there was no mention of the Nazi attempt to exterminate the Jews. "In the United States: Opinion on Germany and Japan," *Public Opinion Quarterly* 9, no. 4 (1945/1946): 533.

TABLE 1
Themes of American "Holocaust" Feature Films, 1945–1959

Theme	Number of Films (26)
Refugee Survivors in DP Camps or as Immigrants to Israel and the United States	7
Hunting and Trying Nazi War Criminals	7
Thwarting Neo-Nazi Conspiracies	6
Jews Escaping or Hiding from the Nazis	4
Allied Liberation of Concentration Camps	2

recorded received less attention in the United States.[14] The verdict issued by the International Military Tribunal established that 6 million Jews had been slaughtered by the Germans, but this offense belonged to a broader litany of charges for crimes against peace, war crimes, and crimes against humanity.[15]

The category of "Holocaust" film in this period includes any movie whose plot or subplots feature or refer to the Nazi internment and racially motivated mass murder of Jews and other subjugated nationalities, evasion of these policies by members of the targeted groups, and the postwar repercussions of Nazi racism for Allied liberators, captured perpetrators, fugitive war criminals, neo-Nazis conspiring to overturn the Allied victory, and survivors of Nazi persecution. Hollywood filmmakers assumed that audiences recognized the images and themes derived from recent headlines, newsreels, and photographs of the carnage and civilian misery the Third Reich left in its wake.

American films produced between 1945 and 1959 usually dealt with the postwar consequences of what had happened to European Jewry rather than with the losses and travails its members incurred during the war. (See Table 1.)[16] From an American perspective, responding to Germany's crimes against humanity meant caring for surviving displaced persons (DPs), ferreting out Nazi war criminals and putting them on trial, supporting Jewish attempts to immigrate to Palestine, and thwarting a resurgence of Nazism. At first, Jews appeared only as minor characters or offscreen victims who were the beneficiaries of American sympathy. By the 1950s, Jewish protagonists started to take center stage in these movies as the precariousness of their wartime existence and the urgency of their postwar situation received fuller treatment.

The early popularization of the Holocaust in American feature films must be correlated to other contemporaneous sources of information available to the reading and viewing public. Reports concerning the German effort to destroy the Jews of Europe had a cumulative impact on many Americans by the end of the war. The extensive coverage of German camps being liberated, the snapshots and personal accounts brought back by returning U.S. troops who had participated in the liber-

[14] Donald Bloxham, *Genocide on Trial: War Crimes Trials and the Formation of Holocaust History and Memory* (New York, 2001), 80–87; Janina Struk, *Photographing the Holocaust: Interpretations of the Evidence* (London, 2005), 124–149.

[15] Michael R. Marrus, "The Holocaust at Nuremberg," *Yad Vashem Studies* 26 (1998): 5–41.

[16] Lawrence Baron, *Projecting the Holocaust into the Present: The Changing Focus of Contemporary Holocaust Cinema* (Lanham, Md., 2005), 25. The figures in this table are not the same as the ones in my book because the latter includes television dramas and fundraising films not intended for theatrical distribution.

ation, and the articles and books spawned by the Nuremberg Trials enhanced public awareness of the "Final Solution" as well.[17] The editors of *Time* presumed that the magazine's readers knew enough to understand the caption inserted below a photograph of German soldiers aiming rifles at a man standing in front of a ditch: "Jew (with Star of David) and Nazi Executioner, *Six million died—one by one, alone.*"[18] Throughout the 1950s, the publication of Holocaust memoirs, most notably those of Anne Frank (1952) and Viktor Frankl (1959), popular novels such as John Hersey's *The Wall* (1950) and Leon Uris's *Exodus* (1958), and historical studies about Nazi Germany such as Willi Frischauer's biography of Heinrich Himmler (1953) and Gerald Reitlinger's study of the SS (1957) elaborated on what Jews had endured in camps and ghettos or while in hiding, and on Hitler's rise to power and his attempt to rid Europe of Jews.[19]

Jeffrey Shandler has surveyed the important role that television played in introducing the Holocaust into American popular culture during the late 1940s and throughout the 1950s. Various documentaries about World War II kept the atrocity footage in the public's eye. Dramatic programming based on Germany's genocide of European Jews and their responses to it appeared frequently in Sunday morning religious fare and primetime theatrical productions. Indeed, Stanley Kramer's heralded *Judgment at Nuremberg* (1961) was originally broadcast on CBS's *Playhouse 90* in 1959.[20]

To be sure, Hollywood movies "Americanized" the Holocaust by plucking positive stories out of a morass of suffering to communicate edifying messages that would be personally touching and politically relevant to their audiences. Most Holocaust scholars decry this process as a trivialization and universalization of the event that dilutes its horror, Jewish specificity, and uniqueness.[21] On the other hand, Doneson insisted that despite these shortcomings, American films served an important function in conveying a semblance of the Jewish calamity to a broad spectrum of the public.[22] While the timeline for the popularization of the Holocaust in the United States proposed here is different from hers, it shares her recognition that repre-

---

[17] Lawrence Baron, "The Holocaust and American Public Memory, 1945–1960," *Holocaust and Genocide Studies* 17, no. 1 (2003): 64–66. Although the press downplayed stories about the decimation of European Jewry, it disclosed key facts during the course of the war in a piecemeal way. See Deborah E. Lipstadt, *Beyond Belief: The American Press and the Coming of the Holocaust, 1933–1945* (New York, 1986); Laurel Leff, *Buried by the Times: The Holocaust and American's Most Important Newspaper* (New York, 2005).

[18] "War Crimes," *Time*, December 24, 1945, 29.

[19] Baron, "The Holocaust and American Public Memory," 66–71, 75–79. See David Cesarani, "Challenging the Myth of Silence: Postwar Responses to the Destruction of European Jewry," The J. B. and Maurice C. Shapiro Lecture (Spring), April 2, 2009, Center for Advanced Holocaust Studies, United States Holocaust Memorial Museum, http://www.ushmm.org/research/center/presentations/lectures/index_all.php?content=2-shapiro (accessed December 27, 2009). Hasia R. Diner, *We Remember with Reverence and Love: American Jews and the Myth of Silence after the Holocaust, 1945–1962* (New York, 2009); Kirsten Fermaglich, *American Dreams and Nazi Nightmares: Early Holocaust Consciousness and Liberal America, 1957–1965* (Waltham, Mass., 2006); Michael E. Staub, *Torn at the Roots: The Crisis of Jewish Liberalism in Postwar America* (New York, 2002).

[20] Shandler, *While America Watches*, 23–79.

[21] Lawrence L. Langer, "The Americanization of the Holocaust on Stage and Screen," in Langer, *Admitting the Holocaust: Collected Essays* (New York, 1995), 157–177; Alvin H. Rosenfeld, "The Americanization of the Holocaust," in Rosenfeld, ed., *Thinking about the Holocaust after Half a Century* (Bloomington, Ind., 1997), 119–150.

[22] Doneson, *The Holocaust in American Film*, 199–209.

---

sentations of a crime so heinous boggled the imagination of Americans and therefore had to be framed in idioms and terms familiar to them. This recognition is predicated on the constructivist model articulated by Alan Mintz, which assumes that "historical events, even the Holocaust, possess no inscribed meanings; meaning is constructed by communities of interpretation—differently by different communities—out of their own motives and needs."[23]

The pioneering "Holocaust" films naturally bear the imprint of the cinematic styles and narrative practices of Hollywood productions from this era. Their treatment of violence is less graphic than in American movies made since the 1960s.[24] They possess a linear structure, deliver a moral message, treat individuals as the primary agents of historical change, and simplify the causal complexity of history. They elicit admiration for heroes, antipathy toward villains, and sympathy for victims. Robert Burgoyne, Marnie Hughes-Warrington, Robert Rosenstone, and Robert Brent Toplin have shown how the vicarious historical experience imparted to viewers by well-wrought movies renders filmed history more emotionally engaging, but less intellectually complicated, than its academic counterpart.[25]

In the interim between the end of World War II and the Eichmann trial, Hollywood generated a cinematic repository of what Alison Landsberg terms "prosthetic memories." Using the analogy of an artificial limb, she maintains that "prosthetic memories originate outside a person's lived experience and yet are taken on and worn by that person through mass cultural technologies of memory." Like prosthetic devices, these vicarious memories "often mark a trauma" so excruciating that it needs to be buffered for those who have not sustained it. Cognizant of the tendency of feature films to manipulate emotions, she nonetheless asserts that their accessibility "makes images and narratives widely available to people who live in different places and come from different backgrounds, races, and classes." Hence, movies personalize the abstract forces of history and engender empathy for past and present victims of oppression.[26]

IT DID NOT TAKE LONG for the atrocity footage of liberated camps to appear in an American feature film. Orson Welles's *The Stranger* (1946) holds the distinction of being the first to employ such clips. Welles modeled its sinister SS villain Franz Kindler after Martin Bormann, the highest-ranking Nazi to elude capture by the Allies. Kindler, as played by Welles, uses his fluent English and forged credentials to attain a position as a German history professor at a New England college under the alias Charles Rankin. Edward G. Robinson plays Detective Wilson of the Allied

[23] Mintz, *Popular Culture and the Shaping of Holocaust Memory in America*, 37–40.

[24] J. David Slocum, "Film Violence and the Institutionalization of the Cinema," *Social Research* 67, no. 3 (2000): 654–660.

[25] Robert Burgoyne, *The Hollywood Historical Film* (Malden, Mass., 2008); Marnie Hughes-Warrington, *History Goes to the Movies: Studying History on Film* (New York, 2007); Robert A. Rosenstone, *Visions of the Past: The Challenge of Film to Our Idea of History* (Cambridge, Mass., 1995); Rosenstone, *History on Film/Film on History* (New York, 2006); Robert Brent Toplin, *Reel History: In Defense of Hollywood* (Lawrence, Kans., 2002).

[26] Alison Landsberg, *Prosthetic Memory: The Transformation of American Remembrance in the Age of Mass Culture* (New York, 2004), 18–22. See also Anna Reading, *The Social Inheritance of the Holocaust: Gender, Culture and Memory* (New York, 2002).

War Crimes Commission, who tracks Kindler down. At a dinner party thrown by Kindler, Wilson listens intently as his host lectures about the innate authoritarianism of the Germans and their lack of a philosopher who championed freedom. When Kindler's son-in-law suggests that Karl Marx disproves this generalization, Kindler scoffs at the suggestion that a Jew such as Marx could be considered a German. To enlist the cooperation of Rankin's unwitting wife, Wilson shows her films of corpses, a gas chamber, a burial pit, and a skeletal survivor and charges that Kindler, a.k.a. Rankin, "conceived of the theory of genocide, the mass depopulation of conquered countries."[27]

With hindsight, it is easy to fault *The Stranger*'s overly broad definition of genocide and its failure to specify that Jews were targeted for extermination. The latter flaw typifies the narration in early documentaries such as *Nazi Concentration Camps* and *Night and Fog* (1955), which barely mention the victimization of the Jews in order to stress the multinational scope of German war crimes.[28] Despite *The Stranger*'s vagueness, its clue about Rankin's antisemitism, the inclusion of concentration camp footage, and the reference to genocide indicate an awareness of what the Third Reich's racial policies entailed.[29] Joseph Breen of the PCA did not object to the graphic atrocity footage, but he advised the studio to replace the word "cyanide" with "poison" when Wilson describes the gas to Mary.[30] Most reviewers noted that Kindler planned Nazi atrocities and mass murder.[31] The film's tagline labels him "the most deceitful man a woman ever loved," reinforcing the belief that a few wicked men "were to blame for Nazi excesses."[32]

Not all screen Nazis died while trying to escape like Kindler. Those who were apprehended became the subject of courtroom dramas. Although during the war the percentage of Americans in favor of summarily executing Nazi leaders far exceeded the percentage who favored putting the worst offenders on trial, 75 percent approved of the International Military Tribunal at Nuremberg after its establishment. While they were certain the defendants were guilty, they believed that the IMT afforded the defendants the same legal safeguards as an American trial.[33]

Even before the end of the war, André de Toth's *None Shall Escape* (1944) previewed what a war crimes trial would look like. Some ads and posters for it quoted the Moscow Declaration of 1943, pledging international trials of Nazi leaders after

[27] *The Stranger*, dir. Orson Welles (U.S., 1946); Palmer R. Barton, "The Politics of Genre in Welles' *The Stranger*," *Film Criticism* 9, no. 2 (1984–1985): 2–14.

[28] Struk, *Photographing the Holocaust*, 150–158; Ewout van der Knaap, "The Construction of Memory in *Nuit et Brouillard*," in van der Knapp, ed., *Uncovering the Holocaust: The International Reception of Night and Fog* (London, 2006), 17–19.

[29] Baron, *Projecting the Holocaust*, 27–28; Caroline Joan (Kay) S. Picart and David A. Frank, *Frames of Evil: The Holocaust as Horror in American Film* (Carbondale, Ill., 2006), 25.

[30] Letter from Joseph I. Breen to William Goetz, September 18, 1945, *The Stranger*, Special Collections, Margaret Herrick Library, Academy of Motion Picture Arts and Sciences [hereafter MHL-AMPAS], Beverly Hills, Calif.

[31] Bosley Crowther, "*The Stranger*," *New York Times*, July 11, 1946; Jack D. Grant, "Welles, Young, and Robinson Score Hits," *Hollywood Reporter*, May 21, 1946; "The New Pictures," *Time*, June 17, 1946, http://www.time.com/time/magazine/article/0,9171,793120,00.html (accessed December 27, 2009); "Movie of the Week: *The Stranger*," *Life*, June 3, 1946, 78.

[32] William J. Bosch, *Judgment on Nuremberg: American Attitudes toward the Major German War-Crime Trials* (Chapel Hill, N.C., 1970), 111.

[33] Ibid., 90–112.

the cessation of hostilities.[34] The courtroom testimony of witnesses against the Nazi governor of a district in Poland occasions flashbacks to the origins of his bitterness as an ethnic German residing in a town that fell within the borders of the new state of Poland created by the Treaty of Versailles; his joining of the Nazi Party in the 1920s; his suppression of dissidents, including his own brother, once the Nazis were in power; and his reign of terror over his former hometown, where he burns the synagogue and orders the shooting of Jews who resist deportation. The reviewer for the communist *Daily Worker* lauded the film for presenting "the most militant indictment of anti-Semitism in the history of Hollywood."[35] The picture proved to be a box-office hit and received an Oscar nomination for Best Original Story.[36]

The attempt to be unbiased toward an ostensibly guilty Nazi is the theme of the second American film about war crimes trials, Lewis Allen's *Sealed Verdict* (1948).[37] It opens with newsreel footage of Justice Robert Jackson's opening statement at the Nuremberg Trials: "They (the accused) are the living symbols of racial hatreds, of terrorism, and violence, and of the arrogance and cruelty of power. We must never forget that the record on which we judge these defendants today is the record on which history will judge us tomorrow."[38] Major Robert Lawson, played by Ray Milland, watches this clip to prepare for his prosecution of General Otto Steigmann, who is being tried for the reprisal executions of sixty Czech hostages in the town of Leemach when he was the military governor of Bohemia. This incident is obviously modeled on the Nazi massacre of Czechs at Lidice as retaliation for the assassination of Reinhard Heydrich in 1942. Lidice had attracted much coverage in the American press and inspired two other feature films, *Hangmen Also Die!* (1943) and *Hitler's Madman* (1943).[39]

Lawson easily wins a conviction and death sentence against Steigmann. Themis, the daughter of a French resistance leader whose life was spared by Steigmann, accuses Lawson of sending an innocent man to his death. Although initially suspicious of Themis because the French government has demanded her extradition for collaborating with Steigmann, Lawson has pangs of conscience over having failed to produce two key pieces of evidence: a Night and Fog Decree signed by Steigmann and a commendation letter from Hitler for the Leemach killings. Moreover, Lawson's commander pressures him to execute Steigmann quickly, because rumors of his possible acquittal are becoming a rallying point among restive Germans. Lawson discovers that Steigmann's mother may possess the missing documents. She lives at the home of a family friend, a rabbi whose wife and daughters were gassed at Buchenwald and whose son's skull was crushed by an SS guard there. Mrs. Steigmann burns

---

[34] *None Shall Escape*, dir. André de Toth (U.S., 1944); "Clippings," *None Shall Escape*, Special Collections, MHL-AMPAS; "Scrapbook 1," Joseph Than Collection, MHL-AMPAS.

[35] J. Hoberman, *Bridge of Light: Yiddish Film between Two Worlds* (Philadelphia, 1995), 324. Hoberman's claim that this film originally was a Yiddish production that was dubbed into English in 1944 is contradicted by various drafts of the script and the studio correspondence with the PCA. For example, see Burt Kelly to Jeff Sherlock, April 14, 1943, *None Shall Escape*, Special Collections, MHL-AMPAS.

[36] "Scrapbook 1"; Lester Cole, *Hollywood Red: The Autobiography of Lester Cole* (Palo Alto, Calif., 1981), 205–206.

[37] *Sealed Verdict*, dir. Lewis Allen (U.S., 1948).

[38] Jonathan Latimer, "Sealed Verdict: Release Dialogue Script," March 10, 1948, Special Collections, MHL-AMPAS.

[39] *Hangmen Also Die!*, dir. Fritz Lang (U.S., 1943); *Hitler's Madman*, dir. Douglas Sirk (U.S., 1943).

the incriminating papers shortly before Themis and the rabbi arrive to confiscate them. She castigates Jews as "filthy pigs" who will be liquidated when the Nazis regain power. Pretending that he has found the two documents, Lawson confronts Steigmann in his cell. The latter confidently retorts, "We will rise again and exterminate all sub-humans throughout the world. All countries must be liberated from the degenerate races."[40]

Although Bernard Dick credits *Sealed Verdict* with being "the first American film to speak of the camps specifically as death camps," most reviewers and scholars have criticized its convoluted plot, its portrayal of the rabbi as too forgiving, and the unfaithful adaptation of the novel on which it was based.[41] Whatever its deficiencies as a film, it inextricably linked Nazi reprisals against enemy civilians with racist rationalizations for the eradication of "inferior" races, including Jews. Heeding Robert Jackson's advice, Lawson hesitates to hang a possibly innocent man until Steigmann confesses to the charges against him. The movie premiered several months after the Soviet Union had blockaded West Berlin, and during the American, British, and French airlift to supply the city with necessities.[42] Despite speculation that Hollywood avoided the subject of the Holocaust to appease West German public opinion, the PCA's review of the script never censures it for broaching the topic of German war crimes.[43] Paramount vouched for the authenticity of the trial scenes by hiring Jackson's press secretary, Gordon Dean, as a consultant. The studio's publicity campaign hyped the issue of fraternization, since Lawson falls in love with Themis, but also mentioned the "dramatic war-crimes trials," "the mass murderer of Leemach," and the decree legitimating "the murder without trial of countless Europeans."[44]

Ex-Nazis who evaded capture or trial onscreen remained menacing foes hatching plots to foment revolution, inventing weapons of mass destruction, or trying to clone Aryan supermen.[45] Not all thrillers about the ongoing threat that Nazis posed to the free world limited themselves to their current machinations. Some thrillers about clandestine Nazi activities discredited their villains by reminding audiences of the shameful record of the Third Reich. Andrew Marton's *The Devil Makes Three* (1952) drew on a true story about a smuggling operation conducted by former Nazis. When Lieutenant Jeff Eliot, played by Gene Kelly, returns to Munich in 1947 to search for

[40] Latimer, "Sealed Verdict: Release Dialogue Script," Reels 4A–5A. The Night and Fog Decree, issued by Hitler on December 7, 1941, authorized the *Wehrmacht* to arrest those suspected of endangering German occupation troops and submerge them in the "night and fog" of secret extralegal trials and incarceration in Germany. See "Night and Fog Decree," in United States Holocaust Memorial Museum, *Holocaust Encyclopedia*, http://www.ushmm.org/wlc/article.php?lang=en&ModuleId=10007465&print=y (accessed December 27, 2009).

[41] Bernard F. Dick, *The Star-Spangled Screen: The American World War II Film* (Lexington, Ky., 1985), 209; Bosley Crowther, "*Sealed Verdict*," *New York Times*, November 3, 1948; Herbert G. Luft, "The Screen and the Holocaust," in David Platt, ed., *Celluloid Power: Social Film Criticism from "The Birth of a Nation" to "Judgment at Nuremberg"* (Metuchen, N.J., 1992), 378.

[42] "Release Dates," *Sealed Verdict*, Internet Movie Database, http://www.imdb.com/title/tt0040764/ (accessed September 7, 2008). The movie premiered in November 1948. The blockade and airlift began in June of that year.

[43] Letter from Joseph I. Breen to Luigi Luraschi, August 21, 1947, Production Code Administration File, Special Collections, MHL-AMPAS. Breen objected to the script primarily on the grounds that it implied an illicit sexual relationship between Lawson and Themis and that Themis might be a prostitute.

[44] *Sealed Verdict*, Paramount Press Sheets–Releases Season 1948–1949, Group A-8, Special Collections, MHL-AMPAS.

[45] Lawrence Baron, "Holocaust Iconography in American Feature Films about Neo-Nazis," *Film and History* 32, no. 2 (2002): 38–40.

the family who hid him after his plane was shot down over Germany during the war, he learns that all but their daughter Willie perished in bombing raids. He manages to track her down, and finds her soliciting drinks in a bar. Accepting his invitation to go to Salzburg, she rents a car from the owner of the bar. Willie regularly carries contraband over the Austrian border in vehicles supplied by her boss, but does not realize that these cars are plated with looted Nazi gold masked with a fresh coat of paint. The Criminal Investigation Division of the U.S. Army recruits Eliot to infiltrate the smuggling ring. The CID chief tells him that the gold must "have been collected over the years from the hundreds of thousands of men and women who were exterminated in concentration camps, from their teeth, jewelry, wedding rings, et cetera."[46] *The Devil Makes Three* continued the wartime practice of vilifying Nazis rather than Germans.[47]

Reviving the postwar scare that German women were using their liaisons with American soldiers to subvert the Allied occupation, Samuel Fuller's *Verboten!* (1959) centers on the relationship between a wounded American GI named David and the German woman, Helga, who hid him and nursed him back to health near the end of the war.[48] He marries her and takes a job with an occupation relief agency. Unbeknownst to either of them, Helga's brother Franz belongs to the Nazi Werewolves, who assassinate American officials and disrupt the distribution of food and medicine. Ashamed of her brother's bigotry and subversive activities, Helga forces him to attend the Nuremberg Trials and watch footage from *Nazi Concentration Camps*. In a ten-minute excerpt, the narrator describes how the Third Reich persecuted Christian Germans, euthanized the infirm, and killed citizens of every European country. Then he declares, "Perhaps the greatest crime the Nazis committed was against the Jews whom they used as a scapegoat to make Hitler God and *Mein Kampf* the bible." Mortified by what he has seen, Franz professes to have known nothing about these policies. He steals a list of safe houses used by the Werewolves to smuggle war criminals out of the country and gives it to David. A combat veteran of World War II, Fuller despised Nazism, but cautioned viewers not to stereotype Germans as pro-Hitler or anti-American as David unjustly does twice in quarrels with Helga.[49]

HOLLYWOOD FILMS INITIALLY DEPICTED Jewish victims of the Nazis as traumatized displaced persons dependent on American or Israeli aid to heal from their mental and physical wounds. The prominence of the DP issue in American films mirrored the refugee crisis in postwar Europe, where millions of people flocked to the American, British, and French zones in Germany after its surrender in 1945. Jews con-

[46] *The Devil Makes Three*, dir. Andrew Marton (U.S., 1952). See script by Jerry Davis, *The Devil Makes Three*, Special Collections, MHL-AMPAS.

[47] Clayton R. Koppes and Gregory D. Black, *Hollywood Goes to War: How Politics, Profits, and Propaganda Shaped World War II Movies* (New York, 1987), 278–316; Robert L. McLaughlin and Sally E. Parry, *We'll Always Have the Movies: American Cinema during World War II* (Lexington, Ky., 2006), 100–119.

[48] *Verboten!*, dir. Samuel Fuller (U.S., 1959); Christina von Hodenberg, "Of German Fräuleins, Nazi Werewolves, and Iraqi Insurgents: The American Fascination with Hitler's Last Foray," *Central European History* 41, no. 1 (2008): 71–92.

[49] Samuel Fuller, *A Third Face: My Tale of Writing, Fighting, and Filmmaking* (New York, 2002), 354–374.

stituted a minority of this influx.[50] Most Jewish DPs refused repatriation to countries where few Gentiles had protected them or resisted Nazi antisemitic measures, and where others had collaborated with the Germans.[51] Compared to Gentile DPs, Jews usually had spent longer periods in captivity or hiding, lost more family members, and suffered greater harm, as documented in the Harrison Commission Report in September of 1945.[52]

Since many Jewish DPs were demanding to go to Palestine, President Truman endorsed the commission's recommendation that the British government permit 100,000 of them to immigrate there immediately. Worried about exacerbating the volatile tensions between Arabs and Jews in the region, England rejected the proposal, but eventually deferred to the UN's decision to partition Palestine into an Arab and a Jewish state.[53] American public support for Jewish immigration to Palestine and the creation of Israel increased as the revelations of Germany's decimation of European Jewry sank in. Whereas only 36 percent of those surveyed backed the establishment of a Jewish state in 1944, that figure climbed to 42 percent in late 1945, and then to 65 percent in 1947, shortly before the UN's vote on the matter.[54] For American filmmakers, the dramatic reversal of Jewish impotence in Europe to Jewish empowerment in Israel made Zionism "a progressive cause that was also a safe one in a time of fear in Hollywood."[55]

Fred Zinnemann's *The Search* (1948) documented the plight of DP children in Europe and the preparations for some of them to settle in Palestine. Zinnemann had experienced antisemitic discrimination in his native Vienna and immigrated to the United States in 1929. During World War II, he directed *The Seventh Cross* (1944), starring Spencer Tracy as a political dissident who escapes from a prewar concentration camp and encounters ordinary Germans who variously help, ignore, or threaten to betray him. After the war, Zinnemann learned that his parents had perished at the hands of the Nazis.[56] Swiss producer Lazar Wechsler approached Zinnemann to direct a movie about children languishing in DP camps. The United Nations Relief and Rehabilitation Administration (UNRRA) allowed Zinnemann and his team to tour DP shelters in Germany. They based *The Search* on UNRRA case files and interviews conducted with young DPs. Zinnemann cast children from the camps in all but the leading juvenile role and shot the outdoor scenes in the rubble of German cities.[57]

[50] Mark Wyman, *DP: Europe's Displaced Persons, 1945–1951* (Philadelphia, 1989).

[51] Angelika Königseder and Juliane Wetzel, *Waiting for Hope: Jewish Displaced Persons in Post–World War II Germany* (Evanston, Ill., 2001), 9–53.

[52] Harry Reicher, "The Post-Holocaust World and President Harry S. Truman: The Harrison Report and Immigration Law and Policy," http://www.schnader.com/files/Uploads/Documents/post-holocaust .pdf (accessed August 2, 2009).

[53] Arieh J. Kochavi, *Post-Holocaust Politics: Britain, the United States, and Jewish Refugees, 1945–1948* (Chapel Hill, N.C., 2001); Abram Leon Sachar, *The Redemption of the Unwanted: From the Liberation of the Death Camps to the Founding of Israel* (New York, 1983).

[54] Eytan Gilboa, *American Public Opinion toward Israel and the Arab-Israeli Conflict* (Lexington, Mass., 1987), 15–21.

[55] Deborah Dash Moore, "*Exodus*: Real to Reel to Real," in J. Hoberman and Jeffrey Shandler, eds., *Entertaining America: Jews, Movies, and Broadcasting* (Princeton, N.J., 2003), 209; Neal Gabler, *An Empire of Their Own: How the Jews Invented Hollywood* (New York, 1989), 350.

[56] Fred Zinnemann, *A Life in the Movies: An Autobiography* (New York, 1992), 7–55.

[57] Ibid., 56–73; Gabriel Miller, ed., *Fred Zinnemann: Interviews* (Jackson, Miss., 2005), 42–43, 87–88. Vincent Brook has recently asserted that Ivan Jandl, the boy who played Karel, was also a concentration

As a train pulls into a station at night, a narrator describes its cargo as a "tiny handful of millions of orphaned, homeless, bewildered children, children who had a right to better things—a right taken from them by the war." Not distinguishing between the DP shelter and concentration camps, the new arrivals steal bread and slavishly obey orders. A faded swastika and German eagle painted on a wall loom as relics of Nazi persecution. When interviewed by UNRRA social workers, the children recall internment in concentration camps and the deaths of family members there. A blond boy named Karel bears an Auschwitz ID number on his forearm. He replies "I don't know" to questions about his identity. Flashbacks clarify that his Czech parents were arrested as political enemies by the Gestapo and that he last glimpsed his mother as she was being escorted away from Auschwitz by the SS. His amnesia signifies his repression of traumatic memories.

Karel's caseworker decides to transfer him to another facility for therapy. An ambulance picks up Karel and other troubled youngsters. To them, it resembles a German gas van. Suspecting the worst, the children panic and escape. Karel and a companion leap into a river, where the former hides and the latter drowns. In the meantime, Karel's mother, Hannah, has been trekking along a deserted autobahn searching for her son. She reaches the shelter where he was staying until he ran away. When his cap washes up on the riverbank, Hannah believes that her son is dead, but she stays at the shelter to care for his peers. Montgomery Clift radiates decency as a GI named Stevenson who spots Karel scrambling over debris and tosses him a sandwich. At first the youngster spurns Stevenson, but eventually he overcomes his distrust of anyone wearing a uniform. Stevenson decides that he wants Karel to come live with him in America, but Hannah and her son are reunited shortly before the adoption can be finalized.[58]

Zinnemann and screenwriter Peter Viertel originally intended to make a film that would indict the United States for "locking the Jews together with their murderers" and abandoning the goal of de-Nazification to ingratiate itself with the Germans living in its occupation zone. The assurances of the UNRRA officials who guided Zinnemann's visits to the DP shelters shifted his focus to the plight of the children residing there. Since his impressions of the DP camps were more positive than Viertel's, Zinnemann chose a less controversial script by David Wechsler and Richard Schweizer.[59]

The Search alludes to the past ordeals of the young DPs and mentions that the majority of them are Jewish. A Hungarian Jewish girl named Miriam recalls that her parents were gassed at Dachau. A boy named Joel Markowsky feigns that he is Catholic because his mother warned him never to tell anyone he is Jewish. A Zionist youth group celebrates its departure to Palestine by singing a Hebrew song in a classroom where a placard on an easel gives the death toll as 6 million. The impact of the

---

camp survivor. Brook, *Driven to Darkness: Jewish Émigré Directors and the Rise of Film Noir* (New Brunswick, N.J., 2009), 207.

[58] Jorg Thunecke, "Flotsam and Jetsam: Fred Zinnemann's *The Search*, 1947, and the Problem of 'Unaccompanied Children' at the End of World War II," *Modern Austrian Literature* 32, no. 4 (1999): 271–286.

[59] Brian C. Etheridge, "In Search of Germans: Contested Germany in the Production of *The Search*," *Journal of Popular Film and Television* 34, no. 1 (2006): 34–45.

FIGURE 1: Karel's mother, played by Jarmila Novotna, celebrates the departure of the Zionist youth. From *The Search* (1948), directed by Fred Zinnemann. MGM/Photofest. © MGM.

testimony of the children and their tremulous behavior is disconcerting. Zinnemann admitted that he chose "to soften the truth to a certain extent, because to show things as they really were would have meant that the American audience would have lost any desire to face it."[60]

The Search garnered many accolades and awards. It won two Golden Globes for Best Screenplay and Best Film Promoting International Understanding, a special Oscar for young Ivan Jandl's poignant performance as Karel, and the United Nations Award from the British Academy of Film and Television Arts.[61] The National Board of Review named it one of the ten best films of 1948.[62] Reviewing the movie for the *New York Times*, Bosley Crowther praised it for its "vivid and convincing representation of how one of the 'lost children' of Europe is found" and its "graphic, overwhelming comprehension of the frightful cruelty to innocent children that has been done abroad."[63] *Life* magazine devoted a pictorial spread to *The Search*, juxtaposing stills from it with photographs of DP children.[64]

[60] Fred Zinnemann, "A Different Perspective," *Sight and Sound* 17, no. 67 (Autumn 1948): 113.
[61] "Awards and Nominations," *The Search*, http://www.imdb.com/title/tt0040765/awards (accessed June 30, 2007).
[62] Miller, *Fred Zinnemann*, 87.
[63] Bosley Crowther, "*The Search*, Arresting Drama of Europe's 'Lost Children' Film at the Victoria," *New York Times*, March 24, 1948.
[64] "Movie of the Week: *The Search*," *Life*, April 5, 1948, 75–79.

George Sherman's *Sword in the Desert* (1949) was the first mainstream Hollywood film to portray Holocaust survivors as the rightful heirs to Israel's struggle for sovereignty.[65] Adrift in longboats, refugees of all ages, some wearing striped uniforms with a Jewish star on the back, look up at David, the Zionist organizer of their surreptitious landing. David pleads with the mercenary American captain of the freighter from which they have disembarked to accompany them to the beach. His soliloquy enumerates the names of the infamous German camps they survived and where their loved ones died. Astounded that his father is waiting for him on the beach, a son asks, "How long did it take you to get here?" David answers in the other man's stead: "Two thousand years." The bravery of David and his comrades ultimately wins the admiration of the cynical American captain. Lester Friedman's characterization of *Sword in the Desert* as "little more than an American war movie" in which "the Jews are the good guys and the British the enemy" elides the film's significance as a forerunner of American motion pictures such as *Exodus* (1960) and *Cast a Giant Shadow* (1966), which popularized the Zionist interpretation of the Holocaust as the culmination of antisemitism in the Diaspora and Israel as the sanctuary for persecuted Jews.[66]

Edward Dmytryk's *The Juggler* (1953) delves more deeply into the inner turmoil of a Holocaust survivor who arrives in Haifa in 1949. At the registration center for new immigrants, the former juggler and clown Hans Mueller hallucinates that his deceased wife and children are peering at him from a window. When asked what vocational skills he possesses, he replies, "I can smile while being beaten by fists, foot straps, and long lengths of hoses. I can be used as a guinea pig for new drugs and old poisons." Chafing against being confined even in a transit camp, he escapes from the facility and beats up a police officer whose attempt to check his identification papers stirs up memories of Nazi interrogations. Roaming the countryside, Hans befriends a boy named Yehoshua and a woman named Ya'El, who belong to a kibbutz and invite him to stay there. Upon glimpsing the numbers on his forearm, Ya'El wonders why he has not talked about his imprisonment in a concentration camp. He points to a small room and tells her, "Pretend you're seeing a place one-quarter the size—nothing but walls, a floor, and a ceiling, quite a lot of air for one man. That's where I lay with ten others when they told me my wife and children had been burnt in their ovens." Hans blames himself for their deaths because he was counting on his fame and German citizenship to shield them from persecution. When the police come searching for him, he barricades himself in a room. Assured by Ya'El that they won't harm him, Hans surrenders and finally acknowledges that he is sick and needs help.[67]

The Juggler prefigures the trope of the survivor as a psychologically wounded soul, which found its most powerful expression in Sidney Lumet's *The Pawnbroker* (1965). Hans differs from Lumet's Sol Nazerman in that his flashbacks are verbal and not

---

[65] *Sword in the Desert*, dir. George Sherman (U.S., 1949).

[66] Lester D. Friedman, *Hollywood's Image of the Jew* (New York, 1982), 100–103; Michelle Mart, *Eye on Israel: How America Came to View Israel as an Ally* (Albany, N.Y., 2006), 25–28; Moore, "*Exodus*," 207–209.

[67] Patricia Erens, *The Jew in American Cinema* (Bloomington, Ind., 1988), 215–217; Friedman, *Hollywood's Image of the Jew*, 160–162. Avisar, Doneson, and Insdorf do not discuss *The Juggler* in their books.

FIGURE 2: Hans, played by Kirk Douglas, barricades himself in his room to keep the police from arresting him. From *The Juggler* (1953), directed by Edward Dmytryk. Columbia Pictures/Photofest. © Columbia Pictures.

visual, and that he remains an affable character capable of friendship and love.[68] Hans repeatedly remarks that "home is a place you lose," but slowly discerns that Israel is a homeland for Jews fleeing oppression. A physician at the immigration center tries to assuage Hans's fear of authority by explaining Israel's raison d'être: "Listen, every person is precious to us. That's why we go on half rations and crowd our homes to bring in the people from the ghettos of Europe and Africa. That's why we have an Israel, for no other reason."[69]

Like their real-life counterparts, Jewish DPs in American films also immigrated to the United States. Maxwell Shane's *The Glass Wall* (1953) is a plea for liberalizing immigration policy. In the movie, American officials deny a Hungarian refugee named Peter Kaban permission to enter the United States because he stowed away on the ship that has brought him to New York. During his interrogation, he discloses that he was interned at Auschwitz, where the rest of his family was gassed in 1944, the year several hundred thousand Hungarian Jews were deported to Auschwitz and

[68] For recent analyses of *The Pawnbroker*, see Bartov, *The "Jew" in Cinema*, 94–100; Joshua Hirsch, *Afterimage: Film, Trauma, and the Holocaust* (Philadelphia, 2004), 85–110; Mintz, *Popular Culture and the Shaping of Holocaust Memory in America*, 107–125; Alan Rosen, " 'Teach Me Gold': Pedagogy and Memory in *The Pawnbroker*," *Prooftexts: A Journal of Jewish Literary History* 22, no. 1–2 (2002): 77–117.
[69] Mart, *Eye on Israel*, 25–27.

killed.[70] Citing a law guaranteeing residency to anyone who helped Allied soldiers during the war, Peter says that he qualifies because he rescued a wounded American—a pilot named Tom who was a jazz clarinetist from New York. Given the vagueness of Tom's identity and whereabouts, the officials decide to send Peter back to Europe, but he jumps ship and combs the city's nightclubs in search of Tom. Along the way, he is sheltered by a Hungarian-American woman, who chides her son for urging her to turn him away because he is a "lousy foreigner"—the same epithet with which the boy's dead father was once stigmatized. Finally, Peter goes to the United Nations Headquarters, the site of the glass wall in the title, and states his case to an empty conference room: "As long as there is one man who can't walk free where he wants, as long as there is one displaced person, there won't be peace, because to each man, he's the world." Having read about the police hunt for Peter in the newspaper, Tom finds him and saves him from committing suicide, assuring him that he can stay in the United States.

The film adaptation of Irwin Shaw's novel *The Young Lions* (1958) has provoked the ire of Holocaust scholars, who inveigh against its apologetic portrayal of the main German character, Christian Diestl.[71] In the book, Diestl degenerates from an apolitical German attracted to Hitler's promises of restoring Germany's standing in the world and creating opportunities for social mobility into a ruthless killer who obeys orders.[72] Director Edward Dmytryk and screenwriter Edward Anhalt felt that the "dyed-in-the wool Nazi heavy" had become a "cliché" and changed Christian into a fundamentally decent man who is gradually disillusioned by his nation's wartime truculence. When Brando proposed that his character follow his rejection of Nazism by denouncing injustices endured by African Americans and Native Americans, Dmytryk wisely quashed this idea.[73]

Dmytryk did indulge Brando's absolution of Christian toward the end of the film. In the book and the first draft of the screenplay, Diestl happens upon an inmate rebellion that has broken out in a concentration camp after most of the SS guards have retreated. He knocks out a prisoner and steals his uniform. To allay suspicions of his real identity, he cuts the throat of the camp commandant before fleeing into a forest, where he ambushes two American soldiers. In the final version, Christian abhors what he discovers about the camp's grisly purpose from its commandant, and he walks off into the forest. Although he aims his rifle at the GIs, he decides to smash it instead and approaches them unarmed. They shoot him, and he tumbles into a thicket and dies face down in a brook.[74] Brando's vanity and Dmytryk's aversion to the hackneyed Nazi villain rather than Cold War diplomacy influenced this redemptive finale.

Shaw's outrage over Nazi barbarism is displaced onto Captain Hardenberg, played by Maximilian Schell. He is as arrogant and brutal as Diestl is humble and

---

[70] Randolph L. Braham, *The Politics of Genocide: The Holocaust in Hungary* (Detroit, 2000), 133–154.

[71] Avisar, *Screening the Holocaust*, 111–116; Lipstadt, "America and the Memory of the Holocaust," 200–201.

[72] Irwin Shaw, *The Young Lions* (New York, 1948).

[73] Edward Dmytryk, *It's a Hell of a Life, but Not a Bad Living* (New York, 1978), 220–230.

[74] Edward Anhalt, "The Young Lions. First Draft," April 25, 1957, Core Collection, MHL-AMPAS, 170–174.

humane. Hardenberg declines Diestl's request to be relieved of his duty arresting fugitives for the Gestapo in Paris by lecturing, "When you became a soldier, you contracted for killing in all its forms." Both serve on the North African front, where Hardenberg presides over the massacre of British soldiers who have signaled their surrender. Disgusted by Diestl's refusal to execute a wounded Englishman, Hardenberg fires the fatal bullet. Later, as they escape on a motorcycle from the advancing Allied forces, Hardenberg rebukes Diestl for still being "infected with a little human feeling." During the 1950s, American movies such as *The Desert Fox: The Story of Rommel* (1951) and *The Desert Rats* (1953) differentiated between honorable German officers such as Rommel and sinister Nazis.[75] Brando's portrayal of Diestl fits the first category, Schell's performance as Hardenberg the second. Hardenberg's condoning of war crimes in North Africa contradicts the apologetic thrust of the Rommel movies.

The concentration camp scene arraigns Germany for crimes against humanity. Dmytryk rented an abandoned concentration camp for the set and watched unedited U.S. Signal Corps footage to re-create what American troops saw when they liberated camps.[76] The SS commandant explains to Diestl the difficulty of running the camp, "with all the gas chambers, target ranges, and doctors with their experiments." He proudly takes credit for meeting his quota of exterminating 1,500 inmates daily from among the "Jews, Poles, Russians, French, and political prisoners" and predicts that government policymakers will deny that there "was a national policy to kill 12,000,000 people." Citing a death toll higher than 6 million to encompass Gentile casualties typifies not only contemporary American movies such as *Verboten!* but also the statistical tactic that Shaw employed in refusing to endorse Brando's exculpatory portrayal of Christian and his ilk.[77] The commandant's admission reveals far more about Nazi intent than what is disclosed in the same scene in Shaw's novel and the original script.[78] It appears that Dmytryk compensated for Brando's exoneration of Diestl by stressing the scope and severity of Germany's extermination of European Jews and its ruthless repression of vanquished Gentile populations.

The second half of the liberation scene is devoted to the Jewish survivors. When American soldiers fling open the doors of a barracks and see pallid faces staring back at them, a lone survivor with a bare, sunken chest shuffles toward them and raises his empty bowl. A rabbi in prison garb subsequently interrupts a meeting between Captain Green, who heads the American platoon, and the mayor of a nearby German village who has offered to help clean the camp for upcoming visits by dignitaries. The rabbi requests permission to conduct a memorial service for the Jews who perished at the camp. The mayor advises the captain against agreeing, since it would offend non-Jewish prisoners. Green grants the permission and sternly warns the mayor never to return to the camp. Dmytryk's final version implicates the Germans more

---

[75] Beverly Crawford and James Martel, "Representations of Germans and What Germans Represent: American Film Images and Public Perceptions in the Postwar Era," in David E. Barclay and Elisabeth Glaser-Schmidt, eds., *Transatlantic Images and Perceptions: Germany and America since 1776* (Cambridge, 1997), 295–297.

[76] Dmytryk, *It's a Hell of a Life*, 237–238.

[77] Avisar, *Screening the Holocaust*, 114–115.

[78] Shaw, *The Young Lions*, 660–671; Anhalt, "The Young Lions: First Draft," 170–174.

FIGURE 3: Concentration camp inmates upon their liberation by American soldiers. From *The Young Lions* (1958), directed by Edward Dmytryk. 20th Century Fox/Photofest. © 20th Century Fox.

than Shaw's novel, in which it is an interned Albanian diplomat who objects to the memorial service.[79]

The lead American characters, Noah and Michael, witness this exchange and then leave. Noah, played by Montgomery Clift, has persistently been fending off antisemitic harassment by his fellow soldiers to gain their respect, and he has overcome the reluctance of his Gentile girlfriend's father to allow his daughter to marry a Jew. The concentration camp exposes him to a more virulent strain of antisemitism. Noah and Michael walk away from the camp as a truck filled with corpses drives by them. Noah wonders whether Michael ever imagined that such places existed, adding, "My father's brother died in one of those." Noah returns home to his wife and baby, comforted by the thought that decent men such as Green will now be in charge of the world. Dmytryk deleted a line about Noah's thirst for revenge that was articulated in the original script: "The people who built these camps—you have to shoot them, of course, the way you'd shoot a wild animal or a poisonous snake."[80] The liberal faith in humanity espoused by Noah at the end of the film echoes Shaw's dialogue and was not an interjection of "Hollywood's incurable optimism," as Avisar

[79] Shaw, *The Young Lions*, 674–677.
[80] Anhalt, "The Young Lions: First Draft," 177; Shaw, *The Young Lions*, 679–680.

has charged.[81] Dmytryk considered Noah's personal growth and not Christian's "the heart of the story."[82]

FOLLOWING THE EXAMPLE of television programming in the 1950s, Hollywood belatedly broached the plotline of Jewish characters caught in the throes of the Nazi maelstrom by the end of the decade.[83] *Me and the Colonel* (1958), Peter Glenville's adaptation of Franz Werfel's play *Jacobowksy and the Colonel*, starred Danny Kaye as the enterprising S. L. Jacobowsky.[84] His odyssey across Europe epitomizes the fate of European Jewry under Hitler:

My earliest recollections are of Poland—shots, screams in the night. My poor mother took her candlesticks and pillows, her most cherished possessions and fled to Berlin . . . I was a citizen, a patriot; I belonged, but a certain housepainter had different ideas. So I packed my belongings in five trunks and fled to Vienna, the city of waltzes, but the waltz soon changed into a goosestep. I packed my belongings in two trunks and fled to Prague, but the German army seemed to take absolute delight in following me. Once again, this time with no trunks, I came to Paris, the city of light. Now the lights are going out, so I embark on migration number five.

When Jacobowsky offers to combine his own resourcefulness with the military prowess of a Polish colonel in hopes that together they can evade the Germans, the haughty Colonel Prokoszny, played by Curt Jurgens, will not deign to entertain the idea. He envisions only one possibility: an honorable death fighting for his nation. Jacobowsky believes that there are two possibilities in every situation: "If there is only one possibility, I'd have died I don't know how many times. What about an honorable life?" The Colonel intimates that he cannot associate with a Jew, prompting Jacobowsky to expound on the intractability of antisemitism: "I understand perfectly; the Colonel does not like Jews. He cannot help it, that's the way he was brought up. I'm Jewish; I cannot help it, that's the way I was brought up." As Jacobowsky repeatedly manages to outfox their German pursuers, the Colonel comes to appreciate his ingenuity. Werfel disliked the Broadway version of his play upon which the film was based because it did not sufficiently accentuate the tragedy enveloping European Jewry during World War II.[85] Despite its comic tone, however, *Me and the Colonel* leaves little doubt that Nazi antisemitism was implacably lethal even if the Colonel's aristocratic contempt for Jews was not. The film earned Kaye a Golden Globe for Best Actor in a Comedy and a spot on *Time*'s Top Ten Movie List for 1958.[86]

Although Werfel had firsthand experience as an émigré from Nazism, his play

[81] Shaw, *The Young Lions*, 680; Avisar, *Screening the Holocaust*, 114–116.

[82] Dmytryk, *It's a Hell of a Life*, 220.

[83] Shandler, *While America Watches*, 41–69.

[84] *Me and the Colonel*, dir. Peter Glenville (U.S., 1958); Franz Werfel, *Jacobowsky and the Colonel*, American adaptation by S. N. Behrman (New York, 1944).

[85] Lionel B. Steiman, *Franz Werfel: The Faith of an Exile—From Prague to Beverly Hills* (Waterloo, Ont., 1985), 174–177.

[86] "Awards," *Me and the Colonel*, http://www.imdb.com/title/tt0051915/awards (accessed August 7, 2009); "Top 10 Movie Lists," http://www.geocities.com/aaronbcaldwell/dimtime.html (accessed August 9, 2009).

could not match the popularity of *The Diary of a Young Girl*, which became an instant bestseller when it was released in the United States in 1952. It inspired a television program and a radio drama the same year.[87] Anne Frank's father, Otto, originally granted Meyer Levin permission to write a play based on the diary, but he changed his mind and went instead with the husband-wife team of Frances Goodrich and Albert Hackett because they had a successful box-office record. *The Diary of Anne Frank* premiered on Broadway in 1955. Its optimistic and universal themes pleased Otto Frank and resonated with American audiences and critics alike. Articles about Anne's life and death appeared in popular magazines such as *Reader's Digest* and *Life*.[88] *Look*'s cover story for its first issue of 1959 featured a photographic essay about the Third Reich and concluded with a quotation from Anne's diary: "I can feel the sufferings of millions, and, yet, if I look into the heavens, I think that it will all come out right, that this cruelty too will end."[89]

George Stevens secured the movie rights for the diary in 1956. As the head of the U.S. Army's Special Motion Picture Unit in Europe, he had directed the filming of the liberation of Nordhausen and Dachau. The experience had profoundly affected him: "I know there is brutality in war, and the SS were lousy bastards, but the destruction of people like this was beyond comprehension."[90] He consulted with Otto, who guided him through the Amsterdam building where the Frank family and their friends had hidden. Stevens meticulously replicated a vertical cutaway of the rooms on each floor to simulate the claustrophobic atmosphere of living in such close quarters. He visited Bergen-Belsen to get an idea of what Anne had endured there, then returned to Dachau to rekindle his indignation over what he had beheld at the site twelve years earlier.

Stevens grappled with how to convey Anne's ebullient personality without neglecting her tragic destiny. He considered closing the film with a shot of her standing in the midst of listless camp inmates with a "tiny expression on her face indicating a note of optimism among all the dreary faces around her." In keeping with the diary and the Goodrich and Hackett play, Stevens focused on Anne's relationships with the other residents who shared the family's hiding place in the attic, which Anne dubbed the "Secret Annexe."[91] In an interview he gave in 1963, he articulated his intention: "I wanted to make a film about a human being who knew how to conduct herself in a time of overwhelming misfortune, even though the audience knows from the outset what Anne doesn't know: her ultimate fate."[92]

As knowledge of the Holocaust has increased, scholars have excoriated the play and movie versions of *The Diary of Anne Frank*. They resent that Anne's recognition that Jews had suffered perennially is eviscerated when she tells Peter in both ad-

---

[87] Shandler, *While America Watches*, 62–63; Lawrence Graver, *An Obsession with Anne Frank: Meyer Levin and the "Diary"* (Berkeley, Calif., 1995); Meyer Levin, *The Obsession* (New York, 1973); Ralph Melnick, *The Stolen Legacy of Anne Frank: Meyer Levin, Lillian Hellman, and the Staging of the "Diary"* (New Haven, Conn., 1997).

[88] Louis de Jong, "The Girl Who Was Anne Frank," *Reader's Digest*, October 1957, 115–120; Ernst Schnabel, "A Tragedy Revealed: Heroine's Last Days," *Life*, August 18, 1958, 78–90.

[89] John Hunt, "The Insane World of Adolf Hitler," *Look*, January 6, 1959, 43.

[90] Paul Cronin, ed., *George Stevens: Interviews* (Jackson, Miss., 2004), 65–67; Marilyn Ann Moss, *Giant: George Stevens, a Life on Film* (Madison, Wis., 2004), 115–118.

[91] Moss, *Giant*, 230–247.

[92] Cronin, *George Stevens*, 22–23.

aptations, "We're not the only people that have had to suffer. There always have been people that have had to—sometimes one race, sometimes another."[93] This is cited as the most egregious example of minimizing Anne's Jewishness so that Gentile Americans could identify with her. Critics of the play and movie contend that confining the action to the attic insulates the audience from the sufferings of Jews who failed to find such a haven. The hard realities of the Holocaust are allegedly glossed over by the film's concluding voiceover of Anne affirming her belief that "people are really good at heart."[94]

Although Stevens portrays Anne as an ecumenical martyr of prejudice, he makes it clear that the Franks and their friends were victims of antisemitism. Reading the first entry in the diary, Otto's voice segues into Anne's as she recalls that her family fled Germany when Hitler came to power because they were Jewish. She enumerates the restrictions imposed on Jews by the German occupation government in Holland. Jewish stars appear conspicuously on the fronts of their coats. When Peter cuts his star off, Anne refuses to emulate him because, "after all, it is the Star of David." The peril facing Dutch Jews is underscored when Dussel joins the group. He agitatedly tells them that "right here in Amsterdam every day hundreds of Jews disappear." After Anne ponders how fortunate she and her cohort are, Jews wearing stars are marched away by armed German guards on the street below.

The charge that Stevens minimized Anne's Jewish identity is predicated on an exaggeration of how religious she was and how ethnically assertive American Jews were in the 1950s. Anne hated antisemitism and believed that Jewish suffering and survival possessed redemptive meaning.[95] She described herself as "not orthodox" and found value in any creed that obligated its adherents to act ethically.[96] The Chanukah celebration in the movie is more elaborate than Anne's diary entry about it: "We didn't make much fuss about Chanukah. We just gave each other a few little presents and then we had the candles."[97] Although the characters in the film recite the blessings in English, implying that they were speaking Dutch and not Hebrew, Otto refers to the Jewish uprising that inspired the holiday: "We kindle the Chanukah light to celebrate the great and wonderful deeds wrought through the zeal with which God filled the hearts of the heroic Maccabees two thousand years ago." John Stone, who headed the Jewish Film Advisory Committee, a group that lobbied the movie industry to promote positive images of Jews, gushed over Stevens's approach to Anne's Jewish identity: "You have given the story a more 'universal' meaning and

[93] Compare Anne's comments about Jewish suffering in Anne Frank, *The Diary of a Young Girl* (New York, 1952), 221, with her dialogue in the play *The Diary of Anne Frank* (New York, 1956), 168.

[94] Christopher Bigsby, *Remembering and Imagining the Holocaust: The Chain of Memory* (New York, 2006), 219–257; Pascale Bos, "Reconsidering Anne Frank: Teaching the Diary in Its Historical and Cultural Context," in Marianne Hirsch and Irene Kacandes, eds., *Teaching the Representation of the Holocaust* (New York, 2004), 23–46; Cole, *Selling the Holocaust*, 23–46; Judith E. Doneson, "The American History of Anne Frank's Diary," in Hyman A. Enzer and Sandra Solotaroff-Enzer, eds., *Anne Frank: Reflections on Her Life and Legacy* (Urbana, Ill., 2000), 123–138; Cynthia Ozick, "Who Owns Anne Frank?" in Ozick, *Quarrel and Quandary: Essays* (New York, 2000), 76–87; Alvin H. Rosenfeld, "Popularization and Memory: The Case of Anne Frank," in Peter Hayes, ed., *Lessons and Legacies: The Meaning of the Holocaust in a Changing World* (Evanston, Ill., 1991), 243–278.

[95] Frank, *The Diary*, 57, 139, 220–222, 252–253.

[96] Ibid., 270–271; Robert Alter, "The View from the Attic," *New Republic*, December 4, 1995, 41–42; Lawrence L. Langer, "The Uses—and Misuses—of a Young Girl's Diary: 'If Anne Frank Could Return from among the Murdered, She Would Be Appalled,'" in Enzer and Solotaroff-Enzer, *Anne Frank*, 204.

[97] Frank, *The Diary*, 68–69.

FIGURE 4: SS guards march Jews away. From *The Diary of Anne Frank* (1959), directed by George Stevens. 20th Century Fox/Photofest. © 20th Century Fox.

appeal. It could very easily have been an outdated Jewish tragedy by less creative or more emotional handling—even a Jewish 'Wailing Wall,' and hence regarded as mere propaganda."[98] Much of the criticism of the universalizing treatment of Anne in the play and film retrospectively stems from the overt ethnic and religious pride that has evolved among sectors of American Jewry since the 1960s.[99]

The violence that the Germans meted out to the Jews looms menacingly in the background. The film opens with Otto sitting on the back of a truck with other survivors, one of whom still wears a striped uniform. He tells his Dutch rescuers Kraler and Miep that he has returned alone. The moments of serenity in the Secret Annexe alternate with jarring radio broadcasts of Hitler's speeches and external noises such as jackboots clattering on the pavement and the whining of sirens. The night Anne learns that her best friend has been deported, she envisions the other girl in a nightmare sequence lethargically swaying in the midst of women inmates. She wakes up, crying "No! No! Don't . . . don't take me!" Before declaring her faith in human goodness, Anne admits how difficult it is to maintain hope when people are doing such horrible things. The strident sound of sirens and screeching tires heralds the arrival of the police, who furiously break down the door to the attic to get at their prey. The diary's pages symbolically flip from written to blank.

[98] Letter from John Stone to George Stevens, December 23, 1957, Goodrich-Hackett File, Wisconsin Center for Film and Theatre Research, Madison, Wis.

[99] David Barnouw, "Anne Frank and Film," in Enzer and Solotaroff-Enzer, *Anne Frank*, 165–172; Diner, *We Remember with Reverence and Love*, 365–390; Matthew Frye Jacobson, *Roots Too: White Ethnic Revival in Post–Civil Rights America* (Cambridge, Mass., 2006).

Otto's closing recollections reconfirm that he is the sole survivor. He recounts how the men went to Auschwitz and the women to Belsen. When Auschwitz was liberated, he was among its few surviving prisoners. From there, he embarked on a journey back to Holland. Along the way, he queried former camp inmates whether they knew anything about the fate of his loved ones. He gradually was apprised of their deaths. The day before he returned to Amsterdam, he met a woman who informed him that Anne had died in Belsen. As he immerses himself in her diary, a dissolve segues to gulls soaring in the clouds while Anne's voice reiterates her conviction that "people are really good at heart." Otto's soliloquy and Anne's faith in humanity manifest the dichotomy between doom and hope that hangs over the movie.

Most contemporary responses to the play and movie applauded the vibrancy of Anne's outlook, but did not disregard the dire circumstance in which she and her compatriots were trapped. In a review tellingly titled "Two Hearts at the Edge of Doom," *Newsweek* advised moviegoers to focus on the positive aspects of the film so as to avoid being stunned and depressed by it.[100] *Look*'s coverage featured stills with captions that left no doubt about the religious identities of the characters holed up in the Secret Annexe and what ultimately happened to them: "Anne regards her Star of David as an honor"; "Peter and Anne looking out from the bombed garret at people delivered into the hands of the cruelest brutes that walk the earth"; and "Anne, Peter, and her parents hear Nazi soldiers below as they come to take them to concentration camps."[101]

Writing after the premier of the play, a high school English teacher from Georgia described what her students culled from reading the diary:

My classes, faced with problems of desegregation in the South, have caught my enthusiasm for the diary. As seen through Anne's eyes, the evils of discrimination have made a terrific impact on these young people's minds ... Though not living under the grim shadow of gas chambers, the Gestapo, and death in a concentration camp, high school boys and girls in America are very close to Anne's experience.[102]

This sounds more like a prosthetic memory than a Panglossian diversion from a disturbing past. Similarly, Alan Mintz credits the diary with building "a bridge of empathic connection, even identification" between Hitler's Jewish victims and Americans.[103]

HISTORIANS NEED TO PLACE THESE FILMS in the chronological perspective of American cinema in general and the evolving consciousness of what the Holocaust entailed in particular. Directors such as Zinnemann, Dmytryk, and Stevens operated under the PCA, which regulated how violence could be depicted onscreen.[104] After those restrictions were no longer heeded, movie violence intensified "in the effort to restore

---

[100] "Two Hearts at the Edge of Doom," *Newsweek*, March 30, 1959, 98.
[101] "Movie Review," *Look*, May 26, 1959, 105–106.
[102] Mary Lane, "On Anne Frank," *The English Journal* 45, no. 5 (1956): 269–271.
[103] Mintz, *Popular Culture and the Shaping of Holocaust Memory in America*, 17.
[104] Stephen Prince, *Classical Film Violence: Designing and Regulating Brutality in Hollywood Cinema, 1930–1968* (New Brunswick, N.J., 2003).

the possibility of having an effect, creating a shock, provoking a response."[105] In the immediate postwar period, Hollywood introduced characters belonging to different ethnic, racial, and religious minorities, but expected them to blend into the melting pot.[106]

The first wave of American "Holocaust" cinema contributed to an incremental process of raising public awareness of the human toll that Hitler's policies had taken. To achieve a semblance of authenticity, some movies excerpted or re-created the images and symbols of Nazi crimes gleaned from the atrocity footage of the liberated camps. They simulated a documentary look by establishing the convention of using black and white stock to film stories set in the Holocaust or its immediate aftermath. This latter practice was standard in the late 1940s, during the heyday of film noir, but marked a departure from the Technicolor epics produced at the end of the 1950s. It provided a model for subsequent films, including *The Pawnbroker*, *The Odessa File* (1974), and *Schindler's List* (1993). The pioneering "Holocaust" films focused on uplifting narratives, but alluded to an ominous offscreen evil that reduced Jewish characters to traumatized refugees, survivors, and fugitives. What has changed since 1960 is not the disappearance of edifying endings, as is evident in the miniseries *Holocaust* (1978) and the feature films *Schindler's List* and *The Pianist* (2002), but rather the foregrounding of the deadly forces arrayed against predominantly Jewish protagonists.[107]

The number of American films with Holocaust themes pales in comparison to Hollywood's total movie production between 1945 and 1959.[108] Yet critically acclaimed and commercially successful motion pictures such as *The Search*, *Me and the Colonel*, *The Young Lions*, and *The Diary of Anne Frank* enabled American audiences to shift their perspective from citizens of a country that prided itself on defeating the Third Reich, bringing its perpetrators to justice, and rehabilitating its survivors to that of innocent Jews such as Jacobowsky, the Franks, and their friends, whose only crime was their religious affiliation. These movies accustomed Americans to the idea of the "Final Solution" by keeping its savagery offscreen or within existing conventions for movie violence. They portrayed acculturated Jewish characters whose appearance and actions did not seem foreign to Americans. By domesticating the Holocaust, these early films laid the visual and thematic foundations of a prosthetic memory for audiences who fortunately never experienced its horrors. Subsequent cinematic representations of the Shoah featuring gorier images and stressing its Jewish specificity should not be construed as the surfacing of a repressed trauma, but rather as a reworking of familiar subject material by a motion picture industry freed

[105] Leo Charney, "The Violence of a Perfect Moment," in J. David Slocum, ed., *Violence and American Cinema* (New York, 2000), 49.

[106] See Judith E. Smith, *Visions of Belonging: Family Stories, Popular Culture, and Postwar Democracy, 1940–1960* (New York, 2004).

[107] Stephen J. Whitfield, *In Search of American Jewish Culture* (Hanover, N.H., 1999), 188–189.

[108] See figures 6 and 7 in Lary May, *The Big Picture: Hollywood and the Politics of the American Way* (Chicago, 2000), 276–277.

Lawrence Baron

of the limitations imposed by the PCA and more attuned to the ethnic, racial, and religious identity politics that have competed with the melting pot paradigm in the United States since the 1960s.

Lawrence Baron is Abraham Nasatir Professor of Modern Jewish History at San Diego State University. He received his Ph.D. from the University of Wisconsin in 1974 and taught at St. Lawrence University from 1975 until 1988, when he accepted his current position. He is the author of *Projecting the Holocaust into the Present: The Changing Focus of Contemporary Holocaust Cinema* (Rowman and Littlefield, 2005) and served as the historian for Sam and Pearl Oliner's *The Altruistic Personality: Rescuers of Jews in Nazi Europe* (Free Press, 1988). He is currently editing an anthology on depictions of modern Jewish history in world cinema.

AHR Forum
Going Visual:
Holocaust Representation and Historical Method

SARAH FARMER

THE ARTICLES IN THIS FORUM take up the challenge for historians to use visual material as the basis for historical evidence, argument, and interpretation. They set aside, if not completely to rest, questions that vexed scholars and intellectuals in the late 1980s and early 1990s: Can and should the Holocaust be represented more than forty years after the Judeocide? If so, how? The dovetailing of postmodern concerns about the nature of representation, and an acute awareness that Holocaust survivors who had lived into old age were dying, instigated debates about the "limits of representation."[1]

The articles presented here, on the other hand, address contemporaneous acts of representation so embedded in the unfolding of the Holocaust that they do not stand outside it. They drive home the fact that the Holocaust was being visually represented by victims, perpetrators, and bystanders even as it was happening; the "Holocaust" has never not been "represented." The scholars in this forum are contending with the opportunities offered—demanded, even—by the density of this visual evidence. Their work establishes a potent role for the visual (accepting, of course, that filmmaking, photography, and building memorials are different enterprises) in the emergence of a notion of a specifically Jewish catastrophe that came to be known as the "Holocaust." To the extent that they underscore the pervasive impact of photography and film in shaping twentieth-century ways of seeing, knowing, and feeling, they invite historians working on this period to ask what visual sources could inform their subject of inquiry and what new avenues these sources might open. They raise our awareness of particular qualities that make the photographic image function differently than the written documents on which historians traditionally rely.

A Florence Gould Foundation Fellowship at the National Humanities Center (Research Triangle Park, N.C.) in 2008–2009 provided ideal conditions for the reading, viewing, and discussion with colleagues across disciplines that went into preparing this essay. Vanessa Schwartz and Randolph Starn gave careful and responsive readings of early drafts.

[1] Saul Friedlander, ed., *Probing the Limits of Representation: Nazism and the "Final Solution"* (Cambridge, Mass., 1992).

HISTORIANS OF THE WESTERN EXPERIENCE in the nineteenth and twentieth centuries still overwhelmingly depend on text-based archives, although interdisciplinary research projects, conferences, and publications in the last ten years indicate a "visual turn" in the scholarship.[2] Of course, historians of the ancient and medieval worlds, for which sources are relatively scarce, have always relied on visual and material evidence, and the image has long been given its due in Renaissance studies, where divisions between history and art history have not been drawn so sharply as for later periods. The historiographical context for the essays in this forum is a growing literature on the visual history of the Holocaust pioneered by scholars of photography and communications as well as members of a generation of historians indebted to the new cultural history.[3] This visual turn explores how images work in history and includes (but is not limited to) putting visual sources at the center of analysis (as opposed to using them solely for content or illustration); considering how visual materials make history; reflecting on how they engage questions of temporality; and taking into account, and employing in historical work, the ways in which modern visual culture shapes the way we construct historical narratives.[4]

Many reasons account for the reluctance of most historians to place images at the center of their work. Much of it can be laid at the door of habit and training tied to the nineteenth-century origins of the discipline and its focus on the state-produced archive. This archive has traditionally been thought of as a collection of written and printed documents; yet the more we look, the more we find that it contains records in visual form (photographs, film, maps, etc.).[5] Some make the case that our reverence for the word goes back to the birth of Renaissance humanism founded on the recovery and criticism of biblical and classical texts. Art historian David Freedberg argues that images engage us cognitively to produce both identification and emotion

[2] In an effort to define the field of "visual culture," scholars have published anthologies and readers: John A. Walker and Sarah Chaplin, *Visual Culture: An Introduction* (Manchester, 1997); Nicholas Mirzoeff, *The Visual Culture Reader* (London, 1998); Marita Sturken and Lisa Cartwright, *Practices of Looking: An Introduction to Visual Culture* (Oxford, 2001); Barnard Malcolm, *Approaches to Understanding Visual Culture* (New York, 2001); Richard Howells, *Visual Culture* (Cambridge, 2003); Vanessa R. Schwartz and Jeannene M. Przyblyski, *The Nineteenth-Century Visual Culture Reader* (London, 2004). In 2005–2006, the Eisenberg Institute for Historical Studies at the University of Michigan took as its theme history and the visual. In September 2006, the electronic mailing list for German history, H-German, published a forum titled "German History after the Visual Turn," http://www.h-net.org/~german/discuss/visual/visual_index.htm.

[3] Scholars of communications and photography include Barbie Zelizer, *Remembering to Forget: Holocaust Memory through the Camera's Eye* (Chicago, 1998); Janina Struk, *Photographing the Holocaust: Interpretations of the Evidence* (London, 2004). For historians of photography, see Clément Chéroux, "Du bon usage des images," in *Mémoire des camps: Photographies des camps de concentration et d'extermination nazis, 1933–1999* (Paris, 2001); Detlef Hoffmann, "Fotografierte Lager: Uberlegungen zu einer Fotogeschichte deutscher konzentrationslager," *Fotogeschichte*, no. 45 (1994): 3–20. For work by historians of film, see Sylvie Lindeperg, *"Nuit et Brouillard": Un film dans l'histoire* (Paris, 2007); Christian Delage, *La vérité par l'image: De Nuremberg au procès Milosevic* (Paris, 2006). Arno Gisinger brings together artistic and historical sensibilities in his photographic work for *Inventarisiert: Enteingnung vom Möbeln aus jüdischem Besitz* (Wien, 2000). Sybil Milton was among the first historians to consider photographs as a source for writing the history of the Holocaust; Milton, "Images of the Holocaust," *Holocaust and Genocide Studies* 1, no. 2 (1986): 193–216. For a review of Holocaust photography in the German context, see David F. Crew, "What Can We Learn from a Visual Turn? Photography, Nazi Germany and the Holocaust," at http://www.h-net.org/~german/discuss/visual/visual_index.htm.

[4] Vanessa R. Schwartz, "Film and History," in James Donald and Michael Renov, eds., *Sage Handbook of Film Studies* (Los Angeles, 2008), 199–215.

[5] For recent work on the nature and history of archives, see Ann Blair and Jennifer Milligan, eds., *Toward a Cultural History of Archives*, Special Issue, *Archival Science* 7, no. 4 (December 2007).

more viscerally than text—which can make historians uncomfortable, believing as we do in the specificity of historical conditions to shape response.[6] Be that as it may, this forum suggests that historians have a role to play in how we understand the "power of images" by showing how, historically, the visual was made, deployed, and received. It is also the case that when brought to bear on the history of the Holocaust, visual evidence brings the emotional impact and truth claims of the visual into greater relief—often painfully so.[7]

Two landmark photographic exhibits made the case by example that there is too much visual evidence of the Holocaust for historians not to engage it. "War of Extermination: Crimes of the Wehrmacht, 1941 to 1944," organized by the Hamburg Institute for Social Research, opened in 1995 and traveled for four years throughout Germany and Austria, where it was seen by 900,000 visitors. The exhibit presented photographic evidence from the eastern front of the mass murder of Jews and extermination of other civilians, accompanied by extensive excerpts from official army documents and soldiers' personal letters and diaries. Almost all of the 1,000 photographs in the exhibit were taken by German soldiers for propaganda purposes or for their personal use (to send home or to keep as souvenirs).[8] The exhibit generated enormous public debate about the wartime conduct of the Wehrmacht; the fact that much of the controversy crystallized around errors in the captions of several photographs highlighted the cardinal role of words in the framing of visual evidence.[9]

The exhibit "The Memory of the Camps: Photography of the Nazi Concentration and Extermination Camps (1933–1999)," held in 2001 at the Hôtel de Sully in Paris, aimed to historicize the photographic record of life and death in the camps. It emphasized the diversity of images and the range of sources that visually document the Holocaust: the camps' internal photographic services (which served bureaucratic, "scientific," and propaganda purposes); photo reporting by the German press; photo albums created to document the history of individual camps; "the Auschwitz album" compiled by SS photographers to record the triage of Hungarian deportees in the summer of 1944; personal albums made by Nazi camp officials; aerial photographs taken by the U.S. Air Force; and photographs taken at the Liberation by professionals and amateurs.

These images were not unknown. For Clément Chéroux, a historian of photography who organized the exhibit, the point was to cast an "analytical and critical" gaze on this "immense, ill-defined, iconographic lexicon of infamy" by bringing the

[6] David Freedberg, *The Power of Images: Studies in the History and Theory of Response* (Chicago, 1986).

[7] This is true as well for other images of human degradation and violence such as lynching. James Allen et al., *Without Sanctuary: Lynching Photography in America* (Santa Fe, N.Mex., 2005); Dora Apel and Shawn Michelle Smith, *Lynching Photographs* (Berkeley, Calif., 2007).

[8] Hamburger Institut für Sozialforschung, *Vernichtungskrieg: Verbrechen der Wehrmacht 1941 bis 1944: Ausstellungskatalog* (Hamburg, 1996).

[9] See Hannes Heer, "The Difficulty of Ending a War: Reactions to the Exhibition 'War of Extermination: Crimes of the Wehrmacht, 1941 to 1944,'" trans. Jane Caplan, *History Workshop Journal*, no. 46 (Autumn 1998): 187–203; *Jenseits des Krieges*, a documentary film by Ruth Beckermann, records veterans' confrontation with photographs and each other as they take in the exhibit. For a detailed discussion by an organizer of the exhibit of controversy over mistaken captions, see Bernd Boll, "Zloczow, July 1941: The Wehrmacht and the Beginning of the Holocaust in Galicia," in Omer Bartov, Atina Grossmann, and Mary Nolan, eds., *Crimes of War: Guilt and Denial in the Twentieth Century* (New York, 2002), 61–99.

photographs themselves to the fore as historical objects. According to Chéroux, "one must return to these pictures their documentary value, which generally has been buried under generations of reproductions or under multiple layers of their use for symbolic value. One needs, in sum, to undertake a true archaeology of the photographic document."[10] This entailed presenting the pictures in their original format, writing precise captions, identifying the context in which the pictures were taken, and noting the names of the photographers. This exhibit proposed that those who follow the historian's imperative to contextualize can effectively mine the vast, scattered, complex, distressing visual archive of the Holocaust to yield significant information and insights.

Debates about representation of the Holocaust and the use of images in shaping historical understanding have by no means been settled. Critics of the 2001 Paris exhibit recalled French filmmaker Claude Lanzmann's famous rejection of the use of any historical footage or archival images in favor of the testimony of survivors in his 1985 documentary masterpiece *Shoah*.[11] Susan Crane has proposed that atrocity photography from the Holocaust be removed from easy viewing in order to protect these images (taken without the subjects' consent, and therefore "ethically compromised") from "banal attention."[12] Nonetheless, as this forum indicates, historians of the Holocaust are increasingly employing visual sources in their work as well as making the visual record of the Holocaust a subject of study.

David Shneer takes an archaeological approach to Dmitrii Baltermants's photographs of the December 31, 1941, atrocity at Kerch and Evgenii Khaldei's photograph of a Jewish couple in Budapest at the Liberation. Digging in a range of archives, he tracks down when the photographs were taken, where they appeared, and how, when published, they were framed and defined by layout, captions, and surrounding text. In the Russian-language press, the text that accompanied the photographs stressed that the Nazis had killed Soviet civilians indiscriminately. Editors in the Yiddish-language press informed their readership that the victims had been preponderantly Jewish. Shneer teases out the connotations embedded in captions to show how the same sets of images, combined with different texts, were used to create overlapping narratives of suffering (Soviet and Jewish) that, during the war, informed each other. Over time, the use of the most famous Kerch image ("Grief") to commemorate the wartime sacrifices and suffering of the Soviet population erased specific and nuanced understandings of the Kerch images and, instead, nourished competing narratives—one "Soviet," and the other Jewish. The possibility that so many meanings can be attributed to an image (in this case a grieving widow) lies at the heart of what makes historians wary of visual sources. (Since this is no less true for oral and written sources, the question remains why photographs provoke this

    [10] Chéroux, "Du bon usage des images," 16.

    [11] Jacques Mandelbaum, "La Shoah et ces images qui nous manquent," *Le Monde*, January 25, 2001. Lanzmann also rejected Steven Spielberg's historical enactment of the Shoah in *Schindler's List*. "A propos de 'la liste de Schindler,' dernier film de Steven Spielberg: Holocauste, la représentation impossible," *Le Monde*, March 3, 1994. The debate over Lanzmann's versus Spielberg's approach has been extensively addressed in the scholarly literature as well as in the more public forum of the press and film criticism. Yosefa Loshitzky, ed., *Spielberg's Holocaust: Critical Perspectives on "Schindler's List"* (Bloomington, Ind., 1997); Stuart Liebman, *Claude Lanzmann's "Shoah": Key Essays* (Oxford, 2007).

    [12] Susan Crane, "Choosing Not to Look: Representation, Repatriation, and Holocaust Atrocity Photography," *History and Theory* 47 (October 2008): 309–330.

response.) Shneer deftly turns the photograph's malleability to his advantage; by taking an archaeological approach, he uses the polyvalence of the image to historicize the subtleties and paradoxes of historical interpretation and understanding in the Soviet Union of the nature of the Nazi war on the East.

Shneer raises tantalizing questions, as yet unexplored in the scholarship, about the fact that Jews made up 50 to 75 percent of the wartime Soviet press corps. Both Baltermants and Khaldei were Soviet Jews. It would appear that the photographers themselves lived out overlapping narratives of personal identity; this emerges dramatically in the contradictory accounts Khaldei gave about his encounter with the Jewish couple he photographed in 1945 in Budapest. (Did he address them as a Soviet citizen or as a Jew? Did he speak German or Yiddish?) By including evidence of Khaldei's own shifting identity and understanding of his photographs, Shneer highlights the contingency of authorial intention. His original research on Baltermants and Khaldei underscores the value of finding out as much as possible about who is behind the camera. It recognizes that the photograph is taken from the perspective of a historical participant and observer of the period and deserves consideration like other commentaries on a place and time.

Shneer's discussion of the aesthetic and ideological conventions that governed Soviet war photography leaves one wanting to know more about the history and impact of these practices and how they might fit into a longer history of war photography that goes back at least to the Crimean War.[13] It also reminds us that we know much more about the traditions and norms practiced by the reporters who shaped how Western Europeans and Americans pictured the Holocaust: Robert Capa, Margaret Bourke-White, Lee Miller, George Rodger. Shneer's article provides an excellent example of the steps historians can take to read visual language as skillfully as we do more familiar kinds of sources.

Lawrence Baron, writing about what he calls the first wave of American "Holocaust" films, and Harold Marcuse, exploring the emergence of memorial sites, engage visual sources as indices of popular consciousness of public discourse about the Holocaust. Baron makes the case that well before the 1960s (when most scholars consider a concept of the Holocaust to have taken hold in the United States), Hollywood movies had raised public awareness of the "human toll" of Nazi policies. In order to argue a case about the periodization of Holocaust awareness in America, Baron sets his definition of what constitutes a "Holocaust" film so broadly that it seems to work at cross-purposes with the term itself, which aims at specificity. (Having read this forum, readers are surely aware that the term was coined to refer to the Nazi effort to eradicate the Jews entirely—a fate not intended for other groups who were to be diminished by murder, starvation, and enslavement.) Baron's detailed discussions of the plots of films made between the end of the war (1945) and the trial of Adolf Eichmann (1961) succeed in showing that Hollywood directors embedded stories of the fate of European Jews in films about the war. But to characterize these movies as Holocaust films seems an overstatement that does little to

---

[13] Ulrich Keller, *The Ultimate Spectacle: A Visual History of the Crimean War* (London, 2002). For discussions of this and on photography and reality, see Errol Morris's *New York Times* blog, http://morris.blogs.nytimes.com.

push forward understanding of how these films informed or shaped American awareness or understanding of the Judeocide.

Baron notes that many scholars and critics consider Hollywood's treatment of the Holocaust to be tainted by commercialism ("Shoah business") and trivializing of its subject. Baron, on the other hand, embraces cultural critic Alison Landsberg's optimistic assessment of mass culture's ability to create in the consumer "prosthetic memory": "deeply felt memory of a past event through which he or she did not live."[14] Movies such as *Schindler's List* and *The Pianist* or a visit to the United States Holocaust Memorial Museum, which produce "prosthetic memory" for the case of the Holocaust, demonstrate the ability of mass culture to generate empathy and alliances among the public. This provocative idea is worthy of consideration; one might place it in line with work that considers cultural practices and emotion in the rise of humanitarianism or the invention of human rights.[15] In order to do more than just assert that these films created empathy for Jewish victims, Baron needs to tell us something about their reception by audiences and film critics. Furthermore, his application of the notion of "prosthetic memory" leaves no room for responses other than empathy for victims of oppression. Any consideration of Holocaust memory needs to at least acknowledge the possibility of prosthetic memory that would not be reverential. What about the possibility of a viewer who sympathizes with the perpetrator? Or the person who, in an award-winning memoir, fraudulently presented himself as Binjamin Wilkomirski, a child deported from Poland who survived the death camps as an orphan?[16] One cannot help but wish that Baron the historian would resist the conflation of narrative, history, and memory to argue for the potential of feature films to foster an understanding of history rather than the appropriation of memory.

Baron makes tantalizing references to the use within the plots of early "Holocaust" feature films of documentary footage to prove the existence of Nazi crimes of mass murder. For example, he tells us that in Sam Fuller's *Verboten!* Franz, a diehard Nazi sympathizer, is forced to attend the Nuremberg Trials and watch footage of the documentary *Nazi Concentration Camps*. As a result, Franz turns against the war criminals he has been helping to harbor. Baron's work would be deepened by analyzing how these films operate in ways other than by the unfolding of plot. Disappointingly, he misses the opportunity to explore the imbrication of the documentary and fiction genres in the films as well as the vital role of the Hollywood film industry in early postwar filmmaking (as well as during the war itself). At the behest of Supreme Court Justice and Chief American Prosecutor Robert H. Jackson, Hollywood director John Ford led a team that filmed the sessions of the International Military Tribunal at Nuremberg to create a historical record of the trial. Ford also produced two films (including *Nazi Concentration Camps*) from U.S. Department of Defense sources that were shown at Nuremberg as proof for the prosecution and to elicit demeanor evidence from the accused.[17] Consideration of the role of Hollywood directors in making this evidence, as well as the long history of the film

[14] Alison Landsberg, *Prosthetic Memory: The Transformation of American Remembrance in the Age of Mass Culture* (New York, 2004).

[15] See Lynn Hunt, *Inventing Human Rights* (New York, 2007).

[16] Philip Gourevitch, "The Memory Thief," *New Yorker*, June 14, 1999, 48–68.

[17] Film historian Christian Delage has analyzed in writing the use of filmed evidence at Nuremberg

genre of the courtroom drama, could illuminate the intentions of the directors of first-wave "Holocaust" films as well as the possible impact of their work on postwar American audiences.

ALL THE ARTICLES PRESENTED HERE take us back to the origins of representation of the Holocaust in overriding concerns to amass evidence of the genocide. Even if, as Chéroux tells us, images of the camps have been used primarily for their symbolic value, they were originally taken to be used as evidence—whether the photographer was a perpetrator or the object of annihilation. A searing example is four images taken at the site of the gas chambers at Auschwitz in August 1944 by members of the *Sonderkommando* and smuggled out to London by members of the Resistance.[18] Shneer shows that the images of Soviet war photographers first served to prove to Soviet citizens the nature of Nazi crimes. The films that Baron discusses share a preoccupation with evidence and proof. Before the first efforts, described by Marcuse, to erect memorials to the victims of Nazism, the remains of concentration camp sites were kept as physical proof of Nazi crimes. Representation at the camps first took the form of presenting the site as unmediated evidence that could speak for itself. Didactic and symbolic elements were not added until the 1960s.

Marcuse looks at a range of early memorial expression, including a rudimentary sculpture erected at Majdanek and plans for monuments in Warsaw and in New York to the heroes of the Warsaw Ghetto Uprising. In charting the emergence of the Holocaust memorial as a new genre, he analyzes the intentions of the memorializers and consciously refrains from analyzing how the memorials function as representations. (It remains unclear why he considers an analysis of how the memorials function to be a theoretical problem and not a historical one.) Marcuse does note that until 1970, no abstracted representation went up at Majdanek because substantial ruins remained.

The concentration camp site itself served as physical proof of the Nazi persecution and mass murder. By being seen, it could prove guilt and make viewers acknowledge the atrocities perpetrated. This is why, when the British army liberated the concentration camp of Bergen-Belsen, it required the local German population to tour the camp and view corpses. Marcuse sees the classical forms of the memorials first erected at Bergen-Belsen and Buchenwald as an indication that the memorializers had not yet formulated the meanings they wished to represent. Be that as it may, it seems that the first meanings assigned to the places where mass murder took place were forensic: the site itself served as proof of the crimes to be prosecuted, and this meaning was seen to speak for itself. In the 1960s, memorializers layered onto this bedrock of evidence self-conscious efforts at artistic or symbolic interpretation that, Marcuse notes, diverged sharply from "traditional forms of war memorials" to "abstract, avant-garde forms." James Young has shown, for example, that

---

and has also made a documentary film about the trial using the filmed footage. Delage, *La vérité par l'image*; *Nuremberg: Les Nazis face à leurs crimes*, DVD (Montreal, 2006).

[19] Georges Didi-Hubermann, "Four Pieces of Film Snatched from Hell," in Didi-Hubermann, *Images in Spite of All: Four Photographs from Auschwitz*, trans. Shane B. Lillis (Chicago, 2008).

the 1964 monument at Treblinka, made of broken fragments of rock surrounding a giant cracked obelisk, "emblematizes both the destruction and impossibility of recovery" of Jewish life in Poland.[19]

This forum not only underscores the critical importance of visual material as a source and subject for writing twentieth-century history, but also provokes reflection on where historians might move next in the ongoing "visual turn." The first implication of the "visual turn" has been to challenge historians to look, find, see, and interpret visual sources. The next step is to explore the relationship between the visual, the spoken word, and the text.[20] The modern historian's inclination is to view sources as either visual or verbal, either image or text. Medievalists, for example, are more attuned to texts that are illustrated, pictures that contain words, visual signs that function as words, and texts that describe images. Yet a photographic image, a film, and perhaps a memorial site are also embedded in language. We know from historians of photography that photographic images have never been far removed from print culture. By the mid-nineteenth century, most photographs were taken to be placed in a book (the family album) or, by the 1880s, published in a newspaper. By the 1930s, the modern photography book (produced by photographers themselves, carefully edited to create a visual narrative in book form) had come into its own.[21] Baron's work reminds us that most feature films follow the conventions of popular print narratives such as the detective novel or thriller. In fact, the intimate interaction between the image and the word played a cardinal role in the heated discussions of Holocaust representation in the 1980s and 1990s. Lanzmann's images of survivors recollecting the Shoah brought enormous attention to the nature of oral testimony.[22] The three articles in this forum, while bringing our attention to the visual, also remind us not to overstate the independence of word and image and place in the making of narratives—the written often relies on the visual, and the visual often relies on the word.

[19] James E. Young, "Broken Tablets and Jewish Memory in Poland," in Young, *The Texture of Memory: Holocaust Memorials and Meaning* (New Haven, Conn., 1993), 185.

[20] On the relationship and interaction between text and image, see W. J. T. Mitchell, *Picture Theory: Essays on Verbal and Visual Representation* (Chicago, 1994).

[21] Andrea Nelson, brochure for the exhibit "Reading the Modern Photography Book: Changing Perspectives," held in conjunction with "Looking In: Robert Frank's 'The Americans,'" National Gallery of Art, January 18–April 26, 2009.

[22] This spurred Lawrence Langer's groundbreaking exploration of the different ways that testimony is construed and framed by the act of writing or the act of being filmed. Langer, *Holocaust Testimonies: The Ruins of Memory* (New Haven, Conn., 1991).

Sarah Farmer is Associate Professor of History at the University of California, Irvine. She is the author of *Martyred Village: Commemorating the 1944 Massacre at Oradour-sur-Glane* (University of California Press, 1999). She is currently writing a book on cultural and social responses to the demise of peasant society in postwar France. This work seeks implications that go beyond the French case for understanding how societies make sense of their traditions in light of dynamics of change particular to the twentieth century.

The December 2007 issue led off with an article by David Eltis, Philip Morgan, and David Richardson titled "Agency and Diaspora in Atlantic History: Reassessing the African Contribution to Rice Cultivation in the Americas." Making extensive use of calculations from the Trans-Atlantic Slave Trade Database, the authors not only challenged recent interpretations of the origins of rice cultivation in the New World but also commented on the nature of exchange and innovation in the Atlantic world. In addition, they offered some methodological suggestions for how we should think about the cultural transmission in a diasporic context. Because of the challenging nature of that piece, we opened our pages to specialists in this field to comment on the authors' substantive and methodological claims.

In the first of three comments, "Beyond 'Black Rice': Reconstructing Material and Cultural Contexts for Early Plantation Agriculture," S. Max Edelson essentially agrees with Eltis, Morgan, and Richardson that the case for the African origin of rice in the American South is dubious. He argues, however, that our focus should be less on the slave trade and more on the developing plantation economy. In the Carolina Lowcountry, his case study, he finds that rice cultivation emerged as Africans and Europeans improvised ways to eat and work on a rough plantation frontier. Rice, and the plantation world based on this crop, resulted from responses to contingent material conditions rather than from a culturally specific "contribution" that generated a particular developmental course. Edelson urges investigations of slaves' adaptive agricultural practices as a more promising path toward understanding black agency in plantation America.

The focus of Gwendolyn Midlo Hall's critique, "Africa and Africans in the African Diaspora: The Uses of Relational Databases," is primarily methodological. She argues that the database employed by Eltis, Morgan, and Richardson is inadequate, citing calculations from her own database, the Louisiana Slave Database, which she claims is superior insofar as it includes information not only on the slave trade voyages but also from documents found throughout the Amer-

icas. Indeed, she calls for the creation of a Western Hemisphere Slave Database based on the extensive archives on this side of the Atlantic. Hall's own view supports the claim for the African slave origin of American rice cultivation, and she calls Eltis, Morgan, and Richardson to task for what she judges as unfair criticism of this analysis.

The final comment, "From 'Black Rice' to 'Brown': Rethinking the History of Risiculture in the Seventeenth- and Eighteenth-Century Atlantic," by Walter Hawthorne, is also primarily methodological in emphasis. Hawthorne argues that both the "black rice thesis" and the analysis of Eltis, Morgan, and Richardson are flawed, as each is based on a particular evidentiary approach. He calls for a modified interpretation, one that recognizes the contributions of both Africans and Europeans to rice cultivation, processing, and cooking on both sides of the eighteenth-century Atlantic.

In their response, Eltis, Morgan, and Richardson answer the specific criticisms of these commentators and defend their own methodology and analysis. They begin by challenging once again the assumption that risiculture was established in the Americas by African slaves, claiming that the evidence they have assembled makes this a doubtful proposition. They insist, however, that their analysis is not meant to undermine claims for African slaves' agency. "In challenging the 'black rice' thesis," they conclude, "we sought to place transatlantic slavery in an Atlantic context and to remind readers how imbalances in power between the enslaved and their owners molded the history of emergent American plantation societies under the influence of changing market conditions."

AHR Exchange
Beyond "Black Rice": Reconstructing Material and Cultural Contexts for Early Plantation Agriculture

S. MAX EDELSON

IN PURSUIT OF THE IDEA THAT enslaved African farmers introduced rice agriculture to the Americas, scholars have constructed an elaborate argument to make the case for this transatlantic transfer of knowledge and practice. They have traced the passages of captives from Upper Guinea to the labor camps of the Carolina Lowcountry, drawn parallels between cultivation methods in Africa and America, and speculated about how slaves who understood how to produce a valuable article of trade might have shaped plantation society in colonial South Carolina and Georgia. This argument was first advanced in a speculative formulation by Peter H. Wood and then developed by Daniel C. Littlefield, both historians of African America.[1] Geographer Judith A. Carney has recently added new links to this chain of reasoning, vouched for its soundness, and made the most far-reaching claims for the significance of what might be called the "black rice thesis" after her 2001 book, *Black Rice: The African Origins of Rice Cultivation in the Americas*.[2]

In "Agency and Diaspora in Atlantic History," David Eltis, Philip Morgan, and David Richardson mobilize statistics to refute this argument's claims about how rice farmers passed through the slave trade to reproduce an African agricultural system on the western shores of the Atlantic Ocean.[3] Although their critique of Carney makes a convincing case that few skilled rice farmers figured among the enslaved population of the early Carolina Lowcountry, and perhaps elsewhere, it leaves unanswered the question of how rice became the region's staple commodity. Driving this debate is an underlying disagreement about whether or not slaves exerted significant influences on economic formation in South Carolina, and by implication throughout the Americas. This point of contention has set the stakes for rice's significance in terms of its role as an export into the transatlantic marketplace. This emphasis on commercial outcomes, however, distorts the crop's earliest meanings

I thank my colleague Joseph C. Miller for his perceptive comments on and criticisms of this essay.

[1] Peter H. Wood, *Black Majority: Negroes in Colonial South Carolina from 1670 through the Stono Rebellion* (New York, 1974), chap. 2; Daniel C. Littlefield, *Rice and Slaves: Ethnicity and the Slave Trade in Colonial South Carolina* (Baton Rouge, La., 1981), chap. 4.

[2] Judith A. Carney, *Black Rice: The African Origins of Rice Cultivation in the Americas* (Cambridge, Mass., 2001).

[3] David Eltis, Philip Morgan, and David Richardson, "Agency and Diaspora in Atlantic History: Reassessing the African Contribution to Rice Cultivation in the Americas," *American Historical Review* 112, no. 5 (December 2007): 1329–1358.

within the dynamic domestic economy of the recently settled colony. Instead of counting heads and untangling contributions, we can attempt to reconstruct the specific conditions under which African slaves and European colonists first practiced agriculture in New World environments. These adaptations reveal a world of unintended consequences and surprising collaborations that shaped the emergence of American plantation societies.

Critics of the black rice thesis look skeptically on the idea that the enslaved entrenched an African system at the heart of the planters' economy. Its advocates have been compelled by the revisionist implications of this very idea to demonstrate that it was true. Both perspectives take for granted that the best explanation for the Carolina Lowcountry's expansive plantation society must locate the most probable point of origin that leads, step by reasonable step, toward this outcome. The debate has thus focused a great deal of attention on gauging the demographic probability that significant numbers of Africans familiar with rice came to the colony and put their knowledge to use there. Establishing such a critical mass is not necessary, however, to account for the integration of African methods within a European-directed commercial farming economy. A single African farmer may have demonstrated viable ways to grow and process rice that others observed, emulated, and disseminated.

Contingency, not destiny, gave the region its staple commodity. Without distorting the social and economic dynamics that governed this early plantation society, we can explain the rise of rice in ways that account for the roles played by Africans as well as Europeans. To do so means abandoning a single-minded focus on awarding Africans credit as the propagators of rice culture. It also means shifting the context of explanation from the transatlantic market economy, in which sustained demand for rice provides the ultimate reason why it became an important commodity, to the spatial scale of the swamp field and the temporal scale of the agricultural season, in which colonists and slaves came to focus on rice to reconstitute material life in the harsh setting of an accelerating plantation economy. We have much to gain by channeling the drive of the black rice thesis to reveal African sources for American development into new investigations of agricultural adaptation that took place long after this plantation society came into being. As the expanding rice economy grew to consume their labor in the eighteenth century, enslaved farmers gained a measure of material control over their lives by planting seeds, tending crops, and trading commodities.

THE BLACK RICE THESIS HAS BECOME a commonplace, widely invoked as an emblematic story of colonial South Carolina's beginnings as well as a surprising truth about Africans' influential roles in the development of American plantation societies.[4] Carney's elaboration of its core idea accounts for much of this renewed popularity. *Black Rice* features Alfred Crosby's concept of the Columbian exchange to consider how

---

[4] See, for example, textbook treatments of this issue in James Henretta et al., *America's History*, 5th ed. (Boston, 2004), 84–87; Pauline Maier et al., *Inventing America: A History of the United States*, 2nd ed. (New York, 2005), 114. A popular online source for information about American slavery states simply that "some of the earliest African arrivals had shown English settlers how rice could be grown in the swampy coastal environment." PBS, "Africans in America," Part I: The Terrible Transformation, The Growth of Slavery in North America, Narrative, http://www.pbs.org/wgbh/aia/part1/1narr5.html.

people, themselves traded as commodities across the Atlantic, could direct the process of long-distance species diffusion; it makes the gendered division of labor in West African farming communities and its disruption in the slave trade a centerpiece of analysis; and by offering detailed investigations of rice cultures on three continents and the connections among them, the book provides a capacious Atlantic perspective. Carney's detailed descriptions of West African floodplain agriculture picture rice in new terms as a complex cultural inheritance. These systems rested on a series of ingenious adaptations to specific African environments that, improved over centuries of refinement, revealed rice culture to have been a deeply rooted collective enterprise. The sophistication required to grow rice along a landscape gradient in central Gambia, for example, was not merely a technical achievement. It required the wholesale cultural engagement of men and women who learned how to select seed, maintain irrigation systems, and process harvested grain, among other tasks, and passed on this knowledge to their children. Carney's claim in *Black Rice* that slaves brought a transformative agricultural system to South Carolina is not an original insight. But she has investigated the African dimensions of this story most rigorously and drawn together multiple currents of recent historical inquiry about slavery and American colonization to make a new case for its relevance.

Recent attention to how plantation societies diverged because of the different material demands of producing specific commodities has provided a good reason to articulate a new version of the black rice thesis since the publication of Wood's *Black Majority* in 1974 and Littlefield's *Rice and Slaves* in 1981. Once considered an adjunct region to the dominant Chesapeake, the Carolina Lowcountry (along with the neglected British Caribbean) has emerged in recent scholarship as a distinctive slave society.[5] The unique cultivation, processing, and transportation requirements of making and exporting tobacco, rice, and sugar distinguished British plantation America's three major regions from one another in important ways. As much as the production of these place-defining staples structured these societies internally, the surging commerce they initiated drew these colonial places into connection with the larger Atlantic economy, fueling their growth and territorial expansion and opening them to myriad influences. In light of this new appreciation of regional economic diversity in colonial America and the multiple and diverse "slaveries" that took root around it, the claim that African rice farmers introduced rice culture to the Carolina Lowcountry attempts to tell a new story about a critical American founding.[6] In South Carolina, sometime around 1700, enslaved Africans did more than persevere with their humanity intact. Their impact extended beyond the intermittent shocks

[5] See, for example, Joyce E. Chaplin, *An Anxious Pursuit: Agricultural Innovation and Modernity in the Lower South, 1730–1815* (Chapel Hill, N.C., 1996); Robert Olwell, *Masters, Slaves, and Subjects: The Culture of Power in the South Carolina Low Country, 1740–1790* (Ithaca, N.Y., 1998); Philip D. Morgan, *Slave Counterpoint: Black Culture in the Eighteenth-Century Chesapeake and Lowcountry* (Chapel Hill, N.C., 1998); Andrew Jackson O'Shaughnessy, *An Empire Divided: The American Revolution and the British Caribbean* (Philadelphia, 2000); Trevor Burnard, *Mastery, Tyranny, and Desire: Thomas Thistlewood and His Slaves in the Anglo-Jamaican World* (Chapel Hill, N.C., 2004); Russell R. Menard, *Sweet Negotiations: Sugar, Slavery, and Plantation Agriculture in Early Barbados* (Charlottesville, Va., 2006); S. Max Edelson, *Plantation Enterprise in Colonial South Carolina* (Cambridge, Mass., 2006).

[6] Ira Berlin and Philip D. Morgan, eds., *Cultivation and Culture: Labor and the Shaping of Slave Life in the Americas* (Charlottesville, Va., 1993); John J. McCusker and Russell R. Menard, *The Economy of British America, 1607–1789* (Chapel Hill, N.C., 1985).

of black resistance to white rule. By bringing rice culture across the Atlantic, the black rice thesis has asserted, they set this society in motion along its expansive developmental course. Like the tale of Squanto teaching Pilgrims to plant maize, the image of black slaves instructing their white masters in the intricacies of sowing seeds, culling weeds, and irrigating fields is a multicultural origin story designed to make a pedagogical point. Establishing the Lowcountry rice economy was an achievement for which blacks appear to deserve credit that white colonists as well as white scholars have long denied.

Beginning with its strong assertion of African technological and cultural continuities, Carney's argument incorporates the key points of the revisionist reinterpretation of American slavery by which historians have demonstrated the power of black self-definition despite relentless white repression and exploitation. The black rice thesis describes slaves as conscious bearers of unique agricultural skills rather than as workers reduced to their capacity for physical labor. These skills, according to Carney, armed slaves with a bargaining chip in their negotiations with their masters, enabling them to claim time for independent production under the terms of the region's distinctive task labor system. The ability to grow rice prior to enslavement, it is claimed, provided a material center around which family life could be reassembled, nurtured, and reproduced within slavery. With the important exception that introducing rice to the Americas fostered collaboration with, rather than resistance against, slave-owning colonists, the black rice thesis illustrates the major elements of this revised portrait of culturally independent slave agents.

Carney's bold extension of the black rice thesis capitalized on the spirit of inversion at the heart of this reinterpretation to make a mark on scholarship about plantation societies in the Americas. Following her lead, a new generation of historians will plunge into the documentary record of African source cultures and American destinations to show that African ways and African people must be reckoned with as full participants in a more inclusive story of American accomplishment. They will read against the grain of neglected texts and into the logic of material processes in search of new revelations that other unacknowledged black contributions shaped the foundations of the modern West. The impact of *Black Rice* has had little to do with seeds, water, and soil, the means by which African rice farmers, it is claimed, set a course for economic expansion in early America. Its appeal centers on a vision of slave agency as a capacity to project power outward, beyond a defensive preserve of autonomy, to constitute societies as they began and leave an indelible stamp on them as they developed. Such an amplification of influence for enslaved Africans has sounded a compelling chord for those devoted to extending this revisionist moment in the historiography of American slavery, now four decades old, into the future.

Awarding Africans credit for initiating this important transatlantic trade from colonial British America also changes the tenor of slavery's meaning as a national story. The black rice thesis softens the antagonism of valiant, if often futile, resistance against exploitative rule by white Europeans and their American successors. For contributing their part to the future expansion, power, and prosperity of the United States, Africa and Africans receive due acknowledgment and respect. By the light of the black rice thesis, ingenious colonial slaves can appear alongside pioneering white colonists as protagonists rather than rebels, fellow founders in a narrative of national accomplishment distinguished by long-term economic growth.

In "Agency and Diaspora," Eltis, Morgan, and Richardson work to sever the interpretive links that support the black rice thesis. Basing their analysis on the Trans-Atlantic Slave Trade Database as well as other sources, they lay bare the lack of documentary support for the claim that a large group of slaves with rice-farming knowledge clustered in South Carolina around the time that the rice industry began (ca. 1690–1710). What little evidence exists for this period suggests that rice farmers composed a small minority of the Lowcountry's black population. Eltis, Morgan, and Richardson show that planters did not draw slaves with knowledge of rice cultivation to the Lowcountry by expressing a preference for them; nor did they pay a premium to obtain them. The article synthesizes recent scholarship that demonstrates that African knowledge was not an indispensable source for successful rice-planting techniques in Carolina. Planters had access to a generic range of solutions to the challenges of wetland farming developed by several Old World agricultural traditions, including English ones. Many were eager to experiment with promising crops because of their exotic potential and despite a lack of firsthand experience growing them. These findings cast considerable doubt on Carney's definitive claims that "the origin of rice cultivation is indeed African, and that slaves from West Africa's rice region tutored planters in growing the crop."[7] Those who still suspect that the black rice thesis offers a compelling explanation for the rise of the plantation economy in the Carolina Lowcountry will have to find new ways to demonstrate and document its premises.

The authors of "Agency and Diaspora" launch a critical, quantitative broadside that seems disproportionate to the looser, more associative style of reasoning that Carney offers in *Black Rice*. They deploy unforgiving statistics against a process of inferred cultural transmission that could, because the documentary record omits African perspectives, leave only the faintest impressions in the archives. Instead of sympathy for the quest to credit slaves for their ingenuity, they seem almost churlish in their unwillingness to admit that Africans might have deposited this significant stratum in colonial British America's economic foundation. It would be unfair, however, to assume that the authors critique the black rice thesis because they are unwilling to see Africans as contributors of such foundational knowledge. They take issue not with the possibility of African agency on this scale, but rather with characterizations of the slave trade made to demonstrate it.

Carney's version of the black rice thesis depends on the idea that large numbers of Upper Guinean rice farmers endured the Middle Passage to arrive together in the Carolina Lowcountry, as well as in rice-producing regions of Brazil and Suriname. In these low-lying, waterlogged places, they found themselves very much at home despite the constraints of their enslavement. Forced to grow their own food and surrounded by like-minded agriculturists from home, they seem to have had all they needed in such a familiar landscape to reconstitute a sophisticated African system of rice farming. "Agency and Diaspora," by contrast, depicts the slave trade as a cruel lottery, a centrifugal rather than centripetal force for social formation in the Western

[7] Carney, *Black Rice*, 81.

Hemisphere. Eltis, Morgan, and Richardson critique the black rice thesis in defense of this bleak vision of diasporic contingency by which Africans were scattered into plantation America by capricious market forces.[8] Their article brings the slave trade into more precise temporal and geographic focus to show how ill-suited it was to support the mass transplantation of this coherent, culturally specific agricultural system from West Africa to South Carolina, Brazil, or Suriname.

REPRESENTING THIS PROCESS as a human bridge across the Atlantic large enough for rice farmers to travel across en masse with their agricultural system intact also requires problematic distortions of life and labor in the early Lowcountry. The black rice thesis pictures South Carolina planters as strangers to rice, utterly lacking in the knowledge to produce it, when in fact early colonists had identified the commodity as a desirable article of commerce and were steeped in a European culture of agricultural innovation stocked with techniques used to grow the crop in inland and tidal swamps. Two critical technologies used to irrigate rice in the Lowcountry, freshwater swamp reservoirs and tidal floodgates, have European, not African, origins.

Carney has asserted that slaves who brought rice to America as a group bargained with planters as a group to gain "leverage to negotiate and alter some of the terms of their bondage."[9] Specifically, she claims that they traded the secrets of rice cultivation for the benefits of the Lowcountry's task labor system, which allowed individual slaves time for independent production after they had completed a set amount of daily work. Not a scrap of documentary evidence suggests that this was so, only the logic that those who possessed such lucrative knowledge would attempt to get something of commensurate value in exchange for it. Such speculation about a literal process of negotiation over labor makes it seem as if colonists acknowledged slaves' cultural standing, respected their knowledge, and gave up a measure of their authority to obtain it. Violence, not diplomacy, however, was at the heart of the master-slave relationship in turn-of-the-century Carolina. This was an era in which whites inflicted unspeakable tortures and subjected those they enslaved to extreme material privation. As one new colonist observed bluntly in 1711, those among the first generation of rice planters who could "get a few slaves and can beat them well to make them work hard" prospered in South Carolina. We should not confuse this brutal and entrepreneurial society with the more unconstrained place imagined in *Black Rice*, in which newly arrived slaves put new systems of production into operation on plantations and bargained collectively for better working conditions in exchange for their expertise.[10]

Despite varied attempts to demonstrate that Africans transplanted rice culture to the Carolina Lowcountry, the black rice thesis now appears like a horizon that will continue to recede no matter how avidly scholars try to reach it. To hold fast to such a specific point of causation from such a sparse documentary record is to court dis-

[8] Eltis, Morgan, and Richardson, "Agency and Diaspora in Atlantic History," 1339–1346.
[9] Carney, *Black Rice*, 81.
[10] St. Julien R. Childs, "A Letter Written in 1711 by Mary Stafford to her Kinswoman in England," *South Carolina Historical Magazine* 81, no. 1 (1980): 4; Edelson, *Plantation Enterprise in Colonial South Carolina*, chap. 2.

appointment. The glare of this critical scrutiny has exposed mischaracterizations of the slave trade's demographic flows, misunderstandings of planters' economic culture, and misreadings of the meaning of "negotiation" in master-slave relations. The project of assigning explicit origins itself focuses so narrowly on establishing a chain of causation that it forces readers to accept or deny its premises and claims in toto.

To say that the case has not been made is not, however, to dismiss all of the insights that have been gathered in building it. The black rice thesis encapsulates the revisionist sensibility of Wood's *Black Majority*, forcing us to look at early Carolina as an imperial frontier characterized by social and racial flux. It was the means by which Littlefield illustrated the dynamic centrality of African ethnic diversity to British America. It led Carney to profile the agricultural backgrounds of African slaves with new range and detail. After *Black Rice*, it is impossible to see enslaved field workers as the brute laborers of racist myth. Other questions, whose answers build on more carefully documented material contexts, can help generate a more compelling scenario about the origins of plantation agriculture in the Carolina Lowcountry.

How, for instance, did rice become South Carolina's staple commodity? During the colony's first decade, its most ambitious planters experimented far more enthusiastically with ginger, silk, wine, indigo, and cotton than with rice, while most rank-and-file settlers contented themselves with growing maize, harvesting lumber, and raising cattle. As economic historian R. C. Nash has shown, rice was a relatively cheap substitute for European grains in times of dearth, far more mundane than exotics such as those that founded plantation fortunes in the West Indies and the Chesapeake. Those slaves who knew how to cultivate a crop that was so sensitive to drought might have avoided rather than pursued it, given the limited time and resources they had to produce their own food. Familiarity alone did not privilege rice as a likely candidate to become one of the Atlantic world's premier staple commodities.[11]

At a time when black and white Carolinians alike focused more on getting enough to eat than on producing transatlantic commodities, the early role of rice as food suggests how it first entered into plantation agriculture. Maize, called "Indian corn" by the English, was the longstanding dietary staple in plantation America. Even as it provided essential nourishment, this "coarse and meane fare" at first offended white as well as black palates.[12] When wheat plants failed to flourish, English colonists mixed maize with rice flour in Carolina and with cassava flour in Barbados to whiten and refine a creole bread. When their masters served them yet another bowl of maize mush (called "loblolly" after the sailor's gruel), Africans in seventeenth-century Barbados protested, "O! O! no more Lob-lob." Where they had access to well-watered wastelands at the edges of plantation fields, slaves throughout the greater Caribbean grew rice for themselves. In contrast to less palatable rations of maize, sorghum, and yams, rice's flexibility as a starch appealed to slaves in Jamaica,

[11] Ibid., 60–63; R. C. Nash, "South Carolina and the Atlantic Economy in the Late Seventeenth and Eighteenth Centuries," *Economic History Review* 45, no. 4 (1992): 677–702; Wood, *Black Majority*, 61.

[12] Quotation from John Stewart, "Letters from John Stewart to William Dunlop," *South Carolina Historical Magazine* 32, no. 1 (1931): 22; Edelson, *Plantation Enterprise in Colonial South Carolina*, 69–71; on maize aversion, see also Trudy Eden, *The Early American Table: Food and Society in the New World* (DeKalb, Ill., 2008).

Brazil, Suriname, and Martinique, among other places, regardless of whether most of them had grown or eaten it in Africa. In Barbados, where such land and water resources were scarce, Africans apparently did not grow rice, although there were probably many who knew how to do so. Long after rich Charlestown planters could afford to import all the wheat they could eat from Philadelphia, New York, and South Carolina's rapidly settling Backcountry, they still breakfasted on thin rice-and-maize wafers that tasted vaguely of almonds. As early white and black colonists scratched out subsistence and sought to cobble together good meals from the materials at hand in tropical and subtropical America, they were drawn to rice.[13]

Perhaps an enslaved woman prepared the first bread made from such mixed flours to serve a European master, introducing him to the promise of risiculture. Perhaps a planter saw the viability of rice affirmed when he looked down from the arable highlands to notice a single slave tending thriving plants in the wetland patch in which he grew his own food. Perhaps a few enterprising Europeans experimented with the crop, after which slaves took some seed to add to the repertoire of grains and vegetables they grew to fill their cooking pots. Each of these scenarios of an inadvertent, incremental path for rice's rise to commodity status is plausible. None assumes what we cannot and need not prove: that the first rice grown in South Carolina was anything more than one of many attempts to see what might thrive there, or that large numbers of Africans who knew how to grow it came to the colony at a particular moment in time.

There are only three contemporary references before 1700 to rice-growing in South Carolina, none of which suggests a unilateral African role in the commodity's introduction. By 1674, according to an English runaway in Spanish St. Augustine, some rice that had been "grown on the soil" of South Carolina was shipped to Barbados. Agricultural improver John Stewart's letters about his own rice experiments documented that by 1690, colonists had directed slaves to cultivate the crop on multiple sites in at least two different parts of the province: the banks of Goose Creek and the upper Cooper River. Some among the slaves whom Stewart directed no doubt contributed to his success by putting their farming experience, with rice or other crops, into practice on these experimental fields. Years later, slaves planting rice continued to press holes with their heels and cover seed with a sweep of the foot in the West African fashion. In 1699, at the close of a decade in which colonists conducted these successful crop trials, customs collector Edward Randolph reported that rice had moved from provisions grounds and experimental plots to the heart of plantation agriculture. Hundreds of slaves that year planted, cultivated, and processed some 330 tons of rice to ship to England and the West Indies, launching it as a long-distance commodity. Every grain exported into the Atlantic economy was pounded in African-style pine mortars and winnowed in African-style coiled grass baskets before being packed into barrels for export.[14]

Planters in South Carolina never grew rice without African slaves to perform the labor. Slaves never grew rice in the colony outside the plantation system that planters

[13] Quotation from Richard Ligon, *A True & Exact History of the Island of Barbados* . . . (London, 1657), 31; Edelson, *Plantation Enterprise in Colonial South Carolina*, 67–69, 71, 90.
[14] Edelson, *Plantation Enterprise in Colonial South Carolina*, chap. 2; Morgan, *Slave Counterpoint*, 151.

controlled. Planters never relinquished control of this process of commodity innovation, even as they reconfigured and amalgamated European and African traditions to exploit a unique subtropical environment and produce a crop that could be sold for profit abroad. What is compelling about this moment of agro-economic genesis is how open it was to cross-cultural improvisation on both sides of the Lowcountry's emerging racial divide.[15] Once European colonists had found their staple commodity and mastered the techniques of rice production, they would never again be so interested in what American Indians and African slaves sowed and reaped, with the possible exception of their therapeutic uses for wild plants.

Many of the enslaved who had planted and processed those first barrels of rice exported in 1699 survived to endure this plantation economy's harshest transition. It was from slaves' "wounds," as one sympathetic Anglican minister put it, that planters were able to "extract their estates." As the rice economy expanded in the 1710s and 1720s, Peter A. Coclanis has demonstrated, planters forced slaves to work more days every year hacking through swampy forests and more hours every day weeding rice plants.[16] As the commodity's demands encroached on slaves' time, masters insisted that workers continue to provide their own food and clothing. Slaves endured this new material impoverishment in rags, hunger, and despair, often running away from their deprivation and occasionally burning down the pounding barns in retaliation. By mid-century, two pervasive new customs emerged to stabilize this wrenching shift to intensive commodity production. The regular provision of plantation rations eased slaves' desperate quests for food, and the task system gave the most productive workers time away from plantation labor to produce food on their own. With these ameliorative compromises between procuring subsistence and procuring commodities in place, the rice economy expanded into the Lowcountry's northern and southern coastal frontiers, where subsequent generations of slaves labored on isolated tidal rice plantations. The material consequences of the successful establishment of rice as a transatlantic commodity were extremely negative for enslaved workers. Some Africans in seventeenth-century Carolina had probably grown the crop for their own physical and cultural sustenance before planters coerced their collaboration in the first commercial rice fields. Once planters appropriated these African agricultural contributions, they inverted the meaning of this work for the enslaved: rice was now a crop that consumed them.

To SURVIVE THIS HARROWING economic context, African farmers made use of the time and space for independent production that the task system allowed, cultivating crops that had originated across the vast coastlines and archipelagos of the Atlantic world,

[15] On this point, see T. H. Breen, "Creative Adaptations: Peoples and Cultures," in Jack P. Greene and J. R. Pole, eds., *Colonial British America: Essays in the New History of the Early Modern Era* (Baltimore, 1984), 220–221.

[16] See S. Max Edelson, "The Nature of Slavery: Environmental Disorder and Slave Agency in Colonial South Carolina," in Robert Olwell and Alan Tully, eds., *Cultures and Identities in Colonial British America* (Baltimore, 2005), 26–31; Brian Hunt (1727), quoted in Frank J. Klingberg, *An Appraisal of the Negro in Colonial South Carolina* (Washington, D.C., 1941), 52; Peter A. Coclanis, *The Shadow of a Dream: Economic Life and Death in the South Carolina Low Country, 1670–1720* (New York, 1989), chap. 3.

and by doing so, making them their own. Making sense of how enslaved farmers exploited this agricultural autonomy after rice's emergence as a commodity can invoke a variety of West African agricultural backgrounds beyond the Senegambian mangrove swamps. More precise environmental studies of how they adapted African, Native American, and European crops and methods under the constraints imposed by part-time farming on marginal lands could reveal new portraits of slave cultures centered on the garden patches of Virginia and Barbados, the "little plantations" of South Carolina and Georgia, and the upland polinks of Jamaica. Given the scarcity of early colonial records and accounts, the potential for unearthing documents that can help register slaves' ongoing engagement with agricultural innovation in the Atlantic world, both as bearers of African knowledge and as creative synthesizers of what they encountered in the Americas, is promising.

A 1784 deposition to the British Board of Trade, for example, describes the thriving commerce that had connected colonial slaves on the mainland to the voracious provisions markets of the West Indies. This testimony, collected to help determine whether Caribbean colonies should be allowed to import food directly from the United States, revealed the extent to which enslaved farmers had become enmeshed in this system of multilateral exchange as independent agents. In the decade before the outbreak of the American Revolution, the captains of New England fishing vessels had made a practice of navigating south to the Lowcountry during the off-season. After assembling "Assorted Cargoes" of dried fish, sugar, molasses, lathed wooden pieces called "Turnery ware," and other "articles of coarse Household Furniture," they sailed "up the Rivers and Creeks in the Carolina's and Georgia, and the Master opened a kind of retail Shop on Board for Bartering with the lower planters and Negroes for Corn, Rice, Lumber and other produce of the Country." Although the "planters had often cause to complain of the Masters of these small Vessels encouraging their Slaves to Rob their Barns," the rising demand for all of these Carolina products in the resource-dependent Caribbean enlarged the trade and created a channel of unregulated access to the Atlantic economy. Removed from their masters' oversight, enslaved farmers traded rice and other crops that they grew on their own time for these simple goods and participated directly in the Atlantic world's producer and consumer revolutions. Such consumption enhanced, but did not displace, adapted African material culture.[17]

The moment when the first rice plant sprouted in a cleared Lowcountry swamp, its signature panicle drooping under the weight of filling grains, inaugurated a long history of African American agricultural enterprise that falls beyond the interest in singular origins of the black rice thesis. When an enslaved man sold some tobacco and rice to naturalist John Lawson in 1700, another important "first" was recorded.[18] How slaves made use of interiors just beyond the pale of English plantation settlement, how they exploited marshlands, swamps, and forests to collect plants and

[17] Minutes, March 30, 1784, West India and American Intercourse, Records of the Great Britain Board of Trade, Box 5, Volume 1: March 1, 1784–May 31, 1784, Manuscript Division, Library of Congress, Washington, D.C., 122–123. On the persistence of African-style colonoware ceramics excavated from Lowcountry slave sites, see Leland Ferguson, "Struggling with Pots in Colonial South Carolina," in Randall H. McGuire and Robert Paynter, eds., *The Archaeology of Inequality* (Cambridge, Mass., 1991), 28–39.

[18] John Lawson, *A New Voyage to Carolina*, ed. Hugh Talmage Lefler (Chapel Hill, N.C., 1984), 16.

hunt game, and how they occupied the spaces in between the boundaries of plantation fields to make an autonomous living for themselves are topics ripe for new investigation. Moving beyond "black rice" means setting aside specific one-to-one correspondences between source and destination regions to describe the character of New World cultures. It means following the tangled borrowings and adaptations by which Europeans, Africans, and American Indians remade material life in the wake of colonization. Far from diminishing the idea that Africans and their descendants were calculative, innovative, and responsive participants in early agriculture, this line of inquiry opens up new opportunities to document a long history of meaningful black agency in plantation America.

S. Max Edelson is Associate Professor of History at the University of Virginia. He is the author of *Plantation Enterprise in Colonial South Carolina* (Harvard University Press, 2006). He is currently working on a history of cartography and empire in eighteenth-century British America and developing a new digital tool for map analysis, the Cartography of American Colonization Database (CACD).

AHR Exchange
Africa and Africans in the African Diaspora: The Uses of Relational Databases

GWENDOLYN MIDLO HALL

> African American Studies, better labeled Negro American Studies, are for the most part superficial and incomplete, referring to black people without knowing them. The typical researcher cannot disengage from the tendency to present them as fragmented and superficial, without seeing Africans as individuals coming from a society with rules and values of its own . . . as someone torn from a particular culture that could not be erased by the simple act of crossing the Atlantic. From human beings full of culture and knowledge, they have been transformed into mere merchandise: tons of ebony.
>
> Nicolás Ngou-Mve, "Historia de la población negra en México"

IN THEIR 2007 *AHR* ARTICLE "Agency and Diaspora in Atlantic History," David Eltis, Philip Morgan, and David Richardson make two major claims: (1) that the article presents a new, superior model for interpreting the formation of culture in the Americas, and (2) that it challenges the belief that Africans played an important role in the introduction and technology of rice cultivation and processing in the Americas. For their conclusions about rice, they rely mainly on calculations from the Trans-Atlantic Slave Trade Database, Version 2 (referred to hereafter as TSTD2) as a tool

I owe a deep debt to the National Endowment for the Humanities and the taxpayers of our country, who funded the expansion of my Louisiana Slave Database as part of National Endowment for the Humanities Collaborative Research Contracts numbers RO-22619-1901 and 1993, "Africans in Spanish and Early American Louisiana," with Patrick Manning as co-investigator. I also received major financial support from the Guggenheim Foundation, as well as generous contributions from the French Ministry of Culture, the Program for Cultural Cooperation between Spain's Ministry of Culture and United States Universities, and the Louisiana Endowment for the Humanities. Steven Mintz has given generously of his enthusiasm, time, and support for nearly a decade now, including with this article. Paul E. Lovejoy, Director of the Harriet Tubman Institute for Research on the Global Migrations of African Peoples, York University, Toronto, Canada, and his graduate students and our colleagues in this network have played a very special role. I am grateful to Maureen Hewitt, Editor-in-Chief at LSU Press, for her foresight and enthusiastic work in preparing the CD-ROM version of the database for publication (*Databases for the Study of Afro-Louisiana History and Genealogy, 1699–1860: Computerized Information from Original Manuscript Sources*, 2000). Other colleagues have given their time and attention to help and encourage me after Katrina and to make this article much better than it was: O. Vernon Burton, Rina Cáceres, Yvonne Captain-Hidalgo, Judith A. Carney, Douglas B. Chambers, Matt D. Childs, Howard Dodson, Joseph C. Dorsey, Christopher Dunn, David Hackett Fischer, Michael A. Gomez, Rebecca L. Hall, Joseph E. Harris, Susan Heywood, Joseph E. Inikori, Aondofe Joseph-Ernest Iyo, Eileen M. Julien, Jane I. Landers, Juan Manuel de la Serna, Joseph C. Miller, Nell Irvin Painter, Ibrahima Seck, Ned Sublette, Ibrahim K. Sundiata, and John K. Thornton.

FIGURE 1: Mandinka women displaying bundles of African and Asian rice, 1987. Photo by Judith A. Carney.

to study the distribution of enslaved Africans from rice-growing regions in Africa to regions in the Americas that exported rice to Europe.[1]

The authors claim to have made a great new discovery about culture formation in the Americas. They then revive and reprise an unrelated discussion from a 1991 forum in the *William and Mary Quarterly*, criticizing a book by David Hackett Fischer titled *Albion's Seed*. Fischer's book is about British colonizers of the United States. Scholars have never claimed that British cultures were erased by the transatlantic crossing. Its methodology has not served as a model for African diaspora studies.[2]

The article distorts the work of the many scholars it criticizes. Our varied methodologies are reduced to a monolithic advocacy of static "seed" cultures brought over from the Old World and continued as "enclave cultures" in the Americas. "Rather than frame the issue as solely one of transfers and conduits," the authors write, "we should also think of transformations and overlapping circuits. Rather than posit that slaves and planters always acted knowingly, we should entertain the possibility that they often responded to unseen market forces. Rather than assume that migrants remained conservatively attached to traditional ways, we might also view them as experimenters and improvisers" (1332).

The scholars criticized in "Agency and Diaspora" share only one interpretation:

[1] David Eltis, Philip Morgan, and David Richardson, "Agency and Diaspora in Atlantic History: Reassessing the African Contribution to Rice Cultivation in the Americas," *American Historical Review* 112, no. 5 (December 2007): 1329–1358.

[2] "Albion's Seed: Four British Folkways in America—A Symposium," *William and Mary Quarterly*, 3rd ser., 48, no. 2 (1991): 224–308.

that the knowledge and culture of Africans from particular coasts and ethnicities were not erased by the transatlantic crossing. This historian, for example, has written that the process of culture formation (creolization) responded to various, changing factors in the Americas, including the patterns of introduction of Africans from particular regions and ethnicities; gender proportions and patterns of mating and parenting; how rapidly migrants began to procreate and the extent of biological merger among diverse peoples; the demographic and military strength of the Native American population; whether the geography facilitated runaway slave (maroon) communities; the economic, strategic, and military priorities of the colonizing powers; the extent of manumission of former slaves and their demographic strength and social status; military and police uses of slaves and free people of color; the labor demands of the major exports as the economy evolved; and policies of social control reflected in various European political and religious traditions and institutions and how effectively they were enforced. Concepts and definitions of creolization in the Americas vary among the scholars whose work is criticized in "Agency and Diaspora." The most recent version is Linda Heywood and John Thornton's conclusion that the Charter Generation of Africans who molded the Creole cultures of British and Dutch America before 1660 were largely Europeanized, Catholic West Central Africans.[3]

The rest of the article minimizes the significance of African technological transfer to the Americas in the planting and processing of rice. Although some anecdotal qualitative sources are used, the argument relies overwhelmingly on calculations made from TSTD2. David Eltis, Stephen Behrendt, David Richardson, and Manolo Florentino deserve great credit for their tireless work on this database, including its impressive technological advances over the first version, TSTD1. Thousands of new Brazilian and Portuguese voyages have been added, correcting the Anglo-focused distortion of TSTD1. The database has been made more user-friendly and is accessible to the public free of charge as an open-source work. It enables users to make calculations, corrections, and additions. It can answer many important questions about the transatlantic slave trade. But when it comes to certain kinds of questions, its limitations must be taken into account. It cannot answer the questions about rice posed in "Agency and Diaspora."[4]

Historical databases are wonderful, innovative tools. They can integrate huge amounts of detailed, concrete data into broad patterns allowing for analysis over time and place. The vast quantity of information they can contain and analyze is a great advantage, especially in making broad, comparative studies. Databases can answer questions that cannot be answered using more traditional methodologies, can partially or tentatively answer others, and can help answer still others, combining quantitative calculations with the findings of other disciplines, including archaeology, anthropology, linguistics, and geography, as well as traditional history. But there are some questions that are simply beyond their capabilities. It all depends on the

[3] Gwendolyn Midlo Hall, *Slavery and African Ethnicities in the Americas: Restoring the Links* (Chapel Hill, N.C., 2005), 166–167; Linda M. Heywood and John K. Thornton, *Central Africans, Atlantic Creoles, and the Foundation of the Americas, 1585–1660* (Cambridge, 2007). See my review of Heywood and Thornton's book in *Journal of Interdisciplinary History* 39, no. 3 (Winter 2009): 463–464.

[4] TSTD2 calculates 5,099,816 enslaved Africans landed by Portuguese and Brazilian voyages and 2,733,323 by British voyages.

questions that a given database is designed to answer. Databases can be more rigid than qualitative sources. In using them, scholars must keep in mind that just because something is not included in a historical document or a database, that does not mean that it did not happen. There is important information that has never been documented; there are documents that have not yet been found and studied. TSTD1 and TSTD2 were designed to contain only documented and studied voyages of slave trade ships that crossed the Atlantic. "Agency and Diaspora" hardly considers the redistribution process that took place when these new Africans were first sold in the Americas, then reloaded onto other ships and subsequently moved by water and/or land to other places before reaching their varied final destinations. In this process, they were sometimes clustered by their region of origin and/or ethnicity when buyers were able to purchase the new Africans they preferred.[5]

There are problems with rigidity as well as the omission of important data in TSTD2. It was created from research into original manuscript documents carried out by many historians during the past forty years or more. Each record covers a specific transatlantic slave trade voyage. The fields in a database contain information about the individual records that it includes. They are designed to answer the questions the creators of the database want to ask, not necessarily to provide the information contained in the original documents. Unless a database has been designed to be flexible, once the fields have been defined and a substantial amount of data has been entered, adding new fields can be laborious, time-consuming, and expensive. TSTD2 remains locked into the same questions that scholars have asked since the publication of Phillip D. Curtin's *The Atlantic Slave Trade: A Census* in 1969, but with a notable limitation: there is no field for the entry of data on African ethnicities. Except for a few entirely quantitative questions, such as gender, age category, and deaths when this information was recorded in the documents and then noted and published by the historians who studied them, TSTD2 does not focus on information about the enslaved Africans on the ships. The fields were not changed between TSTD1 and TSTD2.

Obviously, historians record only what they think is important, and we cannot tell what those who did the original research chose not to record. In some cases, information that indeed was recorded by the scholar who conducted the initial research will not be entered into the database because no field was created for it. Such omissions may have included information about African ethnicities that Eltis, Morgan, and Richardson dismiss as inaccurate and perhaps therefore unimportant (1349). Was information about the ethnicities of Africans on transatlantic slave trade voyages documented? Yes. To what extent? Without consulting the original documents, we cannot know. If there were no fields in TSTD2 in which this information and the contents of these original documents could be recorded, this data is not available to us. Thus a crucial advantage of using original manuscript documents is lost. Perhaps there is very little information in transatlantic slave trade documents about the Af-

---

[5] Joseph E. Inikori, "The Known, the Unknown, the Knowable and the Unknowable: Evidence and the Evaluation of Evidence in the Measurement of the Trans-Atlantic Slave Trade" (unpublished paper presented at the Conference on the Trans-Atlantic Slave Trade Database, Williamsburg, Virginia, September 1998); Hall, *Slavery and African Ethnicities in the Americas*, 68–79; Douglas B. Chambers, "Slave Trade Merchants of Spanish New Orleans, 1763–1803: Clarifying the Colonial Slave Trade to Louisiana in Atlantic Perspective," *Atlantic Studies* 5, no. 3 (2008): 335–346.

ricans aboard the ships; or perhaps, as Nicolás Ngou-Mve observed, those who conducted the research using the original documents did not consider this information important enough to record. Thus when the editors of TSTD2 did not do the initial research themselves, the information in the database is twice removed from the original sources. Ngou-Mve calls on historians to look at all the documents again, even if other historians have already studied them. This writer's experience with transatlantic slave trade voyage documents is limited to Louisiana, but it supports Mve's conclusion.[6]

Historical databases and new media need to go beyond purely quantifiable questions. As Daniel J. Cohen suggests, "Focusing on the full potential of the medium and being sure that digital history is not simply an echo of quantitative processes or algorithms to the abundant digital record in the service of source discovery and analysis is extremely important . . . and equally important are the networking and collaborative possibilities of the medium—that is, focusing on human rather than machine activities."[7] The search and visualization capabilities of advancing technology facilitate these advances. Visualization will allow us to consult the original documents whose contents have been filtered out by rigid, purely quantifiable databases and their questions.

During the past two decades, there has been a seismic change in perception about documents relating to Africans and their descendants throughout the Americas. The shift has been from a belief that original manuscript sources did not exist or were extremely rare to a recognition of the truly extraordinary abundance of documents in archives, courthouses, ports, museums, and private collections housed throughout the Americas. This writer's database about Louisiana slaves was initiated in 1984. Focusing on people who were enslaved, it was created almost entirely from original manuscript documents. It contains almost all of the information about each description of a slave entered into the database from original documents, including unquantifiable data.[8]

THE LIMITATIONS OF TSTD2 call into question Eltis, Morgan, and Richardson's critique of Judith A. Carney's well-known work about the transfer of rice cultivation from Africa to the Americas. She carried out a truly impressive range of varied and exhaustive research and used it judiciously and well. Carney is a multilingual, multidisciplinary geographer who was inspired to study original historical documents by the pioneering work of historians Daniel C. Littlefield and Peter H. Wood. Her grasp of geography and agricultural technology enhances her insights into the meanings

---

[6] Nicolás Ngou-Mve, "Historia de la población negra en México: Necesidad de un enfoque triangular," in María Elisa Velázquez Gutiérrez and Ethel Correa Duró, eds., *Poblaciones y culturas de origen africano en México* (México, 2005), 39–64, 51; Gwendolyn Midlo Hall, *Africans in Colonial Louisiana: The Development of Afro-Creole Culture in the Eighteenth Century* (Baton Rouge, La., 1992), 56–95.

[7] Remarks by Daniel J. Cohen in "Interchange: The Promise of Digital History," *Journal of American History* 95, no. 2 (September 2008): 463.

[8] The Louisiana Slave Database can be found at http://www.ibiblio.org/laslave. The search engine can be used for many fields, and the entire database can be downloaded free of charge in several formats. For a discussion of its origin and possibilities for other databases to be created from various types of original manuscript documents housed throughout the Americas, see http://afropop.org/multi/interview/ID/76/Gwendolyn+Midlo+Hall-2005.

of such primary sources. From the earliest manuscript sources and publications of Portuguese observers, beginning with the mid-fifteenth century, she thoroughly documents the well-established, widespread, complex cultivation of rice in varied environments along the coasts of Upper Guinea and up its rivers. She makes use of a variety of approaches, including documentary sources on both sides of the Atlantic throughout the five centuries of the Atlantic slave trade and in-depth field work in Africa and the Americas. In contrast, Eltis, Morgan, and Richardson base their conclusions on the flimsy evidence of what they found documented for twenty voyages of the Royal African Company visiting Gambia and Sierra Leone between 1779 and 1788. The sample of voyages they used is very small and limited in time because there was no field to record such information in TSTD2; thus they had to consult original documents. Nevertheless, they state: "From this evidence, women did not mill rice on the Middle Passage" (1347).

It is possible that women milled rice on slave trade trips but that those activities were not recorded in the documents; or that documents survive but have not yet been found; or that the original researchers did not record this information; or that they did record it, but it was not included in TSTD2. Carney has evidence of women pounding seed rice on a slave trade ship in 1796, pointing out that it is only one such clearly documented case. She speculates about how rice seeds could have been introduced into the Americas without drawing firm conclusions. She discusses evidence for multiple and varied directional introduction of rice between Africa and the Americas over the centuries. Carney could not possibly have claimed, as Eltis, Morgan, and Richardson state, that "a single enslaved African woman carrying a few grains of rice in her hair can become all that is necessary to sustain the thesis" (1357). One of the major points she makes in *Black Rice* is that the Columbian exchange involved the transfer not only of seeds, but of systems of cultivation as well, including processing techniques from places of domestication to elsewhere in the Atlantic world. That is why she uses the word "systems." Eltis, Morgan, and Richardson take the word "systems" out of context (1333) and then dismiss her entire work with unsupportable criticisms.[9]

"Agency and Diaspora" is correct in stating that "Part of the strategy for keeping valuable property alive on the transatlantic crossing was to ensure that slaves received food to which they were accustomed" (1347). The authors say that more millet than rice was placed on the twelve slave trade ships they studied, which left Upper Guinea between 1779 and 1788. But rice, not millet, was an important food crop in the Americas. The authors suggest that Africans as well as Europeans might have improvised their eating patterns in the Americas, minimizing enslaved Africans' preferences for rice (1354). Did the need to enable enslaved Africans to follow their traditional eating patterns in order to keep them alive disappear after the Atlantic crossing?

Eltis, Morgan, and Richardson criticize Carney for overstating the role of women in rice production in the Americas. They point to the relatively high male ratios on voyages arriving from Upper Guinea. But these calculations tell us nothing about sex ratios among slaves from rice-producing ethnicities, or about masters' preferences

---

[9] Judith A. Carney, *Black Rice: The African Origins of Rice Cultivation in the Americas* (Cambridge, Mass., 2001), xii, 66–67, 144–145, 154–157, 164–167.

TABLE 1.
Gender Balance of Upper Guinean Ethnicities in Louisiana (age 15–39), 1719–1820

	Male	*Female*	*Total*
Bamana	n = 205 87.2%	n = 30 12.8%	235
Mandingo	n = 353 67.9%	n = 167 32.1%	520
Nar/Moor	n = 49 70.0%	n = 21 30.0%	70
Poulard/Fulbe	n = 80 69.6%	n = 35 30.4%	115
Wolof/Senegal	n = 225 61.5%	n = 141 38.5%	366
TOTAL	n = 912 69.8%	n = 394 30.2%	1,306

Calculated from Gwendolyn Midlo Hall, Louisiana Slave Database, 1719–1820.

for women of these ethnicities. They write that "the number and percentage of Africans with rice-growing experience must have been far below the total number of slaves leaving Upper Guinea" (1348). This is no doubt true, but therefore their studies of gross gender ratios among slaves leaving the entire Upper Guinea coast are not clarifying with respect to rice producers. Throughout most of the eighteenth and early nineteenth centuries, enslaved warriors were sent down the Senegal and Gambia rivers in large numbers, mainly Bamana (Bambara) during the 1720s, before the designation "Bambara" took on wider, vague, generic meanings. Many captured warriors were shipped to the Americas from Senegambia and Sierra Leone, tilting gender ratios toward males. Male ratios were highest among the ethnicities most often captured in warfare, as well as among cattle herders. Gender ratios among Africans from Upper Guinea varied in accordance with ethnicity. Some captured warriors came from rice-producing ethnicities, for example Bamana (Bambara) and Mandingo. The male ratios on slave trade ships that the authors present (1350–1351, Tables 5–7) tell us nothing about whether masters cultivating rice in Carolina, Georgia, and northeast Brazil preferred women from rice-producing ethnicities.

A stronger case can be made about preferences for women who knew how to produce rice by focusing on mean prices by gender among rice-cultivating ethnicities. In Louisiana during the 1770s, the mean price for women from two rice-producing ethnicities inventoried on estates, Mandingo and Wolof, was higher than that for men. Among the Bamama (Bambara), another rice-producing ethnicity, the mean price was slightly lower for women than for men during the 1770s and higher for women than for men between 1810 and 1820. The mean price for Wolof women was higher than the price for men throughout the Spanish period (1770–1803). The rice-producing skills of these women might at least partially account for this atypical price pattern.

Eltis, Morgan, and Richardson claim that calculations from TSTD2 prove that Africans from Upper Guinea could not have introduced rice or systems for its cultivation and processing to the Americas, nor did masters who planted rice prefer them or choose them (1335–1338, Tables 1 and 2). They argue that few slaves from Upper Guinea arrived in rice-exporting regions when this crop began to be cultivated. For later periods, they dismiss the significant impact on transatlantic slave trade patterns of the relatively high proportion of enslaved Africans brought from rice-producing regions in Africa to rice-exporting regions in the Americas, pointing to factors other than the preferences of slave buyers (1335, 1342, 1345). This is not

TABLE 2.
Mean Price by Gender of Rice-Producing Ethnicities Inventoried on Estates in Louisiana, 1770–1820

Decades	Ethnicity	Number of Males	Mean	Standard Deviation	Number of Females	Mean	Standard Deviation
1770–1779	Bamana	7	282.66	26.904	3	266.67	61.101
	Mandingo	18	297.78	87.753	5	312.00	45.497
	Wolof	9	235.56	107.251	5	288.00	56.619
1770–1803	Wolof	96	321.87	236.861	188	331.23	260.229
1810–1820	Bamana	45	420.22	261.008	7	511.43	316.882

Calculated from Hall, Louisiana Slave Database, 1719–1820. Explanations of price data, price conversion formulas, and studies of mean prices by gender and ethnicity by decade for Africans inventoried on Louisiana estates can be found in Hall, *Slavery and African Ethnicities in the Americas*, Appendix A, 173–179.

news. This writer's book, *Slavery and African Ethnicities in the Americas: Restoring the Links*, cited several times in "Agency and Diaspora" in other contexts, has an entire chapter devoted to various evolving patterns in the entire Atlantic slave trade, including market forces. Preferences among buyers for slaves of particular ethnicities are treated as only one factor.[10]

It is unclear what the calculations from TSTD2 cited by Eltis, Morgan, and Richardson can prove about whether there was an African impact on rice production and processing in the Americas. How many people did it take to introduce and develop rice in varying environments? Was there only one introduction of rice, after which the masters knew everything they needed to know about its cultivation despite the varied and changing environments and ecosystems used in its production over time? Did there have to be a majority, or a large minority, of enslaved Africans arriving from Upper Guinea at the time rice began to be produced, or a higher percentage of Upper Guineans among all slaves arriving in both the Caribbean and the Atlantic Coast colonial United States, even though rice was rarely exported from the Caribbean, and the colonial East Coast United States was a marginal region for the transatlantic slave trade (1337, 1338, Table 2)? Documents from Louisiana show that the Company of the Indies asked only for several slaves who could teach them how to cultivate rice.[11]

Carney perhaps understates, and Eltis, Morgan, and Richardson do not mention, the possible role of Madagascar in the introduction of rice to America. Immigrants from Ceylon began to populate Madagascar in about 800 A.D., bringing with them Asian sativa rice and techniques for its cultivation and processing. TSTD2 contains records for ten voyages arriving in Barbados from Madagascar between 1664 and 1683, and seventeen voyages arriving in the East Coast colonial United States from Madagascar between 1686 and 1721. There were also slave trade voyages from Madagascar by smugglers, privateers, and pirates of several nationalities that are not re-

[10] Hall, *Slavery and African Ethnicities in the Americas*, 55–79.

[11] "Instructions pour le sieur Herpin, commandant du vaisseau *l'Aurore*, destiné pour la traite des nègres à la coste de Guynée," July 4, 1718, Section Marine, Archives Nationales, Paris, series B42B, folios 201–204.

corded in the database. Aside from the voyages from Upper Guinea entered into TSTD2, any one or more of these voyages or one or more of the 749 voyages whose provenance is listed in TSTD2 as "Africa port unspecified" could have brought seed rice and enough Africans who knew how to cultivate and process it and who could have taught their masters these skills. Conclusions about the role that Africans played or did not play in the introduction of rice into the Americas cannot be drawn from TSTD2, whose calculations are based on African regions, not African ethnicities. Carney's careful, exhaustive, multilingual, multidisciplinary field work and studies of documents in several languages over the wide sweep of time and place in the Atlantic world are much more convincing. In addition, Edda L. Fields-Black's book *Deep Roots*, which uses mainly sociolinguistic evidence along with traditional historical sources, establishes the time depth and variety of rice cultivation involving inheritance, innovation, and borrowing among several ethnicities living along the Rice Coast of Upper Guinea and their transfer to the Americas over time.[12]

Eltis, Morgan, and Richardson conflate rice production with the export of rice to Europe. This narrow definition enhances their argument that masters fully controlled the decisions relating to the production, processing, and marketing of rice. Production by maroon (runaway slave) communities is dismissed as unimportant. The domestic market for rice is dismissed as subsistence production, or a "system that generated exports rather than the export itself" (1343). Food crops were introduced and exchanged throughout the Atlantic world. Slaves worked their own garden plots, and they produced and sold all types of foods, including rice, corn, beans, fruits, vegetables, eggs, poultry, pork, ham, and smoked beef. In South Carolina, Jamaica, and Louisiana, slaves were the major suppliers of food to towns and cities. Europeans and Africans—especially the first generation—and Native Americans preferred to eat the cereals they were accustomed to. In Louisiana, Europeans preferred wheat, Native Americans preferred corn, and Africans preferred rice. But those preferences did not always determine the types of cereals they consumed. Everyone ate whatever they could get during the frequent wars, when imported food was cut off and food was hoarded by speculators, and also during hurricanes and floods, when rice survived better than any other crop. Even for the Carolina plantations that produced rice for export to Europe, the authors of "Agency and Diaspora" exaggerate the power and control that masters had over their slaves. Europeans were not all-powerful, certainly not in matters of economy and culture. They, too, were strangers in a strange, dangerous, and hostile world. Control was not always firmly in their hands, especially during the early, most crucial stages of the formation of the economy and culture. William Dusinberre's study of life on the rice plantations of Carolina and Georgia demonstrates that masters and their families were often absentees from that environment of deadly fevers. Masters could not get white overseers to work in the rice swamps. During the nineteenth century, black slave overseers were the supervisors of the slave laborers. But the most trusted slave overseers were often the leaders of slave conspiracies and revolts.[13]

---

[12] Edda L. Fields-Black, *Deep Roots: Rice Farmers in West Africa and the African Diaspora* (Bloomington, Ind., 2008).

[13] Hall, *Africans in Colonial Louisiana*, 21, 24, 123–124, 343–375; William Dusinberre, *Them Dark Days: Slavery in the American Rice Swamps* (New York, 1996); Robert L. Paquette, "The Drivers Shall

FIGURE 2: "Planting the Rice," from T. Addison Richards, "The Rice Lands of the South," *Harper's New Monthly Magazine*, November 1859, 726.

"Agency and Diaspora" minimizes the interest of buyers in the skills of new Africans: "Buyers of slaves in the Americas wanted a cheap supply of undifferentiated labor for field work, and transatlantic suppliers sought locations in Africa where they could obtain large numbers of slaves quickly and at reasonable cost" (1339). The Louisiana Slave Database records an impressive range of expertise among African-born slaves. Thousands of the Africans arriving in Louisiana came from regions that were well known for certain skills. Although we can query the Louisiana Slave Database about the skills listed for African-born slaves, it cannot tell us that they brought such expertise with them, even though we know that particular skills were

Lead Them: Image and Reality in Slave Resistance," in Robert I. Paquette and Louis A. Ferleger, eds., *Slavery, Secession, and Southern History* (Charlottesville, Va., 2000), 31–58.

widely practiced in their African homelands. But it is highly suggestive of skills transferred by enslaved Africans arriving in the Americas.

Timing gives us even stronger evidence for the transfer of African technology and skills. Having complained for years that they could not find anyone who knew how to produce and process indigo, the Louisiana colonial authorities asked French colonial authorities to send someone who possessed such knowledge. Shortly after Africans began arriving from Senegambia, Louisiana started to produce indigo, beginning in 1721 on an experimental basis, and soon as the major export crop. In French Louisiana, the captains of the first two Atlantic slave trade ships that arrived from the African coast in 1719 had both been officially instructed "to try to purchase several blacks who know how to cultivate rice and three or four barrels of rice for seeding which they were to give to the directors of the Company of the Indies upon their arrival in Louisiana." The first ship, *l'Aurore*, stopped at Cap Lahou on August 28, 1718, where these instructions could have been carried out, and then went on to Whydah to buy slaves. Rice production in Louisiana expanded rapidly thereafter, as almost all transatlantic slave trade ships began coming from Senegambia. During the French administration (1699–1769), rice was shipped from Louisiana to the French Caribbean and to Spanish Pensacola. It was widely cultivated in swampy soils, which did not require irrigation, while indigo, corn, and other crops were cultivated on the same farms and estates on higher lands near the rivers. During the Spanish administration (1770–1803), rice was shipped to the French Caribbean and to Havana as Cuba's sugar monoculture expanded. Louisiana began to satisfy Cuba's needs for foods of all kinds, including rice. Did whites teach clueless Africans all these skills? It seems obvious that the diverse peoples of Louisiana—Africans, Creoles, Cajuns, Canadians, French, Germans, Spanish, Canary Islanders, and Native Americans—taught each other.[14]

Eltis, Morgan, and Richardson seriously overstate what we can know from calculations derived from TSTD2 about the distribution of Africans in the Americas. We have seen that newly arrived Africans were often sold and then transferred to final destinations outside the colony where they first landed. Documents created and housed in the Americas show that at each stage of their redistribution, buyers could, and often did, select Africans from particular coasts and/or ethnicities. In Cuba, Manuel Barcia and Matt D. Childs have found clustering of African ethnicities on plantations, among cabildos de naciones, and among slave rebels. In St. Domingue/ Haiti, Gabriel Debien and David Geggus found clustering of African ethnicities on individual estates. In Spanish Louisiana, Upper Guineans were clustered dispro-

[14] The practitioners of such skills include cowboys, breeders of cattle and horses, horse trainers and groomers, leatherworkers, tanners, saddlers, shoemakers, butchers, cooks, bakers, confectioners, pastry chefs, chocolate makers, rum makers, cigar makers/tobacco stemmers, goldsmiths, silversmiths, potters, indigo makers, tailors, hat makers, charcoal makers, basket makers, oven makers, barbers, wigmakers, spinners, coach/cart drivers, plantation managers, overseers, foremen, masons, painters, plasterers, chimney builders, stone engravers, millers, blacksmiths, tool makers, tool sharpeners, metalworkers, makers of fireworks, wheelwrights, cart makers, woodsmen, hunters, fishermen, lumbermen, carriers and squarers of timber, sawmill workers, carpenters, cabinetmakers, locksmiths, brick makers, sailors, navigators, sounders, shipbuilders, sail makers, oar makers, caulkers, coopers, innkeepers, street vendors, butlers, domestics, personal servants, seamstresses, laundresses, hospital workers, nurses, midwives, doctors, dentists, surgeons, musicians, and linguists/interpreters of languages. Calculated from Skill fields in the Louisiana Slave Database.

FIGURE 3: Acadian girl with mortar and pestle used for hulling rice. From the *Rowley Signal*, January 20, 1904.

portionately in St. Charles Parish, which produced rice, and in St. Landry Parish, where cattle were raised. St. Landry Parish contained a far higher proportion of Upper Guineans among African-born slaves than any other parish: 67.9 percent (73 percent male) among slaves with identified birthplaces. In West Africa, breeding and herding were not practiced east of Upper Guinea because of the tsetse fly. St. Landry Parish remains the traditional place of Afro-Creole cowboys and zydeco music. Transatlantic slave trade voyages alone cannot tell us nearly as much as Eltis, Morgan, and Richardson claim about the gender proportions among African ethnicities or the distribution of Africans at their final destinations in the Americas.

HISTORICAL DATABASES ARE EXTRAORDINARY new tools, and more scholars should learn to use them and to create them. They should be used widely, but wisely and judiciously, with an understanding of their limitations. But depending on how they are designed and the questions they are programmed to answer, they can be rigid and inflexible, locking in outmoded research and questions and not allowing for new ones. Databases are not a higher form of knowledge that can somehow trump other kinds of research. Scholarship is not a zero-sum game. When scholars overstate the questions that a database can answer and criticize others' work through the use of irrelevant calculations, it seriously undermines our difficult but essential task of informing our colleagues about the unique value of historical databases in producing broad, comparative studies. We need to appreciate what others have done and encourage diverse scholars to use a variety of methodologies in doing the important work they do best. Despite the vast complexities of these questions, the long list of senior scholars and the new generation criticized in "Agency and Diaspora" are constantly making new discoveries, the value and impact of which will be enhanced by rapidly advancing technology.

There has been much progress in historical methodology since World War II. We have developed social history: history from the bottom up. Concepts of the positive values of race mixture and creolization have been introduced through the work of José Vasconcelos of Mexico, Gilberto Freyre of Brazil, and Edward (Kamau) Brathwaite of Barbados.[15] Our greatest strength is our growing acceptance of diversity. We live in a rapidly shrinking world where ethnic and religious conflicts are stirred up and exploited by ambitious political, military, and religious bureaucracies and economic elites. It is not so much that people are intolerant of "the other" as that social systems and their ideologues provoke and exploit these conflicts. History is applied art, science, and literature that can teach mutual appreciation and respect among peoples. The authors of "Agency and Diaspora" have taken a great leap backward in this task. As TSTD2 is revised and improved, its editors need to make it more flexible and avoid drawing invalid conclusions from evidence that is indirect, incomplete, and flawed, or our work will be discredited by overreaching. The calcu-

---

[15] José Vasconcelos, *The Cosmic Race: A Bilingual Edition*, trans. and annotated by Didier T. Jaén (Baltimore, 1997; Spanish ed., 1920); Gilberto Freyre, *The Masters and the Slaves (Casa-Grande and Senzala): A Study in the Development of Brazilian Civilization*, trans. Samuel Putnam (New York, 1946; Portuguese ed., 1935); Edward Kamau Brathwaite, *The Development of Creole Society in Jamaica, 1770–1820* (Oxford, 1971).

FIGURE 4: Women pounding rice in Mandinga, Mexico, 1988. Photo by Judith A. Carney.

lations from TSTD2 that Eltis, Morgan, and Richardson cite in their article might seem impressive, but these historians do not look at what they do not want to see, and they cannot look at what they do not have. Their conclusions far outrun their evidence.

Gwendolyn Midlo Hall is Professor Emerita of Latin American and Caribbean History at Rutgers University and an International Advisory Board Member of the Harriet Tubman Resource Centre on the African Diaspora, York University, Toronto, Canada. Her awards include the Distinguished Service Award, Organization of American Historians (2004); Knight of the Order of Arts and Letters elected by the National Assembly of France (1997); and John Simon Guggenheim Fellow (1996). Her book and database publications include *Slavery and African Ethnicities in the Americas: Restoring the Links* (University of North Carolina Press, 2005); *Africans in Colonial Louisiana: The Development of Afro-Creole Culture in the Eighteenth Century* (Louisiana State University Press, 1992), which won nine book prizes; *Social Control in Slave Plantation Societies: A Comparison of St. Domingue and Cuba* (Johns Hopkins University Press, 1971); and the Louisiana Slave Database and the Louisiana Free Database, 1719–1820, http://www.ibiblio.org/laslave. Her works in progress are her memoirs, "Daughter of New Orleans: Crossing the Color Line, 1929–2009"; "Diversity, Race Mixture, Slavery, and Freedom: Louisiana, 1699–1820"; and the Western Hemisphere Slave Database. She has lectured internationally in English, French, and Spanish.

AHR Exchange
From "Black Rice" to "Brown":
Rethinking the History of Risiculture in the
Seventeenth- and Eighteenth-Century Atlantic

WALTER HAWTHORNE

IN THE DECEMBER 2007 ISSUE of this journal and in the first major piece of scholarship to make use of the recently launched second version of the Trans-Atlantic Slave Trade Database (TSTD2), David Eltis, Philip Morgan, and David Richardson challenge what has come to be known as the "black rice thesis."[1] Developed over several decades by Peter H. Wood, Daniel C. Littlefield, and Judith A. Carney, the thesis posits that skilled rice farmers from Upper Guinea introduced technology important for the establishment and expansion of lowland South Carolina and Georgia's eighteenth-century rice-based plantation system.[2] Carney extends the argument by applying it elsewhere, including Maranhão, Brazil.[3] Underlying Eltis, Morgan, and Richardson's challenge are two assertions. First, they state that most of the Africans shipped to South Carolina, Georgia, and Amazonia (by which they mean the eighteenth-century captaincies of Maranhão and Pará) during "crucial" periods in the development of plantation rice agriculture were not Upper Guineans but were Af-

Thanks to Martin Klein, James Sweet, Emily Osborn, Peter Alegi, Patrick Griffin, Edda Fields-Black, Chris Duvall, Beatriz Mamigonian, Marina Padrão Temudo, Benjamin Lawrance, Lynn Schler, David Bailey, and two anonymous reviewers for comments or responses to inquiries.

[1] David Eltis, Philip Morgan, and David Richardson, "Agency and Diaspora in Atlantic History: Reassessing the African Contribution to Rice Cultivation in the Americas," *American Historical Review* 12, no. 5 (December 2007): 1329–1358. For another critique, see S. Max Edelson, *Plantation Enterprise in Colonial South Carolina* (Cambridge, Mass., 2006), 53–91. The TSTD2 is at http://www.slavevoya ges.com. The term "black rice" is often applied to *O. glabberima*, a dark-grain rice indigenous to West Africa. Carney uses the term to refer metaphorically to rice of any strain (especially white-grain *O. sativa* varieties) that was produced by Africans using technologies developed in Africa. Judith A. Carney, *Black Rice: The African Origins of Rice Cultivation in the Americas* (Cambridge, Mass., 2001). I discuss the "black rice debate" in an interview conducted by Peter Limb and Peter Alegi for the Africa Past & Present Podcast, Episode 12, August 30, 2008, http://afripod.aodl.org/?m=200808.

[2] Peter H. Wood, *Black Majority: Negroes in Colonial South Carolina from 1670 through the Stono Rebellion* (New York, 1974); Daniel C. Littlefield, *Rice and Slaves: Ethnicity and the Slave Trade in Colonial South Carolina* (Baton Rouge, La., 1981); Carney, *Black Rice*. More recently, see Edda L. Fields-Black, *Deep Roots: Rice Farmers in West Africa and the African Diaspora* (Bloomington, Ind., 2008). The definition of "Upper Guinea" has changed over time. Here I use Eltis, Morgan, and Richardson's delineation—Senegal to Liberia, including the Senegambia, Windward Coast, and Sierra Leone slave-trading regions.

[3] Judith A. Carney, " 'With Grains in Her Hair': Rice in Colonial Brazil," *Slavery and Abolition* 25, no. 1 (2004): 1–27; Carney, "Rice and Memory in the Age of Enslavement: Atlantic Passages to Suriname," *Slavery and Abolition* 26, no. 3 (December 2005): 325–347.

FIGURE 1: Inundated rice fields in Maranhão, Brazil. Photo by Walter Hawthorne, 2005.

ricans with no previous knowledge of rice cultivation.[4] Second, they write that, more than the "basic farming knowledge" that African slaves possessed, planter power and a broad Atlantic economy and culture shaped how rice-based plantation systems emerged. A "subaltern role" in the making of New World agricultural systems "should be highlighted," they instruct, "where it is attested," but Africans were not, they conclude, "the primary players in creating and maintaining rice regimes."[5]

Though Eltis, Morgan, and Richardson demonstrate that some of Carney's ancillary arguments should be rethought, I am not convinced that we should throw the black rice out with its husks—discard, that is, the "black rice thesis" altogether. Embracing the trio's approach, I fear, risks writing Africans and their descendants in the Americas once again out of history. If planters "called the shots," they did not necessarily know more than their slaves about particular crops. If planters "experimented keenly," their experiments were not necessarily better than the ones that African farmers had been conducting for hundreds of years. If we do no more than "highlight" the agricultural initiatives of African slaves where white people "attested" to them, black people will necessarily occupy positions in the backgrounds of our studies. Following Eltis, Morgan, and Richardson's thoughtful essay, we should recognize that over the course of the eighteenth century, on all of the Atlantic's coasts but at a different pace in different places, rice became metaphorically "brown," as light- and dark-skinned people responded to market forces, devised new methods for planting and processing the grain, and created new dishes that featured

[4] Eltis, Morgan, and Richardson, "Agency and Diaspora in Atlantic History," 1334.
[5] Ibid., 1335, 1357.

it.[6] But before the eighteenth century, rice, to the extent that it was known in the Atlantic world, was "black." In this period, Upper Guineans—and not Europeans—were the Atlantic's master rice producers. Evidence that Eltis, Morgan, and Richardson call on to refute the claim that Upper Guineans introduced rice technologies to parts of the Americas is not always as revealing as they claim, and at times it is contradicted by alternative sources from Maranhão.

ELTIS, MORGAN, AND RICHARDSON'S CRITIQUE of Carney's work is founded on their different understandings of what constitutes sound evidence for historical reconstruction. Following an Africanist tradition of seeking non-archival approaches to construct knowledge about people who did not leave written records, Carney adopts what she calls a "geographical perspective focused on culture, technology, and environment." Her assumption is that the Columbian exchange involved more than the transfer of seeds. "People and plants together migrated," and it was people who brought with them knowledge of how to plant seeds, cultivate crops, and process, store, and cook what they harvested. Since "the only people in South Carolina" possessing knowledge of how to grow rice in wetlands were West Africans, one must look to them, she argues, "for adapting the crop to challenging New World conditions."[7] Although she can cite no contemporary observer who attested that West African technologies were responsible for the establishment and expansion of rice agriculture in South Carolina, Georgia, or Maranhão, she reads the landscapes of rice-producing regions on both sides of the Atlantic, finding parallels in techniques of production, processing, and cooking that she argues are evidence in support of her thesis.

Eltis, Morgan, and Richardson are not impressed with Carney's geographical perspective. Taking an archival approach to historical evidence, they see script penned on paper as the stuff of source material. For them, it is all the better if that paper holds data that can be quantified. And quantifiable data is what they have—records of the voyages of more than 35,000 slave ships contained in the TSTD2.

As its predecessor was, the TSTD2 promises to be an invaluable tool for the crafting of innovative studies about the early modern Atlantic. But databases have limitations, and the limitations of the TSTD2 make it a dubious source for a critique of the "black rice thesis." First, its data are most thorough for periods when bureaucracies capable of tracking shipments from particular African ports and to particular American ports were well established. But bureaucracies were not well established in early colonial North America. It is odd, indeed, that the first publication to focus attention on the TSTD2 dwells on a period (pre-1700) in South Carolina

[6] Ibid., 1358. Here the trio makes this point clearly: "Atlantic history was the result of the creolization of peoples from four continents." I agree, but I argue for more attention to time and place. Rice slowly became an Atlantic crop in the eighteenth century, with people from many places reshaping how it was grown, processed, and cooked, but it was not so much an Atlantic crop in the seventeenth century.

[7] On Africanist approaches to evidence, see Jan Vansina, *Living with Africa* (Madison, Wis., 1994), 40–59; Steven Feierman, "African Histories and the Dissolution of World History," in Robert H. Bates, V. Y. Mudimbe, and Jean O'Barr, eds., *Africa and the Disciplines: The Contributions of Research in Africa to the Social Sciences and Humanities* (Chicago, 1993), 182; Joseph C. Miller, "History and Africa/Africa and History," *American Historical Review* 104, no. 1 (February 1999): 1–32. Quotations from Carney, *Black Rice*, 6–8, 81–82.

and Georgia's history for which the dataset records no slave arrivals.[8] A second limitation of the TSTD2 is that it contains a range of information about slave shipments from Africa and only from Africa. Yet most of the slaves who arrived in the Lowcountry and Chesapeake when experiments with rice agriculture were first being conducted were transfers from other American colonies. Many were "saltwater" slaves—Africans—who touched briefly at Barbados.[9] These transfers are not recorded in the dataset. At best, then, the TSTD2 provides only a fuzzy snapshot of the makeup of North America's African population during the "crucial formative period" in the history of North American rice farming.

Finally, the TSTD2 does not reveal where slaves forced onto ships at African ports hailed from. That is, while it allows users to determine the number (among other things) of slaves embarked at particular African ports and disembarked at particular American ports, it does not enable them to determine the birthplaces of the Africans aboard any given ship. Eltis, Morgan, and Richardson rightly note that Upper Guinea "was never uniformly committed to rice production," and that the nature of rice cultivation there and across the ocean was not fixed but was in great flux in the eighteenth century.[10] But without data on Upper Guinea slave origins, they rely on speculation as the basis for one of their central arguments—their claim that "the number and percentage of Africans with rice-growing experience must have been far below the total number of slaves leaving Upper Guinea."[11]

WERE THERE NECESSARILY "FEW" RICE PRODUCERS on "many of the vessels from Upper Guinea"?[12] Although research into the British and French trades is needed to fully answer this question, written sources indicate that Eltis, Morgan, and Richardson's speculation is wildly off the mark for the eighteenth-century Portuguese trade. The first source is a registry from the slave ship *S. José*, which departed Cacheu in 1756.[13] The total number of captives was ninety-seven, of which fifty-two had been seized in a swampy "lowland" coastal strip not far from the ports of Bissau and Cacheu. This strip was occupied by small communities composed of people from a range of ethnic groups. Those listed on the registry were Balanta, Bijago, Floup, Brame, and Papel. The remaining forty-five captives hailed from farther inland or north, and most were identified as Mandinka.[14] Lands that Mandinka occupied were higher in

---

[8] From a search of TSTD2 (accessed September 22, 2009). The database lists thirty ships arriving in Virginia. Of the twenty-two identified by region of embarkation, eight were from Senegambia (Upper Guinea) and eight from Bight of Biafra. Two were from West Central Africa, two from the Gold Coast, one from Southeast Africa, and one from Benin.

[9] John Coombs, "Building the 'Machine': An Episode in the Development of Plantation Slavery in Colonial Virginia, 1630–1730" (Ph.D. diss., William and Mary, 2006), 103–104. Eltis, Morgan, and Richardson assume that since many slaves arriving in South Carolina were transfers from Barbados, the slave population in the two places must have looked the same. Yet for many of the ships the TSTD2 lists as disembarking at Barbados in the period before 1700, the African port of embarkation is unknown.

[10] Eltis, Morgan, and Richardson, "Agency and Diaspora in Atlantic History," 1345–1346.

[11] Ibid., 1348.

[12] Ibid., 1349.

[13] Biblioteca Nacional de Lisboa [hereafter BNL], Collecção Pombalina, codice 628. Of the hundreds of ship registries from Upper Guinea departures that I have examined for the eighteenth century, this is the only one that lists the ethnic origins of the captives held on board.

[14] For a history of the region, see Walter Hawthorne, *Planting Rice and Harvesting Slaves: Trans-*

elevation than those of the coastal strip, and thus are often called "uplands." A second source is a database (the Maranhão Inventories Slave Database, or MISD) derived from inventories of slave populations in Maranhão that were recorded between 1767 and 1832.[15] It dovetails with the ship's records. Isolating the period 1767 to 1800, it shows that Upper Guineans made up the largest single group of slaves in Maranhão (followed by *crioulos* or Brazilian-born slaves), and that almost two-thirds of Upper Guinean slaves had been born in the lowland coastal strip. They were from the same ethnic groups as the slaves listed on the registry from the *S. José*, and there were also some Biafada. The other third of Maranhão's Upper Guinea–born slaves were overwhelmingly Mandinka.[16]

From the late seventeenth century, all of the people from the Upper Guinean coastal strip who were represented on the registry from the *S. José* and in the MISD had some commitment to rice agriculture on uplands or lowlands. Some of the most proficient producers of rice in lowland mangrove swamp areas were Floup and Brame, whose agricultural sectors approached paddy rice monocultures. Moreover, from about the mid-eighteenth century, the commitment of Papel and Balanta to mangrove swamp cultivation increased considerably, as most coastal dwellers turned to the crop because it could be grown in places that slave raiders could not easily reach, and it could be marketed in growing urban centers and to ship captains.[17] Although, as Eltis, Morgan, and Richardson note, not all Mandinka were rice producers in the seventeenth and eighteenth centuries, many did produce rice, particularly those who lived only sixty to one hundred miles east and north of Cacheu and Bissau around the towns of Farim and Geba, and tens of miles to the north along the Casamance River. Contemporary observations indicate that it was these Mandinka who accounted for the bulk of Mandinka forced onto ships such as the *S. José* that left Cacheu and Bissau from the mid-eighteenth century.[18] To be sure, as Eltis, Morgan, and Richardson write, rice producers were not "easy prey" for slavers.[19] In Upper Guinea's coastal strip, few communities were eradicated as a result of slaving. Overall, rice-producing communities defended themselves well. However, individuals from coastal communities were taken captive and sold abroad. They became slaves as a result of tensions within communities that resulted in witch-

---

formations along the Guinea-Bissau Coast, 1400–1900 (Portsmouth, N.H., 2003); and Hawthorne, "Nourishing a Stateless Society during the Slave Trade: The Rise of Balanta Paddy-Rice Production in Guinea-Bissau," *Journal of African History* 42, no. 1 (2001): 1–24.

[15] I assembled the MISD at the Arquivo Judiciário of the Tribunal de Justiça do Estado do Maranhão (TJEM). It contains information about the names, gender, region of origin, age, marital status, and health of most of the approximately 8,500 slaves listed in it. Inventories at the TJEM have not been catalogued. There are 342 slaves listed in the database for the period 1767 to 1800.

[16] The percentages of people from coastal and interior (mainly Mandinka) groups remained almost identical from 1801 to 1832.

[17] Hawthorne, *Planting Rice and Harvesting Slaves*, 35–39, 155–157.

[18] On rice around Farim and Geba and near the Casamance, see Arquivo Histórico Ultramarino [hereafter AHU], Guiné, cx. 11, docs. 57 and 63; cx. 12, doc. 3-A; Arquivo Nacional da Torre do Tombo [hereafter ANTT], Junta do Comércio, mç. 63, cx. 203; Olga F. Linares, "From Tidal Swamp to Inland Valley: On the Social Organization of Wet Rice Cultivation among the Diola of Senegal," *Africa* 51, no. 2 (1981): 577–578. On the capture of Mandinka near Cacheu and Bissau, see AHU, Guiné, cx. 9, doc. 55, cx. 11, docs. 20 and 63; cx. 12, doc. 13. On violence in the region, see Boubacar Barry, *Senegambia and the Atlantic Slave Trade* (New York, 1998), 92.

[19] Eltis, Morgan, and Richardson, "Agency and Diaspora in Atlantic History," 1346.

craft accusations and kidnappings and tensions among communities that gave rise to small-scale raids.[20]

There were, then, many rice producers on Portuguese vessels bound for Maranhão and Pará. Since the Portuguese and British concentrated their efforts at different Upper Guinea ports, data for the Portuguese trade does not necessarily reflect the British trade bound for South Carolina.[21] Nonetheless, data from the Portuguese trade raises an important question: Is Eltis, Morgan, and Richardson's archival evidence more accurate than the evidence that Carney derives from a "geographical perspective"?

Unlike tobacco, sugar, and cotton, rice was a crop that African farmers had cultivated long before European seafarers reached the Upper Guinea coast in the fifteenth century. It was also a crop that African farmers adapted to a variety of ecological conditions by drawing on indigenous knowledge. On upland (dry-land or rainfed) areas, farmers could produce rice with relatively little labor and by using crude tools. When planted on lowlands (wetlands), however, and particularly on tidal floodplains, rice demanded an incredible amount of technological sophistication and tremendous inputs of labor. In tidal zones in West Africa, rice farmers had to clear mangroves, build and maintain dikes with specialized tools, leach salt from soils, carve paddies out of the land, and manage freshwater levels. Planting, harvesting, processing, and storing rice required considerable effort, too, much more, perhaps, than any other staple of eighteenth-century Atlantic Rim diets.[22]

Recognizing the differences between the demands of upland and lowland rice agriculture, Carney develops in *Black Rice* an argument that is more nuanced than Eltis, Morgan, and Richardson acknowledge. She shows (and the trio does not dispute) that the sophistication of rice production in South Carolina and Georgia increased as the number and ratio of Upper Guinean slaves in the region increased.[23] From close readings of descriptions of agricultural landscapes, she argues that upland rice was "emphasized" from the late 1600s through the early 1700s, when Upper Guineans were present but Angolans constituted a majority of slaves. It was "from the 1750s," she writes, that "the even more productive but labor-demanding tidal floodplain system . . . would dominate Carolina and Georgia rice plantations until the Civil War."[24] And, indeed, the calculations that Eltis, Morgan, and Richardson

[20] Hawthorne, *Planting Rice and Harvesting Slaves*, 91–110; Robert Martin Baum, *Shrines of the Slave Trade: Diola Religion and Society in Precolonial Senegambia* (New York, 1999), 108–129. I explore this data in greater depth in my forthcoming book.

[21] In Upper Guinea in the eighteenth century, the Portuguese were based at Bissau and Cacheu, though they obtained some slaves from farther south, transshipping them on small vessels. The British and French dominated other ports, obtaining a considerable but unknown number of slaves from Bissau, Cacheu, and the neighboring Bijagos Islands by breaking Portuguese monopolies at will. Hawthorne, *Planting Rice and Harvesting Slaves*, 67–82; Jean Mettas, "La traite portugaise en Haute Guinée: Problèmes et méthodes," *Journal of African History* 16, no. 3 (1975): 343–363; Walter Rodney, *A History of the Upper Guinea Coast, 1545–1800* (New York, 1970), 122–151.

[22] Hawthorne, *Planting Rice and Harvesting Slaves*, 159–166; Baum, *Shrines of the Slave Trade*, 28–31; Linares, "From Tidal Swamp to Inland Valley," 557–591.

[23] Nowhere do Eltis, Morgan, and Richardson acknowledge the technical sophistication required in paddy rice production. They focus only on the possibility that "some" Africans "introduced Old World customs of sowing, threshing, and winnowing" to the New. They ignore similarities in diking and water and saline management practices on both sides of the Atlantic. "Agency and Diaspora in Atlantic History," 1335.

[24] Carney, *Black Rice*, 82–85.

make with the TSTD2 confirm Carney's contention that for a period after 1750, Upper Guineans arrived in South Carolina and Georgia in greater numbers than slaves from other regions of Africa.[25]

WITH RESPECT TO THE LOWCOUNTRY, the "black rice thesis" should not, then, be discarded. A paucity of archival evidence about early colonial South Carolina and Georgia should not be enough to trump knowledge gained through a "geographical perspective." It appears possible that in the formative years of the upland rice complex, and likely in the formative years of the lowland complex, Upper Guineans were, as Carney points out, the only people in South Carolina who knew how to produce rice on a large scale. Nowhere has that point been disproved.[26]

Is the same true of Maranhão? Did Africans introduce the technology required for the establishment and expansion of agriculture there? In their examination of this region, Eltis, Morgan, and Richardson make two flawed arguments in an attempt to downplay the significance of rice in the eighteenth century. First, they state, "Rice was not . . . the major crop of Amazonia." It "always lagged behind cotton and cacao."[27] On this point they are correct, but in fact, what Eltis, Morgan, and Richardson have dubbed "Amazonia" comprised two captaincies— Maranhão and Pará. If we disaggregate exports from Maranhão (where rice was a significant crop) from exports from Pará (where it was not), we must draw a very different conclusion. Rice was the largest single export from Maranhão for most years between 1774 and 1811. Cacao exports from Maranhão lagged far behind those from Pará. Cotton was an important export from Maranhão, but it did not surpass rice in pounds exported. Some years the valuation of rice exports was higher than the valuation of cotton exports. Moreover, rice was consumed in Maranhão, meaning that export figures do not give a full picture of the crop's centrality to slaves' working lives.[28] Contemporary

[25] Ibid., 89; Eltis, Morgan, and Richardson, "Agency and Diaspora in Atlantic History," 1336.

[26] Edelson argues that planters brought knowledge of channeling water from England to South Carolina. However, he does not show that the same farmers who mastered water-control technologies in England moved to South Carolina. Moreover, I am not convinced that the technologies applied in England were all that similar to those necessary for paddy rice agriculture anywhere—particularly on tidal flats. This is not to say that planters did not learn rice technologies over time. Clearly, Edelson shows, planters wrote about the crop. They were innovators. Edelson, *Plantation Enterprise in Colonial South Carolina*, 53–91; Eltis, Morgan, and Richardson, "Agency and Diaspora in Atlantic History," 1353–1354.

[27] Eltis, Morgan, and Richardson, "Agency and Diaspora in Atlantic History," 1342.

[28] Maranhão exported more than twice as much rice as Pará from 1776 to 1780, just under half as much from 1781 to 1785, and about two-thirds more from 1786 to 1790. When the period 1796–1811 is looked at as a whole, the value of cotton exports from Maranhão was higher than the value of rice exports. However, cotton was not more valuable every year. For example, foodstuffs (most of which was probably rice) accounted for 65.1 percent of the value of all exports in 1802, and in 1811 they were 65 percent. The trio errs when reading Portuguese sources for rice export data. Eltis, Morgan, and Richardson say that rice could not have accounted for more than 10 percent of the value of Maranhense exports from 1796 to 1811. From the sources they cite, the figure should be 20 percent. "Agency and Diaspora in Atlantic History," 1342. They cite José Jobson de A. Arruda, *O Brasil no comércio colonial* (São Paulo, 1980), Table 28, which is of *imports into* and not *exports from* Maranhão. My calculations are from Arruda, *O Brasil*, 245–247; Raymundo Jozé de Souza Gayozo, *Compendio historico-politico dos principios da lavoura do Maranhão* (Paris, 1818), 182; Manuel Barata, *A antiga producção e exportação do Pará: Estudo historico-economico* (Belem, 1915), 3; M. Nunes Dias, *Fomento e mercantilismo: A Companhia Geral do Grão Pará e Maranhão (1775–1778)* (Belém, 1970), 430; C. M. dos Santos, "Cultura, indústria e comércio de arroz no Brasil colonial," *Lavoura Arrozeira* 32, no. 315 (1979): 6–20; Dauril Alden, "Late Colonial Brazil, 1750–1808," in Leslie Bethell, ed., *Colonial Latin America* (Cambridge,

observations leave little doubt that slaves in Maranhão spent considerable time growing rice in the second half of the eighteenth century.[29]

Second, Eltis, Morgan, and Richardson attempt to downplay the importance of rice in Maranhão by demonstrating that exports from South Carolina were far greater after 1785 (the period when Maranhense exports reached a high point and then plateaued and South Carolina exports recovered from a decline during the Revolutionary War).[30] This claim is correct, but it should be put into historical perspective. Before the mid-eighteenth century, Maranhão was an underdeveloped outpost of the Portuguese empire. Its exports were few, and the colonial population was small.[31] After mid-century, policymakers fostered economic expansion in Amazonia by encouraging white immigration and African slave imports (principally from Upper Guinea). Rice was first exported from Maranhão in 1767, and its production grew steadily over the next fifteen years, leveling off at about 9.1 million pounds per year after 1785.[32] By that time, South Carolina had been exporting rice for ninety years. Too, South Carolina had a considerably larger population than Maranhão by 1785. In 1787, the governor of Maranhão figured the region's colonial population at 61,699, of which an estimated 18,894 were white and 35,963 were black.[33] The population of South Carolina in 1790 was more than four times larger, standing at 249,073, of which 140,178 were white and 108,895 black.[34] Given this, it is not all that impressive that South Carolina's rice exports were four times higher than Maranhão's from 1785 to 1789, the period for which Eltis, Morgan, and Richardson provide data. Lower export totals from Maranhão are not evidence that rice was an insignificant crop in the captaincy.

With respect to Maranhão, Eltis, Morgan, and Richardson do not, then, provide

---

Mass., 1984), 601–660; and César Augusto Marques, *Dicionário histórico-geográfico da Província do Maranhão* (Rio de Janeiro, 1970), 207; supplemented with data from AHU and BNL. On rice consumption, see AHU, Maranhão, cx. 45, docs. 4458 and 1772; Marques, *Dicionário histórico-geográfico da Província do Maranhão*, 93.

[29] Among many others, see AHU, Maranhão, cx. 43, doc. 4264; AHU, Maranhão, cx. 51, doc. 4938. Also Marques, *Dicionário histórico-geográfico da Província do Maranhão*, 93.

[30] Eltis, Morgan, and Richardson do not provide export figures for South Carolina during the American Revolution. They argue that Lowcountry exports between 1770 and 1774 were seven times those of Amazonia after 1785. "Agency and Diaspora in Atlantic History," 1340–1341.

[31] In 1720, white Maranhense numbered 1,378, and there were few Africans among them. Jerônimo de Viveiros, *História do comércio do Maranhão, 1612–1895* (São Luís, 1954), 63.

[32] Calculated from Gayozo, *Compendio historico-politico dos principios da lavoura do Maranhão*, 182; Barata, *A antiga producção e exportação do Pará*, 3; Dias, *Fomento e mercantilismo*, 430; Santos, "Cultura, indústria e comércio de arroz no Brasil colonial," 6–20; Alden, "Late Colonial Brazil," 601–660; and confirmed by sources from AHU. Portuguese consumers did not like the dark-grain indigenous rice that was native to Maranhão, so until a new strain introduced from South Carolina was substituted for it in farmers' fields in the mid-1770s, Maranhão's rice export sector did not thrive. AHU, Maranhão, cx. 46, doc. 4528. This does not necessarily mean, as Eltis, Morgan, and Richardson state, that the introduction of a new rice strain and "not the arrival of slaves from Upper Guinea" was responsible for an export-based risiculture. Following Carney's logic, someone had to have knowledge of rice production. "Agency and Diaspora in Atlantic History," 1342.

[33] There were Indians counted in the census, too. Figures presented here do not count Piauí, a small captaincy that Maranhão controlled. Maranhão and Piauí had a combined population of 98,743. ANTT, Ministério do Reino, mç. 601, cx. 704. In 1777, when Maranhão's economic expansion was beginning, its total population stood at 47,410, which was far below South Carolina's. Dauril Alden, "The Population of Brazil in the Late Eighteenth Century: A Preliminary Survey," *Hispanic American Historical Review* 43, no. 2 (1963): 191.

[34] Walter B. Edgar, *South Carolina: A History* (Columbia, S.C., 1998), 327.

FIGURE 2: Man in Maranhão, Brazil, gathering unmilled rice that has dried in the sun. Photo by Walter Hawthorne, 2005.

adequate evidence to undermine the foundation of the "black rice thesis." However, they do show that parts of the thesis are problematic. First, they make convincing arguments against Carney's claims that rice-producing slaves in the Americas used skills developed in Africa as a bargaining chip in negotiations with planters over work. Simply put, there is no evidence that Upper Guineans agreed to apply specialized knowledge to rice production in exchange for better labor conditions.[35] Second, with data from sales and an impressive array of contemporary observations, Eltis, Morgan, and Richardson show that Carney, like many before her, is incorrect in stating that South Carolina planters were willing to pay a premium for Upper Guinean women because they possessed particular knowledge of rice.[36] Data from the MISD supports the same conclusion for Maranhão, where the values of slave women between the ages of 18 and 37 were, on average, less than those of men of the same age.[37]

Finally, Eltis, Morgan, and Richardson present compelling evidence that planter preference does not account for the proportionately large presence of Upper Guineans among slave imports into South Carolina and Georgia in the period after 1750.[38] And evidence supports the same conclusion for Maranhão.[39] At times Amazonian landowners expressed a desire for slaves from specific places, but their reasons for doing so had nothing to do with perceptions of skill levels and everything to do with the health, size, and age of slaves arriving from particular ports at particular times. The journey to Amazonia was shorter from Upper Guinea than from Mina, Angola, and Mozambique, meaning that Upper Guineans generally arrived in better condition than others, and thus often fetched higher prices. But such was not always the case. In 1774, Maranhão's governor claimed that "the best slave is a Mina, which is the nation of the most value selling here for 100,000 reis, and those of Angola and other nations very much cheaper."[40] The governor was writing in the midst of Maranhão's rice boom, and Mina slaves arrived with no knowledge of rice agriculture. That same year, planters complained that slaves arriving on several ships from Cacheu, who were likely skilled rice producers, were "very old and worthless."[41] In 1787, a different governor expressed a different opinion. "The common price for slaves in Maranhão," he said, was "150,000 reis for those of top quality from Cacheu and Bissau and for those of first quality from Angola 120,000 reis."[42] Yet evidence from the MISD shows that differentials in the average values of slaves from various places in Africa disappeared once the slaves became acclimated to life in Maranhão. From

[35] Eltis, Morgan, and Richardson, "Agency and Diaspora in Atlantic History," 1356; Carney, *Black Rice*, 99–101.

[36] Eltis, Morgan, and Richardson, "Agency and Diaspora in Atlantic History," 1334, 1350–1353; Carney, *Black Rice*, 107; Wood, *Black Majority*, 106–107; Littlefield, *Rice and Slaves*, 56–57. The argument was first made in Elizabeth Donnan, "The Slave Trade into South Carolina before the Revolution," *American Historical Review* 33, no. 4 (July 1928): 804–828.

[37] Calculated from the MISD for the years 1767–1832.

[38] Eltis, Morgan, and Richardson, "Agency and Diaspora in Atlantic History," 1338–1339; Carney, *Black Rice*, 88–97.

[39] Upper Guineans arrived in Amazonia in large numbers for the reasons that Eltis, Morgan, and Richardson explore—favorable winds and currents. A metropolitan desire to reestablish influence at Bissau and Cacheu and develop the economy of northeastern Brazil is also an explanatory factor. Carney erroneously cites Gayozo's work as a source attesting that Upper Guinean slaves commanded a higher price, with planters "selecting" them for their skills. However, Gayozo's discussion was centered on the price that African sellers wanted for their captives in Africa, not the price that captives were sold for in Maranhão. Where Gayozo derived his information is unclear, and I suspect he was wrong. Carney, " 'With Grains in Her Hair,' " 14; Gayozo, *Compendio historico-politico dos principios da lavoura do Maranhão*, 244.

[40] AHU, Maranhão, cx. 48, doc. 4665.

[41] Ibid., cx. 47, doc. 4618.

[42] ANTT, Ministério do Reino, mç. 601, cx. 704.

FIGURE 3: Woman pounding rice in Maranhão, Brazil. Photo by Judith A. Carney, 2002.

1767 to 1800, the average inventory valuation of slaves in Maranhão who had been born in the Upper Guinea coastal zone was not different from that of slaves from the Angola-Congo region.[43]

That Upper Guineans were not, over time, more valuable to rice planters in Maranhão is not surprising given the relatively low level of technological sophistication applied to rice farming there, which is a topic that Eltis, Morgan, and Richardson do not explore. Accounts from Maranhão indicate that most rice was of the upland variety. Slaves cleared forests by burning them, and they used tools and

---

[43] Calculated from the MISD. Calculations made for groups delineated by age and gender and adjusted for inflation over time in the price of slaves.

techniques similar to those applied to rice agriculture in Upper Guinea for planting. But little that slaves did in fields required a skill set that approached the skills required for paddy rice production in mangrove swamp areas.[44] Angolans and Minas, who brought no rice knowledge from their homelands, labored beside those who did, performing the same tasks under a hot equatorial sun. This is not to imply that Upper Guinean knowledge was valueless. Before mechanical mills were established throughout Maranhão, slaves, the majority of whom were from Upper Guinea, processed rice the same way they had in their homelands—with mortars and pestles.[45] Moreover, Upper Guinea women slaves introduced rice-cooking techniques and rice-based dishes to Amazonia, many of which are popular today.[46]

Why a rice-producing region with high concentrations of coastal Upper Guineans did not make the leap from upland rice to higher-yielding paddy rice is a question that should be addressed in future studies. In addition, there is much left to understand with regard to why rice agriculture of any type emerged in some parts of the Americas that had concentrations of Upper Guineans but not in others.[47] Further, advocates of the "black rice thesis" should address questions about why Upper Guineans introduced technologies to a slave system that brutalized them.[48] And, finally, if planter preference does not explain why Upper Guineans were found in concentrations in two rice-producing regions of the Americas, scholars need to focus more attention on the role of unanticipated contingencies—forces "seen and unseen"—in the making of the Atlantic world.[49]

Although there are questions yet to be answered, the "black rice thesis" itself should not be discarded. To be sure, the nature of rice production—and of the cultural systems in which rice was central—transformed in the eighteenth century on both sides of the Atlantic, as light- and dark-skinned people met and mixed. On the Upper Guinea coast, the introduction of large quantities of iron, the spread of violence associated with slaving, and the development of urban and Atlantic markets for rice sparked massive changes in rice systems as people sought ways to produce sustenance and to garner a share of the goods brought on oceangoing vessels.[50] In

[44] For descriptions of Maranhense rice production, see Dias, *Fomento e mercantilismo*, 443; Antonio Bernardino Pereira do Lago, *Estatistica historica-geografica da provincia do Maranhão* (Lisbon, 1822), 54–56; F. A. Brandão Júnior, *A escravatura no Brasil: Precedida d'um artigo sobre agricultura e colonisação no Maranhão* (Brussels, 1865), 31–38; printed in Robert Edgar Conrad, *Children of God's Fire: A Documentary History of Black Slavery in Brazil* (University Park, Pa., 1984), 96–99; Carney, "'With Grains in Her Hair,'" 15–16.

[45] By 1772, there were only five small and unreliable mechanical mills in all of Maranhão, so most milling was done by hand. AHU, Maranhão, cx. 46, doc. 4514; cx. 45, docs. 4458 and 4460.

[46] Personal observations; Matthias Rohrig Assuncão, "Maranhão, terra Mandinga," *Boletim da Comissão Maranhense de Folclore* 20, no. 4–5 (August 2001): 4–5.

[47] Eltis, Morgan, and Richardson point to Chesapeake as an example of a place with a concentration of Upper Guineans but without a history of rice agriculture. However, many factors—ecological, economic, cultural, political, demographic, and technological—determined what commodities were produced in particular places at particular times. That rice did not emerge as an important crop in Virginia does not necessarily undermine the foundation of Carney's argument. "Agency and Diaspora in Atlantic History," 1337.

[48] Ibid., 1356. Upper Guineans may have grown rice in the Americas in part because they could not contemplate a meal without it. Further, that Africans applied technologies from their homelands to crop production is not surprising. When given a task, Upper Guinean slaves did it the only way they knew how.

[49] Ibid., 1358.

[50] Hawthorne, *Planting Rice and Harvesting Slaves*, 119–143, 151–171.

parts of the Americas, Upper Guineans applied technologies developed in their homelands while toiling in slave systems, growing rice for white masters who sought new technologies and labor organization schemes to make those systems more efficient. Over time, rice-producing cultures in the Americas became "creolized"; they transformed as the result of many forces "relating to both inheritance and experience."[51] By 1800, America's "black rice" was "brown." But acceptance of this point does not require rejection of the argument that the roots of American rice cultures can be traced to Africa. Rice, particularly paddy rice produced in tidal areas, required too much technological sophistication to be developed and sustained by people who knew nothing about the crop. Through a "geographical perspective," Carney finds an innovative way to construct knowledge about people who left no written records. Eltis, Morgan, and Richardson point historians of the Atlantic in a new and promising direction and correct some of Carney's few mistakes, but they do not undermine the foundation upon which the works of Carney, Littlefield, and Wood are built.

[51] Quote from Eltis, Morgan, and Richardson, "Agency and Diaspora in Atlantic History," 1358.

Walter Hawthorne is Associate Professor of African History at Michigan State University. He is the author of *Planting Rice and Harvesting Slaves: Transformations along the Guinea-Bissau Coast, 1400–1900* (Heinemann, 2003). With funding from a National Endowment for the Humanities Faculty Fellowship, he has written a book manuscript titled "From Africa to Brazil: Culture, Identity and an Atlantic Slave Trade, 1600–1830" (forthcoming from Cambridge University Press), which explores linkages between the Upper Guinea Coast, Portugal, and Amazonia. His research was funded by a Fulbright-Hays Faculty Fellowship.

AHR Exchange
Black, Brown, or White? Color-Coding American Commercial Rice Cultivation with Slave Labor

DAVID ELTIS, PHILIP MORGAN, and DAVID RICHARDSON

WE ARE GRATEFUL TO THE EDITOR of the *American Historical Review* for this chance to reply to these three comments on our article. Our respondents run the gamut: S. Max Edelson is broadly supportive, Walter Hawthorne somewhat critical, and Gwendolyn Midlo Hall largely dismissive. That readers see matters differently is nicely encapsulated in these varied reactions, but it makes a reply difficult. Rather than building our response around praising Edelson, qualifying Hawthorne, and combating Hall, perhaps it would be best to restate the central division in this exchange, as we see it, before tackling some of the ancillary themes underlying the three responses.

The fundamental split can be posed counterfactually. Was it possible for a rice export economy to have existed in the Americas without input from the rice-growing cultures of Africa? We think the answer is yes. Prior experience of growing rice was not essential to the emergence of the export economy of South Carolina. Indeed, Europeans organized the production of a wide range of crops in the Americas—including indigo, cotton, tobacco, cacao, and coffee—for which there was no established template in either Europe or Africa.[1] Furthermore, while the sugar complex passed through the Mediterranean, it was scarcely full-formed when it entered the Atlantic in the fifteenth century. Why alone of these products would rice, which clearly had an African (but also an Asian and European) heritage, have been beyond the adaptive reach of an aggressive and exploitative plantation system? For Hall such a possibility is inconceivable, but all her empirical evidence is drawn from Louisiana, not from a rice-exporting region. Louisiana was hardly mentioned in our essay because it exported no significant quantities of rice. The debate to which we thought we were contributing is not what Africans grew when they arrived in the Americas (indeed, we are not aware of any such debate), but rather whether rice plantations could have developed without drawing captives from the rice-growing regions of

---

[1] Tobacco was grown in England as well as Continental Europe about the time that it became a cash crop in Virginia, but this was a relatively recent innovation in Europe. Joan Thirsk, "New Crops and Their Diffusion: Tobacco-Growing in Seventeenth-Century England," in Christopher W. Chalklin and Michael A. Havinden, eds., *Rural Change and Urban Growth, 1500–1800: Essays in Regional History in Honour of W. G. Hoskins* (New York, 1974), 76–103. In England the cultivation of tobacco was associated with "free" white labor. A mix of free and indentured white labor dominated tobacco cultivation in the Chesapeake through the mid-seventeenth century. Thereafter, enslaved Africans became increasingly important.

Africa. Whatever plantation owners learned from their slaves in Louisiana, how to set up a rice-exporting culture was not one of them. Two of the most important pieces of evidence we offered in support of our position are the following. First, during the formative years of the rice plantation system, tobacco planters in the Chesapeake drew on the rice-growing coasts of Africa just as much as did South Carolina's planters. This pattern seems unlikely if rice-growing in the Americas was supposedly dependent on skills available only from Upper Guinea. Second, from the mid-eighteenth century onward, Upper Guinea slaves became more widely available as a component of the Atlantic slave trade, but again this growing share was not exclusive to the Lowcountry. Our critics have largely failed to address either of these key pieces of evidence.

This fundamental division masks three polarities that we see as explicit, and sometimes implicit, in the critiques. One is the reliance that ought to be placed on documentary versus nontraditional sources. Another is the well-worn debate about African origins versus creolization. And, finally, despite the commitment to objectivity and the use of pure reason in reaching conclusions, which we all share, differences owe something, we contend, to optimistic versus pessimistic tendencies. This reply will explore these three issues in turn.

One general concern is how much reliance scholars should place on documents—and the databases drawn from them—compared to other sources. In a number of places, Hawthorne draws a distinction between our "archival" orientation and Judith Carney's "geographical perspective." This "geographical perspective," he claims, offers a way to "construct knowledge about people who left no written records." Indeed, he asks at one point whether our archival evidence is "more accurate than the evidence that Carney derives from a 'geographical perspective.'" Similarly, Edelson notes how we "deploy unforgiving statistics against a process of inferred cultural transmission that could, because the documentary record omits African perspectives, leave only the faintest impressions in the archives." Finally, Hall views the Voyages Database interface of the new Transatlantic Slave Trade website as an "inflexible" tool that "lock[s] in outmoded research and questions," by which she means that it fails to include information about African ethnicities.[2] But African ethnicities are rarely reported in slave-trading documents, and we certainly cannot tell precisely which captives carried off from Upper Guinea came from risicultures and which did not. No source—documentary or otherwise—will systematically help in this regard. It would be easy to add such information to the Voyages database, except for one significant problem: for the most part, it simply does not exist.[3]

Both Hawthorne and Hall highlight the limitations of databases—a position with which we readily concur—but then they quickly foreground the value of their own datasets. Hall thinks our sample for vessels for which we have information on provisions is too small, but neither she nor Hawthorne gives us a sense of the relative importance of their own number of observations. For Louisiana, given the century-long span of her database, the 80,000 black population present in 1820, and the probable 40,000 African arrivals after 1719, the 1,306 slaves in Hall's Table 1 and the 383 in Table 2 (the sum of columns 3 and 6) must constitute a sample size of

---

[2] http://www.slavevoyages.org/tast/database/search.faces

[3] A rare example is provided by Walter Hawthorne in his critique, which we mention below.

well below 1 percent. Indeed, the true numbers in her tables must be even smaller than those reported, given that several individuals were certainly counted twice.[4] For Amazonia, nearly 60,000 captives arrived from Africa between 1767 and 1800; the numbers Hawthorne reports—totaling less than 400—are therefore a small fraction.

To set traditional and nontraditional sources in opposition to each other is to pose a false dichotomy. Obviously, scholars should combine *both* archival documents and a range of disciplinary insights, the geographical being just one. In our larger works, we have tried to do just that. In the smaller compass of a journal article, naturally we had to constrain our scope. Numbers obviously matter—they can give a sense of scale and proportion—but gross statistics must always be interpreted and contextualized. Furthermore, we do not see "script penned on paper" (Hawthorne's term) as the only source material, but then again historians quite naturally gravitate—as do our critics—to archival documents. Where it is possible to deploy numbers to answer questions, we believe it is the responsibility of the scholar to do so. It is true that our article rested largely, though not entirely, on the evidence drawn from a single multi-source database. Much of the argument of our critics revolves around the limitations of that resource.

Both Hawthorne and Hall, for example, point out that we offer no information on where captives brought to the Americas eventually lived and worked. Thus, Upper Guinea slaves brought to areas in the Americas other than South Carolina and Georgia could have been sent to the Lower South via the intra-American slave trade. But as we noted in our essay (1336), there is now a way of taking this movement into account. Few could have traveled to Charleston or Savannah by land, but for the seaborne traffic, Gregory O'Malley (referred to in footnote 17 of our article) has assembled a large database tracking the movement of 7,000 vessels carrying slaves between ports in North America (including the Caribbean) between 1619 and 1807. He estimated that about 16 percent of all captives brought into mainland North America arrived indirectly via the Caribbean—a conclusion with which we are in agreement.[5] Between 1700 and 1740, only about 10 percent of all slaves arriving in South Carolina did not come direct from Africa, and before 1776, South Carolina and Georgia attracted fewer captives by this route than did the Chesapeake. In the formative years of South Carolina, 1671 to 1710, for every slave arriving in South Carolina from the British Caribbean, seven were taken to the Chesapeake. O'Malley is not able to track the African coastal origins of those on board the voyages he recorded. Some would not have been African at all, and many others would have been African but not from rice-growing cultures.

---

[4] About constructing her own database, Hall has written: "We did not delete the same slaves duplicated over time because, aside from the difficulties and uncertainty of such an undertaking, it would have eliminated much data, which demonstrated changing patterns and made it impossible to trace particular slaves in time depth. When estates were inventoried and then sold immediately afterwards, we recorded slaves only once, indicating the date of the inventory and the date of the sale and both the inventory and the sale price. In cases where months and, at times, years elapsed between inventory and sale of estates, we recorded slaves separately in order to be able to calculate changes over time in the same estate." Gwendolyn Midlo Hall, "The Louisiana Slave Database and the Louisiana Free Database, 1719–1820," http://ibiblio.org/laslave/AcksandIntro.html.

[5] Gregory E. O'Malley, "Beyond the Middle Passage: Slave Migration from the Caribbean to North America, 1619–1807," *William and Mary Quarterly*, 3rd ser., 66 (2009): 125–172, esp. 166; David Eltis, "The U.S. Transatlantic Slave Trade, 1644–1867: An Assessment," *Civil War History* 54 (2008): 347–378.

The Voyages database allows us to go beyond O'Malley's work and infer something about the African backgrounds of those sent to the North American mainland from the Caribbean. As noted in our original essay, Upper Guineans formed a very small share of the captives arriving in the British Caribbean between 1671 and 1710. Arrivals from Sierra Leone and the Windward Coast averaged about 200 a year in those years, compared to 1,500 from Senegambia. Voyages also shows that almost three-quarters of all Upper Guinea arrivals left from the Gambia River alone.[6] How many of this group came from risicultures? The information we offered on the provisioning of slave vessels leaving the Gambia provides a clue: provisions reflecting the diet to which the captives would have been accustomed. We cited twenty slave voyages that carried off no fewer than 3,800 slaves during 1679–1688—the busiest of the four decades between 1671 and 1710. That equates to about one in every five slaves carried off to the British Caribbean from the Gambia, or 18.3 percent from Upper Guinea as a whole in this decade. As noted in our original article, 70 percent of the provisions leaving the Gambia consisted of millet, not rice; and even in Sierra Leone and on the Windward Coast, Nicholas Villault noted millet and "mays" in great abundance, as well as rice, at the outset of this period.[7] Thus as risiculture in South Carolina was beginning, the colony could have had very few slaves with rice-growing experience. As we have seen, when South Carolina planters did turn to the direct traffic with Africa for their labor, they showed no more preference for Upper Guineans than did Chesapeake tobacco growers. Neither Hawthorne nor Hall grapples with this evidence.

Hall claims that in the redistribution process—which often involved being reloaded onto other ships after a transatlantic voyage and then being moved to another location—Africans "were sometimes clustered by their region of origin and/or ethnicity when buyers were able to purchase the new Africans they preferred." This reading of what might have happened is not supported by the one scholar who has looked systematically at this subject. For "many captives," O'Malley argues, "the extensive inter-colonial trading meant that the journey continued after they survived the Middle Passage, adding to the risk of mortality and the likelihood of separation from kin, colinguists, or shipmates." Wherever extensive transshipment occurred, a "polyglot assortment of African peoples" was likely.[8] Furthermore, it strains credulity to think that enough people with a rice-growing background arrived via the Caribbean to change the regional mix of Africans coming into the Lower South derived from looking at transatlantic arrivals alone.

Hawthorne is mostly interested in the connections between northeastern Brazil

[6] http://slavevoyages.org/tast/database/search.faces?yearFrom=1671&yearTo=1710&mjbyptimp=60100.60200.60300&mjslptimp=33200.33400.33500.33600.33700.34200.35100.35200.35500. Arrivals in the British Caribbean from Upper Guinea averaged just over 200 a year.

[7] *A Relation of the Coasts of Africk Called Guinee; with a Description of the Countreys, Manners and Customs of the Inhabitants; of the productions of the earth, and the Merchandise and Commodities it affords; with some historical observations upon the coasts. Being collected in a voyage by the Sieur Villault, Escuyer, Sieur de Bellefond, in the years 1666, and 1667*, 2nd ed. (London, 1670), 45, 61, 107. We are indebted to Philip Misevich for drawing this source to our attention. Estimates of the proportion of rice in the provisions for slaves from Upper Guinea earlier in the century are even smaller—10–15 percent; see Linda A. Newson and Susie Minchin, *From Capture to Sale: The Portuguese Slave Trade to Spanish America in the Early Seventeenth Century* (Leiden, 2007), 78–84.

[8] O'Malley, "Beyond the Middle Passage," 165–166.

and Upper Guinea. He provides two pieces of information that are valuable additions to knowledge. We are grateful to him for sharing this information in this exchange. It adds something of substance to the debate. At the same time, of course,
one piece of his information is a fragment—a useful fragment, nevertheless. He has
found evidence of the ethnic origins of ninety-seven captives from one ship that
arrived in Brazil in 1756. As he notes, about half of the enslaved were from the
coastal areas and might well have known something of rice cultivation; the other half
came from farther inland or north, and were probably not as knowledgeable about
rice but nevertheless perhaps had some experience of the crop. Furthermore, he also
has ethnic origins for some of the 342 slaves listed in inventories between 1767 and
1800. He does not report how many Upper Guineans there were among this group
of 342, but they were the largest single group, and about two-thirds of them were
from the lowland coastal strip. This suggests that a connection between the kinds of
Upper Guineans swept into Atlantic trading and rice-growing was certainly possible,
perhaps even likely. But Maranhão's rice exports were only one-fifth those of the
Lower South, in part because of, in Hawthorne words, "the relatively low level of
technological sophistication applied to rice farming there."

Was the rice that was carried as provisions still in the husk and thus capable of
germinating in the Americas? And were women employed in its cleaning? Almost
all of the rice and millet leaving the Gambia in the 1680s had already been cleaned
prior to loading. On the basis of this evidence, which is considerably more than the
proponents of the black rice hypothesis have offered, we are skeptical of the claim
that women regularly milled rice on slave ships. Two examples of this practice have
been cited. One was the ship *Mary* in 1796, on which women cleaned rice before the
transatlantic voyage began.[9] The most likely explanation for this practice is that the
vessel was not yet at sea. Removing the husk without breaking the grain was a skilled
task, and one not easily carried out on a small, pitching vessel during an ocean voyage. A second instance derives from a contemporary painting—a nontraditional
source—of the Danish slave ship *Fredensborg*, in which a profile of two women can
be discerned pounding what is likely grain. But this cereal was almost certainly not
rice. In 1785, this vessel boarded sixty slaves in small groups at various locations
along the Windward, Ivory, and Gold Coasts before embarking the bulk of its human
cargo, 230 individuals, at one of the Danish forts on the eastern Gold Coast. At best,
then, less than 10 percent of the captives would have been accustomed to eating rice.
The grain on the *Fredensborg* was more likely to have been millet, or what the English
at the time called corn. Thus, as the evidence now stands, women did not mill rice
on board slave ships once the voyage was under way, and captains preferred to load
rice that was already "clean," that is, without its husk.[10]

[9] Elizabeth Donnan, *Documents Illustrative of the Slave Trade to America*, 4 vols. (Washington, D.C.,
1930–1933), 3: 376. The *Mary* (id 36631 in Voyages) was on the Gold Coast at the time of this report
but had on board 116 slaves purchased from various locations in Upper Guinea.

[10] See id 35,035 in Voyages, and for the image see Leif Svalesen, *The Slave Ship Fredensborg* (Bloomington, Ind., 2000), 40–41. This conjunction highlights, of course, the value of using documentary evidence when available, including that contained in datasets, to assist in the interpretation of the meaning
of nontraditional sources. It raises a wider issue, too, namely the alleged role of women in the transatlantic diffusion of rice cultivation and Carney's claim that because of their peculiar importance, female
slaves fetched relatively high prices in South Carolina. We disputed this claim. Evidence presented by
Hawthorne for Maranhão supports our position on this issue.

Another general issue raised by all three respondents concerns the question of how much Africa should be credited with the development of export rice cultivation in the Americas. Hall accepts the African role without question; Hawthorne is more qualified; and Edelson is skeptical. Hawthorne occupies a middle ground, acknowledging specific African ethnic expertise, but conceding that whites as well as blacks contributed to rice's development in the Americas. For him, chronology is critical. Before 1700, rice was "black," in that Africans were the Atlantic's "master rice producers"; only later did the crop go "brown" as whites learned how to cultivate it. For him, rice at first "required too much technological sophistication to be developed and sustained by people who knew nothing about the crop." By contrast, Edelson advocates "abandoning a single-minded focus on awarding Africans credit as the propagators of rice culture" and replacing it with a broader inquiry into how whites and blacks "reconstitute[d] material life in the harsh setting of an accelerating plantation economy." In his view, many so-called African techniques were "generic . . . solutions to the challenges of wetland farming developed by several Old World agricultural traditions." As he points out, "Two critical technologies used to irrigate rice in the Lowcountry, freshwater swamp reservoirs and tidal floodgates, have European, not African, origins." As we noted in our article, the primary African influences were in "sowing, threshing, and winnowing the crop." Rice culture in the Americas was a hybrid form of agriculture, grafting different Old World practices together to produce a distinct New World crop.[11]

Hall offers a specific role for a part of Africa not normally mentioned in the debate about the continent's contribution to American rice-growing. She suggests that rice growers might have come from Madagascar. Ideally, it would be good to know from which part of the island they came: if from the east, the likelihood of some knowledge of rice cultivation would have been much higher than if from the drier west, where rice was a much less important component of the diet and agricultural economy. Hall mentions some voyages from Madagascar into early Barbados and North America. In fact, before 1750, the Voyages database reveals 14,000 captives arriving in the Americas from Madagascar. Of these, 1,440 went to the Chesapeake, but the largest number went to Brazil and the Rio de la Plata. Not one went directly to the North American mainland south of the Chesapeake. Malagasy slaves would seem an unlikely source for rice-growing in South Carolina and Georgia.[12]

As Edelson points out, the "black rice" thesis is widely accepted by textbook writers, and sanctioned by a popular PBS series. If any doubt remained about the general acceptance of the African origins of rice-growing in the Americas, consider Edda L. Fields-Black's 2008 book *Deep Roots*. Her starting point is that "historians have established the importance of West African rice-farming technology to the plantation economies of the U.S. South." She later adds that "after thirty years of research by Peter Wood, Daniel Littlefield, and Judith Carney, there is little credibility to notions that enslaved Africans did not play an important role in the trans-

[11] For a recent article that endorses our view, echoed by others, that scholars should "break free" from the straitjacket of creolization versus survivals, see James H. Sweet, "Mistaken Identities? Olaudah Equiano, Domingos Álvares, and the Methodological Challenges of Studying the African Diaspora," *American Historical Review* 114, no. 2 (April 2009): 279–306.

[12] http://slavevoyages.org/tast/database/search.faces?yearFrom=1500&yearTo=1750&mjbyptimp=60800.

mission of rice cultivation and processing technology to and in the development of commercial rice production in South Carolina and Georgia." With that established, her goal, as she sees it, is "to discern the antiquity" or the "deep roots" of the West African "rice knowledge system," to which end she employs historical linguistics in order to demonstrate that in the Rio Nuñez region—her chosen area of study— migrants from the interior "sowed the seeds of the coastal rice knowledge system" by circa 500 to circa 1000 C.E., as they interacted with prior coastal dwellers who had long since adapted to the floodplains and mangrove swamps of the littoral. Even so, as she acknowledges, "just how West African farmers developed coastal rice-growing technology remains unexplored." Whether historical linguistics can truly illumine this question seems doubtful. She recognizes that the Upper Guinea Coast was "a minor player in the trans-Atlantic slave trade," and that slaving vessels rarely came to the Rio Nuñez region, and even more rarely disembarked slaves in South Carolina or Georgia. Nevertheless, she claims that ship captain Samuel Gamble's description of tidal rice farming among the Baga in the early 1790s was the "spitting image" of tidewater rice production in South Carolina. She adds that "South Carolina colonists may have had experience draining swamps and using irrigation in England, but they lacked experience creating the delicate balance between fresh and brackish water." The evidence on this last point is sketchy, and the claim that such knowledge was a "unique feature" of the "West African rice knowledge system" is thus an exaggeration.[13]

One last divisive issue concerns what might be termed temperamental disposition: the separation is between those who take a sunny, optimistic view and those who adopt a darker, pessimistic standpoint. Thus Edelson characterizes our view of the slave trade as a "cruel lottery," offering a "bleak vision of diasporic contingency," with "capricious market forces" determinative. He detects an "almost churlish" unwillingness on our part to admit that Africans contributed their expertise to rice culture in the Lowcountry. Edelson is inclined toward this stance himself, since he emphasizes colonial South Carolina's "brutal and entrepreneurial society," which he thinks minimized the role that slaves could play in rice cultivation. South Carolina masters, in Edelson's view, "inflicted unspeakable tortures" on their slaves, whom they subjected to "extreme material privation." Early Carolina, he maintains, was emphatically not an "unconstrained place" where "newly arrived slaves put new systems of production into operation on plantations and bargained collectively for better working conditions in exchange for their expertise." His is an even more harrowing depiction of Lowcountry life than our own. Hawthorne and Hall tend to the

[13] Edda L. Fields-Black, *Deep Roots: Rice Farmers in West Africa and the African Diaspora* (Bloomington, Ind., 2008), 8, 10, 51, 77, 80, 112, 48–49, 50, 159; see also her "Untangling the Many Roots of West African Mangrove Rice Farming: Rice Technology in the Rio Nunez Region, Earliest Times to c. 1800," *Journal of African History* 49, no. 1 (2008): 1–21. Fields-Black is not the only scholar to claim the "black rice" thesis as an article of faith. See Paul E. Lovejoy, "Extending the Frontiers of Transatlantic Slavery, Partially," *Journal of Interdisciplinary History* 40, no. 1 (2009): 57–70, in which he insists that the Voyages database "provides convincing proof that many people who knew how to grow rice in Africa were deliberately taken to such rice-producing areas in the Americas as South Carolina, Louisiana, and Amazonia; the connection is not a mere unhappy coincidence" (66). In our view, Voyages alone does not prove what Lovejoy claims, though it does show that South Carolina and Maranhão were among the various places in the Americas to which slaves from rice-growing areas of Atlantic Africa were taken. By itself, of course, this does not demonstrate a transatlantic diffusion of rice-growing cultures in Africa to the Americas, which is the core claim of the "black rice" thesis.

opposite pole. Hawthorne concurs with Edelson that "Upper Guineans" did not agree "to apply specialized knowledge to rice production in exchange for better labor conditions," but he still clings to an upbeat reading of the African contribution. Otherwise, he says, the minimalist approach "risks writing Africans and their descendants in the Americas once again out of history." Hall wholeheartedly supports the position that Africans successfully transferred technological expertise in the planting and processing of rice to the Americas. She lauds the contributions of Africans to New World cultures. As she states in her work on the "clustering of African ethnicities," the "clearest example of African technology transfer to the Americas is the production of rice." For her, "Africans from Upper Guinea were prized in Carolina and Georgia because of their skills in rice cultivation" and "were less feared" there "than in the demographically imbalanced Caribbean sugar islands." In our view, this is an essentially optimistic reading of the Lowcountry milieu.[14]

We return to our opening counterfactual and to our belief that it was possible for rice-exporting economies to have existed in the Americas without input from the rice-growing cultures of Africa. Edelson's response, which acknowledges that the notion of intact agricultural systems crossing the Atlantic "requires problematic distortions of life and labor in the early Lowcountry," making the black rice thesis seem "like a horizon that will continue to recede no matter how avidly scholars try to reach it," is quite consistent with our stance. For Hall (and Carney), by contrast, African technology was what made the South Carolina rice export economy possible. Hawthorne's position on this issue is unclear. An agnostic attitude would place him closer to our view than to that of Hall and Carney. If, indeed, he is simply arguing for an African influence on the risiculture of the Americas, then there is no fundamental difference between us; and we are certainly grateful to him for providing information on the ethnicity of Africans entering Maranhão.

It is a huge step to infer from our argument that we seek to erase the contribution of Africans to the history of the Americas. When placed alongside other evidence, the Voyages database has shown unequivocally the importance of Africans to the re-peopling of the Americas after Columbus. Their enslavement made an enormous contribution to wealth creation in the Americas. In challenging the "black rice" thesis, however, we sought to place transatlantic slavery in an Atlantic context and to remind readers how imbalances in power between the enslaved and their owners molded the history of emergent American plantation societies under the influence of changing market conditions. These asymmetries in power relations meant that whites were the principal drivers of changes in life and labor in such societies, and reaped the major share of the ensuing rewards. This was the harsh reality facing the overwhelming majority of enslaved Africans taken to the Americas, regardless of the cash crop they were forced to produce. In the end, enslaved Africans' contribution to commercial risiculture may have been greater than their role in other American plantation crops that had no cultural antecedents in Africa, but highly profitable rice-growing certainly did not depend on African expertise.

[14] Gwendolyn Midlo Hall, *Slavery and African Ethnicities in the Americas: Restoring the Links* (Chapel Hill, N.C., 2005), 66–67. Cf. Alexander X. Byrd, *Captives and Voyagers: Black Migrants across the Eighteenth Century British Atlantic World* (Baton Rouge, La., 2008), esp. 85.

Featured Reviews

THOMAS N. BISSON. *The Crisis of the Twelfth Century: Power, Lordship, and the Origins of European Government*. Princeton: Princeton University Press. 2009. Pp. xxviii, 677. $39.50.

For almost a century now more or less everyone who has written about the twelfth century has portrayed it, correctly, as a time of great constructive endeavor when the foundations of Europe's future predominance were laid. A signal and salutary achievement of this book is to remind us how nearly they were not, but that is not Thomas N. Bisson's chief purpose. Rather he wants to show us the Latin Europe of the period in its own terms, *wie es eigentlich gewesen ist*. Above all that means—as indeed it must for any age—understanding the exercise (or, as Bisson prefers, the experience) of power from the perspective of those who suffered it as well as of those who possessed it. To do so, he rightly insists, we must discard all thought of consequences, and jettison the vocabulary, as well as the priorities, of hindsight—the anachronistic notions of government (as consciously directed to public ends), of politics (strictly understood as the reconciliation of legitimately conflicting interests), of rational or efficient administration. In their place stands lordship ("personal command over dependent people . . . peasants, knights or vassals" [p. 3]), effectively alone, as the form that power assumed and the means by which it was exercised, self-aggrandizement its sole object. Thus, to take one example among many far less obvious, however excitably posterity may have hailed Henry I as an architect of the English state, Henry himself, Bisson maintains, sought or envisaged no higher or broader goal than the maintenance and extension of his personal lordship. He did not conceive of his kingly status as conferring an office (in Bisson's vocabulary, the antithesis of lordship) that might impose obligations on him, or endure independently of him. His men, including those famous "new men," were not officers held to account for their discharge of acknowledged functions, but "those with whom he was content to share the proceeds of his lordship," including "for practical purposes, an inner, curial circle of trusted aides, and an outer circle of tenants-in-chief" (p. 180).

This is not, of course, a new idea. What is distinctive about Bisson's use of it is the explicitness with which it excludes alternative frames of reference, the constancy with which it pervades the thought and action of his protagonists, and the consistency with which it is applied to the description and elucidation of a turbulent and often seemingly inchoate century and a half of European history. Bisson's object is not so much to convince us of particular propositions—his major ones are neither new nor, for the most part, particularly contentious—as to teach us to think differently about the twelfth century by showing us how it was, not what it was going to become. Appropriately to that end, his presentation is less forensic than impressionistic (his own metaphor is the kaleidoscope [p. 578]), and his book is best, and most enjoyably, read in that spirit.

The weight of the exposition, following a preliminary characterization of "The Age of Lordship, 875–1150," is borne by two pairs of chapters dealing respectively with the period from the middle of the eleventh to the middle of the twelfth, and with the later twelfth and early thirteenth centuries. The third and fifth, "Lord-Rulership, 1050–1150" and "Intrusions of Government, 1150–1215," present in unconventional ways what in conventional terms might be called an interpretative essay on the political and administrative history of Western Europe. The masterly fourth presents a classic series of "Crises of Power, 1060–1150," among them vivid and penetrating discussions of the Saxon revolt against the Emperor Henry IV and its consequences, the murder of Count Charles the Good of Flanders, and Stephen's reign in England. "Celebrations and Persuasions, 1160–1215" (chapter six) includes a variety of ways in which changing perceptions of power among various groups were reflected, a remarkable and fascinating comparison of confrontations between monarchy and nobility in Catalonia and England, and a broader discussion of the fragmentary emergence through such conflicts of something like a sense of common interest, which a brief epilogue reminds us not to mistake for the appearance of a political culture like our own. The weight of the argument throughout rests, as will be expected, on Spain, France, and England, but it is conducted on a genuinely European front, the imperial lands in particular receiving careful attention, with the result that while regional differences are scrupulously and acutely registered the universality of the domination and culture of lordship is brought out unforcedly, but very forcibly.

This is a long book and a generous one, the fruit of a command of both the narrative and the record sources equalled by no recent anglophone scholar, to be taken at leisure, and often, no doubt, in parts, and it is rich enough, as well as thoughtful and provocative enough, handsomely to reward such treatment. If we stand well back from the myriad vivid accounts and close discussions of great and small events, a clear outline emerges in which the turbulent and chaotic conditions of the eleventh and early twelfth centuries give way slowly to a more ordered world in which central authority—that is, the greatest lords—imposes itself more effectively and begins to sense the possibility of broader, even common interests. It is a slow and painful business, much slower and more piecemeal than ordinary accounts, especially recent ones, have brought out. This is an important corrective to the many who, like the present reviewer, have been tempted to hail the distant shore the moment the clifftops are sighted, at the risk of overlooking the breakers between.

It is also, especially in the earlier part, a restatement of a classic view. As such it inevitably raises again the question that Bisson has already ventilated with classic pungency, of the so-called (though no longer by him) "feudal revolution." His thorough and vigorous treatment of the issue here sets the scene for the main concern of the book, and displays both the strengths and the limitations of his method. In concluding—and it is powerfully argued—that (leaving aside the metaphor of revolution as "lacking explanatory cogency" [p. 48]) the vocabulary, as well as the character, of usurpation and harassment in early eleventh-century sources described a new level of lawless violence, profoundly disruptive in itself and representing a decisive break with the past, he reiterates a familiar position with great clarity. Other perspectives in the debate are warmly acknowledged but not always absorbed sufficiently to enrich this account as much as they might have done. His description of the maintenance of order in the late Carolingian world, for example, gives welcome emphasis to what Bisson calls "associative power," that of "natural communities of interest that must often have functioned autonomously to determine agrarian customs and collective rights" (p. 27) in ways seldom recorded or reflected in the record, and brutally overwhelmed by the proliferation of castles and knights. This is brilliantly and exhaustively described but explained only in very general terms as a function of the crumbling of an old order and, less insistently but perhaps more usefully, of the opportunity and capacity to exploit the profits of agrarian intensification. Certainly this implies the sharper social differentiation that must surely be key to the case

for the rapid increase in the pace of change around the millennium that Bisson maintains, but it does not go far enough to account for it; the consequences of the cost of up-to-date military equipment and training, for instance, are surprisingly little considered. Social differentiation was both expressed and resisted in the many forms of ritual power that so much recent work has uncovered. The humiliation of relics, the curse of the holy man, the excommunication carefully prepared and collectively articulated by regional synods, the claim and counterclaim that eventually knit together an accepted pattern of neighborhood landholding around a monastery: all represented ways in which the unarmed community rallied in defence against the storms whipped up by Bisson's chief protagonists. Feeble as these devices were in the face of naked force, they were not entirely without immediate or cumulative effect. This was part of the experience of power, and Bisson's assessment is incomplete without it. It is a chink in his case, as it was in Thomas Hobbes's, that so many even of the blackest-hearted villains crave legitimacy even in the eyes of their humbler neighbors; why else did the status of those new men of Henry I whose unbridled self-aggrandizement he shows so graphically depend on "the unshakable future of *royal* lordship" (p. 180; reviewer's emphasis)? It was part also of the culture of power, and of the reason why, although ecclesiastical lordship was little different from any other in the earlier part of the period as Bisson shows so well, there are growing indications that by the second half of the twelfth century bishops were beginning to develop a model of lordship increasingly different in style, and perhaps also in substance, from that of their secular counterparts.

It is hard to be sure that such reflections as these do justice to a complex and densely argued work. This one has the deeply collegial character of a searching and meditative dialogue with fellow scholars of many generations and traditions—most often with the legacy of the great tradition that culminated in Charles H. Haskins and Joseph Reese Strayer—and indeed with the author himself. There is a price in thought and language that leaves him vulnerable to misunderstanding and even distortion. Nothing is more difficult after long immersion in a complex subject—and few have been immersed more deeply or for longer than Bisson—than to return to the everyday knowledge, and even the vocabulary, of a prospective audience, and it must be said that this book is not always easy reading. Nor, in a sense, should it be, for it does not deal in easy questions or offer simple answers. But its impact will inevitably be reduced, and its message misinterpreted, in consequence. This reader, for example, is by no means confident, after rereading pp. 310–321 several times, that he has grasped correctly the concept of a "shadowed peace," which according to the map on p. 315 covered most of Europe in the second half of the twelfth century. Yet it is an insight of fundamental importance, both in itself and to Bisson's thesis. It is a phrase, he says, used by several writers, though he names and quotes only Aldebert, bishop of Mende (1151–1187), who described (rather more intelligibly to my mind) as *umbra pacis* the situation that existed after he had succeeded in evicting various usurping lords from the lands of his bishopric and replacing them by his own officials. What he had achieved, Aldebert is surely saying, looked like peace—the shadow on the wall, as it were—but was not the substance because his appointees continued to behave exactly as the usurpers had done before them. It was not the replacement in itself, but the ultimately successful struggle of Aldebert and other lords to compel or persuade such men to exercise the restored powers differently—responsibly—that constituted Bisson's crisis. This is a theme whose variations are compellingly

explored and most illuminatingly compared across the continent, and through a series of particular crises as complex, notable, and portentous as any in European history. It seems petty to cavil at the phraseology that introduces it, but it is the key to one of the most searching and serious reappraisals of the twelfth century in our time, which will and which must be long debated. It is very much to be hoped that Bisson will provide the entry-level summary for undergraduates that must otherwise come from clumsier hands; they would not be alone in their gratitude.

R. I. MOORE
University of Newcastle upon Tyne

BRUCE R. SMITH. *The Key of Green: Passion and Perception in Renaissance Culture.* Chicago: University of Chicago Press. 2009. Pp. 326. $39.00.

We are cognitively hungry. We know well how needy we are. Our survival depends on our learning as much as we can about our surroundings, and thus we are always actively searching for usable information from the environment that can be integrated with memory and applied to current need. We accommodate different kinds of information through different sensory systems: ears take in sound waves, for example, and eyes light waves. That much is universal. Different cultures, however, rank the different sources of knowing differently, and allocate both brain and cultural space according to their own scales of value. In Western cultures, children spend many years in school (*a fortiori*, those who become academic historians and philosophers), so it is not surprising that in academia knowledge is virtually identified with the written word. Recent new histories—cultural, social, gender—have awakened us to the distortion caused by the identification of word and knowledge and fortunately the picture is changing slowly. Pictures, in fact, are becoming respectable even in history books.

Welcome, then, Bruce R. Smith's attractive and interesting book, which aims to help Renaissance scholars move beyond words to an understanding of meaning as emerging from the dynamic interaction of human bodies and all their senses with their natural and cultural ambience. One of the reasons that this study should help us to overcome our wordy biases, we are told right off, is because green "is not a thing; it is a relationship . . . 'Green' invites us to consider that subjects, especially *thinking* subjects, don't exist apart from the objects amid which they live, move, and think" (p. 1). This is not Smith's first exploration of sense knowledge. In 2000 he proposed "historical phenomenology" as a method of studying knowledge available from all the senses ("Premodern Sexualities," *PMLA* 115, no. 3).

In *The Acoustic World of Early Modern England: Attending to the O-Factor* (Chicago, 1999), he was already engaged in reorienting scholars from words toward a wide range of acoustic phenomena, asking "what sounds would have filled the air in Early Modern England and what would sounds have meant to people in that largely oral culture?"

Both books are compendia of sense phenomena, many of which have either been entirely unnoticed or insufficiently studied because fitting them into traditional historical understanding presents a real challenge. Smith's approach is encouraged by recent neuroscientific work demonstrating the interconnection of our bodies, our emotions, and what we are used to thinking of as rational decision making. Antonio Damasio's work (e.g., *Descartes' Error: Emotion, Reason, and the Human Brain* [New York, 1994]) is becoming known in the humanities, and there is wide confirmation of his argument for the interdependence of aspects of mind that were considered distinct in the Renaissance, such as the faculties of reason and desire or will.

Smith overwhelms the reader with his examples of "green stuff": large amounts of briefly analyzed or unanalyzed data which, on his hypothesis, should be integrated into our understanding of early modern ways of thinking. He has visited English manor houses and searched museum collections. He has consulted gardening manuals, alchemical treatises, books on painting and dying and on color symbolism in heraldry. From these sources and many others he draws references to green gems, green bile, green wall hangings, green men, green dyes, green lions, green sickness, green turf, not to mention greenish, green-blue, yellow green, and verdure, and on and on. Although the book's aim is to unword us, Smith has had no choice but to scour as many written sources as possible for clues to the phenomenal life of green. Many sections of the book are little more than lists, but in fact invite us to search with him for previously unnoticed patterns. The richness of the book, thus, is to be found in the imaginative combination of new "stuff" with Smith's often startlingly original and suggestive hypotheses of what he calls ambient meaning.

In a chapter called "Between Black and White," for example, Smith hypothesizes the material and symbolic importance of green by noting its place at the midpoint of Aristotle's color spectrum, which (unlike ours) extended from black at one end to white at the other, with the colors in between. Smith constructs a parallel spectrum of sixteenth and seventeenth-century thinkers according to their distrust of, or tolerance, or even affection for ambiguity. He suggests that the centrality of green eludes the binary, allowing nuance or "play." The color spectrum, he then argues, is by analogy a key to a "crisis of consciousness" in the mid-seventeenth century. Michel de Montaigne and Edward Herbert, two men who occupy the centrist "green" position, are "writers who think with their bodies as well as their brains and are not afraid to say so" (p. 106). Green, thus, wherever it appears, may be understood to express sympathy with a middle way. Smith does not hide his appreciation of this position, for it is clearly *sensible* in both senses of that word: not extreme, and not merely brainy. Yet he often has to stretch the evidence to meet his claim, sometimes beyond credibility. The argument can become circular, as for example, when he attempts to hear green (p. 203) or uses green as a verb (p. 173).

For example, in the course of his searches for green things that might be read as displaying an intelligence open to sense knowledge, Smith studies the description of a painting of the fall of Troy in William Shakespeare's "The Rape of Lucrece" (1594). He must have been disappointed to find no mention of green, yet because he finds other evidence of openness to sense knowledge, he argues that the author is looking through "green spectacles," metaphorically, that is. Having asserted the meaning of green as just this willingness to learn from the senses, he himself seems to see through green spectacles. It is not that the argument cannot be made; on the contrary, it becomes too easy to make. Green witnesses a habit of mind, and that habit of mind, found with or without coloring, is "green."

Patience with Smith's flights of green imagination is often rewarded. Studying Andrew Marvell's garden poems, seeking connections beyond the usual outdoor and abstract connotations, he examines indoor greens, asking what the apparent frequency of green wall and table coverings in the private rooms of aristocratic homes can tell us about pastoral poetry. Were these rooms for private reading? The book is scattered with new and insightful if undeveloped suggestions like this one. In short, I am grateful for Smith's speculative and groundbreaking exploration of the way philosophical and literary texts, paintings, works of plastic art, and aristocratic house furnishings can be understood to collude with written texts. They help us, the argument goes, to calibrate conceptual and sensory phenomena and wrest meaning from their convergences. This work carries on the work of Elaine Scarry's *Dreaming by the Book* (1999), also an exploration of how nonverbal evanescent communications of sensation and emotion can become part of our historical understanding.

ELLEN SPOLSKY
Bar-Ilan University

NEIL SAFIER. *Measuring the New World: Enlightenment Science and South America*. Chicago: University of Chicago Press. 2008. Pp. xviii, 387. $45.00.

In 1669, the French abbé Jean Picard, using the methods of cartographic triangulation developed by the Dutch mathematician Willebrord Snell, measured one degree of latitude along an arc of the meridian passing through Paris. King Louis XIV, upon seeing the Picard map years later and realizing that his royal territory had been greatly reduced, bemoaned that the new scientific measurements had cost him more territory than he had previously lost in war. In an engaging and well written book, Neil Safier explores the transatlantic legacies of this early Enlightenment explosion of interest in cartography. Safier traces the cultural history surrounding Charles-Marie de la Condamine's 1735 expedition to South America and subsequent publication of scholarly studies related to this exploration. Combining rigorous archival and field work with methodologies drawn from the historiography of the book, Safier elucidates the relationship among maps, mimesis, and imagination as they related to scientific goals of measuring the New World.

Safier begins with an anecdote that summarizes a common theme studied throughout his book: during the annual festival held at Quito in celebration of the Spanish reconquest of the Iberian peninsula, Condamine noticed a group of young mestizos mimicking the scientific activities of the French academicians. This burlesque was performed with such accuracy, Condamine stated, "that it was impossible for us not to recognize ourselves" (p. 3). As Safier argues, "the pantomime portrayed science as a socially circumscribed and materially bounded spectacle" (p. 5). It is this constellation of phenomena that Safier so assiduously submits to review. His interests lie in exposing the particular social activities that gave rise to scientific texts. In doing this, Safier builds upon the work of earlier studies of this episode, such as Antonio Lafuente and Antonio Mazueco's *Los caballeros del punto fijo: Ciencia, poli?tica y aventura en la expedicio?n geode?sica hispanofrancesa al virreinato del Peru? en el siglo XVIII* (1987), and of histories of cartography and culture in general, such as Ricardo Padrón's *The Spacious Word: Cartography, Literature, and Empire in Early Modern Spain* (2004). However, Safier develops the important thesis that Enlightenment science, as a branch of human culture, "is a reflection of the people that carry it out and ultimately depends for its meaning on the audiences to which it is addressed" (p. 18). Throughout his book, Safier reveals how various publications created spaces and opportunities for social interaction. While these texts and maps could serve to make new ideas known, they could also suppress and silence the sources and criticisms of this knowledge.

But how does one uncover what Michel-Rolph Trouillot has referred to as "the silences of the past"? Safier accomplishes this brilliantly by making use of the tools of the sociology of the text, as developed by Robert McKenzie and Roger Chartier. In each of his seven chapters Safier studies a particular text and the social activity that accompanied its creation. In doing this, Safier presents a version of science as theater, with scientific investigation understood as a performance in which the individual creating the narrative wielded power over knowledge. Safier's first two chapters study what we might call Condamine's orientalist conceptualization of America. Here Safier looks at, "how the geographical conceptions of the European travelers were fueled by their previous reading and how literary memories intertwined with local observations in the narrative construction of South American geography and mythology" (p. 62). In chapter one, "The Ruined Pyramids of Yarquí," he studies Condamine's 1751 publication of the *Histoire des Pyramides* and looks at the work that went into constructing similar structures in Quito for the purpose of providing a fixed point of reference for geodetic triangulation. In chapter two, "An Enlightened Amazon, with Fables and Fold-out Maps," he focuses on the 1745 *Relation abregee* and studies the politics and polemics related to map making. Of interest here, when unable to observe locations along the Orinoco and Amazon, Condamine relied on indigenous testimonies, the attribution of which he subsequently suppressed.

In chapter three, "Armchair Explorers," Safier further develops the argument that writing should be seen as a polemical practice that retains embedded traces of social negotiations. He proves this by exploring the crit-

icism brought against Condamine by European intellectuals, such as the Dutch Jew Isaac de Pinto and the Ecuadorian Creole, then living in Europe, Pedro Vicente Maldonado. In chapter four, "Correcting Quito," Safier looks at the mapping of Quito and draws attention to the silences of map-making: that is, the omitted corrections suggested by Maldonado, who had accompanied Condamine during his voyage through Brazil. In chapter five, "A Nation Defamed and Defended," Safier switches his focus from France to Spain and studies Jorge Juan and Antonio de Ulloa's 1748 publication *Relación histórica del viaje á la América Meridional*. Juan and Ulloa had been ordered by King Philip V's minister José de Patiño to accompany Condamine to South America. Upon their return, the subsequent Spanish publication was intended to serve as a statement of the nation's scientific prowess. However, the work was criticized at home in an anonymous critique entitled "Juicio Imparcial." Safier breaks new ground here by bringing the existence of this polemical piece to light for the first time (p. 184). In chapter six, "Incas in the King's Garden," Safier studies the 1744 French republication of the Inca Garcilaso's *Histoire des Incas*. Among other insights, Safier reveals how chapter twenty-eight of the history was converted via editorial maneuvers into a "virtual tour" (p. 218) of the Royal Garden or *Jardin du Roi*. In his last chapter, "The Golden Monkey and the Monkey-Worm," Safier studies Denis Diderot's *Encyclopédie* and the process of selection of non-European scientific information. Although travel narratives were considered unreliable, writers in Europe "needed these 'ignorant liars' in order to write authoritatively about the world beyond Europe's shores" (p. 237). However, the *encyclopédistes* erroneously included three discrete references to the same indigenous group, the Omagues, variously listed as "Aguas," "Homagues," and "Omagues" (pp. 248–249).

To conclude, Safier reminds us that Maldonado, like other South American Creoles, "seemed to understand that from the perspective of Paris, the Andes would appear flattened and their features diminished" (p. 165). Ironically, in his preface, Safier presents us with a different outcome. Upon summiting the 2,824-meter peak of Cerro Francesurco in Tarqui, Safier claims to have been "largely disappointed with what [he] found" (p. xii). If Condamine had flattened the Andes, Safier had arrived there with heightened expectations of this landscape. To his credit, Safier never loses this exuberance and passion for his topic. His breakthrough study reconstructs this important historical moment and reminds readers that cartography consisted not only of projections on maps. As with all science, people affect the objects under their investigation. In uncovering this human agency, Safier provides scholars in history, literature, and cartography with many new directions upon which to embark in the study of the European Enlightenment and its legacies throughout the transatlantic world.

JONATHAN CARLYON
Colorado State University

JULIE GREENE. *The Canal Builders: Making America's Empire at the Panama Canal*. (Penguin History of American Life.) New York: Penguin Press. 2009. Pp. 475. $30.00.

ALEXANDER MISSAL. *Seaway to the Future: American Social Visions and the Construction of the Panama Canal*. (Studies in American Thought and Culture.) Madison: University of Wisconsin Press. 2008. Pp. xii, 267. $34.95.

The movement to bring cultural and social approaches to bear on American empire has resulted in pathbreaking studies on places such as the Philippines, Hawai'i, Haiti, Cuba, and Puerto Rico around the turn of the twentieth century. With the publication of the two books under review, Panama is at last winning recognition within this emerging scholarship as a leading outpost of American power in the early twentieth century.

There are several points of convergence between these two noteworthy accounts. Among other things, both treat Theodore Roosevelt's 1906 visit to the Panama Canal as a significant public relations coup that revitalized a struggling endeavor, both suggest that the canal served nation-building purposes as readily as military and commercial ones, both delve into the governance of the Canal Zone by executive order, and both examine racially discriminatory practices. Yet in the end, they lean in different directions: Alexander Missal emphasizes the utopian visions affixed to the Panama Canal, and Julie Greene focuses on the anything but utopian experiences of the remarkably cosmopolitan laborers who built it.

Starting from the premise that the canal was "filled not only with mud and water but with meanings as well" (p. 4), Missal takes a discursive approach to his subject. To find the canal's meanings, he turns to what he terms "Panama authors," meaning an assortment of journalists, administrators, and travelers who penned accounts of the canal's construction (between 1904 and 1914) for white, middle-class U.S. audiences. Missal finds this pool of writers to be a fairly cohesive bunch, motivated by a search for order, guided by optimism, and dedicated to the competing goals of collectivism and segregation.

Following the structure that typified his main texts, Missal begins with prehistories of the waterway, going back to Spanish explorers and a failed French effort to dig a canal. He moves on to accounts of the canal's construction, assessments of the Canal Zone state, visual depictions of the construction project, and San Francisco's 1914 Panama-Pacific International Exposition. In each of these cases, he finds that U.S. writers used the Panama Canal as a point of reflection for somewhat vague domestic concerns about disorder. Not all assessments were positive—most notably, Poultney Bigelow faulted the enterprise for political favoritism, discriminatory labor policies, poor sanitation conditions, and prostitution after a 1905 visit.

Canal boosters responded to Bigelow's critique with vigor. Roosevelt made his famous visit to the construction site (the first time a sitting president left the United States) in large part to counter Bigelow's criticisms. His gambit paid off when images of the white-clad president, sitting at the controls of a massive steam shovel, displaced charges of corruption, injustice, disease, and immorality. The official effort to spin the canal for domestic audiences continued after Roosevelt's departure with the employment of a government photographer. As a result of his labors, there are around 16,000 Panama Canal photographs in the U.S. National Archives, ranging from sublime vistas to shots depicting the primitivism of native life. When these are added to the lithographs made by Joseph Pennell, the result is a visual record that heralded the achievements of construction and, as seen in before and after pictures, the beneficent impact of the United States on Panama. Further efforts to shape the image of the canal can be seen in efforts to control the sightseeing experience through official guides and tightly organized train excursions.

Although Missal pays some attention to official efforts to sell Panama to domestic audiences, aside from Bigelow's critique he does not provide much explanation for the need for such a campaign. His focus on utopian depictions appears to result, in part, from his source base. In comparison to government reports, letters from workers, and postcards from travelers (18,972 of whom toured the Canal Zone in the first half of 1913 alone), the Panama texts he selected reached comparatively large audiences. Yet they lacked the critical edge of some of the reports cited by Greene, including those by African Americans who deplored the Jim Crow conditions found in the Canal Zone.

Although Panama served as source material, Missal finds that it was not really the main focal point of the writings he considers. Rather, Panama's importance lay in its significance for U.S. culture and intellectual life. The same holds true for Missal's interpretation, which he describes as "an alternate history of the construction of the seaway, which takes place not on the Isthmus but within the United States—not in excavations of dirt but in people's minds" (p. 19). To show how ideas about Panama intersected with preeminently domestic concerns, Missal situates his group of Panama authors in intellectual contexts defined by writers such as Brooks Adams, Frederick Jackson Turner, Edward Bellamy,

Frederick W. Taylor, and Walter Lippmann. He finds ample evidence to support his argument that the Panama Canal project served as a utopian touchstone. Following the lead of Roosevelt, Panama authors applauded the canal not only for its military and commercial utility but also for the manhood-building challenges it presented and its symbolic importance in the quest for national greatness. Panama authors found much to celebrate in the defeat of yellow fever, re-engineering of the landscape, and U.S. ability to succeed where the French had failed. From these accomplishments, they drew lessons about good governance, social welfare provisioning, public ownership, and national will.

Yet instead of lauding the Canal Zone as a socialistic experiment reeking of working-class rule, the Panama authors cited in this book saw it as an example of what could be attained under the firm command of engineer-soldiers. In reporting on everything from the efficiencies of the commissary system to the enviably light domestic duties enjoyed by U.S. housewives, enthusiastic Panama authors depicted the Canal Zone as, in Missal's apt words, a "suburban fantasy" (p. 132).

One of the greatest strengths of this book is Missal's ability to recognize the fantasy for it was and to shine a more critical light on the practices that captivated his sources. Rather than serving as a model of democratic practice, the Canal Zone was an autocratic state. As the effusive accounts of the pleasant working and living conditions that ignored West Indian workers suggest, the supposed utopia was based on exclusionary principles. Furthermore, despite efforts to associate the Panama Canal with peace, Missal notes that by serving as a symbol of American attainment and progressive promise, it helped legitimate further American expansion abroad.

Missal tracks the positive lines of writing on Panama superbly, but his tight focus blocks off other interpretive paths. This can be seen in statements such as "What American middle-class families were supposed to see through their stereoscopes were not the details of the work or the Panamanian landscape but a vision, a metaphor, of the future America" (p. 121). It is not necessary to argue that the *only* messages from Panama were futuristic visions for the United States in order to make the case that these were important messages. Indeed, by emphasizing domestic lessons, Missal overlooks Panama's imperial lessons. If, as Missal claims, Panama writers had to build a case for the Canal Zone's relevance to the United States, that may have been because some of the most obvious points of contrast were other imperial outposts. The utopian visions that Missal explores so well can be seen as extending far beyond the United States to the future of the world under U.S. leadership.

Julie Greene's book joins Missal's in countering earlier writings that celebrated the engineering and medical challenges surmounted in the course of constructing the Panama Canal. Like Missal, Greene finds that the canal "became an icon of what a strong, progressive federal government could accomplish in world affairs" (p. 7). However, in Greene's eminently readable account, the Canal Zone is not so much the basis for utopian fantasies as it is a site of hard work and bitter struggles. By joining the history of U.S. imperialism to the history of labor, Greene makes significant contributions to both fields.

The workers who built the Panama Canal came from a stunningly wide array of places. More came from Barbados than any other nation, followed by Jamaica. The 1912 census listed 9,721 U.S.-born workers (including six from the Philippines and forty-three from Puerto Rico), 4,030 from Spain, and close to 7,000 from Panama. More surprisingly, the census revealed workers from places like Algeria, Denmark, Egypt, Greece, India, Japan, Madagascar, New Zealand, Russia, Sierra Leone, Turkey, and Uruguay.

Greene builds on a rich body of literature on canal workers, mostly on the experiences of the West Indians who constituted nearly half of the Canal Zone's 62,000 inhabitants in 1912. But in contrast to histories focusing on workers from particular nations, Greene weaves the experiences of several groups together in chapters focusing on the officials who oversaw the canal's construction and workers from the United States, the West Indies, and Spain. Additional chapters focus on women in the Canal Zone and Panamanians on its edges.

The underlying research is both broad and deep. Greene mined government archives in Panama, the United States, and the United Kingdom; records from the National Civic Federation and Panama-Pacific International Exposition; and a wide array of published materials, including not only hearings and Isthmian Canal Commission reports but also newspapers and magazines published in Panama, the United States, and Jamaica.

The result is a richly textured account that makes the variegated social history of canal building come alive. For example, Greene tracks the high pneumonia rates in the Canal Zone to the perpetual soddenness endured by workers who toiled in water all day, never having a chance to dry out their clothes. The cross-group comparisons are especially illuminating. Among other things, Greene finds that Spaniards had more limited occupational opportunities than West Indians, some of whom had entered the artisanal track during the failed French effort to construct a canal across the isthmus.

This book explains well George Washington Goethals's claim that the greatest challenge that faced him as director of the construction project was not conquering nature but controlling the people who labored in the Canal Zone. This control did not come easily. Workers strove to improve their conditions via everything from labor and residential mobility to absenteeism and sit-down strikes. Workers from the United States lobbied the Isthmian Canal Commission in Washington, D.C., and had their allies in U.S. unions advocate on their behalf. They played up their rights as American citizens, as white men when they could, and as representatives of American empire. Unable to claim these rights, West Indian workers appealed to British and French consuls to advocate for their rights as imperial subjects, and they made use of the Canal Zone's legal system, a complicated mishmash of U.S., Spanish, and Colombian law. Along with purposeful challenges to official control, workers disrupted Goethals's efforts to maintain order through unruly behavior, including drunken sprees, domestic violence, and rioting.

Goethals had extraordinary powers to wield in response. Chief among them was the gold and silver system, in which some workers, mainly from the United States and Europe, were paid in gold currency and others, mainly workers of color from outside the United States, in Panamanian silver. Over time this system became the basis for a segregated society that pitted workers against each other on the bases of race and nationality. When skilled U.S. workers came to seem the greatest threat to their management policies, officials brought them under control by replacing them with silver men. Officials also took advantage of their ability to deport labor organizers and others who stirred up too much trouble. Relying on a network of spies and police enforcers, they fined those who failed to show up for work. They also punished loiterers, vagrants, beggars, and disorderly people with hard labor. Some utopia.

Whereas in Missal's study, Panama became a model for U.S. Progressivism, in Greene's book, U.S. Progressivism tackled Panama. Like Missal, Greene discusses Roosevelt's trip to the isthmus, but she notes that negative publicity did not end as a result. Roosevelt sent reformer Gertrude Beeks of the National Civic Federation to inspect conditions in the Canal Zone and make suggestions (based on her expertise in corporate welfare) for improvement. Beeks found much to praise, but she also found much wanting. Her call for a labor commissioner was not heeded, but her visit resulted in reforms such as drying sheds, lower commissary prices, and the establishment of women's clubs. It did not affect the racial hierarchies of the Canal Zone because these had not struck her as a problem. In summing up the episode, Greene concludes that administrators had sought to create a "progressivism for the world," but insofar as they created a utopia, it only became apparent in contrast with the dystopia of Panama.

The American-controlled Canal Zone was highly permeable. Canal workers passed easily from the ten-mile-wide Canal Zone to Panama and back. Many workers preferred to live in Panama so as to escape official scrutiny and regulation; U.S. soldiers and marines shared the preference for Panama's entertainment districts, known for their saloons and brothels. It is not easy to uncover the on-the-ground relations between canal workers and Panamanians in these border cities, but Greene provides enormously illuminating insights in a chapter on the 1912 Cocoa Grove riots. Greene sets the context for these (and later) conflicts by reviewing the history of U.S. military interventions into Panama

prior to 1904 and the subsequent efforts to control Panamanians via governmental advisers and public health inspectors. The Panamanian policemen who figured largely in the riots had their own particular grievances, having to do with the humiliations of being disarmed and subjected to U.S. supervision. For their part, the U.S. soldiers who clashed with the Panamanian police in raucous Fourth of July celebrations felt that their privileged standing as white men and representatives of the United States was on the line. The result was a violent explosion that, according to Greene, "profoundly challenged the image of the United States as an effective, beneficent, and peaceful power on the Isthmus of Panama" (p. 333).

The utopians got the last word, however, in the 1914 Panama-Pacific International Exhibit. Coinciding with the outbreak of war in Europe, it presented the United States as a benevolent technological force. It did so most notably in a mechanical model of the canal. Like other exhibits, the scale model erased the histories of those who had built the canal and who were, in many cases, in the process of being repatriated or seeking plantation work elsewhere in Central America.

This book makes an important contribution to the history of U.S. empire by approaching it through the lens of labor. In Greene's compelling rendering, the U.S. presence in Panama was far more than a matter of contestation between nations; it was also a racialized struggle for dominance between managers and workers. This finding leads to questions of the wider significance of the Panamanian case. Like Missal, Greene sees Panama as a model, but not so much a utopian one as a template for "how to exercise power" (p. 367). Yet if it was a model, it was also the result of prior experiences, not all of them located in the United States, and some stretching back to earlier U.S. railroad building efforts and French undertakings on the isthmus. Furthermore, just as domestic Progressivism helped determine Panamanian policies, the larger reach of U.S. empire at the turn of the twentieth century also made its mark on the Canal Zone. Greene is sensitive to this wider context—recognizing, for example, that many of the U.S. workers in Panama had prior experience in Cuba, Puerto Rico, and the Philippines—but her work suggests the value of further mappings of the circuits that passed through Panama.

As for the typicality of the Canal Zone, Greene finds that it differed from other sites of U.S. empire around the world because it was cut off and distinguished from the Republic of Panama. Yet as an enclave controlled for much of the construction period by a military officer, Panama seems a harbinger of the U.S. bases that came to dot the globe later in the twentieth century. The massive engineering works undertaken in Panama may make it seem exceptional, but more attention to the labor of U.S. armed forces and that of the Panamanians affected by the U.S. presence may reveal ways in which it was not so unusual after all.

Greene's book concludes with an epilogue that covers the 1977 treaties that eventually placed the canal in

Panamanian hands and the heated opposition these elicited within the United States. In the end, her work powerfully counters the sentiment that "we bought it, we paid for it, it's ours" (p. 373) by revealing that the Panama Canal was never a strictly U.S. enterprise and

by prompting reflection on whether the ability to acquire something necessarily makes its purchase just.

KRISTIN HOGANSON
University of Illinois,
Urbana-Champaign

THOMAS J. SUGRUE. *Sweet Land of Liberty: The Forgotten Struggle for Civil Rights in the North.* New York: Random House. 2008. Pp. xxviii, 666. $35.00.

Seeing the reviews of Thomas J. Sugrue's epic study of the civil rights movement in the North in the *New York Times* and *Washington Post*, I felt we had finally made it. After more than a decade of scholarship by historians including Adina Black, Martha Biondi, Matthew Countryman, Jack Dougherty, Johanna Fernandez, Douglas Flamming, Dayo Gore, Patrick Jones, Peniel Joseph, Matthew Lassiter, Annelise Orleck, Wendell Pritchett, Brian Purnell, Robert Self, Josh Sides, Clarence Taylor, Quintard Taylor, Heather Thompson, Craig Steven Wilder, and Komozi Woodard, a book providing a mountain of evidence on the varied battles and myriad figures of the northern civil rights movement along with extensive documentation of racial injustice and segregation in the North had commanded the attention of the *Times* and the *Post*.

The disquiet apparent in the newspaper reviews seemed to be evidence of the significant intervention that Sugrue's book was making and the important shift that an examination of the northern movement requires to our understandings of the postwar period. The reviewers' criticisms seemed to stem partly from their desires to hold onto a much simpler tale of postwar America with recognizable "good guys" (moral, upstanding southern blacks and their northern white allies) and "bad guys" (racist southern whites and alienated northern blacks) and decisive happy endings (the 1964 Civil Rights Act, the 1965 Voting Rights Act, the 2008 election of Barack Obama). Sugrue's text, however, forces us to move past a morality tale of social change to a more sober examination of the nation's race problem. In the midst of a presidency being hailed by pundits as "post-racial" and in an age awash in public celebrations of the civil rights movement (including the Martin Luther King Jr. memorial on the National Mall) that include no recognition of northern-based activists, *Sweet Land* is a book needed now more than ever. (I choose to shorten the book's title in part to evoke Toni Morrison's use of Sweet Home in *Beloved*—to get at the northern feign of racial innocence captured by Gunnar Myrdal and quoted by Sugrue in the introduction: "The social paradox of the North is exactly this, that almost everybody is against discrimination in general but, at the same time, almost everybody practices discrimination in his own personal affairs" [p. xv].)

Sweet Land begins in the 1930s and 1940s, highlighting the importance of the black Left and its white allies

in raising the intertwined issues of jobs and racial justice during the Great Depression and World War II years. It moves through the heroic period of the civil rights movement with an examination of the many movements in northern cities and towns that grew up alongside their more famous counterparts in Nashville, Birmingham, Jackson, and Montgomery. It then traces the various outgrowths of Black Power and militant protest in the late 1960s and 1970s. The book proceeds with thematic chronology through some of the key battle issues of the northern movement: jobs, housing, public accommodations, education, policing, and public assistance.

Sugrue is strongest in his handling of the variety of places whose movements he chronicles throughout the text. Like a master juggler, he does not just detail struggles in Detroit, Philadelphia, New York, and Chicago but also adds dozens of small cities, suburbs, and towns (schools in New Rochelle, New York; interracial housing developments in Deerfield, Illinois; lunch counters in Wichita, Kansas; pools in Cleveland, Ohio), thereby showing the dramatic sweep of the movement for racial justice across the entire United States. For anyone who might think the actions of Harlem mothers who kept their kids home in 1958 to protest New York's segregated schools were anomalous, Sugrue shows us parent boycotts in Long Branch, New Jersey, and walkouts in Hempstead, New York. He also reminds us that the move for community control in New York City in the late 1960s looks much different after acknowledging the longstanding movement for desegregation and educational equity headed by black mothers who had been thwarted time and again in the city.

One of the best chapters, "No Place for Colored," begins with Martin Luther King Jr.'s experience of being denied service in a restaurant in New Jersey in 1950 and chronicles the segregated nature of public accommodations in the North. The chapter offers a devastating rebuttal to the idea that the desire to segregate and the fear of race-mixing was a southern compulsion. "For colored only" signs were not needed at many pools, beaches, amusement parks, and movie theaters across the Northeast, Midwest, and West Coast for black patrons to be barred from these establishments. Sugrue also shows the ways in which local, state, and federal officials "mixed the gravel of racism into the mortar of public policy" (p. 203) regarding schools, housing, jobs, and public services—a stark reminder that the racism imbedded in these policies was not an accidental flaw but rather a constitutive element of New Deal and Veterans Administration home loans, the drawing of school and electoral district boundaries, and the parceling out of government contracts, jobs, and public assistance. The book takes issue with the distinction between northern "de facto" segregation and southern "de jure" segregation, tracing the work of activists like black lawyer Paul Zuber who litigated many northern school cases. Zuber had his first major win in 1961 in New Rochelle when Federal Judge Irving Kaufman (who had ordered the Rosenbergs' executions a decade earlier) sided with the plaintiff's case challenging New Rochelle's unequal schools. Judge Kaufman contested the government's legal justification of "neighborhood schools," which "cannot be used as an instrument to confine Negroes within an area artificially delineated in the first instance by official acts" (p. 197). Sugrue persuasively argues that the cheaper the change, the more likely it was to happen—so northern public accommodations desegregated but on the whole schools and housing did not. One exception was welfare rights, and Sugrue includes a marvelous section on the campaign by poor women to open up public assistance, which helped reduce black poverty rates in the 1960s and 1970s.

Sweet Land captures a fifty-year chronology of the nation's Second Reconstruction (incomplete the first time not only in the South but throughout the nation) and the indefatigable nature of activists of varying ideology who, year after year, decade after decade, continued to press for equality and justice in the promised land of the North. In one twenty-page stretch, Sugrue describes the political philosophies of Urban League president Whitney Young, Nation of Islam leader Elijah Muhammad, and former communist and reparations advocate Queen Mother Moore. He is particularly adept at analyzing what people conceived of doing rather than falling into the familiar trap of writing about what they should have done. Resisting the recent tendency to commemorate not-angry activists (as in the public funerals of Rosa Parks and Coretta Scott King), Sugrue is not afraid to show the considered and considerable reasons behind many organizers' outrage. A number of them held allegiances to communism, racial separatism, or armed self-defense—ideologies more difficult for public celebration (and national mythology) than the life of a tired seamstress who refused to give up her seat on a bus.

Unfortunately Sugrue does not use this history of northern struggle to rethink the stories of the period that we assume we already know (Rosa Parks, for instance, also believed in self-defense and spent more than forty years fighting northern injustice from her Detroit apartment). He does not show us the African American riot in Birmingham in May 1963 after segregationists bombed the Gaston Motel where King and other Southern Christian Leadership Conference (SCLC) members were staying—an incident that pro-

vides an interesting counterpoint to the northern riots of the mid-1960s and that factored into President John F. Kennedy's endorsement of the Birmingham agreement the next day. We never see the parallels between the difficulties the SCLC encountered in Albany, Georgia, in 1962 and in Chicago in 1966 (and the ways in which officials in both cities reneged on their promises, drawing little national outrage of the sort the firehoses and police dogs in Birmingham did). We avoid reckoning with how Congress passed the 1964 Civil Rights Act only after its northern sponsors deliberately exempted northern schools by stipulating that " 'desegregation' shall not mean the assignment of students to public schools in order to overcome racial imbalance." We miss King being called a communist in 1964 for his opposition to California's Proposition 14, whose passage (which would overturn the state's recently passed fair housing law), he argued, would be "one of the most shameful developments in our nation's history." Nor do we see his attack on official claims of "surprise" surrounding the Watts Riots, given the conditions in Los Angeles and white intransigence to the demands of civil rights activists there. The book includes no analysis of how the New Right's allegiance to "taxpayer rights" and "law and order" and opposition to "forced busing" and "government interference" which gestated in the campaign around Proposition 14 and Ronald Reagan's election as governor in California eventually became the lexicon of conservatism in the South.

Sugrue's book provides much detail of the various battlegrounds of the northern struggle but does not always take enough time to step back and consider the wider canvas. While its subtitle highlights the "forgotten struggle for civil rights in the North," it does not fully explain how, even at the time, the northern movement was obscured. The idea of the South and the movement unfolding there—and its presumed *difference from* the North—served as a constant reference point that bedeviled northern activists in the 1940s, 1950s 1960s and 1970s. The obfuscation of the northern freedom struggle happened by design, not oversight, in part because of a strategic response by public officials and northern residents at the time to deny black grievances. In cities across the North, public officials regularly refuted black demands with the claim that "this is not the South" and expressed their shock at rising militancy and urban uprisings in the mid 1960s—all while willfully forgetting decades of civil rights struggles in their own cities that had produced negligible change.

Deep into the book, Sugrue zeroes in on northern claims of racial innocence: "[R]acial liberalism did bequeath to suburban whites a new language of color blindness that allowed them—despite the long history of deliberate racial exclusion in housing—to claim that they had overcome their racist past and to profess their innocence" (p. 248). But he does not fully explain how this process worked. Indeed, by the 1960s, there was a growing incentive for white northerners to support change in the South while resisting civil rights movements in their own backyards. As they viewed the public support of racial segregation as the distasteful purview of southern racists, "culture of poverty" discourse provided a socially acceptable rhetoric to harness many northern whites' opposition to housing, school, and job desegregation. Unlike many of their southern counterparts who defended segregation in the 1950s and early 1960s, northerners celebrated "colorblindness," were "surprised" by black anger, but still maintained school systems where the pupils and the resources were deeply segregated. To explain these discrepancies, they cast African American and Latino youth as "problem students" whose behavior (along with their parents) hampered their educational success— and framed their resistance to desegregation through a language of "neighborhood control," "taxpayer's rights," "free enterprise," and "forced busing." Such a frame proved to be a supple and effective means of thwarting the large-scale desegregation of schools or housing in the urban North. It continues to have currency today.

Deriving partly from the mid-century sociological theories of E. Franklin Frazier and Gunnar Myrdal (and gaining further prominence with the 1965 Moynihan Report), this culturalist formulation cast "northern blacks" as undone by the structural landscape of northern cities and untethered from the values of religion, family, and community that anchored southern black communities. The phrase "northern blacks" thus came to signify a different kind of black community from those in the South, one now hampered by dissolution and dysfunction. Arguing that the structures of American racism and urban political economy produced black cultural responses that led to educational and job underattainment, many white liberals, with support from some black middle-class leaders, sponsored programs addressing juvenile delinquency, job readiness skills, and cultural remediation to facilitate black educational and economic attainment. They could thereby claim attention to racial concerns while maintaining that educational, housing, and job structures in these cities were not discriminatory.

Attempting to counter this discourse of cultural pathology, northern civil rights activists regularly pointed out the similarities between their actions and those of the southern movement. They stressed the righteousness of the southern struggle not only because they were inspired by the bold actions taking place there but also because they were trying to demonstrate the national character of racial inequity and to challenge the cultural frame that rendered the problems of their own communities so very different from southern ones. Indeed, highlighting the moral urgency of Southern battles became, for many northern activists, a way to demonstrate the righteousness of their own struggles.

This cultural paradigm also helped shape the very different way that the press covered southern and northern civil rights struggles. Northern movements garnered quite a bit of media coverage (even on the front page) but were treated as episodic (individual events rather than as a cohesive movement) and often described less righteously (as "protests," "disturbances," or "clashes"). While many young journalists like Howell Raines, Claude Sitton, and David Halberstam built their reputations by chronicling the southern movement, much of the celebrated journalism about the North took its cues from a new wing of urban sociology that sought to plumb the depths of black ghetto culture. Because a sharecropper could occupy a place of dignity in the American imagination that a welfare mother did not, a very different story of race in the North emerged in the nation's top newspapers.

The previous observations are not meant to detract from the importance of Sugrue's book. *Sweet Land* provides an opening for a much broader discussion of race and democracy in postwar—and even "post-racial"—America. Let us hope that we are listening.

JEANNE THEOHARIS
Brooklyn College

Reviews of Books

METHODS/THEORY

NANCY G. SIRAISI. *History, Medicine, and the Traditions of Renaissance Learning.* (Cultures of Knowledge in the Early Modern World.) Ann Arbor: University of Michigan Press. 2007. Pp. ix, 438. $75.00.

Medicine has always had a historical component. A patient's history has been an essential part of diagnosis, and nowadays long-term population trials chart changes across time whilst the more esoteric subject of evolutionary medicine brings history into science and medicine. In the early modern period, as Nancy G. Siraisi makes clear in this original and scholarly study of medical men and history writing, history was even more important for learned medicine, the medicine taught in the universities. For many physicians classical medicine held the key to medical knowledge. It had been corrupted, they argued, by the Arabs and then in medieval Europe. In the sixteenth century it was in the process of being retrieved by humanist scholarship. Within this framework Siraisi has brought into focus a number of medical men ranging from the well known such as Gerolamo Cardano and Geronimo Mercuriali to the relatively obscure Dr. Peter Memm of Rostock whose commentary on the Hippocratic *Oath* "supplied the adolescent Hippocrates with a whole curriculum of studies," even though Memm admitted that he had no evidence for his conjectures (p. 84).

Siraisi has looked at two types of history writing produced by early modern learned physicians: histories that have medicine as their subject and non-medical history. Siraisi's awareness of the developments in the writing of history and how they influenced physicians is a major strength of her book. For instance, the move from medieval chronicles and hagiography to classical models of history retrieved and then further developed by humanists such as Jean Bodin made history more of a research activity based upon inquiry. However, history still served to provide moral examples. Although, as Siraisi points out, the physician Cardano was ambivalent about the value of historical exemplarity. In his view what created history were the hidden "treacheries . . . corruption of ministers favourites . . . ancient enmities, hatreds" (p. 155). These were not good exemplars. He believed that historians, such as Herodotus, could be biased liars. Cardano used history to provide

examples, but he did so with a skepticism that emphasized their secular nature and, to use a word that recurs in Siraisi's book, their "particularity." Case histories from the past needed verification, while Cardano's encomium on the noble origins of medicine was tempered by his recognition of the avarice of some of its practitioners. Moreover, Cardano's sense of history was made more complex by his acceptance of the relativity of value judgments, thus making any moral examples to be learned from history even more debatable.

Some well-known topoi are discussed by Siraisi. For instance, the issue of whether the human body had changed over time, a critical question given Andreas Vesalius's criticism of Galen's observational anatomy, is given new life by relating it to the historiographical views of the participants in the debate. Anatomy in Gabriele Fallopio's view progressed through the accumulation of knowledge, whilst Vesalius had argued that he was going back to a time before Galen when anatomy and medicine were perfect and had then deteriorated. Here, history helps to justify new particularities and *autopsia*, seeing for oneself, which as Siraisi shows throughout the book also became part of the evolving nature of history writing.

The learning in this book is immense and is put to good use. We are shown how the political and cultural contexts in Paris, Milan, Rome, and Vienna influenced the work of medical writers. Different types of history are presented to the reader; the enthusiasm for collecting material objects, antiquities, was one such type, which is often ignored. Siraisi shows how ancient remains helped Mercuriali to reconstruct classical gymnastics whilst still giving priority to textual evidence. In Rome Andrea Bacci in *Del Tevere* (1599) wrote that the flooding of the Tiber could be prevented by using ancient techniques. He tried to recreate them by examining the remains of locks and by taking on board the "experiences" contained in ancient texts.

Vienna provides a setting for some of the non-medieval history written by physicians. The imperial court was central to the work of Johannes Cuspinianus (1473–1521), Wolfgang Lazius (1514–1565), and Johannes Sambucus (1531–1584); the last two were appointed imperial *historici*, whilst Cuspinianus was a diplomat as well as poet, professor of medicine, and historian. Their histories served the interests of the

court: Cuspinianus's biographical studies of the Cae-
sars both ancient and modern (with the patriotic declaration that Charlemagne was not a Gaul but a Frank
and that France had never possessed the empire), Lazius's histories of Austria and its nobility, and Sambucus's
editions of histories of Hungary. As with the rest of the
book, the Viennese chapter is immensely rich in detail
and context, so that the personal politics, the intellectual contexts, and political history of the time are all
presented to the reader, as when Hugo Blotius, the imperial librarian, implicitly accused Sambucus, an invet-
erate collector of manuscripts, of not returning to the
library the famous sixth-century Anicia Juliana codex of
Dioscorides that had recently arrived in Vienna.

Historians of medicine and intellectual historians will
enjoy reading Siraisi's book. She relates the medical
histories of physicians to early modern trends and debates in medicine, for instance, the different *fortuna* of
Hippocrates and Galen or the question of whether
Egypt was the true origin of medicine. Moreover, the
intellectual history of history writing is put into its social
and cultural contexts, and this broadening of intellectual history is something that is much to be welcomed.
All in all, this is an outstanding book.

ANDREW WEAR
*Wellcome Trust Centre for the History of Medicine,
University College London*

ANDRÉ TURMEL. *A Historical Sociology of Childhood:
Developmental Thinking, Categorization and Graphic Visualization.* New York: Cambridge University Press.
2008. Pp. xii, 362. Cloth $110.00, paper $39.99.

André Turmel's book provides a valuable account of
the study of childhood from 1850 to 1945. The subtitle
indicates the main themes. According to Turmel, there
emerged across the period studied a scholarship of
childhood that defined normal childhood as progress-
ing or developing sequentially through a series of age-
graded stages from birth to adulthood. He indicates
that there was a "historical seizure" of the study of
childhood by developmental thinking, with developmental thinking becoming the dominant approach for
understanding and acting upon children.

Turmel states that interest in observing children and
in studying uniform stages of development existed
among the Enlightenment thinkers of the eighteenth
century. During this period and during the nineteenth
century, scholars observed individual children, often
their own, and documented individual changes occurring in various aspects of physical stature and behavior.
In the second half of the nineteenth century a new
methodological emphasis emerged that focused on the
collection of information about very large numbers of
children. This research emphasized a population approach to the study of childhood and the reporting of
information about aggregates rather than individuals.
Turmel reports that these studies produced extensive
data about many aspects of childhood, including physical and mental measurements. One result of these
large data collections was the production of numerous
tabulations, graphs, and charts describing childhood.

According to Turmel, the emphasis on statistical regularities led to thinking about the matter of normalcy,
with the normal child being defined in various ways.
Central to normalcy was the idea of a population average. The concept of normalcy was also expanded from
the idea of average to include the ideas of healthiness
and acceptability. An element in this description of normal childhood was the association between age and
physical and mental attributes. This emphasis on age
was followed by a division of childhood into a series of
sequential stages, or a developmental trajectory, that
led from birth to the achievement of adulthood. Such
trajectories of change became seen as normal child development, forming developmental standards, with
some children identified as precocious and others as
slow in their development. According to Turmel, by the
1930s such developmental thinking was the master
framework for thinking about and dealing with children. In the last part of the book, Turmel discusses several convincing critiques of developmental thinking.
The critiques focus on several problematic assumptions
of the developmental approach: that it ignores history
and culture; that it is individualistic; that it is universalistic; that it is teleological; and that it assumes a natural biological process.

Turmel's documentation of the influence of developmental thinking in the study of children and the changes
individual children experience across their lives parallels research showing the power of developmental
thinking in the study of a different kind of change—
societal-level change across historical rather than individual time. Several studies have demonstrated the
dominance for at least two centuries of developmental
thinking in analyses of sociohistorical change (see Robert Nisbet, *Social Change and History* [1969]; Maurice
Mandelbaum, *History, Man, and Reason: A Study in
Nineteenth-Century Thought* [1971]; Arland Thornton,
*Reading History Sideways: The Fallacy and Enduring Im-
pact of the Developmental Paradigm on Family Life*
[2005]). The parallels between the history of thinking
about individual-level change and about societal-level
change are fascinating and demonstrate the overwhelming power of developmental models in the history of scholarly research concerning various types of
change.

Turmel provides an important account of the history
of the study of childhood and the powerful role of developmental models in that history. From my perspective, the main limiting feature of the book is its focus
on the period from 1850 to 1945. Turmel acknowledges
that many elements of the story exist in the writings of
the eighteenth century, but he does not systematically
investigate how the ideas and assumptions of that period were used and modified in subsequent periods.
Also, I found myself wanting more information about
the period after 1945. While the study of childhood in
psychology is still often labeled as developmental psychology, there has been an abandonment of many of the

developmental assumptions. Perhaps the author will extend his considerable talents to future books about the periods before 1850 and after 1945.

ARLAND THORNTON
University of Michigan

MURRAY G. MURPHEY. *Truth and History*. Albany: State University of New York Press. 2009. Pp. x, 213. $60.00.

ROBERT F. BERKHOFER, JR. *Fashioning History: Current Practices and Principles*. New York: Palgrave Macmillan. 2008. Pp. xi, 270. $84.95.

Both of these books, each written by a historian about the writing of history, aspire to keep the profession on the straight and narrow. Each champions the centrality of evidence to the enterprise, but each sees the enterprise differently. For Murray G. Murphey, developing causal explanations, which he takes to be about "how and why events and actions took place" (p. 47), is what matters. For Robert F. Berkhofer, Jr., the enterprise has to do with "producing facts about past persons, their ideas and actions, their experiences and institutions, and the events involving them" (p. 24). Readers may be skeptical about just how narrow these interests are if they are to do justice to the field. Be that as it may, such concerns should not prevent one from reading the books on their own terms. For both authors, those terms lead into philosophical underbrush as they strive to establish the key distinctions they think they need to ground their core theses.

Bertrand Russell famously declared in 1913 that "causation . . . is a relic of a bygone age, surviving, like the monarchy, only because it is erroneously supposed to do no harm." That view was shared by many philosophers of science in the twentieth century who followed Carl Hempel in treating causal explanation as no more than an incomplete sketch of what really counts as explanation, accounts grounded on laws. Murphey understands that the challenge this view poses is to provide a robust account of causation that stands apart from the notion of lawhood. In his book, he valiantly (if impatiently) marches the reader through the alternatives in play in the literature. I say "impatiently" because when he is done, he throws up his hands and declares the he "has no idea what causation is, and as far as I can see, no one else does either" (p. 60). Unbowed though, he goes on to defend three ways in which we can collect evidence of causation at work: regularities, the application of John Stuart Mill's methods of similarity and difference, and what Murphey calls "counterfactual truths" but what I would prefer to think of as "robust counterfactual claims." Murphey then appeals to Charles Sanders Peirce's account of abductive reasoning: to the extent that positing a cause is implicated in the best explanation of such evidence, we have reason to believe in the existence of that cause. I am broadly sympathetic with this line of argument, even if there are disquieting aspects to how Murphey gets there.

I am also sympathetic with Berkhofer's interests. The late (great) historian, Timothy W. Mason, used to talk about striving to understand the "horizon of possibility" of historical actors. Even if you eschew the *"eigentlich"* in Leopold von Ranke's realist dictum about history (*"wie es eigentlich gewesen ist"*), it seems to me that philosophers of history pay far too little attention to the challenge of constructing the view from the inside when it comes to constructing the past. Unfortunately, however, Berkhofer gets off on the wrong foot when he relies on the philosophical distinction between methodological individualism and methodological holism. The idea that group behavior (or collective institutions) cannot be reduced to the sum of the actions of the individuals that make up that group was perhaps the defining point of contention in late-nineteenth and early twentieth-century debates about whether the social sciences and the natural sciences shared a common methodology. But the distinction needs to be handled with care. Berkhofer writes that "individualism asserts . . . the primacy of the individual in determining what happens in human affairs, while holism declares the dominance of the social whole in explaining human affairs" (p. 57). He goes on to classify historical accounts on this basis between those that rely on individual consciousness and voluntary action in contrast to those that rely on a conception of society that is taken to shape the "reality of the various lives within it" (p. 58). Puzzlingly, Berkhofer deploys this distinction to ground different methods in history only to assert that in fact "scholars in practice attempt to avoid the dilemmas posed by individualism and holism by seeking some middle way" (p. 61). That does not necessarily make the appeal to the holism-individualism distinction a wild goose chase. But does the distinction enhance our appreciation of historical practice in the "middle"? I suspect not, because Berkhofer's approach is too insensitive to the variety of questions that interest historians and how dependent historical method is on those questions. The tension between individual autonomy and more collective explanations is thus contextually dependent. I have another reservation about Berkhofer's paradigm as well. To associate methodological individualism with the individual as an autonomous agent is to confuse a methodological claim with a substantive claim. A crowd may be no more than the sum of the individuals that make it up, but that is not inconsistent with the fact that people are at risk to lose their autonomy in crowds. This is not a matter of holism; rather it is a psychological fact about individual action in the presence of (many) other individuals.

There is much more in these ambitious books that I have not touched on. Murphey offers an extensive treatment of how the picture of Peircean inference to the best explanation plays out in narrative and confirmation. Berkhofer devotes much space to a discussion of exhibitions and films as both sources for the historian and loci for the practice of history. That said, I am left with a sense of disappointment by what both of these books ignore if one is to attend to the practice of historians.

History marches to two different drummers. One is our aspiration to understand how it was for "them." But this forward-looking history has to compete with our access to their world looking back and knowing what they could not know. This tension is the source of the inexhaustible creativity of the discipline, and any comprehensive treatment of the discipline is incomplete without attending to it.

MARTIN BUNZL
Rutgers University

PETER CHARLES HOFFER. *The Historians' Paradox: The Study of History in Our Time*. New York: New York University Press. 2008. Pp. xi, 215. $30.00.

This book is a rattlingly good read. I cannot recall quite so much wisdom and experience so amusingly and efficiently expressed since F. M. Cornford's *Microcosmographia Academica: Being a Guide for the Young Academic Politician* (1908). I am reminded too of W. K. C. Guthrie's foreword to the 1949 edition, stating that "the business world itself was in urgent need of its counsel" (p. ii), for this is also appropriate for Peter Charles Hoffer's chapter seven, "Historians in the Marketplace," packed with theoretically informed advice about what sells. But that chapter, just right for the youthful historian wondering about publishing, is merely one of nine that together cover an immense range and address readers at various stages of their careers.

There is fun for all, and Hoffer is proud of it: anyone who, as he does, describes David Hackett Fischer's *Historians' Fallacies: Towards a Logic of Historical Thought* (1970) as "relentless and somewhat humorless" (p. 33) has to be seriously into being amusing. Allan Megill, in a book for a readership at first sight similar to Hoffer's (*Historical Knowledge, Historical Error: A Contemporary Guide to Practice* [2007]), implicitly disagrees with Hoffer when he disclaims being able to "rise to the level of Fischer's refreshing wit" (p. ix). Who is the wittiest? Can there be a right answer? Does it matter? Yes. A simple judgment: effectiveness of presentation is crucial when teaching, and students will enjoy this book. But it is not just the pace and the anecdotes. I strongly recommend this book in any teaching context where students of history are being asked to reflect philosophically upon the nature of their subject. It may seem that there are two judgments here: first, that I like the presentation (but then my choice of comedian may be different from yours); second, that I distinguish presentation from academic content and that I like the latter, too.

However, the distinction is not that obvious. Here we may raise a philosophical question about historiography: is history anything other than what we say it is? Perhaps being amusing is a paradigmatic part of an inevitably sophistical presentation. Chapters on "Historians and the Loaded Question," "One of Us Is Lying," and "Uncertainties" will help the student begin to recognize such philosophical issues. Moreover, Hoffer seeks to help the student answer them, with the first

chapter on logic and the second on argument, and useful references to many of the great names of Western philosophy. Throughout there are well-presented, simple explanations of central issues in logical reasoning and analysis and in the theory of knowledge, with a glossary of the terms involved at the end. What is the philosophy that holds all of this together? Eventually, his editor asks that question, and Hoffer replies that "we are the stuff of history. It is that single, necessary fact that enables us to know about the past and demands that we seek out its truths" (p. 182). More helpfully, "American pragmatism fits a philosophy of history for our time" (p. 155), and the book, in being broadly consistent with that approach, stays on what is, for our current understanding, fairly safe philosophical ground. Yet it does more: works on the philosophy of history usually restrict themselves to epistemological issues, while here we have a sophisticated chapter on "The Politics of History and History in Politics" and a rather surprising theological one called "Historians Confront the Problem of Evil." If philosophy is best understood as the finding of questions rather than the finding of answers, its range alone makes this book good philosophy.

Despite these commendations, I do not trust the book. If you teach with it (and I would), ensure that you supplement it with sound philosophical material. The glossary (of bold print words in the text) is correctly introduced as follows: "The definitions below refer to the use of the words on those pages" (p. 183). No doubt they accurately reflect Hoffer's understanding of them. But his understanding of many of the terms is not that of my fellow philosophers. For example, an argument is not "a statement or series of statements," an empiricist is not "someone who reasons from inference," the problem of evil misses the assumptions that God is all-powerful and all-knowing, and pragmatism does not assert that "meaning can be based only on empirical verification." The claim that "you can always logically substitute things that are identical for one another" (p. 49) is wrong. Are these complaints mere "logic chopping," as defined in the glossary? Some may indeed be philosophical small print and irrelevant to historical understanding, but some are big.

JONATHAN GORMAN
Queen's University Belfast

CHRIS WICKHAM, editor. *Marxist History-Writing for the Twenty-First Century*. (British Academy Occasional Paper, number 9.) New York: Oxford University Press, for The British Academy, London. 2007. Pp. viii, 187. $26.95.

This volume consists of eight essays bound together by the assertion that "Marx's insights (continue) to provide powerful tools for critical historical analysis" (p. 139) even after the intellectual and political collapse of Marxism. The introduction by W. G. Runciman points out the character of this consensus in the context of a world at the beginning of the twentieth-first century fundamentally different from that in which Karl Marx wrote. "By the end of the twentieth century," he writes, "it had become a virtual commonplace that there are narratives but no master narratives, theories but no grand theories ... no authoritative prophecies of the destiny of humanity" (p. 1). Marx can no longer be read as a "prophet," but, Runciman continues, it is still possible for "Marxist historians to credit Marx with an original and fundamental insight into the process of historical change as such" (p. 2). Nevertheless there are other reasons why Marx is alleged to have lost the relevance to historiography he once had. Runciman lists three reasons that are recognized by all the contributors to this volume. The first is that Marx's teleology has lost its credibility. The second is his neglect of culture. Why, Runciman asks, "did he give so little attention to the experience of women and colonial peoples in favor of the experience of the European, white, male working class" (p. 3)? And finally, how does the apparent success of capitalism fit into Marx's scheme of historical development? All of the contributors, with the possible exception of Robert Brenner, question the applicability of Marx's historical materialism. They agree that economic phenomena, while important, or even crucial, can never be understood without the role of cultural, including ideological factors, and of political contexts, which are not a mere reflection of the economy. In short, there are class conflicts, but there are also other conflicts.

Five of the ensuing essays pursue these themes. These considerations are central to Andrea Giardina's essay on Marxist perspectives on Roman history and the nature of slavery. The same trend away from an economic interpretation of history marks Chris Wickham's essay on the role of Marxism in medieval history. But Marxist ideas, he notes, are far from dead. "Marx simply becomes a major social theorist of the past whose ideas can be drawn on, just like Malthus, or Smith, or Weber" (p. 35). Catherine Hall seeks to demonstrate through her examination of British domestic and imperial policies in the period of reform between 1827 and 1832 that historical analysis requires a conjunction of Marx's theories and those derived from "feminist, poststructuralist, and post-colonial theory" (p. 135). And since about 1970 there has been a turning away from social and economic history, Marxist as well as non-Marxist, if the distinction still holds, to cultural history, gender history, and discourse analysis. Hall, Gareth Stedman-Jones, and Alex Callinicos all conclude that the direct connection between a class and its political representatives is gone in "The Eighteenth Brumaire of Louis Napoleon" (1852). Stedman-Jones goes further and argues that Marx moved away from his earlier materialist determinism and found it impossible to move beyond the first volume of *Capital* (1867), which remained a torso of the work he had originally planned. Stedman-Jones then considers how Marxists, notably Perry Anderson and Eric J. Hobsbawm, have sought since 1989 to make sense of the twentieth century as a whole in the face of Francis Fukuyama's pronounce-

ment of the definite and final victory of capitalism over socialism.

In contrast to the other relatively short chapters, Brenner's essay covers approximately one third of the book. It offers a clear presentation of his thesis of the transition from feudalism to capitalism, which has been a center of discussion and debate among medieval and early modern historians, Marxists and non-Marxists. But Brenner goes in a somewhat different direction from the other essays. After arguing that Adam Smith's concentration on the market and Thomas Robert Malthus's and David Ricardo's focus on population, who assumed that economic behavior follows laws independent of a historical context, failed to offer adequate explanations for the transition from feudalism to capitalism, Brenner concludes: "It is at this point that historical and materialist theory come into their own ... [and] offer a way to resolve ... the problems" (p. 57). Hobsbawm's essay, "Marxist Historiography Today," is a fitting conclusion to the volume. The essay contains an emphatic critique of the relativism of postmodernist theories that argue that the limitations of language are impenetrable. In his view, "it is time to re-establish the coalition of those who want to believe in history as a rational enquiry into the course of human transformation" (p. 185).

All of the essays make strong arguments for both the continued validity of Marxist forms of historical analysis and their limitations in the face of a world that has fundamentally changed since Marx's days. The economic core, they argue, is still valid if it is integrated with non-economic factors, foremost culture and gender. Only Brenner's essay goes in a somewhat different direction, concluding that social and economic inequality remain fundamental but that a much more complex character of class and social conflict than that offered by Marx and Friedrich Engels must be taken into consideration. I think that all eight authors would agree with Hall that "the ghost of Marx is still necessarily with us. [But] Marx needs those Others [i.e. non-Marxist theories] and those Others need him" (p. 139).

These essays are excellent, and yet there are regrettable limitations. Except for the article by Giardina, translated from the Italian, they center on discussions in Great Britain; debates elsewhere are ignored almost entirely. It would have been important to deal with Marxist theory outside the Western world, in Latin America, India, and post-Mao China. The volume is also narrowly academic and surprisingly apolitical. Yet as Hobsbawm rightly points out, "Most intellectuals who became Marxists from the 1880s on, including Marxist historians, did so because they wanted to change the world" (p. 180). But this important aspect is totally missing in the volume, which is largely a debate among university-centered scholars. Badly needed is an additional volume, or rather a series of volumes, that deal with the relevance of Marxism for history writing today from a broader global and interdisciplinary perspective. The present collection would fit in well in this series.

GEORG G. IGGERS
State University of New York,
Buffalo

HENRY E. HALE. *The Foundations of Ethnic Politics: Separatism of States and Nations in Eurasia and the World.* (Cambridge Studies in Comparative Politics.) New York: Cambridge University Press. 2008. Pp. xiii, 278. Cloth $85.00, paper $27.99.

To say that this book is theoretically informed or rich would be a massive understatement. Henry E. Hale takes political science theorizing on the theme of ethnicity and politics motivated by ethnic imperatives to new heights of abstraction. Sophisticated and weighty, this is an extremely well-organized and tight presentation of the basis for organized ethnic expression and frequent human desires to live in surroundings that are increasingly administered and ruled by "people like us." Even if the reader is not an ethnicity or identity specialist and finds lengthy reviews of the extant social science literature on the essence of ethnicity to be uninteresting, he or she will find that Hale does a reasonably good job of keeping his narrative moving and accessible. More importantly, he constantly reminds his readers about his topics and conclusions. This proves helpful when one has to digest phrases about ethnic feelings being tied to "uncertainty reduction," something that seems to mean the comfort of the familiar for those who speak (or read) political science poorly.

Hale's book contains eleven chapters in two basic parts. The first four chapters review and synthesize theoretical ideas and works devoted to the phenomenon of ethnicity and separatist politics along ethnic lines. The first 100 pages mark the most challenging read for those unversed in this literature, which also discuss the need (according to Hale) to revamp theorizing on these topics. The author settles, rather convincingly according to this reviewer, on a relational theory of ethnic politics favoring separatism because an organized body politic simply finds multiethnic cooperation untenable. Why try to fit in with other constituencies when the stakes are better served through the creation of a new, more homogeneous entity (p. 62)? The second part of the book befits a typical political science model by dealing with case examples. Here readers will become more engaged, mainly because we are all familiar with various countries and their recent histories of ethnic politics and separatist movements. In boldly dealing with Eurasian case examples of Ukraine and Uzbekistan, by contrast, Hale opens himself up to the criticism that one needs to know a situation empirically via "being there" (a theme of Clifford Geertz to which he pays little heed) rather than through Ukrainian and Uzbek periodicals, locally based official and academic data, polls, or various sources of political analysis. Knowing what state or regional leaders do and to what extent they truly rep-

resent popular interests is immeasurably more problematic that Hale appears to admit.

Overall, chapter seven on framing effectively demonstrates why predictions about who would and would not side with the idea of preserving the USSR during the crucial 1990–1991 period were misguided. Framing basically means that political leaders control the expression of ethnic politics, and in the late Soviet context this means that they either helped manipulate popular expression to preserve relations with the USSR or to break from it completely. Based on Cold War assessments, the general thinking proceeded as follows: Ukrainians are much like Russians—sharing similar languages, customs, economies—and would tend to side with continuation of the Union whereas Uzbeks, who are dissimilar to Russians in terms of language, religion, culture and who have felt oppressed by the Russians' chauvinistic attitudes, would opt out of any union if given the chance. Of course, the opposite turned out to characterize both cases, and Hale intelligently shows why with reference to historical events and the positions and developments of both territories and peoples within the Soviet context. Furthermore, there also has long been a virulent, anti-Soviet Ukrainian exile or émigré literature that should have disabused any prognosticator long ago of the idea that Ukrainians would act in any other way than separatists if given the chance to voice their feelings. Then again, students of the Soviet Union know that Ukraine is an enormous country where separatist feelings cleave along regional lines, most specifically between west (hearth of separatist ambitions) and east (long peopled by Russians and representatives of other minority populations who were never pro-Ukrainian).

Where Uzbekistan positioned itself with regard to separation reflects significant political manipulation of mass interests, according to Hale's reading of Uzbek terms for notions of "independence," "sovereignty," and "strength." The analysis here (p. 156) reflects a sophisticated reading to be sure, but why should we assume, as the author seems to do, that the state leadership under President Islam Karimov worries much about how the masses will react to its decisions about crafting questions for a referendum? Perhaps this was one way in which it built its road to dictatorial power, which has now lasted for nearly two decades. However, the reader expects the presentation in this instance of more convincing evidence that such repressive elites felt such a need to meet mass expectations. What we now know from the earliest years of Uzbekistan's independence is that any perceived challenge to political authority has been met with harsh measures that rarely seem to have any effect whatsoever on the leadership's future course of action based on concerns of mass opinion.

On the whole, Hale furnishes a terrific revisionist take on ethnic politics and mass mobilization by sinking his teeth into the morass of the Soviet breakup. Curiously, today millions of ex-Soviet citizens continue debating the necessity or inevitability of this collapse. In this sense, Hale's work should serve specialists of separatist movements and the Soviet collapse partly based on ethnic motivations for many years to come. While this text may be seen as limited to political scientists, consideration of his arguments will greatly benefit other social scientists and historians of the Soviet period each time we encounter the now divisive, now beneficial aspects of separatist actors in world affairs.

RUSSELL ZANCA
Northeastern Illinois University

COMPARATIVE/WORLD

ANNE HAOUR. *Rulers, Warriors, Traders, Clerics: The Central Sahel and the North Sea 800–1500.* (British Academy Postdoctoral Fellowship Monographs.) New York: Oxford University Press, for The British Academy, London. 2007. Pp. xiv, 178. $60.00.

From different hemispheres around 900 A.D., a European and an African could have wound up in Old Cairo on the same slave dealer's block. Inspired by parallels and even links between the central Sahel and early medieval Europe, this is a brave book. In Europe's comparative light, Anne Haour synthesizes archaeological investigation of a vast zone between the tropics and the Sahara. Although written records run thin and late compared to contemporary Europe, scrutiny of medieval Africa's material culture is advancing rapidly. Africanists will make their own judgments but Haour, who has excavated in southern Niger, is impressively informed about recent work in post-Roman Europe. Medievalists readily look to their Africanist colleagues for methodological insights. Africanists, Haour argues, gain by returning the favor.

The Sahel's late medieval integration into international trading systems emerged from much older developments. Haour's argument parallels the new vision of Europe's economic development which has moved away from the 1960s consensus of sudden take-off around 1000, toward a much longer expansion beginning around 700 A.D. The intellectual itinerary is explicitly mapped. If that reads rather awkwardly, it is not unwise given the book's innovative complexity. Highlighting similarities, Haour lays out the argument for comparison. Centuries of dialectical investigation of medieval Europe prove intellectually liberating for the Sahelianist, since broad changes in medievalist opinion should encourage flexibility among Africanists. The most productive comparison between two roughly coeval societies aims not so much to prove things as to provoke interesting questions in unexpected new directions.

From Darfur to the Niger river, Haour surveys all Sahelian archaeological sites whose calibrated radiocarbon midpoint dates fall between 800 and 1500, and a few without scientific dating. An appendix tabulates some 130 radiocarbon dates and challenges chronologies derived from oral tradition and late king-lists. The Sao settlement pattern in southern Cameroon resembles northwestern Europe: growth until 1000, then stasis until settlements drop sharply between 1300 and 1500. Specialists have seen here pressure arising from environmental change driven by historical developments. I wonder about the impact on the Sahel's fragile ecology of the rapid climate change known in Europe as the Little Ice Age. And did the fourteenth-century global plague pandemic also reach the Sahel? From about 890 Arab geographers mention Gao and the Niger river downstream from Timbuktu; various tenth to twelfth-century indices signal a "boom in trans-Saharan trade." As in Europe, the trade probably began earlier, judging from ninth-century reports of slaves and gold, and the cache of fifty hippopotamus tusks collected at Gao around 850, presumably for sale to the workshops of North Africa and Spain or beyond. Long-distance trade reached this area about the same time that Europe's economy was surging back to life.

Comparative chapters summarize the title's themes in both worlds. Anything but conventional states, Europe's first great polities ruled people rather than land, which should steer Africanists away from forcing transpersonal state models onto Sahelian evidence. Identifying control with influence over people, concretized by tribute, implies boundaries more fluid than those traditional history imagines. Similarly, growing medievalist doubt whether kings launched the new trading networks (which, Haour notes, is not the same as royal eagerness to tax new wealth) may challenge Africanist opinion about Sahel rulers and rising commerce. Since social and political benefits now explain European princes' perpetual motion (rather than economic shortcomings that supposedly obliged kings to eat their way across their countries), she wonders whether a Kanem Borno ruler's movements reflect the social requirements of peripatetic rulership as well as military ambitions. The horse's role in decentralized early medieval Europe challenges the link posited between its introduction and centralized polities in Africa, e.g., among the Hausa. Horses, or at least ponies, archaeology now argues, are older in Africa than centralizing polities and medieval Magyars show that horse raiding needs no state.

Haour compares two early trading settlements: Jutland's Haithabu and, slightly later, Sahelian Marandet. Similar biases shape the evidence: archaeology uncovers some durable goods and written sources document small amounts of costly items, while the bulk of perishable wares remains invisible. Although both disciplines have debated substantivist vs. formalist economic history, in Europe the idea of exchange unrecognizably embedded in an alien culture has lost steam. Haour and the reader are struck by the parallel currents of trade, particularly slaving, that flowed from the Islamic economic powerhouse southward into the Sahel and northward into Europe. Indeed, seen from that tenth-century Cairo slave block, northwestern Europe and the central Sahel might appear parts of a related network.

"Animist" religions—the label avoids the theological

value judgment implied by the traditional "pagan"—yielded to new monotheisms. Both new faiths connected with new elites and comparable syncretisms. The better, teleologically recorded conversion process in Europe hints in the Sahel at multiple waves of Islamic influence and conversion. The new religions undermined the leaderships of locally rooted belief communities to the advantage of a transcendent god and his representatives on earth when both Boniface of Fulda and the Sahel's Muslim proselytizers felled the trees that focused animist worship.

Looking at similar questions in dissimilar but comparable societies sharpens the sense of what one cannot see directly and opens up explanations beyond those entrenched in the historiography. Notwithstanding the successes stemming from fields that increasingly narrow, broad-gauged historical investigation demands perspectives beyond our microscopic fields of expertise and the world we live in. More than just mastering the special field, twenty-first-century historians must acquire competence in areas remote from the main focus. Only that transcendent competence creates the intellectual freedom to imagine other ways of writing the history one knows best. Haour makes this argument and shows its value.

MICHAEL MCCORMICK
Harvard University

FRANCESCO BOLDIZZONI. *Means and Ends: The Idea of Capital in the West, 1500–1970.* New York: Palgrave Macmillan. 2008. Pp. viii, 221. $69.95.

An enormous historical and conceptual gap separates the claim that money is not a living plant, and therefore it is unnatural to expect it to bear fruit, from the claim that money as such is not capital. As Francesco Boldizzoni demonstrates in his engaging survey, it took Western thought a long time to free itself from the distinction between the sterility of money and the fecundity of organic nature, which had its authoritative source in Aristotle, and arrive at an understanding of how it is possible to make money out of money. The idea of capital has a technical history central to the development of economics as a discipline, and Boldizzoni ably traces the broad contours of this progress in the understanding of how money can be productive. His story encompasses late medieval and Renaissance figures, seventeenth-century Jesuits, William Petty, the Physiocrats, Adam Smith, Thomas Malthus, David Ricardo, Karl Marx, Alfred Marshall, J. B. Clark, a host of German institutionalists, and twentieth-century thinkers like John Maynard Keynes, Joan Richardson, and Robert Solow.

Alongside the history of investigations into the nature of investment, rents and interest, the various modalities of capital, and the social movement of capital, Boldizzoni is at least as concerned with the ethical dimension that has accompanied the entire development of the idea of capital. A crucial aspect of that value-laden discussion was, of course, the church's longstanding misgiving about usury. That scruple was overcome, partly through the relentless development of economic practices and partly through the arguments of Renaissance and early modern thinkers, including numerous clerics. However, concerns persisted about the proper moral relationship between profit from investment and gain from productive labor, the nexus of capital, land, and labor, Marx's concern about value and expropriation, and the relative merits of accumulation and spending. The latter issue persisted into the twentieth century, with Marshall defending the moral value of accumulation and Keynes insisting that, because in the end we all die, it is immoral to accumulate when spending would bring improvement in the here and now. (Surprisingly absent from Boldizzoni's discussion is Max Weber's treatment of the Protestant ethic, which surely holds an important place in the modern debate over the moral grounds of accumulation.) The wide range of ethical meanings attached to the notion of capital is nicely encapsulated in the book's title, namely the tension between means and ends that Boldizzoni names the "old unresolved question" (p. 151).

Using exemplary figures to trace out a long and complicated history of ideas, this book admirably achieves its main goal, which is "to put economic ideas into the context of the history of facts" (p. 6). Given the scope of the endeavor and the brevity of the book, the discussion remains surprisingly accessible, clear, and concise, despite instances of extreme compression. The tendency toward compression becomes more conspicuous and somewhat more problematic in the later chapters covering the decades from Marx to the post-Keynesians. For even as Boldizzoni tries to deal with an increasingly complicated "history of facts" that involves among other things the second industrial revolution, the economic rise of Germany and America, European imperialism, and British decline, he also has to grapple with an increasingly rarefied technical and scientistic economic discourse. A non-specialist will find these later chapters heavier going than the earlier.

Although Boldizzoni treats the various modern theories of capital evenhandedly and without much critical commentary, he signals a polemical intent in the opening pages. There, he describes the state of the science after around 1970: "Making of economics an 'imperial science', allowing a mainstream in the service of an ultraliberal ideology to prevail, removing the ethical basis of economic discourse and replacing it with operational concepts or facile epistemologies which have arisen out of the degeneracy of pragmatism have resulted in constructive debate being stifled, and the way opened to a desolate state of rudeness" (p. 6). This judgment, along with Boldizzoni's belief in the contemporary value of the history he has excavated, returns on the book's final page, where he calls attention to "how damaging it is to forsake an abundance of ideas," lose a diversity of national traditions of economic thought, and reduce economic theory to "a small number of opposing positions" (p. 169). Boldizzoni's sharp criticism would have been better supported had he delved deeper into the recent and present condition of academic economics, particularly the development of neo-liberalism. One also wishes he had expanded his observation that since the interwar period finance has tended to free itself from production "in ways that did not always operate in harmony with the general logic" (p. 161), an assertion that is particularly resonant in the wake of the economic turmoil that coincided roughly with the book's publication. The nature of that financial crisis suggests that the present idea of capital could use a tempering dose of Aristotle's seemingly naïve observation that money neither grows on trees nor is a tree. Boldizzoni's small but ambitious book reminds us that unlike the closed circularity of much recent thinking about capital, the centuries-long attempt to understand the productive power of money has been embedded in a dense web of ideas about nature, society, labor, and culture.

WARREN BRECKMAN
University of Pennsylvania

FRANCES E. DOLAN. *Marriage and Violence: The Early Modern Legacy*. Philadelphia: University of Pennsylvania Press. 2008. Pp. 235. $47.50.

The central ideal of marriage in early modern England as an indissoluble union in which man and wife became "one flesh," whether symbolically in the Christian view of matrimony or legally through the common law of coverture, in which husband and wife became one legal agent by means of the husband's "subsumption" of his wife into himself, has been documented in social and cultural histories of marriage. But while historians have often viewed the "one flesh" model as being particular to the early modern period, Frances E. Dolan argues that this figuration of marriage has a lasting legacy and informs understandings of marriage in modern America. Imported from England by America's seventeenth-century Puritan settlers, this ideal of marriage—which seems to promise a kind of equality but is riddled with contradictions, ambiguities, and, ultimately, the prospect of violent conflict—acts as a persistent drag on marriage fulfilling its potential as a meaningful union of autonomous individuals. This model of marriage creates an "economy of scarcity" in which there is only room for one "full person" rather than two individuals. Since marriage is still conceived of as a patriarchal hierarchy, for wives this means a surrendering of selfhood.

The book places center stage the relationship between the early modern English past and the American present, eschewing conventional chronology by juxtaposing the two. It aims to analyze modern marriage's burdensome early modern legacy as a means of laying the basis for change to a more equal partnership. While Dolan is always sensitive to the fact that, as social histories of early modern marriage have revealed, "couples often negotiate their relationships in ways for which legal and moral prescriptions cannot account" (p. 70), her aim is to demonstrate the cultural ties that link us to the early modern past. It is only by recognizing these, she argues, that we can "clear space" for "imagining connection" in more meaningful ways (p. 25).

Dolan begins by reading late twentieth-century evangelical Christian advice books on marriage against sixteenth- and seventeenth-century Puritan conduct books to explore the persistence of the "one flesh" model and its implications. While the fusion of individuals in marriage is meant to overcome differences between the two spouses, in fact this process whereby two become one is only accomplishable, Dolan argues, through compromise, conflict, and loss. Early modern wives were counseled to surrender their individual wills and subscribe to male headship else the union be rendered meaningless and fall apart. Such was the stranglehold of these ideas that wives trapped in dysfunctional marriages are portrayed as only becoming independent beings by either imagining their husbands dead or actually killing them. Dolan explores this aspect of marital violence by comparing seventeenth-century accounts of wives convicted of "petty treason" with modern movie portrayals of battered wives.

While the book's main focus is on the husband-wife dyad, Dolan also examines the broader context of domestic conflict by examining relations between masters and mistresses and other household subordinates. She shows how the shared duty of admonishing servants or slaves, including violent physical correction, in the early modern period simultaneously caused tension in marriages and also—by granting women some authority (a concession in the "battle for the breeches")—made it possible to begin to imagine the wife as her husband's "companion." The book ends with a discussion of the influence of early modern models of marriage on popular historical fiction, focusing on Philippa Gregory's novels about the marital travails of Tudor queens.

The resulting analysis is both challenging and provocative, and the book provides one of the most subtle and articulate studies of the early modern "one flesh" model of marriage yet published. Although the historical grounding of the work is impressive, occasionally some evidence is treated rather selectively. For example, Dolan contrasts the yoking together of unequal partners in marriage with the true union of equals in (male) friendship, suggesting that the two were viewed as qualitatively different in early modern England. Yet she does not examine the conceptualization of marriage as the "Queen of friendships" in works such as Jeremy Taylor's influential *Discourse of the Nature, Offices and Measures of Friendship* (1657). While the parallel examination of past and present is effective in illuminating overlooked continuities in understandings of marriage and its conflicts, the book's approach will not satisfy all readers. Students of early modern marriage may find its chronological experimentation frustrating, while those reading it as a political treatise for rethinking the marital union today may find its historical discussions too dense and distracting. Nevertheless, this book makes an impassioned case for historical understanding as a means of effecting political change, and as such deserves a wide readership.

DAVID M. TURNER
Swansea University

YU LIU. *Seeds of a Different Eden: Chinese Gardening Ideas and a New English Aesthetic Ideal*. Columbia: University of South Carolina Press. 2008. Pp. x, 208. $39.95.

In this searching, stimulating, but sometimes chauvinistic book, Yu Liu has compressed what are essentially two separate studies into just 200 pages and nine monochrome illustrations. He first aims to prove that in the eighteenth-century interchange between Europe and China, the leader in garden design was China. While thought provoking, his argument is flawed in two respects, to be examined shortly. However, his second theme—Chinese religion and the problems that European Christian missionaries faced when confronted by the formidable interlocking of Confucianism and Taoism—is handled with sensitive and revealing brilliance.

The first of two flaws in Liu's account of the Sino-European garden exchange is that European gardeners ignored the most important central elements of Chinese garden design while accepting China's relaxed and natural garden asymmetry. The other is that Liu is unaware of the extent to which seventeenth-century English gardeners had already anticipated the natural layouts of Chinese gardens several decades before Sir William Temple introduced the Chinese principle of *Sharawadgi* in his celebrated essay *Upon the Gardens of Epicurus: Or, of Gardening in the Year 1685*.

To take Liu's first error, he makes no mention of the central features of Chinese garden design: reverence for grotesquely shaped stones and interpenetration of house design, with miniature garden courts enclosed by living rooms and small lakes winding around wings of single-story palaces. Neither twisted stones nor interior courts made any impact on European gardens. Missing from Liu's excellent bibliography is the one recent book, Maggie Keswick's *The Chinese Garden: History, Art and Architecture* (1978), which would have provided him with the designs that he fails to analyze.

Lui's second error can be exposed by a reading of Sir Henry Wotton's *The Elements of Architecture* (1624). Wotton, a provost of Eton and a distinguished diplomat, wrote: "as Fabriques should bee *regular*, soe Gardens should bee *irregular*, or at least caste into a very wilde *Regularitie*" (p.109). One of his Etonians, John Beale, had formulated exactly the Chinese garden ideal of naturalness, urging that gardeners should never impose a plan "to any particular phantsy, but to apply unto it the best shape that will agree with the nature of ye place" (Hartlib Manuscripts, University of Sheffield, 25/6/3). Such advice might well have come straight from Taoist writing. When John Milton's description of Eden in *Paradise Lost* was published in 1667, a devoutly Christian England was assured that God's ideal garden was wild, natural, and beautiful. So when, in his 1685 essay, Temple described the superior flowing aesthetic

of Chinese gardens, it was welcomed in England, not so much as a garden innovation as a confirmation that another civilized nation was gardening in the same way.

In another excusable error, Liu claims William Kent's garden revisions for Lord Burlington at Chiswick as the first instance of an English garden on natural Chinese lines. In fact, Stephen Switzer had popularized a relaxed garden chaos of fields, lakelets, canals, avenues, and woods in his *Ichnographia Rustica: Or, the Nobleman, Gentleman, and Gardener's Recreation* (1718), and given the credit for such informal garden planning to a classical grove, which he had seen and admired in 1710 at the Duke of Shrewsbury's Heythrop in Oxfordshire. It is a romantic confusion of nymphaeum, cold bath, winding paths, and streams in damp woodland some distance from the house. Switzer described this as "the first attempt of this kind, I ever saw," adding "there is an inexpressible Pleasure in these Natural Twinings and private Walks, to a quiet, thoughtful, studious Mind" (p. 197). But neither Thomas Archer, its probable designer, nor Switzer made any Chinese connection; Italian gardens in Rome were most likely Archer's model.

Liu makes some perceptive suggestions about the classical influences behind English garden innovators like Joseph Addison and Alexander Pope, but the book's most rewarding subtext is his ruthless and detailed analysis of how Christian missionaries came up against Chinese religiosity as they tried to convert a country already possessed by two highly sophisticated and happily interlocking faiths. Confucianism had laid down wise guidelines for domestic life and political actions, while Taoism was virtually Platonic philosophy carried to its muscular logical conclusion. It explained Earth as the mirror image of Heaven and a continuum to Heaven's substance, capable of spontaneous self-regeneration, with no need for a directing God. Faced with Chinese assumptions of superiority to Western barbarism, the leading Jesuit, Matteo Ricci, steered missionary efforts away from Christ to stress the supposed links between Christian transcendentalism and the Chinese belief in an all-pervading Heaven.

Chinese gardeners never attempted to impose straight lines upon topographies that already reflected Heaven. Only sensitive readjustments to the existing lines of lakes, hills, and woods were permitted. This was exactly Wotton's "wilde *Regularitie*," urged in 1624, and the bland beauty that Lancelot Brown laid out all over England so successfully after his 1741–1751 apprenticeship as head gardener at Stowe.

TIMOTHY MOWL
University of Bristol

JESSIE GREGORY LUTZ. *Opening China: Karl F. A. Gützlaff and Sino-Western Relations, 1827–1852*. (Studies in the History of Christian Missions.) Grand Rapids, Mich.: William B. Eerdmans. 2008. Pp. xix, 364. $45.00.

The German-born missionary Karl F. A. Gützlaff (1803–1851) was an important yet controversial figure in Sino-Western relations in the second quarter of the nineteenth century. Long dismissed as an impostor and an agent of imperialism by Chinese and Westerners alike, he has been given a more balanced treatment recently, with a number of scholars pointing out his role as a cultural mediator. Still lacking was a comprehensive biography that conformed to the standards of modern scholarship. Jessie Gregory Lutz has written that biography. It is based on a vast amount of source material, which she collected in the course of over two decades, partly together with her husband, the late Rolland Ray Lutz, whose role in transcribing the handwritten German documents is acknowledged in the preface.

Lutz's biography advances the study of Gützlaff in a number of ways. First, she manages to maintain a balance between her protagonist and the overall context of Sino-Western relations. On the one hand, Lutz demythologizes Gützlaff's carefully crafted public image. Contrary to what the flamboyant missionary declared, he was not so much a daring pioneer who ventured where none had gone before, but relied on pre-existing structures and networks. On the other hand, Lutz manages to decipher Gützlaff's often enigmatic personality. Tracing his career from his childhood in Germany to his deathbed in Hong Kong, she shows that Gützlaff was a loner with a striking ability to convince, but incapable of establishing any lasting attachment to other people. This detachment was probably the key to the multiple roles he managed to fulfill: undogmatic missionary, opium dealer, spy, government employee, autodidact, incurable Romantic, somewhat patronizing "lover of the Chinese" (according to one of his pen names), and frantic worker.

Second, Lutz undertakes a careful analysis of Gützlaff's publications, especially his writings in Chinese, which have largely escaped scholarly attention. She admits the ephemeral character of Gützlaff's religious tracts, but points to some technological and stylistic innovations that he helped introduce to China, such as movable type, punctuation, influence on *baihua*, and the romanization of dialects. She also discusses Gützlaff's secular Chinese writings as a futile attempt to spread Christianity through the transmission of Western culture. Information provided by Gützlaff was digested and processed by a few open-minded Chinese scholars such as Lin Zexu, Wei Yuan, and Xu Jiyu, while the majority of the Chinese literati remained unresponsive. It was only after Gützlaff's death and a series of further military blows that Western knowledge made deeper inroads into Chinese culture.

Third, Lutz traces the web of Gützlaff's extensive and in fact transnational and transcultural relationships, which included fellow missionaries, mission officials, clerics, publicists, donors, and politicians from various European countries and the United States, as well as Chinese language teachers, catechists, and Christians. The character of these relationships varied to the extent that Gützlaff depended on them or was able to adopt a patronizing attitude (particularly vis-à-vis Chinese).

Of particular interest is Lutz's analysis of Gützlaff's connections with heterodox groups in China, such as the Taiping, although these interactions were mostly indirect.

In interweaving these different trajectories into a coherent narrative, Lutz leaves enough room for the ambivalent character and roles of Gützlaff. There is no easy way to understand a man who, on the one hand, spread a religious message based on the notion of the equality of people and served as an intellectual bridge between China and the "West" and, on the other, became an agent of imperialism. In pointing to the multiplicity, complexity, and irreducibility of Gützlaff's roles, Lutz avoids any of the oversimplifications that have characterized Gützlaff's image not only among his contemporaries but also in historical scholarship. Her analysis is probably weakest where she discusses Gützlaff's role within the missionary movement, juxtaposing the unbound, nondenominational, and experientially oriented "evangelical" type of Gützlaff with the more disciplined and institution-oriented "confessional" type. Here, she underestimates the common background and outlook shared by both varieties. And though Lutz is certainly right that Gützlaff's understanding of Christianity is still pretty much alive in Chinese house churches today, she fails to explain why this is so, especially given the fact that these churches have no historical links to Gützlaff, his native assistants, or even the Taiping. All told, however, Lutz has written a book that is much more than a conventional biography in that it addresses many fundamental problems in Sino-Western contacts in the early nineteenth century. It should therefore become a standard reference not only for mission historians but for all scholars interested in questions of cultural transfer, imperialism, and Sino-Western relations.

THORALF KLEIN
University of Erfurt

SALONI MATHUR. *India by Design: Colonial History and Cultural Display*. Berkeley and Los Angeles: University of California Press. 2007. Pp. xi, 219. Cloth $50.00, paper $19.95.

Saloni Mathur's book takes the "red-hot status of contemporary Indian art in the West" as an impetus to explore the evolution of cultural forms and cultural debates that developed out of the crucible of colonialism (p. 5). In this savvy and engaging book, Mathur offers a series of five interlocking case studies, all of which loop between India and Britain as they track the development of the craftsman, the exhibition, the oil painting, the postcard, and finally, the discourse of repatriation. These "representational phenomena," all hallmarks of modernity, helped to make India visible in the West (p. 170). To show as much, Mathur, an anthropologist who now teaches in an art history department, adeptly uses the tools of historicism, postcolonial criticism, and visual analysis as she charts the development and fracturing of these forms at three discrete yet conjoined moments: the colonial, the national, and the postcolonial.

Mathur demonstrates particular skill and panache in tracking the development of cultural forms and ideals, as well as their ironic reconfigurations and redeployments, across historical moments and geographical boundaries. This is especially evident in her delineation of the ideal of the Indian craftsman. Developed in quintessentially colonial institutions like Liberty's Department Store and the South Kensington Museum, the craftsman had a second life as an avatar of Indian nationalism, most apparent in Gandhi's use of this role. Ironically, Mathur notes, this recycling attests to the limits of liberation within a colonial dialectic of nationalism. Although it aimed to challenge colonial rule, "Indian nationalism" remained constricted by the very "conceptual frameworks that it repudiated" (p. 49). Other chapters similarly engage with cultural forms and hierarchies by placing aesthetic forms in a distinctly "global field" (p. 80). For instance, Mathur considers the development of oil painting in India against the backdrop of the travels of European artists, the rise of exhibitions, and the institutionalization of art education on the subcontinent. As with the figure of the craftsman, the aesthetic prototype of the watercolor both enabled and contained. In the later nineteenth century, the transnational movement of education and talent enabled the rise of a discrete genre of oil painting on the Indian subcontinent, yet painters found their works categorized as ethnography rather than as art at international exhibitions.

Mathur is concerned with art and craft, but she notes that both were linked inextricably to industrial regimes of education and production. The postcard, a seemingly ephemeral and essentially transnational form, enjoyed its golden age thanks to the rise of photography and the modern firm. "Mass-produced, dispersed, and always in motion," Mathur writes, "it was the quintessential traveler of the modern age" (p. 115). Industrial modernity contained and produced several ironies, as Mathur's treatment of the living village at the Colonial and Indian Exhibition of 1886 attests. There, thirty-four ethnographic subjects provided a display of craft production. In truth, Mathur points out, the alleged craftsmen at the Exhibition were inmates recruited from Agra Jail who had learned their putative crafts while in custody. No simple embodiments of craft culture, the artisans were a tribute, instead, to "the modern realities of industrialization and the perversities of prison reform" (p. 88). In a final irony, this group included the Punjabi peasant Tulsi Ram, who, in making his way to London to petition the Queen, entered the ranks of the criminal classes himself.

In her conclusion, Mathur notes that her book aims to "historicize" a set of cultural forms and epistemological debates in the service of understanding the visual and material regimes "through which our modern understandings of the Indian subcontinent have been formed" (p. 170). She expertly uses the insights of postcolonial theory to construct a usable history with great relevance to the present. In the process, she manages to offer new archival finds and new cultural arguments. Her final chapter, which discusses Buddhist relics in London, challenges our understanding of repatriation, which is often considered to be a product of the postcolonial age. Mathur cannily contravenes this orthodoxy by showing that repatriation debates began in the nationalist era, when they often took on surprising directions and made for unsuspected alliances. Largely episodic, Mathur's history is often skilful. Yet there are silences and omissions in this narrative, leaving readers to wonder what has happened in the epochs between the punctuating moments of empire, nationalism, and postcolonialism laid out herein. Similarly, the institutionally and geographically grounded narrative that is in play at the outset tends to thin on some occasions. These shortcomings may be pitfalls of the sorts of cultural studies and histories from which Mathur understandably takes her lead. Ultimately, Mathur offers us an effective, elegant, and engaging history which crystallizes the ways in which imperial exchanges gave rise to "contemporary entanglements" of a postcolonial kind (p. 6).

LARA KRIEGEL
Florida International University

MARTIN J. WIENER. *An Empire on Trial: Race, Murder, and Justice under British Rule, 1870–1935.* New York: Cambridge University Press. 2009. Pp. xiv, 255. Cloth $80.00, paper $25.99.

"British Power in India is like a vast bridge . . . Strike away either of its piers and it will fall, and what are they? One of its piers is military power: the other is justice, by which I mean a firm and constant determination on the part of the English to promote impartially and by all lawful means, what they (the English) regard as the lasting good of the natives of India. Neither force nor justice will suffice by itself." Perhaps it is no surprise that James Fitzjames Stephen, legal adviser to the government of India (1869–1873), should dignify the world of Indian legal practice in this manner. Less to be expected is the fact that distinguished historians of empire 150 years later should share something of Stephen's outlook. For Martin J. Wiener, author of this fascinating book, "Law lay at the heart of British imperial enterprise," not in India alone but increasingly throughout the colonial empire. That it did so owes much to the scholarship of legal writers themselves, not only Stephen but others such as Henry Maine and the Mills. They were outstanding members of Britain's nineteenth-century intellectual elite, constantly crossing the frontiers of law, jurisprudence, custom, anthropology, and history. All were fit subjects for detailed biographical study, as illustrated in *The Victorian Achievement of Sir Henry Maine: A Centennial Reappraisal* (1991).

In recent years, however, as even the briefest of glances at the historiography demonstrates, the perspectives of historians of law have greatly widened. General collections of essays have explored multiple themes in specific regional settings. These range from *Law, History, Colonialism: The Reach of Empire*, edited by Diane Kirby and Catharine Coleborne (2001) to *The Grand Experiment: Law and Legal Culture in British Settler Societies*, edited by Hamar Foster, Benjamin L. Berger, and A. R. Buck (2008). Colonial and postcolonial legal activities, notably relations between white settlers and "first nations," have been explored in magisterial works such as P. G. McHugh's *Aboriginal Societies and the Common Law: A History of Sovereignty, Status, and Self-determination* (2004) and Peter Karsten's *Between Law and Custom: "High" and "Low" Legal Cultures in the Lands of the British Diaspora—The United States, Canada, Australia, and New Zealand, 1600–1900* (2002). All focus in varying degrees on several central questions. What was the "rule of law," extolled by the British as a central plank in their civilizing mission? What relation did it bear to liberal ideals, above all notions of equality before the law? How was it institutionalized, and what did this mean in practice?

In addressing these issues, Wiener starts by challenging the continuing crudity of so much writing on empire: comment that ignores the diversity and ambiguity of empire, or the role and capacity of law as a force for resistance and change. He rejects polarized interpretations, the juxtaposition of celebratory accounts, and unquestioning indictments as well as exclusive talk of any single "imperial project." Wiener ranges widely, scrutinizing an imaginative selection of seven colonies—Queensland, Fiji, Trinidad, the Bahamas, India, Kenya, and British Honduras. These colonies exemplify those with a mainly non-European population as well as those where white settlers were growing in number. The book also includes a chapter on "the High Seas," bringing out the degree to which homicide was a serious issue on British ships in an ever more cosmopolitan or global naval and commercial fleet.

Looking at the critical issue of murder trials and capital punishment, Wiener asks what determined sentencing: for what reasons might one escape the extreme penalty or become a virtually certain candidate for the death penalty? While avoiding any comment on martial law, Wiener suggests that three areas of life were in particularly prone to generate cases of homicide: plantations, the armed forces, and contract labor. In each of these three areas of life, but also elsewhere, the predominance of white authority, the absence of effective or adequate supervision, and the liability (fueled by race prejudice, fear, or even sadism) to abuse any power also fed extreme colonial violence. In examining these broader themes Wiener often illuminates generalizations already familiar at least in part. At the same time, however, he offers a masterly account that brings out the great variety of colonial settings. The well-known abuses of the jury system, for example, were by no means always fatal; the possibilities of appeals could often bring out divisions in colonial society as well as hostility between civil authorities and legal officers, executive and judiciary, or legal professionals and lay antagonists, with resultant clashes in interpretations of

the law. Most cases carried with them their own ambiguities and a mass of political interests and bias. Terminology and institutionalization created confusion. Rape, for example, was rarely "rape," but more usually "wrongful confinement." The scarcity of English police and the oppressiveness of local policemen produced unusual combinations of liberality and perversity. Finally, Wiener offers a thought-provoking interpretation of the shifting influence of racism, at a peak between the 1870s and 1890s and broadly declining thereafter. This is an excellent study and will surely get the wide readership it deserves.

ANDREW PORTER
King's College London

GREGORY D. SMITHERS. *Science, Sexuality, and Race in the United States and Australia, 1780s-1890s.* (Routledge Advances in American History.) New York; Routledge. 2009. Pp. xvi, 298. $95.00.

In the last ten or so years, historians have increasingly used a global perspective when exploring the histories of settler societies. Gregory D. Smithers's argument that white identity from the 1780s to the 1890s in the United States was a fragile biological category, while in Australia it was seen as robustly transformative, is an important contribution to this body of scholarly research. By interrogating scientific theories and using focused, comparative case studies, his book shows how fluid and fickle the category of "whiteness" could be, even as it nominally united many different settler groups.

Smithers utilizes both comparative and transnational analytical frameworks. Transnational history is often seen as the successor to comparative history, but Smithers shows how well they can work together, particularly with carefully selected case studies. As he points out, "the United States and Australia featured prominently in the popular literature and international scholarly debates about the biological and cultural meaning of whiteness" (p. 1). By examining them together and not shying from the vast, often seemingly incomparable particularities of each site, Smithers offers a comprehensive discussion of the global circulation of ideas about race and reproduction. He also demonstrates how the best of comparative/transnational history is anything but neat.

The first three chapters offer internal comparisons, exploring which of the globally circulating social, humanitarian, and scientific ideas were drawn upon by white Australians and Americans. Smithers covers a wide range of ideas, discussing phrenology, assimilation, biological absorption, debates about human evolution, ideas of "good breeding," and the fixity of racial types. He firmly situates these ideas against the social changes and events that occurred before and during their formation. For historians of Australian colonialism, the first section's examination of biological absorption (whitening through interracial "breeding") in the early years of Australian colonies will be particularly appealing. Only a few Australian historians have explored biological absorption in the lead-up to the "White Australia" policy of 1901, and Smithers's work is thus helping to fill a significant gap in the literature. Our understanding of the origins of the effort to create a "white" Australian nation will be enhanced by Smithers's global argument about the importance of reproduction to the development of "whiteness" in settler colonies.

The second part of the book details Australian and U.S. ideas of whiteness in specific locations, showing how "Whiteness . . . was defined in historically and temporally specific settler colonial contexts, just as an 'indian,' 'Negro,' and Australian 'native' were defined and redefined over time and in different geographical locations" (p. 192). This section also offers a "subaltern perspective," showing how Cherokee, mixed-race Indians, and slaves responded to hardened racial boundaries and efforts to control their sexual reproduction. Smithers was not as successful in locating "voices" of Aborigines, which are rarer in part because of the fewer Aborigines with a European education and in part because of the unforgivable violence directed at the Aboriginal population. Undeterred by the difficulty of matching his American indigenous "voices" with similar written Australian sources, Smithers utilizes missionary materials to provide his Australian account. Indeed, a welcome feature of this book is the attention it pays to the importance of missionaries to the development of Australian and North American colonial practice.

Smithers ultimately argues that "ideas about humankind's place in nature and reproductive sexuality were intimately entwined in a transnational debate about the importance of racial categories to social order" (p. 192). These ideas were expressed in very different ways. In Australia, "evolutionary theories transformed the idea of a well-bred individual into a quest to breed out color" (p. 87). In the United States, "whiteness came to represent a fragile biological category that needed legal protections to prevent the dilution—or even extinction—of the imagined purity of the white races" (p. 163). Smithers convincingly traces these diverging paths from the origins of each nation through the development of their vastly different social orders in the eighteenth and nineteenth centuries.

In his acknowledgements, Smithers calls his work "a very strange dissertation, and now a very odd book" (p. xv). Smithers might not have felt that way if it had been written in Australia, where histories that look outward and across national borders are becoming more and more common, perhaps more so than in the United States. Histories that truly look and compare beyond national borders such as this one are rare. The insights Smithers draws from such a study show what a pity this is. This book makes contributions to the growing field of comparative and transnational histories that see the story of imperialism as a global phenomenon, has much to say to the troubled area of whiteness studies, and

offers a shining example of how to do comparative/transnational history.

KATHERINE ELLINGHAUS
Monash University

VAL COLIC-PEISKER. *Migration, Class, and Transnational Identities: Croatians in Australia and America*. (Studies of World Migrations.) Urbana and Chicago: University of Illinois Press. 2008. Pp. xii, 252. $45.00.

In this book, Val Colic-Peisker examines different patterns of integration into host societies and forms of transnationalism among members of two waves of Croatian immigration to the city of Perth in Western Australia: rural Dalmatians who arrived in the 1950s and 1960s and became blue-collar workers in local manufacturing and services, and urban professionals who followed in the 1980s and 1990s and whose high-power human capital allowed them to maintain or improve their socioeconomic status in the receiver country. Based on her collection of ethnographic data, Colic-Peisker contests theories of ethnicity and immigrant transnationalism that inform current immigration research in the United States, a model implicitly but incorrectly presumed to apply also to other parts of the world. As she distinguishes between Perth's working-class Croatians' territorially anchored and *gemeinschaftlich* ethnic mode of membership in the host and home societies and their professional fellow-nationals' cosmopolitan or deterritorialized and "portable" identities, Colic-Peisker argues for the importance of class, understood in the Weberian tradition as market-regulated life chances based on educational credentials and skills (pp. 17–18), as the crucial factor shaping people's identities, life orientations, and forms of social participation.

Well informed about the current research agenda and theoretical debates of immigration studies (primarily in the United States), engagingly written, and with proposed arguments supported by extensive citations from interviewees, the book is an evident accomplishment. This historical sociologist also appreciated the premise of time and place specificity and, therefore, the inherent diversity of the examined social phenomena informing the analysis, and its author's attention to the temporal dimension of social and cultural life—in particular, her careful examination of how the immigrants' home-country traditions and lifestyles (chapter one) affect the transformation of the same in Australia (chapters six and seven)—both effectively combined with a theoretical interpretation of the investigated issues. The proposition of context—here, class-specific ethnic and cosmopolitan types of immigrants' transnationalism—an equivalent of sorts of the concept of "segmented assimilation" (Alejandro Portes and Min Zhou, "The New Second Generation: Segmented Assimilation and Its Variants," 1993) recognized by the sociologists of immigration—is an additional and welcome contribution.)

The book is not without weaknesses. I note three such shortcomings. First, the subtitle is misleading. There is nothing in the study about American Croatians, and, excepting a short passage about white ethnics (pp. 80–84), the information about the general experience of immigrants in America is derived exclusively from current sociological theories. These theories can perhaps be taken as suggestive but certainly not as representative of immigrants' experience. My second reservation concerns the too-strong language of the author's theoretical claims vis-à-vis the empirical basis of her study. Having interviewed a mere ten men and ten women in each of the two immigrant cohorts (p. 24), Colic-Peisker's assertive conclusions about ethnocentric versus liberal-universalist value profiles of working-class and professional respondents are not very convincing when based on tabulations where an apparently impressive difference in answers to a particular question—between, say, fifty percent and thirty percent—corresponds to five and three persons (pp. 181, 187). This type of exploratory ethnographic study, based on a small and unrepresentative sample, is perfectly legitimate in qualitative social science research, but it calls for a "soft" style of narrative of the findings and tentative conclusions in the form of hypotheses or heuristic guideposts for future studies. My third complaint is Colic-Peisker's unjustified reduction of her theoretical assessment of the form and "contents" of immigrant transnationalism to one factor: class. It contradicts an elegant multilevel empirical account in chapters one through three of the transformation between the 1950s and 1990s of the immigrants' home country, Australian society, and the world in general, which clearly implies not one but a constellation of circumstances as contributing to the emergence of international migrants' "vagabond" identities, and it does not agree, either, with the idea of the inherent complexity of the social world announced in the introduction as the premise of the analysis.

Despite these reservations, Colic-Peisker's book will certainly be a good read for immigration specialists, not only in Australia but also North America and Europe, and elsewhere around the globe where migration studies are beginning to thrive.

EWA MORAWSKA
University of Essex

MICOL SEIGEL. *Uneven Encounters: Making Race and Nation in Brazil and the United States.* (American Encounters/Global Interactions.) Durham, N.C.: Duke University Press. 2009. Pp. xxii, 386. Cloth $89.95, paper $24.95.

Carmen Miranda and barely clad *mulata* women dancing samba are among the varied stereotypical images of Brazil that have circulated internationally in the twentieth century. A parallel foreign fascination has focused on Brazil's racial configurations, as historians, social scientists, and journalists have visited the continent-sized country to decipher its understandings of racial categories, identities, hierarchies, and discrimination. Numerous scholars have written comparative studies of

how these racial systems operate differently in Brazil and the United States. Most of these analyses argue for the existence of alleged all-encompassing, nationally bound social and cultural configurations of skin color and their relationship to class, status, and people of mixed races. In embarking on a self-described transnational history of interactions among North Americans, Brazilians, and Europeans that rejects this comparative methodology, Micol Seigel seeks to uncover the complex webs of interchange that were spun in the 1920s as Afro-Brazilians sought to occupy larger political, cultural, and social spaces in the decades after abolition. As the title of this broadly conceptualized study proclaims, power relationships framed these exchanges, placing Brazilians, and particularly Afro-Brazilians, on an unequal playing field with those with whom they interacted at home and abroad.

Drawing widely from postmodern, postcolonial, feminist, diasporic, and queer studies, Seigel approaches this topic through a bold use of sources, archives, and theoretical approaches, arguing quite convincingly that Afro-Brazilians played an active role in the international circulation of ideas and cultural expressions in the tumultuous 1920s. In a whirlwind tour of U.S.-produced Brazilian coffee ads, the ephemeral *maxixe* dance craze, the appropriation of jazz by Rio's musicians, and interactions between Afro-Brazilian and African American newspapers, the author documents how members of the African diaspora maneuvered through varied notions of race, skin color, and individual and national identities. At times these interactions came from traveling abroad. Riding the tide of "Negro fever," Afro-Brazilian dancers and musicians performed in Europe, promoting themselves as exotic others. When they returned to their homeland, they used elites' pro-European proclivities to affirm and legitimize their cultural creations and their own social status by pointing to the warm reception they enjoyed in centers of "civilization."

These encounters, however, did not always require individuals to cross the Atlantic or travel north to engage in cross-fertilization. Debates about race also circulated transnationally through print. Seigel examines Afro-Brazilian newspapers that flourished in the 1920s and 1930s to show how these exchanges unfolded. Like many scholars unpacking the constructions of race in Brazil in the early twentieth century, Seigel points to discursive transformations that revolved around the nature of race, the role of Afro-Brazilians in Brazilian society, and the strategies they used to overcome discrimination. While Afro-Brazilian editors were outspoken critics of the lingering marginalization of people of color, they also embraced emergent ideas that later scholars have compacted into the code term "racial democracy" and that have been dismantled by intellectuals and activists in recent decades. Just as Afro-Brazilian entertainers used European prominence to show that racial hierarchies were "uncivilized," so, too, Afro-Brazilian writers used the emergent claim that racial discrimination was minimal in Brazil to set a standard against which to point out inconsistencies in everyday practices. Seigel deftly captures this strategy by tracking the debates in the Afro-Brazilian and African American presses about proposals for African American immigration to Brazil and the movement to erect a monument to honor the *"Mãe Preta"* (Black Mother). Despite a seemingly common diasporic strategy to attack racial discrimination and recognize the lasting legacies of slavery, however, the U.S.-Brazilian dialogue often got lost in translation.

Seigel is adamant in arguing that comparative studies about national ideological and social systems can become discursive tropes that flatten complexities and ambiguities. Among the important contributions of this outstanding study the ways it identifies international exchanges, complex circulations of people and ideas, and the ways they influenced and transformed the local. Yet, at times the author is forced somewhat uncomfortably into national comparisons, recognizing, for example, that African American newspaper editors had a uniquely different agenda and understanding of Brazil than did their Afro-Brazilian counterparts. In large part, both were shaped by distinct national narratives, agendas, and identities. The local many times took precedent over the transnational. As Seigel points out, the reified "other" could serve as a useful political strategy for setting standards and making useful comparisons to buttress arguments, and it was precisely this approach that Afro-Brazilians and African Americans employed to promote national agendas. News of lynchings in the U.S. South could reassure Brazilians of all colors that race relations in their country were superior to those of the allegedly civilized giant to the north. Embracing that notion also served as a measure against which to emphasize discrepancies between discourse and reality. Similarly, Brazil's supposed racial paradise served as a foil for African American intellectuals who used it as an argument against racism and segregation in the United States.

JAMES N. GREEN
Brown University

WILLIAM J. HAUSMAN, PETER HERTNER, and MIRA WILKINS. *Global Electrification: Multinational Enterprise and International Finance in the History of Light and Power, 1878–2007.* (Cambridge Studies in the Emergence of Global Enterprise.) New York: Cambridge University Press. 2008. Pp. xxiv, 487. $80.00.

I read this book with great interest and with great pleasure. The subject is important and the story is well told. As is not always the case, the title is a very good reflection of its content. William J. Hausman, Peter Hertner, and Mira Wilkins's monograph deals with the role played by multinational enterprises and international finance in the development of the light and power industry throughout the world from the 1870s to the 1970s, by which time this role virtually came to an end; an epilogue brings the story up to date. This story is not new, as it is part of the general history of international

business (with which it has much in common). But it has never been told in this way.

Three features make this book a new and original work. First, it combines two or even three sets of writings in business and economic history that have had little interaction with each other: the history of the electrical industry, the history of multinational enterprises, and the history of banking and finance. Second, it encompasses the whole world and offers a truly comparative perspective. Third, it provides an excellent analysis of the first globalization of the world economy, not by sacrificing to current fashions but by closely looking at the activities of the global players in a global industry.

One interesting and extremely valuable aspect of this scholarly undertaking is that it is the collective effort of a group of highly distinguished business and economic historians, as opposed to an edited volume gathering essays written by individual authors. Moreover, the authors maintain a unity of purpose from beginning to end. The book is more concerned about the complexities of historical events than grand but approximate generalizations. However, the historical past is analyzed through a series of original and operational concepts defined for the purpose of the study by making ample use of the business, finance, and economics literature.

The book is divided into seven chapters. The first two deal with concepts. Chapter one provides a broad analytical survey of the development of the electrical industry, mainly at technical and economic levels, from the early nineteenth century to the 1930s. Chapter two critically reviews the literature on international business (with particular attention to portfolio and direct investments, freestanding companies, and corporate governance) before defining a typology of foreign direct investments in the power and light industry that is then employed throughout the remainder of the book. Chapters three through seven follow a fairly uncontroversial chronological order: 1880–1914, 1914–1929, 1929–1945 (with these three eras forming the core of the book); and 1945–1978 and 1978–2007 (with these last two, shorter chapters being conceived as a conclusion to the story with, so to speak, the death and rebirth of multinational enterprise in the electrical industry).

This monograph is primarily concerned with the major players in the field: the manufacturers in the electrotechnical industry; the banks and other finance companies, such as investment trusts; and the holding companies. The authors pay particular attention to the networks of relationships existing within and between these players, their cooperation as well as their competition, and the making and unmaking of business groups. The text provides a fairly comprehensive view of the actors who mattered, as witnessed by the list given in Appendix A, which contains some 300 entities. Several of these companies, groups, and networks are followed across several chapters, with their names becoming familiar to the reader as the story unfolds. In that respect, this thoroughly researched book succeeds in combining relevant details with general trends and broad explanations.

This is a great piece of scholarship written by three leading economic and business historians, with another eight eminent experts contributing indirectly to the volume. Given the importance not only of electrification but also of big business and high finance, it should be of interest to all historians of the modern and contemporary world.

Youssef Cassis
University of Geneva and *London School of Economics*

Erika Kuhlman. *Reconstructing Patriarchy after the Great War: Women, Gender, and Postwar Reconciliation between Nations.* (The Palgrave Macmillan Series in Transnational History.) New York: Palgrave Macmillan. 2008. Pp. xiv, 246. $74.95.

Erika Kuhlman sets an ambitious goal: to expand our understanding of the process and meaning of peace both between and within nations by exploring not only the words and actions of official peacemakers but also the ways in which "ordinary people—soldiers, housewives, business people, social workers, clergy, and especially women—conducted their lives in the face of a watershed international event such as the Great War and its aftermath" (p. 3). The author of *Petticoats and White Feathers: Gender Conformity, Race, the Progressive Peace Movement, and the Debate over War, 1895–1919* (1997), Kuhlman continues her engagement with complex questions of war and peace, nations and citizenship, and identity and hierarchy. The author succeeds admirably in providing her readers with a nuanced and comprehensive understanding of the process of international and domestic reconciliation in the postwar period in Germany and the United States and the complex ways in which the reestablishment of patriarchy was woven into this process.

Kuhlman begins with an exploration of the American occupation of the Rhineland and efforts to control women's sexuality conducted by both Americans and Germans in the occupied zone. She documents the important assertion of, and interplay between, two systems of domination—patriarchy and the international power of the war's victors—as the two countries, and in particular American soldiers and German civilians, navigated their postwar relationships. According to Kuhlman, patriarchy was similarly bolstered in the "Rhineland Horror" campaign, an international, and indeed transnational, propaganda campaign against French use of African troops in the occupation, a protest initiated by Germans but soon successful in recruiting whites across the political spectrum and across national borders on the basis of white supremacist beliefs. Turning to American attitudes toward peacemaking, Kuhlman discovers the dominance in the United States of a traditional approach to the war's outcomes, an approach that claimed the victor's role in controlling and redeeming the conquered foe and framed those actions

in distinctly masculine terms. It is in this context that Kuhlman's explication of the transnationalist thinking of the Women's International League for Peace and Freedom (WILPF) provides an example of an alternative vision of the war's end, as American and German members imagined a reconciliation process in which both women and men, and both the vanquished and the victors, might work together toward lasting peace. Although official peacemakers had little trouble dismissing WILPF's call for a role for women, particularly given the essentialist position of women's natural pacifism the group wielded in making its claim, women's efforts to exert influence through unofficial channels, including in the provision of relief, illustrated the possibilities of a different kind of peace based in true reconciliation. In the end, militarism and patriarchy won out. On the homefront, too, women advocating for a new world of women's full equality found militarism, nationalism, and patriarchy too powerful to overcome as Germans and Americans alike commemorated only the masculine heroism of war and found a much-sought-after normalcy in returning women to a dependent and subordinate female role. Patriarchy ruled the day domestically, while victors ruled the vanquished in the international realm.

Appropriately published as part of the Transnational History Series, Kuhlman's work succeeds in complicating our understanding of what constituted the peacemaking process following World War I. Exploring the role of non-governmental actors as diverse as the American Legion Women's Auxiliary and WILPF, the "Rhineland Horror" propagandists and the civil rights activist Mary Church Terrell, and giving voice to countless other individual writers, thinkers, and activists from the United States and across Europe, with special focus on Germany, Kuhlman helps us to recognize that peacemaking is not exclusive to policymakers but also involves the process of reconciliation among human beings across and within national borders. In such a process after World War I, transnational identities and issues necessarily played a significant role. By restoring this broader understanding of the postwar process, Kuhlman acknowledges the agency of individuals and organizations that attempted to shape the future, and illustrates as well the wide range of competing visions that surrounded official leadership even as they nevertheless constructed a notably traditional peace.

With an enormous subject and complex ideas, the clarity and grace of Kuhlman's work are especially praiseworthy. Given her explicit organizational scheme, Kuhlman might have eliminated the sometimes too frequent internal references to previous or forthcoming discussions in her text. But this is a very minor distraction in a book that is otherwise scrupulously polished and well presented. Kuhlman's argumentation is cogent and her evidence thorough. The book is well grounded in the surrounding historiography, proving attentive to both complementary and competing interpretations. It is also richly documented with a wide range of primary sources from both sides of the Atlantic, especially news-

papers, magazines, journals, and government and organizational archival materials. Kuhlman's balanced
and effective presentation of both the German and
American stories is particularly impressive.

Having begun her study with an interest in "how . . .
wars end" (p. 2), Kuhlman suggests an important contemporary lesson about the limits of the peacemaking
process, a lesson outlined in her provocative epilogue.
The process of postwar reconciliation, she says, is not
a promising forum for creating meaningful and lasting
change in women's place in the world, given the powerful attraction of "normalcy" and patriarchy's central
role in it. To resolve the crises that confront women's
lives across national boundaries and around the
world—violence, hunger, and exploitation, for instance—we must not wait until wars are fought and concluded but seek such transformation against the backdrop of peace. Such a conclusion suggests again the
significance of this superb work of transnational history.

NANCY K. BRISTOW
University of Puget Sound

MARTIN SHIPWAY. *Decolonization and Its Impact: A
Comparative Approach to the End of the Colonial Empires*. Malden, Mass.: Blackwell. 2008. Pp. xi, 269. Cloth
$86.95, paper $36.95.

Despite their variegated beginnings, Europe's empires
came to an end with remarkable speed at roughly the
same time. Surviving World War II largely intact, the
two largest empires, the British and the French, had all
but disappeared by the early 1960s. It is this surprisingly
quick, if complex, process of decolonization that is the
subject of Martin Shipway's useful new work. Shipway
carefully analyzes what he considers to be the "twenty
year crisis" (borrowing E. H. Carr's phrase) of European empires following 1945, showing the war to have
been instrumental in making some form of decolonization inevitable. But just *what* form was anyone's
guess. As Shipway shows, outcomes were often neither
intended nor envisioned, and players on both sides of
the colonial divide were commonly left disappointed.

There is a sizable body of literature on decolonization, but what makes Shipway's study novel is its effort
to present a history of the end of empire from somewhere between above and below. Noting the tendency
to see decolonization as either an act of surrender by
weakened European states or a hard-won triumph for
anti-colonial independence movements, he "triangu-
lates" between "top-down" and "grass roots" explanations of the process. Central to this method is a comparative approach that explores the similarities and
differences between the French and British experiences. Comparisons also allow Shipway to form broad
generalizations about the postwar contexts of European imperialism.

Shipway argues that the impact of World War II on
colonialism was essential, though largely indirect. The
war certainly changed the ordering of the international

system, the management of colonial rule, and the economic prowess of colonial powers. But in few cases did
it spell the immediate end of colonial rule, India being
a notable exception. Shipway shows that both France
and Britain emerged from the war with a "new conviction" about the importance of the empire to the health
of the metropole, and both undertook a "second colonial occupation" to increase economic production, a
process that was well underway during the war itself.
This reinvigorated enthusiasm for empire in Europe
met with increased opposition not only from nationalist
anti-colonial movements, but also from administrators
of the late colonial state who often found the "collab-
orator system" of rule to be taxed by changing postwar
mentalities and political realities.

The regional studies that make up the bulk of the
book follow a logical trajectory and explain how various
paths to decolonization took shape in specific contexts.
Several chapters explore the first wave of decolonization in South Asia immediately after the war, as well as
the rise of nationalism in Southeast Asia, especially In-
dochina, Malaya, and Indonesia. Three rich chapters
depict the road to independence in Africa. Here, Shipway's "triangulation" method is perhaps at its clearest
as he maps the rise of African nationalist organizations
alongside shifts in European attitudes and strategies regarding self-rule. In a particularly original chapter,
Shipway devotes much needed attention to the impact
violence and war had on the process, a subject too often
dealt with cursorily in works on decolonization, offering
a pair of valuable comparisons of Madagascar and Kenya and Algeria and Cyprus.

While based almost exclusively on secondary sources,
this book offers both original insights and a meticulous
engagement with the existing historiography on the
subject. The reliance on secondary sources has one
downside: Britain and France, the two countries that
have received the most attention from scholars, are the
real focus of the book. Anyone looking for a discussion
of decolonization in the Belgian or Portuguese empires
will likely be disappointed. While unfortunate, this
omission does not undermine the central arguments of
the book. That decolonization was a process accelerated by World War II certainly holds true in European
empires beyond Britain and France. The inclusion of
Belgium and Portugal would have made the study richer
in evidence but likely would have done little to make
Shipway's observations more persuasive. As it stands,
scholars in the field will welcome this book for its innovative methodology and valiant attempt to unite European and non-European perspectives on events. Advanced students will also find it to be a useful overview
of the major issues of the period and an excellent introduction to the key historiographical debates on the
subject.

Perhaps Shipway's most significant achievement is
his fidelity to historical contingencies and his refusal to
rely on overarching models of decolonization that unnecessarily simplify the past. Here decolonization is a
series of separate, though sometimes parallel, pro-

cesses over which few participants, be they European administrators or anti-colonial nationalists, felt they had much control. The result, ironically, was that disillusionment was keenly felt by almost everyone involved.

J. P. DAUGHTON
Stanford University

MARC J. SELVERSTONE. *Constructing the Monolith: The United States, Great Britain, and International Communism, 1945–1950.* Cambridge: Harvard University Press. 2009. Pp. xi, 304. $49.95.

In the summer of 1954, Clement Attlee and other leading members of the British Labour Party went to China. The professed purpose of their controversial visit was to help raise the bamboo curtain, which had isolated the People's Republic of China since the Liberation of 1949. During the course of their visit, the former British prime minister conversed over tea with Chairman Mao Zedong. It was said to be the first time that Mao had met with any Western leader since taking power. Predictably, he used the occasion to rail against the United States and to insist that China was not merely a "catspaw" of the Soviet Union, as American policy makers apparently liked to think. Attlee, whose visit had been fiercely condemned in the United States, replied that "it was rather frightening to other nations who often had disagreements among themselves, to see a group of countries acting as a single monolithic bloc," adding that this sort of behavior "actually gave the whole of the case to those elements in the United States who argued that the world was divided into two blocs."

This polite assertion, which exploited the idea of the communist monolith at the same time as dismissing it as a crude oversimplification, is a late example of the way of thinking explored so convincingly in this closely argued and yet broadly illuminating book. Marc J. Selverstone sets out to show how, in the five years following World War II, Americans and Britons came to see communism as a "monolithic force," even though the history of that movement suggested it was in fact no such thing.

As it emerged in 1945–1946, the Cold War seemed firmly of its moment. And yet many of the ideas and images with which policy makers on both sides of the Atlantic tried to make sense of the polarized postwar world were inherited from the early twentieth century. Just as the iron curtain actually emerged as a political metaphor during World War I and had then been wrapped around Bolshevik Russia by 1920, so the "monolithism" of the international communist movement had been loudly proclaimed by its advocates in the 1920s and 1930s. Other habits of thought shown to have been carried over from earlier in the century included a fear of collaboration, a sense of communism as a contagious virus or plague, and the infernal rhetoric of "Red Fascism," in which fascism and communism were treated as more or less identical forms of totalitarianism.

Having traced these lines of descent, Selverstone shows how the idea of the communist monolith came to be reestablished in Anglo-American policy during the opening months of the Cold War. From the start, the image prompted doubts in the minds of various diplomats and officials, but it was also deliberately projected into the public mind by governments using advertising and other techniques to override opposition and dissent. The tensions this commitment to the "iron-controlled" monolith could produce are particularly well elucidated. During the years of the hard-line Truman Doctrine, U.S. officials found themselves having to play up the "monolith" threat in order to get Americans to come into line over Europe. In the process, they unleashed an anticommunist sentiment they would then "struggle to manage." The same sort of complexity came up in 1948 when Josip Broz Tito's Yugoslavia was kicked out of the Cominform, a "first crack" in the idea of the communist monolith, as Selverstone agrees, but one that was successfully used to concentrate the image around the Soviet Union and its loyal satellites: a break, in other words, that proved the monolith stronger, even as it gave encouragement to the designers of the "wedge" strategy that would later be applied in Asia as well as in Europe.

Some of Selverstone's best pages concern the maneuvers of policy makers who saw the dangers of "monolithic" thinking and tried to steer their governments away from it. A telling example is found in American Policy Planning Staff member John Paton Davies, who was unconvinced by the propaganda about communist China being a mere stooge of Moscow and worried that the employment of "monolithic" imagery in describing this relationship might actually be "emboldening" the Kremlin and "contributing to Soviet success." In 1949, therefore, Davies and his colleague, Ware Adams, wrote a paper calling for a change in U.S. propaganda, insisting that, while the Kremlin may indeed have wanted to create exactly such a monolith, the communist parties and nations around the world did not amount to any such thing. They advocated that a new distinction be made between "communism" and "Russian imperialism."

This is an important and largely persuasive book, which raises more questions than it can possibly answer. Despite Selverstone's skillful use of archives, there are times when he seems rather schematic in his arguments. The suggestion, for example, that the "monolith" was supported by a shared "Anglo-American historical consciousness" involving a perception of "a long line of threats to freedom and liberty" seems to generalize a perspective that, to a British reader at least, seems the much contested possession of Winston Churchill and, perhaps, the Conservative mythmaking historian, Arthur Bryant. There were others, after all, and not just adherents such as Agnes Smedley, for whom Mao Zedong stood in the tradition of American democracy, a kind of Benjamin Franklin in a blue shirt. Similarly, it is really only in passing that Selverstone suggests that the "monolith" prepared the way for the "axis of

evil"—an intriguing hypothesis to which he might usefully return in the future.

PATRICK WRIGHT
Nottingham Trent University

STEPHANIE COOKE. *In Mortal Hands: A Cautionary History of the Nuclear Age*. New York: Bloomsbury. 2009.
Pp. 488. $27.00.

As Stephanie Cooke notes early in her invigorating
book, "The civilian nuclear enterprise is more politi-
cized than any other industry, even oil, because of its
close link to nuclear weapons" (p. 5). This is an observation worth thinking about. Immediately after World
War II, the hope for civilian nuclear power—energy
"too cheap to meter," in the words of Lewis Strauss,
President Dwight D. Eisenhower's chairman of the
Atomic Energy Commission (AEC)—promised both
bounty and redemption for American scientists and
politicians. Yet this vision of a utopian future was but
the outer surface, masking the vast archipelago of sites
involved in nuclear weapons production. The AEC
mostly made bombs, but it did not talk about that part
much. Historians have sniffed out the military side of
the story, and the historiography of nuclear weapons
has (pardon the pun) mushroomed in recent years.

Yet nuclear power, the civilian face of the military
juggernaut, has not received comparable attention.
Cooke's great merit is to take a journalist's trained eye
(she has covered the industry for almost thirty years) to
the history of nuclear matters with power generation
front and center. Instead of nuclear energy being
tacked onto a history of weapons, the weaponry is subordinated here to a history of power generation. All of
the usual stops of the American weapons narrative are
here: the Manhattan Project, testing in the South Pacific, the Cuban Missile Crisis. But we also get Atoms
for Peace, Three Mile Island, Yucca Mountain, and a
worldwide tour of nuclear power: Soviet (with Chernobyl); British (with Windscale); Israeli, Indian, and
Pakistani (with bombs); and Iran's ventures into the
dark nucleus of uranium and plutonium atoms.

Cooke's text is a work of advocacy. In an age of concerns about global warming and dwindling fossil fuel
reserves, nuclear power may be experiencing a renaissance. Her purpose here is to show how the promise of
"the peaceful atom" has been tainted, in three senses,
from the very start. The first taint, indicated by Three
Mile Island and Chernobyl, is the persistent danger of
nuclear accidents. It is noteworthy that the nuclear
weapons side of the atomic complex had a lot fewer
accidents, with consequently less catastrophic environmental and health consequences, than the supposedly
sunny side of fission.

Industry advocates respond that there are plenty of
safeguards, and proper regulation will tame the atom's
dangerous consequences. This is the second taint: regulatory capture by the nuclear power industry. The
AEC had two major functions aside from its primary
one of producing atomic bombs: promoting nuclear

power and regulating it. The conflicts of interest eventually led to the fracture of the AEC in the 1970s,
spawning the Department of Energy (bombs and promotion) and the Nuclear Regulatory Commission
(oversight). But the centrality of atomic fuel to American national security and the narrowing of expertise to
industry stalwarts meant that regulators were consistently biased in favor of permitting questionable practices. (The International Atomic Energy Agency
[IAEA] is in the same quandary, minus the bombs.) Accordingly, no nuclear nation has managed to solve the
problem of waste storage. Nuclear power may be in
abeyance now (the last operating license was granted in
1996, when reactors produced about a fifth of American
energy), but calls abound for a return to the boom.
Cooke disagrees with such suggestions.

Consider the third taint: nuclear proliferation. Every
single nuclear weapons program, with the exception of
the first two (American and Soviet), stemmed from the
clandestine transformation of civilian power plants into
sources of high-grade weapons fuel. By 1959, Cooke
notes, the United States' "Atoms for Peace" program
had provided *forty-two* countries with reactors and fuel,
some of them unstable dictatorships like Vietnam and
the Belgian Congo. The Soviets, British, French, and
Chinese followed. Iran, for example, acquired the uranium now fueling its program in the final years of the
Shah through the loophole in IAEA regulations that
excluded mining. As a result, the London firm Rio
Tinto-Zinc moved material from Namibia to Tehran.
Cooke lays bare many of the apparent lacunae in today's non-proliferation regime by showing how those
holes were deliberately inserted by the power industry:
"Yet even the best safeguards system in the world cannot guarantee 100 percent protection from a determined country or group pursuing and achieving its objectives, because people cheat, money talks, and the
technology is now widely available" (p. 381).

Although Cooke does engage in some archival research (especially surrounding the nuclear tests at Bi-
kini in 1946), most of her evidence is drawn from extant
scholarship, published sources, and decades of fascinating interviews. The stories presented here may not be
utterly new, but their juxtaposition into a compelling
narrative packs a punch, making this book a valuable
introduction to the global history of nuclear power.

MICHAEL D. GORDIN
Princeton University

DAVID CORTRIGHT. *Peace: A History of Movements and
Ideas*. New York: Cambridge University Press. 2008.
Pp. xii, 376. Cloth $90.00, paper $29.99.

A peace movement organizer turned peace studies academic, David Cortright has produced an overview of
peace campaigning—part one of his book—and its associated ideas and inspirations—part two. He has firsthand experience of the American peace movement over
several decades, reads widely, organizes material carefully, writes elegantly, shows sensitivity to chronological

and cultural variations, and exudes moral seriousness. His survey therefore deserves a bright future as an ambitious and multiskilled introduction to an important subject.

Even so, it has its limitations. A reviewer for a historical journal such as this one must immediately point out that it occasionally resorts to anachronistic oversimplification, as in its presentation of Immanuel Kant as a believer in the eirenic effect of democratic, as distinct from republican, regimes, and is heavily dependent on secondary sources, often of a quite general kind. Some of its historical judgments lack balance; thus, Cortright writes of "the success of non-violent resistance in winning independence for India . . . without stirring the rancor and bitterness that often result from revolutionary change" and of "the peaceful and even amicable way in which Britain handed over power in 1947" (pp. 211–212), yet he fails to mention the Hindu-Muslim massacres that followed what was, for the former imperial power, in part a decision to scurry away from a predictable bloodbath. Likewise he describes the Danish and Norwegian experiences of Nazi occupation in World War II as "examples of nonviolent success" without pointing out that the attempted "mass noncooperation" of some Scandinavians was not the same as the disarming of a would-be conqueror by means of that technique, which had been the criterion of success set by advocates of nonviolent resistance during the 1930s (p. 228).

A reviewer with theoretical interests must also note a slight analytical looseness. Cortright is aware that peace movements have always comprised two distinct elements: a minority seeking the abolition of war through the immediate and total renunciation of armed defense, and a majority pursuing the same goal through reforms of the international system or the states composing it and, in the meanwhile, allowing military force provided it is used in a defensive and progressive manner. He is also aware that the term "pacifism" is now normally applied only to the minority, although when first coined it included the majority as well. Even so, he uses the word to describe peace activism of a non-absolutist kind, too, sometimes without using an adjective such as "pragmatic" to distinguish it from pacifism as now more commonly understood in its absolutist form. This occasionally proves problematical: for example, the statement "Pacifism (broadly understood) includes internationalism" is followed seven lines later by the assertion that "Internationalism embodies a narrower and more conservative outlook than pacifism" (pp. 45–46), which left this reader a little puzzled as to the relationship being claimed between the two ideas. And although aware that the goals of peace and justice sometimes conflict, Cortright has a tendency to run with the hare and hunt with the hounds on this issue. At times, notably in his sympathetic accounts of conscientious objectors and nonviolence, he can sound like an advocate of absolute pacifism, but at others, as when denouncing "the pusillanimity of Britain and France" (p. 82) in the face of Benito Mussolini's seizure of Ethi-

opia, he appears to be more of a humanitarian interventionist. Disarmingly, he owns up to "a tendency towards utopianism" (p. 334), which prepares the reader for his sanguine expression of confidence in "an emerging science of peace-building" (p. 337) with which the book concludes.

MARTIN CEADEL
New College,
University of Oxford

ASIA

HILDE DE WEERDT. *Competition over Content: Negotiating Standards for the Civil Service Examinations in Imperial China (1127–1279)*. (Harvard East Asian Monographs, number 289.) Cambridge, Mass.: Harvard University Asia Center. 2007. Pp. xvi, 495. $49.50.

This book aims to answer the following questions: how did Zhu Xi's "Learning of the Way" (*daoxue*) succeed in determining the examination standards of the civil service examination field, and how did the examinations assist in shaping the course of the development of scholarly learning? How did the Southern Song examination content *cum* intellectual history differ from the Northern Song and set the paradigm of the competition over examination contents in later dynasties? The last question has been ably explored by Benjamin Elman in his *magnum opus* on the late imperial period. Hilde De Weerdt has now competently investigated the earlier Southern Song period.

The questions are all important, but they have been asked before. The distinct strength of this book is that De Weerdt seeks answers in works hitherto little examined: examination preparation books. Their existence has been known for a long time, but modern historians have generally ignored them, considering them not worth studying because they represent "little tradition" works. However, De Weerdt uses them effectively to demonstrate that they faithfully reflected popular intellectual trends in examination questions and standards. Any thinker who wished to compete successfully in the scholarly arena first had to succeed in getting publishers to adapt or adopt his writings into examination preparation books. In the beginning of the Southern Song period, the "ancient prose" style and the so-called "Yongjia" scholarship had dominated the "bounded space" of the examinations. Yongjia utilitarianism was a powerful ideology against which Zhu Xi fought; the competition between Zhu's learning and Yongjia thinking was evident in the twelfth century, during which the Song government prohibited the former and even persecuted Zhu and his followers. Nonetheless, by the time of Zhu's death and the immediate decades thereafter, the Zhu school prevailed, as demonstrated by the popular examination books then in print.

The victory of the Zhu school is a reflection of Zhu and his followers' significant gift for synthesis, although De Weerdt does not stress this point. Rather, she uses the content of the examinations to show that the rise of the Zhu school was due to its ability to compete in the examination field. From the viewpoint of a social historian, this is an acceptable interpretation, although I am somewhat inclined to think that the process was a patient effort over a sustained period of intellectual negotiation. It would otherwise be odd that Zhu and his followers did not seek to wipe out the influence of the ancient prose advocates and the Yongjia thinkers.

To consider the examination field as a space in which different schools of thought competed to dominate is a positive step toward understanding the power of the imperial Chinese government and how the principle of "equality," or at least "impartiality," was carried out. It used to be that historians considered the state the sole arbiter in the field of examinations, but De Weerdt questions whether this was actually true. She does not openly state that the field was an open one, or that the state participated equally with other forces—examination book publishers, intellectual leaders, the examinees, and examiners with personal intellectual agendas—and I suspect that her intention is not to argue that these were equal participants in the field, but one still gets the impression that this is her point. I think that this impression is incorrect.

De Weerdt argues that examination practices differed between the Northern Song and the Southern Song. She argues the "localist turn" in debates about the two regimes. I think that this turn, which I accept as real, is a development that from the Northern Song to the Southern Song had more continuity than discontinuity. The state participated in the field as a player "more equal" than others, and this was as true for the Northern Song as it was for the Southern Song. There were intellectual changes in the eleventh century, and these were equally as acute as in subsequent centuries. In both cases, the state remained the ultimate arbitrator. De Weerdt argues that the Southern Song government chose to retreat and let the other participating forces work out their conflicts. This is to me an idealization of the Chinese state and its exercise of power.

In all, this is a very important book, especially for its delineation of the importance of the examination field to the course of intellectual development. Errors and mistranslations aside, the book is a serious and eloquent piece of scholarly research.

THOMAS H. C. LEE
National Chiao-tung University

TONIO ANDRADE. *How Taiwan Became Chinese: Dutch, Spanish, and Han Colonization in the Seventeenth Century.* (Guttenberg-e Online History Series.) New York: Columbia University Press. 2007. Electronic book. Site access $49.50.

Tonio Andrade's electronic book is at the same time a study of the successive colonization of Taiwan by Spanish, Dutch, and Chinese mercantile powers from circa 1623 to 1683, and a story of the "co-colonization" of the island by agents of the Dutch East India Company (VOC) and Han Chinese agricultural colonists, financed largely by Chinese entrepreneurs. In its accounting of global encounters characteristic of the early modern period, this monograph is both a detailed regional history and a foray into world history.

In framing his work, Andrade raises the perennial question: "How do we understand the great colonial movements that have shaped our modern World?" (p. 2). The answer he gives is that "colonialism—at least in East Asia—has less to do with superior technology or military prowess than with motivation. European states were eager to sponsor overseas adventurism. East Asian states were, for the most part, not" (p. 2). He draws this conclusion from the relative ease with which both Spanish and Dutch traders established bases on the island and the alacrity with which a Chinese pirate *cum* Ming loyalist in turn ousted the Dutch in 1662 when he recognized Taiwan as a desirable base for his own activities. Lest such sweeping generalizations produce discomfort, I should hasten to add that Andrade quickly moves from this general picture into specific accounts of historical interactions on the ground.

Following a general introduction, the opening chapters describe Taiwan prior to European colonization; challenges to the Dutch presence in the form of Chinese pirates, Japanese traders, and Portuguese interests in the region; and ultimately Dutch efforts to subdue and make peace with the aboriginal populations of the island. The focus then shifts to the Spanish settlements to the north. Andrade brings out contrasts in Spanish and Dutch approaches to colonization and their relationships with the indigenous populations. The fall of Spanish Taiwan, we learn, was the result of economic policy decisions that left the settlement ill equipped to face challenges from the Dutch.

The core of the book is a detailed study of Dutch rule of the island. In short, the VOC encouraged Chinese agricultural settlement, offering protection and government to the new influx of settlers in exchange for a share of the profits, taken via taxation. Notwithstanding some competition from Chinese pirates and tensions between aborigines and settlers over deer hunting, the Dutch ran a profitable operation for nearly three decades. However, when challenged by a strong Chinese maritime power in the form of Zheng Chenggong (Koxinga)—who first implemented a successful blockade of the island and then won over the loyalty of the Chinese population through their relatives in his base in Fujian—Dutch rule ended. When a Chinese maritime power took interest in Taiwan, the European show was over.

Andrade's careful mining of archival sources and letters allows him to tell a number of important stories that are nested in the larger narrative sketched above. A major strength of the work is his careful tracking of the formation of Dutch policy with regard to the delicate balance of taxation, production, and governance of both native aboriginal groups and the influx of Chinese settlers. In fact, the Dutch developed two distinct systems for governing these two groups of people. Through an institution called the Landdag, the Dutch state invested the aborigines with local authority and allowed them a certain amount of representation. Colorful vignettes about individual historical figures, from Salvador Diaz—a Portuguese-speaking prisoner of the Dutch with ties to Chinese pirates—to Zheng Chenggong's father who, after being baptized a Christian, went by the Romanized name of Nicholas Gaspard, show the opportunities and hazards of the hazy space created when lines of ethnic affiliation, language, and national identity were crossed.

Publication as a Gutenberg-e book has afforded the author the opportunity to include a wide variety of illustrations. Period maps of both Dutch and Spanish origin, ethnographic album leaves of Taiwan's aborigines, contemporary photographs, and even an eighteenth-century aboriginal land deed recorded in roman letters all grace the site. These illustrations add interest and color and bring to our attention the existence of documents that might otherwise be overlooked. Yet, highlighting both the strengths and weakness of publication in this form, these illustrations are in most cases only diffusely related to the textual argument; they are incorporated because they can be rather than as actual visual evidence for an argument.

Andrade's book is important and should not be overlooked by scholars of Qing history, comparative colonial processes, or world history. Hopefully its electronic publication will make it accessible to scholars rather than denying it a place on the shelf next to other equally important but more conventionally published works.

Laura Hostetler
University of Illinois at Chicago

Neil J. Diamant. *Embattled Glory: Veterans, Military Families, and the Politics of Patriotism in China, 1949–2007.* (State and Society in East Asia.) Lanham, Md.: Rowman and Littlefield. 2009. Pp. xiii, 463. $90.00.

For much of its modern history, China has been convulsed by warfare. Tens of millions of men have served in its military forces; China today has the largest standing army in the world. The scale of military service and warfare makes it ironic that two of the areas least covered in Western histories of China are the military and war. Neil J. Diamant's excellent study of Chinese veterans goes a long way toward correcting this neglect. His book joins a number of distinguished new contributions to the social history of the military: Stéphane Audoin-Rouzeau and Annette Becker's *1914–1918: Understanding the Great War* (2002), Drew Gilpin Faust's *The Republic of Suffering: Death and the American Civil War* (2008), and Catherine Merridale's *Ivan's War: The Red Army, 1939–1945* (2006).

Diamant is ideally suited for the topic, having been a soldier in the Israeli Defense Forces before he was an academic. Diamant's work shows a deep compassion and sensitivity to veterans in China and in other societies. His descriptions of the disappointments of veterans who come home from military service to find that they are not particularly welcome are very moving. He has found their stories from trawling through great caches of recently opened local archives that recount the sad lives of many veterans.

From the early 1950s on Chinese veterans had high expectations for their post-military lives. They knew they were the men who had liberated China from the shackles of the past, the heroes who brought the Communist Party, the workers' and peasants' party, to power. They expected good treatment for themselves and for their families but were disappointed. Veterans from the lower ranks of the People's Liberation Army (PLA) encountered constant problems in finding work, acquiring land, arranging marriages, and getting health care. Some suffered from what would now be called Post Traumatic Stress Disorder (PTSD) but was then referred to bluntly as madness (the army's most celebrated general, Lin Biao, himself showed every symptom of PTSD). Veterans discovered on their return to civilian life that their families had had a hard time while they were away serving the nation; they had lost out on opportunities to take advantage of the land reform of the early communist period, and those who were married found that their wives had often been "fair game" for local officials.

They were discovering something fundamental about the status of soldiers in Chinese society: the old, low status of soldiers had not changed in China's new political order. Soldiers might have won the civil war, but they still came from the lowest echelons of society and were poorly educated. They soon gave way in political influence to well educated civilians who won dominance in the Communist Party and government at every level. Only senior officers fared well after demobilization. The PLA seems to have accepted its subordinate role; in spite of its size and importance, it has rarely challenged the civilian elite for power. It has not even shown much concern for its veterans, turning their care over to a toothless catch-all bureaucratic stream, the Civil Affairs system, an indication of the "failure of the state to cultivate a sense of respect for military families—or for veterans."

The veterans did not accept the loss of their expectations easily. The book is full of examples of veterans' protests, both in writing to bureaucrats and occasionally in the streets. Veterans' protests are frightening to any state because veterans know how to fight and to use weapons. Nevertheless, the discontent of Chinese veterans has not translated into better treatment but rather into worse. Since the introduction of "socialism with Chinese characteristics" (i.e. primitive capitalism) in the early 1980s, veterans and their families have been even more marginalized in a society that has minimal belief in providing social welfare for its citizens.

Diamant's book is about Chinese veterans, but it is informed by comparisons with the treatment of veterans in many other societies. The comparisons are so rich that they make the book a general study of the treatment of veterans, not just a book about China. One group of veterans is not covered in this book, however: the hundreds of thousands of Nationalist soldiers who were left on the mainland in 1949 when their govern- ment fled to Taiwan. Some went over to the Commu- nists, but many were sent to prison camps or took to the hills, where some were active into the mid-1950s. The Nationalist veterans became pariahs, enemies of the new state, as the communist advent to power brought a tragic end to their eight years of patriotic service in the Resistance War against Japan. They, like the PLA veterans, thought that they were patriots, as Diamant's subtitle suggests, but patriotism turned out to be a more complex matter than they imagined.

DIANA LARY
University of British Columbia

AYESHA JALAL. *Partisans of Allah: Jihad in South Asia.* Cambridge: Harvard University Press. 2008. Pp. xvi, 373. $29.95.

Contemporary concerns around political Islam, the mo- bilization of jihad, and terrorism have produced a plethora of policy-driven writings and analyses that of- ten tend to single out Islam as a religion of aggression. Ayesha Jalal's book is therefore an important scholarly intervention that challenges reductive understandings of jihad as "holy war" against non-Muslim infidels by providing a rich intellectual history of the shifting, di- verse, and contested meanings of jihad in South Asia.

As Jalal points out, the focus on South Asia is a par- ticularly valuable one not only because the Indian sub- continent is the most populous Muslim region in the world but because Islamic intellectual traditions in the region have been shaped over a millennium in a context where Muslims have lived as a minority in a predom- inantly non-Muslim society. With the present Taliban- ization of the northwest frontier, the book aptly begins with the story of Sayyid Ahmad and Shah Ismail, who ventured from north India to the northwest frontier to wage a jihad against its Sikh rulers from 1826 to 1831 and went on to become the legendary martyrs of Bala- kot. Jalal places their jihad in the context of the ideas of Shah Waliullah, a Delhi-based scholar writing amidst the decline of Mughal sovereignty, and reveals the dis- cursive and imaginative power of this failed venture as it animated subsequent reflections on jihad. Jalal ex- amines the political and intellectual challenges that Muslim thinkers faced with the rise of Western impe- rialism and the production of colonial knowledge about Islam, the different articulations of the universal claims of jihad for purposes of an anticolonial territorial na- tionalism, and finally the entangled relationship among postcolonial states, the ulema, and Cold War mobili- zation of jihad—bringing us back to the extraordinary challenges of understanding jihad in the age of Al- Qaeda and the Taliban.

Drawing on a breadth of Urdu and English secondary and primary sources, Jalal brings together legal and theological writings with those of reformers, philoso- phers, and poets. She thus revisits the works of major figures like Sayyid Ahmad Khan, Abul Kalam Azad, Muhammad Iqbal, and Mirza Asadullah Khan Ghalib,

as well as the writings and careers of lesser-known fig- ures such as Mirza Ghulam Ahmad (the founder of the Ahmadiya sect), Obaidullah Sindhi, Chiragh Ali, and Maulana Fazal Ilahi Vazirabadi. More generally, her critique of Orientalist scholarship of Islam, which has privileged legal and theological perspectives, and her argument for placing ideas of jihad within the historical specificity of imperialism, are important. The book also shows the extent to which the northwest frontier, a cru- cial battleground today as it was through much of the colonial period, animated Islamic political thought in the rest of India.

In making her analysis, however, Jalal makes a dis- tinction throughout the book between a correct under- standing of jihad and "hopeless distortion" (p. 3). She privileges an understanding of jihad as a spiritual en- deavor, an ethical and moral struggle, taking words from the poet Ghalib, "to be human" (p. 5). Thus, while on the one hand the book forcefully recovers a nonvi- olent humanist tradition in Islam, on the other hand such judgment forecloses other lines of enquiry; despite the diversity of interpretations, why and how do some interpretations gain greater authority and political force? For instance, while W. W. Hunter's description of Muslims as seditious and fanatical had an enormous impact on colonial governance, G. W. Leitner's nu- anced scholarship on Islam was simply ignored by the colonial state. Jalal's brief explanation, that this was the result of the "inequality of discursive authority in late nineteenth century colonial India" (p. 162), does not help us to understand the nexus between knowledge and power. Furthermore, as an intellectual history the study does not engage with the social life of ideas, or how text-based interpretations impact popular reli- gious beliefs. In the particular case of the martyrs of Balakot, it would be interesting to interrogate how Sayyid Ahmad of Rae Bareilly in Uttar Pradesh trans- mitted his ideas of jihad to Pathan tribesmen, and the process by which the social memory of their failed jihad was formed. Nonetheless, this is a concerned and so- phisticated contribution to the effort to historicize ji- had, and one which should be read widely in an effort to rethink the politics of jihad in the present.

VAZIRA FAZILA-YACOOBALI
Brown University

GUY N. A. ATTEWELL. *Refiguring Unani Tibb: Plural Healing in Late Colonial India.* (New Perspectives in South Asian History, number 17.) Hyderabad: Orient Longman. 2007. Pp. xvi, 316. Rs. 695.00.

Although scholarly writings on medicine in colonial In- dia have done justice to Ayurveda, there has been a paucity of literature on Unani medicine over the same period. Guy N. A. Attewell's inspiring study fills this void by providing a comprehensive assessment of the reconstitution of medical identities by Unani practitio- ners and patients under the rubric of contesting medical authorities. In this respect, Unani medicine was subject to similar sociopolitical pressures as its Ayurvedic counterpart. This resulted in changes in medical paradigms to fulfill colonial models of legitimacy and recognition.

The book also highlights major themes relevant for an understanding of the evolution of healing systems more generally. One theme that emerges is the dynamic dialectical relationship between learned spheres of knowledge, the local elite, and the popular domain. Attewell provides a new dimension to the entire process of reconfiguring Tibb, and hence of its reconstruction. He argues that the move to reform Unani rested largely on elite practitioners for whom professional identity, successful practice, and social honor were equally indispensable to justify their medical credibility. Hence, popular acceptance and recognition heralded the reformation of Unani medical knowledge in late colonial India.

Unani medical practitioners saw epidemic diseases as enabling their claims to professional credibility in the public domain. In chapter two, Attewell convincingly demonstrates how the spread of plague, which, although defying colonial medical practices, enabled learned tabibs to "claim historical, moral and medical legitimacy to deal with this disease" (p. 52). It also opened up opportunities for making their legitimacy public and open for negotiation. This also resulted in conflicts over the nature of Unani Tibb, whether it was a communitarian profession or akin to some form of commercial practice not acceptable to learned practitioners.

The dynamics of reform in Unani Tibb in the late nineteenth century are a significant focus of Attewell's study. Chapter three focuses on the creation of teaching institutions as a means of achieving these dynamics. In Hyderabad, the rise of Unani schools for the first time marked a disjuncture in locating Unani Tibb because it questioned the fundamentals of Tibb medical knowledge and practice, which were dismantled with the establishment of formal teaching institutions. While the author discusses these changes at length, he falls short of explaining whether this disjuncture led to the emergence of different strata of practitioners and patrons, and if so, whether it resulted in hostility between patrons, and at what levels? After all, what were the Tibb practitioners trying to achieve: to exhibit power through traditional means of medical instruction, or to reform the medical art to achieve more power in the medical and public spheres?

Nationalism has been a major force in reframing medical traditions throughout South Asian history. Chapter four unravels the various sociopolitical events that set off waves of revitalization of Unani Tibb. However, it could have provided a more complete picture with explanations of the concept of nationalism, which has often been viewed as a creation of colonial expectations. While the rise of national and professional associations did much to establish professional uniformity, the emerging religious issues resulting from nationalistic politics led to conflicts in the medical profession in late colonial India. Nevertheless, religious

connotations became useful when, by the early twentieth century, Unani Tibb came to be seen as an "important element in the education . . . of Muslim women" (p. 194), as chapter five demonstrates. This coincided with overall changes in the sociopolitical milieu, when women and their social environment became a new focus of study for medical women.

Demonstrating professional authority to the public was part of the establishment of medical claims and authenticity in colonial India. This is the focus of chapter six, where the author demonstrates how close interactions between practitioners and patients allowed the latter to understand their own bodies and ailments. The development of print culture and the rise of medical journals facilitated publicity for some of these basic queries from patients, thus acting as a medium through which disparate trends in Tibb practices became visible. The author has provided the reader a broad swath of rich sources including journals, pamphlets, and various texts written in Urdu and Arabic, some by Tibb practitioners themselves.

Overall, this study makes a significant contribution to the increasing scholarship in the social history of medicine and the evolution of healing systems in colonial contexts. It also provides new perspectives in disassociating traditional forms of knowledge from their political frame to understand the formation of professional authority in the public sphere.

POONAM BALA
University of Delhi

SHABNUM TEJANI. *Indian Secularism: A Social and Intellectual History, 1890–1950*. Bloomington: Indiana University Press. 2008. Pp. xvi, 302. Cloth $65.00, paper $24.95.

There is a large and exhaustive body of research on Indian secularism. For the most part, scholars confine themselves to the post-independence period and relate secularism to the policies and practices of the sovereign Indian nation-state. Although opinions differ as to whether secularism is "good" or "bad," indigenous or alien to the Indian context, there is for the most part a shared consensus that secularism is a temporally delimited phenomenon—a postcolonial project—that is primarily statist and institutionalist in its provenance and orientation.

Shabnum Tejani's recent monograph offers a different approach. The book promises to be a "study of the historical emergence of the idea of secularism in India" (p. 2) through an investigation of six key historical moments between 1890 and 1950, when particular and shifting meanings were attached to this concept. When and why did secularism become a foundational term in Indian politics? What did the term signify at the moment of its emergence, and what were the various meanings and alternative political vocabularies that it drew upon and synthesized? By addressing these important but largely overlooked questions, Tejani draws our attention to the evolution of secularism as a polit-

ical concept in colonial India, and to the often unexpected conceptual anchors that continue to exert a determinative, though hidden, influence over secular
politics up to the present day.

Tejani argues that late nineteenth to early twentieth-
century understandings of an upper-caste, Hindu nationalism, and early to mid-twentieth-century understandings of communalism as a problem of "Muslim
minority separatism," informed the Indian Constituent
Assembly's debates on secularism in the late 1940s. In
this genealogy, the constitutional structure of postcolonial secularism reflects the preoccupations of "overwhelmingly middle-class, upper caste Hindu men" (p.
15) who deployed secularism in the effort to shore up
their position as the national majority in a new and
democratic nation-state.

Although provocative, this argument about the
Hindu majoritarian core of Indian secularism is a familiar one that has already been made by several scholars and public intellectuals in India. It is Tejani's second
proposition about what exactly this strategic deployment of secularism entailed that stands out for its orig-
inality and is the major innovation of this book. According to Tejani, the deployment of secularism in the
project of creating and consolidating a unified upper-
caste Hindu majority entailed the production of a particular kind of minority politics. Specifically, secular
ideas and policies delinked caste and religious minorities, such that the needs and interests of caste minorities such as Dalits and religious minorities such as
Muslims would henceforth be seen as fundamentally
distinct.

Tejani argues that at the time of the Constituent Assembly debates socioeconomic equality was regarded as
the primary demand of Dalit groups, while the demand
for the recognition of their distinct identity was the
main demand of Muslims. Secularism played a key role
in establishing and upholding this bifurcation between
"equality" and "identity" and the corresponding distinction between caste and religious minorities. Designed as a non-interventionist policy of respecting and
recognizing the distinct religious identities of minorities, Indian secularism effectively "required religious
minorities to forego any claims to inequality" (p. 264).
With this, Indian secularism aided the transformation
of religious politics into an "identity question," whereby
religious minorities, Muslims in particular, were seen to
require the state's protection rather than political representation. In contrast, the newly independent state
committed itself to an active, although temporally delimited, policy of "reservations" or affirmative action
for caste minorities that legitimized their concerns
about inequality but denied their demands for recognition as a distinct identity group. Both of these maneuvers—the legitimization of religious identity and
the denial of separate caste identities—consolidated a
Hindu upper-caste majority that could rule India, the
former by neutralizing a separate Muslim politics and
the latter by assimilating lower-caste groups to a unified
Hindu identity.

What explains this particular outcome? Tejani does
not provide an answer, and in fact argues that there was
no predetermined reason for Indian secularism and the
politics of religion and caste to have taken this particular form in the closing decade of the colonial era. Indeed, the burden of her book is to show that there were
many different and competing understandings of secularism, religion, and caste over time, and the crystal-
lization of one particular set of normative meanings—
secularism as "minority protection"—was essentially a
contingent outcome.

However, this crucial notion of contingency remains
unexplored as a result of the high politics approach that
informs the book; national-level institutional and constitutional maneuvers on the part of political elites take
precedence over a fine-grained analysis of the complex
and varied dynamics of political transformation over
time. The reader is provided with static snapshots of
Indian politics at different moments in time over a sixty
year period, without any explanation of how these moments are linked or why these particular moments have
been selected for investigation. In a similar vein, the
particular regional focus of the study—why Tejani focuses on western Indian politics in her quest to understand the national-level phenomenon of secularism—
remains unexplained.

The monograph would benefit from a concluding
chapter where these analytical choices, as well as the
broader comparative and theoretical implications of
the argument, are discussed in further detail. For instance, there is considerable theoretical convergence
between Tejani's discussion of the "identity versus
equality" distinction and the work of scholars such as
Nancy Fraser on the limits of identity politics in the
United States. By locating her discussion in a comparative theoretical field, Tejani would be able to achieve
more effectively her own goal of broadening discussions
of Indian secularism.

SRIRUPA ROY
*University of Massachusetts,
Amherst*

ANDREW SARTORI. *Bengal in Global Concept History:
Culturalism in the Age of Capital.* (Chicago Studies in
Practices of Meaning.) Chicago: University of Chicago
Press. 2008. Pp. ix, 284. Cloth $55.00, paper $22.00.

Andrew Sartori's book is a study of the rise to importance of the concept of culture and the multiple ways
in which it was discursively employed in nineteenth and
twentieth-century Bengal. Culturalism was by no means
confined to Bengal, but in the course of the nineteenth
and twentieth centuries it "achieved the status of a truly
global concept" (p. 4). Thus Sartori writes, "My account
of Bengali culturalism will also be an attempt to account
for Bengali culturalism—to understand why the logic of
culturalism's most fundamental organizing categories
were plausible within a particular historical milieu" (p.
5). The author's answer to the question of why culturalism became a global concept in very diverse settings

is global capitalist modernity. A particular and peculiar mode of social abstraction engendered by the globalization of commodity production is what made culturalism an intellectually plausible way of regarding and responding to a changing scene in Bengal, and elsewhere. This book, its author declares, is situated "squarely in the non-economistic tradition of Hegelian Marxism" (p. 63), and it defines itself, in part, in opposition to currently influential studies of south Asia, especially those labeled postcolonial, which Sartori argues are unable or unwilling to seek the conditions of possibility of the discursive tropes they critique, are too willing to label and criticize certain concepts and discourses as "Western" (and therefore as derivative, when employed in non-Western contexts), and commit the mistake of treating as "indigenous," and as oppositional to Western modernity, that which has in fact been produced by global capitalist modernity.

The book thus has two major strands, one of them an intellectual history of the rise of culturalist discourse in Bengal, and the other an elaboration of a theory about the relation of this discourse to its conditions of existence. Both of the main arguments are thoughtful and interesting. The attempt to develop a sophisticated Marxist approach to intellectual history contains moments of insight. The re-readings of Bengali intellectual history, including iconic figures such as Rammohun Roy, Bankim Chandra Chatterjee, Rabindranath Tagore, and others are original and provocative. Indeed, the more conventional intellectual history is the better part of the book, for I am not convinced by the materialist/Marxist attempt to trace culturalism back to the logic of capitalism.

In the very limited space available, I can only register my disagreements and reservations. The question of what made culturalist discourse plausible across very different histories is a good one, but for Sartori this immediately becomes a question about the *material* conditions that made culturalist discourse possible. At the heart of this book is a distinction between the discursive/ideational and the material/social, and the presumption that the material/social domain is "logically prior" to the discursive/ideational domain, and that the latter must in some sense originate in, and derive its intelligibility from, the former. This claim is sometimes made as an assertion, as when the author declares that the appropriation of Western concepts in Bengal "must have had its roots in moments of social transformation" (p. 19); elsewhere, we are told that the "referential dimension" must be accorded logical priority over the "hermeneutic dimension" if historical explanation is to succeed (p. 63). Posed in these terms, there is an intuitive reasonableness to according the material explanatory priority over the ideational, but it is this metaphysical opposition that warrants problematization. But even if we grant that the world is divided into reference and discourse, or the material and the ideational, and that the former must explain the latter, the actual demonstration of how global capitalism enabled culturalism in Bengal is not always very convincing.

Sometimes the author makes this argument by invoking Karl Marx's distinction between real and formal subsumption to capital. By the nineteenth century Bengal had become integrated into global circuits of capital, and therefore, even if old ways of life continued, "the sheer fact of their being embedded within the new social context of a capitalist social formation" meant they were, more or less by definitional fiat, "fundamentally transformed" (p. 52), and this material/social transformation is what explains Bengali culturalism. But if in important respects lifeworlds had not been transformed, then surely formal subsumption is, in this context, a moot point; if lifeworlds were the same as before, why would Bengalis need the culture concept or find it plausible? In other places Sartori endeavors to show that Bengali society, including peasant production, was transformed in important ways by Bengal's integration into a global capitalist order and that these material changes were intimately connected to the rise of Bengali culturalism. However, the arguments for the transformation of Bengali society rely heavily upon a selectively used secondary literature, and for the most part the attempt to relate these changes to intellectual developments is forced.

These critical comments should be read in the knowledge that the reviewer's own critical coordinates are in important respects shaped by postcolonial theory, an approach the author finds wanting and seeks to surpass. My criticisms notwithstanding, this is a highly intelligent and original book, one that will be read with profit by anyone interested in Bengali intellectual history and in methodological questions of how intellectual history should be written.

SANJAY SETH
Goldsmiths, University of London

OCEANIA AND THE PACIFIC ISLANDS

BAIN ATTWOOD. *Possession: Batman's Treaty and the Matter of History*. Assisted by HELEN DOYLE. (Miegunyah Volumes, Second Series, number 115.) Carlton, Victoria: The Miegunyah Press. 2009. Pp. xv, 415. $54.99.

In 1835, John Batman produced a document that he claimed as proof that he had purchased a large tract of land from the Aboriginal people in the area that is now Melbourne. The document and the transaction it evidenced would have been unexceptional in many other parts of the British Empire, particularly North America, where settlers and colonial officials had been acquiring land in similar transactions with indigenous people for two centuries. In Australia, however, where British practice was to occupy land without regard to its prior Aboriginal inhabitants, Batman's treaty was the very first. It was also the last. The imperial government refused to recognize the treaty, and the British continued to take land by force. Batman died, disfigured by syphilis, a few years later.

Bain Attwood's book is about both the treaty and the way the treaty has been remembered over the years. The first of the book's three parts, and in my view the best, is a wonderfully nuanced and contextualized account of the treaty itself. Despite little direct evidence from the purchasers' point of view, and even less from the sellers', Attwood does an exemplary job of reconstructing how the transaction would have been understood from both sides. Batman's treaty has always presented some puzzles. Why would a group of adventurers have bothered to negotiate it, when there had never been any such transactions in Australia before? What meanings would the Aboriginal sellers have attributed to it? Why did the would-be purchasers put so much time and effort into what seems, at least in retrospect, to have been the hopeless task of trying to convince the imperial government to recognize the treaty's validity? In providing the most comprehensive answers to these questions to date, Attwood makes good use of the recent burst of scholarship on the legal relations between settlers and indigenous people throughout the empire, especially the work of Paul McHugh.

The second part of the book traces the rise of Batman's posthumous reputation. Nearly forgotten in the 1850s, Batman became an honored founder of Melbourne by the end of the century. This section is a chronicle of patriotic settler historians spinning tales of the brave and farsighted pioneers who had come before them, of historical societies erecting suitable monuments, and of all the paintings, plaques, and busts imagining Batman anew in each generation. Attwood's purpose here is to show how Batman came to be remembered not for trying to dispossess Aborigines of land but rather for choosing the location of a great city, something he probably never did. Batman serves as a symbol of popular white historical memory, as a leading player in a story from which the Aborigines had been largely erased. This part of the book culminates in Victoria's centennial celebration of 1934–1935, which included a Batman impersonator and an exhibit of Batman relics at the National Gallery of Victoria.

In the last part of the book, memories of Batman turn darker, as Aborigines re-enter colonial history. Batman and his treaty play an ambivalent role, and ultimately a minor one, in the campaign for Aboriginal land rights. The treaty could be viewed as just another sorry episode in a long history of mistreatment, or it could be seen as the sole occasion on which settlers respected Aboriginal property rights and tried to purchase land rather than seize it. Batman drops out of Attwood's story for long stretches in these chapters, which are really about the general relationship between whites and Aborigines in the second half of the twentieth century. When Batman does appear, it is clear that the popular memory of him is beginning to fade. Shoppers pay little attention to Batman's memorial, now stuck in the corner of a market's parking lot. As Attwood notes, "perhaps the cult popularity of another Batman narrative, one about a detective with cape, cowl and bat logo, which circulated in comic books and film serials, made it increas-ingly difficult for the city's cultural elite to take a local historical figure with the same name seriously" (p. 279).

The Melbourne University Press deserves applause for the lavish design of the book, which is published under its Miegunyah imprint. There are approximately ninety pictures, many in full color. Because much of the book is about depictions of Batman rather than Batman himself, the pictures are particularly valuable.

STUART BANNER
University of California,
Los Angeles

CANADA AND THE UNITED STATES

PHILLIP BUCKNER, editor. *Canada and the British Empire.* (The Oxford History of the British Empire, Companion Series.) New York: Oxford University Press. 2008. Pp. xiv, 294. $70.00.

This book is on a mission to restore the British Empire to Canadian history. Since the 1960s widespread amnesia has developed with respect to the imperial dimension of Canadian history. Phillip Buckner, in his vigorous yet scholarly introduction, emphasizes that the volume's contributors are not apologists for now-discredited aspects of imperialism, yet he is critical of the way in which the empire has been air-brushed from current presentations of Canada's past. "Most Canadian historians," he complains, "continue to believe that Canadian participation in the Empire was an elite preoccupation, and that the support for the Empire did not have deep roots in Canadian soil. This volume essentially refutes that proposition" (p. 20). The approach is refreshingly comprehensive both in terms of chronology and themes, going right back to the earliest European contacts with the Aboriginal peoples, and covering everything from "Women, Gender, and Empire" (by Adele Perry) to "Economy and Empire: Britain and Canadian Development, 1783–1971" (by Douglas McCalla) and "British Justice: English Law and Canadian Legal Culture" (by Philip Girard).

Most chapters are written by seasoned specialists which gives substance to the arguments made. When John G. Reid and Elizabeth Mancke, for example, write on the "Emergence of British North America to 1783," they place the "Canadian" parts of the story within the current literature on the Atlantic world. Even more broadly, they place this North American case in the context of tensions between commerce and settlement that existed in all the European empires of that era as they pursued their interests from the Great Lakes to the Indian Ocean.

It was during the 150 years following the American Revolution that the empire had its most wide-ranging impact on the remaining British colonies, and on what became, after 1867, the Dominion of Canada. The migration of loyalists from the United States and the burst of British emigration between 1815 and the 1840s confirmed the British colonial cast of anglophone Canada, which made it quite different in terms of values and institutions from the republic to the south. Even most French Canadians during this era willingly accepted the empire in spite of some rough moments because, from the 1774 Quebec Act onward, imperial policies helped preserve their language and religion when the only alternative seemed absorption into the aggressive, excessively individualist, and assimilationist United States. This core period is authoritatively dealt with by J. M. Bumsted ("The Consolidation of British North America, 1783–60"), Buckner himself ("The Creation of the Dominion of Canada, 1860–1901"), and John Herd Thompson ("Canada and the 'Third British Empire,' 1901–39"). Each shows clearly, with abundant evidence, that loyalty to the empire never signified unthinking deference to British policies or British mores. Pride in being Canadian—the first and most important dominion—was inextricably intertwined with pride in the empire.

Colin M. Coates's chapter on "French Canadians' Ambivalence toward the British Empire" is the first reminder of why the empire eventually became so problematic in Canada. French Canadian willingness to accept their place in the empire took a different direction when the empire called on Canadians to fight imperial wars overseas. During the South African War, for example, French Canadian sympathies lay with the Boers, whom they chose to see as a community struggling for survival against the military might of the empire. When a more assertive Québécois nationalism emerged during the 1950s and 1960s, one obvious way to counter its claims was to remove the remaining symbols of an empire-shaped identity and replace these with exclusively Canadian symbols (such as the new maple leaf flag in 1964). Thus in the history of Canada that began to be reconstructed from the 1960s onward the empire faded away. This tendency was given additional impetus as the Canadian population was transformed by non-British immigrants, many of them from the Indian sub-continent, whose ancestors had often suffered at the sharp end of British imperialism.

Buckner and his fellow authors are well aware of the forces that have led to the marginalization of empire but they do a first-rate job in forcing readers to consider the manifold ways in which empire has been a core element in Canadian history. The Aboriginal peoples, for example, often looked to the imperial authorities in London for some leverage against local colonists. By the 1800s, as in other parts of the empire, the London government could often be more sensitive (at least rhetorically and on paper) than the settler population. "The flag of the Siksika (Blackfoot) nation," Sarah Carter points out, "features a tipi fashioned out of the Union Jack, signifying their 1877 treaty and their enduring connection with the British Crown, their treaty partner" (p. 218). In the 1980s the Aboriginal peoples worked successfully to delay the patriation to Canada of the 1867 British North America Act in protest against a new constitutional arrangement that did not entrench their rights as recognized by imperial Britain. The manner in which bringing in the empire nicely complicates Canadian history is also evident when it comes to women and empire. Perry shows that while it is possible to find women who were critical of imperial polices, mainstream women's movements were eager to promote Canada's links with the empire. One example was the founding in the 1890s of the Imperial Order Daughters of the Empire (its membership reaching 50,000 by the outbreak of the Great War in 1914).

This book succeeds splendidly in its stated goal. It shows that Canadian history without the empire is stunted and flawed. This curious turn of events in the presentation of Canada's past raises fundamental issues about the uses and misuses of history. One of the things at work in creating the problem addressed by this book is the changing nature of the field of history itself. National histories were at one time standard approaches to the past, but this is no longer the case; in most university history departments single-country courses are now outnumbered by topical, thematic, regional, comparative, or global offerings. It is worth noting in this context that the work of Reid and Mancke on early Atlantic Canada fits much more readily (and more interestingly) into the fields of Atlantic history and seventeenth and eighteenth century imperial history than it does into the framework of Canadian national history.

But there is an even bigger issue at work than these new directions in academic history writing. The relationship between history and national identity is always fraught with tension; this is particularly problematic in all the former settlement colonies within the British Empire. Canadians nowadays like to see themselves as tolerant, committed to diversity, civic-minded, and international in outlook. Keeping the British Empire in the story of Canada's past makes such decent and diffident self-images more difficult to sustain. That is why, for most ordinary Canadians, the empire has well-nigh disappeared from Canadian history. In spite of their immense knowledge, historians, alas, have much less influence than they would like in determining how the past is remembered by the general public. But this fine book challenges professional historians in Canada not to join in the forgetting.

GORDON T. STEWART
Michigan State University

ANNMARIE ADAMS. *Medicine by Design: The Architect and the Modern Hospital, 1893–1943.* (Architecture, Landscape, and American Culture Series.) Minneapolis: University of Minnesota Press. 2008. Pp. xxv, 169. $27.50.

Current efforts in the construction of hospitals directed toward "healing by design" recognize the fact that health care facilities providing medical services must also take into consideration the social and psychological needs of patients. Annmarie Adams has written a thought-provoking book highlighting the active role played by architecture in the development of twentieth century medicine. She rightly condemns medical historians for their tendency to privilege written sources while considering artifacts such as buildings mere embodiments of medical concepts. Although both the scope and length of her work are modest—it only covers a few Canadian hospitals from the 1890s to World War II—this publication provides a wealth of detail and helps readers understand the importance of hospital buildings during a critical period in the evolution of scientific medicine. Indeed, the interwar years witnessed the dramatic transformation of hospitals into professional workshops. Their new image allowed them to become institutions of first resort not only for the poor, but also for the middling and upper classes.

Through a close reading of plans and descriptions, the author's stated goal is to present a few examples of hospital architecture and depict their designs as products of a contested, dynamic enterprise not only involving medical experts but also the architects themselves. Chapter one features a snapshot of the Royal Victorian Hospital in Montreal that opened its doors in 1893, followed by a second chapter describing the addition of the Ross Memorial Pavilion, built in 1920 for the purpose of attracting a middle-class clientele. Chapter three deals with issues of social class, discussing private patients—with emphasis on women requiring obstetrical services—and children. Next comes a section on nurses and their spatial confinement, followed by another on architects and physicians. A final chapter summarizes the new architectural features of modernism.

The book prominently features the life and work of the American architect Edward F. Stevens (1860–1946), who, together with his partner Frederick Lee from Chicago, was responsible for the construction of nearly a hundred hospitals during their twenty-one-year association. Stevens embodied the new twentieth-century architect with special expertise in the design of hospitals based on his familiarity with the demands of modern medical practice. Well-traveled, he assiduously visited European institutions to learn about novel divisions of hospital labor, equipment and procedures, and the impact of professional nursing. From the Pasteur Institute, Stevens took home cost-efficient strategies to promote antisepsis and mitigate institutional contagion. Moreover, he was keenly aware of the critical importance of kitchen and laundry facilities together with power plants for running an institution. With a previous background in designing large private dwellings, Stevens came to be uniquely qualified for the tasks that would replace older monumental, pavilion-type complexes such as the Royal Victoria Hospital in Montreal—the "castle for the poor"—with new structures designed from the inside out with priority given to spatial arrangements that facilitated and enhanced the hospital's functions.

Adams deftly juxtaposes the old with the new, first describing the location and configuration of the Royal Victoria, a civic landmark and general hospital for Montreal's poor. She then shifts "from castle to hotel" to consider the Ross Memorial Pavilion adjacent to the Royal Victoria, designed and built in 1920 by Stevens and Lee for housing private, paying patients. With its

outside appearance of another medieval castle, the interior hotel ambience sought to appeal to the throng of middle-class patients now ready to experience the luxuries of large, paneled rooms with balconies, fine furnishings, overstuffed chairs, and private telephones. A gated entrance, formal garden, and teahouse contributed to the appeal. Physicians and surgeons, for their part, came to enjoy ample operating and working suites.

The panorama presented by the author is one of creative architects familiar with the shifting needs of medical practice and the financial constraints of administrators faced with escalating costs. These men competed with physicians who had acquired some expertise in architectural design and sought, as "hospital consultants," to keep design issues within the realm of the medical profession. Both groups, often working together, went on to shape a wave of old hospital conversions, additions, and new constructions extending into the present. Readers will detect similarities with the current situation. After a post-World War II period of sterile "matchbox on a muffin" hospitals designed to accommodate expanding diagnostic and therapeutic technologies, designers are once more busy attempting to recreate homelike environments. For historians interested in the dynamics of hospital design and its reflection of changing aesthetic, social, and medical values, this book provides an instructive case study.

GUENTER B. RISSE
University of California,
San Francisco, and
University of Washington,
Seattle

H. SOPHIE BURTON and F. TODD SMITH. *Colonial Natchitoches: A Creole Community on the Louisiana-Texas Frontier.* (Elma Dill Russell Spencer Series in the West and Southwest, number 29.) College Station: Texas A&M University Press. 2008. Pp. xiii, 216. $39.95.

Anyone interested in community formation will find this book a joy to read. A model local study, it is also a tribute to teamwork. F. Todd Smith brings to the task extensive knowledge of the Native Americans in the Old Southwest, so the reader is often reminded of the town's situation in Indian country. The body of evidence is gathered from a wide variety of French and Spanish manuscript sources. The statistical evidence of the town's social profile is presented in no less than fifty tables.

Established in 1714 on French Louisiana's frontier with Spanish Texas, Natchitoches (pronounced "nak-a-tish") began as a racially heterogeneous society "on a relatively equal basis" (p. x), but that soon changed. While the town always remained mixed like other North American towns, it soon developed "a higher percentage of free people of French descent" (p. x) than the rest of Louisiana. All free people were French throughout the colonial period, sharing their Catholicism and Creole lifestyle with the rest of French Louisianians. That is Smith and H. Sophie Burton's first major finding. The second finding is that the Indian trade did not dominate the town's economy throughout the colonial period, contrary to historians' assumptions in the past. Finally, the town developed into a true slave society dominated by a tobacco planter class (by the 1770s), and it was a typical North American slave regime that kept a nearly all-black slave population in subjugation by force. (There were a few dozen Chitimacha and Apache domestic slaves.)

There are no signs here of fluid racial categories that allowed for social mobility, and certainly no racial intermarriages, except for a handful of peripheral men married to Indian women, usually by Indian rites. The French planters married strictly among themselves and those newcomers known to have impeccable, unmixed ancestry. When Spain took over the colony in the 1760s, Spanish officials made a modest formal attempt to ameliorate the day-to-day treatment of slaves, and allowed a few who had the money to purchase their freedom, but Burton and Smith are not able to discover any measurable change in the condition of most slaves. In short, it was just like the slave regime in New Orleans.

Implied with the racial conclusions are two other generalizations. First, Indians were far less visible in the town itself than one might expect in a frontier community, although the product of their labor in tens of thousands of skins and furs sustained the annual economy in the early years. Second, unlike the French or English, the Spanish directly encouraged colonial economic development in the era of Charles III, with remarkable success.

Just a small expense by the Spanish governor (in subsidizing the cost of freight to New Orleans) led almost overnight to the production of huge quantities of tobacco and to the appearance of a substantial slave-owning class. The government encouraged the African slave trade to the province, and even offered to subsidize the purchase of slaves. But the resulting economic boom had the effect of fastening slaves and arrogant slave-owners on the town, generally "exacerbating class differences and increasing the gap between rich and poor" (p. 126).

The planter class was vibrant and growing along with its slave population before the Louisiana Purchase in 1803. In 1791, the slaves of eighty-three planters produced 700,000 pounds of tobacco (p. 18). However, the Spanish stopped buying tobacco in 1789 because of oversupply, and the planters were momentarily flummoxed and rebellious against Spanish rule. Then they quickly made the transition from tobacco to cotton, along with the Anglo-American planters in the upcountry of the Deep South. It bears emphasis that the Anglo-Americans who took over the province in 1803 did not make it over according to their own supposed strict regime of slavery, for the local planters had established the same repressive order at the beginning. As in the rest of the South, moreover, their slave population was growing by natural reproduction, for the town received few of the new slave imports between 1769 and 1808. In

1803, the population comprised 948 slaves and 900 free people.

A special chapter on free blacks describes them as a growing segment of the population, but never large enough—nor sufficiently prosperous nor free enough from dependency on whites—to form a cohesive or happy community of their own.

Other chapters cover the traders in the commerce with Indians and the cattle ranchers. Over time, the Indian trade declined and ranching became less profitable as the state stopped promoting the sale of beef to Mexico at the end of the 1780s. Both the traders and ranchers formed less reputable groups, among whom the planters were unlikely to seek spouses.

All historians of the early Deep South should put this book on their essential reading list.

THOMAS N. INGERSOLL
Ohio State University

ROSALIND J. BEILER. *Immigrant and Entrepreneur: The Atlantic World of Caspar Wistar, 1650–1750.* (Max Kade German-American Research Institute Series.) University Park: Pennsylvania State University Press. 2008. Pp. xii, 208. $55.00.

This book provides the reader with a serious picture of German immigration to eighteenth-century Pennsylvania. It has nothing to do with the "quaint Dutch," hex signs on barns, or painted marriage chests. Instead, although the argument is never explicitly presented as revisionist, the emphasis is on the ways in which German political, religious, and business practices exerted influence in colonial Pennsylvania, forming the roots of what has usually been considered American exceptionalism. Through meticulous research and careful analysis, and aided by a plethora of maps, figures, and tables, Rosalind J. Beiler makes a convincing case.

In eight chapters, evenly divided between old world and new, the work introduces the reader to a detailed picture of the seventeenth-century Palatine from which the majority of Germans immigrated to Pennsylvania, and an equally comprehensive narrative of the rags-to-riches life of Caspar Wistar, unquestionably one of the most successful of these immigrants.

The first two chapters are filled with minutiae relating to the lives of Wistar's grandfather and father, the villages in which they lived, the trials and tribulations of foresters and hunters in a bureaucratic electorate that suffered under war and scarcity, and in which petty local quarrels could destroy a family's livelihood and honor. They also provide a clear picture of how one might operate in such an environment—advancing through ability rather than birth or education, learning mediation skills, and developing business techniques for producing and marketing commodities.

Chapter four deals with the history of immigration in general and Wistar's experience in particular. Much of this is speculative since there is very little evidence about Wistar's own situation, and there are a great number of "must haves" and "probablies." What personal material does exist gives a moving sense of the emotional wrench that such leave-taking involved.

Most interesting perhaps is chapter three, which traces the ways in which religious diversity in the Palatine flourished despite a nominally established church. There religious affiliation was chosen more for social and economic reasons than doctrinal ones. Reared in a family whose members included Lutherans, Reformed, Roman Catholics, and a brother who dabbled in Pietism, Wistar, who himself became a Quaker, adjusted readily to the Pennsylvania scene.

The second half of Beiler's work details Wistar's American world and the ways in which he both adapted to and changed it. The impression is of an opportunistic man who used his knowledge and experience of the German world to achieve his ends. Chapter five follows Wistar's youthful steps (uncannily like those of Benjamin Franklin in his autobiography) as he joined the Quaker establishment through marriage, political, and professional connections.

The remainder of the book focuses on Wistar's business acumen and the ways in which he became a very rich and powerful man. His understanding of land as a marketable commodity made him both a patron of the German American community and a leader in shaping the ethnic landscape of Pennsylvania. His activities as a merchant helped to form a German-speaking Atlantic world by facilitating trade in the goods the newcomers were accustomed to, assisting them in dealing in all sorts of problems of living in the new land, and keeping up communication between old world and new.

Finally, in a stunning chapter on business practice, Beiler shows how, rather than being an example of American exceptionalism, the glass company Wistar founded borrowed German business ways, developing workers' contracts that resembled those of a modern corporation and creating an environment that functioned like a nineteenth-century factory town. The workers depended on the company for food and housing, they bought goods on credit against the profit of the glass they would make that year, and the bosses ran the general store and the grist mill.

The major flaw in an otherwise exemplary work is the lack of any description or analysis of the everyday nature of the lives of Germans in their homeland or in Pennsylvania. A look at the material world of these folks would help to bring the eighteenth century alive and humanize the book's central figure. There are tantalizing hints: the importation of shirt clasps decorated with hearts; hairpins like "those the Mennonite or Swiss women wear" (p. 145); Wistar's use of an English signature even on German documents, although it is clear he spoke with a heavy German accent. Finally, one wishes for at least as much concentration on the American family Wistar created as on the German one he left behind.

This aside, Beiler's book should be of interest to historians who seek to understand the relationship between early America and the rest of the Atlantic world.

STEPHANIE GRAUMAN WOLF
McNiel Center for Early American Studies
University of Pennsylvania

EMORY G. EVANS. *A "Topping People": The Rise and Decline of Virginia's Old Political Elite, 1680–1790.* Charlottesville: University of Virginia Press. 2009. Pp. x, 266. $55.00.

Sometime during the evening of January 1, 1777, William Byrd III—son and grandson respectively to two of the wealthiest and most influential men of colonial Virginia—took his own life. Overwhelmed with debt, Byrd had recently borne the insult of having his offer to serve as an officer during the American Revolution rejected: first by the British, then by Virginia's patriots. Even Byrd's seat on the Council of State seemed increasingly superfluous. Earlier that same day Royal Governor Dunmore had ordered the burning of Norfolk as he fled Virginia on a British warship. It was a long fall for a family that had held a seat on the Council for almost a century and that had often intrigued on both sides of the Atlantic to get its way. Now that the war had begun, Byrd was left with nothing of worth to offer either side.

Emory G. Evans examines the wealthiest and most influential of Virginia's families, a much more exclusive group than the better-known first families of Virginia. The study focuses on twenty-one families—including the Byrds, Carters, Lees, Nelsons, and Randolphs, among others—who dominated the Old Dominion's political, economic, and social life. In almost every case, each family's progenitor—typically a younger son of the English gentry—arrived in the Old Dominion well before 1680. Other traits common to these foremost families included two or more men serving on Virginia's powerful Council of State, the colony's twelve-member upper house. This select group also served as the colony's highest court and advisors to the governor. The first generations were blessedly long-lived, a relatively rare trait in early Virginia. These same families were inter-related to an astonishing degree. Large families were the norm, and it was common for several generations to live together in one great house. All of them made money from tobacco. Uncommonly acquisitive, these men "operated stores, loaned money, served as agents and factors for English firms in both the tobacco and slave trades, managed estates for absentee owners, rented land, owned parts of vessels in the Atlantic trade, operated ferries and ironworks, and held a variety of remunerative public positions" (p. 92).

Evans begins his study in 1680, shortly after Bacon's Rebellion when the crown was actively striving to reassert its authority in Virginia. During this time, the Council just as strenuously fought to protect its own interests, especially the custom of granting its members many thousands of acres. This battle of wills continued from the arrival of Governor Effingham in 1684 until 1722, when Hugh Drysdale replaced Alexander Spotswood as the king's representative in Virginia. The next three decades, by contrast, were marked with "calm and usually amicable relations" between the governor and the Council (p. 71). Politically the Council gradually lost influence to the House of Burgesses, where the top families were also well represented. The families continued to acquire land, hatch schemes of profit and improvement, and marry one another's children, widows, nieces, and nephews. In the midst of an active social life of dancing, cards, and visiting, most of them were slipping further into debt.

Virginia's first families lived similar lives. While individual members could be famously competitive, their overall interests were broadly similar, as were their attitudes, measures of success, and anxieties. While the Council was generally successful in its contest with the governors over the practice of granting its members land, they rarely succeeded in their land speculation schemes. Overproduction and the resultant low prices for tobacco hurt many of the families, even as they attempted to diversify to other crops. Falling income rarely led the first families to curb their purchases or their lifestyles. Accustomed to the ready credit offered by London factors, the families continued spending until alarmed creditors limited their ability to borrow just before the American Revolution. By 1776, two-thirds of the twenty-one families were in "serious financial trouble" (p. 114), in stark contrast to 1700, when nineteen of the families had been financially secure. Evans's assessment of William Byrd III in the latter eighteenth century could easily apply to many of the other families: "Unable to escape an enormous debt and unwilling to give up an extravagant lifestyle, he long since had lost the independence so important to him" (p. 193).

Evans deftly balances the complexities of Virginia's elite families—especially their multilayered interconnections—with a compelling story of intrigue and competition. It is divided into topical chapters on politics, economics, and society. A thoughtful introduction and epilogue, ten black and white portraits, and several tables, together with over fifty pages of notes complete the volume. This book is strongly recommended to everyone interested in Virginia history and historians of the eighteenth century.

L. SCOTT PHILYAW
Western Carolina University

JEWEL L. SPANGLER. *Virginians Reborn: Anglican Monopoly, Evangelical Dissent, and the Rise of the Baptists in the Late Eighteenth Century.* Charlottesville: University of Virginia Press. 2008. Pp. viii, 288. $45.00.

In this deeply researched and well-argued book, Jewel L. Spangler offers an important reconceptualization of the early history of evangelicalism in the American South. Focusing on the rise of the Baptist denomination in late colonial Virginia, Spangler rejects the widely held notion that evangelicalism constituted a class-inflected insurgency against the hierarchical values of the southern gentry (an interpretation most closely associated with the innovative work of Rhys Isaac in the

1970s and 1980s). Spangler argues instead for the basic compatibility of Baptist practices with those of "the dominant social and political order" (p. 4) and concludes that the Baptists ultimately "participated in preserving and carrying forward the old colonial hierarchies into the postwar era" (p. 8).

The first half of Spangler's book makes the case that the rise of evangelicalism in the colony was not primarily a product of underlying social or cultural tensions but rather of "a subtle interplay of something like religious supply and demand" (p. 48). Spangler demonstrates that the inconsistent geographic and institutional development of Virginia's Anglican establishment allowed first Presbyterians and later Baptists to gain a "toehold" (p. 3) in the colony by providing underserved Virginians with access to worship and Christian community in areas where the establishment was weak and by offering alternative forms of worship and community to those dissatisfied with the establishment in areas where it was stronger.

The success of the Baptists in the 1760s and 1770s prompted hostile reactions from defenders of the establishment, and historians have often used such reactions as evidence of the social and cultural radicalism of the evangelical upsurge in Virginia. But in the book's central chapter, "The Baptists and the Dominant Order," Spangler delves deeply into church minutes and local records to paint a picture of a movement that was neither as socioeconomically marginal nor as socially radical as this rhetoric suggests. Although converts came predominantly from the ranks of small farmers, Baptists claimed members from across the social spectrum—including the relatively wealthy—and the strict moral discipline of their churches echoed broader concerns in the colony about virtue, order, debt, and self-discipline.

Most importantly, Baptists embraced the same basic presumptions of white male patriarchal authority that had structured Virginia society for more than a century. Baptists saw women and slaves as spiritual equals in theory, but in practice the white male-controlled churches treated white women as "decidedly unequal persons" (pp. 152–153) and slaves of both sexes as "household dependents of the lowest order" (p. 158). Antislavery sentiment in the churches was weak, conflicted, and easily contained, and by allowing non-slaveholding white men to participate in the discipline of enslaved members Baptists may even have given poorer whites "the necessary direct experience to form their own version of proslavery ideology" (p. 164). The "primacy of the patriarchal household" (p. 152) and the perpetuation of slavery thus constituted powerful continuities between Baptist practice and Virginia's traditional order.

Within these limitations, however, Spangler still finds Baptists distinctive in important ways. The emotional experience of conversion constituted a deeply meaningful personal transformation that created communities of believers across worldly boundaries even as formal church membership reinstated and reinforced those boundaries. The process of collective discipline and the demand for converts to submit to both God and church resulted in an attenuation (though not an erasure) of hierarchical distinctions among white men, an innovation that became more palatable to many Virginians as the political and cultural changes of the Revolutionary era moved the mainstream in a similar direction. Indeed, the American Revolution reshaped Virginia's dominant order in ways that undermined opponents' primary critiques of the Baptists and made the movement's areas of convergence with the mainstream more apparent. Ultimately, through their intertwined commitments to patriarchy, self-government, and white male equality, Baptists joined other Virginians in "an ongoing process of incorporating revolutionary principles into a slaveholding society" (p. 228).

Spangler's emphasis on the contingency of the Baptists' rise and her careful attention to the specifics of chronology and local variation are particularly impressive and welcome. By focusing attention on the compatibilities rather than the conflicts between Baptist values and those of the Virginia mainstream she inverts the traditional approach and provides critical new insights. Occasionally, however, the book's argument seems too starkly drawn. Both the Baptists themselves and the Virginia mainstream sometimes appear unproblematically monolithic, when each was rife with power struggles and internal contradictions. The book's focus on white men and the effectiveness of their domination of dependent white women and slaves creates a top-down model of Baptist culture that could be leavened with greater attention to diversity and conflict within that culture. Although these issues suggest additional complications, they do not invalidate the book's argument or central insights. This very fine study deserves to serve as a touchstone for emerging new interpretations of the rise of evangelicalism and its place in the origins of the Old South.

RANDOLPH FERGUSON SCULLY
George Mason University

KONSTANTIN DIERKS. *In My Power: Letter Writing and Communications in Early America.* (Early American Studies.) Philadelphia: University of Pennsylvania Press. 2009. Pp. xviii, 358. $45.00.

Konstantin Dierks has used letters from over 300 collections of eighteenth-century family papers on America's eastern seaboard to address now familiar transatlantic topics: empire, commerce, migration, consumption, revolution, and race. Devoting a chapter to each, and personalizing each topic through at least one contemporary letter writer, Dierks retells the story of America's founding as a transatlantic narrative about the "rise to ascendancy" of the "British and American middle class" (p. 1) through letter-writing, conceived as a form of personal agency and as a manner of making history that unconsciously disempowered Africans, Indians, and anyone who was not middle class.

Chapter one, "Communications and Empire," which

begins with Edward Randolph arriving in Boston with a letter from the king, touches on British universities, conduct books, the establishment of local and transatlantic infrastructure (post office, roads, packets, and paper making), and the institution of the Lords of Trade and Plantation to argue that the only people "required" (p. 49) to communicate across the Atlantic in the seventeenth century were royal officials, who in this account used letters exclusively to exert authority over others. Letter-writing as a form of personal agency is identified with men of business in chapter two, "Letter Writing and Commercial Revolution," which describes the vast array of printed matter (business, accounting, penmanship, and letter manuals) available to teach transatlantic tradesmen the requisite skills, and personalizes transatlantic commerce through the careers of Henry Laurens and Joseph Crittenden. Chapter three, "Migration and Empire," describes letters by immigrants trying to stay in touch with family members throughout the empire and uses the career of Henry Bouquet, a mercenary Swiss officer employed by the British, to discuss interactions with Indians on the frontier and describe the intercolonial postal service. Chapter four, "Letter Writing and Consumer Revolution," gives a short account of the ubiquity of the letter form in all genres of eighteenth-century print from politics and science to the epistolary novel, discusses the ambiguous relations between middle-class familiar letters in America and the prescribed epistolary forms, and returns to questions of paper-making to castigate the middle class for its myopia about its exploitation of others. Chapter five, "Revolution and War," describes the patriot takeover of the American postal system and establishment of wartime communications. The final chapter, "Universalism and the Epistolary Divide," shows the American middle class ensuring that its children acquired skills which it denied others on racial grounds.

The new material here—the little-explored letters from the 300 American family collections—appears only as snippets within Dierks's generalizing descriptions of what they were like. But Dierks repeatedly insists that his larger narrative about the role of letters, infrastructure, and printed manuals in the ascendancy of the middle class is something of which eighteenth-century letter-writers were completely unaware, and which would be validated only in the nineteenth century. Together with his emphasis on "writing history forward through imagination and effort" (p. 11), this creates an admirably readable, wide-ranging, yet streamlined historical narrative that integrates letters into the American story and opens the way for others to do more nuanced work. It would be interesting to know, for instance, how different segments of the American middle class—artisans, tradesmen, merchants, and professionals—used letters; whether differences in style or use prevented some segments of this class from rising to ascendancy while enabling others to constitute themselves as a ruling elite; and why, in the nineteenth century, when the middle class was in the ascendancy, letters ceased to be the dominant, all-pervasive genre of public and private documentation and communication they had been in the eighteenth century.

It would be good too to have more close studies of neglected family letters *as* letters, and to learn how missives actually written by the letter-writing middle ranks related to those of other letter-writing sectors of the population such as plantation owners in the South, farmers in the North, religious communities of different denominations, and indentured servants and migrant workers, many of whom also had transatlantic links. If, as Dierks argues, we need "a cultural, social, economic and political history of communications and letter writing in the eighteenth-century Anglophone world, a history that is fully comprehensive across a matrix of social groups and cultural domains" (p. 3), we also need a clearer sense of differences between the situation of the letter-writing middle ranks in America and those in British Canada, the West Indies, and Britain, where the letter-writing gentry and aristocracy did not become irrelevant in 1700 and the letters of "the meanest persons" were swelling the post as early as 1674 (p. 33). It is to be hoped, therefore, that this book will stimulate and empower a whole new generation of work on letters in the Atlantic world.

Eve Tavor Bannet

University of Oklahoma [All reviewers of books by Indiana University faculty are selected with the advice of the Board of Editors.]

Richard Godbeer. *The Overflowing of Friendship: Love between Men and the Creation of the American Republic.* Baltimore: Johns Hopkins University Press. 2009. Pp. xii, 254. $35.00.

Historians have long been aware of the existence of profoundly romantic, emotionally and physically expressive friendships between women in nineteenth-century America, friendships that confound modern categories of identity and sexual orientation. This new book by Richard Godbeer will surprise many, for it explores the romantic friendships that were common among *men*, particularly well-educated white men during the American Revolutionary era.

Godbeer presents abundant evidence of the ubiquity of intense, loving, emotionally expressive bonds among educated middle and upper-middle-class young men in mid-eighteenth-century America. These men imagined their friendships as redemptive and ennobling influences that would inspire them to behave virtuously. They expressed passionate feelings of adoration and longing for their friends, toward whom they were physically affectionate and demonstrative. They usually formed loving friendships when they were young, although Godbeer finds that these friendships often persisted for a lifetime. Incongruously (to us), men did not usually think of these friendships as involving sexual attraction or sexual lust. In fact, they imagined their loving friendships with men as entirely compatible with their loving marriages to women.

The ideal of loving male friendship, Godbeer suggests, emerged from the confluence of several intellectual influences in colonial American culture. A model of redemptive friendship had existed among seventeenth-century Puritans, who imagined loving relationships between redeemed Christians emerging from powerful feelings of their shared love for Christ and for one another. Prerevolutionary evangelical Protestants revived the notion that re-born men and women were bound together in intensely emotional bonds of love and sympathy. And eighteenth-century moral philosophers associated with the Scottish Enlightenment, including Francis Hutcheson, David Hume, and Adam Smith, helped to popularize the notion that mutual sympathy and love between friends could provide a basis for social harmony and morality. Friendship would teach individuals to cultivate sympathetic feelings and benevolence and, in turn, make them behave virtuously toward all of mankind, making possible a truly harmonious society in which people pursued the public good rather than their selfish individual interests.

While Godbeer is not the first historian to notice the ideal of romantic male friendship in eighteenth-century America, his beautifully crafted book breaks important new ground by connecting the ideal of sympathetic fraternal love to the reconceptualization of politics and political community in revolutionary America. Various scholarly trends, not least a Whiggish tendency in American historical writing, have made us imagine the American Revolution mostly as a struggle by individuals resisting domination or seeking autonomy. In fact, the revolutionary struggle also involved a rethinking of the basis for mutual solidarity and community, including political community. Prerevolutionary Americans imagined themselves as bound together by their shared loyalty to the king. Before repudiating their shared bond with England, they had to find a way to re-imagine the moral obligations on which community could be based. The basis for those obligations would be mutual sympathy and benevolence, and loving friendship was understood as one of the experiences through which sympathy could be nurtured.

Godbeer's argument makes an important contribution to the question of how it became possible to create a functioning civil society in the early American republic. As he argues here, friendship provided a metaphor for the conceptualization of a civil society on benevolence and mutual trust.

What is most interesting and provocative about this book is that it focuses on ideals of love between men while devoting only a few pages to ideals of love between men and women. This focus may leave the unwarranted impression that male friendship had *greater* ideological importance than romantic heterosexual love in creating an American "republic of sympathy." In fact, the intellectual roots of the two ideals were closely interwoven, and the legitimization of heterosexual romantic love was arguably a more radical development than the idealization of male friendship because it challenged centuries-old traditions of suspicion toward women and female sexuality. To compare these developments, it would be useful to read this book alongside Ruth Bloch's "Changing Conceptions of Sexuality and Romance in Eighteenth Century America" (*William and Mary Quarterly*, 3d ser., 60: 1 [January 2003]: 13–42).

Yet the elision of women from the discussion of love is the point of this book, not an unintended oversight, for Godbeer wants us to think about the historical constructedness of love and gender. Eighteenth-century Americans developed an emotionally expressive, erotic vocabulary that enabled individuals to express feelings of love and longing for one another without being hedged in by modern taboos against same-sex desire. That ability was lost with the invention of twentieth-century categories of sexual identity. Godbeer's book could not be more timely in asking us to reflect upon the costs of that loss.

ANNE S. LOMBARD
California State University,
San Marcos

CHRISTOPHER P. MAGRA. *The Fisherman's Cause: Atlantic Commerce and Maritime Dimensions of the American Revolution.* New York: Cambridge University Press. 2009. Pp. x, 243. $75.00.

Filling a significant gap in the study of the American Revolution's origins, Christopher P. Magra's book places the New England cod fishery in an Atlantic world context and demonstrates how the salted cod trade with the Iberian peninsula and the West Indies helped build economic relationships with these locales. Further, by stressing the importance of the cod trade in Atlantic commerce and the colonial economy, Magra complicates notions that agrarian interests alone sparked the revolution. Instead, Catholic fasting and sugar plantation slavery made New England salted cod one of the most important commodities in the Atlantic world. This lucrative trade gave rise to colonial fortunes but eventually attracted the attention of English bureaucrats and politicians, who closed the cod fishery to punish rebellious colonists. The loss of the cod trade had a ripple effect from the sugar islands to rum distilleries in New England, and when faced with economic ruin, both fish merchants and fishermen joined the revolutionaries.

Magra devotes the first section of the book to fish, fish merchants, and fishermen, providing the necessary background and labor-versus-capital interactions without being heavy-handed. At times, though, his fishermen seem faceless cogs in the industry's wheels rather than historical actors. Part two concerns the Atlantic economy of cod, trade routes and markets, and competition with English migrant fishermen. In the eighteenth century, when salted cod was used to feed slaves on sugar plantations, the volume and direction of the cod trade shifted and commerce between New England and the West Indies increased.

Magra's best work comes in part three, where he demonstrates how commercial relationships were converted into wartime resources. Trade routes became supply lines, fishing schooners were converted to fighting craft, and newly out-of-work fishermen enlisted in both coastal defense forces and the regular army. Magra makes a solid case that five Marblehead, Massachusetts, fishing schooners leased directly to the Continental Congress constituted the "first American navy" (p. 178). Differentiating these craft and their operation from the more celebrated revolutionary-era privateers represents new thinking in the naval history of the American Revolution and will surely spark debate and renewed attention to the revolutionary navy.

Several areas are cause for concern. While discussing salt cod's preparation, Magra uses the terms "fillet" (p. 22) and "filet" (p. 67). Filleting describes the process of removing flesh from bones. Instead, traditional cod fishermen "split" cod, removing about two-thirds of the backbone and leaving most bones intact to provide structure to the salted product. One of his sources mentions rum's use in the "Guinea trade" and notes that although the cod fishery used more rum, "both [fishing and slaving] will take off great quantity" (p. 90). However, he treats fishing as the sole cause of increased New England rum production. Declining to consider slaving as an additional factor is a perplexing omission. Data regarding colonial measurements, wages earned, and price comparisons could have been better presented through charts or tables. Deeper knowledge of traditional-rigged sail's operation would have also clarified several areas. Moreover, Magra repeatedly reminds readers of the cod trade's centrality to New England's economy, and, at least three times in eight pages, that his is the first "book-length academic study" (p. 9) or "systematic examination" (p. 16) of the cod fishery's influence on the revolution. More rigorous editing could have eliminated some of these redundancies. These points are minor, though.

The greatest concern with Magra's work is that he may be overstating his case. A more appropriate subtitle would have been "The Cod Fishery and the American Revolution," as he is talking about the salted cod trade, rather than whaling, other fishing, or trade exchanges of raw materials and manufactured goods. Magra leaves no doubt that cod was "New England's most significant contribution to the Atlantic economy" (p. 100), most of its trade was with the Caribbean by the revolution, and that connections established through the cod trade were important during wartime. However, he also notes that most New England commodities—from grain and flour to timber and livestock—followed similar patterns (p. 87), and that on voyages seeking military stores, vessels were laden with many New England products beyond salted cod (p. 173). General oceanic trading, not simply the cod trade, helped build the webs of commerce that supplied the revolution.

Magra's book ultimately rests on established economic explanations for the revolution. He reminds readers, however, that it was not simply farmers and agrarian laborers who revolted when their livelihoods were threatened. By exploring the business of salted cod within the Atlantic world, Magra demonstrates the contribution of fish, fishermen, merchants, and markets to the American Revolution. Without the codfishing industry's vessels, manpower, and capital, Massachusetts's revolutionary fervor might not have risen to such a fevered pitch as quickly or with such conviction. His study of cod fishing shows one way that the New England maritime world played an important, if heretofore understated, role in achieving American independence.

GLENN M. GRASSO
U.S. Coast Guard Academy

DOUGLAS R. EGERTON. *Death or Liberty: African Americans and Revolutionary America*. New York: Oxford University Press. 2009. Pp. x, 342. $29.95.

Since the 1960s, there has been an explosion of scholarship on the experiences of African Americans in the era of the American Revolution. Much of the most recent work has taken as its mission dismantling the stubbornly held belief that enslaved and free people of color were overwhelmingly supportive of the colonists in this struggle; surely freedom-seeking blacks and freedom-seeking whites must have been on the same side. But as several scholars—most notably Gary B. Nash, Simon Schama, and Cassandra Pybus—have reminded us, the side fighting for freedom from British "slavery" was not the side that offered liberty to actual slaves, and a great majority of the latter knew it and acted accordingly. Nor did the ultimate independence of the American colonies translate into immediate freedom for more than a handful of slaves who actually had fought with the Patriots and survived the war. Very slow, hesitant, and partial postrevolutionary progress toward abolishing the institution of slavery in the northern states left a virulent racism directed at free blacks in its wake, and even these gingerly steps had ceased from Virginia south by the early 1830s, leaving the nation fatally divided on slavery and united on race.

This is the story told in Douglas R. Egerton's comprehensive synthesis of the last half-century of scholarship on black American experiences of enslavement and freedom from the onset of the crisis with Britain through the American Revolution. Egerton defines the revolutionary era as the lifespan of the "ideal of liberty" (p. 272), and his book explores how blacks waged their own struggles to enact this ideal.

Each chapter opens with the story of a different African or African American whose revolutionary-era circumstances and actions in some way epitomize an important aspect of black experience, as the author moves from the rising hopes of the 1760s to the increasingly disappointing realities of the postrevolutionary period. The names of most of these men and, in one case, a woman—Olaudah Equiano, Absalom Jones, Denmark Vesey, Elizabeth Freeman (Mum Bett)—will be familiar to Americanist scholars and some students, although many of the fascinating and telling details of their lives included here may not be. In each chapter the exemplary character's life serves as a kind of scaffolding on which the author builds a complex story peopled by hosts of other black men and women in similar and contrasting positions. For the most part this strategy works well, although in a couple of cases the protagonist disappears so quickly that his role as a device becomes obvious.

The prologue and each of the first six chapters examine how blacks made and seized opportunities to negotiate, circumvent, endure, protest, litigate, rebel against, and flee the constraints of enslavement. The next two chapters explore the postrevolutionary efforts of free blacks to recover families, find employment, establish churches, and generally build strong communities in the face of rising racism. One focuses on urban settings in the U.S. North and South; the other follows a former slave's odyssey to Nova Scotia and then to Sierra Leone.

By 1800, the backsliding on black freedom had begun in earnest, and here the author switches the narrative perspective to two white men: Thomas Jefferson, whose speculations in *Notes on the State of Virginia* (1781) fueled the rise of racism and the codification of black inferiority, and Eli Whitney, whose cotton engine fostered the rapid expansion of cotton production and the consolidation of slavery. An epilogue switches back to a black perspective again, suggesting that the failed revolt of the Virginia slave named Gabriel represented the end of the revolutionary dream for Blacks.

This book covers an amazing amount of ground. One of its many strengths is that it carefully places the American Revolution and its aftermath in a larger Atlantic frame, introducing the great diversity of Africans and black creoles who populated the British Empire by tracing the travels of Equiano and then returning periodically with various of its characters to Canada, Africa, and the Caribbean as the American Revolution unfolds.

It would be difficult to produce a narrative of this scope without errors of fact, and there are a few minor ones here. For example, it was not the case that immediately after the revolution "[t]he thirteen united colonies began to write thirteen new state constitutions" (p. 94); eleven of them did, but it took Connecticut and Rhode Island until 1818 and 1842, respectively, to abandon their colonial charters. It also would have been helpful, especially for graduate students, for the author to have provided more explanatory footnotes where brief mention is made of scholarly debates on matters such as the evolution of paternalism. But these are very small points. This book offers an engaging and persuasive view that, on balance, the American Revolution was a disillusioning failure for the Africans and

African Americans who struggled to make it meaningful for themselves.

JOANNE POPE MELISH
University of Kentucky

ANNETTE GORDON-REED. *The Hemingses of Monticello: An American Family.* New York: W.W. Norton and Company. 2008. Pp. 798. $35.00.

What remains to be said about Annette Gordon-Reed's masterpiece? Early newspaper reviews applauded the sophistication of her analysis and the transcendent meaning of her book for Obama-era America. It won the National Book Award in 2008 and the Pulitzer Prize in 2009. By the time this review is published, surely more honors will have accrued.

Gordon-Reed writes with the nuance and confidence of having fully immersed herself in every part of the Hemingses' world. She has achieved an extraordinary mastery of eighteenth-century sources and scholarly writing about that era. She adeptly moves from law to psychology to architecture, recreating the fullness of her subjects' lives. This is no easy task, given the sparse extant records from the Hemingses. Gordon-Reed is forthright about the evidentiary limitations, and she invites her reader to reason with her, to imagine what the sources cannot tell us definitely. When did Thomas Jefferson and Sally Hemings begin their sexual relationship? Did they care for one another? Why did Sally and her brother, James, return from Paris (where they would have been free people) to Virginia? What was it like to be reunited with their Virginia relatives—and with Virginia slavery? Gordon-Reed shows that just because we cannot know for certain the answers does not mean we ought not to ask such questions. She offers her reasoned assessment of these and a myriad of other matters only after carefully considering alternative theories. Gordon-Reed's curiosity is infectious, and her candor inspires confidence.

The book is an achievement of particular note for early Americanists. It brings specificity of time and space, and it enlivens with emotional resonance a field of inquiry—colonial slavery studies—often characterized by analyses of demographic or cultural patterns. To be certain, Gordon-Reed could not have crafted her family history without the path-breaking work of scholars like Philip Morgan, Ira Berlin, and Kathleen Brown. The text reveals how the patterns uncovered by historians such as these played out in individuals' lives. Moreover, Gordon-Reed shows how fully interwoven the lives of these slaves and slaveowners were. The African Americans are not simply reactive to the whites; their fates are inextricably linked. The relationship between Jefferson and Hemings is only the most prominent of the intimate connections between blacks and whites at Monticello. Gordon-Reed reminds us that Elizabeth Hemings was the only constant female presence in Martha Wayles Jefferson's life. Elizabeth was there at Martha's birth, watched over her after the death of her mother and two stepmothers, and attended

to her as she lay dying. Elizabeth was also, of course, mother to Martha's step-siblings. And so it would be for Elizabeth's daughter, Sally, and Martha's daughter and namesake, Martha, living in closest proximity—and in shared intimacy, since one woman's father was the other's lover.

Gordon-Reed deserves the widest readership in the scholarly community. Historians—including those without any particular interest in early America, or slavery, or even the history of the United States—can learn a valuable lesson from this book. It is exactly the kind of writing more of us should attempt. Historians regularly lament—with good reason—how little Americans know about the past. And too often, the refrain goes, the reading public learns about history from journalists and popular writers, not scholars. We should own our part of that and focus more on writing as a craft, rather than principally as a mechanism for conveying a thesis. This book is beautifully written; it is poignant, gripping, lively, and clear. It is a story—deeply rooted in historiography, reliant on a sophisticated reading of evidence and written by as serious a scholar as one can find—but still, a story.

If DNA evidence did not do it, Gordon-Reed's 662 pages (not counting notes) will not convince the naysayers. And some readers will not be persuaded by her assessment of the romantic tenor of the Jefferson-Hemings relationship. More important, the narrative imposes a subtle but nonetheless powerful moral arc to the story of life at Monticello: the resolve and nobility of the Hemingses. It would be harder to quarrel with this framing if we did not know how, in her earlier work, Gordon-Reed struggled to challenge an analogous, deeply entrenched narrative built around the dignity and morality of the Sage of Monticello. Still, as a closing testimony to the book's beauty, I was most disappointed by its ending so soon, in the early nineteenth century. Hopefully when the awards season ends Gordon-Reed will hurry back to the archives and tell us what the future held for this fascinating American family.

LORRI GLOVER
Saint Louis University

JANE E. CALVERT. *Quaker Constitutionalism and the Political Thought of John Dickinson.* New York: Cambridge University Press. 2009. Pp. xiv, 382. $99.00.

Generations of American historians have slighted and misunderstood the Society of Friends, which was a significant presence in the seventeenth and eighteenth-century British Atlantic world. Over time, however, there has been a gradual accretion of good historical literature that takes Quakers seriously and tries to understand who and what they were and what we might make of their place in early America. Jane E. Calvert's book is the culmination, to date, of that collective effort, the keystone in an arch of scholarly writings that opens the way to a thoughtful and stimulating reconsideration of Quakerism.

Calvert's book "has three overarching purposes—to

describe Quaker constitutional theory; to identify the practical expressions of this theory; and to explain the thought and action of Founding Father John Dickinson, within this tradition" (p. 6). The first is in many ways the most important, because if one can understand the origins of Quakerism many insights follow, since Quakerism has a logic, which was and is palpable. The sense that this is so is what has made it so seductive to some and deeply repugnant to others. In her early chapters Calvert succinctly identifies the environment in which the Society of Friends came of age as one that fired a bubbling cauldron of writings on religion and government. She makes the case that, along with better-known political philosophers, William Penn, Robert Barclay, Isaac Pennington, and other Quakers were major contributors to the cacophony of debate. In fact, they were extraordinarily creative in developing a core set of ideas that Calvert very aptly calls "Quaker constitutionalism." These ideas revolved around a conjoining of the religious and political, which gained expression in the organization, practice, and structure of the Society of Friends and in a theory of government which held that the contract between people and government should never be broken but was "a continual process of negotiation" (p. 89). In practice that meant Quakers were charged with the obligation to act out "peaceful resistance to government to effect constitutional change," and civil disobedience was the most extreme form of that obligation (p.6).

Having articulated this central insight, Calvert goes on to explore how these ideas played out in Pennsylvania. Both in the context of the many constitutional changes that Pennsylvania underwent in its early years and in the later decades of Quaker governance, the author markedly clarifies our understanding of the Quaker new world. For example, she points out Quaker recognition of the practices of trimming and balancing as positive strategies; she strengthens the case for understanding the Quaker regime as one that embraced a distinctive conjoining of politics and religion; and she illustrates the power of "Quakerization," the expressions of which were most palpable among fellow-travelers in Pennsylvania but which also allows us to better understand the influence Friends had, and fears they generated elsewhere.

Quakerization, a concept the colonists themselves identified, is critical in building a bridge to Dickinson, who was not a meeting member but who, in so many ways, acted the part of a Quaker. As the author points out, Dickinson generated frustration not only in John Adams but also in every historian who subsequently tried to comprehend his role in the revolutionary era. But they did not have what Calvert brings to the table. Her theory of Quaker constitutionalism makes perfectly comprehensible why Dickinson acted the way he did. It explains what he was trying to say in the *Letters from a Pennsylvania Farmer* (1767), his tones of urgency and incitement along with his placatory petitioning, his refusal to sign the Declaration of Independence, his political career through the late 1770s and mid 1780s in-

cluding his drafting of the Articles of Confederation, and his role at the Constitutional Convention. This is a scholarly accomplishment of note and it will, I hope, generate some restating of revolutionary history.

For all its success, the book is not entirely satisfying. The most striking section is the first 200 pages on Quaker theory and practice. This part has coherence because it is a contextualized exploration of Quaker constitutionalism. In comparison, context is missing in the section on Dickinson, and it is vitally important for our understanding of the Quaker legacy to locate him not just relative to his public career but also in terms of the fragmentation and evolving character of Quaker meeting and polity. A short narrative line projecting a Quaker heritage in the form of civil disobedience is a weaker conclusion than this very insightful and rewarding study deeply deserves.

ALAN TULLY
University of Texas,
Austin

ERIC SLAUTER. *The State as a Work of Art: The Cultural Origins of the Constitution*. Chicago: University of Chicago Press. 2009. Pp. xii, 373. $40.00.

Eric Slauter undertakes a reconstruction of the complex conceptual and semantic shifts that found expression at the moment of the adoption of the United States Constitution. One immediate benefit of such a focus is a heightened sense of just how contentious, confused, even seat-of-the-pants much of the debate was. Slauter is well informed about the back-and-forth of the convention itself, making fascinating use of a range of notes, diaries, and reports. And indeed, his observations about how James Madison's posthumously published handwritten notes were selectively edited is another salutary reminder of how thoroughly mediated our access to the "founding" is. Slauter's assiduous recourse to primary documentation is an understandable response to the saturated nature of historiography of the founding, although this reader would also have liked more direct engagement with the many powerful analyses of this moment already on the table.

Slauter's central thesis can be grasped by changing "as" to "is" in the book's title. His view is that the debate over the Constitution and its eventual adoption reveals to what extent a new view of society and politics had taken hold. With roots in Montesquieu and the Scottish Enlightenment, this view made it possible to view the "Constitution as simultaneously an artificial creation and an outgrowth of the culture of the people" (p. 16). The "art," or artifice, involved in the Constitution maintains a complex relationship to the "culture" of Slauter's subtitle, the latter term designating the "vortex of words and concepts" concerning "manners, morals, beliefs, opinions, customs, genius, and tastes" (p. 11). "Culture" is the crucially ambidextrous term here, mediating between the realm of artifice and that of the organic and natural: "At stake in such debates was the question of how the recognized artifice of

Reviews of Books

law and politics could be used to help people be more natural . . . and to help citizens see their lives under a political state as if politics was simply an extension of nature" (p. 11). There is perhaps less genuine transformation of underlying political ideology in this story than it seemed to its actors: Alexander Pope's famous couplet from *An Essay on Man* (1733)—"For Forms of Government let fools contest; / Whate'er is best administer'd is best"—may have been roundly repudiated in the era, as Slauter documents, but the idea that a natural "fit" between government and people was best decided by those on top is still intrinsic to much of the thinking of the era, as is suggested by Samuel Stanhope Smith's unapologetic invocation of Solon's answer to the question of whether he had given the Athenians the best constitution: "*he had given them the best they were able to bear*" (p. 12). What Slauter exposes to view, and does so with lucidity, in precise detail and with rich variety, is how social and political change takes place as a kind of leveraging of ambiguity. He opens his book with a lovely account of the "Speaker's" chair in which Washington sat during the Convention, and which prompted Benjamin Franklin to the observation, recorded by Madison, that it had long been unclear whether the sun on the back of the chair was rising or setting, but that Franklin now felt relieved that the sun was rising. As Slauter points out, while Franklin's wordplay obviously takes the emblem of the chair as an allegory for the state, it also makes the "unsettled ambiguity" (p. 8) of that emblem during the debates an allegory of the necessity of interpretation itself, as if to say, "Part of what we have done here, gentlemen, is played productively with ambiguity."

All this is to say that Slauter's book does not exactly provide a new historical narrative about the founding, or even a new account of its ideological origins. Rather, it shows the ways in which the Constitution, as artifice and as ("natural") emanation of the "people," could be understood and packaged as an object of aesthetic experience. In a series of well-proportioned chapters, Slauter reviews the waning of the metaphor of the body politic and its replacement by the architectural idiom in which constitutions are "erected" and can be beheld (the bodily figure going underground to serve primarily as a punning subtext); he considers the historical practice and ideological usefulness of the "miniature" and the "transcript" as ways of imagining the work of representation; he offers a new way to conceive the era's ability to disarticulate chattel slavery from its central assertions about natural rights (the revolt against neoclassicism made "slavish imitation" something subhuman—Phillis Wheatley is his text here); and he explores the fascinating popularity of hermit stories as a refraction of political thought. The book is extensively and inventively researched, and written with grace and clarity.

JONATHAN ELMER
Indiana University,
Bloomington

PRISCILLA H. ROBERTS and RICHARD S. ROBERTS. *Thomas Barclay (1728–1793): Consul in France, Diplomat in Barbary.* (Studies in Eighteenth-Century America and the Atlantic World.) Bethlehem: Lehigh University Press. 2008. Pp. 407. $62.50.

Thomas Barclay lived a remarkable life as an Irish immigrant to America, prominent merchant, revolutionary patriot, and one of the United States' earliest and most important diplomats. Nevertheless, because he left virtually no papers, he is nearly unknown today, even among historians. Therefore, this biography is a welcome addition to the literature of the early republic.

Born in County Tyrone in 1728, Barclay immigrated to Philadelphia, probably in 1764. Drawing on his Irish connections, his mercantile firm prospered, particularly during the decade before the American Revolution. Priscilla H. Roberts and Richard S. Roberts calculate that he managed twenty-two percent of Philadelphia vessels leaving for Ireland and forty percent of those arriving from Ireland in 1774, and that in 1767 he invested in thirteen of the fifteen Philadelphia ships trading with southern Europe.

With economic success came influence in the Philadelphia patriot movement, which Barclay seems to have strongly supported, perhaps because his Irish and southern European connections made him less attached to and dependent on Britain than many other merchants. He served on nearly all the city's revolutionary committees, and his summer house near Trenton was briefly George Washington's New Jersey headquarters in December 1776. In 1780 he was nominated to be America's first consul in France (in fact, the first anywhere).

In France, Barclay's mercantile background proved useful as he spent the bulk of his time settling America's accounts, including those with the playwright-spy, Pierre Augustin Caron de Beaumarchais. At the same time, Barclay looked after his own business, making useful contacts in the small community of American merchants overseas.

After the war, Congress appointed Barclay to negotiate a peace treaty with Morocco, whose sultan had been the first potentate to recognize American independence but had more recently captured an American ship and its crew. Barclay managed to negotiate a treaty at very little cost, unlike his counterpart in Algeria, which continued to harass U.S. shipping for many more years. Finally, on the verge of a new mission to Algeria, he died suddenly in Lisbon, the first American diplomat to die abroad in his country's service.

Barclay's career created a fair amount of controversy in his day and later. Samuel Flagg Bemis suggested that he may have been a British secret agent during the American Revolution, a charge that Roberts and Roberts find unconvincing. Barclay also got into trouble for mingling his personal and diplomatic business, particularly when his arrest by creditors in Bordeaux threatened to create a diplomatic rift between the United States and its most important ally. The authors blame the French creditors and praise Barclay for "giving priority to his public responsibilities" to the extent that his business suffered greatly after the Revolution. Barclay was an "exemplar of the Puritan ethic," they conclude somewhat cryptically (p. 265).

Roberts and Roberts have nicely overcome the lack of surviving Barclay papers to provide a readable and remarkably full account of their subject's life, most notably his business and diplomatic careers. Uncommonly tenacious researchers, they have delved into state papers; the letters of Thomas Jefferson, Benjamin Franklin, and other patriot leaders; and a number of more obscure archival sources, most notably the papers of Barclay's European business partner, Matthew Ridley of Baltimore.

Because of the nature of these sources, Barclay's personal life and inner thoughts, especially during his early years, are understandably hard to know. The authors' tendency is to provide large chunks of context to get around the problem of missing texts. Sometimes, as with their interesting descriptive passages on Morocco, this technique works quite well. In other cases, such as in their long descriptions of the well known events in Philadelphia leading up to the revolution, it can become a bit burdensome.

In general, Roberts and Roberts eschew analysis in favor of narrative. Barclay's life touches on a number of subjects that have recently interested the historical profession and the general public, including American interaction with the Islamic world and the United States' engagement with the broader Atlantic world. Readers looking for explicit analysis of these issues will be disappointed, but this biography will certainly offer fodder for anyone interested in exploring them further.

LAWRENCE A. PESKIN
Morgan State University

LAWRENCE A. PESKIN. *Captives and Countrymen: Barbary Slavery and the American Public, 1785–1816.* Baltimore: Johns Hopkins University Press. 2009. Pp. ix, 256. $55.00.

Historians have long struggled with placing the Barbary Wars within the larger context of American history. A few college textbooks do not even mention the conflicts, and those that do usually relegate them to a paragraph focused on the war against Tripoli. Lawrence A. Peskin offers a corrective to this yawning gap in our knowledge by arguing that the Barbary Wars were central to the emergence of an American national identity during the early republic.

He develops this thesis along several lines. First, Peskin examines how the news of the captivity of American seamen spread in the 1780s and 1790s. When Algiers seized two American merchant ships and twenty-one crewmen in 1785, there was little the United States could do for the captives, and although the incident was reported in the newspapers, the American public hardly took notice. In 1793, the situation was different as an animated press decried the loss of eleven ships and the

enslavement of over 100 seamen. The difference in reaction reflected differences within the United States. By 1793, a more extended diplomatic corps had developed, with both ministers and consuls funneling information back to the United States at a much more rapid pace than the letters sent by the captives themselves during the 1780s. Second, an integrated news network provided a vehicle to distribute information to an eager public interested in a world beyond their own immediate community. Finally, a stronger national government had created a more effective entity to deal with foreign policy.

The Barbary conflicts both challenged and strengthened American pride. Since at times the nation appeared impotent to aid its captives, Barbary seizures of American shipping were an embarrassment, but the willingness to militarily confront the Barbary states of North Africa came to be a source of pride—the Marine hymn phrase "to the shores of Tripoli" is relevant here—since the United States established a navy to meet the crisis in the 1790s and succeeded in defeating both Tripoli in a war from 1801 to 1805 and Algiers in 1815. The result was an enhanced sense of identity and an extended global reach unimaginable a generation earlier.

The Barbary Wars also spoke directly to slavery, the central internal problem confronting Americans before the Civil War. The fact that dark-skinned North African Muslims enslaved white (and some black) Americans allowed abolitionists to offer an appeal that reached beyond the racist assumptions of the day. The conflicts with the North African states thus contributed to the dialogue that helped to make slavery a national issue.

Although Peskin provides an important contribution to the understanding of the development of American nationalism, his analysis is marred by efforts to place his work in the context of too many recent trends in historiography. Perhaps some reviewers may applaud this effort; however, I prefer history that is less jargon-laden and not forced into analytical boxes that may or may not fit. For example, Peskin couches his discussion of the spread of information about the Barbary captivities in the context of a "public sphere," using the concept as if it were a historical actor itself (p. 3). Similarly, national identity is cast as a result of "imagined communities," yet citing this idea may obscure more than it illuminates (p. 2). Challenges to national pride are portrayed as threats to "masculinity," although few if any of the quotations Peskin uses refer to a male identity (pp. 137–162). Interest in the Islamist East in American literature becomes "Orientalism" (p. 163), and the entire book is a contribution to the history of "globalization" (p. 212). Peskin also sprinkles his texts with a few anachronistic phrases, referring to the spread of news as "the late-eighteenth-century worldwide web" (p. 22) and the building of coastal fortifications as "homeland security" (p. 128).

These criticism aside, Peskin has done much to correct our understanding of the Barbary Wars. He also suggests that, amid the "naval triumphalism and sense of a mission to protect commercial and individual liberty" after the War of 1812, the American experience with North Africa became something of an embarrassment and was therefore easily forgotten (p. 209). Our modern concerns with the Muslim world and the good history written by Peskin and others will erase that historical amnesia. Ultimately, the Barbary Wars will work their way into our textbooks not just because they represent the first sustained intersection between the United States and Muslims, but because the conflicts were crucial to the emergence of an American national identity.

PAUL A. GILJE
University of Oklahoma

SHEILA L. SKEMP. *First Lady of Letters: Judith Sargent Murray and the Struggle for Female Independence.* (Early American Studies.) Philadelphia: University of Pennsylvania Press. 2009. Pp. xvi, 484. $39.95.

Judith Sargent Murray is surely more than the "virtually unknown commodity" her new biographer claims (p. xi). She appears in every biographical dictionary of American women writers, and is included in both the Norton and Heath anthologies of American literature, which means thousands of students have read her important essay on the equality of the sexes. Exactly this reputation, however, justifies Sheila L. Skemp's detailed and scrupulously fair-minded biography.

The biography is divided into three sections: first comes Murray's life until around the age of forty, then her years of literary productivity, and finally the declining years. When, as a widow, she moved to Natchez, Mississippi with her married daughter in 1818, the written record ceases, but Murray took with her to Natchez nine letter books containing many years of carefully redacted correspondence. Long thought to have disappeared, they were unearthed in 1984 (confusingly, Skemp says they were found in the 1990s) by Unitarian-Universalist minister Gordon Gibson and turned over to the Mississippi State Archives. (They are available in microfilm and will eventually be published by the Judith Sargent Murray Society.) Skemp's method is to work through the letters almost one by one, summarizing, quoting, and contextualizing, making her book a revealing guide to Murray's own self-presentation.

Hoping for literary fame and literary income, Murray (1751–1820) contributed many essays to Massachusetts magazines during her years in Gloucester and then Boston. These essays used the going conventions of eighteenth-century essay writing, with numerous personae, allegorically named characters, didactic fictions, and the like. The three plays she wrote were performed in Boston, although they did not do well on stage. As though to vindicate their quality, Murray published two of them in *The Gleaner*, her massive three-volume miscellany combining previously published and new pieces published in 1798. *The Gleaner* is one of the high points of female literary production from the early years of the new republic.

Literary scholars see Murray as one of the most important American women writers of her era, not only for her productivity but because of her Enlightenment belief in the mental equality of the sexes and her description of the sad results—for self, family, and nation—of keeping women ignorant. She elaborated a detailed curriculum for female education, arguing that uneducated young women could not control the passions that so often led them astray, nor fend for themselves economically if conditions required, nor manage their domestic affairs. If educated, they could participate, through the stabilizing force of "republican motherhood," in forming the emerging nation. Unfortunately for Murray, her belief that enlightened motherhood was the be-all of an elite woman's existence had to wait until she was almost forty years old before she herself became a mother, at which time (as is so often the case) her practice and her principles often went in different directions.

Moreover, as Skemp admirably shows, Murray's views of social class and entitlement were deeply conservative. She believed in "subordination" of the classes if not of the sexes and deplored lower-class revelry and bawdiness. Despite inconsistencies between her program and her practice, she was consistent throughout her life in her need to write and her desire to publish, which implies much about American ideas of female possibility at the turn into the nineteenth century.

Skemp describes some of Murray's published work—especially the serialized novella "The Story of Margaretta" (1798)—but has no descriptions of the plays. Readers hoping for sustained discussion and analysis of Murray's literary output, not to mention an informed consideration of the literary context both national and international from which she drew, will have to turn to *The Gleaner* itself. This is not Skemp's fault so much as it is that of Murray's letter books, which say little about literary motifs and form though much about unfavorable reviews and inadequate compensation.

Skemp repeatedly shows how Murray's strong sense of entitlement—she came from one of Gloucester's elite families—clashed with the reality of her two economically disadvantageous marriages. In that her first husband, John Stevens (a seafaring merchant), was a terrible businessman and her second, John Murray (the premier Universalist minister of his time), was no businessman at all, one can comprehend the deep sense of insecurity which, coupled with her sense of class privilege, made her life (at least insofar as the letters are accurate) one of constant anxiety. Many of her letters appeal for support to her two brothers or complain about the poverty in which she was forced to live.

Accessibly written, and with contextual material involving both Murray's times and up-to-date historical thinking about Enlightenment women and the early republic, the book will become the starting point for all future work about Murray and women writers before the Jacksonian period.

NINA BAYM
University of Illinois

SHIRLEY ELIZABETH THOMPSON. *Exiles at Home: The Struggle to Become American in Creole New Orleans.* Cambridge: Harvard University Press. 2009. Pp. 362. $49.95.

Shirley Elizabeth Thompson's precision of insight, depth of archival research, and accessible narrative make her book a superior undertaking and a wonderful read. Thompson's narrative explores how pre-1803 Spanish/French New Orleans viewed the concept of "race" so differently from Ango-American definitions of the same elsewhere that New Orleans was essentially a foreign territory. This distinguished it from other "empty" regions elsewhere in the Louisiana Purchase and other lands newly acquired by the new nation. While farther north, groups such as the Métis could be easily removed, ignored, or erased, in New Orleans generations of interracialism, forgotten genealogical trackings, and entrenched entanglements with multiracial communities throughout the Caribbean (especially Saint Domingue/Haiti and Cuba) made the assignment of specific racial identity—increasingly necessary in the decades leading up to the Civil War—nearly impossible. Thompson maps out these conditions through the experiences of individual families. Her archival ambit ranges from diaries and letters to court transcripts, property records, published narratives, Creole-of-color poetry (*"Les Cenelles": A Collection of Poems by Creole Writers of the Early Nineteenth Century* [1979]), and white fiction, such as George Washington Cable's *The Grandissimes* (1898).

In that sense, the book falls well within the methodological traditions of American Studies, even though that field originally stressed unity while Thompson's story is of the persistence of diversity. She seeks support for her conclusions in the work of scholars ranging from African Americanists such as Henry Louis Gates Jr. and Gayraud Williams and cultural historians John Ernest, Karen Halttunen, and Russ Castronovo. However, the best elements of the book are the novelistic sequences when Thompson tells the stories of individuals caught between the shifting color lines. The book opens with the story of Anastasie Desarzant's efforts to rebut Pierre LeBlanc and Eglantine Desmaziliere's claim that she was "colored." Thompson traces this and other cases, pitting the idiosyncratic legality of the Spanish and French traditions concerning race, identity, family, nationality, gender, and ownership against the sterner and more "modern" American definitions whose enforcement had been lax in the first decades after statehood. With more and more "white" and Protestant Americans and their "black" slaves moving to the city—especially during the Union occupation and Reconstruction (1862–1878)—the cultural conflicts over civil rights, property ownership, and inheritance took some tortured and convoluted twists, resulting in a period when those who had once sought to be identified as "white" now self-identified as "colored." Desarzant's case even led to folk songs ("Toucoutou") and public debate, and Thompson recreates the public spectacle of private lives with lively pacing and appropriate commentary.

What sets Thompson's book apart from other narratives of the assimilation of New Orleans is her particular awareness of gender as a contributing factor to the stories of both specific individuals and the city as a whole. The practice of *placage*—the de facto bigamy of French men who kept "quadroon" women as concubines—is addressed not only as a complicating factor in the resolution of inheritance issues but also for its reverberating effects on, for example, the excluded male *gens de couleur*, and their search for redemption in the affectation of class-based privilege. In tracing their stories, this book develops a transnational dimension in that many of the men emigrated to Cuba, France, or Haiti. However, with the occupation of New Orleans by the Union Army, this population—which had briefly fielded a Confederate regiment—ironically found itself empowered in the new ways.

The final sections of the book trace the gradual recontainment of New Orleans's mixed-race population, leading toward the staging of the case that would become *Plessy v. Ferguson* (1896), the ultimate denial of American multi- and interracialism. Thompson's story, then, is finally that of the displacement of the entangled and contradictory colonial paradigm by the sterner binaries intrinsic to "Americanization." This book is about America and its failure to accommodate anything other than a rigid model of national identity as the nineteenth century progressed, a lively addition to a body of scholarship defined by the work of Reginald Horsman, Bruce Dain, and many others. Yet despite the enormity of her task, Thompson has written a clear and entertaining book, an excellent contribution to a number of subfields within American history. Even before I finished reading the first chapter, I was recommending the text to my students, and I will continue to do so.

EDWARD WATTS
Michigan State University

JUDITH KELLEHER SCHAFER. *Brothels, Depravity, and Abandoned Women: Illegal Sex in Antebellum New Orleans.* Baton Rouge: Louisiana State University Press. 2009. Pp. xiii, 221. $32.50.

In researching *Becoming Free, Remaining Free: Manumission and Enslavement in New Orleans, 1846–1862* (2003), Judith Kelleher Schafer discovered numerous legal cases on prostitution. Intrigued by what they reveal about sex, vice, and the local courts, she combed through two thousand trial transcripts and sixteen years of the *New Orleans Picayune*, beginning in March 1846, to flesh out details of the city's infamous sex trade. This prodigious research effort stands as the greatest strength of her new study, which, like her other works, places Louisiana, its case and statute law, and its people at center stage. Nine topical chapters illuminate, in minute detail with myriad examples, the business and practice of prostitution, the disinclination of judges and district attorneys to restrain it, the attempts of municipal officials to police and profit from it, and the precarious lives of those women embroiled in it.

As in most states, selling sex was not a crime in antebellum Louisiana. Consequently, in chapter one, Schafer describes the panoply of charges levied against public women. These ranged from the expected—vagrancy, indecent exposure, drunk and disorderly behavior, insulting a white person—to the less-well-documented offense of cross-dressing. What emerges is a city very similar to other southern ports in that prostitution remained a contentious and contested business in the antebellum era, but not one that was targeted for elimination.

Two chapters focus on sex across the color line and the sexual exploitation of children, well-documented topics in the historiography of New World slave societies. Schafer recounts examples of sex between white men and women of color as well as the more elusive cases of white women and men of color. As elsewhere in the antebellum South, this practice was common—in brothels and private homes—as were the ubiquitous public denunciations of it. Schafer's work adds to our knowledge of the sex trade by revealing slave women managing establishments owned by wealthy, white slumlords; and white and enslaved men patronizing the same brothels. By mining records of the newspaper reports of municipal recorder's courts, she has unearthed multiple cases of teenagers and young girls entering or being forced into prostitution. Schafer aptly acknowledges the hard economic reality that poor southern girls, like their northern counterparts, could "earn more in an hour [selling sex] than a seamstress earned in a day" (p. 54). Like other historians studying port cities from Bridgetown, Barbados, to Charleston, South Carolina, the author also documents how slaveowners, female and male, capitalized on a ready market for sex by forcing girls and women into prostitution either directly or by hiring them out to other urban residents.

Prostitutes' lives were fraught with tumult, danger, larceny, and violence, various aspects of which Schafer details in three chapters. Although somewhat repetitive—accounts of assaults by customers, physical violence at the hands of pimps and other prostitutes, murders, petty theft—she provides rich detail of daily life among those in the lowest ranks of society who barely scraped by. Schafer also reveals convincing evidence of corrupt court recorders and wealthy, "respectable" businessmen and city landlords colluding to perpetuate the sex trade while making a show of prosecuting individual prostitutes. In a rare bit of interpretive commentary, Schafer contends that, contrary to Marilyn Wood Hill's articulate, well-supported argument in *Their Sisters' Keepers: Prostitution in New York City, 1830–1870*, New Orleans prostitutes competed against, stole from, and attacked each other. "If a sisterhood among prostitutes existed, as some have suggested, it is difficult to see. In fact, the overwhelming weight of the evidence is to the contrary" (p. 107). Zealously refuting the notion of camaraderie and mutual support among prostitutes, Schafer loses sight of the obvious: the two

propositions are not mutually exclusive. As she notes, public women "lived by their wits, struggled to survive, and hoped to escape as much violence as they could" (p. 73). They did so by mobilizing diverse survival strategies. Hackneyed as it sounds and annoying as it likely is to some, reality does not always conform to tidy categories of bad or good, white or black, all or nothing.

Schafer focuses so heavily on Louisiana's alleged distinctiveness and its law that neither her evidence nor her weakly articulated argument is fully anchored in the historiography of the slave South or that of prostitution. Some scholarship is cited but many relevant works are missing. This weakness is manifest in the narrative style, which tends toward a recitation of examples. Nonetheless, court records wonderfully illuminate social relations, as many historians of slave societies have demonstrated over the past two decades. In Schafer's presentation of the facts, economics, and legal and political machinations surrounding the practice of prostitution in New Orleans, fascinating nuggets of information emerge about the seamier aspects of urban life in a slave society; about how the law impinged on people's lives; and about the nature of gender, race, and class relations in antebellum America.

CYNTHIA M. KENNEDY
Clarion University of Pennsylvania

SUSAN INGALLS LEWIS. *Unexceptional Women: Female Proprietors in Mid-Nineteenth-Century Albany, New York, 1830–1885*. (Historical Perspectives on Business Enterprise.) Columbus: Ohio State University Press. 2009. Pp. xx, 203. Cloth $44.95, CD-ROM $9.95.

Susan Ingalls Lewis's new book explores the scope and complexity of women's business enterprises in nineteenth-century Albany. A meticulous statistical study of one community, the work contributes to broader scholarly efforts to reframe American business history, which until recently accepted individualistic, ambitious, and successful businessmen as the norm. Although her study includes the most prominent among nineteenth-century Albany's female proprietors, Lewis underscores that such women were not "exceptional pioneers" but were the most successful among a much larger group of "women [who] were unexceptional contributors to their family economies and local communities" (p. 2). To make her case, Lewis draws upon city directories, credit reports of the R. G. Dun Mercantile Agency, census records, and advertisements from local newspapers. Linking and comparing the information in these different sources, she compiled detailed databases describing the businesses and lives of Albany's female proprietors. Identifying more than two thousand individual businesswomen active between 1830 and 1885, she leaves little room to doubt that "businesswomen abounded in the nineteenth-century United States" (p. 2).

At a time when prescriptive literature depicted respectable women as outside the marketplace, significant numbers of Albany's women engaged in commerce. And yet Lewis does not celebrate these activities as evidence of women's entry into the public sphere. Instead she notes that women's businesses were truly "private enterprises"—small, privately held, and very often home-based. This rejection of easy dichotomies between private and public, home and market, is representative of Lewis's analysis overall. She repeatedly lays bare the messiness of her findings and rethinks "the definitions, standards, and categories used by historians to examine businesswomen" (p. 11). While making the case for the vital connections between women's and business history, she reveals her project's inherent analytical challenges: How do we even define "business" in the context of nineteenth-century women's enterprises, many of which generated little, if any, profit? How can we accurately measure the length of a woman's business career when contributions to a family-run business were so often undocumented? Where exactly can historians draw the line between workers and owners in the small businesses that were typical of women's commercial enterprises?

Although occasionally dizzying in its embrace of complexity, Lewis's book is well organized into eight manageable chapters. In addition, several charts and an appendix highlight the results of her quantitative analyses. Most important, throughout the book Lewis balances numbers with narrative. For example, in chapter two, which focuses on the decade between 1875 and 1885, Lewis ranks women's business ventures from most to least common and describes typical Albany businesswomen as "middle-aged, widowed, white, foreign-born mothers with several children living with them in the same household" (p. 36). To give greater meaning to this demographic profile, Lewis provides brief biographies of statistically representative women in each of the major trades, introducing a diverse cast of characters: "A single native-born dressmaker, a married Irish-born grocer, a remarried German saloonkeeper, and two widowed British-born proprietors: one the keeper of a boarding house and the other of a fancy goods/variety store" (p. 42). The stories of these and many other businesswomen animate Lewis's study, ground her statistics, and integrate the multiple threads of her analysis.

Noting that "no letters or diaries . . . no commercial ledgers or company records . . . no investigative reports or union records . . . appear to have survived" (p. 25), Lewis builds stories from faint traces in her sources and supplements her local focus by drawing upon journalism and fiction. She uses credit reports to uncover women's motivations for entering business, making the most of credit examiners' tendency to comment on businesswomen's family arrangements. For example, the report on widowed milliner Charlotte Armington mentioned her large and "expensive" family as well as two sons who caused her "a great deal of trouble" (p. 54). Not surprisingly, married women supported their families when husbands refused or were unable to work. In these cases, credit reports recorded husbands who were "shiftless," "lazy," "poor cuss[es]," or "in bad health"

(p. 55). Many reports also noted that married women supplemented their husbands' wages, and Lewis's findings make clear that "marriage did not necessarily mean the end of a [woman's] business career" (p. 56). Again and again, Lewis asserts that not all businesswomen were victims of circumstance. Many were talented and ambitious and saw proprietorship as a choice. R. G. Dun described such persons as a "hardworking good bus[iness] woman," "making a nice profit," "sharp as a thistle," and even "the man of the concern" (pp. 57–58).

Lewis reveals nineteenth-century Albany as a place of small, home-based businesses in which ordinary women and men shared the marketplace and formed local networks—a city where working-class women owned and ran businesses, sought and gained credit, survived, and crafted their own definitions of business success. In the end, she leaves the reader with a vivid and excitingly unfamiliar picture of the nineteenth-century urban economy and a richer understanding of working women's lives.

AMY G. RICHTER
Clark University

JAMES P. DELGADO. *Gold Rush Port: The Maritime Archaeology of San Francisco's Waterfront.* Berkeley and Los Angeles: University of California Press. 2009. Pp. xiv, 238. $45.00.

James P. Delgado's impeccably researched and highly innovative history lays out quite clearly the centrality of San Francisco to U.S. control of the Pacific and explores how the city rose to dominance as a strategic port. The author's methodology blends *Annales* School social history and world systems theory "with urban and mining-site historical archeology and with new western history" (p. 167).

Delgado's mission here is two-fold: to break away from the tradition of investigating preciosities inherited from pioneer marine archeologist George Bass, quoting Immanuel Wallerstein to the effect that "in the long run, staples account for more of man's economic thrusts than luxuries" (p. 110); and to extend marine archeology to the excavation of some of the vast number of ships buried beneath the landfill that makes up much of the waterfront of the city of San Francisco.

Many of the crews that sailed to California after the discovery of gold deserted. So many unusable ships crowded into the harbor that they became a floating city used for offices, accommodation, and storeships (warehouses). The British had pioneered the use of such hulks to house French prisoners in the Napoleonic Wars and as storeships off Chinese ports in the 1830s to avoid Chinese interference in the opium trade. Much of this city of hulks was razed in the fire of 1851, and the area along Market Street from First to the Embarcadero subsequently infilled. Today's financial district sits atop this razed city.

The conventional history of American westward expansion has a landward bias owing much to Frederick Jackson Turner's frontier thesis. Delgado here identifies what we might call a "merchant's frontier" in the Pacific basin, connected strongly by sea by the 1840s into a genuinely global economy stretching back into the North Atlantic. Home base for American ships bound for the Pacific was Boston, with an important way station at Valparaiso, Chile. The connections were all maritime, the Pacific Coast Range and the Rockies making for an impermeable barrier to affordable transportation of the bulk goods central to global trade.

Modern archeology during building construction in the financial district of San Francisco allows Delgado to use the contents of several buried storeships, most notably *General Harrison*, to analyze the patterns of the burgeoning bulk trade of the late 1840s, demonstrating how much global trade was already under way, how much China had collapsed as a player in the global economy, and how powerful the American presence in the Pacific was before the discovery of gold in California. The goods aboard the *General Harrison*, detailed in appendix three, were not preciosities, but rather the huge quantities of basic tools, foodstuffs, and clothing without which California gold could never have been exploited. But there was also a leavening of such luxury goods as wines (1,000 cases of claret) and champagne (400 cases) to reward those who "struck it rich."

And it was the gold that ultimately mattered most. Gold confirmed the centrality of San Francisco to the emerging Pacific trade system. Gold built a port on razed ships and fill. Gold built a set of powerful merchant houses trading around the world. Gold built comfortable homes for the rising elite of the new city. California gold made the United States the premier power in the Pacific at a point when the Pacific was still up for geopolitical grabs.

Although this is a great book, it just misses a broader context. It fits California into a developing American global system, in particular by the geopolitically prescient acquisition of San Francisco Bay at the treaty of Guadalupe Hidalgo that finally settled the Mexican War. Where it lacks in a world-system context is in its consideration of three things: competing U.S. mercantile settlements in Portland and Honolulu; the geopolitical struggle with Britain and France, all contesting control of Hawai'i in the 1840s; and the geopolitical struggle with Britain, which had powerful presences in Australasia and on the coast of Asia by the early 1850s. To make San Francisco's fascinating story complete, we need those broader contexts, but Delgado's account of San Francisco's rise is a welcome start.

PETER J. HUGILL
Texas A&M University

AARON W. MARRS. *Railroads in the Old South: Pursuing Progress in a Slave Society*. Baltimore: Johns Hopkins University Press. 2009. Pp. xi, 268. $55.00.

The character of the antebellum slave South remains a controversial historiographical topic. An older tradition considered the region a slow-paced, precapitalist holdover from colonial times, while more recent his-

torians see the slave states cheerfully participating in the nation's mid-nineteenth-century market revolution. Aaron W. Marrs certainly belongs to the latter group. In this study he sees little difference between antebellum northerners and southerners in laying out railroads, providing for their management, encountering and overcoming technical problems, and confronting legal and community issues. The difference between the two sections lay in their labor systems, but Marrs quite successfully argues that southerners had easily incorporated slavery into the Age of Progress. Marrs has produced important interpretations that antebellum historians will have to include in their generalizations about pre-Civil War southern society.

The study proceeds by laying out five essential themes connected with antebellum southern railroads: the technical and managerial problems the railroad presented, the use of slavery in the railroad labor force, the imposition on the public of an awareness of time, the demands that different communities required, and a comparison of southern experience with northern experience. In the last category, Marrs is persuasive and undoubtedly correct; northerners and southerners found common ground in exploring the problems and solutions to railroading in the antebellum era, and he even points out that engineers developed a national network to share information; they tended to move between North and South without much cultural friction. His treatment of the different communities in the South (such as ministers, the post office, urban officials, travelers) is interesting, although one wishes that he might have done more with legal issues, especially the doctrine of public carriers. The subject of time and its new requirements in a highly agricultural setting is informative but unremarkable.

Marrs looks at antebellum southern railroading from a social history perspective, thereby explaining why some of the themes dominate, but he provides excellent economic information. Two aspects stand out. One is the commercial role of the southern railroads. Marrs makes it clear how quickly antebellum southerners adopted—usually with enthusiasm—the railroad, how they financed it, how it connected the coastal areas with the interior, how the finances of the roads depended upon more than just cotton, and how large southern railroad construction was in the 1850s. But the author only partially recognizes the great limitation of railroad construction in the antebellum South: the lack of urban areas. Railroads depended on urban areas for their existence; the population of the countryside was secondary. The financial problems of railroading in the nineteenth-century South had much to do with the failure of large and medium cities to emerge.

The second aspect, and the one that will interest most readers, is Marrs's treatment of slaves in the railroad workforce. Marrs finds slaves in all areas of railroad work, save engineering. He presents much information on the wage rates of free white workers, free blacks, and slaves. He describes well the advantages, and some of the disadvantages, to using slaves, and gives an illuminating discussion of the railroad owners' debates about hiring slaves versus purchasing them. Marrs believes that by 1860 southerners had successfully incorporated slavery into the railroad workforce without encountering social upheaval between free white labor and black slave labor.

Marrs's conclusions concerning slave labor deserve a wide reading and general approbation—with some reservation. Although he determines that slaves were about one-half the cost of white labor (p. 81), the data given are so individualized and disparate that a firm conclusion is hard to figure out. One suspects, contrary to Marrs's depiction, that occupations were racially segregated, with slaves being tossed more to the grunt labor side of work and the semi-skilled and skilled positions going to free whites. Finally, a great reservation has to be made that the conditions allowing a nearly frictionless use of slave labor and free labor together resided in the circumstance of the immature nature of the southern economy and its labor shortage. As population grew and the supply of free labor became more plentiful, free and slave labor could not have coexisted without increasingly explosive antagonisms.

JAMES L. HUSTON
Oklahoma State University

JOHN MAJEWSKI. *Modernizing a Slave Economy: The Economic Vision of the Confederate Nation*. (Civil War America.) Chapel Hill: University of North Carolina Press. 2009. Pp. xiii, 240. $39.95.

In this bracing, sophisticated, and persuasive revisionist account, John Majewski reminds us that studies of the Old South's political economy are making something of a comeback.

Majewski's argument is at once original and simply expressed. Secessionists in South Carolina and Virginia—his two sensibly selected states—envisioned and, indeed, actively promoted state-sponsored manufacturing and commerce in an effort to secure economic independence for the new southern nation and preserve its political and cultural authority. Secessionists imagined a Confederacy that braided slavery, manufacturing, and commerce. Political independence, therefore, "would unleash the South's economic potential that the Union had restrained through discriminatory taxes on southern commerce and unfair subsidies to northern industry" (p. 3). What amounted to a Confederate, Hamiltonian state activism in the form of deliberate, focused, and sustained sponsorship of southern commerce and manufacturing was essential to the elaboration of this vision.

Majewski engages in something approaching litotes when he writes that his study "presents an interpretation of the Confederacy that is at odds with much of the Civil War literature" (p. 4). Most historians of the Confederacy and secession see states' rights animating secessionist behavior and explain the burgeoning authority of the Confederate government in terms of military necessity. Emory M. Thomas, for example, has long maintained that the establishment of a powerful, robust, tariff-supporting Confederate state was a product of military, wartime necessity, not desire. Majewski disagrees. The Confederate government was activist, he maintains, because "the strong Confederate state was not a radical disjuncture but a natural outgrowth of southern attitudes established during the antebellum period" (p. 7).

In making that argument, Majewski joins and extends an important historiographical trend. In recent years, some scholars have argued that southern planters especially and southern society generally were far more modern in their outlook than their precapitalist slave mode of production would suggest. Scholars have pointed to the adoption of modern labor techniques on plantations, state support of nascent southern industrialization, and the emergence of a modest but healthy southern bourgeoisie. Majewski builds on these insights and makes a persuasive case that South Carolina and Virginia sponsored internal improvements that were expressly dedicated to the modernization of their society. Although Majewski believes such efforts were less than successful, courtesy of the enduring habit of shifting cultivation, a good deal of this study details in fine and compelling fashion substantive moves on the part of planters and the state to modernize along lines that were being actively pursued in free wage labor societies. Reform-minded planters lobbied for state-sponsored agricultural schools, state support for scientific agricultural societies, as well as heavy state investment in railroads and manufacturing, all in an effort to make the slave South competitive economically (and therefore more independent politically and culturally) with the free wage labor North. Not all southerners agreed, of course, and Majewski deftly examines tensions within reform groups. Some supported certain aspects of state-sponsored modernization, others fretted over its extent, still others endorsed state-sponsorship of particular projects and rejected others.

If Majewski is right, we might well need to redefine what we understand southern secessionists to have meant when they invoked the term "states' rights." For Majewski, it sometimes seems a hollow phrase, one inconsistent with the state activism antebellum and Confederate southerners sponsored. Majewski believes that most secessionists "used states' rights doctrines in selective fashion," that "they readily abandoned them" when they proved inconvenient (p. 144). Certainly, there is some truth to this. But that might not necessarily be the whole story. States' rights could coexist within the context of an activist state government. States' rights thinking embraced a robust notion of individual liberty and, especially, freedom of individual states from a federal authority. Southern slaveholders were, after all, prepared to accept limitations placed on their behavior and even their property by their states—witness the strictures against the rights of many slaveholders to manumit their slaves. In this respect, they understood states rights within a very particular context, and the emergence of a powerful Confederacy did not necessarily require them to "jettison" states rights but, rather, required them to redefine it. To argue otherwise—especially given the strength of Majewski's evidence—is to suggest that they understood states' rights as a mere rhetorical device or, in fact, that they did not understand it at all. There is just too much evidence from thoughtful southern politicians to comfortably embrace that interpretation.

Above all, Majewski's fine study sheds much-needed light on what is still a deeply underappreciated aspect of the Old South: the extent to which state activism was an important part of the southern fabric. His study will be read with enormous profit by scholars of the Civil War and the Old South.

MARK M. SMITH
University of South Carolina

JAMES M. GILLISPIE. *Andersonvilles of the North: The Myths and Realities of Northern Treatment of Civil War Confederate Prisoners.* Denton: University of North Texas Press. 2008. Pp. vii, 278. $24.95.

The purpose of James M. Gillispie's study is to show that harsh circumstances experienced by Confederate prisoners of war in northern prison camps were not the result of a cruel Union policy that emerged from a cancellation of prisoner exchanges during the war. He claims that there was nothing intentional about causing the suffering of Confederate prisoners; indeed he argues that their treatment, as prison camps go, was often generous in several respects.

Gillispie rightly points out that by the time many captured Rebels came to prison camps, they were already in bad health from deprivations caused by service in the Confederate Army. As the war dragged on, supplies of food, clothing, shoes, and other necessities dwindled. Confederates marching to and from battles often went barefooted in freezing weather, certainly a detriment to maintaining a healthy body.

Also, as many previous studies have demonstrated, the diseases that plagued soldiers in both armies defied the knowledge of doctors to treat them. The existence of germs was unknown, and treatment of smallpox, dysentery, and other diseases challenged doctors' abilities to deal with hundreds of cases at one time. Of course, these factors contributed to sick and death rates in camps where men, forced into close confinement, were more likely to be victims of contagious illnesses.

Questions raised by Gillispie's methodology are the caveats to an otherwise worthwhile reinterpretation of Union treatment of enemy prisoners. Gillispie contends that post-Civil War accounts written by Confederates who survived the camps are tainted with a Lost Cause mentality that exaggerated bad, even sadistic treatment by the Federals. The question is, can all such writings be dismissed as such? Surely words written in diaries at the time a prisoner was incarcerated would tend to be more honest, but that, too, is a stretch. What would happen if guards took the diaries, saw condemnation of the prison by Rebels against the guards, or,

more likely, the prison commander? Generalizations in either case must be handled with care and not dismissed or accepted based on when they were written. Gillespie seems to feel that accounts in the *Official Records of the Confederate and Union Armies, 1861–1865* are more truthful, but Civil War historians who have spent much time with those records know better.

Another problem is that just because officials in Washington, D.C., did not sanction revenge-type treatment of Confederate prisoners does not mean that local commandants did the same. Gillespie does show that the worst of these were often removed from command, but there were those whose sadism was more subtle, and the power guards and their commanding officers had over prisoners certainly played out in often despicable acts. Of course this was true in both armies, but the author is focusing on Federal prisons, and he often seems much too kind. Yes, some prisoners were treated better than others, and statistics, always questionable in war, and certainly disputed in almost all cases in the Civil War by historians, would indicate that northern prisons had decent survival rates better than those of southern prisons. A detailed look at the personalities of prison commanders might have either strengthened Gillespie's case or detracted from it. He touches on this issue, but in-depth analysis is lacking.

Appendixes show that Union prisons discussed by Gillespie had mostly comparable or better recovery rates from disease, Elmira Prison in New York being the exception. Gillespie does not try to gloss over the hellish conditions at Elmira. Gillespie also includes a chart that lists the leading medical killers of Confederate prisoners at the various Federal institutions. They are too numerous to list here, but he does list the top three: diarrhea/dysentery, pneumonia, and eruptive fevers, which resulted in 14,460 deaths.

Gillespie freely admits that Confederates faced "unpleasant and potentially dangerous" (p. 246) residences in Union prison camps, but he argues that there was no concerted, official effort by the Union to create these kinds of prisons and subject the enemy to miserable conditions. His argument is that the lack of medical knowledge had more to do with illness and fatalities than prison conditions. Certainly he makes a cogent point, for just being in either army was likewise unpleasant and potentially dangerous. The conditions of war, he concludes, played a greater role in Confederate deaths in Union camps that any planned system of making the Rebels suffer.

The author knows, and does not intend to argue otherwise, that this work is not the final word on the subject. He challenges historians to look closer at the issue, and hopefully that challenge will be answered. Certainly, and to his credit, Gillespie has given historians food for thought on the issue of Civil War prison humanity.

MICHAEL B. BALLARD
Mississippi State University

Mark L. Bradley. *Bluecoats and Tar Heels: Soldiers and Civilians in Reconstruction North Carolina*. (New Directions in Southern History.) Lexington: University Press of Kentucky. 2009. Pp. xi, 370. $50.00.

What role did the United States military play in Reconstruction? Army officers staffed the Freedmen's Bureau; soldiers supervised the political process; and it was often left to the army to battle white supremacist terrorists and protect Republican state and local governments. In this book Mark L. Bradley examines what happened in North Carolina when military personnel oversaw the process of Reconstruction.

Bradley picks up the story in 1865, when William T. Sherman's armies and the fall of Fort Fisher brought Confederate North Carolina to its knees; by April of that year, Sherman had accepted the surrender of Joseph E. Johnston's Confederate forces. At the end of the next month, President Andrew Johnson chose North Carolina to commence in earnest his own policy of reconciliation and restoration with minimal provision to protect recently freed blacks. Military commanders coexisted somewhat uneasily with William W. Holden's provisional government and Jonathan Worth's successor regime, although they were not always eager to protect the freedpeople—indeed, there were numerous instances of friction between white soldiers and both black soldiers and civilians. In 1867, the passage of the Reconstruction Acts inaugurated a second round of civil-military friction, as Daniel Sickles and Edward Canby supervised the process of constructing a new state constitution and government. Even with the restoration of civil rule, the military found itself called upon to subdue terrorists, but it did not engage in this process in earnest until the Democratic Party gained control of the state in 1870. The following year saw progress in subduing violence, as the Republicans enjoyed a temporary resurgence, but the victory proved temporary, and by the mid-1870s the scattered military units still on duty seemed more eager to work alongside local whites than to protect blacks and their white allies from violence.

Bradley's basic argument is that, for all the tales about the supposed repressive brutality of military occupation that remain a staple of outdated Reconstruction narratives, United States military personnel tended to facilitate reconciliation with southern white conservatives and were erratic and sometimes halfhearted when it came to dealing with violence against African Americans. As he points out, it proved something of a "juggling act" (p. 6) to promote reconciliation with whites and protection for blacks, as each worked at the expense of the other. While Bradley rejects more recent claims that the military sided far too often with their former enemies, he admits that most commanders favored moderation, and all too few proved vigorous proponents of a more forceful response to anything less than overt violence.

This detailed study takes note of variations in place, time, and circumstance, for it is at times hard to make generalizations that hold equally across the entire state. Moreover, directives from Washington changed over time, as Johnson's plan gave way to the mandates of Congressional Reconstruction, followed by the policies of the Grant administration. If Bradley is surely correct in pointing out how state studies reveal critical differences from state to state, it is also true that those differences highlight the challenges confronting national policymakers, who soon discovered that one approach did not suit in all instances. Unlike most other studies, Bradley's text does not abandon the subject with the coming to power of the Democrats; his book is one of the first to look with care at what happened after the triumph of this party, which in North Carolina was not initially quite so enduring or conclusive as it would later become. If the men in blue did not spearhead a radical revolution in race relations, it is in part because their primary responsibility was pacification and reconciliation. They were there to restore order, not to establish a new one; white officers and men often shared the racial prejudices of the recently defeated.

Overall, this is a most helpful examination of how military commanders wrestled with the problems posed by Reconstruction. Additional studies focusing on other states may help us understand why the revolutionary potential of Reconstruction might have fallen short of what many scholars today ardently wish it had been; furthermore, it may finally be time to drop the stereotypes of military repression and oppression still favored by a few people who apparently regret that Reconstruction happened at all.

Brooks D. Simpson
Arizona State University

Gregory J. Renoff. *The Big Tent: The Traveling Circus in Georgia, 1820–1930*. (Kenneth Coleman Series in Georgia History and Culture.) Athens: University of Georgia Press. 2008. Pp. x, 235. $34.95.

For over a hundred years southerners embraced the circus. Now considered primarily a children's amusement, it once was the most popular of live entertainments. No one could resist the lure of Circus Day, whether it was the more marginalized members of society—drunks, grifters, prostitutes, gamblers, and pickpockets—or the elite—church elders, merchants, politicians, matrons, and educators. Some claimed to abjure the circus because it was immoral and scandalous. Even as they nodded solemnly from the pews in support of the pulpit's denunciations, however, the same citizens thrilled with cheers and gasps from their seats in the circus bleachers. It was a space like no other where men and women, black and white, rich and poor, planter and merchant all came together to laugh, exclaim, and marvel at a thrilling spectacle.

Gregory J. Renoff documents this now vanished but once ubiquitous phenomenon. His book, while never losing sight of the circus as live performance, describes in exacting detail the circus as a productive site to explore the social, cultural, political, racial, gender, spatial, and financial economies of the emerging New South. The enthusiasm on every page for the subject is infectious; however, this is no sentimental portrait or jeremiad for a lost utopia. Class and racial violence are thoroughly explored, as are the ways in which women's sexual behavior (of both performer and spectator) was constructed and policed. The role the circus played in the commercial growth of the New South and the attendant emphasis on consumer capitalism are also major trajectories. Renoff draws from a diverse array of sources—memoirs, newspapers, archives, fiction, government documents, and other scholarly works—to provide a multi-perspective portrait of a germinal enterprise.

The book's structure carefully traces the circus's journey to performance, starting at the literal and figurative beginning to get the show on the road. The circus's historical antecedents are accounted for, as are the politics and economics of touring. The next three chapters deal with getting the audience into the bleachers. Circuses were quick to exploit postwar regionalism, whether by directly addressing the veterans in the audience or by relentlessly promoting their performances as entirely regionally defined. This played well as the circus was forced to address religious and political objections to its presentations, whether on moral, gendered, or racial grounds. Like other popular entertainments at the time, the circus promoted itself as entirely appropriate for the most genteel and refined of spectators with nothing that might offend delicate middle-class sensibilities. Objections that the circus diverted revenue that might otherwise have flowed into local coffers was another continuing challenge. Such complaints faded away as the nineteenth century wore on and the merchant class expanded.

With the audience finally in the tent, Renoff turns his attention to the audience's experiences. Those were unique for southerners, as nowhere else did the races, classes, and genders mix so freely, particularly outside and as people entered the tent. Once seated, the spectators' behaviors are evidence of how they constructed and understood their world. Whether starting fights or turning their backs at morally suspect moments, audiences had no doubt as to their agency. Concomitantly, circus managers and performers were never in doubt as to what their audiences thought about the show in front of them. But what really mattered was the show itself. There was nothing like it. One moment audiences were paralyzed with fear that acrobats or equestrians might be killed as they executed their daring feats; in the next they were indulging in erotic fantasies about the scantily clad performers. But always they were riveted by what happened around them in the ring and in the bleachers.

The touring tent circus came to a quick end. As soon as it found itself considered all-American in the 1920s, worsening economic conditions, growing audience sophistication and mobility due to radio and the automobile, and the rapid transformation of public space by the emerging suburbs made touring difficult and then impossible. But circuses reinvented themselves, emerging in the form familiar to twenty-first-century audiences.

This book has much to offer readers who want to understand the tensions that shaped regional southern life and the role live performance played in exacerbating and relieving them. The study could have been even stronger had it contextualized the circus more fully as live performance. While I take Renoff's point that circuses were not commensurate with other forms of performance, his isolation of circus from popular touring forms like vaudeville, Chautauqua, and medicine shows makes the circus appear more singular than it was, and audience experiences less polyphonous. Much live entertainment in the nineteenth and twentieth centuries struggled with the same issues that circuses did; a greater recognition of this would have made this significant book even more valuable.

CHARLOTTE M. CANNING
University of Texas,
Austin

STEVEN M. AVELLA. *Sacramento and the Catholic Church: Shaping a Capital City.* (The Urban West Series.) Reno: University of Nevada Press. 2008. Pp. xv, 368. $39.95.

Religion, a powerful and often overlooked motivating force, deserves investigation, but its ephemeral nature makes it an elusive and difficult subject. Making sense of religion's influence in the life of the capital city of the most populous and arguably most powerful and influential state in the United States over the course of 150 years is a task even more worthwhile and difficult. Steven M. Avella brings considerable and unique talents to this inquiry into the Catholic Church's influence in the history of his hometown from 1850 through 2000. This crisply written, engaging book shows how Sacramento and the Catholic Church shaped each other and offers a model for writing about religion's influence in western cities.

This book amounts to a dual biography. It tells Sacramento's history and the Catholic Church in Sacramento's history sometimes simultaneously, but most often alternately. In some sections it tells the city's story better than the church's and in others the roles reverse, but in the end the reader leaves knowing each much better and appreciating their coexistence. Avella focuses on the roles played by Catholic Sacramentans who actively and deliberately aligned with what he calls the "urban agenda" or the "urban consensus" set by the city's leaders. That agenda, present from the city's origins to the present, includes economic development, city modernization, and social stability. The book also addresses the influence of religious institutions, with attention paid to roles of important leaders. Avella justifies book-length scrutiny for the topic by pointing to the church's expansive civic footprint. The founding generation's Roman Catholics ranked as the largest denomination in the city, the church has maintained large membership and a high rate of participation by members, and it has a breadth of civic involvement represented by schools, hospitals, an orphanage, a settlement house, and other institutions unmatched by any other denomination.

The author's case slowly becomes convincing. Avella introduces the Reverend John F. Quinn—pastor of the Cathedral of the Blessed Sacrament 1899–1906 and at the same time a real estate investor and all-around booster—as evidence of the church acting in concert with community leaders bent on economic development and urban beautification during the Progressive era. From the perspective of secular Sacramento history, did it matter that Quinn was Roman Catholic? Maybe. During the Depression the Catholic Ladies' Relief Society provided a number of services to the needy. They could not keep up with demand, but they make good evidence for the significance of the Catholic fiber in the city's social safety net. This argument continues to strengthen as Avella moves through the mid and late twentieth century discussing the church's links to the Latino community and in a remarkably compelling chapter, arguably the book's strongest, on the issue of homelessness, which marked the most notable episode of discord between city and church as the latter followed its calling to aid the poor.

In addition to the church-city relationship, Avella found evidence of a church-region relationship wherein Sacramento's Catholics enjoyed a more inclusive and less contentious history than their counterparts in the East and the Midwest. Avella attributes this to unique characteristics of the American West and writes that Sacramento Catholics followed a path similar to their coreligionists in western cities such as Portland, Cheyenne, Phoenix, and Seattle. This becomes especially striking in his discussion of growth and sprawl fueled by World War II and the postwar boom in the military-industrial complex. Referring to this era as " 'pioneer' days," Avella reminds us of the continuity of themes in western history and argues convincingly that new parish communities played an important role in dramatically changing previously "empty" spaces (p. 206).

Avella's insider status, both as a Catholic and a Sacramentan, raises questions about his objectivity, but he handles both subjects evenhandedly. His impeccable research in both secular and ecclesiastical archives and his storytelling and measured interpretations betray passion but not bias. Given that the book focuses on the capital city of the nation's most important state and deals with a hugely significant theme, this reviewer hoped for some discussion of the twin topics' greater importance. But that should not detract from the author's tight and successful treatment of Sacramento and the Catholic Church. Those interested in western urban history, U.S. religious history, and the intersection of city, region, and religion would do well to consult Avella's fine work.

TODD M. KERSTETTER
Texas Christian University

AVIVA BEN-UR. *Sephardic Jews in America: A Diasporic History*. New York: New York University Press. 2009. Pp. x, 321. $35.00.

Successful explorations of ethnic history achieve two sorts of results. Ethnic historians must enhance the visibility of the group whose experience they wish to highlight. Enhanced visibility leads to a second and even more important achievement. The most effective treatments of ethnic history remind their readers that ethnic groups are continually dialectical, not only as they relate to their "host" cultures but also through the interaction of their own sub-ethnic constituencies. Aviva Ben-Ur's book makes a strong case for the consideration of Sephardim and other non-Ashkenazic Jews (who currently constitute four percent of the United States' total Jewish population) in any larger picture of the American Jewish experience. Of even greater significance, however, is Ben-Ur's effort to complicate our overall sense of who these Sephardim are and how they have both adapted to and helped to transform the "mainstream" of American (Ashkenazic) Judaism. Indeed, the author's most telling contention is that their "minority within a minority" status renders non-Ashkenazic Jews worthy of attention because "the study of the margins" can be an effective "tool for shedding light on broader society" (p. 4). Ben-Ur's book is a valuable contribution to American Jewish historiography, within which treatments of the Sephardic experience have either focused exclusively on the "Old" Sephardic "Grandees" who came to the America before 1776 or, in a contemporary context, have limited themselves to a primarily ethnographic concentration on the folkways of particular communities.

Ben-Ur's primary attention is given to the largely unsung history of the "Eastern Sephardim" and Mizrahi Jews, whose initial arrival in the United States occurred concurrently with that of the great eastern European influx. These immigrants, very few of whom were any more prosperous than the "Russian Jews" who entered the United States at Ellis Island, hailed from such far flung locales as Salonika, Istanbul, Cairo, and Aleppo. Rather than being a strictly chronological rendering of Sephardic history in America, Ben-Ur's book takes shape as a series of case studies, each of which explores the Sephardic *legacy*, often enough as it was filtered through the presuppositions of the non-Sephardim who have so long constituted the majority of American Jews. By reputation, Sephardim could be standoffish and aristocratic or poverty-stricken and racially inferior. Their Jewish practice was either worthy of wonder and reverence for its fidelity to "ancient" Hebraic custom, or it was alarmingly out of touch with what might pass for genuine orthodoxy. In some instances the Sephardic "influence" over the east European majority was entirely inadvertent, as was the case in connection with Hebrew language instruction. With the exception of ultra-Orthodox (Ashkenazic) Jews, most synagogues and Hebrew schools long ago adopted what they termed the Sephardic pronunciation of Hebrew. As Zionists sought to restore an untainted Hebrew to modern use in the land whose settlement was meant to bring an end to the diaspora, American Jews wishing for their own normalization within gentile society overwhelmingly favored a "Sephardic" pronunciation as an antidote to centuries of exile and degeneration. The irony attendant upon this preference was that what the Ashkenazim labeled as Sephardic pronunciation was itself an artificial construct; Sephardim had as many pronunciation schemes as lands of origin. Had the overwhelmingly Ashkenazic promoters of this revival been asked whose language they were speaking or "what exactly was a Sephardic Jew," many of them would have been at a loss to answer the question meaningfully.

When Eastern Sephardim began arriving in New York in large numbers at the turn of the twentieth century, their arrival created a crisis for the Sephardic establishment. Some "Grandees" suggested the term "Oriental Jews" as a measure of the distance between themselves and the newer immigrants. If linguistic practice was an indicator of cultural origin, however, the newcomers' retention of Ladino marked them as no less "Western" than the wealthier Sephardim whose ancestors had come to North America in the colonial era. In the eyes of the even more powerful Ashkenazic majority the members of this broad assortment of *non-Ashkenazic* Jews bore one trait in common: they were hardly recognizable as Jews. Ben-Ur's chapter on "Ashkenazic-Sephardic Encounters" recounts an episode in which an Ashkenazic inquisitor insisted on imposing the ultimate test upon a dark-skinned claimant of Jewish heritage. "They took me to the lavatory," recounts one of Ben-Ur's interview subjects of his arrival at what was to have been a Jewish house of refuge in New York (p. 115).

Even as most "Oriental" and "Arab" Jews have found greater acceptance in contemporary America, a Jewish majority long accustomed to an Ashkenazic norm remains unresolved in its relationship to the Sephardic minority. Two recent phenomena have further complicated Sephardic Jewish identity: first, the cultural divide among Israeli Jews, among whom Sephardim and Mizrahi formed the majority until the recent upsurge in Ashkenazic migration from the former Soviet Union; second, the growing size and influence of Hispanic culture within the United States. Both cases suggest the prospect of non-Ashkenazic Jews in America finding common cause with cultural outsiders. American Sephardim challenge any fixed notion of Jewish identity by inhabiting an awkward point of encounter, not only between Jewish culture and America's Christian majority, but between East and West, as well as a racial and linguistic margin beyond which Ashkenazic Jews, at least in the years since they became "white folks," have rarely ventured.

MICHAEL HOBERMAN
Fitchburg State College

JEFFREY S. GUROCK. *Orthodox Jews in America.* (The Modern Jewish Experience.) Bloomington: Indiana

University Press. 2009. Pp. x, 381. Cloth $65.00, paper $24.95.

Jeffrey S. Gurock never defines Orthodoxy in his new book. This is a careful, well-written work, and I suspect that Gurock consciously decided not to offer a definition. In fact, his point is that a single definition would be unable to encompass the breadth of Orthodox Judaism in the United States. Starting with a portrait of Gurock's own Orthodox upbringing in the Bronx, the book emphasizes the multiple and often clashing ways that Jews have lived observant lifestyles in the United States. Indeed, readers of this book will be hard pressed to find a common thread that links Orthodox Jews across time or space. The question, then, is whether the category "Orthodox" is meaningful at all?

Gurock notes struggle beginning with the earliest evidence of Jewish religious observance in the United States. A miniscule population, the Jews in colonial America encountered a religious environment that was hospitable to religion but suspicious of religious difference. Furthermore, the demands of Jewish observance were not easily met in the new environment, where Jews lived apart from longstanding Jewish communities and where economic pressures forced certain religious transgressions. None of this is too shocking. What is surprising, and what Gurock documents with meticulous detail, is the attention that so many early American Jews paid to observance. Even those who married non-Jews and flouted Jewish laws often remained tied to synagogues. Furthermore, synagogue leaders with aspirations for punctilious observance accommodated a variety of lifestyles and religious choices within their gates. It is important, however, for the reader to appreciate that there was nothing particularly ideological about these examples of tolerance.

Gurock maintains that even as Jewish intellectuals in Europe were gripped by ideological revolutions and calls for religious reform, American Jews tended to be practical minded. One can observe a host of reforms to synagogue life: mixed seating, mixed-sex choirs, and leniency in membership laws. Yet these were not ideologically driven reforms. Gurock, agreeing with other scholars, argues that American Jews were searching for ways to reconcile their Jewishness with their aspirations to Americanize. As the American Jewish population spiked at the turn of the century, this pragmatic approach to Judaism frayed. New congregations were formed and a new self-consciousness about being observant—or Orthodox—emerged.

Education was crucial to the rise of an Orthodox movement. Gurock draws on his past research to illustrate the central role that educational institutions played in defining the parameters of Orthodoxy. At root was the insecurity that many immigrant Jews felt about their ability to transmit Judaism and a Jewish identity to their children. Led by a new professional class of Jews, the Jewish education movement came to define Orthodoxy as the one branch of Judaism committed to religious learning as at least on par with secular learning.

If education came to define Orthodox Judaism, it also very quickly came to splinter it. Jewish leaders could not agree on how or even whether to balance secular and religious learning. Linked to this was a larger debate about the proper relationship between observant Jews and non-Jewish—or, in some cases, simply non-Orthodox—society. Gurock promises the reader an "unflinching" examination of ethical misconduct among Orthodox Jews and, although more could be said on this topic, his point is that some Orthodox Jews see little connection, ethical or otherwise, to those outside their community. For others the opposite is true, and Gurock fruitfully discusses gender politics to show how some high-profile rabbis have reached far beyond their religious world to make a case for rethinking elements of Orthodox Judaism.

Despite Gurock's attention to moderate voices within the Orthodox world, religious fundamentalism appears to have a considerable influence upon Orthodoxy. Many of the hallmarks of American religious fundamentalism—an uncompromising rigidity, an attitude of censoriousness toward the non-religious world, and the desire to create a politics that favors religious values—are present in Gurock's description of post-World War II Orthodox Judaism. Gurock, however, chooses not to emphasize the fairly obvious comparison between Orthodoxy and religious fundamentalism. Instead, he leads the reader to a different conclusion: that Orthodox Judaism remains a big tent and that, in fact, most people within it are "tentative," hardly the vocal espousers of fundamentalist ideologies (p. 315). One gets the sense by the end of the book that Gurock, who tells the reader that he attends a notably progressive Orthodox synagogue, is writing in hopes of preserving the breadth of Orthodoxy. In my mind, this goal shapes the history he tells but does not undermine it; Gurock is the unrivaled expert on Orthodox Jews and Judaism in the United States, something he proves ably with this book. It does explain, however, his reluctance to define Orthodox Judaism, in the end, a defining decision.

LILA CORWIN BERMAN
Temple University

MARGARET LYNCH-BRENNAN. *The Irish Bridget: Irish Immigrant Women in Domestic Service in America, 1840–1930.* Foreword by MAUREEN O'ROURKE MURPHY. (Irish Studies.) Syracuse, N.Y.: Syracuse University Press. 2009. Pp. xxii, 232. $39.95.

Irish maids were a prominent feature of American life in the nineteenth century, so familiar an aspect that the term for an Irish maid was often "a Bridget"—thus the title of this book. The scholarship on Irish domestics has frequently portrayed the life of a maid as virtual slavery and humiliation. In juxtaposition to this portrayal, caricatures and the popular literature of the day depicted Irish maids as uppity and holding the real power in the household. Margaret Lynch-Brennan presents sufficient evidence here to permit scholars to draw their own conclusions.

This book is important because it mobilizes evidence from firsthand accounts of the lives of Irish women as maids in middle-class American households and so is not solely an ideological view. While Lynch-Brennan argues strongly that American women employed domestic servants primarily for conspicuous consumption, there is little evidence from the accounts she uses to support this view. A contrary reality emerges from the 1999 British Broadcasting Corporation (BBC) production called *The 1900 House*, which illustrated the complexity of tasks necessary to operate the most basic of households before the introduction of vacuum cleaners, washing machines, and electric light necessitated some kind of help. In the series, when the lady of the household became a feminist, it proved impossible to manage her household without her maid of all work.

While Irish men tended to live in communities with their fellow Irish, Irish women lived in close contact with American families and this affected the outcome of their future personal histories. Americans in particular have attached both racial and gendered meanings to servitude and this may help explain the nature of the complicated relationship between American mistresses and their Irish servants, thereby making any study of household help in America fraught with difficulty. This is hardly surprising, given that industrialization and urbanization were changing the role of American women, many of whom lacked the skills to manage a household adequately.

The book places some emphasis on the negative aspects of the lives of socially marginalized Irish women as servants. Yet the author fails to engage with academic literature on servitude as upward mobility, including my "'Come You All Courageously Together': Irish Women Write Home," in Kevin Kenny, ed., *New Directions in Irish-American History* (2003), 209–226. The papers of Vere Foster, who sponsored the emigration of thousands of Irish women to the United States, reveal women as eager to leave Ireland and become successful in America. Mary Harlon wrote to Foster that, when one mistress would not raise her wages, she had only to consult the newspaper to find another position. The author does conclude, however, that domestic service provided an acculturating experience for Irish domestics, thereby facilitating their rise into the American middle class.

The decline of the dowry system pushed women out of Ireland. For marriage to be contracted, women needed to bring a dowry and men to bring land. The consequence of population growth and the decline of domestic industry was that Irish families could no longer furnish dowries to all their daughters, and therefore some were "raised to emigrate." It was not the most impoverished who emigrated, but rather those who saw their prospects diminishing. Women in particular took the best option available and left Ireland for the United States, most to become domestics. By living in households where food and shelter were provided, young Irish women could improve not only their own lives but the lives of their families in Ireland, to whom they remitted phenomenal sums of money. Those who married stressed education for their daughters, as the work of Janet A. Nolan emphasizes (See Nolan, "Education and Women's Mobility in Ireland and Irish America, 1880–1920: A Preliminary Look," *New Hibernia Review* 2:3 [1998]: 78–88).

Lynch-Brennan has produced a thoroughly workmanlike book, densely documented with personal accounts, drawing on interviews and letters to let the women tell their own stories. As the first full-length scholarly book on female Irish servants, it will be a valuable text for educators.

RUTH-ANN M. HARRIS
Boston College

LUCINDA MCCRAY BEIER. *Health Culture in the Heartland, 1880–1980: An Oral History*. Urbana and Chicago: University of Illinois Press. 2009. Pp. xviii, 242. Cloth $75.00, paper $25.00.

This is an absorbing study of the century-long transformation of health and medical care in one Illinois county. Lucinda McCray Beier uses oral and other sources to compile a richly detailed portrait of what she calls a "community health culture."

In Beier's definition, "health culture" encompasses a broad variety of factors, including the environment, individuals' experiences of disease, public health policy, medical institutions and professions, and health care practitioners. This inclusive approach is a useful one, allowing for a fuller picture of the meanings of health and medicine than do discrete studies of particular aspects of the system.

The author dug deeply into local source material. She conducted twenty nine interviews of McLean County residents, who commented on events from the late nineteenth century through the 1980s. The book's introductory discussion of the benefits and pitfalls of oral history is excellent and could profitably be used for classroom discussions of methodology. In addition, Beier taps into extant oral histories and the holdings of the local historical society, medical society, and hospitals.

The book's overarching goal is to take the standard paradigm of U.S. medical history—the transformation from domestic, holistic views of health and healing in the nineteenth century to the overwhelming acceptance of "biomedicine," the hospital, and physician authority in the twentieth century—and examine whether and how quickly a less urbanized community participated in this transformation. Overall, Beier finds that the paradigm holds true for McLean County, although she sees a temporal lag in the adoption of some major trends, such as the creation of a public health and sanitation infrastructure and the move from home to hospital. McLean County reflected similar changes happening in major urban centers, but changes happened somewhat more slowly in McLean.

Mid-nineteenth-century McLean County was an unhealthy place known for "fevers," primarily malaria. The draining of swamps for agriculture had the unintended consequence of drastically reducing the threat of mosquito-borne illnesses, and health conditions improved even more when the city of Bloomington began building a sewage system in 1874 (previously, human and animal waste was dumped into sloughs bordering the town, draining directly into the citizens' drinking water). Most medical care took place in the home and was provided by women. Physicians were called only when home treatment failed, but Beier finds that "[e]ven the smallest communities supported physicians" by the late nineteenth century (p. 18).

McLean County's first hospital was St. Joseph's, opened in 1880 and supported by charitable donations and patient fees. It was administered by nuns who also ran a farm that fed both patients and staff. Soon the county was home to several charitable hospitals that charged sliding scale fees to patients of modest means, while the county paid for the hospitalization of "paupers." Local hospital records yield some fascinating insights. Beier finds that alcoholism and injuries were the most commonly identified reasons for admission to St. Joseph's, and that the average length of a hospital stay in 1891 was fifty-two days, indication of the hospitals' custodial role. Hospitals also served as retirement homes for the respectable middle-class elderly, who could purchase accommodations for the remainder of their lives. Early in the twentieth century McLean County was home to a diverse array of medical institutions, but by the 1980s, cost pressures and mergers left the region with only two hospitals. Subsequent chapters on nursing, the medical profession, public health, and patient experiences are similarly rich with fascinating anecdotes and insights about how health care transformation took place at the local level.

This book is a superb model of analytical local history and of social history. Its potential impact on scholarly debates in the history of medicine is less clear; overall, Beier uses new evidence to confirm what historians have long defined as national trends. Still, this is useful in itself, and should encourage additional research that continues to uncover the richer and deeper evidence that is only available through local sources. The author should be commended for undertaking this study that successfully brings a community and its people to life.

BEATRIX HOFFMAN
Northern Illinois University

NATHANIEL DEUTSCH. *Inventing America's "Worst" Family: Eugenics, Islam, and the Fall and Rise of the Tribe of Ishmael*. Berkeley and Los Angeles: University of California Press. 2009. Pp. xiv, 253. Cloth $60.00, paper $24.95.

Scholarly texts on the eugenics movement in the United States have appeared with great regularity during the past decade, and Nathaniel Deutsch has produced a valuable and important addition to that canon. His book is a beautifully written and meticulously researched work that traces three stages of the historiography of the "Tribe of Ishmael" from the 1870s to the present. But this brief description does not capture the range of Deutsch's ambitious project, which is not only a history of the eugenics movement but also a history of Orientalism in the United States *and* a history of upland southerners in the Midwest.

The first stage in America's fascination with the Ishmaels began when Oscar McCulloch, a Congregationalist minister, armchair Orientalist, and proponent of the Social Gospel in Indiana, discovered a number of (supposedly) related families in the slums of Indianapolis whose high rates of unemployment, crime, and degeneracy were, he believed, congenital. "The Tribe of Ishmael: A Study in Social Degradation," McCulloch's article in the 1888 *Proceedings of the National Conference of Charities and Correction*, alerted the American public that this group of itinerant, atavistic savages was living in the heart of darkest Indianapolis, and the Ishmaels, like the Jukes and the Kallikaks, entered the lexicon as a catchphrase for the undeserving poor in Gilded-Age America.

We learn from Deutsch that the Ishmaels were indeed one of many pauper families in Indianapolis in the nineteenth century; he shows that McCulloch chose to refer to the entire underclass of that city as "the Tribe of Ishmael" in order to appeal "to the contemporary craze for things Oriental while still exploiting overtly negative stereotypes of Islam" (p. 54). Indeed, throughout the book Deutsch successfully demonstrates that "each stage of the Tribe of Ishmael's story corresponds to a different phase in [the] fascinating but largely unwritten history of American Orientalism" (p. 14).

The public perception of poor people in the United States entered a second phase in the 1920s when eugenicists like Harry H. Laughlin and Arthur Estabrook of the Eugenics Records Office manipulated the Muslim-sounding surname of the Ishmaels in order to transform the cacogenic family into a symbol of the need for immigration restriction, anti-miscegenation legislation, and widespread sterilization. The eugenicists continually argued that the Ishmael family's pauperism, criminality, and licentiousness were due to their inferior germ plasm, which caused inherited feeblemindedness. It is one of Deutsch's great coups that he is able to prove that the Ishmaels were, in fact, descended from hardworking, patriotic, upland southerners who were simply doing their best to survive during an era of rapid industrialization and urbanization. Deutsch persuasively concludes that it was their poverty and lack of education, "rather than any genetic predisposition toward criminality, wandering, or feeblemindedness, [that explain] the . . .behaviors that became associated with the so-called Tribe of Ishmael" (p. 199).

The Ishmaels entered a third—and thoroughly unexpected—stage in the wake of the Black Power movement, when a white minister named Hugo Leaming (who later joined an African American Islamic temple) published a chapter entitled "The Ben Ishmael Tribe:

A Fugitive 'Nation' of the Old Northwest" in *The Ethnic Frontier: Group Survival in Chicago and the Midwest* (1977), in which he claimed that the Ishmaels were actually descended from escaped slaves who had established the first Muslim community in the United States. Leaming argued, for example, that the sexual promiscuity of some of the Ishmaels was not a mark of wantonness but rather a sign of polygamy, a practice descended from Islamic tradition. Again, Deutsch's historical detective work reveals that Leaming's widely repeated and influential version was based on little more than fantasy and wishful thinking. And that, of course, is the point of Deutsch's book: every generation of American scholars has projected its own ideological and psychological needs and fantasies onto the Ishmaels, a group of "families" who never even existed as a family and were never "degenerate," "cacogenic," or Islamic.

The trope that social scientists see what they want to see has appeared in many recent books on the eugenics movement, including my biography of the leader of the eugenics movement: *Defending the Master Race: Conservation, Eugenics, and the Legacy of Madison Grant* (2009). Like Deutsch, I also argue that the eugenicists were scientific-minded reformers who, like wildlife managers, believed that the good of the individual was subservient to the good of society and thus sought to use the power of the state to bring about the ultimate progressive reform: regulating human evolution. It is fitting, therefore, that Deutsch concludes his wide-ranging book with a scathing indictment of the eugenicists. While recognizing that they "possessed good intentions—at least in their own eyes—when they wrote about the Tribe of Ishmael," he notes the damning irony that from our modern perspective "it is the eugenicists themselves, not the Ishmaels . . . or any of the other supposedly cacogenic groups, who appear to us like an antisocial tribe that once threatened the fabric of the Unites States" (pp. 203–204).

JONATHAN PETER SPIRO
Castleton State College

LINDA DOWLING. *Charles Eliot Norton: The Art of Reform in Nineteenth-Century America*. (Becoming Modern: New Nineteenth-Century Studies.) Hanover, N.H.: University Press of New England, for the University of New Hampshire Press. 2007. Pp. xxi, 221. $39.95.

In this book Linda Dowling provides a revisionist portrait of Charles Eliot Norton, best known as the first professor of fine arts at Harvard University, as an impassioned reformer. What is fascinating about Dowling's account is not so much that she refutes the caricature of Norton that first emerged during the Progressive era, summarized as a "carping, hypocritical, neurasthenic elitist" (p. 143), as that she challenges present-day readers to assess his actions and writings in light of his entire life's work rather than his later public reputation. For this reason, Dowling focuses her attention on the period before Norton's Harvard appointment in 1874. Her book is not a biography—she acknowledges the groundbreaking work of James Turner's *The Liberal Education of Charles Eliot Norton* (1999) in this respect—so much as an intellectual history of Norton and the strain of nineteenth-century liberal thought that he represents.

In order to establish Norton's lifelong commitment to reform, Dowling prefaces this book with a discussion of his sustained public criticism of the Spanish-American War and of U.S. imperialism. She argues that Norton saw contemporary American foreign policy as a betrayal of the moral and civic ideals underpinning the Union cause during the Civil War. She emphasizes that this position made him reviled by many. The subsequent five chapters go back in time to explore the formative impact of the Civil War on Norton, his religious beliefs, and his participation in Anglo-American debates about the role of culture in civic life.

Dowling analyzes relationships and events that radicalized Norton as well as sources of his disillusionment. Through his direct interactions with John Ruskin and the English Pre-Raphaelite artists during the mid-1850s, Norton discovered a model for an alliance between visual culture and social reform. During the subsequent decade, his roles as a propagandist for the Union and a supporter of the Sanitary Commission provided an outlet for his abolitionist beliefs, to which he was a late convert. Dowling juxtaposes Norton's conviction that Union victory would usher in a higher stage of American civilization with his misgivings about the country's rampant materialism. She also links Norton's crisis of faith, which became pronounced after the premature death of his wife, Susan, to his devotion to artistic beauty as the only source of immortality. The author presents Norton as increasingly out of step by the end of the century, bewildered by American society, wary of the aesthetic movement (with which his ideas about art are often equated), and hardening in his habits and judgments. As Dowling puts it succinctly, Norton, like many of his generation, was "mourning a larger belief about the world that had animated his young manhood and middle age: the idea of progress" (p. 153).

Throughout her nuanced analysis of Norton's thought, Dowling challenges the reductive vision of him as simply a prisoner of his class and the ivory tower, whether in his characterization by Van Wyck Brooks during the 1950s or in the more recent assessment of Louis Menand in *The Metaphysical Club: A Story of Ideas in America* (2001). There are a few areas in which Dowling herself seems to perpetuate the myth of Norton, describing without irony his escape from physical discomfort during New England winters to more forgiving climates or recording the simple grace with which Susan Norton entertained at their country home, but her insights into Norton's place in cultural history far outweigh these lapses.

The compactness of Dowling's book makes for a focused profile of Norton; it also leaves the reader eager for more information, for example, about his early work as a housing reformer in Boston or his advocacy of women's rights. Given that Norton believed in art as a means of social reform, Dowling presents a limited examination of his involvement with art and architecture in the United States, whether as a collector, curator, critic, or educator. The catalogue from a recent exhibition, *The Last Ruskinians: Charles Eliot Norton, Charles Herbert Moore, and Their Circle* (2007), and Michael W. Brooks's essay "New England Gothic: Charles Eliot Norton, Charles H. Moore, and Henry Adams" (*Studies in the History of Art* 35 [1990]: 113–125) develop Norton's links with John Ruskin and the Pre-Raphaelites by tracing their American legacies. Future studies could also build on Dowling's portrait of Norton when investigating the institutionalization of culture in Boston during the late nineteenth century.

In summary, Linda Dowling offers a generous reexamination of Charles Eliot Norton, one that both highlights his singular activities as well as the ways in which he was representative of his time, place, and class.

MAURA LYONS
Drake University

MORRIS L. DAVIS. *The Methodist Unification: Christianity and the Politics of Race in the Jim Crow Era.* (Religion, Race, and Ethnicity.) New York: New York University Press. 2008. Pp. viii, 197. $45.00.

Slavery split the Methodist Church into separate northern and southern organizations even before the Civil War split the nation. From 1869 to 1935, race and racism bedeviled the many attempts of Methodists to reunite their denomination. In this well-crafted monograph, Morris L. Davis provides a racial exegesis of an important part of the process that eventually resulted in the formation of the United Methodist Church. Davis focuses this study on the six meetings of the Joint Commission on Unification that took place between 1916 and 1920.

The "primary question" addressed in this work is, "how did so many of these Methodists understand race and Christianity together?" Davis moves beyond standard narratives that merely describe and lament racism. He attempts "to examine race itself as a historical phenomenon." He explores how, during the Commission's deliberations, the language of racism, power, and white privilege was translated into Christian discourse. Davis believes that previous scholars have put too much emphasis on doctrine and theology. He approaches Methodism primarily as a "cultural category," and for that reason he suggests that his work "has an anthropological or ethnographic feel to it."

In order to craft an acceptable plan for reunion, the Commission had to reconcile divergent regional understandings of the significance of race, but some views were held in common. Neither northern nor southern commissioners ever proposed the integration of local churches. Even the two black commissioners felt obliged to join their forty-eight white colleagues in rejecting "social equality" and denouncing miscegenation. Further, none of the commissioners even contemplated changing the existing policy whereby all black churches were grouped together in separate Annual Conferences, which were the basic administrative bodies of Methodism. The only issue in dispute was whether separate black Conferences should have equal standing with white Conferences in matters related to denominational governance—but reaching agreement on that point proved to be extraordinarily difficult.

It was difficult because white Methodists professed to believe that guidelines for the "status of the Negro" could not be found "in any doctrine of salvation through Jesus Christ." So, some vexing questions had to be answered without the benefit of Scripture. Should relationships between white and black Christians be paternal or fraternal? Were racial characteristics fixed or fluid? Would the achievement of "race consciousness" and manhood make blacks want greater inclusion, or more independence? Could a biracial denomination be the bulwark of white American civilization? One of this book's greatest strengths is Davis's very thoughtful analysis of the answers that northern and southern commissioners gave to those questions and others.

On December 1, 1916, the Joint Commission on Unification met for the first time in Baltimore, the city where the Methodist denomination had been officially organized in 1784. It was hoped and expected that Methodist unity would be restored in the city where the denomination was founded. That hope foundered, ebbed, and then died during the deliberations. The meeting in Baltimore turned out to be only the first in a series of inconclusive meetings held in different cities over the next three years. The sixth and "final" meeting of the Commission took place in Louisville, Kentucky, in 1920. A proposal was produced at that meeting, but with little enthusiasm. The commissioners stated simply that it was "the best that we have been able to agree upon, under the circumstances."

That proposal was not accepted by either the northern or southern denomination. The process had reached an impasse. Efforts to resume negotiations moved forward but soon sputtered and were then put on hold, not to be revived for over a decade. In 1935, a new plan was proposed and this time it was accepted and celebrated, to the dismay of many blacks. The new plan created the Central Jurisdiction, which became the administrative home for all black churches in the reunited Methodist denomination, regardless of where they were located. The racially separate Jurisdiction continued to exit until 1968, fourteen years *after* the United States Supreme Court ruled against segregation in public schools, and four years *after* the passage of the Civil Rights Act of 1964.

The Methodist Unification is an engaging and illuminating volume. The 132 pages of text will captivate serious students of Methodism, as well as readers with a general interest in the history of race and religion. Still, it could have had even wider significance and appeal if its analysis was not concentrated on just six meetings and four years of a process that took about a century to work out. Certainly, more attention could have been paid to the final negotiations that took place in 1935, in the midst the upheavals of the Great Depression and the New Deal. In addition, Davis could have extended his analysis to help readers understand why Methodism lagged behind secular society in putting an end to racial separation. In sum, the analysis presented in this study is sharp, ambitious, and original, but the scope of the book is too modest.

REGINALD F. HILDEBRAND
University of North Carolina,
Chapel Hill

CRAWFORD GRIBBEN. *Writing the Rapture: Prophecy Fiction in Evangelical America*. New York: Oxford University Press. 2009. Pp. xi, 258. $29.95.

Over the past decade, Crawford Gribben has established himself as one of the leading experts in the area of what has come to be called, by him and others, "prophecy fiction." With his newly published work, he solidifies his position alongside Amy Frykholm and Paul S. Boyer as one of the most insightful researchers in this field. "Prophecy fiction" (or as some denominate it, "rapture fiction") is a loosely defined genre concerned with a brand of Protestant theology founded on the belief that before Christ comes again, the faithful will be taken to heaven so that they need not experience the Tribulation (a period of time in which the Antichrist comes to rule the earth). Gribben's book is a must read for any scholar interested in prophecy fiction specifically and twentieth and twenty-first-century Protestant fiction more generally.

Worth the price of admission is Gribben's introduction, in which he lays out a careful and nuanced outline of the complicated development of prophecy fiction over the past century. He pays particular attention to the genre's emergence in the United States, and its relationship to various strains of dispensational premillennialism, evangelicalism, and Protestant fundamentalism. In its broadest contours, Gribben's book is a history and historicization of prophecy fiction and how such fiction is one of the best "barometers of evangelical cultural change" (p. 68). Also of great value to scholars is the bibliography Gribben includes at the end of his book, in which he provides a host of valuable primary and secondary source citations related to prophecy fiction and dispensational theology.

Three arguments emerge from Gribben's overview of the development and circulation of prophecy fiction. First, Gribben argues that prophecy fiction has moved from being a genre embraced by various adherents of dispensational theology to the mainstream of the American culture, creating a unique and pervasive American myth in the process. Second, prophecy fiction has become a powerful means of religious cultural critique. It may be a genre that purports to be about the future, but its main concerns are firmly planted in the present. Most pointedly, it has been a genre that has focused its energies on exposing the spiritual dangers of "modernity," as concerns with wealth and rank re-placed more righteous appetites for the things of God. Finally, prophecy fiction shows a trend in American (and some British) Protestantism away from didactic nonfiction as a means of doctrinal education in favor of fiction.

Gribben's study begins in the early twentieth century with a constellation of books that approach rapture theology differently, yet provide the foundation for the general impetus of this genre to seek to impose theological order and meaning on the chaos of an increasingly modern and godless world. Little known yet vastly important authors such as Joseph Birkbeck Burroughs, Milton H. Stine, Joshua Hill Foster, and Sydney Watson occupy central roles in his opening chapters. A central insight revealed in Gribben's engaging study of these authors is their commitment to the "supremacy of white Americans" (p. 29). Racism played a key role in how writers of prophecy fiction both understood their God and his redemptive plan for the world.

Gribben then moves on to study the genre in its World War II and Cold War contexts and argues that prophecy fiction became one of the staunchest advocates for the messianic role of the United States in the war against godless Communism. Gribben's later chapters are then largely devoted to the tremendous popularity and influence of the *Left Behind* series written by Jerry B. Jenkins and Timothy LaHaye. (Particularly noteworthy here are the insights offered through Gribben's interviews with Jenkins.) In these novels one sees the maturation of certain prophecy fiction themes: the moral threats of modernity, the larger civic responsibilities of Christians, and the didactic role fiction might play in converting the world to Christianity. Gribben is even good enough to offer a final chapter on "Prophecy Fiction after *Left Behind*" wherein he explores the continuing evolution of the genre and its pronounced interests in Protestant political involvement, warring theological commitments among various Protestants, and the changing nature of the "evangelical condition" as Christians continue to attempt to triangulate their own positions as both citizens and believers amid the earthly realities of everyday existence (p. 145).

Gribben's work sometimes suffers from his greater familiarity with the British Protestant context over the American one, but this book will become a standard work for all interested in more contemporary Protestant publishing. Religious and cultural historians, as well as literary critics, will find great rewards nestled on almost every page of this work.

PAUL C. GUTJAHR
*Indiana University
Bloomington*

JAMES E. KLEIN. *Grappling with Demon Rum: The Cultural Struggle over Liquor in Early Oklahoma*. Norman: University of Oklahoma Press. 2008. Pp. x, 238. $34.95.

James E. Klein offers a good case study of the prohibition issue in Oklahoma, focusing primarily on the ac-tivism and cultural mores of the state's Anti-Saloon League in the early twentieth century. Informing the study throughout is Klein's argument that the prohibition battle was "a conflict between middle-class and working-class definitions of social propriety," with the result that the "cultural contest over respectability lies at the heart of the liquor question in Oklahoma" (pp. 8, 9). After noting Oklahoma's hard-drinking frontier phase, Klein details the efforts of white, middle-class reformers to achieve official prohibition in referendums of 1907 and 1910 and to enforce nationwide prohibition from 1920 to 1933. These anti-alcohol efforts were seriously hampered, however, by the continual resistance of working-class drinkers and saloon keepers. The conflict produced "two Oklahomas" in Klein's estimation, a duality that was class-based and culturally expressed (p. 183).

While Klein argues for the primacy of class identity in Oklahoma's prohibition battle, he also considers other factors including race, ethnicity, religion, and gender. Particularly interesting is his examination of the Five Tribes of Oklahoma. Both tribal leaders and white reformers were troubled over the stereotype of the "drunken Indian," but jurisdictional conflicts among federal, state, and local authorities bedeviled policy-making and enforcement efforts. African Americans also suffered from the stereotype of the drunken, lascivious black man, which helped prompt oppressive Jim Crow laws and Ku Klux Klan attacks. In addition, white ethnics, particularly German immigrants, endured considerable prejudice for their drinking proclivities. The religious affiliations of white ethnics also entered into the liquor controversy. The lack of prohibitionist fervor among such groups as Roman Catholics, Lutherans, and Jews was taken as proof of cultural inferiority by mainstream evangelical groups such as Southern Baptists and Methodists. The vocal and determined Anti-Saloon League was closely allied with these dry Protestant denominations.

Klein's discussion of gender focuses on female activists in the Woman's Christian Temperance Union (WCTU). This organization mobilized mostly white, middle-class women to fight the alcohol problem on all fronts, from domestic abuse to health problems to criminal activity. The male-dominated Anti-Saloon League soon surpassed the WCTU's influence, relegating women activists to a supporting role as the men zeroed in on the single issue of greatest concern to them: the working-class saloon.

In his portrayal of the saloon, Klein makes a commendable effort to present a fair and balanced account. In doing so, he avoids the tendency of all too many prohibition historians to accept uncritically the dry crusade's negative caricature of the institution. It might have been advisable to provide a bit more explanation of the saloon's appeal beyond its social attractions, for a great many establishments nationwide also functioned as the poor man's bank, message center, labor bureau, political headquarters, and meeting hall. If middle-class pressure suppressed these functions in

Oklahoma's saloons, they should still be discussed to provide a full picture of the workers' anti-prohibition stance.

My principal criticism of this book is that the middle class is too often portrayed as a monolithic group with little internal dissention or change over time. Klein does provide hints regarding the defection of some middle-class people from the dry bourgeois culture: those who drank at home or in private clubs and those who supported the few pro-alcohol organizations in Oklahoma (pp. 141–146, 163, 166). But more analysis of diversity within the middle class is needed, perhaps in the light of such secondary studies as Catherine Gilbert Murdock, *Domesticating Drink: Women, Men, and Alcohol in America, 1870–1940* (1998). Murdock observes that changing cultural attitudes *within* the middle class by the 1920s were creating havoc in the prohibition crusade nationwide. As otherwise respectable men and women began serving drinks at domestic social gatherings, middle-class drys howled about the new traitors while wets grumbled about the old-fashioned extremists (pp. 102–113). Even if the evidence on home drinking in Oklahoma is scarce, some discussion of this burgeoning cultural earthquake seems needed.

Indeed, there are a number of ideas from the secondary literature on alcohol that Klein might have introduced to bolster his analysis. These would include, for example, the "status politics" argument in Joseph R. Gusfield, *Symbolic Crusade: Status Politics and the American Temperance Movement* (1980) and the discussion of the saloon as "alternative culture" in Roy Rosenzweig, *Eight Hours for What We Will: Workers and Leisure in an Industrial City, 1870–1920* (1983). Klein does not engage such well-known scholars directly in the text, although they do appear in the bibliography. While his primary research appears excellent, he might have augmented his analysis with more vigorous use of secondary sources.

In sum, Klein has added much to our understanding of the "two Oklahomas"—one dry, one wet—whose "competing cultures coexist uncomfortably . . . into the twenty-first century" (p. 183).

MADELON POWERS
University of New Orleans

KATHLEEN SPROWS CUMMINGS. *New Women of the Old Faith: Gender and American Catholicism in the Progressive Era*. Chapel Hill: University of North Carolina Press. 2009. Pp. xvii, 278. $45.00.

American history has long been written under the assumption that Catholics are different and that the difference matters. Yet apart from historians of Catholicism, most scholars have tended to discuss this alternative religious community in a cursory way, if at all. Kathleen Sprows Cummings's beautifully written book is a part of a growing body of secondary literature that should help to make this neglect less acceptable in the future. As Cummings's book demonstrates, Catholic women's struggles during the Progressive era speak to larger questions of American identity encompassing gender, citizenship, and faith. These women insisted that they were not "New Women," and critiqued this emerging model of gender as too individualistic—too neglectful of family and tradition. Yet it was their condemnation of the New Woman that enabled them to emulate her, staking a claim for greater opportunities for power, education, and careers within the church.

Even as Catholic women chose to reject the New Woman label and emphasize their religious identity, they strove to interpret their religious tradition in ways favorable to their goals. They created a useable past that enabled them to demonstrate their loyalty to the church while expanding opportunities for themselves and other women. Cummings's subjects include prominent journalists like Margaret Sullivan and Katherine Conway, and leaders in Catholic education like Sister Julia McGroarty and Sister Assisium McEvoy. These women asserted that it was largely the Protestant Reformation that had limited opportunities for women in the first place. They pointed to scholar saints like Theresa of Avila to argue that Catholic higher education for women was merely a logical extension of the past. They cited heroines such as Joan of Arc to advocate that women needed to take a more active role in American society. Even Mary was an elastic symbol who could be marshaled by some in support of domesticity, or by others to praise female courage and achievement outside the home.

Cummings argues that for her subjects, questions of gender were inseparable from issues of citizenship. Nativist organizations claimed that Catholics could never be loyal Americans because of their allegiance to the pope in Rome. Catholic women also faced vocal hostility to their religion from some activists in the suffrage and feminist movements. At the same time, within the church a conflict over "Americanism" raged among the hierarchy, encompassing questions of the church's proper relationship to the emergence of modernity and the liberal democratic state. Cummings argues that as a result of such pressures, her subjects felt far more marginalized in their status as Catholics than as women. The struggle to reconcile gender and religious identity limited their ability to effect change within the church and to cooperate with women outside their faith. Yet one of Cummings's more revolutionary conclusions is that before the changes of Vatican II and the late 1960s women's movement, Catholic women had many more opportunities within the church than outside it. At a time when the options of all women were limited, they established careers for themselves in religious orders, the parochial schools, and the Catholic press. Accordingly, their lack of cooperation with non-Catholic feminists did not hold them back as much as it would later in the century.

Cummings's book demonstrates that it is time for the story of religious minorities to be more deeply integrated into "mainstream" American history. While Catholics were struggling to define themselves at the turn of the century, "mainstream" Americans were also struggling to define themselves relative to religious and other minorities. As scholars examine pieces of this puzzle, the ultimate goal should be to bring the fragments closer together to glimpse a larger image. Cummings gives us an important piece of this puzzle. She draws upon recent scholarship that explores the links between gender and other forms of identity, such as class and race. Her work should inspire further scholarship on such questions as how might Catholic women's struggles over identity relate to issues of "whiteness," to labor union membership, and to their service in the public schools and in government? Not surprisingly, given the Irish dominance within the American Church and the growing secondary literature of American Catholicism, Cummings's work focuses primarily on women of Irish heritage. As this literature expands, it will need to uncover and incorporate the stories of more ethnic and racial groups. The history of American Catholics has begun to provide important insights into subjects like women and gender, reform and social welfare, race and ethnicity, and citizenship and the state. As Cummings's book demonstrates, this history can also reveal how new ideas can foster social change, even within communities that consider themselves to be "conservative" upholders of tradition.

DEBORAH A. SKOK
Hendrix College

CHAD HEAP. *Slumming: Sexual and Racial Encounters in American Nightlife, 1885–1940.* (Historical Studies of Urban America.) Chicago: University of Chicago Press. 2009. Pp. xii, 420. $35.00.

This is a beautiful book that will be a milestone in our understandings of sexuality, race, normalcy, and metropolitan American modernity. Chad Heap's study spans six pivotal decades, the 1880s to the 1930s. He argues that, during this time of enormous cultural flux marked by nativism, the rise of the Ku Klux Klan, the Great Migration, the entrenchment of consumerism, paradigm shifts in New Womanhood, and the professionalization of men, the complicated practice of "slumming" helped portions of the urban populations in Chicago and New York City negotiate concurrent shifts in heterosexuality, homosexuality, whiteness, and blackness. By "slumming," Heap refers to the physical act of a middle-class body touring working-class, immigrant, or non-white metropolitan enclaves. While slumming excursions occurred before this period, he convincingly charts how a succession of new slumming vogues responded to alterations in sexual, racial, and socioeconomic classification and helped to usher in novel categories of identity.

Heap clusters these vogues into four groups. He first examines slumming tours into working-class immigrant environments around the turn of the century and then turns to what was called bohemian "thrillage." Next, he looks at slumming in Harlem, or the "Negro vogue." And finally, he explores the "pansy and lesbian craze." As vice reform watered down each vogue, another

popped up in its place, and the book brilliantly outlines "the crucial role that slumming played both in making visible and in facilitating the transition from one racial and sexual regime to the next" (p. 10). Thus, slumming enabled heterosexuals to declare themselves against homosexuals, whites to pit themselves against blacks, and "'in-between'" populations such as Italians and Jews to define themselves as white (p. 221). Yet Heap also traces various resistances to these physical and ideological acts: "'reverse-slumming' expeditions into elite New York neighborhoods" (p. 141); minorities profiting from their racial and sexual exploitation by "stacking the check" (p. 150); and formulaic shows rather than novel sights.

Heap divides his thesis—and the book—into two sections that support his primary claims, and he marshals an encyclopedic range of resources. The first part provides a general overview of each city vogue, and the second exhaustively details their respective characteristics. No cobblestone is left uncovered. When the author turns to New York City, he presents close readings of how slumming fostered sexual and racial differences in the Tenderloin, Harlem, Greenwich Village, the Bowery, Chinatown, and Times Square. In his analysis of Chicago, he describes nightlife ventures in the West Side Levee, Towertown, Bronzeville, and the Near North Side. The book then closes with a turn to the suburbanization of white populations, the decline of slumming as a leisure activity, and a nod to slumming's "second wave" inside and outside the United States—in Mumbai, through gospel tours in Harlem, and in drag king shows of the 1990s and the present day (p. 282).

Taken as a whole, Heap's book does a fine job of elaborating upon issues raised in George Chauncey's *Gay New York: Gender, Urban Culture, and the Making of the Gay Male World, 1890–1940* (1994). In that monumental tome, Chauncey also saw the Negro vogue in Harlem followed by a "pansy craze," and he stressed that it was shut down by 1940. Heap, however, pays especially close attention to the myriad queers who fell outside the purview of that earlier work: mannish women, bulldaggers, and heterosexual female slummers looking for same-sex escapism, to name but a few. He explores the intricacies of his two-sided thesis to highlight "slumming queers" (p. 273) and the "affluent blacks" who slummed "to shore up their class position within the black community" (p. 227). Thus, Heap and his book join company with other scholars of modern American history and American studies who explore connections among race, ethnicity, and sexuality, such as Kevin J. Mumford (*Interzones: Black/White Sex Districts in Chicago and New York in the Early Twentieth Century* [1997]), Siobhan B. Somerville (*Queering the Color Line: Race and the Invention of Homosexuality in American Culture* [2000]), Lewis A. Erenberg (*Steppin' Out: New York Nightlife and the Transformation of American Culture, 1890–1930* [1981]), Marlon B. Ross (*Manning the Race: Reforming Black Men in the Jim Crow Era* [2004]), Mason B. Stokes (*The Color of Sex: Whiteness, Heterosexuality, and the Fictions of White Supremacy*

[2001]), and Nayan Shah (*Contagious Divides: Epidemics and Race in San Francisco's Chinatown* [2001]).

Any critique of this work can only be the tiniest of quibbles. Near the end of his narrative, Heap somewhat reifies urbanism and modern queerness in his explorations of "vibrant urban community" development (p. 233), and post-1940 slumming ventures continued in various forms prior to the "second wave" of the 1990s in mediums such as print culture and cinema. These are, however, minor points of qualification for the many achievements that this book makes. The text offers up lasting contributions to queer studies, whiteness studies, and to studies of straight urbanity that helped normalized whites expand "the repertoire of the modern cosmopolitan" (p. 194). The metronormativities of the Progressive era and its jazzy follow-up have now been indelibly reconfigured.

SCOTT HERRING
Indiana University,
Bloomington

CATHERINE S. RAMÍREZ. *The Woman in the Zoot Suit: Gender, Nationalism, and the Cultural Politics of Memory.* Durham, N.C.: Duke University Press. 2009. Pp. xxvi, 229. Cloth $79.95, paper $22.95.

A short skirt, fishnet stockings or bobby socks, a tight v-neck sweater, a fingertip-length boxy jacket, heavy eye makeup and dark lipstick, hair teased and piled into a high bouffant: these were the signature fashion elements of the young Mexican American women who participated in the zoot suit subculture in Los Angeles in the World War II era. These women were just as daring and dissident as their brothers, with whom they shared both a style politics and the disapproval of white society. However, the women, sometimes called *pachucas*, remained largely invisible and unintelligible in comparison to their male, *pachuco* counterparts. Police, white servicemen, newspapers, and the courts cast male zoot suiters as unpatriotic, criminal delinquents during the Sleepy Lagoon incident of 1942 and the zoot suit riots of 1943; Chicano nationalists reinterpreted them as icons of resistance during the Chicano movement of the 1960s and 1970s. In an innovative twist on an old question, Catherine S. Ramírez asks, "Where were the pachucas?" By this, she means to investigate both the subculture of the historical subjects and the role of the iconic representation—*la Pachuca*—as it figured into World War II nationalism as well as later, insurgent Chicano nationalist and Chicana feminist reinterpretations. The result is a fresh interdisciplinary history that tells us as much about nationalisms, gender, race, and culture from 1942 to the present as it does about young women who embraced a defiant public style.

Ramírez argues that women who participated in zoot suit culture challenged the gendered expectations of their parents as well as those of the wider society. Their extreme fashions and overt sexuality—exaggerated versions of glamorous Hollywood styles—appeared to many to represent a monstrous femininity. At the same time, their assertiveness, presence in public space, and use of *pachuca/o* slang marked their behavior as transgressively masculine. In addition, some wore pants or the male zoot suit ensemble, and some joined girl gangs. Ramírez shows that the achievement of these styles at considerable expense could signal class mobility within the subculture. However, in the context of World War II celebrations of Rosie the Riveter and the soldier's pretty and faithful girl back home, mainstream representations of the "zoot girls" cast them as inherently delinquent and even treasonous in their refusal of traditional domesticity. Both young men and women in this subculture, then, appeared as the internal enemy during wartime in the mainstream press. Ramírez conducted oral interviews with women who were teenagers during the World War II era and found some who recalled their subculture with pride. Many others, however, disavowed *la pachuca* and continued to experience her as a deviant figure.

While *la pachuca* remained disavowed, Chicano nationalists redeemed *el pachuco*, reinterpreting him as an icon of resistance to U.S. nationalism and racism. Ramírez analyzes a number of Chicano nationalist documents, including *Lowrider Magazine* and Luis Valdez's 1978 play *Zoot Suit*. Valdez's play retold the story of the zoot suit riots (ten days of urban violence between white servicemen and Mexican American youth) and the Sleepy Lagoon incident (the "zoot suit murder trial" that convicted seventeen Mexican American young men for the death of another Mexican American, overturned on appeal two years later). Valdez's rendition traced the origins of the Chicano Movement of the 1960s to zoot-suit-wearing *pachucos*, and they appear as defiant heroes in his play. As Ramírez reveals, however, Valdez positions Chicano insurgent nationalism in opposition to the *pachuca*. Ramírez shows that the Chicano notion of the community as *la familia de la raza* positions the heteropatriarchal family as its nationalist foundation, similar to the way that U.S. nationalism rooted itself in the white normative family. While *el pachuco* could be incorporated into the family as father or son, *la pachuca* was excluded because of her dissident gender expression and sexuality. In a compelling discussion, Ramírez analyzes the testimony of Bertha Aguilar at the Sleepy Lagoon trial against that of Valdez's character Bertha Villarreal, who was clearly based on Aguilar. Ramírez shows that Aguilar courageously refused to be bullied by prosecutors and was "self-possessed, clever and articulate" on the witness stand. In contrast, "*Zoot Suit* reduces her to a boisterous buffoon and 'cheap broad' . . . [and] makes this extraordinary young woman intelligible by transforming her into a whore" (p. 106).

Some Chicana feminists of the 1970s and 1980s, however, reclaimed *la pachuca* as a way to reimagine Chicana/o community and its subjects (p. 119). Examining poetry and visual art, Ramírez charts this third moment in the career of *la pachuca*, demonstrating that her feminist incarnations do not create a static notion of *la familia de la raza* but configure community as constructed,

244

Reviews of Books

"fragile, messy, temporal, and imperfect" (p. 136). Ramírez's book restores *pachucas* to history and also provides astute analysis of the role of cultural production in emerging political formations. It is an excellent accomplishment and a superb model of truly interdisciplinary history.

NAN ENSTAD
*University of Wisconsin,
Madison*

ANITA CLAIR FELLMAN. *Little House, Long Shadow: Laura Ingalls Wilder's Impact on American Culture*. Columbia: University of Missouri Press. 2008. Pp. xi, 343. $34.95.

Since the 1932 publication of *Little House in the Big Woods* (the first in what was to become known as the Little House series), few authors have maintained a more steady presence in the field of American children's literature than Laura Ingalls Wilder. Anita Clair Fellman's book explores the persistence of the Little House series in the American cultural scene, from the home to the classroom, in public life, and, most surprisingly perhaps, in the arena of politics. Arguing that Wilder's celebration of values widely associated with an ethos of the American pioneer functioned in part as a critique of the New Deal policies of the 1930s and 1940s, Fellman examines the possibilities of a formative relationship between childhood reading and adult political worldviews. Readers of this book will likely assent to the claim that, from within an oppositional discourse at odds with the collectivism of New Deal philosophy, "other sources besides mainstream political rhetoric were responsible for maintaining an individualist vision among the populace at large" (p. 3). This book's central challenge, however, lies in its assertion that children's literature is an effective venue for the advocacy of political views and that the Little House series itself retained a strong influence in the lives of adults who read Wilder's books as children. Fellman is well aware of these problems, and while her examination effectively explores Wilder's political beliefs during the period in which the Little House series was published, it is also largely concerned with the persistence of individualist, anti-statist thought among the American populace into the Reagan years and beyond. Thus, Fellman argues, her interests lie with "exploring the overlap between the ideas present in the Little House books and the particular form that contemporary conservatism in the United States has taken" (p. 9).

The monograph's subtitle is perhaps a bit misleading since the two most interesting chapters provide a rich account of the collaborative relationship between Ingalls Wilder and her daughter, Rose Wilder Lane. Anchored in shared political convictions, yet strained by Ingalls Wilder's dependence on Lane for assistance with writing, editing, and promoting the Little House series, the mother-daughter relationship as revealed by Fellman provides for an engaging read. The extent of collaboration involved in these staples of children's lit-

erature will be a surprise to those who are unfamiliar with the behind-the-scenes details of their authorship. Chapters one and two are carefully researched studies based largely on correspondence; letters written between Ingalls Wilder and Lane clearly state their opposition to New Deal politics, while those between Lane and her friends explore the nuances of a mother-daughter relationship often troubled by periods of economic hardship and interdependence. These two chapters also provide important biographical information about the Ingalls family history.

It is the Ingalls family life itself that provides the subject matter for the Little House series, and chapter three, "Revisiting the Little Houses," is devoted largely to close readings designed to reveal the anti-government, individualist views that, according to Fellman, underwrite each of the books. Heavily dependent on a Turnerian typology of the pioneer spirit, she makes a case for Wilder's and Lane's investment in rugged individualism and family self-sufficiency as a consistent paradigm for representational strategies utilized by the authors in their writing. Taking advantage of several historical resources, Fellman makes good use of the authors' omissions from, and revisions to, genuine historical detail; much of what has been reworked in the Ingalls family history clearly reinforces those values that both Ingalls Wilder and Lane held in opposition to New Deal politics.

The close readings of chapter three are stronger in their exploration of individualism and traditional family values than they are with respect to clear anti-government sentiments; the latter seem isolated aspects of the series' ideological agenda, though, again, Fellman makes a convincing argument. Where the book struggles most is in its final four chapters, which explore the "impact" of the Little House series in the classroom, the home, the public sphere, and in politics. Given the broad popularity of Ingalls Wilder's books and their ubiquitous presence (as Fellman aptly demonstrates) in the American cultural landscape, it becomes hard to link them specifically to conservative agendas, and there is a self-conscious tendency in the writing that acknowledges the problematic nature of speculation on the relationships between readers' emotional attachment to books and their political convictions. One feels much more convinced, in other words, of Ingalls Wilder's and Lane's political views than of the impact of the Little House series itself on American culture. Still, this book offers a welcome exploration of the powerful influence of the imagery of the American frontier on the childhood imagination, and it is a strong addition to scholarship that explores both the ideological potential of children's literature and the political implications of nostalgia for a heavily mythologized version of the pioneer spirit.

JOEL DAEHNKE
University of Northern Colorado

AMERICAN HISTORICAL REVIEW

FEBRUARY 2010

NANCY C. LUTKEHAUS. *Margaret Mead: The Making of an American Icon*. Princeton: Princeton University Press. 2008. Pp. xviii, 374. $29.95.

Practically everyone has heard of Margaret Mead, America's most famous anthropologist. Even people who do not quite know what anthropology is have heard of Mead, seen her name in print, or heard her mentioned on PBS specials. Others know her famous, empowering words, "Never doubt that a small group of thoughtful, committed citizens can change the world," a motto that has spurred on grassroots activists around the globe. Mead is an American icon, as Nancy C. Lutkehaus states in the title of her book. But why exactly is she an icon, and how did she become one that is so multivalent in nature? What was the process behind this transformation, and how did the media affect it? And how does an individual remain an icon, a figure of meaning and consequence through time for diverse groups of people? In other words, how does each generation perceive and find new meanings in a woman like Mead and her legacy?

These are the questions that Lutkehaus asks in her fascinating book. They are inquiries about process, changing values, meanings, social critique, the power of the media, and American society during the twentieth century, which in many ways are more important than Mead and her own story, fascinating though it is. Lutkehaus honors Mead for her seminal work as an ethnographer and public anthropologist but also shows how she was a masterful and active agent in creating her own fame. Furthermore, the author skillfully analyzes how the world has seen and used Mead, her scholarship, and her image by examining a wealth of documentary materials—newspapers, magazines, and scholarly journals—as well as Mead's photographs, films, and television appearances. Most important, she tells us how and why. Lutkehaus uses her sources to uncover processes of celebrity and fame, to demonstrate how these powerful social practices actually worked in twentieth-century America, and to reveal how Americans viewed and found value in anthropology as a professional endeavor that supplied meaningful knowledge. She concludes that Mead the anthropologist became a complex cultural heroine through four distinct yet overlapping images: the new woman, the anthropologist/adventurer, the scientist/scholar, and the public intellectual who wanted to improve American society. Lutkehaus shows how these chronologically based images are intertwined with institutions and structure. Of great importance for American historians is Lutekhaus's analysis of how Mead elucidated the problems and issues faced by Americans as they adjusted to change.

The author is aptly situated to write this book. She is a specialist in visual anthropology and has written about the cultural meanings and images of *National Geographic* magazine. Like Mead, Lutkchaus has conducted ethnographic research in Papua New Guinea, and she even worked for Mead while still a student. In addition, Lutkehaus is one of the country's foremost authorities on the media and cultural invention, and, like Mead, is an erudite, accessible writer who can bring a story to life and engage in public anthropology while providing a wealth of evidence for her theories. She spent fifteen years gathering data from archives scattered across the country while writing articles and ensuring that new editions of Mead's works were published. This book is the culmination of her dedicated and insightful efforts.

For those interested in the history of science, the nature of celebrity and fame, and the roles of women in anthropology, Lutkehaus's volume is a welcome and important addition to our understanding of the place of professions and noteworthy professionals in American society and culture. In the introduction to *Hidden Scholars: Women Anthropologists and the Native American Southwest* (1993), I asked why anthropology, which has been called the most welcoming of sciences for women, has never come to grips with charismatic and highly successful figures like Mead, Ruth Benedict and Bronisław Malinowski even as it remains fascinated by them. Had I been able to turn to Lutkehaus's book then, I would have understood better the processes that transform people into icons and, more specifically, Margaret Mead's own unique place in American cultural history and anthropology.

NANCY J. PAREZO
University of Arizona

SUSAN K. FREEMAN. *Sex Goes to School: Girls and Sex Education before the 1960s*. Urbana and Chicago: University of Illinois Press. 2008. Pp. xvii, 220. Cloth $60.00, paper $25.00.

As I sat down to write this review, the Sex Education Week of Action was coming to a close and the Senate Finance Committee had approved a proposal by Orrin Hatch to restore $50 million in federal funding for abstinence-only sex education programs. Susan K. Freeman's book shows that those on the front lines of the current sex education wars have a lot to learn from those who brought sex education to U.S. schools during the postwar era.

Freeman fills an important gap in scholarship on the history of sex education by examining the period between the release of the notorious Kinsey Reports and the so-called sexual revolution of the 1960s, an era that has received scant attention from other historians. Then as now, support for sex education emerged amid intense concern about the consequences of adolescent sexual behavior: juvenile delinquency, increasing rates of "illegitimate" pregnancies, and a skyrocketing divorce rate among those who hid these pregnancies by marrying while still in their teens. Although many of these anxieties targeted young people of color and low-income whites, the "declining morals" of white, middle-class, suburban teenagers were also a cause for concern.

Freeman observes that, unlike the situation today, the creation of sex education programs following World War II "inspired very little popular dissent until the

1960s, when parents and adults outside the schools organized a movement to eliminate it" (p. 3). This was partly due to the content of sex education programs in the immediate postwar era. These courses stressed abstinence before marriage and aimed to prevent divorce by ensuring the sexual compatibility of married couples.

Freeman builds on earlier work by Jeffrey P. Moran, who demonstrated how sex education campaigns in the twentieth century helped to shape the modern concept of adolescence. Yet Freeman departs from Moran's top-down approach, which focused on public health experts and educational professionals. Instead, she looks at how adolescent girls reacted to and processed the messages transmitted through sex education during this period.

Freeman is also the first to examine specifically how gender shaped sex education theory and practice. Not only were gender assumptions at the center of sex education content and methods, she argues; gender ideologies were not as rigid as one might think: although sex education was shaped by a "shared belief in normative heterosexuality" and the nuclear family headed by a male breadwinner, the antifascist and anticommunist ideals of the postwar period also challenged authoritarian, patriarchal families, instead favoring cooperative, democratic marital partnerships. Although sex educators reinforced masculine and feminine gender roles, they also employed a group discussion method in which young peoples' voices found expression and even predominated. Freeman convincingly demonstrates that the "ethic of fairness" in class discussions was a "necessary precursor to feminist consciousness." Although sex education and family life courses reinforced the gender prescriptions of the day, these classes also empowered girls by giving them an opportunity to discuss their confusion and frustration with the sexual double standard. Freeman confirms earlier work by Beth Bailey and Joanne Meyerowitz that shows important continuities between the allegedly "repressed" 1950s and the "liberated" 1960s. Rather than being a radical departure, the feminist concept of the "personal is political" that formed the centerpiece of the modern women's movement had its roots in the gender consciousness of postwar sex education.

Sex education programs came under increasing attack not during the conservative 1950s, but rather during the 1960s as the discussions in sex education classes became more sexually explicit. Freeman observes that attacks on sex education were "mobilized by anticommunist organizations and the early beginnings of an organized religious right" (p. 147). By the end of the twentieth century, controversial topics such as condoms, HIV/AIDS, and gay/lesbian/bisexual/transgendered sexual identities were included in sex education courses. This prompted a backlash and the creation of the abstinence-only programs we are familiar with today. Missing from this new emphasis on abstinence are the positive outcomes of sex education programs of the 1940s and 1950s. Freeman concludes that while postwar sex education stressed heterosexual marriage as the so-

cial norm, these programs nevertheless fostered openness of discussion, less shame about the body, respect for diversity of opinion, and emotional satisfaction provided by romantic and sexual relationships.

This book not only provides important messages for current debates about sex education but does so in an accessible manner. Although Freeman draws on important work by other scholars, the text is free of academic jargon and is highly readable. It would be suitable for both undergraduate and graduate courses in women's history, girls' studies, and the history of sexuality.

HEATHER MUNRO PRESCOTT
Central Connecticut State University

DAVID WARD. *Alcatraz: The Gangster Years*. With GENE KASSEBAUM. Berkeley and Los Angeles: University of California Press. 2009. Pp. xxvii, 548. $34.95.

David Ward (with the assistance of Gene Kassebaum) has produced an engaging history of the federal penitentiary on Alcatraz Island that will be of interest to social historians, sociologists, and criminologists. Ward gained unprecedented access to federal government archives from which hundreds of files of Alcatraz prisoners were randomly selected for systematic coding. Information from these files was supplemented with lengthy oral histories from one hundred former Alcatraz inmates, prison employees, and officials. The book focuses on the "gangster years" from 1934 to 1948, the era when the facility first gained its notoriety as America's toughest prison.

Ward places Alcatraz in historical context. Federal officials, most notably FBI Director J. Edgar Hoover, created Alcatraz as a response to a crisis of legitimacy. In the late 1920s and 1930s, with Prohibition and the Great Depression as backdrops, highly publicized violence by organized crime, official corruption, and a wave of robberies and kidnappings embarrassed local and federal law enforcement agencies. The media focused on the threat of notorious "public enemies" as well as on the incompetence or unwillingness of corrupt officials to deal effectively with crime. In response to this political crisis and public relations disaster, the federal government initiated its first war on crime. Alcatraz, with its reputation for toughness, was both a symbolic part of the war on crime and a practical response to real incompetence and corruption in the prison system.

For most of its history Alcatraz remained shrouded in mystery, partly because of deliberate federal policy to keep journalists and others away from the prison. As a result, wild rumors and gross inaccuracies fed the public imagination of Alcatraz as being America's "Devil's Island." The key contribution of Ward's book is that, for the first time, the shroud is lifted and many myths about Alcatraz are exploded. We receive an objective, well-researched view of what life was really like in Alcatraz. While certainly oppressive and psychologically demeaning, the prison environment was not defined by physical brutality. Life on "the Rock" was one of ex-

treme deprivation and shaped by a boring, mind-dull-
ing, highly regimented routine. Dramatic escape attempts and other forms of individual and collective
resistance occasionally broke the monotony.

The detailed accounts of such incidents make for sus-
penseful and engaging reading. But the author is careful not to let his study devolve into sensationalism. Instead, he carefully shows how the tightly controlled
regime shaped the character of resistance at Alcatraz.
Resistance was key to psychological survival in this
highly regimented environment. It was shaped by the
convict code, which contained a strong proscription
against informing and clear expectations of how to act
toward guards and fellow convicts. The convict code
(adhered to more completely at Alcatraz than at any
other prison or at any time since the "gangster years")
formed the basis for a united front against authorities'
attempts at maximum control. Ward expertly draws on
sociological literature to demonstrate how this struggle
between control and resistance shaped the internal history of Alcatraz.

Within its larger narrative about the federal penitentiary the book provides thorough case histories of several celebrity gangsters, including Al Capone and
George "Machine Gun" Kelly, but it also details the
lives of prisoners who were not as well known. These
case histories examine individuals' lives prior to Alcatraz (which for some indicate why officials considered
them "the worst of the worst"), their experiences in Alcatraz, and their lives after prison. Here Ward presents
some surprising findings. Despite inmates' incarceration in this highly controlled prison environment, the
evidence compiled by Ward and his team shows that
nearly two-thirds of the prisoners led productive, law-
abiding lives after release. This research demonstrates
that the prisoners were not, contrary to the labels given
to them by officials, incorrigible.

Inmates who ultimately "went straight" on the outside had two key characteristics. First (and perhaps surprisingly), they were more likely to have engaged in misconduct while in Alcatraz. Ward notes that the
discernable relationship between misconduct and post-
release success was unique to Alcatraz. The tightly controlled environment and lack of any viable underground
prison economy meant that misconduct at Alcatraz
took the form of individual and collective resistance.
Because of this resistance to regimentation, these inmates did not lose their capacity for self-determination,
which was essential to success in the world outside the
prison walls. Inmates who were not involved in misconduct at Alcatraz (i.e., those who acquiesced to regimentation and submitted to control) were more likely to fail
in free society. Second, the author notes that successful
inmates tended to have greater social support from
family, employers, and others (including prison officials) after release from prison.

Ward's remarkable book is a landmark in the study
of prison history. It is a carefully researched, well-
crafted account of the experience and meaning of the
notorious prison on Alcatraz Island. Because Alcatraz

remains an enduring cultural symbol, the book also contributes to the general history of the United States during the "gangster years" from the 1920s through the
1940s.

MARK COLVIN
Kent State University

ALICIA BARBER. *Reno's Big Gamble: Image and Reputation in the Biggest Little City*. Lawrence: University
Press of Kansas. 2008. Pp. x, 319. $34.95.

Alicia Barber's book, which explores the history of
Reno, Nevada, as a tourist destination from the late
nineteenth to the early twenty-first century, is a welcome corrective to the prevalence of studies that cover
much narrower periods. She introduces a wide cast of
actors—politicians, casino operators, divorcées, and
gamblers among them—who shaped a city known for
gambling and divorce. Her book joins a small but growing number of historical studies of urban tourism. Focusing on the interplay between the way that local
boosters tried to promote Reno and the reputation the
"Biggest Little City in the World" garnered among outsiders, Barber seeks to understand how civic reputation
forms, how it responds to booster efforts, and how the
results remake both the physical city and locals' sense
of place. Barber rejects the simplicity of a prominent
thread in the historiography of tourism—Hal K. Roth-
man's assertion that tourism invokes a "devil's bargain"
made by communities that embrace profit-minded outsiders who transform their physical and social fabric,
often with deleterious effects—by arguing that Reno's
leaders were fully complicit in recasting their city to satisfy evolving consumer desires.

Barber reveals a city first seen in the late nineteenth
century as a colorful frontier outpost in a barren setting.
Between failed ventures as an agricultural center and
health resort and the rise of casino gambling, Reno's
leaders seized upon Nevada's unique legal permissive-
ness to attract well-heeled easterners in search of quick
divorces. With its staid University of Nevada, affluent
divorce colony, and an emerging collection of fashionable downtown retailers, Reno tried to cultivate a reputation as a cosmopolitan city able to transcend its
rough-and-tumble frontier origins. A countervailing
trend toward embracing Reno's differences from other
places, however, proved to be more successful. By the
1920s, no other city (including Las Vegas, which
emerged as a major destination only after the 1930s)
could match Reno's freewheeling reputation, one furthered by a fateful transformation of city hall from fa-
cilitator of progressive reform to handmaiden of wide-
open entertainment. With the national allure of
celebrity sightings and its around-the-clock casino action, Reno serviced both Americans' materialistic, individualistic yearnings and their efforts to escape the
strictures of conformist culture in the "first modern decade." Yet the city remained a place where locals, tourists, and "pseudo-tourist" divorce-seekers intermingled

Reviews of Books

to a surprising degree, especially in a downtown that bucked the national pattern of decline in the 1930s.

Prior to World War II, Reno's promoters hardly had to advertise their city because its divorce colony attracted steady press coverage. As Las Vegas began to compete in the postwar years, however, Reno's boosters became more aggressive. Through the 1970s, Reno managed to expand its roster of casinos, which in turn made a larger footprint in the downtown area and gradually emptied city streets of local residents. Only then, more than a half-century after Reno's initial rise as a tourist destination, did the city really begin to see large outside corporations and investors displace local ownership of tourism-oriented businesses. By the 1970s and 1980s, Reno, like Atlantic City, devolved from an urban playground to a place benighted by urban problems. As Barber observes, in the past two decades Reno's leaders have had to rethink their approach to economic development. Once a powerful national magnet, Reno could no longer compete even within its own state. With Las Vegas becoming a fantasia of replicas of world-renowned landmarks and renewing its embrace of adult transgressions, Reno turned to a seemingly unlikely alternative: adventure tourism. In contrast with its developmental strategy a century before, modern Reno has come to rely on its setting in the Sierra Nevada Mountains near Lake Tahoe, transforming a setting once seen as challenging and uninspiring into one with potential for outdoor adventures. Less surprising has been the city's recent embrace of a more conventional type of revitalization that includes downtown living, entertainment districts, and riverfront redevelopment. Once known as a resting place for cast-off wedding rings in a fabricated divorce ritual, the Truckee River now supports whitewater rafting and riverside pedestrian walks.

Barber devotes relatively little attention to the impact of tourism on ordinary Reno citizens and is virtually silent about the experience of African Americans in the city's divorce trade and tourism industry. If her book misses opportunities to broaden the scope of the social impacts of Reno's economic development, it still does an admirable job of situating Reno within many national trends, including the demise of the western frontier, progressive reform, the emergence of mass culture, economic depression, and the upsurge of postwar consumerism. Her work makes a compelling case for more nuanced scholarship on the role of image in the history of managing cities in growth and decline.

J. MARK SOUTHER
Cleveland State University

WENDY L. WALL. *Inventing the "American Way": The Politics of Consensus from the New Deal to the Civil Rights Movement.* New York: Oxford University Press. 2008. Pp. xi, 320. $35.00.

The significant contribution this book makes is the way in which it identifies the creation and circulation of a framework of consensus as a "political project," one that originated as one side of an argument in the 1930s and then became a widely, though not universally, accepted form of common sense in the 1950s. Wendy L. Wall shows how the project took shape through wide-ranging discussions in three distinct periods with different dynamics: the late 1930s contests over the direction of New Deal labor and economic policies; wartime debates over national purpose and especially over what needed to be subordinated to the ideological demands of national unity for the war effort; and new postwar fears of totalitarianism and the resulting social requirements for fighting a national cold war against communism. Wall identifies the most important groups that actively participated in the thirty-year-long "cultural conversation" of building support for this consensus: "business and advertising executives, interfaith activists, government officials, and other cultural elites" who "seized on the notion of a unifying and distinctive 'American Way' and sought to define it in ways that furthered their own political and social agendas" (p. 5).

Language was an important battlefield in this political project, with "free enterprise" coming to substitute for the more pointed language of "private enterprise" utilized by the advocates of various New Deal forms of economic security and industrial democracy. Debates regarding the cultural definition of "American" fell between a more robust ethnic, pluralist, and potentially racially diverse framing of the country as a "nation of immigrants" on the one hand and the foregrounding of a common Judeo-Christian identity that proposed civility and tolerance as substitutes for demanding racial equality on the other. Wartime and left-wing discussions that identified the external threat of fascism gave way to frameworks that subsumed fascism and communism under the overarching label of totalitarianism and accused these ideologies of endangering the "American Way."

Wall notes that, "more often than not, those with money and influence 'won' the cultural battles of the 1940s and 1950s by shaping the terms of public debate" (p. 11). Her book is most persuasive in documenting the central role of the business community in spearheading specific campaigns that called for tolerance, pluralism, and unity to defend their vision of market-based capitalism, thereby emphasizing individual freedom, rights, and opportunities rather than democracy or egalitarian economic or social values. These campaigns proved to be enormously successful in rallying diverse constituencies, including national interfaith coalitions like the National Conference of Christians and Jews. A 1939–1940 National Association of Manufacturers (NAM) campaign explicitly linked the protection of free enterprise to freedom of speech and religion. One postwar campaign attempted to mobilize "Letters to Italy" from Italian Americans to encourage their relatives to vote for the Christian Democrats rather than the Communists in the 1948 elections. Similarly, another campaign lobbied ethnic community newspapers and organizations to support a "Letters from America" program and a "Crusade for Freedom" to emphasize

American political freedom and consumer abundance in contrast to the stark postwar conditions in Europe.

Wall's research makes extensive use of the records of the NAM and the Advertising Council during and after World War II as well as the papers of Advertising Council leader Thomas D'Arcy Brophy, the American Heritage Foundation, and its president Winthrop Aldrich. Brophy, president of an advertising agency, was an active promoter of a mild form of ethnic, religious, and (sometimes) racial tolerance as a means of garnering support for American-style capitalism and anticommunism. He effectively led the Advertising Council as it arranged White House conferences, roundtables, and public service campaigns in pursuit of his goal of "resell[ing] Americanism to Americans." Aldrich, an opponent of the New Deal and the conservative chairman of Chase National Bank, led the effort to mobilize private-sector support for Brophy's public service campaigns, particularly the 1947–1949 Freedom Train. Under the leadership of Brophy and Aldrich, what had begun as a postwar traveling exhibit of key documents from the National Archives abandoned an emphasis on unfinished democracy in favor of a more explicit promotion of free enterprise and freedom of religion as bulwarks of anticommunism.

Wall's claim that the business-promoted efforts to "define a unifying national consensus" gave many working-class ethnic and black Americans "a powerful lever with which to pry open some doors of America's mainstream culture" is less convincing (p. 11). Making this case more persuasively would require different sets of sources, especially those exposing the differing debates and contested political agendas within ethnic and black communities, in addition to Wall's accounts of the efforts of leaders such as author Louis Adamic, the NAACP's Walter White, and the National Urban League's Lester Granger. The consensus focus on tolerance as a civic virtue ran the risk of negating citizenship demands altogether, as a black journalist wrote in the Baltimore *Afro-American* on December 31, 1949, remarking that "[t]here is nothing to be tolerant of. All people should be treated equally not because it is the 'nice thing to do' but because they are equal."

JUDITH E. SMITH
University of Massachusetts,
Boston

JEFFREY G. BARLOW. *From Hot War to Cold: The U.S. Navy and National Security Affairs, 1945–1955.* Stanford, Calif.: Stanford University Press. 2009. Pp. xii, 710. $65.00.

As early as the spring of 1943, Jeffrey G. Barlow observes, military planners in the United States viewed the direction of World War II with so much clarity that they began planning for the postwar peace. Yet within two years of the bombing of Hiroshima, the same planners were faced with a new enemy with seemingly limitless reach and power. That the certainty of victory over fascism failed to reveal with the same clarity a coherent strategy to defeat the Soviet Union is perhaps the thorniest of the many problems in Cold War history. With this book, Barlow offers an important examination of American foreign and military policy during the Truman and Eisenhower administrations. The United States Navy, he contends, offers an extremely useful lens through which the transformation of American policy from "national defense" to "national security" can be understood.

Barlow points out that many of the antecedents of the United States' Cold War national security policy lay in World War II. Franklin D. Roosevelt and his service chiefs faced the dual problems of fighting a global war against fascism and a battle for the direction of grand strategy with their more polished British counterparts. The solution to both problems lay in organizational reforms. FDR brought his service chiefs together as the Joint Chiefs of Staff and provided them with a support system that streamlined the distribution of resources while also increasing U.S. control over the direction of strategy. The navy, Barlow argues, proved itself to be extremely adept at recognizing and adapting to the necessity for the services to act jointly. At the same time he points out that Commander in Chief, U.S. Fleet, and Chief of Naval Operations Admiral Ernest King and his staff were equally adept at positioning the navy as the country's principal force for securing the postwar peace.

Peace with Japan and Germany was soon overshadowed by the threat emerging from Soviet Russia and Joseph Stalin. Barlow argues that ambiguities surrounding Soviet foreign and military policies resulted in a level of forward American military presence and engagement incongruous with traditional peacetime policy. Uncertainty abroad was only exacerbated by the recently revealed power of the atomic bomb and the short-lived American monopoly on such weapons. Ambiguity, however, extended beyond plans for a future war with the Soviet Union, for the bomb proved to have an even greater destabilizing effect on the traditional roles and missions of the armed forces.

Barlow observes that naval officers successfully navigated service policy to deal with both the Soviet threat and the interservice debate over roles and missions. The branch moved beyond its original suspicions of defense unification and used the redefined national security structure to reorganize its own Office of the Chief of Naval Operations framework in ways that would serve both the nation and the navy. A decade of forward-looking naval officers proved instrumental in shaping the direction of national security policy away from the newly created U.S. Air Force's strategy of atomic blitz and toward a strategy in which aircraft carriers and conventional operations appeared the most reasonable means of engaging Soviet proxies without setting off a nuclear war.

With a strong evidentiary base drawn from extensive primary source material, Barlow's text offers a fascinating and important examination of organizational reform within a military organization and the ways in which that reform can influence the direction of national policy. The book should resonate with historians from various fields as well as political scientists interested in the policy-making process. Barlow's arguments also provide grist for re-energizing a debate long overdue in Cold War historiography. Air power historians, for example, should take issue with his treatment of the relationship between the U.S. Navy and the Air Force. They may have to concede that the former was accurate in its criticism of the latter's blinkered vision of national security policy. But a case can also be made that so-called "visionary" naval officers such as Admiral Arthur W. Radford were no less immune to the allure of nuclear weapons and were as willing to conflate service interests with national security interests as their brethren in the air force. Perhaps the early struggle over roles and missions was an unavoidable consequence of the policy-making process in the early Cold War. The uncertain nature of a future war with the Soviet Union clouded any notions of victory, relegating America's armed forces to proxy wars abroad and locking them in a struggle for legitimacy at home.

CRAIG C. FELKER
U.S. Naval Academy,
Annapolis, Maryland

ROBERT JUSTIN GOLDSTEIN. *American Blacklist: The Attorney General's List of Subversive Organizations.* Lawrence: University Press of Kansas. 2008. Pp. xix, 361. $34.95.

This book describes the historical and political contexts in which the Attorney General's List of Subversive Organizations (AGLSO) was created, gained support, and came to limit the development of mid-twentieth-century political discourse. Established in 1947, for the next twenty-seven years the AGLSO functioned as a quasi-secret blacklist used to damage the lives and careers of Americans believed to be members of the 280 organizations appearing on its rolls. Robert Justin Goldstein draws upon an impressive number of court documents, archival materials, and records released under the Freedom of Information Act to trace the rise, heyday, and fall of the Attorney General's List. His book is an enthralling tale that may compel many readers to question similar government tactics in use in the post-9/11 era.

The AGLSO contained organizations of both the radical Left (e.g., the Communist Party and the Socialist Party) and the radical Right (e.g., the American Nazi Party and the Ku Klux Klan), although it attacked more groups on the Left. It was itself un-American insofar as it undermined fundamental notions of lawful assembly and association. However, Goldstein demonstrates how both Republican and Democratic presidents made use of the list for political advantage by adopting stances that made them appear strongly anti-communist.

After much debate with his peers in the Truman administration, Attorney General Tom Clark decided not to make the names of organizations appearing on the AGLSO available to the public, arguing that "this would lead designated groups to go underground." Thus, the list acquired an aura of mystery, and the National Lawyers Guild denounced it in 1947 as "heresy hunting of the worst kind" that had no constitutional authority whatsoever. Goldstein establishes that the criteria for inclusion on the list were never clear and that personal taste and distrust of progressive organizations held sway in an era in which J. Edgar Hoover's Federal Bureau of Investigation successfully limited political discourse.

The list stigmatized relatively obscure organizations like the Photo League, whose membership included Ansel Adams, Dorothea Lange, Richard Avedon, and Paul Strand. Goldstein shows that many of the listed groups were short-lived and had few members; to illustrate, he mentions the Committee for the Negro in the Arts (disbanded three months after its 1954 listing), Everybody's Committee to End War (disbanded ten months after its 1954 listing), and the Abraham Lincoln School in Chicago (disbanded half a year after its 1947 listing). At the same time, other blacklisted groups, like the American Committee for the Protection of Foreign Born and the Washington Bookshop Association, had larger memberships and political power. Finally, there were well-known groups like the International Workers Order (which counted over a million members at its peak) that were crushed by the list.

Goldstein's narrative details a series of court fights that challenged the political biases and arbitrary procedures that attorneys general used for listing specific groups. For example, a congressional effort to ban members of AGLSO groups from being eligible for publicly subsidized housing was not upheld by the courts. In response to such efforts, one *Washington Post* editorial asked, "why not extend the loyalty oath to cover all applicants for books in the public library or to all those who benefit from publicly supported trash collection?"

Goldstein's chronicle of the Attorney General's List details how its influence took a toll on the lives and liberties of countless Americans. One notable case is that of James Kutcher, a World War II soldier who lost both legs to Nazi shelling and was later fired from his job at the Veterans Administration—and even denied his veteran's pension—because of his longstanding membership in the Socialist Workers Party. His hard-won legal victory eight years later was a setback for the power of the Attorney General's List.

Ironically, it was a conservative Republican senator, Harry Cain of Washington, whose 1955 denunciation of the federal loyalty program and the AGLSO began a process that led to the list's demise. (Cain had distinguished himself thirteen years earlier when, as mayor of Tacoma, he had spoken out against the internment of Japanese Americans by the War Relocation Authority.) In time, even the conservative Senate Internal Security Subcommittee turned on the AGLSO, which nevertheless remained in a diminished capacity and with much less importance until its official termination in 1974.

The resurgence of powerful and sometimes secretive lists—for example, terror watch lists, no-fly lists, and lists of suspected terror funding groups—in the post-9/11 United States highlights the political importance of Goldstein's careful scholarship and clarifies the dangers that these lists present to the promise of democracy. This book deserves our careful attention as a cautionary tale.

DAVID H. PRICE
Saint Martin's University

KEVIN ROZARIO. *The Culture of Calamity: Disaster and the Making of Modern America*. Chicago: University of Chicago Press. 2007. Pp. x, 313. $27.50.

The apocalyptic imagination has played a prominent role in American culture since long before the founding of the United States. As Kevin Rozario shows in his wide-ranging book, the sermons of the Puritans were merely early instances of a fascination that remains central to American economics, domestic policy, and cultural production. Drawing on a number of disciplines and a variety of primary sources, Rozario provides a nuanced reading of several key moments that shaped both the institutions designed to cope with disasters and the representation of disasters in popular media.

A bizarre American optimism regarding disasters is evident in the sermons and writings of colonial ministers such as Cotton Mather. As Rozario shows, some ministers came to see calamities not simply as divine punishments but also as unique events that caused a "state of agitation" necessary to prepare people for "moral reformation and conversion" (p. 42). Disasters brought about states of affairs that allowed for both spiritual and financial gain. Rozario traces the rise of the belief in "creative destruction" central to modern capitalism by using the examples of the New Madrid earthquake of 1811, the New York fire of 1835, and the San Francisco earthquake of 1906. By the nineteenth century, the growth of insurance providers led to increased risk-taking and a new type of wealth-building in the aftermath of disasters. Capitalism thrived on replacing old infrastructure, tearing down worn and outdated buildings and factories while building newer, more efficient ones. Disasters accomplished the tearing down more quickly, causing many to consider disasters an economic boon. As Rozario notes, however, only those survivors who were economically or socially privileged usually found themselves in a position to benefit from disaster.

Another thread of the author's argument explores responses to disasters in the public sphere. Here he deftly walks a tightrope, explicitly addressing the limitations of reception studies scholarship while still trying to grasp the varied responses of disaster survivors, commentators, and consumers of media representations. He distinguishes between those who were suffering the horrible consequences of disaster and those who experienced the disaster from a safe distance. The euphoria produced among survivors of the 1906 San Francisco earthquake, for example, was understood by some in Darwinian terms as an eruption of the real, an imposition of raw nature that stirred something primal in individuals who had been dulled by the artificiality and monotony of modern life. At the same time, Rozario shows that the responses of disenfranchised groups were quite different from this euphoric response, which was predicated on a life of relative privilege and security.

The distance provided by representations of disaster also gave consumers the thrill of the event while allowing them to remain at a safe remove from the horrible consequences. Citing the sensationalized reporting of disasters in news media, the reenactments of disasters in amusement parks, and the rise of disaster films, Rozario argues that "modernity created a 'love' of disasters" that helped drive "the corporate reconstruction of American society" in the twentieth century (p. 103). It also contributed to an increasingly centralized response to disasters that culminated with the creation of federal emergency management during the Cold War. Here Rozario overstates his case by saying that "Americans had been prepared by over two decades of government activism (and, more recently, by civil defense propaganda) to believe that it was the responsibility of the government to protect them from sudden catastrophe" (p. 157). The doctrine of self-help, which emphasized the limitations of the federal government to respond to disasters, was central to the civil defense programs and publications of the 1950s.

Such an oversight is probably to be expected with an interdisciplinary work of this scope, however, and it does not detract from the observation that the rise in federal emergency management went hand in hand with the increasing appetite for images of natural and man-made disasters. Rozario's final two chapters drive home the immediate importance of this cultural history, as the "corporate reorganization of network news"—to emphasize affecting spectacles of disaster at the expense of depth or understanding—had a major impact on American responses to the events of September 11, 2001. In colonial New England, disasters inspired charity for the unfortunate, but giving to disaster victims was not just a Christian act of compassion; it was also understood as a wise form of social control that kept society stable. As in the past, affecting images of 9/11 were used as a catalyst to "implement a broad program of political initiatives" that once again centralized power and did little to enhance security (p. 201). Rozario's analyses of 9/11 and Hurricane Katrina provide a sobering conclusion to this well-written and thoughtfully researched examination of our twisted fascination with catastrophe.

PATRICK B. SHARP
*California State University,
Los Angeles*

CRAIG R. PRENTISS. *Debating God's Economy: Social Justice in America on the Eve of Vatican II*. University

Park: Pennsylvania State University Press. 2008. Pp. xii, 267. $55.00.

Craig R. Prentiss's very worthwhile contribution to the history of American Catholic social thought departs from the typical focus on popes and bishops and instead emphasizes debates led by priests and activists from the 1930s through the 1950s. A particular contribution is the emphasis on debates focused on rural life. There is considerable discussion of the priest-led National Catholic Rural Life Conference as well as views expressed in the *Catholic Worker* concerning the evils of industrial society. Most discussions of the Catholic Worker movement focus on its urban origins and houses, just as most discussions of Catholic approaches to social justice emphasize issues of labor organization and poverty with an implicitly urban twist.

While the book occasionally makes broad assertions based on thin evidence, it is mostly well documented. Because Prentiss follows such discussions during a period of turbulent economic times and quickly changing political landscapes, there is a rich portrayal of debates over the nature and role of the state in pursuing or obstructing economic justice. While Catholics on the Right made laissez-faire arguments not obviously consistent with papal social thought, Catholics on the Left divided over whether progress was ever possible in a capitalist, industrial society.

To Prentiss, the book's contribution is its rejection of an insider perspective advocating a particular normative reading of social thought, which in the Catholic context refers primarily to issues of economic justice and economic morality. Here he has a point about a great deal of Catholic scholarship, though his critique is less persuasive given strides in such scholarship in recent years. And it neglects the fact that histories that do not focus specifically on Catholic social *thought*, including those by Jay P. Dolan, John T. McGreevy, and Leslie Woodcock Tentler, have provided broad historical and social context about Catholic approaches to social justice and have not been oriented toward promoting one particular, normative approach.

In ways Prentiss's work is not really a break from the main trends of previous scholarship on Catholic social thought. For instance, it is not difficult to see that he favors the anti-monopolist, pro-union politics of the National Catholic Rural Life Conference. More significant, like a great deal of previous discussions of Catholic social *thought*, this book is primarily an intellectual history. We read little of what the *Catholic Worker* actually *did* but a great deal about the ideas of Peter Maurin and Ammon Hennacy (and thus the book does not make clear how urban the actual *work* of the movement has been). We read about English Catholic redistributionists not because they actually influenced American Catholic social action or even social thought—Prentiss says they did not—but because their ideas had some similarities to dominant ideas in the German Central Verein (an organization of German American Catholics) and the National Catholic Rural

Life Conference. It is difficult to know from the book whether committed Catholics on the Left or Right ultimately did much to influence labor movements or even the politics of many American Catholics, but we do learn in detail what critics and advocates of the Association of Catholic Trade Unionists *thought* of right to work laws.

In a pattern not uncommon when historians borrow from sociological and anthropological theory, Prentiss's introduction suggests that he will use certain concepts to frame the book, but the text then rarely refers to these supposedly central concepts. The opening discussion focuses on "ideology" and "myth" to indicate the naturalization of historically and culturally specific symbols, hierarchies, and narratives. Without being invoked much in later chapters, the concepts remain underspecified, not getting far beyond the general assertion that understandings of reality are socially constructed. Further, Prentiss's initial theoretical discussion gives no hint of the large amount of disagreement about the meaning of Catholic social thought, which is actually well documented in the book's historical discussion. Supposedly key concepts of Catholic social teaching, such as "subsidiarity," are vague and inconsistently applied by Rome and by many theologians, so that there is no easy way for those debating issues of social justice to justify one interpretation over another. A more developed discussion of cultural myths could explain that use of the same terminology allows different Catholics to battle over who speaks for the church and what the church has to say. One book can do only so much, but once Prentiss invokes sociological concepts, it would be good to look more closely at work from outside his discipline. Considerable scholarship in sociology, political science, and theology precisely emphasizing Catholic thought on a range of issues has been highly contested. Given the nature of the Catholic Church as an institution, continual battles—over, for instance, social thought, gender and sexuality, and war and peace—are inextricably intertwined with debates over the meaning of even the most basic elements of the faith.

GENE BURNS
Michigan State University

NICHOLAS DAGEN BLOOM. *Public Housing That Worked: New York in the Twentieth Century*. Philadelphia: University of Pennsylvania Press. 2008. Pp. viii, 354. $39.95.

Nicolas Dagen Bloom's rigorous, comprehensive, and fluidly written history of the New York City Housing Authority (NYCHA) adds to an impressive new scholarship that is reassessing much of the conventional wisdom about American public policy and metropolitan development since the New Deal. More specifically, it is an important addition to an exciting list of new histories of the U.S. experiment with public housing. Here Bloom focuses little on tenants and their efforts to secure resources, sustain their communities, and negotiate often hazardous conditions—a hallmark of the best recent ethnographic studies and oral histories; instead he details the motives and performance of the officials, planners, and management staffers who built and literally maintained the city's public housing infrastructure. The result is a story that will no doubt be unfamiliar to many readers but is essential to understanding the history of metropolitan politics and equity in the United States.

By the 1960s, simply managing New York City's public housing was no small task: the NYCHA was responsible for 2,600 high-rise towers that were home to 400,000 residents, representing a considerable percentage of the *nation's* public housing stock. Bloom attributes the authority's enduring "success"—which he contrasts repeatedly with the "failures" of other municipal housing authorities—to its commitment to good management practices. The measure of that success? "[I]ts projects were better built, the tenants more carefully selected, and the buildings better managed than those in other cities" (p. 109).

Bloom divides NYCHA history into three discrete periods, focusing most of his energies on an era that saw the agency dedicated to "the idea of model housing as a municipal service," which dated from its creation in 1934 until 1968. Briefer sections then explore a period of "welfare-state public housing" that lasted until the 1990s and finally the authority's recent return to its "early management principles," which envision public housing as "affordable housing" (p. 5). Along the way Bloom provides a series of important challenges. To Robert Moses-centered narratives of New York City development and urban renewal, Bloom convincingly responds that the NYCHA's institutional dynamics and its leaders' guiding principles are just as important to understanding the balance struck by city officials between bulldozing and social provision. To critics of public housing's architectural monotony, he demonstrates that cost-effective designs enabled the authority to efficiently manage and maintain its housing stock. "New York," he contends, "understood the difference between basic and shoddy" (p. 64).

Because Bloom views management as a key factor, the book offers an exhaustive and always revealing reconstruction of public housing's less public, more mundane side: the work involved in locating appropriate sites, securing funds, staffing police forces and maintenance crews, fixing elevators, selecting and monitoring tenants, and painting stairwells. This is an unapologetic institutional history that offers important insights into NYCHA administrators' strategic decision making. On one level Bloom has written a biography of a unique public service commission, one justifiably attentive to "business principles" and public perceptions. This focus persuasively documents why so many New York City projects tended to be more appealing (or at least acceptable) both to tenants and their neighbors.

Bloom understands that New York City's experience was unique. Nonetheless, it is difficult to weigh the relative importance of housing officials' competence and foresight, on the one hand, and the variables that made the city's experiment quite exceptional, on the other. Partly because the NYCHA was committed to a more expansive vision of public housing than even federal officials were and also because it had municipal and state funding streams to aid with development, by 1965 only forty-one percent of the city's structures had been built with the aid of federal funds. The result was well-built and more attractive structures able to support tenants with higher income levels. New York City offered other "advantages," too: a traditional commitment to high-rise, multi-unit residences, a well-established and often entrenched progressive leadership, access to private-sector funding or community groups interested in setting up shop on NYCHA properties, and, of course, the concentration of an employed working-class population in dire need of affordable housing. Restricted neither by the limits of federal funding nor federal income guidelines for tenants, NYCHA created and sustained for several decades a public housing system that catered to working-class families of modest income. One possible reading is that this model "worked" because it consciously decided not to serve the city's most needy populations. NYCHA was both able and willing to focus on the "affordable housing" model in the early years. This leads to questions of whether the authority's "commitment to professional housing management" (p. 10) is sufficient to explain its success and whether New York City's experience "illustrates that housing management practices, broadly defined, are the most important factors in the long-term shape of public housing communities" (p. 20).

DAVID M. P. FREUND
*University of Maryland,
College Park*

GUIAN A. MCKEE. *The Problem of Jobs: Liberalism, Race, and Deindustrialization in Philadelphia.* (Historical Studies of Urban America.) Chicago: University of Chicago Press. 2008. Pp. ix, 384. $39.00.

In contrast to the trajectory of postwar liberalism in the United States on the national level, Philadelphia's liberal reformers of the 1950s and 1960s recognized early the destructive potential of deindustrialization. They sought out activist public solutions to structural economic problems and were acutely aware of the central importance of jobs to the future viability of their city. The liberal project in Philadelphia eventually succumbed to the effects of racial division, insufficient funding, the machinations of local politicians, the whirlwinds of global economic change, and perhaps even its own limited vision. But its forays into economic planning and job creation provided an alternative model to the national liberalism that ignored or downplayed structural factors and the need for jobs in its antipoverty programs and its focus on "rights." The myopia of national—and much local—liberalism to the critical problem of jobs has been echoed by the scant attention that has been given to this issue by historians. Guian A. McKee's aptly named book has taken an important step in addressing this gap, and it will certainly influence future work in policy history, studies of liberalism and the civil rights movement, the local history of Philadelphia, and postwar urban history more generally.

McKee begins his book with the hopeful ascendance of Philadelphia's reform Democrats in 1951 and concludes it with the rule of the autocratic and divisive Frank Rizzo in the 1970s. In between, he presents succinct histories of the Philadelphia Industrial Development Corporation (PIDC), local economic planning efforts, and the early experiment in affirmative action for the construction industry known as the Philadelphia Plan. McKee also includes a strong, three-chapter history of Leon Sullivan's initiatives in black self-help and "community capitalism" centered in the Opportunities Industrialization Centers (OIC) and the Progress Movement (PM) and funded by corporations and especially the federal government.

This book is important on several levels. In recovering the history of Philadelphia's attempts at industrial renewal, especially through the quasi-public PIDC, it has added a new subject that henceforth must be considered in any history of postwar Philadelphia. The PIDC arrested the decline in the city's jobs and tax base by creative financing of greenfield industrial development in the city's sparsely populated Far Northeast as well as factory rehabilitation in declining inner-city areas. Its efforts added or saved over 68,000 jobs between 1959 and 1970.

On the conceptual level, McKee's most innovative contribution is his characterization of the bifurcation of Philadelphia's job-focused programs along parallel racial tracks. PIDC's leadership consisted of white planning experts and businessmen, and their economic development programs ignored the social component of industrial decline and the racial discrimination that ran through a large swath of Philadelphia's industries. Leon Sullivan's OIC/PM, on the other hand, created successful job training programs and built new business enterprises, but its efforts were targeted entirely at the city's African American population. The two tracks did not intersect.

McKee attributes the ultimate failures of both sides of this divide to a number of factors: opportunistic administration of programs for political gain; insufficient and declining funding of programs in both tracks; the Nixon-era substitution of block grants in place of earlier support for comprehensive local initiatives like OIC; and OIC's too rapid growth under inexperienced management. He contends, however, that the preeminent cause of failure was the racial bifurcation itself and the ensuing "tragic missed opportunities" (p. 283), although it is not clear that even a unified liberal campaign could have overcome the other obstacles listed above or the effects of deindustrialization—the city lost 139,000 jobs during the Rizzo administration alone.

The research underlying the book's eight chapters is impressive. The conclusion, however, is more speculative and open to challenge. McKee's sympathies clearly lie with the reformers, but he has conceded that control

of the playing field lies with the enemies of reform. In an American political culture that he considers "fundamentally conservative," the best we can do is tinker around the edges, perhaps slowing the loss of jobs and the decline of our cities. This conclusion is inescapable only if we accept the "limits of available resources and political institutions" (p. 288) as immutable, as did the subjects of this study. The PIDC was a joint project of city reformers from elite Philadelphia families and the Chamber of Commerce; Sullivan presented OIC and PM as safe, unthreatening alternatives to emerging black radicalism, generating support from Washington and corporate America. McKee's contention that unity was an essential missing ingredient is unassailable. But he does not address the radical alternatives advanced by others in Philadelphia at the time, except to note that "American liberalism will always require a vital left that creates new opportunities" (p. 289), although admittedly that was not his intended subject. He has succeeded superbly in focusing our attention on the problem of jobs and in relating how local liberalism in one city recognized and tried to deal with this problem.

DANIEL SIDORICK
Temple University

BRIAN LADD. *Autophobia: Love and Hate in the Automotive Age*. Chicago: University of Chicago Press. 2008. Pp. 227. $22.50.

COTTEN SEILER. *Republic of Drivers: A Cultural History of Automobility in America*. Chicago: University of Chicago Press. 2008. Pp. x, 230. $19.00.

The history of the automobile, once thought to be largely the province of historians of business or technology or of popularists, has shown new life of late with the publication of several remarkably insightful interdisciplinary studies that take the car out of the assembly plant and garage. Brian Ladd and Cotten Seiler recognize that the automobile offers a unique window into the twentieth century and what it means to be human. Their books draw on cultural sources in ways that more fully explain the psychological and social aspects of the everyday life of automobile owners and users.

Automobiles feature prominently in contemporary culture wars, with environmentally conscious green cars occupying the middle ground somewhere between the extremes. Ladd's *Autophobia* is an eminently readable, yet at times philosophically deep, work that explores notions of humanity in a machine-age, urbanized civilization. Ladd asks his readers, what are we to fear more: ourselves or the automobile? Ostensibly, his primary aim is to understand why critics of the automobile from its late-nineteenth-century origins to the present were largely ignored, adding his own editorial cry of "haven't we had enough?"—enough of the accident death tolls, the environmental degradation, unsustainable energy use, hidden financial costs, and more? In a style similar to that of environmentalist Bill McKibben, Ladd declares that the United States has indeed had enough of this inadequate transportation technology. He points out the paradox in which our perceptions of freedom have been the consequence of a mobility that has left many of us placeless and the irony of autonomous citizens being prisoners in a steel cage, slaves to a technology upon which they are dependent.

Ladd has organized his work primarily along thematic rather than chronological lines. After an opening chapter that mostly focuses on developments prior to World War II, a second chapter follows on the golden age of the 1950s and what the author calls "buyer's remorse." He proceeds to discuss the tensions between urban life and the automobile. It is here that we encounter what Ladd really wants to talk about: sprawl, urban planning, pedestrians, and the quality of modern life. One of the book's strengths is its ability to include episodes and insights taken from Great Britain, Germany, and France in addition to those from the United States. Perhaps this is an indication of Ladd's transnational interests, which are also reflected in his previous book on urban landscapes and political memory in Berlin. Nevertheless, a subsequent chapter on freeway revolts of the 1960s and 1970s contains little new material, nor does a closing chapter questioning the possibility that the automotive age has now come to an end.

But simply to criticize the content of the book's second half is to ignore an important virtue that is so evident in the beginning chapters: namely, the author's use of cultural history (and literature in particular), which is reflective of one emerging approach to studying the history of the automobile that has been neglected in most previous scholarship. Perceptively and with excellent explanatory power, Ladd reflects upon the writings of such authors as J. G. Ballard, Ray Bradbury, Joan Didion, Ilya Ehrenburg, E. M. Forster, Hermann Hesse, Edith Wharton, and Tom Wolfe, among others. In doing so, his examination of a machine and its social and psychological consequences has a very human touch.

However, this work also has some serious shortcomings. The thematic approach occasionally results in annoying repetition and unnecessary rambling. Ladd's treatment of voices hostile to the automobile invariably forces him also to include defenders of the car, yet in attempting to write a more holistic account he has not been completely faithful to either camp. Indeed, even important critics responsible for autophobia are discussed somewhat superficially. For example, John Keats, the author of *The Insolent Chariots* (1958), who was perhaps the most important of all the twentieth-century critics, demands far more careful study than Ladd provides. And then there is the strident anti-car bias of the author, certainly understandable but at times shrill and unsupported. For example, the reader is constantly reminded of the automobile's death toll—according to Ladd, some 30 million people in the twentieth century and currently some 1.2 million deaths annually. However, these statistics are never referenced. He also fails to place auto accident statistics—admittedly horrific no matter what the absolute number—in their proper context. For example, in 1936 some 37,800 individuals were killed in automobile accidents, yet that same year more than 38,500 Americans died in accidents in the home.

Seiler's *Republic of Drivers* takes a very different approach to the study of automotive history. Rather than mirroring Ladd's transnational focus, Seiler looks solely at the United States and related matters of freedom, mobility, exceptionalism, subjectivity, character, individualism, politics, and social integration of the citizen, all of which are viewed through the lens of the act of driving. In doing so, he crafts a remarkable monograph that offers a fresh look into both the early era of motoring up to 1929 and the golden age of the 1950s, which he adeptly places within the larger sociocultural landscape of the Cold War.

Seiler merges a wide range of approaches in this extraordinary interdisciplinary study, moving easily from the detailed business history and history of technology accounts written by James Flink and John Rae to the more abstract sociological queries of Mimi Sheller and John Urry. And like Ladd, Seiler harnesses literary and film materials as well, in the process bringing a fresh perspective to the subject. Despite his vast number of sources and the complexities of bringing together so much disparate knowledge, Seiler's point is rather simple: the act of driving and the governmental controls associated with this act were (and are) intimately connected with citizenship and personal freedoms, both real and imagined.

According to Seiler, with the rise of early twentieth-century corporate capitalism, Taylorism, and the machine age, American intellectuals perceived that there had been a loss of masculinity, privacy, agency, and autonomy. This challenge to men's identities and traditional perceptions of the world was compensated for during the Progressive era by driving the automobile, an act that empowered, provided mobility, and simultaneously created political stability. The automobile as a freedom machine paradoxically resulted in a system that was constrained by rules and by a government that sought to control the driving population through licensing, taxation, road building, new laws, insurance regulations, and, above all, the expansion of law enforcement. Yet purportedly this paradox gave rise to "new" men and women, individuals renewed and energized by a stultifying environment of abundance and conformity.

These impulses, which played off freedom and individuality on one hand and social and political equilibrium on the other, were attenuated during the Eisenhower administration and the Cold War. With the rise of the interstate highway system, the non-statist Eisenhower could contrast the freedoms accorded to men, women, and minorities in the United States with the Soviet Union's inability to provide its citizens with either cars or the roads on which to drive them. Indeed, the open interstate was *the* symbol of American individual initiative, mobility, and capitalist enterprise. Even so, American drivers of this era were only free to conform in established ways, meaning that they moved from place to place within a social and political status quo.

One problem that I have with both books is that their authors failed to distinguish among the wide variety of automobiles on the market and over time. I would argue that few people have ever loved the ubiquitous Ford Focus—or any cheap car for that matter—or would believe that driving these "econoboxes" can result in any kind of quickening pulse or enhanced ego. Hardly anyone can hate a Mercedes Gullwing 300SL or a Lamborghini. Driving such radically different types of cars can be either dull and non-eventful or absolutely exhilarating. Still, why would Americans put up with any other technology that kills so many of our citizens? Is it our love of the car and its associations with status, power, freedom, and independence that keep us intimately connected to this inanimate, mass-produced thing?

JOHN A. HEITMANN
University of Dayton

WALTER L. HIXSON. *The Myth of American Diplomacy: National Identity and U.S. Foreign Policy.* New Haven: Yale University Press. 2008. Pp. xi, 377. $35.00.

Walter L. Hixson has written an American jeremiad more in the style of Jeremiah than most earlier exegeses on the subject of this book. While relentlessly critical of the essence of U.S. foreign policy, he does cherish the hope that America can reform and create a society that will base its approach to the world on cooperative internationalism. To do so, Hixson maintains, Americans need to rid themselves of the "Myth of America" that has dominated their foreign affairs for generations. This myth, which includes seeing the country as a "manly, racially superior, and providentially destined 'beacon of liberty,'" has led the United States into violent engagements with other countries and destroyed the moral fiber that ought to guide its international affairs (p. 1). There is hope for America, Hixson believes, but it can only be realized if its citizens are willing to dramatically alter their behavior as well as their beliefs.

The author's overview of the history of U.S. foreign affairs addresses three broad themes from the beginning to today, the first being that, ever since its creation, the country has taken on a special destiny of expansion and dominance. Hixson stresses the continuity of the policies that have flowed from this particular national identity. Where many other scholars have seen intense conflict over the direction of U.S. engagement with the world, especially in the nineteenth century, this book sees no such contest. The United States is defined by the project of controlling the world that it encounters, and in this pattern there is a direct line from the Mexican War of the 1840s to the Iraq War of the 2000s.

The violence that comes from the American form of warfare is a second theme in the book. Imbued by a sense of cultural and racial superiority, there are almost no limits to American aggression and the forms that it

may take. Although there have been moments when Americans have questioned the price they have to pay for imposing war on others, it has never taken long before the Myth of America has given license to further violence. Shortly after the Vietnam War, "the United States was back at it again—nation building, succoring vicious regimes, bombing, shelling, contaminating, torturing and killing hundreds of thousands of innocents, and destroying enemy-others—not to save them but to affirm itself" (p. 304).

Hixson's third theme is the debate over how best to analyze the history of American foreign policy. He sees a clear connection between the failure of scholars to criticize a set of self-defeating principles and the way in which traditional diplomatic history presents itself. Instead of an emphasis on interests and threats, Hixson's text underlines the need to understand ideas, identity, and culture. His aim is to embrace within his field what he sees as the main changes that have influenced the study of history over the past generation: the linguistic turn, deconstruction, psychoanalytic theory, and postmodernism. Only a radically new version of U.S. diplomatic history can help the nation break with its past, Hixson believes, and he wants his book to symbolize that break.

It is the latter theme that gets Hixson into trouble. His new history, which is the culmination of years of important work in the field, is buried under layers of postmodern localisms and bad prose. The story of the continuity of a violent form of exceptionalism in American foreign policy—which is an important one and needs to be told—never makes it to the surface here. It is submerged under sentences telling us that the "representation of 'America' can never succeed—it cannot achieve closure—and moreover must always claim its identity as a subject by attaching itself to an other" (p. 318). The content of that criticism may be clear to Hixson, but it is not to me or, I suspect, to most readers who otherwise would welcome a critical approach to the history of U.S. foreign policy.

There is little doubt that the study of the development of American international affairs is in bad need of new perspectives of understanding and new methods of investigation. Many younger scholars are positioning themselves to fill that need through international and interdisciplinary studies or through studies that link the crucial elements of U.S. domestic politics and ideology to foreign relations. Some of this work is inspired by the very same theoretical approaches that Hixson makes use of for his survey. But they avoid the jargon-infested sense of relentless predetermination of policies and viewpoints that sinks the book under review here. Hixson undoubtedly has something important to say. It is a pity that he does not say it better.

ODD ARNE WESTAD
London School of Economics and Political Science

CARIBBEAN AND LATIN AMERICA

DOMINIQUE GONCALVÈS. *Le planteur et le roi: L'aristocratie havanaise et la couronne d'Espagne (1763–1838)*. Foreword by MICHEL BERTRAND. (Bibliothèque de la Casa de Velázquez, number 39.) Madrid: Casa de Velázquez. 2008. Pp. xvi, 460. €43.00.

Dominique Goncalvès seeks to explain why Cuba remained loyal to Spain in the early nineteenth century while Spain's possessions on the American continent dissolved into independent republics. Goncalvès sheds new light on an old question by combining political analysis with an impressive prosopography of the Havana elite. The French scholar argues that this group differed from other Spanish colonial elites by its high degree of endogamy. Few aristocrats from other parts of the empire married into the group, and no titled noble from another Cuban town espoused a Havana aristocrat. The group maintained cohesion through this strategy and thereby controlled the town hall (*cabildo*), the most important political office open to Creoles. Almost all were sugar *hacendados*: that is, great planters.

After the British had occupied Havana from 1762–1763, the king of Spain came to rely even more on the "saccharocracy" as a pillar in the defense of Cuba. Havana's strategic position was vital to the empire, yet the insalubrious location and difficulties of supply and reinforcement forced the king to enlist the elite for help. In exchange the monarchy supported the sugar planters to the detriment of other elites, according to Goncalvès. Acting as arbiter and protector, the king lavishly bestowed upper nobility on the elite. The monarch issued forty-one titles and four elevations into the *grandeza*, the premier echelon of aristocracy, one of them nonhereditary. Goncalvès also underscores the capability of most captains general, who used their political leeway to accommodate the planters' demands. This conclusion reinforces established views according to which the sugar barons shied away from independence for fear it could ignite a race war of the slaves against their masters.

After returning to power from Napoleonic captivity in 1814, Ferdinand VII continued to favor the sugar planters for their loyalist stance. Land disputes with tobacco farmers were resolved to the benefit of the sugar barons, and the king allowed free trade even with other nations. Meanwhile the elite maintained exceptional ties to the court in Madrid, where several Cubans had the ear of the king. Although the liberals took command of Madrid in 1820–1823, and Spanish merchants made inroads by obtaining titles of nobility, the conservative Creole elite kept its cohesion beyond 1838. In that year the crown recalled the disputed Captain General Miguel Tacón y Rosique, who failed to bring the elite to heel. This victory for the sugar planters serves as the cutting off point of the study. The event demonstrates, according to Goncalvès, that the elite was able to withstand the energetic governor and perpetuate its influence well into the mid-nineteenth century.

Goncalvès has scoured parochial, judicial, and municipal sources in Cuba and combined them with communications located in the Spanish Archive of the Indies and National Historical Archive. The scholar has also drawn on and contributed to the massive Fichoz database based in Bordeaux and Madrid that registers social networks, including ties of family, ritual kinship, commerce, and patronage, among the empire's administrators. With this impressive source base, he can demonstrate the endogamy of the elite and trace the multitude of Castilian titles received from the king.

Goncalvès shows an inclination to prefer scholarship in the Romance languages over Anglo-American literature. While these tendencies certainly exist in other national historiographies as well, the author may have wished to include, for example, Sherry Johnson's *The Social Transformation of Eighteenth Century Cuba* in the bibliography.

Regardless, this is a strong book and a reflection of the remarkable recovery that the study of elites and their social networks has staged in Europe. In Toulouse, where Goncalvès defended his dissertation, and Bordeaux, historians analyze power relationships through serial biographies. This book therefore provides access to innovative historiographical currents. Goncalvès has written an excellent, well-researched book in which he proposes a new argument based on an intelligent and laborious methodology. For that reason the book is of interest to professional historians and students alike, for whom Goncalvès provides summaries in English and Spanish. A translation would go a long way to disseminate the work.

CHRISTOPH ROSENMÜLLER
Middle Tennessee State University

IVOR L. MILLER. *Voice of the Leopard: African Secret Societies and Cuba*. Foreword by ENGR. (CHIEF) BASSEY E. BASSEY. (Caribbean Studies Series.) Jackson: University Press of Mississippi. 2009. Pp. xx, 364. $55.00.

Sugar monoculture began to develop in Cuba during the latter half of the eighteenth century, after the Haitian Revolution removed Haitian sugar from the international market. At the same time the ethnic groups enslaved in Africa changed. The sudden, massive introduction into Cuba of several distinct ethnicities had major religious, cultural, and institutional impacts. The Yoruba (Lukumí) introduced Santería; the Kongo introduced Palo Mayombe; and large numbers of Africans enslaved in the Bight of Biafra were brought to Cuba, where they were called Karabalí after two ports on the coast of the Bight of Biafra, Old Calabar and New Calabar. They introduced *Abakuá*, a male secret society identified with the leopard.

Ivor L. Miller attempts to demonstrate that Africans brought to Cuba from the Cross River Valley and Cameroon grasslands established the *Ékpè* (Leopard) secret society, the major governing institution in the Bight of Biafra, in and near Havana during the mid-1830s, and that it continues as an informal governing, religious, and cultural institution to the present day. Discipline, justice, payment of debts, protection of pawned persons, and enforcement of community laws were rapidly implemented by members of *Ékpè* lodges wearing elaborate costumes and wielding arms. In Cuba the *Ékpè* lodges were known as *Abakuá*; in the absence of what Western scholarship defines as a state, governance in the Bight of Biafra was local and segmented, allowing its transfer to Cuba.

This impressive book contains exhaustive comparisons of *Ékpè* in Africa and *Abakuá* in Cuba, relying on photographs and drawings as well as other descriptive materials. Miller compares images of *Ékpè* and *Abakuá* ceremonies, lodge temples, ritual paraphernalia, masks, costumes, and *nsibdibi* (sacred) writing, and examines the creation and use of *Abakuá* drums, dance, and chanting and their enormous impact on Cuban music. He traces the names of *Abakuá* lodges in Cuba to specific *Ékpè* lodges in the Cross River Valley and Cameroon; the author was initiated into an *Ékpè* lodge in Africa after revealing information about *Abakuá* in Cuba and building contacts between *Ékpè* traditions in Cuba and their counterparts in Africa.

Miller also discusses *Ékpè* governing institutions on both sides of the Atlantic. Leading offices in these strictly male secret societies were graded hierarchically. In the Bight of Biafra, *Ékpè* lodges controlled vast networks of regional trade, including the slave trade. Miller argues that without ongoing contact or influence from Africa, these secret societies continued to operate as governing institutions in Cuba. The first lodge authorized others, including those in Matanzas, which were established during the 1860s and survive to the present day. These *Abakuá* lodges were created in Cuba after *Ékpè* leaders from the Cross River Valley were captured in battle and sold as slaves to Cuba, where they recreated their governing institutions, producing their ritual paraphernalia in Cuba from memory. Miller dismisses direct, ongoing influence from Africa. The rules for establishing new lodges were elaborate, expensive, and required a charter from an existing lodge. It is quite possible that the first new lodge in Cuba could not follow these rules, but it enforced them when new lodges were created in Havana and Matanzas. *Abakuá* leaders also joined Masonic lodges, whose elements were introduced into *Abakuá*; these lodges survived the end of the Atlantic slave trade because Creole slaves and free people of color were allowed to join. A lodge of white Cuban Creoles was authorized in Havana during the 1760s.

A better explanation of the meaning of Karabalí in Cuba would help. Karabalí was a port, or at best a coastal region, not an ethnic designation, and it essentially meant any slave coming from the Bight of Biafra. Karabalí included the Igbo, who spoke a Kwa language and were exported mainly through Bonny and New Calabar. They vastly outnumbered the Northwest Bantu language speakers, the Ibibio and their subgroups, who were brought mainly from the Cross River Valley and Cameroon and exported through Old Calabar. Their percentage among slaves arriving in Cuba

from the Bight of Biafra increased during the nineteenth century, but the Igbo remained dominant. Igbo were about half female while the Ibibio were heavily male. The *Cabildos de Naciones Karabalí* included all of these ethnicities. *Cabildos de Naciones*, like *Abakuá* lodges, functioned as mutual aid and protective societies, redeeming their members from slavery and providing savings, health, and life and burial insurance; they also controlled labor on the waterfront. Despite their large numbers, the Igbo were marginalized within *Abakuá*.

This book minimizes some elements of *Abakuá*. Miller exaggerates racial harmony in Cuban history. The word "*Ñáñigos*," commonly used for *Abakuá*, is largely ignored because of its association with criminality. This avoids discussing the myths about *Abakuá* criminality that became ideological fodder for the massacre of about 3,000 Afro-Cubans in 1912; the massacre is not even mentioned. The book offers a somewhat mythical history by posing the same questions to three Cuban informants with access to secret and esoteric knowledge of *Abakuá*. According to Miller's informants, members of the top grades were chosen and installed not only for their wealth and power but also for their reputation, character, and moral standing. The fact that three informants responded with essentially the same answers independently tells us more about myths of the powerful role of *Abakuá* in Cuba's history than about deeply rooted racism in Cuba. This book has truly stunning descriptive material, but it would have benefitted from more attention to changes in *Abakuá/Ékpè* on both sides of the Atlantic over time.

GWENDOLYN MIDLO HALL,
Emerita
Rutgers University

JANA K. LIPMAN. *Guantánamo: A Working-Class History between Empire and Revolution.* (American Crossroads, number 25.) Berkeley and Los Angeles: University of California Press. 2009. Pp. x, 325. Cloth $60.00, paper $24.95.

In a historiographic essay in the February 1977 issue of the *American Historical Review*, David M. Pletcher called on scholars to extend the boundaries of the field of inter-American relations. In addition to analyzing relations between states and dissecting the decisions of leaders, Pletcher recommended that historians consider the economic, social, and cultural features of international relations. North American academics, explorers, investors, soldiers and marines, traders, and tourists had played prominent roles in Latin America. Pletcher urged historians to explore this inter-American social and cultural interaction by writing regional histories of oil camps, mining towns, and banana plantations. Over the past three decades, scholars like Jason M. Colby, Jason C. Parker, Dennis Merrill, Harvey R. Neptune, Mary A. Renda, and Emily Rosenberg have helped transform the study of the interactions between people and nations within the Western Hemisphere.

Jana K. Lipman's "working-class history" of the U.S. naval base near the city of Guantánamo, Cuba, is a worthy addition to those studies.

In contemporary political discourse, the word "Guantánamo" signifies the U.S. military prison for terrorists. But as Lipman reminds us, Guantánamo is a provincial Cuban city of 100,000. The United States has maintained a nearby naval base, known by the military acronym of GTMO, since the War of 1898. As part of the Platt Amendment (1901–1934), Cuba had to compromise its sovereignty, ceding a naval base and granting the United States the right to intervene in Cuba's internal affairs. The United States reaffirmed its hold on the naval base in the 1934 agreement abrogating the Platt Amendment. Lipman focuses her study on the period between 1939 and 1964. During World War II, the United States expanded the base, hiring thousands of Cubans to work there. The twenty-five years of intense Cuban-American interactions ended in 1964 when a dispute over a Cuban fishing boat led Fidel Castro to cut the base's water supply. President Lyndon Johnson responded by turning GTMO into a sealed enclave with little Cuban contact. The United States even created its own water supply, constructing a desalinization plant. Lipman has conducted fabulous research for this study, exploring archives in Cuba and in the United States and interviewing eighteen elderly Cubans who had worked at GTMO.

"Ambivalence" is the word used most often to describe Cuban memories of life and work at GTMO. Cubans resented the discrimination that they encountered, receiving lower wages than did U.S. citizens on the base. One published guide to life at GTMO advised spouses of U.S. military men not to "spoil" Cuban maids with "extra gratuities" (p. 131). Cuban workers also faced constant body searches and encountered racially discriminatory base regulations. Cubans further resented the overwhelming influence that the United States had exercised in Cuba since 1898. Nonetheless, work at Guantánamo offered a path to economic security. As Lipman observes, "although GTMO was a direct affront to Cuban self-determination and a tangible reminder of U.S. dominance, for most workers, economic need far outweighed any possible political objections" (p. 41). The political and social elites and merchants of Guantánamo and the smaller town of Caimanera held similarly conflicted views. While on "liberty," U.S. marines and soldiers created mayhem, brawling, drinking, gambling, and whoring. A Cuban journalist counted 1,000 prostitutes in Guantánamo and Caimanera in 1946. Lipman found U.S. Navy records indicating widespread venereal disease. The local hotel proprietors, restaurateurs, and pub owners, the *fuerzas vivas*, welcomed the trade even as they lamented the human degradation and cultural pollution that it brought.

Cubans were not mere victims of U.S. political and military power. They responded to unfair wages by perpetrating petty theft; they also organized unions and lobbied for better wages and working conditions. As ad-mirers of U.S. ideals and ways of life, base workers tried to shame authorities into applying U.S. standards of labor law. "Neocolonial" is the term Lipman applies to the asymmetrical relationship between Guantánamo and GTMO. Base workers applauded Castro and the Cuban Revolution and secreted supplies from GTMO to Cuban guerrillas, yet most remained loyal to their work at GTMO.

Lipman perceives the history of GTMO after 1964 as a harbinger of U.S. military base policy in the post-Cold War world. The United States holds on to GTMO as a challenge to Castro and communism, but it has as little to do with Cuba as possible. After 1964, authorities replaced fired Cuban workers with workers from Jamaica. Similarly, the military relies on private contractors to provide services on its bases throughout the world. These contractors often recruit Third World nationals, like Filipinos, to do the work. These workers have limited rights and no support from the local population. Lipman concludes that, in an ironic way, Cubans who worked at GTMO had a better chance of shaping their own work lives than those who mop the floors and wash the dishes at contemporary military facilities.

STEPHEN G. RABE
University of Texas,
Dallas

ALLEN WELLS. *Tropical Zion: General Trujillo, FDR, and the Jews of Sosúa.* (American Encounters/Global Interactions.) Durham, N.C.: Duke University Press. 2009. Pp. xxxi, 447. Cloth $99.95, paper $27.95.

This is a remarkable and well-researched book. It traces the history of 750 Jewish refugees who fled Nazi persecution and moved to Sosúa, an agricultural settlement established on the north shore of the Dominican Republic. Analyzing the relevance of the event, Allen Wells, a distinguished historian and the son of one of the pioneer settlers, describes a wide array of events that forced European Jews to move to a promised Caribbean haven in the early 1940s.

The volume explores political, economic, religious, and social issues. Throughout the text, readers learn about the Jewish settlers' experience in their adopted Caribbean land, including the geographic and cultural adaptation, entrepreneurial activities, intermarriage, and interactions with the Dominican people. Wells's compelling stories about the immigrants and their families exemplify their failures and achievements. Bringing sociopolitical problems to the forefront, the author describes the vicissitudes of the pioneers, which included grave disappointments but also great achievements.

Arguing that tiny Sosúa represented a Zion for refugees in the 1940s, Wells calls attention to the desperate situation of thousands of Jews dispersed throughout Europe. The author illustrates the Jewish odyssey with the attention-grabbing story of Heinrich Wasservogel, the author's father, a twenty-two-year-old Austrian who had worked at labor camps, had never heard of the Do-

minican Republic, knew no Spanish, and had no experience as a farmer, but who responded to the call of a
recruitment agent for the Dominican Republic Settlement Association (DORSA), a subsidiary of the American Jewish Joint Agricultural Corporation in charge of
relocating Jews to the agricultural colony of Sosúa.
With no other option, Wasservogel accepted the offer
and began a long journey to the Dominican Republic.
From there, he and most of the other immigrants continued the search for a home abroad.

Within the historiographical context of War World
II, this book provides essential facts not only about the
experience of Jewish refugees, but also about the intricacies of international relations that developed during wartime. In the prologue, the author explains how
the refugees became "pawns on *realpolitik* chessboards"
in Berlin, Ciudad Trujillo, New York, London, and
Washington, D. C. Indeed, the existence of the Jewish
community in Sosúa responded to a variety of complex
issues. Among other details, the author points out President Franklin Delano Roosevelt's concern with the
fate of the refugees, the killing of several thousands of
Haitians in the Dominican Republic in 1937, the United
States' Good Neighbor policy, the international conference held in Evian, France, in 1938, and the desire of
Jewish leaders to design agricultural projects for Jews
in the Dominican Republic.

Analyzing the willingness of the Dominican government to receive Jewish refugees, the book explains how
Rafael Trujillo, who had been in power since 1930, used
an effective propaganda machine to attempt to disguise
the massacre of Haitians. At Evian, the Dominican del-
egates endorsed Roosevelt's initiative to resolve the
refugee problem as presented at the conference and expressed the Dominican government's willingness to accept between 50,000 and 100,000 refugees who would
be granted land and homes in agricultural colonies.
Eventually the colonists could become Dominican citizens. This offer, as Wells discusses, was more than a
case of international grandstanding; it provided Trujillo
with the opportunity to project a positive, non-racist
image, and to strengthen his connections with policy
makers and lobbyists in Washington. The proposal became a vehicle for the regime to achieve domestic goals,
securing economic assistance and military support. In
addition to Trujillo, the author discusses Dominican,
Jewish, and U.S. citizens who were deeply involved in
the negotiations to relocate the refugees, as well as the
disputes, disagreements, and controversies among
many of these personalities.

Methodologically, Wells relies on a wealth of existing
publications, unpublished documents, and interviews
that allow the diverse voices of the immigrants to reveal
both idealistic and realistic accounts of their experiences. The interview with Cecil Hess, the circumcised
son of a Jewish father and a Dominican mother, who
became an engineer in a Catholic University, moved to
California, and became a successful businessman, illustrates patterns of the second phase of Jewish relocation,

which included Wells's father, who moved to New York
in 1947.

Wells also shows his skills with the development of
narrative. He traces the evolution of Sosúa from a Dominican agricultural settlement, to a Jewish colony that
became a dairy production center, and then to a "static"
place as most Jews and their descendants moved away.
After the 1980s the former Jewish colony began a gradual transformation and became an international tourist
resort.

In sum, this book is rich in biographical details, vivid
images, and archival data. The volume, a gift for Dominican, Caribbean, Latin American, Jewish, and
global history, is a useful examination of a small settlement in the Caribbean that became a Zion for Jewish
refugees.

VALENTINA PEGUERO
University of Wisconsin,
Stevens Point

SHERRY FIELDS. *Pestilence and Headcolds: Encountering
Illness in Colonial Mexico.* New York: Columbia University Press. 2008. xxi, 188. $60.00.

This is a welcome addition to the still slim collection of
works on health in pre-Pasteurian Mexico. Deviating
from previous institutional and professional studies,
Sherry Fields seeks to explore contemporary systems of
thought "through the prism of the sick-room" (p. x).
Thus, her main concern is to understand how contemporaries understood disease causation and prevention
and how they fought illness.

The first chapter deals with illnesses that affected the
residents of Mexico in pre-Hispanic and colonial times.
After an introduction on pre-Hispanic disease, the
chapter is divided into three sections on epidemic illness brought by the conquerors; endemic illnesses like
malaria, syphilis, and digestive disorders; and everyday
ailments like scabies, swellings, and toothache. The second chapter concentrates on the medical marketplace
and the various types of medical practitioners offering
their services to the public. The section that deals with
pre-Hispanic times, more substantial in this chapter, is
followed by others on licensed and unlicensed practitioners, *curanderos,* the Catholic Church, and divine
healers.

Fields examines Nahua—not Mesoamerican, as
stated in the introduction—notions of the body, health,
and illness in the third chapter. Based on the works of
Bernardino de Sahagún and Hernando Ruiz de Alar-
cón, as well as more recent and well-known experts like
Carlos Viesca Treviño, Alfredo López Austin, and Bernard R. Ortiz de Montellano, it is a summary of previous scholarship. The fourth chapter examines similar
issues from the European point of view. Sections on
humoralism and perceptions of the environment's role
in health and disease are complemented by another on
colonial beliefs of illness causation and prevention.
Thus, humoralism was the base for both the reinter-

pretation of indigenous beliefs and of European understanding of their surroundings.

The final chapter deals with the "constant proximity of sickness and death" that characterized colonial times, and the efforts of contemporaries to find relief by divine intercession. It includes short, very general and loosely linked sections on "sickness culture" and miraculous cures. Although probably meant as a conclusion, this chapter introduces new issues and material. The concluding subsection is a brief and disappointing summary of the material already discussed.

The main weakness of this work is its minimal use of archival sources. Most of the primary materials have been published, and in some cases translated. The main archival source—the letters of the Countess of Miravalle—is mentioned throughout but is far from being the framework of the book, leaving the reader to wonder whether the letters were exploited to the maximum or simply lack enough information on the topic. Fields seems to have ignored one of the sources with the most potential, Inquisition interrogations, with their wealth of details on popular perceptions and everyday life. The choice of secondary sources reflects the obstacles faced by researchers interested in colonial health. It is limited and uneven, and some sources are extremely difficult to find. Nonetheless, works like Francisco de Asís Flores Troncoso's *Historia de la medicina en México desde la e?poca de los indios hasta la presente* (1886–1888), with its first volume on pre-Hispanic medicine, are conspicuously absent. Other choices are surprising, such as that of non-Mexico specialist Guenter B. Risse over Josefina Muriel for the discussion of hospitals.

The lack of original material and the author's decision not to address the "modes of analysis so dear to the hearts of specialists" (p. xvii) such as class, gender, and ethnic divisions in depth result in a superficial analysis without enough focus. Most puzzling is the indiscriminate use of sixteenth, seventeenth, and eighteenth-century sources with little regard to ideological and social changes, and the resulting portrayal of colonial Mexico as a static society.

The above weaknesses may also be seen as a strength as this book provides a general overview and a good introduction for those interested in this field. The objective of the author, to present "an impressionistic (examination), a preliminary study" (p. xvii), has certainly been achieved.

From an editorial point of view, the work contains various errors, such as the use of "principle" instead of "principal" (pp. 98, 140) and "affect" instead of "effect" (pp. 122, 141). Similarly, some Spanish terms are misspelled, like "*decats*" for "*ducats*" (p. 70), "*cámeras*" for "*cámaras*" (p. 17), and "*noveimbre*" for "*noviembre*" (p. 39, note 109, and p. 88, note 119), as well as the names of Josefina Muriel and Germán Somolinos d'Ardois in the bibliography.

In summary, this is a good general introductory work that can be used for undergraduate or graduate reading on Latin American history or health-related courses.

Although it will hold no surprises for specialists, it may spark interest in future research. Its publication as an e-book makes it more accessible to the public, and the color illustrations of this format will facilitate analysis of the paintings discussed.

Luz María Hernández-Sáenz
University of Western Ontario

Samuel Brunk. *The Posthumous Career of Emiliano Zapata: Myth, Memory, and Mexico's Twentieth Century.* (Joe R. and Teresa Lozano Long Series in Latin American and Latino Art and Culture.) Austin: University of Texas Press. 2008. Pp. x, 353. $45.00.

Images recollecting the famous Mexican revolutionary Emiliano Zapata have since his death been drafted, refurbished, manipulated, and appropriated by myriad groups for their own purposes, a reality that comes as no surprise. Proclaimed heroes frequently serve a large variety of such pick-and-choose interests. But creative memories of Zapata have become especially handy to Mexicans in search of political power; gender, class, and ethnic equality; public and private liberties; better livelihoods; and an acceptable national identity. The index of this book offers a hint of the various identities and diversity of imagemakers under the heading "Zapata, Emiliano": "Adopted at national level, appropriated by national government, as bandit, [physical] body of, and the [U.S.-Mexico] border [embraced by Chicanos and Ceasar Chávez farm workers], as charro, as conscience of the revolution, death of, did not die [messianic], as father figure, as founding father [of Mexico], geographical spread of cult, and 'Golden Age' [of Mexican economic growth], as homosexual, horse of, incorruptibility, as Indian, as macho, as mestizo, and nationalism, and order [national tranquility], as patriarch, and progress and productivity [Zapata as modernizer], as rebel, regional cult of, and revolutionary fighting, statues and monuments of, and [as conqueror and liberator of] women" (pp. 352–353). Samuel Brunk addresses many more adaptations of Zapata and adds them to the swirl. For example, Zapata's presence in art, movies, songs, textbooks, literature, and popular culture all receive their full due.

Brunk suggests that this proliferation of usages was the result of the splintering effect of the revolution itself on Mexican society and subsequent attempts by numerous parties over the following decades to reap the rewards of the new openings created by its original chaos. Opportunists and rivals molded Zapata into an ally for their particular ambitions, producing fierce competition for his support. A one-party political system seemed to triumph for much of the past century at the national level, with its Zapata heralded as rural land reformer, but around 1970 the government faced tumultuous opposition from militants whose Zapata demanded social justice. When the federal government in the 1980s reconfigured its Zapata to favor large-scale private enterprise and the North American Free Trade Agreement (NAFTA) over *campesino* needs and values in the countryside, it lost him for good to an armed Zapatista movement in the south which captured the imagination of urbanites in the country's capital and toppled the long-standing rulers from power.

Throughout this struggle for political hegemony at the national level, Zapata came to be incorporated in many other ways; Brunk imbeds them within his chronology, indicating the persistence of some themes while noting the adjustment of others. Among the most entertaining are those concerning the ongoing struggle over Zapata's remains. The federal government wanted him interred with other national heroes in a monolithic monument in the capital, but the authorities and people of the state of Morelos, where Zapata was born and launched his revolution, were determined to keep their favorite son at home. So far they have been able to do so. Yet, within Morelos itself there is disagreement, fueled by tourism revenue and state-sponsored public works, over an official burial site. Should it be Cuautla, the scene of Zapata's first big military victory; Chinameca, site of his assassination; Anenecuilco, his birthplace; or Tlaltizapán, his military headquarters, where he ordered a mausoleum built to honor his movement's illustrious dead? So far, Cuautla has won the dispute.

For the most part, Brunk traces changing representations of Zapata through an impressive number of newspaper accounts of what speakers said at commemorations of the idol, mainly those recalling his death on April 10, 1919. He also scoured archives for their holdings concerning *Zapatismo* and conducted interviews with principals involved in the movement, including two of Zapata's children. For this book, he judiciously drew upon his own previous research on *Zapatismo* and hero cults in Latin America. The result is an absorbing series of vignettes that reveals the multiple modes in which Zapata's image has been both revered and manhandled over the past century.

The historical tissues with which Brunk connects the sketches, however, are somewhat fragile. His history seems stretched to fit his interpretations of the images in order to give the work an overarching theme. Readers will find the fine illustrations in the book capable of multiple interpretations, many of which do not fit Brunk's model of Mexican history. Furthermore, the author's conclusions about the nature of Mexican political hegemony based on molded and managed memories of Zapata—Brunk finds the federal government's seventy-year hold thinner than suspected but still "quite effective in increasing and perpetuating its power" (p. 257)—seem forced, or at least truncated, as do the supposed contributions of *Zapatismo* to Mexican self-identity—"He [Zapata] became someone remembered as something positive about Mexico, an image that Mexicans could rally around" (p. 264). Nonetheless, such analytical shortcomings are minimized by the finely described and often mesmerizing ways in which Brunk weaves small details and large patches of Zapata's legacy into twentieth-century Mexican history.

PAUL J. VANDERWOOD
San Diego State University

JEFFREY L. GOULD and ALDO LAURIA-SANTIAGO. *To Rise in Darkness: Revolution, Repression, and Memory in El Salvador, 1920–1932.* Durham, N.C.: Duke University Press. 2008. Pp. xxvi, 368. Paper $24.95, cloth $89.95.

This fine new book about the 1932 El Salvadoran massacre known as *La Matanza*, co-authored by Jeffrey L. Gould and Aldo Lauria-Santiago, offers insights into a range of issues—agrarian history, ethnicity, the texture of historical discourse and memory, and the ways in which capitalist elites have acted to repress socialism. The book examines the *campesino* revolt of 1932, when a communist victory at the polls was derailed via fraud and a coup. Other works on the subject have barely tapped the available archival sources; Gould and Lauria-Santiago's careful research allows them to challenge stereotypes and resolve many longstanding questions.

El Salvador's oligarchy consolidated power in what had been a nation of flourishing smallholders; by the 1930s, indigenous people represented only one-fifth of the entire population (p. 104). The other four-fifths defined themselves as ladinos and, together with the creole elites, harbored cultural and racial resentment if not outright hostility toward indigenous people. Wages had plunged to subhuman levels in the Great Depression after a decade of stunning profits, giving rise to the Salvadoran communist movement. Their political victories in western El Salvador inspired the coup that removed President Arturo Araujo from office on December 2, 1931. The new dictator, Maximiliano Hernández Martínez, first tried to achieve the destruction of the left via populist maneuvers. His decision to unleash weeks of repression, according to the authors, may well have been forced by the pressure of the United States to do whatever needed to be done in order to prevent *campesinos* from governing their own affairs.

On January 20, 1932 the communists issued their call to arms. In the hour when their insurrection was ascendant they burned land deeds, put their candidates in office, and shouted "death to capitalism." They were responsible for a mere seven deaths, and paid for these deaths with the lives of 10,000 people (p. 189). Perhaps the book's most incredible finding is that military propaganda about these events subsequently became *campesino* common sense.

To get to the heart of these issues, Gould recorded over 200 interviews, snatches of which emerge in the text. The rebels' rage against elites is palpable, as is the elite's disdain for the poor, but the intricacies of class sometimes receive short shrift. One individual who embodies rightwing loyalties among *campesinos*, a man named Sotero Linares, describes himself as of "mixed blood" and understands the massacre as self-defense. Because Linares was himself desperately poor, the authors say "class had little to do with the problem," thereby discounting the racial dimensions of class loyalty. After *La Matanza*, Linares went on to join "the repressive apparatus" (pp. 205–206), using his ethnic identification with the rich as a currency of privilege.

Women are not foregrounded by the authors, although their evidence suggests intriguing gendered histories. When the coup blocked the left's victories, women emerged at the forefront of the decision to turn to armed resistance. "The only significant insurgent military victory during the insurrection" was led by "Red Julia" Mojica and involved 1,500 to 2,000 rebel troops (pp. 129, 175–176). These details argue for sustained attention to the gendering of resistance; they also cast doubt on one of the authors' central explanatory tools, the relationship between "subaltern violence and machismo." Given that women were the revolt's most significant military leaders and accounted for a good number of the participants and victims, their invisibility is disconcerting.

Genocide is another thread that runs through the book. "Mass killings" took the lives of some 10,000 civilians and "most of the victims of the first wave of executions were Indians, even though ladinos probably composed half of the insurrectionary forces" (pp. 219–220). The authors use Nazism as their measuring rod, although the comparison is not always apt since the targeted populations coincided with the working class in many regions. Using the model of Nazism can obscure the ubiquity of racialized class hatreds that have shaped power structures in Latin America and the Caribbean. On the other hand, Gould and Lauria-Santiago have contributed powerfully to correcting erroneous histories in their analysis of the "military inflected narrative" that has dominated popular memory ever since 1932. "Subaltern acts of violence, coercion, and looting are given symbolic weight equal to, and even confused with, the military massacres" (p. 193). This is a complete inversion of the facts, but a predictable turn in the logic of settler ideologies.

Many of the book's best moments are the fruit of the efforts of an indigenous organizer who participated in the rebirth of the Salvadoran left in the 1970s, Reynaldo Patriz. Patriz opened the doors of memory because he is trusted across the indigenous communities that suffered the worst violence in 1932, and Gould hired him for that reason. With Patriz present, the oral histories "often became three-way encounters" (p. xi); "probably the most interesting discussions about ethnicity occurred when Gould managed to keep quiet" (p. xiii). The book's success challenges us to develop new understandings of authorship.

This is "a book produced in the North American academy about Central American subjects" (p. xii), but the lines of division are perhaps not so clear. The authors sometimes deny their own agendas as they grapple with the power relations in which they are enmeshed. "Patriz's intervention nonetheless made a significant difference to this project," they write, "through his growing analytical skills (despite only an eighth-grade education)" (pp. xii, xiii). A perspective from the global south or the working class would point out that Patriz's analytical skills are sharp precisely because of conditions that condemn people to minimal schooling while sparing them the ideological hammering of more advanced curricula.

In the unfolding narrative of the book, elite voices often take center stage. More space is given to the discussion of the elite "imaginary" of sexual violence perpetrated by "the dangerous classes" than to the very real leadership of women among the rebels. Numerous quotes belong to highly literate and foreign actors such as travelers, Protestants, and diplomats.

This book chronicles *La Matanza* with enormous care, showing that it was a watershed between the oligarchical repression born of nineteenth-century agrarian capitalism and twentieth-century varieties of state terror. Gould and Lauria-Santiago's ambitious history of 1932 does tremendous work to deepen the subtlety of our conversations about such moments. Dimensions of *La Matanza* that await further research and attention include gender, indigenous challenges to patriarchy, and imperial power relations that created the conditions for the slaughter.

CINDY FORSTER
Scripps College
[All reviewers of books by Indiana University faculty are selected with the advice of the Board of Editors.]

JEFFREY C. MOSHER. *Political Struggle, Ideology, and State Building: Pernambuco and the Construction of Brazil, 1817–1850.* Lincoln: University of Nebraska Press. 2008. Pp. xi, 344. $50.00.

Establishing a new state and nation is not easy. In the four decades after Brazil began severing its ties to Portugal in 1808, its independent unity remained seriously in doubt. Pernambuco, a province on the Atlantic-thrusting "bulge" in the country's northeast, was especially jealous of its autonomy and reluctant to accept orders from the new capital in Rio de Janeiro. Revolts against central authority, both minor and major, peppered the history of the province until 1848–1849, after which provincial leaders finally accepted their place within a unified Brazil presided over by a constitutional monarch.

Jeffrey C. Mosher delineates four politically important social groups in the province during this period. One was made up of wealthy sugar planters in the coastal region south of the capital of Recife. Since the sixteenth century this area, famous for its richly irrigated loamy soil so favorable to sugar cane production, had been the center of economic activity. Next were the less prosperous landowners who produced sugar along with other crops, including foodstuffs and some cotton, in the somewhat dryer region north of the capital, where a few large tracts of the original coastal forest still survived. Middling urban residents, shopkeepers, merchants, and artisans, many of whom were mulattos, made up a third group. Finally, both in the countryside and the city, Africans and their descendants—slaves, freedmen, and free-born, many of them also of mixed race—provided the labor. The perceived threat this last group potentially posed to social order meant their looming presence had to be considered in all political calculations, even if their voices were silenced.

As Mosher has it, time and time again the landed elites split over two issues: provincial autonomy and social control. The northern landowners pushed most energetically against central authority and won some support from their counterparts to the south. But to be successful insurgents often appealed to the urban middle sectors, egging them on to vent their grievances against the Portuguese-born merchants, artisans, and civil servants who had chosen to remain in Brazil and were said to be greedy cheaters. When riot and mayhem against the Portuguese resulted, the landed class, especially those in the more aristocratic south, feared this unrest would spread and Brazil would become another Haiti. These men quickly abandoned any effort toward provincial autonomy, appealing to the central government for military aid to maintain order. This was especially the case at the time of the *Praieira* movement of the 1840s, but also characterized a republican revolt in 1817 and the separatist Confederação do Equador in 1824–1825, not to mention numerous minor disturbances in the intervening years.

Mosher provides what is surely the most meticulous political history of the province in this period available in any language, and certainly the only one in English. He has consulted a vast secondary literature and plunged into the documents at the state and national archives with gusto. He challenges the reader to accompany the multiple twists and turns of politics, the changing allegiances of actors, and the many seemingly trivial manifestations of discontent blow-by-blow. The detail sometimes overwhelms the interpretation. The huge number of named participants makes it difficult to form a clear image of any single individual. The exception is Antônio Borges da Fonseca, a firebrand republican who turns out to have been marginal to the main story. A map showing the location of most towns mentioned in the text would have been especially helpful.

Writing specifically about the subsequent period of Brazilian history, I have argued that patronage, not policy or ideology, was the very stuff of its politics, an assertion that Mosher questions. He maintains that real ideological differences separated the parties. For the period he studies few would dispute him. Rich men were especially concerned with order and hierarchy, understanding themselves as defenders of the monarchy, and we may label this position conservative. Yet sometimes these southern planters rebelled against the central government if it backed their local rivals, and sometimes to the same end they even supported banditry. After the central government extended and imposed its authority in 1837 by assuming the right to appoint virtually all local officials, so-called Liberals called for decentralization when out of power, but relished holding the right of patronage when it was theirs to dispense, doing nothing to alter that centralizing structure when they could have done so. Nor did they ally themselves with the few abolitionists, and there is little evidence they encouraged universal education or adopted other measures to advance the status of the free poor. I continue to think that by the end of the

period Mosher examines the actions of both parties reveal a pragmatic approach to power and political action rather than an ideological impulse.

RICHARD GRAHAM
University of Texas,
Austin

GREG GRANDIN. *Fordlandia: The Rise and Fall of Henry Ford's Forgotten Jungle City.* New York: Metropolitan. 2009. Pp. x, 398. $27.50.

Although the number of volumes written about Henry Ford pales in comparison to the number dedicated to Abraham Lincoln, Ford has, in one sense, achieved a status akin to that of the fabled American president. It is difficult to imagine that there is any aspect of these men's personal or professional lives left to be explored, no bit of historical minutia left unearthed. Yet this book explores an aspect of the automotive tycoon's career that has not been fully vetted, and is written with considerable verve and style. Greg Grandin's study of Ford's Brazilian rubber plantation tracks the evolution of a profligate project, driven in part by corporate interests but more importantly by the vision of a fabulously wealthy American eccentric.

The decision in 1927 to create a plantation in the vast Brazilian rainforest initially represented a logical response to the threat of a foreign-controlled rubber monopoly that might raise prices on one of the most critical inputs to Ford's industrial colossus. But even as that threat receded along with the practical possibility of generating commercially viable amounts of rubber from the Amazon, Ford persisted in the project, driven by a grander vision of modern technology's transformative potential. The automotive magnate envisioned a world in which modern capitalism created a material utopia and reconciled the differences between urban and rural society while preserving what he perceived as the values of his own American past. Fordlandia, as the plantation became known, would replicate similar reformist experiments that Ford had launched in the U.S.

The Fordlandia experiment, which endured for more than two decades before its remnants were sold to the Brazilian government for a fraction of the millions invested, conjures up a rich variety of images that Grandin plays upon in his narrative. The author makes references to modern man against unconquerable nature, the naivety of Americans abroad, and the relentless destruction of the natural environment by onrushing multinational capitalism. Fordlandia's raw steel structures, its extravagant, sometimes ruinous investments in technology, its seemingly pristine housing facilities, and its rigid labor discipline, set among the shimmering tropical luxury and threat of the Amazon, lend themselves readily to the treatment of these larger themes. Writing in a fluid and open style, Grandin uses his encyclopedic knowledge of the Fordlandia materials to bring these issues to life with tales of swindlers both American and Brazilian, adventurers who challenged the rain forest and its dangers, and of course the peripatetic initiatives and sometimes loony visions of the plantation's eccentric founder. This approach breathes life into fields of scholarship not generally known for their vivacity.

Grandin's study demonstrates the potential for taking the seemingly mundane events of business history and international relations and infusing them with the excitement of human endeavor and adventure. At the same time the approach is insightful, as the author argues that the vision behind Fordlandia represented a strain of American pastoralism which, rather than imagining modern man pitted against nature, saw the two in a holistic relationship in which nature and industrialization fulfilled each other. But the study's subject narrows the scope of its significance.

In the litany of massive U.S. corporate projects in Latin America, Fordlandia stands out for the enormity of its failure. By comparison, the initiatives of corporations such as the Cerro de Pasco Corporation, General Electric, and ITT not only enjoyed success but also had profound and lasting consequences in the region. Whether positive or negative, Fordlandia's impact pales by comparison. While there are strong parallels between the burn and clear tactics of Ford and the contemporary assault on the Brazilian rainforest, the causative connection is tenuous. On the other hand, the town of Cerro de Pasco in Peru remains, more than one hundred years after the corporation's creation, one of the most polluted population centers on the face of the earth. Fordlandia's contributions to economic change lie rusting in the rainforest, while power generation facilities, telecommunications networks, and consumer markets created by GE and ITT play a central role in the economic life of modern Latin America.

Fordlandia's corporate failure resulted in part from Ford's refusal to rely on the professional expertise that was central to the success of all modern corporations, including his own. Unfortunately, the book's perspective relies too heavily on the same narrow vision embedded in the Ford materials. While recounting the travails of Ford managers in recruiting and disciplining labor, coping with the challenges of a tropical environment, and dealing with the vagaries of local politics and politicians, the author offers few comparative perspectives on these issues from the voluminous scholarship on other U.S. enterprises. Such references would have offered considerable insight into the complex functioning of American corporations in Latin America and broadened the analytical significance of Ford's monumental fiasco.

Yet the limitations of the book are those of an ambitious and accomplished piece of scholarship. The book is a compelling read and hopefully will stir wider interest in the history of corporations and international relations.

THOMAS F. O'BRIEN
University of Houston

DONNA J. GUY. *Women Build the Welfare State: Performing Charity and Creating Rights in Argentina, 1880–1955.*
Durham, N.C.: Duke University Press. 2009. Pp. xi, 252. Cloth $79.95, paper $22.95.

The book under review is, in the words of its author, an attempt to examine "the complex interrelationships between female philanthropic groups and feminists in their advocacy of child welfare programs and family reforms" (p. 1) in Argentina between the late nineteenth century and the first half of the twentieth. According to Donna J. Guy, the welfare state established by Juan Perón in the late 1940s did not constitute a total rupture with the past—as the Peronist discourse would have it—but was built around a pre-existing system of effective, if disjointed, subsidies to private and semi-private philanthropic organizations. One of the merits of this book is that it reconstructs the sometimes confusing mosaic of philanthropic institutions, both lay and religious, Jewish and Catholic, as well as those belonging to particular immigrant communities, all receiving government funds, that provided social services in the pre-Peronist Argentina. This system would end when the Fundación Eva Perón, established in 1947 by "Evita," Perón's wife, absorbed most philanthropic activities.

Recent scholarship has emphasized the traditional weakness of the Argentine state until Perón's rise to power, particularly regarding its ability to establish social policies. According to this view, the works of philanthropic institutions often overlapped with those of state-run organizations, creating an inefficient and expensive conglomerate of institutions catering to different publics. Moreover, the powerful Sociedad de Beneficencia de la Capital, established in the early nineteenth century and run by elite women, had conflicts with (male) state officials and reformers who wanted to "modernize" the whole system of social welfare policies. Interestingly, in almost all cases until the 1930s the women of the Sociedad had their way. Guy shows a somewhat different picture, emphasizing the relative efficiency of a system based on state subsidies and formed by a heterogeneous collection of institutions.

This book is based on impressive research including previously unused primary sources. Given the shape of most Argentine archives, this is not a minor accomplishment. The book reads well and is appropriate for both undergraduate and graduate courses in Argentine history, women's history, and in the history of social policies.

However, it has some serious flaws. First of all, Guy never defines her terms. Thus, concepts like "welfare state" float through the book without the reader ever being informed what exactly the author is talking about. Can the Peronist system built around the Fundación Eva Perón be considered a "welfare state"? Sometimes the answer seems to be yes and sometimes it seems to be no. Similarly, Guy never discusses who exactly the feminists were in late nineteenth and early twentieth-century Argentina. Other topics that should have been discussed more in depth include the "*Ley Agote*" law of 1919, which redefined the power of parents over their children in relation to the state, and which Guy dispatches in less than one page. The conflict between the Catholic Church and the state that took place toward the end of Perón's government, and that determined many of Perón's policies toward families and children, is mentioned one time in the volume with no further discussion. Although the author claims that she also conducted research outside of Buenos Aires in the provinces, the focus is definitely placed on the capital city. The book discusses in length the operation of different institutions for abandoned and delinquent children. However, little is said about how children became inmates of those institutions and even less about the actual experiences of children confined there.

Guy presents a large number of cases but in most instances she fails to extract a conclusion from the material. She does make some unwarranted generalizations. For instance, concluding from a single case of a child born with birth defects who did not become eligible for adoption that the "case demonstrated that the Peronist government continued to discriminate against handicapped children and refused to allow them the opportunity to be adopted" (p. 174) seems a bit of a stretch. Virtually nothing is said about the operation of the Fundación Eva Perón. Finally, the lack of any comparative perspective impoverishes the analysis since the reader would not know to what extent the Argentine case is unique.

There are also some errors sprinkled throughout the book. Just to mention a few, Colonia Carlos Casares is in the Province of Buenos Aires, not in Córdoba, and Dr. Gregorio Bermann is characterized by Guy as "one of the founders of non-Freudian Argentine psychiatry" (p. 135), while in fact he was among the first doctors to introduce Freudian thought in Argentinian psychiatry. He even visited Freud in Vienna.

This book is useful in spite of its weaknesses, and it opens new perspectives for the understanding of almost one hundred years of Argentine history.

MARIANO BEN PLOTKIN
IDES/CONICET-Universidad Nacional de Tres de Febrero

EUROPE: ANCIENT AND MEDIEVAL

VOLKER GRIEB. *Hellenistische Demokratie: Politische Organisation und Struktur in freien griechischen Poleis nach Alexander dem Großen.* (Historia; Einzelschriften, number 199.) Stuttgart: Franz Steiner Verlag. 2008. Pp. 407. €77.00.

This book, based on the author's Ph.D. thesis, addresses an interesting question and displays solid scholarship but comes up with a somewhat disappointing answer. The question concerns the fate of the classical city-state following Alexander's conquests and throughout the so-called Hellenistic Age (323–330 B.C.). The conquests of Alexander brought about a profound change in the political map of the Greek world. In the Classical Age (formally, 478–323 B.C.), that world

consisted of hundreds of independent political units, tiny by our standards, most of which displayed vibrant power structures, intricate social systems, and highly sophisticated cultures. Some of these city-states (*poleis*), notably Athens, developed very special democracies that enabled lower-class citizens to participate directly in the decision-making process in a manner that had never before been possible, nor ever would be again, even in the far more sophisticated representative democracies of the modern age. Following the disintegration of Alexander's empire, these city-states were gradually incorporated within the territories ruled by his successors and then, as these succumbed one by one to the superior power of Rome, within the territories ruled by the Roman Republic.

Volker Grieb seeks to answer the wider question of what happened to the classical city-state when caught in the vortex of these superior power systems by analyzing the history and the political systems of four city-states that were recognized as democracies by their contemporaries: Athens, Kos, Miletus, and Rhodes. Contrary to the widely held view that classical democracy survived only nominally in the Hellenistic Age ("The Greek term *demokratia* became steadily more devalued during the process I have been describing," wrote G. E. M. de Ste. Croix), Grieb maintains that these four cities were genuine democracies at least until the middle of the second century B.C.

Grieb effectively handles the main problem that bedevils his enterprise: the dearth and fragmentary nature of the evidence. We owe him a debt of gratitude for producing the most complete collection possible of the literary fragments and inscriptions pertinent to these cities (see his "Quellenindex"). But even so, considerable lacunae remain. Consecutive descriptions of events over longer periods of time or vivid representations of the aspirations, frustrations, dilemmas, and disputes of the population are not available for these cities in the way they are, for example, for classical Athens. What we have instead are flares of information that illuminate one limited aspect of a city's life for shorter time periods and are then extinguished, giving way to years of obscurity.

This may account, at least in part, for the rigid structure of Grieb's book. Each city is given one chapter, divided into four sections. The first section is concerned with the "people"; the second with political institutions, at both local and city levels; the third with the concepts of democracy, freedom, and autonomy; and the fourth with the decline and demise of democracy under Roman rule. The most satisfactory of these sections are those devoted to the people and to the political institutions, and the least satisfactory are those concerned with the key concepts of democracy.

Grieb convincingly demonstrates that institutions treated by their contemporaries as democratic did indeed exist and were actively involved in international politics throughout the period in question. All four cities had well-articulated concepts for people (*demos*), often with subdivisions; all had popular assemblies (*ekklesia*) and councils (*boule*) whose decisions, as can be seen in surviving inscriptions, were recorded under the heading "decided by the people" (the quintessential emblem of people power in the Classical Age). In all four cities, various executive officials and juries were elected regularly by official bodies; all had political groups within the citizen body, whose existence presupposes ideological and power struggles. But do features such as these, even if operating simultaneously, justify the label of genuine democracy?

Grieb thinks that they do, but the sections devoted to the key concepts of democracy leave some doubts concerning the accuracy of his claim. Rather than making a more determined attempt to assess the presence and intensity of the essential features of a genuine democracy, such as the freedom to vote; the participation, possibly facilitated by payment, of the lower class; the absence of informal foci of power capable of vitiating the results of elections (I, for one, find it hard to believe that those numerous individuals styled in honorary decrees as "friends" of the kings, or as "staying with the king," played the political game in their cities as obedient isonomic democrats), Grieb presents a survey of the four cities' international relations throughout the Hellenistic and early Roman periods with an eye to the "people." Nor is a wide range of scholarship concerning the high theory of democracy, freedom, and related concepts by scholars such as M. I. Finley, Robert A. Dahl, Josiah Ober, and Orlando Patterson brought into play (not that I am suggesting that it could have substantially changed the picture, given the nature of the evidence). Ultimately, Grieb's endeavor boils down to the question of whether democracy in these four cities was merely a matter of form, or also one of substance. He has shown convincingly that it was a matter of form. Due to the nature of the evidence we shall probably never know for sure whether and to what extent it was also a matter of substance.

Gabriel Herman
*Hebrew University,
Jerusalem*

Peter Fibiger Bang. *The Roman Bazaar: A Comparative Study of Trade and Markets in a Tributary Empire.* (Cambridge Classical Studies.) New York: Cambridge University Press. 2008. Pp. xv, 358. $110.00.

Perceptions of the economy of the Roman Empire are dominated by comparisons, explicit or implicit, with the European experience of modernization. For the classical political economists, Rome was the obvious test case, as an equally powerful and sophisticated society, for making sense of contemporary developments. As it became clearer that those developments were unprecedented, and that modern material power far exceeded that of any earlier society, this discourse fragmented; economists largely ignored preindustrial societies (assuming nevertheless that their analyses of economic behavior were universally applicable), while ancient historians embarked on an interminable debate about the

level of development of the Roman economy. Some continued to see Rome as semi- or proto-modern and sought to identify the ancient impediments to full economic take-off; others insisted on the absolute difference between ancient agrarian-aristocratic society and industrial-capitalist modernity. Since the ancient evidence is so fragmentary and ambiguous, "modernizers" and "primitivists" have taken up ever more extreme positions, defining themselves against one another, with every new account falling into the ruts of the old arguments. Blinded, perhaps, by European culture's myth of its own origins in classical antiquity, neither group has questioned the appropriateness of the comparison or the idea that it holds the key to understanding the past, despite the increasingly obvious sterility of the debate. It is time, as Peter Fibiger Bang argues in this provocative and thought-provoking book, "to abandon *the tyranny of Europe over Rome*" (p. 59), to reconceptualize the problem and seek more appropriate comparisons.

Bang's title makes two moves that are echoed in the organization of his argument. Firstly, Rome is defamiliarized, presented not (as in many accounts) as a composite of French country markets, Corsican peasants, and little Italian towns but in terms of the exotic, chaotic, and above all Oriental world of the bazaar. His first two chapters challenge the obsession of earlier accounts with measuring Rome against early modern Europe, and insist instead that we should look to the Chinese, Ottoman, and Mughal empires for concepts and ideal types of economic behavior and structures. The "tributary empire," in which the bulk of production is consumed by its producers and a high proportion of the disposable surplus is controlled by the state and its elite, offers a far superior model for the Roman economy than a proto-capitalist market system. This is the second move; understanding Rome in terms of the bazaar does not make its workings inexplicable, but points us toward a different set of analytical tools. Tributary empires are not solely rapacious; their power depends on the efficient mobilization and distribution of resources, and this explains both the development of inter-regional resource transfers, overcoming the usual "limits of the possible" set by technology and ecology, and also the limited development of regional specialization and the division of labor. In the second half of the book, Bang draws on comparative material, above all from the Mughal Empire, to characterize the world of the Roman trader—risky, fragile, dominated by uncertainty—and to identify the themes that we should be studying: the role of the state as predator, protector, and parasite on trading activity and the operations of communal solidarity, sociability, and informal coercion in the absence of adequate state control of the chaos of the bazaar. Above all, this shift in focus emphasizes the need to understand patterns of consumption in order to interpret the significance and development of particular kinds of trade in their specific context.

This is an extremely rich and stimulating book, based on an impressive knowledge of the scholarship on two different societies; many of Bang's discussions—his characterization of Rome as a tributary empire and his speculative quantification of its economy, his ideas on the "domestication" of risk and imbalances in the bazaar—will be key points of reference for future debates. The book is densely argued and expects a lot of its readers; some of the short, confident dismissals of other scholars' arguments will mean little to anyone without an intimate knowledge of the historiographical tradition on the Roman economy. Bang does, to my mind, spend too much time engaging with that tradition rather than developing his positive characterization of the Roman Empire as a whole and of the workings of trade and exchange within it; he extricates himself from the ruts of the old debate by examining their origins in detail, at the cost of reducing the momentum of the vehicle that is carrying him onto new paths of understanding. Nevertheless, this book makes an important contribution to establishing the specific dynamics of the Roman economy, rather than seeing it as either modern or not modern, and will need to be read carefully by anyone interested in the development of pre-industrial empires.

NEVILLE MORLEY
University of Bristol

ISABELLE ROSÉ. *Construire une société seigneuriale: Itinéraire et ecclésiologie de l'abbé Odon de Cluny (fin du IXe-milieu du Xe siècle)*. (Collection d'études médiévales de Nice, number 8.) Turnhout, Belgium: Brepols, with the Centre National de la Recherche Scientifique, Centre d'études Préhistoire, Antiquité, Moyen âge. 2008. Pp. 732. €55.00.

Odo, although the second rather than the first abbot of the monastery of Cluny (founded 909–910), played a major role in shaping what would become one of medieval Europe's most influential monastic houses. For a long time Odo was considered interesting chiefly because he wrote the first hagiographic "life" of a medieval lay lord (Gerald of Aurillac), but more recently he has been seen as playing a key role in the very foundation of Cluny as well as its subsequent development, especially its role as a reformer of other monasteries. Here Isabelle Rosé provides a detailed biography (or biographical itinerary, as she terms it) of Odo; an appendix gives a year-by-year account of his activities, with citations. She finds it necessary to justify such a biography, as the form is often considered outdated, even artificial, by French scholars. The biographical itinerary is followed in the book's second part by a close study of Odo's thinking on ecclesiology and cosmology, especially the role of monks in a properly organized society.

The "lordly society" of the title is misleading, as Rosé never discusses rents, serfdom, or banal dues (what medievalists normally mean by "seigneurialism") but rather focuses on Odo's belief that secular society, especially the powerful, needed to be guided by monks. She chose the title because she sees Odo in particular

and Cluny in general as standing between the Carolingian age of the ninth century and the so-called seigneurial age of the eleventh century, which they helped to shape. This is an interesting idea, but the author never really makes clear how a cosmology in which churchmen assigned the powerful an important potential role in shaping Christian society led to their political dominance—especially as much recent scholarship has downplayed the supposed independence of eleventh-century lords.

This book began as Rosé's doctoral dissertation. It has all the strengths of a French *thèse de doctorat* as it is a very thorough and well-documented analysis of all points raised. Such a long book, full of extensive historiographic discussions, footnotes in Latin, and complicated charts, can only make an American scholar jealous; would that we could publish something as wide-ranging. And yet the book also has the normal weaknesses of a *thèse*, especially having less to say that is new than the sheer size of the work might promise. Many of Rosé's broader points, such as that one cannot read backward from the eleventh century to understand tenth-century Cluny's origins, or that a Cluniac abbot's reforms of other houses cannot be characterized as the construction of a highly structured order, or that monks saw an important role for laymen in service to the church, were made a generation ago by Barbara H. Rosenwein (*Rhinoceros Bound: Cluny in the Tenth Century* [1982]), in a book that Rosé cites.

Rosé's most original contribution is a close examination of Odo's own liturgical and theological writings, thus making it possible to discuss what he thought were his period's crucial issues, not merely what he did. She does a thorough job of placing Odo's intellectual origins within the context of the scholars of the late Carolingian renaissance, the men who taught him and whose doctrinal questions influenced him. Indeed, the book's most important broad theme is probably Cluny's roots in ninth-century developments, correcting the too-easy assumption that the monastery's foundation constituted a sharp break with the past. She also details Odo's role in reforming Italian monasteries (generally without reference to the pope), a topic treated only superficially by most previous scholars.

The division of the book into two parts is somewhat awkward and results in unnecessary duplication, as when, for example, Rosé discusses Odo's travels to reform monasteries as part of the biographical itinerary and then treats those same reforms again in the context of his ecclesiology. One could certainly have used Odo, as the author intended, to illuminate his changing society without separating his actions quite so thoroughly from his ideas. It is also unfortunate that, although she discusses Odo's theologically inspired views of the world with some thoroughness, she does not do the same with John of Salerno, Odo's first biographer. That is, rather than looking at John of Salerno as deliberately creating an ideal holy monk and abbot, she uses his account as a straightforward record of what Odo did and when, primarily concerned with questions of whether some of his dates might have been off by a year or two. That said, this book will be referenced by anyone studying the early history of Cluny or the broader history of Benedictine monasticism from the ninth to the eleventh centuries.

CONSTANCE B. BOUCHARD
University of Akron

STEPHEN BAXTER. *The Earls of Mercia: Lordship and Power in Late Anglo-Saxon England.* (Oxford Historical Monographs.) New York: Oxford University Press. 2007. Pp. xviii, 363. $150.00.

This book is a thoroughly researched and thought-provoking study that should be read by anyone interested in late Anglo-Saxon aristocratic politics and society. Stephen Baxter uses the careers of the late Anglo-Saxon ealdorman Leofwine and his family as a locus to explore a constellation of issues in tenth and eleventh-century English politics, religious patronage, land tenure, and lordship. Leofwine and his descendents were unique among late Anglo-Saxon aristocrats in maintaining their power from the 990s until the 1070s, surviving all but the last of the crises that affected England in that period. The book seeks to understand and explain this political longevity by examining both the nature of and the limits on the powers wielded by the earls of Mercia in the tenth and eleventh centuries. Baxter clearly shares with James Campbell and the late Patrick Wormald a "maximum view" of the late Anglo-Saxon state, and not every reader will agree with this perspective. Baxter sets the Mercian earls and their powers firmly within the maximalist paradigm, but argues that, though earls enjoyed great wealth and power, their positions were distinctly insecure.

Baxter begins by charting the careers of Leofwine, his sons Northmann, Eadwine, and Leofric, grandson Ælfgar, and great-grandsons Eadwine and Morcar. Opportunism, a knack for astute alliances (e.g., with Gruffudd ap Llewelyn of Wales in the 1050s), and simple good fortune go some way to account for the survival of the house of Leofwine, but Baxter argues that the structures of late Anglo-Saxon politics and society contributed to their success. Having established a prosopographical and chronological framework, Baxter then devotes each of the following four chapters to a different topic: the extent, nature and limits of the earls' power *vis á vis* royal government; their wealth in land and the means by which they acquired it; their patronage of religious houses; and their development, through the complex mechanisms of lordship, of a network of followers.

Baxter sees the earls' powers and interests as closely intertwined with those of royal government, and stresses the degree of control late Anglo-Saxon kings had over the structure of earldoms. He also demonstrates the wide range of judicial, political, and military activities in which earls engaged. In his examination of the Leofwinesons' landed wealth as recorded in Domesday Book, Baxter contends that many of their estates were "on loan" from the king and were held only so long as they stayed in office as earls. He shows that the house of Leofwine was clearly eclipsed in terms of lands by the house of Godwine, but challenges directly Robin Fleming's well-known claim that the Godwinesons controlled more land than Edward the Confessor. Baxter emphasizes the social and political aspects of the Leofwinesons' patronage of monasteries and secular minsters, but also explores ways in which the *Vision of Earl Leofric* provides remarkable insight into the personal religious devotion of a late Anglo-Saxon aristocrat.

The chapter on lordship is, for this reviewer, the most interesting. Through a close analysis of Domesday evidence—in particular, the textual formulae used to describe lordship—Baxter reconstructs the complex arrangement of followers and commended men who supported the earls. In his analysis, Baxter sets out clearly and succinctly the various and potentially overlapping bonds between lord and man in late Anglo-Saxon England. He argues compellingly that Frederic William Maitland's interpretation of commendation as a weak bond was mistaken, and that passages in Domesday usually translated as "mere commendation" were meant instead simply to contrast a commendatory bond with one based on dependant tenure or soke right. The book concludes with a sketch of the events that lead to the downfall of Eadwine and Morcar after the Norman Conquest. Baxter argues that the structures of power that underpinned the Leofwineson earls were irrecoverably eroded in the five years after the battle of Hastings.

It must be pointed out that the factors Baxter highlights as central to the achievements of the earls of Mercia—their exploitation of powers acquired as agents of the king, their accumulation of landed wealth, their use of monasteries and religious patronage as foci for extending their influence, and their cultivation of a body of commended men and other supporters—were not unique to the house of Leofwine. Many late Anglo-Saxon aristocrats employed some or all of the same techniques in the struggle for power and reward, though neither on the same scale nor with the same level of success over the long term. It would be interesting, if challenging, to see the methods and models Baxter applies to the Leofwineson earls used to examine other, lesser members of the late Anglo-Saxon aristocracy.

ANDREW LOWERRE
English Heritage,
Portsmouth, England

ALEXANDRA CUFFEL. *Gendering Disgust in Medieval Religious Polemic.* Notre Dame, Ind.: University of Notre Dame Press. 2007. Pp. xviii, 430. $45.00.

On the outer surface of the monumental Dome of the Rock in Jerusalem, completed by 691 C.E., one finds tiles inscribed in letters as tall as a human being with a blessing that confers peace upon Jesus as God's

Prophet and servant, alongside verses from the Qur'an (Sura Maryam 16:34–37) denying the possibility that God can incarnate. This inscription literally confronts and intentionally affronts the Church of the Holy Sepulchre across the valley and stands both as testimony to the incorporation of Jesus into the line of pre-Muslim prophets and as a strong visual polemic against Christianity.

The abject disgust that Muslims felt about the idea of the incarnation was not merely philosophical but embodied, visceral, and physical. It had to do with birthing, ritual impurity, and the "filth" of the pregnant and menstrual female body. Alexandra Cuffel engages in extraordinarily incisive analysis of a chronologically and linguistically breathtaking range of texts that explore the rhetoric of physical disgust in the polemic literature of Christians, Muslims, and Jews against one another. "Body, gender, and religious deviance," she tells us, "first coalesce [in antiquity] to form a particular form of polemic" (p. 11). Cuffel demonstrates how this mode eventually became common in pagan, Christian, and Jewish discourse as, first, pagans and Jews used the idea of bodily filth to degrade and devalue Christians and to "diminish the dignity of the Christians' god" (p. 132). Christians in turn used similar rhetoric against nascent Islam, inveighing against what they regarded as its abject, sensuous physicality, and Muslims responded with echoes of the ancient Jewish and pagan canards against the possibility of God being born from the corrupt body of woman.

The corrupt female body is at the center of Cuffel's discussion, as it appears again and again in polemics in a way that both exceeds and incorporates the tropes of the animal, the corpse, the sensual/sexual. The very fact that Cuffel pays attention to the gendered nature of the polemics is welcome, as previous writers have tended to look at the material without seeing the distinctly misogynist rhetoric it encloses. Her nuanced treatment of the phenomenon is truly impressive as she exposes the ways in which women's bodies, consistently connected with "dirt, waste, and rot," led to the understanding and construction of "'female' as a negative ontological category in relation to the spiritual world" (p. 26). In the first part of her study she limns for us a picture of late antique differentiation of the male and female and the presentation of women as other, both in terms of their relationship with men and with the divine. In the second part of the book she discusses the high medieval valorization of the figure of the Virgin Mary as the vessel of Christ's humanity and the reaction of Jews and Muslims to this theological development, demonstrating *inter alia* how the rise of scholarly interaction among representatives of the three faiths led to polemics that were more learned and knowledgeable, but simultaneously and as a direct result more intense, incisive, and cruel.

A highlight of Cuffel's analysis and an area in which previous research has also been relatively lacking is her treatment of visual culture, particularly the idea and ideal of animal filth, wildness, and violence in bestiary literature. Having perceptively pointed out at the outset that polemics could take many forms including the physical transport of materials engendering disgust into the sacred space of one's enemy (p. 245), she builds on the work of scholars such as Debra Higgs Strickland and Claudine Fabre-Vassas to illuminate the manner in which the space of illustrated manuscripts and sculpture in the round could also become a site of contestation wherein the polemics of disgust could enable the troping of one's enemy in a manner that was simultaneously bestial and feminizing (p. 200).

Polemics, whether written, spoken, or visual consist of in-group rhetoric that is yet directed outward toward the enemy other. They must be simultaneously comprehensible (and repugnant) to the group that polemicizes and equally recognizable and shocking to the group polemicized against. As such, polemic is inherently a rhetorically violent intervention that involves cross-cultural translation and cross-pollination, demonstrating that intercultural contact involves creativity not only in exchange and cooperation but in canard and vituperation. The study of polemic enables one to see the often ugly interior prejudices of cultures locking horns while simultaneously exposing their most public faces. One cannot help but be impressed with the breadth of Cuffel's analysis and by the manner in which her command of the sources in Latin, Hebrew, Arabic, and various vernaculars enables her to see both surfaces of the polemics at hand. This book is precisely the sort of cross-disciplinary, cross-cultural analysis that is absolutely necessary to make any sense of the complex and fascinating exchange between cultures that both collude and collide.

MARC MICHAEL EPSTEIN
Vassar College

GIULIANO MARCHETTO. *Il divorzio imperfetto: I giuristi medievali e la separazione dei coniugi.* (Annali dell'Istituto storico italo-germanico in Trento, number 48.) Bologna: Il Mulino. 2008. Pp. 500. €32.50.

As is well known, medieval canon law did not allow divorce as we understand it today. What the medieval canonists called *divortium* came in two kinds: *divortium quoad vinculum*, what today we would call annulment, and *divortium quoad thorum*, what today we would call separation. The former was a declaration that the marriage had not been properly formed in the first place. In most circumstances a judgment of *divortium quoad vinculum* allowed the couple to remarry. *Divortium quoad thorum* relieved the couple of the obligation to cohabit but did not allow them to remarry so long as both of them lived. Because of the church's exclusive jurisdiction over matters of the formation and dissolution of marriage, these were the rules that were applied throughout Western Europe in the high and later Middle Ages and, in some places, well into the early modern period.

The basic principle of the indissolubility of marriage and the grounds for annulment of marriages have been the subject of considerable literature, from the point of theology and legal doctrine, from the point of view of the law as applied in the church courts, and from the point of view of their effect on social reality and of feedback from social reality. The same cannot be said of separation. Even the development of the legal doctrine is unclear, and treatments of its application in the courts and the social reality that lies behind the cases are few and scattered.

The grounds for separation remained debatable throughout the classical period of canon law (roughly 1100–1500). Generally adultery, which the canonists called "fornication," was the sole cause mentioned for separation from bed and board. Use of the word "fornication," the word used in the "except" clauses in the Vulgate edition of Matthew's Gospel (5:32; 19:9), rather than "adultery" allowed the canonists to expand the grounds somewhat. They included "spiritual fornication," heresy, or conversion to Judaism or paganism. Rarely, if ever, however, do the canonists mention cruelty, even extreme physical cruelty, as a ground for an action of separation from bed and board.

They do, however, mention cruelty as a defense to the action for restoration of conjugal rights. "A man seeking restoration," Raymond of Peñafort writes, "should not be restored [if] his cruelty is so great that adequate security cannot be provided to the fearful woman, or [if] he is pursuing his wife with capital hate" (*Summa de matrimonio* 4.19 [c.1235]). While similar views on the topic can be derived from other canonists, it has been supposed that it was not until Panormitanus, who died in 1445, that a mainstream canonist held that cruelty was a sufficient ground for an action of separation from bed and board, and that proposition did not become the *communis opinio* until the sixteenth century.

At the same time the records of the church courts in the same period reveal, in some areas, an extensive jurisprudence concerning actions of separation. The grounds were by no means confined to adultery. Separation on the ground of cruelty was available in many places by at least the beginning of the fifteenth century. Some courts were willing to go considerably further. The ecclesiastical courts in the diocese of Cambrai, for example, were willing to grant separations on the ground of *morum discrepantia*, a phrase that seems in application to bear a distinct resemblance to the modern "irretrievable breakdown of the marriage."

The key issue, then, with the medieval canon law of separation, is whether and to what extent what was happening in the courts in such cases is reflected in the development of the legal doctrine in the later Middle Ages. In this regard, Giuliano Marchetto's book disappoints, for he says virtually nothing about what was happening in the courts. The book is valuable, however, as a work of doctrinal legal history. It contains the most detailed description that I know of juristic writing on both the procedure and the substance of separation cases (pp. 327–426), although it is confined mostly to printed sources. It would have been even more valuable had Marchetto continued the story into the sixteenth century when the canonists generally came to recognize

cruelty as an independent cause for a judgment of separation. Almost half the book (pp. 21–231) is devoted to the basic principle of the indissolubility of marriage and its relationship to the way in which the marriage was formed. Marchetto is not breaking new ground here, but his bibliography is up to date, and he writes with clarity. Errors are relatively few and not serious. The documentation in the book is extensive and allows the specialist to check the original sources.

More work clearly needs to be done, but Marchetto has advanced our understanding of the medieval law of separation considerably.

CHARLES DONAHUE, JR.
Harvard Law School

WILLIAM J. PURKIS. *Crusading Spirituality in the Holy Land and Iberia c. 1095–c. 1187*. Rochester, N.Y.: Boydell Press. 2008. Pp. xi, 215. $90.00

This book is a valuable contribution to crusades studies. Following Giles Constable and Jean Leclercq, William J. Purkis sees the crusades as an integral part of twelfth-century religious reform. In that framework, he emphasizes the importance of pilgrimage and the imitation of Christ and the apostolic life to the origins and early development of crusading.

The first two chapters argue that Pope Urban II touched on the deepest devotional needs of his audience in his crusading appeal. The preachers and first historians of the crusade understood the crusaders as imitators of Christ and practitioners of the apostolic life, which also seems to have been the crusaders' self-perception. *Imitatio Christi* and *vita apostolica* were "two foundations of crusading spirituality" (p. 56). Chapter three looks at the first fifty years of crusaders' rule in the East. In that period, the connection between crusading to the East and ideals of apostolic life faded away, while ideas of Christo-mimesis continued to be central to crusading spirituality. Chapter four examines the Cistercian influence on crusading spirituality in the second and third quarters of the twelfth century. As a result of Cistercian preaching, the ideal of *imitatio Christi* was divorced from crusaders and reserved for those who committed their whole lives to following Christ, such as the Templars. Crusaders, in turn, were defined by the "duty to their bloodline" (p. 118). Their duty was to follow the crusading *exemplum* of their fathers. The last two chapters turn to Iberia. As a tribute to the potency of the *imitatio Christi* ideal, which itself was linked to the pilgrimage to Jerusalem, crusading was introduced to Iberia as an alternative route to Jerusalem. But this idea of *iter per Hispaniam* was soon supplanted by the invention of local crusading foundational legends and centers for penitential pilgrimage, such as the cult of St. James, the patron of the fight against the Muslims of Spain, at Compostela.

This book clearly belongs to a particular school of crusades studies. Purkis's research lies within the interpretative framework of his supervisor Jonathan Riley-Smith and some of Riley-Smith's established stu-

dents, notably Marcus Bull, innovating by narrowing
the range of ideas that informed early crusading spirituality and following their development over a longer
period of time. The book is based on a broad range of
primary sources, although its use of secondary literature is more limited. Except for the last two chapters,
most of the sources are in English, and a weighty por-
tion of them is partisan. Divergent perspectives are occasionally mentioned only to be neutralized.

More clarity and conceptual precision in defining the
subject would have strengthened the book's argument.
Is it religious reform that helps us understand the crusades, or does crusading spirituality help us understand
religious reform? If this book on "crusading spirituality" is "specifically focused on the ideology of crusading" (p. 7), what is the distinction between the concepts
of spirituality and ideology, neither of which is clearly
defined? In what sense can "ideology" be used for the
study of early crusading? Purkis also merges the question of spirituality as "the point where faith and action
intersect" with the issue of the crusaders' motivation (p.
8). This raises methodological questions. If crusading
spirituality is about how the faith is lived, can we approach that experience through the study of sources
telling us how "those who organised, promoted or subsequently wrote narrative accounts of the campaigns"
(p. 10)—rather than those who took part in them—associated a specific spirituality with crusading?

Purkis convincingly demonstrates that crusaders
were pious and that their piety was Christo-mimetic.
But what did crusading imitation of Christ make of
Christ? To more fully understand the nature of crusading religion, it is not enough to know how crusaders
translated their faith into action. We also need to understand how that action affected the lives of others. Of
this Purkis says nothing. War is hardly ever mentioned
in this book. Christo-mimesis is posited as a research
alternative to "meritorious warfare" (p. 4) and is, as
individual religious experience, abstracted from the
devastating violence it carried to the "unfaithful."

Purkis contributes to understanding crusaders on
their own terms. That is laudable, as long as the historian reflects on how his efforts to understand crusaders in their own context is informed by contemporary
intellectual and political contexts and how it shapes the
terms on which we understand the crusades. If what we
get is no more than identification with crusaders, then
this outcome is contentious on both scholarly and political grounds. Uncritical use of crusaders' language to
describe their actions is anachronism in reverse. The
merit of writing today of crusaders' "liberation of
Jerusalem" and "custody of the Holy Land" without any
qualifications consists in posing the question of the politics of crusades research itself.

TOMAZ MASTNAK
*Scientific Research Centre of the Slovene Academy of
Sciences and Arts*

ROBERT W. SHAFFERN. *The Penitents' Treasury: Indulgences in Latin Christendom, 1175–1375.* Scranton: Uni-

versity of Scranton Press. 2007. Pp. x, 240. Cloth $40.00,
paper $25.00.

Robert W. Shaffern's book offers a most useful modern
history of the indulgence in the High Middle Ages. Several important articles have been published on this matter (some authored by Shaffern), but an updated, book-
length study has been lacking in English.

The volume begins with a historiographical chapter
that argues that "the confessional, polemical historiographies of the Reformation and Counter-Reformation
still influence today's points of view" (p. 5) and moves
on to give an excellent overview of those lines of
thought before addressing the significant and innovative contributions of Nikolaus Paulus and Bernhard
Poschmann in the first half of the twentieth century.
Shaffern then turns to the origins of the indulgence.
Chapter two ("The Emergence and Variety of Indulgences") confirms that the first pardons were granted in
the eleventh century, as some historians long have argued, and places them within the context of eleventh-
century reforms. It also discusses their precursors in the
penitential regime from the early medieval church onward, including the use of absolutions and redemptions
in the Carolingian and Ottonian churches; the book
thus takes a longer view of its subject matter than implied by its title.

The next chapter is entitled "The Treasury of Merit"
and analyzes the idea of this inexhaustible fund of merit
generated by Christ, the Virgin Mary, and the saints.
Shaffern follows its development to its formulation in
Pope Clement VI's bull *Unigenitus* (1343), emphasizing
that the bull did not represent new papal ideas about
the doctrine of indulgence but rather served as "the endorsement of two centuries of learned theological and
canonistic speculation concerning indulgences" (p.
105). Drawing on a wealth of material, Shaffern discusses the origins of the idea of a treasury of merit and
contests the traditional "top-down" approach that suggests that it was authored by intellectuals. He argues
that the metaphor and imagery came from the Bible
and were transmitted through liturgy, homilies, and religious drama.

Much of the volume focuses on the ideas of theologians and canonists, but chapter four ("Indulgences, the
Saints, and Devotionalism at the End of the High Middle Ages") explores how indulgences were perceived
more generally in the medieval religious imagination
and uses a variety of sources, including saints' lives, to
disprove the nineteenth-century idea that indulgences
and the idea of Purgatory created a "piety of fear" or
"piety of terror." Further explorations of the laity's perception and reception of indulgences and of the preaching and transmission of these spiritual rewards would
have been most interesting, but are outside the scope
of this short book.

Returning to the intellectual elite, the last two chapters of the volume discuss some of the numerous disputes surrounding indulgences at the end of the High
Middle Ages. Chapter five ("Controversy and Indul-

gences Prior to the Great Western Schism I") centres on two forms of pardons that were much debated among fourteenth-century theologians and canonists, namely, indulgences for the dead and pardons from penalty and guilt (*a pena et a culpa*). Chapter six ("Controversy and Indulgences Prior to the Great Western Schism II") analyzes the short treatise *De quantitate indulgenciarum* by the Dominican John of Dambach (1288–1372), which was written to defend his southern German brothers who had been accused of illegally preaching indulgences, accusations that most likely were an element in the conflict between the Dominicans and their enemies within the German church.

In his conclusion ("*Unde indulgentiae?*") Shaffern sums up his position, stressing that "the traditional interpretation, which depicted pardons as spiritually stultifying, ought now to be laid at rest. To be sure, indulgences rarely encouraged great conversion experiences; at the same time, neither did they generally reduce the Christian religion to a sterile series of robotically performed works" (p. 214). He also states that "the fervor of the laity generated most indulgences" as the majority were issued in response to "petitions from devout laity requesting that a bishop or pope grant a desired remission" (p. 211); he thereby joins the many scholars who convincingly argue that the high medieval church and certainly its head, the papacy, was reactive rather than proactive in many of their dealings with the laity and that an exchange of religious ideas and forms of expression between the papacy and the laity provided the impetus for many of the church's actions and policies.

The volume provides an insightful, stimulating, and well-written account of the development of the indulgence in the High Middle Ages and will undoubtedly be well received by scholars and teachers of medieval history who have been wanting an introduction to this important religious practice.

IBEN FONNESBERG-SCHMIDT
Aalborg University

J. S. BOTHWELL. *Falling from Grace: Reversal of Fortune and the English Nobility, 1075–1455*. New York: Manchester University Press. 2008. Pp. xv, 269. £60.00.

On the face of it, the power and position of the medieval English nobility appears strong. Indeed, it was sometimes great enough to undermine royal authority. Yet at base the nobility relied on royal favor. If that favor was lost then nobility itself might be lost. This imaginative study by J. S. Bothwell considers this topic over four centuries, from the revolt of earls against William the Conqueror in 1075 to the beginning of the Wars of the Roses in 1455. The approach is thematic rather than chronological, considering comparatively across time the various stages of royal disfavor. First there are the circumstances under which the nobility might fall foul of the crown and the general context within which this operated. Here a change is seen over the centuries as arbitrary royal will largely gave way to trial by battle, trial by other legal procedures, and subsequently to trial

by peers in a parliamentary context. The importance of the 1352 Statute of Treasons is well emphasized. It is a pity that the author chose not to consider the full exploitation of attainder from the mid-fifteenth century onward. While it is true that others have studied this topic, the book would have been even more useful had it included it.

Bothwell emphasizes that, even with the development of legal procedures, royal arbitrariness was never completely lacking. This theme recurs later in the book when he shows that favor might be restored almost as quickly as it was lost, and that there were relatively few noble lines that were subject to permanent perdition. The various forms of control and punishment are then considered, including excessive mutilation as part of execution. Other ways in which the crown could damage nobles who fell from their grace, such as forfeiture, banishment, and exile, are also discussed, with an appropriate attention to the problems faced by wives and families "left behind." The conclusion presents a dichotomy: despite increased opportunities in the fourteenth and fifteenth centuries for "semi-rational if increasingly regulated political debate" in parliament, the crown turned to greater violence against its noble opponents. Bothwell's explanation is that the development of formal parliamentary contexts removed the possibility of other opportunities for rational debate; if parliament "failed to offer a way to resolve issues between rulers and ruled ... a more angry, violent and bloody form of dialogue developed." This arguably overlooks the ways in which kings used parliament as a means of confirming their actions against their enemies, such as in 1397 and 1399. Again it is a pity that the Wars of the Roses were not included in the study.

That said, the book is already impressive as a wide-ranging and multifaceted study of a topic that has never before been studied comparatively. Bothwell has definitely filled a gap in crown-noble relations, and his book should be essential reading for anyone interested in either or both parties. It is not always an easy read, however. Paragraphs are often long and dense and lacking signposts. The book teems with examples but inevitably the same ones crop up under different themes, and sometimes there is inconsistency, for instance in the names used for the magnates (always a problem when dealing with changing titles in the reigns of Richard II and Henry IV). Referencing also raises an interesting question. Quite often the *Oxford Dictionary of National Biography* is quoted as the source of information. That work is a tremendous achievement but is not footnoted. Therefore the reader of this book, wanting to follow up a particular incident, would not be able to know in which contemporary sources to look. It is also difficult to know how many examples of a particular phenomenon one would need to indicate or prove a trend. At base too it is difficult to assess the impact of personalities on crown-noble relations. But Bothwell has succeeded in producing an imaginative and fascinating study nonetheless, which also has a pleasing in terdisciplinary feel to it through its invocation of literary and artistic sources.

ANNE CURRY
University of Southampton

DEREK G. NEAL. *The Masculine Self in Late Medieval England.* Chicago: University of Chicago Press. 2008. Pp. xiii, 303. Cloth $68.00, paper $25.00.

This is a very clever book. In it, Derek G. Neal tries to tease out varied meanings of masculinity from a combination especially of legal and literary sources between 1350 (the Black Death) and 1530 (the Reformation in England) to examine men from head to toe (an idea that the cover of his book nicely recapitulates). He rejects the "crisis of masculinity" model as too trite— masculinity always seems to be in crisis, he notes—in favor of a model of "double discourse" that he takes from George Devereux, examining external and internal influences on masculine identity or the social and psychological self (p. 6).

Neal's chapters offer varied approaches to this subject. Chapter one describes the spectrum of masculinity between the man who is "true, open, straightforward" and he who is "false, hidden, tricky," seeing these as the fundamentals of men's reputation (p. 47). Chapter two introduces the notion of "husbandry": the male management of the self, of the household, and of public relationships. Chapter three examines the male body and the myriad connections between physicality, sexed bodies, desire, and gender. Chapter four turns to fictional romances as openings into men's minds.

Neal is an elegant and witty writer, and his book is thoroughly entertaining. "Late medieval England was laced through . . . with regulatory forces," he writes, and then adds: "laced, rather than walled; with sufficient agility one could slip through the web for quite some time, but one would probably trip up before long" (p. 24). In the Chancery records he finds that "legal formality cushions endless self-interested whining" (p. 165), and medieval romance is "the nuttiest genre" of the age (p. 187).

Neal clearly wants to set himself apart as a scholar as well as a writer. He refers to other scholars to criticize as readily as to praise. He wants to frame his topic in new ways, with words like "husbandry" for proper masculine behavior and "substance" for what they strove for, meaning not only wealth and property but also status and reputation (pp. 58–59). He is willing to show how he wrestles with his sources. He wants to push the field in new directions. Particularly interesting is his rejection of the notion that the male clergy presented a sort of "third sex" or intermediate gender identity; they were men "whether they liked it or not," he concludes (p. 122).

That cleverness sometimes gets in the way. Neal never explains how he selected the sources he uses, mainly court cases of the diocesan consistories and the court of Chancery, except to say that they are "plentiful and detailed" and reveal the interplay between interior and exterior man "more consistently than others" (p. 28). His bibliography references Canterbury, Exeter, London, Taunton, and York; were these all that survived from the period or are they samples of a larger whole? The cases he describes, likewise, are not representative of what he found but "the more interesting" of them (p. 30). He often neglects to summarize stories in his eagerness to get to his interpretation; a reader of this book might be expected to know Geoffrey Chaucer, but the absence of overviews of Partenope of Blois, Bevis of Hampton, and other more obscure literary tales, not to mention some of his legal cases, is regrettable.

More troubling is Neal's use of Freudian theory in the book's last chapter. He argues that one cannot understand medieval men without studying their psychic as well as their social selves. For Neal, that way is through psychoanalytic theory, since it provides the best language for talking about interiority. It is not anachronistic, he argues, since advances in neuroscience have increasingly demonstrated the relationship between thought patterns and the structures of the brain (p. 184; medievalists may recognize here the influence of his dissertation adviser, Nancy Partner). Neal provides a detailed analysis of psychic conflict with mother and father figures in late medieval English romances; he is not afraid to refer to oedipal complexes, castration anxiety, narcissism, dream theory, and other ideas that he draws from Sigmund Freud, Nancy Chodorow, or medievalist literary scholars. Yet the Middle Ages had a language for talking about interiority, that of religion, although Neal seems uninterested in what that language had to say and dismisses it as "a question for another book" (p. 247). How well these legends reflect the masculine mind is another open question; we know so little about their authorship and some are, as Neal admits, neither English nor late medieval in their origins.

Neal is surely clever enough to realize the gauntlet that his argument throws before historians and to anticipate the reaction of scholars to it. I think I would have liked the book more without that final chapter; the legal cases and Neal's interpretation of them were interesting and insightful enough. Despite my reservations, therefore, I look forward to see what he offers us next.

MATHEW KUEFLER
San Diego State University

JOHN VAN ENGEN. *Sisters and Brothers of the Common Life: The Devotio Moderna and the World of the Latter Middle Ages.* (The Middle Ages Series.) Philadelphia: University of Pennsylvania Press. 2008. Pp. ix, 433. $59.95.

John Van Engen has written a book that provides a welcome reappraisal of *Devotio Moderna*, a movement on the border between medieval and modern forms of Christian life and thought. Almost a century ago Albert Hyma claimed that the Modern Devout characterized a "Christian humanism" that was unique and "a turning point . . . in European history" (p. 3). He was later attacked by R. R. Post, who dismissed the Devotion as basically monastic and thus not innovative. Van Engen's goal is to consider the Modern Devout in a fresh manner, "to have that story bring into focus not the early modern future but the late medieval present" (p. 5), even though he does allow himself to incorporate Benjamin Franklin and George Eliot among the successors of the movement.

The strength of this book lies in its careful, thoughtful, and insightful reading and rereading of primary sources, many of them not previously published. What could turn into an arid historiographical debate remains close to the lived experience of generations of men and women who for one reason or another did not enter formalized religious or monastic environments but found the companionship and inspiration of societies based on friendship. Traditional monastics and religious were often deeply suspicious of these self-made men and women in the urban environments of what we call the Low Countries. But thanks to sympathetic bishops and brilliant theologians such as Jean Gerson, the Modern Devout avoided being stamped as heretical.

To understand these remarkable people, Van Engen begins with their own self-understanding in terms of the process of conversion, the turning of the mind and body towards a new life, inspired by the Gospel: "The Modern-Day Devout were self-conscious converts" (p. 19). In this first chapter and the next we meet the figure of Geert Grote of Deventer, whom Van Engen locates in the urban landscape of the area and who in 1374 gave over his home to "poor women to serve God" (p. 61). The Devout had to cope with "Suspicion and Inquisition" (chapter three) but managed to survive all challenges at a time when other groups such as the Lollards were succumbing to charges of heresy.

The varieties of life covered by the term Modern-Day Devout are reviewed in chapter four: "From Converts to Communities: Tertiaries, Sisters, Brothers, Schoolboys, Canons." Because of pressure from their enemies, many of the Devout accepted the status of Third Order Franciscans and became tertiaries. Van Engen's careful review of the different categories of the Devout is not only useful: he shows the creativity with which groups of men and women met the challenge of a church that was in the midst of crisis, with papal schism and a search for genuine religious experience. Van Engen uses the documents of the Devout themselves to show how they fitted into their urban environments, respected parish life, and yet followed their own way.

The details of this life are found in chapter five: "Inventing a Communal Household: Goods, Customs, Labor, and 'Republican' Harmony." The inspiration came from biblical accounts of the early Christians, and so everything was to be held in common. At the same time, however, the Devout did not take vows and thus distinguished their way of life from that of monastics. They chose to make societies and not corporations, and so they sought what one participant called an "amicable society or companionate friendship" (p. 199).

To live together according to friendship had been the dream of reformed monks of the twelfth century, but they soon developed into an order based on legal structures. The Devout managed to maintain their original inspiration, in spite of challenges from inquisitors. Key members of the Council of Constance defended them (chapter six), and in the remainder of the fifteenth century the writers of the movement explicated their way of life and spirituality (chapters seven and eight).

Van Engen captures the simultaneous complexity and simplicity of the Modern Devout and shows how so influential a tract as the *Imitation of Christ* could have come from this environment. This book is more than a history of the *Devotio Moderna*. It is a presentation of the "long fifteenth century" in Europe as a bond between medieval and modern forms of life. Here we find Gerson, Francis Petrarch, Desiderius Erasmus, Martin Luther, and John Calvin, all seen in their indebtedness and reaction to the Modern Devout.

The book cannot decide on whether or not to downsize the "Middle Ages." In some places the term is capitalized (as I think it should be) and in some places not (p. 120). Sometimes proofreading is lacking (p. 190, "Men wold"; p. 235, "oddly defensiveness way").

This is a grand and important book not only for those bitten by medieval studies but for all interested in Western civilization's transition from medieval to modern.

BRIAN PATRICK MCGUIRE
Roskilde University

DEBRA BLUMENTHAL. *Enemies and Familiars: Slavery and Mastery in Fifteenth-Century Valencia.* (Conjunctions of Religion and Power in the Medieval Past.) Ithaca: Cornell University Press. 2009. Pp. xii, 306. $42.00.

The historiography of slavery has made much of the distinction between the so-called Mediterranean model as opposed to the Atlantic model of ownership and exploitation of slaves. The former held sway during ancient and medieval times, while Atlantic slavery emerged as a central feature of the expansion of European influence in Africa and the Americas beginning in the fifteenth century. The characteristics associated with the earlier regime were its smaller scale, its urban as opposed to rural location, the commitment of slave labor to largely domestic settings, and above all the relative absence of racial justifications for enslavement. In comparison with the horrors of the transatlantic system, most historians have regarded its predecessor as relatively benign. Debra Blumenthal's aim is not so much to challenge this opposition—if anything, she returns a mixed verdict on the Mediterranean experience—as to shift the focus of its study in a different direction. To that end she offers a highly detailed reconstruction of slave experience at a crucial time and place: fifteenth-century Valencia, a prosperous maritime center that was beginning to register the effects of ever deeper Iberian penetration into the Atlantic.

This clearly organized and well-written book opens

with a close look at how persons became enslaved. Late medieval Valencia obtained slaves in three ways. The leading source was the most traditional one: Muslims from Granada or northern Africa captured via wars and piracy. Enslavement could also result from court orders mandating penal servitude, which was reserved for *mudejars*, or local Muslims living under Christian rule. The final source was international commerce. Formerly centered on the eastern Mediterranean, it was now shifting westward, above all toward sub-Saharan Africa and the Canary Islands. After discussing how slaves were procured, Blumenthal then examines how sales were made, and highlights the role of brokers in running a highly informal and decentralized market whose transactions became public only at the final stage when contracts were signed and taxes paid.

The bulk of the book is devoted to the social and economic dimensions of slave life: the sorts of work slaves engaged in, their activities and roles within their masters' households—including the sexual exploitation of women—and the limited but very real means by which slaves could hope to obtain and retain their freedom. The overall picture that emerges is a predictably mixed bag. But between the extremes of cruelty and degradation on the one hand and virtual absorption into the owner's family on the other, one gets a general impression of substantial integration by slaves into Valencian society. While relegated to mostly menial and unskilled tasks, slaves worked alongside free laborers. What is more, an impressive number appear to have been able to accumulate enough wealth to purchase their freedom. Generally positive expectations in regard to manumission, which was widely seen as a fitting reward for long-term loyalty, also seem to have alleviated some of the burden of servitude.

Blumenthal sustains her argument through extensive references to local documentation. That she has carefully trolled through a huge mass of paper is made clear by the generous excerpts from original records in Catalan and Latin that grace her footnotes. Pride of place belongs to two bodies of sources: notarial documents and the registers of municipal and especially royal officials. Prominent among the latter was the *Batlle* or bailiff who certified owners' claims of servile status through public examination of individual slaves. While often perfunctory, the "confessions" these interrogations elicited provide personal information on some 1200 slaves from the fifteenth century. Combining this with depositions from litigation in royal courts and the abundant data on family life and other domestic matters in the notarial records, Blumenthal provides a singularly vivid reconstruction of the rhythms of everyday life at the lower levels of a late medieval city. At the same time she enriches this tight focus on Valencia by keeping a sharp eye open for comparisons with the experience of slaves elsewhere. These range from nearby Catalonia and Castile—the author is clearly familiar with the numerous local and regional studies of slavery in the Iberian Peninsula—to the rest of the Mediterranean, especially southern Italy, and even to the an-

tebellum American South. Not surprisingly, this work shows strong awareness of the major themes of the historiography of slavery in these other latitudes. It is particularly sensitive to the crucial issue of agency and initiative on the part of the slaves themselves who, thanks to the author's skillful use of Valencia's documentary riches, often emerge from the mass to appear as strikingly distinctive personalities. The result is an innovative reconstruction of a significant underside of urban life that usually languishes far beyond historical reach.

JAMES S. AMELANG
Universidad Autónoma, Madrid

EUROPE: EARLY MODERN AND MODERN

JOHN M. HEADLEY. *The Europeanization of the World: On the Origins of Human Rights and Democracy.* Princeton: Princeton University Press. 2008. Pp. xvi, 290. $29.95.

The argument underlying this book is that the European Renaissance was the primary source of the movement toward the creation of a universalistic culture within Europe, and that they ultimately prepared the ground for globalization. John M. Headley, a Renaissance scholar, is aware of the contemporary implications of his claims, and while seeking to avoid polemical and triumphalist claims about the rise of the West, he offers a cautious historical argument on topics that are much discussed in contemporary social and political thought. He draws attention to two distinctive features of European civilization as it emerged in the Renaissance period: the idea of a common humanity that reveals itself in human rights, and the tenability of political dissent that expresses itself in constitutional democracy. The book is organized into three chapters. The first chapter discusses the general context of the Renaissance, setting the terms for the emergence of these two features which are then respectively explored in the following two chapters.

A major dimension of the Renaissance was not only the recovery of classical antiquity but also a fundamental shift in spatial perspective, which was reflected in the exploration of new worlds. Headley is struck by the fact that the earth's habitability has never been subject to much consideration in Renaissance studies. His claim is that the significant factor for the Renaissance was the recognition of the habitality of the new lands that European explorers encountered and that increasingly became more accessible. This was a challenge to the Christian myth of a common human descent and the denial of an inaccessible yet habitable antipodes. The problem of the accessibility of a habitable world beyond the seas required a redefinition of the Christian ecumene in order to affirm the universal redemption of the human race. Headley's examination of the ramifications of this for Renaissance Europe is fascinating. The complex entwinement of cartography, theology, racism, and the history of exploration in the sixteenth century was a ground in which the medieval notions of universal empire and a universal church gradually underwent transformation. The second chapter extends the discussion to the early modern period (1500–1800), where the shift from the religious to the secular occurred more decisively than in the Renaissance. Headley puts forward the bold argument that at the core of Western European civilization is a universalizing principle directed toward the construction of a common humanity. While this universalizing thrust was religious in its inception, it took shape through a process of detachment from religion. Here the story is how in the movement from the Renaissance to Enlightenment cultural, moral, and political ideas came to replace religious ways of imagining the world. This is what Headley calls "the Europeanization of the world," namely the formation of a mind that postulated a common humanity as a goal to be achieved.

Against those who would reduce the universalistic impulse to colonialism and racism, this book offers an interpretation of the European heritage that, while not denying or downplaying the history of violence that was a feature of European history, emphasizes how this universalizing culture provided modernity with two important resources: a political one, based on the recognition of human equality, rationality, dignity, and rights, and an intellectual one, based on respect for scientific and intellectual inquiry. Headley argues that the first of these represents the most attractive feature of the western universalizing principle. Much of the second chapter is devoted to the history of natural rights in the early modern period. Chapter three moves on to look at the emergence of politically constituted dissent in modern Europe. Here the story moves into the domain of political thought, territory that will be more familiar to the political theorist. The key argument advanced in this chapter is that Europe developed a culture of self criticism whose roots lie in Plato's dialogues, medieval Scholasticism, Thomas More's humanism, and philosophical skepticism, out of which came a propensity for toleration and an orientation towards dissent. But dissent was not only something to be tolerated; it was also positively recognized. The challenge, as it was first formulated in the early modern period during the wars of religion, is how to make possible the coexistence of dissenting groups.

There is much in this book for Renaissance scholars, historical sociologists, and students of contemporary history. For the present reviewer, a historically oriented sociologist, the book is an important contribution to understanding the European heritage. The analysis of the Renaissance quest toward universality is undoubtedly the major strength of the book. The later sections are less original but serve the purpose of developing the early arguments around a fuller interpretation of modern European self-understanding. Headley's book can be situated in the context of other works on European civilization that stress the uniqueness of the West. His claim is that the principle of a common humanity based on the quest for freedom and dissent is a direct challenge to postcolonial interpretations of the European heritage and to those that reduce that heritage to one that culminated in the death camps of the Nazis.

GERARD DELANTY
University of Sussex

MONICA H. GREEN. *Making Women's Medicine Masculine: The Rise of Male Authority in Pre-Modern Gynaecology.* New York: Oxford University Press. 2008. Pp. xx, 409. $120.00.

Monica H. Green recognizes the yearning for a usable past, but this book offers neither golden age nor renaissance. Empirically exigent and analytically rigorous, it accounts for increasing male control of "women's medicine" from the twelfth to the seventeenth century not by universities, licensing, humanism, guilds, or forceps but by multiple limitations on women's participation in authoritative knowledge.

For Green, authority is not simply a patriarchal tautology; it is the product of women's relationship to written works on medicine. She deploys old-fashioned philology with great skill, but the work's strength lies in its treatment of texts as objects of material culture that are produced, compiled, revised, owned, and exchanged, and are thus artifacts of social relations and processes. Seen in this light, the issue of women's medical literacy is not whether an individual woman might be able to read (or have read to her) a particular Latin or vernacular work, but whether any group of women constituted a textual community that could create, communicate, and sustain a tradition of medical knowledge. Texts are sites of content and social collaboration over space and time. Thus, although Green enumerates the ways women continued to practice without books and integrates many examples, she does not treat systematically their work or orally transmitted experience. Scrutiny of hundreds of manuscripts on women's health and reproduction, as well as inventories of convent libraries and individual women's possessions, establishes that female ownership of medical works was extremely rare throughout the period, as were texts that purported to address female audiences. One reason, Green argues, is that after late antiquity midwifery, the most plausible social identity around which a textual community might form, had ceased to be a distinct occupation.

To illuminate women's marginalization, the book follows a group of Latin texts dealing with gynecology, obstetrics, infant care, cosmetics, and hygiene that originated in twelfth-century Salerno and are sometimes attributed to, and sometimes entitled, "Trotula." (Green has edited and translated these: *The "Trotula": A Medieval Compendium of Women's Medicine* [2001]). In spite of evidence that one treatise reflects women's knowledge and addresses a female audience and in spite of the existence of a woman author, Trota, whose practical treatments it incorporated, the ensemble became part of a tradition of women's medicine presided over by men. Already in the twelfth century a trend among male authors to embed diagnosis and treatment within a theoretical framework diminished the acknowledgment of practical instruction that characterized work like Trota's. As the *Trotula* texts traveled through medical and clerical circles in the thirteenth and fourteenth centuries, they shed most of their few signs of female influence or audience. The areas that were to become gynecology and obstetrics attracted scant attention in general works of medicine or surgery, but well before the Black Death physicians took up the subject of generation and staked a claim to the treatment of infertility. Indeed, there is evidence that male practitioners increasingly treated female patients, even for conditions affecting parts of the body sequestered by women's modesty and their male relatives' honor.

Green's analysis of the migration and management of shame is one of the most original and elegant aspects of the book. She shows that the literature and practices of male physicians and surgeons gradually shifted the boundaries of taboo, so that their speech, gaze, and touch came to be regarded as respectable and expert. Nevertheless, they often depended on women assistants, giving rise to a paradox: while women's practical knowledge was being denigrated, it was a necessary instrument of men's expanded professional range. At the same time, the dynamic of shame manifested itself in new ways, for example in the association of the *Trotula* texts with a mainly misogynist literature on "women's secrets." Katharine Park has documented the role of these mysteries in the history of anatomy (*Secrets of Women: Gender, Generation, and the Origins of Human Dissection* [2006]); Green's interest is in the ways shame seeped from bodies to texts and morphed into slander, as reading about women's "nature" extended beyond circles of practitioners. The issue of readers' (even boys') illicit uses of such texts became acute with their translation into vernaculars and the rise of literacy in the late Middle Ages. Green detects signs of women's resistance to the presumably prurient abuse of the *Trotula* and other works, and copies of the vernacular books can seldom be linked to women.

Rather it is in connection with new, more specialized works detached from the *Trotula* tradition that midwives, again a profession from the fifteenth century, emerge as an audience. Male professionals' long involvement in reproductive matters led to them to articulate a separate field of gynecology (enhanced by newly discovered Hippocratic works) with women cast as assistants. It likewise gave rise in the sixteenth century to a distinct obstetrical literature, sometimes addressed to midwives and, in the seventeenth century, even produced by them. But by that time, Green argues, the gates were closed: much of the authority women might have claimed was squarely in the possession of men. The new books assumed deference to male professionals and defined midwives' duties narrowly. Thus they represent no triumph of women's medicine. Indeed, only within the non-professional space of recipe collections in household books does Green see a manifestation of women's medical literacy and authority in the early modern period.

Magisterial in scope—chronological, geographical, linguistic, and thematic—this book is a monument not to the mythical medical expert "Trotula" but to mature feminist scholarship. Her scrupulous conclusions permit Green to render this history useful as a way of thinking about health in terms of human rights and about the consequences of structures that exclude populations from the production and control of knowledge about their own health care.

JOAN CADDEN
University of California,
Davis

MARK S. MICALE. *Hysterical Men: The Hidden History of Male Nervous Illness.* Cambridge: Harvard University Press. 2008. Pp. xiv, 366. $29.95.

This hidden history is a story about how, since the Enlightenment, the men of Western medical science contrived to ignore masculine psychological subjectivity. Playing on the title of Elaine Showalter's *The Female Malady: Women, Madness, and English Culture, 1830–1980* (1985), it is a study that confronts a "male malady," that is, a "chronic inability to reflect nonheroically, without evasion and self-deception, on oneself individually and collectively" (p. 282).

After briefly sketching a history of hysteria down through the seventeenth century, Mark S. Micale's story begins by reconstructing eighteenth-century nervous culture in Georgian England. He describes this age of sentiments and autobiography as an oasis of egalitarian diagnosis, sandwiched between older demonic and uterine beliefs, and later Victorian forms of moral profligacy and constitutional degeneracy. He then proceeds to explain how this inclusive Georgian culture fragmented, succumbing to a "great Victorian eclipse" and a "wave of amnesia" (p. 49) that descended over European medicine from 1790 to 1860. Micale interprets this as a vehement and successful neo-Hippocratic backlash against the egalitarian message of the Enlightenment and the French Revolution. As uterine doctrines reasserted themselves, this backlash resulted in the "feminization, sexualization, pathologization, and moralization" (p. 60) of the discourse on hysteria. Micale finds this eclipse of male hysteria in scientific discourse, but not in literary romanticism. In his narrative, the post-1790 fragmentation of the Georgian "synthesis" produced two cultures of hysteria, a scientific and an artistic one, each going their separate ways. Whereas medical science "embraced an exclusionary objectivist ideology, banned women from its professional ranks, and cultivated a new professional persona that was rigorously masculinist," European literary discourses of hysteria remained "open, creative, and exploratory" (p. 114).

If Western medicine had more or less closed down its discourse on male hysteria in the first half of the nineteenth century, then it was largely Jean-Martin Charcot, Pierre Janet, and Sigmund Freud who struggled to reopen it in the 1880s. They did so, according to Micale, by effectively reducing hysteria to neurology, draining it of affective content and thereby desexualizing and demoralizing the discourse. Micale reads this not as a new strategy of social control, but rather a calculated response to older, moralistic interpretations of hysteria. Precisely because Charcot's model of hysteria was so narrowly neurological, it became possible to apply it to men and thereby implicitly challenge the conventional gender roles of the time. Hence, although scientific discourse was decidedly more diverse and ambiguous during this putatively "golden age" of hysteria, efforts to suppress male hysteria continued. Medical practitioners often ignored Charcot's work, misattributed male hysteria to foreigners, or simply circumvented it terminologically.

In his chapter on "Freud and the Origins of Psychoanalysis," Micale marshals considerable evidence to demonstrate that Charcot "impregnated" (p. 233) Freud with the idea of male hysteria. Freud recast Charcot's work in a gender-neutral theory of neurosis and, to a remarkable degree, bridged the gap separating scientific and literary genres. But even Freud—himself struggling with the symptoms of nervousness—suppressed male hysteria in his published work and ultimately never escaped the "historical 'prison of gender'" (p. 275). In Micale's view, it would take the multiple traumas of the twentieth century to make the repressed and hidden history of male hysteria tellable. The rise of psychoanalysis, the undeniable evidence of male emotional collapse in two world wars, and social liberation movements have all helped overcome the "obstacles to masculine self-understanding" (p. 284). The male malady, it would seem, is on the mend.

Most of the problems in Micale's account derive from a narrative that is overinvested in an Enlightenment discourse and haunted by the specter of the "Great Victorian eclipse." And yet, there is plenty that remains eclipsed in Micale's own account. For example, there is nothing on the significance of Mesmerism and virtually no credence given to the important influence of spiritualism. Arguably, these movements played a decisive role in the very literary Romanticism—to say nothing of theories of the unconscious—that are so crucial to his story. It seems as though Micale's laudable attention to gender dichotomies has led him to overlook the crucial role of religion in mid-nineteenth-century Victorian discourse. If indeed there were two cultures of hysteria in Victorian society, the discourse on masculine nervousness stood—as Janet Oppenheim clearly saw—in a far more ambiguously symbiotic relationship to religion than Micale assumes.

The Achilles' heel of Micale's account is likely to be found in his portrayal of Western medical science as a kind of bogeyman threatening enlightened gender relations. If the "exclusionary methodology of positivist science" and its male practitioners' "acts of omission and commission" (p. 279) were in fact so pervasive, then it becomes difficult to imagine why, at the height of scientific prowess in the late nineteenth century, discussions of male hysteria were growing in "diversity and ambiguity" (p. 177). Micale positions Otto Weininger as a pivotal figure who supposedly captured these internal contradictions of biomedical discourse. But Weininger was not so much a representative *of* scientific discourse as he was an example of how rapidly and brazenly ideas were exchanged *between* scientific and literary genres. Micale's juxtaposition of an enlightened literary discourse on male hysteria and a benighted positivistic one has difficulty capturing the intensity of such exchanges.

Nevertheless, this is a major contribution to the history of hysteria. It is a highly readable synthesis that not only incorporates larger political and cultural developments but also delivers an innovative re-interpretation of the early development of Freudian psychoanalysis.

Eric J. Engstrom
*Humboldt University,
Berlin*

Hannu Salmi. *Nineteenth-Century Europe: A Cultural History*. Cambridge: Polity. 2008. Pp. vii, 192. $24.95.

"The nineteenth century cannot be forced into a brief overview, the particulars of which would be valid from the era of the Napoleonic Wars to the decadent atmosphere of the *fin de siècle*," writes Hannu Salmi in the introduction to what is, in fact, a brief overview of nineteenth-century European cultural history, originally published in Finnish. Well aware of the dangers of generalizing about one hundred years of historical development in twenty-odd states (some of which, like Greece, actually did not exist in 1800, others of which, like Hanover, did not survive the century), Salmi chose instead to write an impressionist treatment, one that portrays the period largely through the experience of those who lived it. Drawing especially on literary reflections, Salmi, a Finnish cultural historian who has written extensively on Wagnerism and (strange combination, perhaps) the history of kissing, attempts to give readers the flavor of nineteenth-century cultural experience without claiming any sort of exhaustive coverage. He succeeds, in fact, in his mission to present a rich nineteenth century without the "isms" and not reducible to its great socioeconomic structural changes (p. 1). The question is, however, if this impressionistic version will satisfy those seeking a reliable as well as an engaging new way of presenting this world of unparalleled cultural richness and diversity to their students.

Salmi does not work chronologically, per se, though he begins with industrialization and ends with a chapter on the *fin de siècle*. Nationalism is treated in chapter four, already a problem for places like Russian Poland or Greece, or Finland for that matter, where nationalism came before industrialization and subjects like the department store (chapter six) or colonialism (chapter eight) are essentially irrelevant. I would be tempted to put the chapter on mechanical reproduction of texts and images (chapter seven) before the chapter on trains (chapter two), and to devote at least one full chapter to rural life and one to urban working-class culture rather than periodically reminding readers that these lifestyles were very different than the bourgeois Parisian cultural world that remains, here, still the epitome of nineteenth-century culture, despite Salmi's attempts at diversification. I cannot imagine, either, not wanting to divide all this up into smaller temporal units; nowhere in Europe, not even in rural Transylvania or in Eugen Weber's Limousin, was "culture" the same in 1890 as it was in 1810, and of course for elite writers, artists, composers, and scholars, the world was transformed multiple times over this period. Salmi knows this, to be sure, but the effort at generalizing, and at telling the story essentially without the relevant political contexts, ultimately makes Europe's enormous disparities—in wealth and religion, in freedoms and opportunities, in technology and diet, in musical taste and in home furnishings—disappear. It may just be the case that an impressionistic view of nineteenth-century culture inevitably becomes so subjective a set of juxtaposed elements that it resembles James Thurber's famous sketch, made upon finally succeeding in seeing something in his laboratory microscope—a picture that turned out to represent his own eye.

Of course, some eyes *do* see better than others, and Salmi's insights are often instructive. His passages on gender issues and family life are generally well done, and he provides a nice rereading of Rudyard Kipling's poetry. His Finnish examples are interesting, and help to diversify our sample of nineteenth-century voices. But there are also many generalizations made here that specialists will find objectionable, and choices of subject matter or evidence with which one can quibble. No one who knows Lord Byron well will agree that Romanticism was an escapist movement (p. 22). As a person who has taught both works repeatedly, I object to being told that Johann Wolfgang von Goethe's *Faust* (1808) "tell[s] a story of the constant pursuit of material well-being" (p. 31), and that François-René de Chateaubriand's *Atala* (1801) is an example of the merging of classicism and Romanticism (p. 44). Much recent work has combatted the view that the role of religion "had greatly diminished" by mid-century (p. 56); as usual, here, the rise of antisemitism is treated in the German context, but not in Russian, Austro-Hungarian, or French contexts (pp. 125–126). Phrenology is treated in the *fin de siècle* chapter, despite the fact that its founder, Franz Joseph Gall, died in 1828 (p. 129). The section on Richard Wagner, remarkably given Salmi's earlier work, is deeply problematic; the author asserts, for example, that there were pro and anti-Wagner circles in the 1840s, when he was still an almost unknown composer, and that Wagner was "nearly a predecessor to the Nazis" (p. 66), a controversial statement if ever there was one.

Of course one can always quibble with interpretations or generalizations, and suggest better ways to organize chapters or chronologies. But I think the problem here is the deeper one Salmi himself identified: a short history of nineteenth-century European culture, embracing so many nations, classes, genres, and technological and ideological revolutions, simply cannot do the subject justice. Perhaps I simply love the nineteenth century too much to approve of its compression in this way; but perhaps too there are some histories that just should not be so brief.

SUZANNE MARCHAND
*Louisiana State University,
Baton Rouge*

CHRISTOPHE CHARLE. *Théâtres en capitales: Naissance de la société du spectacle à Paris, Berlin, Londres et Vienne 1860–1914*. (Bibliothèque Albin Michel Histoire.) Paris: Albin Michel. 2008. Pp. 572. €29.00.

Christophe Charle's ambitious book promises a study of the "social, political, and cultural dimensions" of the society of spectacle that developed in Europe in the nineteenth century (p. 7), comparing the theatrical centers of Paris, London, Berlin, and Vienna. The links of these four cities with an international European culture made their theaters sites for the importation of plays from other parts of the continent, demonstrating the cultural hierarchies of Europe in the late nineteenth century. They also experienced the processes of liberalization, commercialization, and growth of alternative avant-garde performing companies and playwrights that marked European culture at that time.

To fulfill his promise, Charle describes in turn different aspects of theatrical history in these four cities. The first section of the book is concerned with business and professional aspects of theaters. He begins with the expansion of the number of theaters in each city, their locations, and potential audiences. He then takes up the different kinds of individuals who made these theaters function, beginning with the director who made aesthetic, entrepreneurial, and political decisions, and who took many of the risks involved in putting performances on stage. The recruitment, training, and hardships that made up the profession of actor are then described, along with the parallel experiences of those who wrote for the stage. This first section concludes with an inquiry into the factors that made some of these individuals a success, a goal so ephemeral that it is no surprise that contemporaries often attributed it to "magic, charm, mystery" (p. 203). Charle, for his part, concludes that while a risky market for older, successful plays existed, the public's attraction to diversity and the reformulation of theatrical genres opened the way for moderate innovation. But this moderation limited the attraction of the radical changes associated with avant-garde theater groups and playwrights such as Henrik Ibsen.

The second half of the book takes up more directly the relationship between theatrical performance and its audiences. A first chapter in this section focuses on the audiences in London and Paris. The changing location of theatrical districts, from the East End to the West End in London and from the boulevards to central Paris are described, along with the late-nineteenth-century difficulties of theaters in these cities. He shows the international domination of Paris, which exported plays that had broken free of the aristocratic Old Regime and portrayed a society dominated by a successful but fallible bourgeoisie. He then examines the content of plays more closely, describing not only the changing portrayal of elites, as bourgeois replaced aristocrats, but also the ways women were represented on stage and, at the end of the century, the emergence of characters from the working class. The conflicts between public authorities, who sought to protect their own version of public morality, and the producers and directors of plays that pushed the limits of what was permissible, provide insight into themes such as decadence, treatment of workers, and the various scandals that marked Parisian theater in the late nineteenth and early twentieth centuries. As a conclusion, Charle discusses the rise of modern theater before World War I, including the naturalist and symbolist styles that changed the content and form of plays. He also considers the transition at the same time from this first "Society of Spectacle" to one dominated not by live performance but by the new medium of cinema.

Charle's book is rigorously thorough in describing the social and economic aspects of nineteenth-century theater in these four cities. But he replicates the Parisian dominance of Europe in that period, with Berlin and Vienna especially fading into the background of his account. He provides invaluable information on the social recruitment of directors, actors, and authors, and important insights into the changing audiences of late-nineteenth-century theaters. But the book is strongly influenced by this emphasis on social history, and seems to give only minimal attention to cultural aspects that might help answer some of his questions about the attraction of audiences to particular actors, authors, and plays. Finally, and perhaps most disappointing, is his narrow definition of spectacle. Restricted to stage performances in legitimate theaters, this takes no account of the many other forms of performance that marked European popular culture at this time, such as cafés-concerts, popular festivals, wax museums, or the increasingly democratic and performative politics of late nineteenth-century Europe.

JAMES R. LEHNING
University of Utah

RONALD HUTTON. *Blood and Mistletoe: The History of the Druids in Britain*. New Haven: Yale University Press. 2009. Pp. xv, 491. $45.00.

Some of the peoples whom the ancient Greeks and Romans designated as "Celts" revered a class of priestly intellectuals called "Druids," whom the Romans eventually suppressed, and there are references in medieval Irish and Welsh sources to magicians or prophets whose names (*druí, derwydd*) are evidently derived from the same Celtic term. This much seems beyond reasonable doubt, but it is almost all that can be said about the Druids without venturing onto more or less controversial terrain. Mysterious, remote, and—depending on

one's perspective—either inspiring or sinister, the Druids have attracted conjectures and projections of all kinds ever since their first appearance in the written record.

If that which is known for certain about the Druids is remarkably exiguous, then that which has been thought about them is unquantifiably vast. This is the topic that Ronald Hutton confronts in this engaging, learned, evenhanded, and abundantly rewarding book: "The raw materials for the construction of ancient Druids, so frustrating for a prehistorian or ancient historian, have resulted in a wonderful subject for a student of modernity" (p. 48). At 491 pages, this is a substantial piece of work—although, as Hutton states toward the conclusion, it required extensive pruning at every stage to keep it from being several times longer. It is a tribute to the subject, and to its treatment here, that one is tempted to regret this authorial self-discipline.

After a chapter that sketches the ancient and medieval "raw material," and another devoted to the Renaissance scholars who, rediscovering the Druids in classical texts, pressed them into the service of emerging European nationalisms, Hutton turns his attention to Britain. Ultimately, "this book is about neither archaeology nor Druidry, but about the British, and the way in which they have seen themselves, their island, their species and their world" (p. xv). The result is a masterpiece of cultural history, which sheds manifold light on the centuries-extended interplay of politics, faith, and identity.

As the Druids represented a spiritual tradition which the Greeks and Romans had contrasted with their own, it was easy for Britain's Protestant denominations to find in them an analogy to their own independence from the Roman church. Nor did they stop with analogy: the idea, already put forward in the seventeenth century, that the Druids had inherited the faith of Abraham, was developed into a claim that they had in fact played a crucial part in shaping a distinctive Celtic Christianity, forerunner to the Church of England. Other agendas found very different analogies. As Britain became an empire, claiming the mandate of a civilizing mission, Rome in turn was seen as an increasingly congenial model; while classical justifications of the suppression of the Druids as perpetrators of human sacrifice could evoke associations with all that seemed most reprehensible in accounts of Hindu ritual.

The eighteenth century saw initiatives to reassert the distinctiveness of Welsh language and culture. Inevitably, this movement came to involve the Druids: not only could the Welsh, as speakers of a Celtic language, claim a more direct connection with the ancient Britons than their Anglo-Saxon supplanters, but the only ancient mention of British Druids (by the historian Tacitus) situates them on the Welsh island of Anglesey. Two figures are especially noteworthy in this connection: Edward "Celtic" Davies (1756–1831), who elaborated a reconstruction of Druidic belief based on contemporary theories concerning comparative religion; and Edward Williams alias Iolo Morganwg (1747–1826), a laudanum addict, fiery political radical, and compulsive forger whose multitudinous fabrications included his own vision of a Druidic theology. The inventions of these men were blended and developed by many successors, giving rise both to the ceremonial of the Welsh national arts festival or *eisteddfod*, and to the teachings of the contemporary Druid groups whose tangled evolution Hutton charts in the book's final chapters.

These paragraphs can only hint at the riches to be found in this fascinating and revealing study. Besides the breadth of its coverage, and the insights of which it is so full, one of the book's most striking features is the fairness, indeed the compassion, with which Hutton regards all of its multifarious protagonists. When placing superseded theories in their broader context, or when tracing the tradition of modern Druidism back to roots in self-delusion and imposture, he writes with patience and understanding, and without the facile contempt which is all too frequent in academic accounts of unconventional thinkers. The same fairness is brought to bear on the academics themselves: thus Hutton shows us how the story of British archaeology—in its engagement with the Druids as in other respects—is itself an often murky battleground of rival prejudices, of the clash of classes and personalities.

JOHN CAREY
University College Cork

MEREDITH ANNE SKURA. *Tudor Autobiography: Listening for Inwardness*. Chicago: University of Chicago Press. 2008. Pp. xii, 301. $45.00.

The study of sixteenth-century English autobiography has made great progress. An informal canon has established itself through such focused studies as Elizabeth Heale's *Autobiography and Authorship in Renaissance Verse: Chronicles of the Self* (2003) and *Early Modern English Lives: Autobiography and Self-Representation, 1500–1660*, by Ronald Bedford, Lloyd Davis, and Philippa Kelly (2007). Meredith Anne Skura's new book concentrates even more closely on the sixteenth century. Its choice of core authors is unsurprising: John Skelton, Thomas Wyatt, John Bale, Thomas Whythorne, Thomas Tusser, Isabella Whitney, George Gascoigne, Robert Greene, plus five authors who contributed to *The Mirror for Magistrates* (some of them more plausible instances than others). The discussions of these authors address various issues, too many to report on in full here, but the book's general methodology deserves our attention.

In her introduction Skura clears a wide theoretical space for herself by "adopting a very loose definition of autobiography" (p. 12). Early modern texts have a bewildering habit of mixing fact and fiction, and of playing authorial peek-a-boo games with the reader, and they may even have been written under a false name. For her part, Skura rejects distinctions between "true" and fictional autobiographies as anachronistic (p. 3), but that stance is not consistently maintained. For instance, her declaration in the introduction that "William Baldwin

could praise the poet who 'feyneth well but never lyeth,' whose fiction was not, as it is often said to be today, a lie" (p. 3) seems to have been forgotten by chapter four, where Baldwin figures as a writer "increasingly concerned with separating true 'historia' from the 'invention', 'conjecture', and biased judgment that had made it unreliable like poesie" (p. 77). The author certainly does believe in truths of some kind, for she undertakes to "retrieve all the information I can from what people did say, as well as what they may have revealed inadvertently" (pp. 2–3). In this strategy, wary of the text, all reliability must come from the researcher's ingenuity, as in an interrogation. The book's subtitle evidently refers to this procedure.

The techniques Skura applies include familiar ones, such as formal literary analyses and factual contextualizations: she compares, for instance, Wyatt's versions of his poems with those of Richard Tottell, and interprets various editions of Tusser's *A Hundreth Good Pointes of Husbandry* (1557) in relation to the documented events of his life. Extending her interpretative scope, she analyzes, more programmatically than previous scholars in the field, "what an author is doing as well as what she says," (p. 9); she also ventures psychoanalytical hypotheses, for instance that "on some level Bale sees himself as an abandoned child" (p. 69), that Whythorne fostered unexpressed rage at the women who hurt him (p. 123), and that Greene felt a need for a father substitute (p. 215). With so many different approaches, it may take the reader some time to develop a feeling for what exactly is being argued. While most chapter titles foreground literary analysis of specific texts—particularly of tell-tale adaptations and revisions—and although those chapters include some close reading, it is evidently not Skura's focal concern to find out how authors devised an idiom of the self or of the heart, as Anne Ferry did in *The "Inward" Language: Sonnets of Wyatt, Surrey, Shakespeare, Donne* (1983). Skura's concluding chapter confirms that the real question has been "Autobiographers: Who Were They? Why Did They Write?" (p. 220), an approach showing more affinity with James S. Amelang's *The Flight of Icarus: Artisan Autobiography in Early Modern Europe* (1998).

Skura's conclusion points out features shared by the authors discussed, showing how they worked under similar circumstances, often as "educated, socially mobile servants" in close interaction with their masters (p. 221). The separate chapters, however, though ordered chronologically and discussing literary models and influences in relation to individual authors, stop short of combining these into ongoing autobiographic traditions like Heale's "narratives of experience." By the end of the sixteenth century, Skura concludes, autobiography had become commonplace, and conventions for it were firmly established (p. 198); but the book's division into modular chapters, rather than foreground interrelationships between authors, serves to emphasize their uniqueness and isolation.

General readers will appreciate Skura's book as a series of information-packed (and abundantly but unobtrusively annotated) introductions to individual autobiographers: the book provides what twenty-first-century people are interested to know about other people. Given the reliance on the researcher's detected truths rather than on the authors' professed ones, such readers should be warned against fancying that this book tells them all they need to know: the original texts still remain to be read. It is not, after all, for us to show Tudor autobiographers how to listen for inwardness: it is they who have taught us.

HENK DRAGSTRA
University of Groningen

JAMES MURRAY. *Enforcing the English Reformation in Ireland: Clerical Resistance and Political Conflict in the Diocese of Dublin, 1534–1590.* (Cambridge Studies in Early Modern British History.) New York: Cambridge University Press. 2009. Pp. xvi, 353. $120.00.

James Murray's groundbreaking study was prompted by the scholarly debate concerning the failure of the Protestant Reformation in Ireland that took place during the 1970s. His introduction is especially useful for scholars embarking upon a study of sixteenth-century Ireland, providing a critical review on the formative impact of the Bradshaw-Canny debate on scholarship in this field and reflections on the implications of developments in English Reformation studies for advancing that scholarship in the Irish context. This is not a standard local study of the Reformation in the diocese of Dublin that examines the minutiae of parish or clerical life at grassroots level. Rather, by focusing on the Dublin diocese, the major ecclesiastical unit within the English Pale, this book explores how initiatives pursued by reforming archbishops of Dublin and successive Tudor viceroys to secure the allegiance of the indigenous community to the established church ultimately ended in failure.

Chapter one details the unique character of Dublin diocese vis-à-vis its cultural, structural, and strategic advantages, and a sense of its anticipated openness to embracing the crown's religious policies is effectively conveyed. However, the Englishness of the diocese is shown to have had a pronounced, longstanding, deeply engrained, and inherent religious dimension that was Catholic in a particular sense. Murray presents fascinating insights into the complexities that characterized the *mentalité* of the "faithful Catholics of the English nation" in the Pale on the eve of the Reformation. Their conservativism and local patriotism, their sense of distinctive identity as a close-knit community that upheld particular values and a way of life since *Laudabiliter* (1155), and the privileges invested in their religious corporations and defended by senior corporate clergy are highlighted. Early on, therefore, the reader is alerted to this community's likely resistance to the perceived threat to their ethos and privileges posed by the crown's religious reforms in the 1530s.

In the first of two chapters on Archbishop George Browne's attempts at enforcing religious reform down to 1542, Murray explains how the Kildare Revolt contributed to the emergence of a culture of indigenous clerical resistance in the Dublin diocese just as the Tudor regime prepared to implement its ecclesiastical reforms. Browne's strained relations with the diocese's corporate clerical elite and with the king's deputy, Leonard Grey, are detailed and his early successes in advancing the Henrician Reformation acknowledged. The notion that Thomas Cromwell's demise effectively silenced Browne is challenged. Murray shows how the archbishop engaged confidently and wholeheartedly with the political reform project launched by the new viceroy, Sir Anthony St. Leger, in the early 1540s. Having identified 1541–1542 as the "high watermark of the Henrician Reformation" (p. 158) in Dublin and the Pale, he traces the rise and fall of St. Leger's settlement, rendering extremely complex developments in an accessible fashion. In support of his contention that St. Leger's successes were built upon "uncertain foundations" (p. 188), reliant on "continuance of a stable political environment, the endurance of a doctrinally conservative religious settlement and the prolongation of St Leger's own viceroyalty" (p. 188), Murray shows how these conditions, together with the viceroy's early successes in implementing religious changes, were swept away in the period 1546–1551.

In examining the restoration of Catholicism under Mary I, he challenges the notion that this alone of all the religious settlements promoted in sixteenth-century Ireland engendered no controversy. The incompatibility between Archbishop George Dowdall of Armagh's strategy based on rejuvenated, independent, and assertive clericalism and St. Leger's mode of government is exposed. Murray reevaluates the career of Hugh Curwen, the man charged with implementing the Catholic restoration in Dublin, and concludes that thanks to Curwen's "efforts, or the carefully contrived lack of them, the old religion was in a very healthy state on his departure" (pp. 259–260).

The final chapter focuses on Archbishop Adam Loftus's efforts to Protestantize Dublin in the period 1567–1590, exploring in particular Loftus's relations with senior conservative clergy of St. Patrick's Cathedral and the viceroy Sir Henry Sidney's role in preventing him from pursuing a progressive reform policy.

Murray concludes that the main reason for the failure of the Tudor religious reforms was the English Irish community's attachment to a survivalist form of Catholicism, an attachment actively defended and cultivated by the corporate clerical elite of the Pale, particularly during the Marian restoration and first decade of Elizabeth I's reign. This impressive study ends with the resonating assertion that "the origin and potency of this religion resided not in the heroic spirit of the Irish nation, not in the ideology of the Counter-Reformation, but in the values and reflexes of a clerical elite, which had long sustained the identity of the old colonial community in a hostile world" (p. 321).

That the thrust of Murray's narrative is deliberately

prospective rather than retrospective is a key strength of this study, ensuring that the reader remains engaged with developments as they unfurled. Aside from some repetition, the book is well structured, coherent in it arguments, and written in a very elegant style. The analysis is appropriately pitched for an academic readership and the discussion is consistently grounded in archival evidence and supported by an extensive scholarly apparatus. In short, this book makes a very important scholarly contribution to our understanding of the history of the Reformation in Ireland and will be essential reading for all scholars of the entire Tudor realm for many years to come.

MARY ANN LYONS
Dublin City University

RORY RAPPLE. *Martial Power and Elizabethan Political Culture: Military Men in England and Ireland, 1558–1594.* (Cambridge Studies in Early Modern British History.) New York: Cambridge University Press. 2009. Pp. xiii, 332. $120.00.

This skillfully written book aims first to dissect the careers of English captains who governed Ireland in self-serving fashion, and second to reveal their dissatisfaction with the Elizabethan regime. They vented social, political, and economic discontent by rationalizing executive intrusions into the judicial realm, denying due process, disregarding trial by jury, and trampling upon the common law (particularly property law). According to the author, the captains' bad behavior reveals their alienation from a royal court that failed to esteem the value, and leadership, of soldiering men.

Rory Rapple's tone conveys disapproval that English captains enriched themselves in the name of the state. Early modern colonization was entrepreneurial, however, and prone to wider autonomy than intended, as illustrated by the bewildering variety of charters granted to settlers of the Atlantic seaboard. The author makes an implicit moral judgment that sixteenth-century crown servants should have observed something like modern office-holding protocols, an anachronism perhaps reflective of Rapple's continuing involvement in professional journalism. Although this study makes an original contribution to our understanding of political culture, its usefulness to a wide scholarly audience is limited by its conceptual framework and research parameters.

Was the *imperium* practiced in Ireland and described by Rapple unique, or characteristic of other occupied dominions? By disregarding this question the author's meticulous rendering of the captains' mental world is partial, indeed two-dimensional. Stephen Webb's 1979 case study of Sir George Carey, an Elizabethan who governed the Isle of Wight, reveals similarities with the captains' autocratic rule in Ireland. Particularly relevant (and absent as well) is the "permissive frontier" concept that Nicholas Canny applied both to English rule in Ireland and to the American colonies. Canny demonstrates that virtually all those who promoted private colonization or state-sponsored plantations in Ireland made deliberate comparisons with North American settlement. However, Rapple ignores civil-military government in the Americas, on the Isle of Wight, in the English-governed "cautionary towns" of Brill, Flushing, and Ramekins (after 1585), and other English outposts (such as garrisoned joint-rule at Ostend from 1586). These omissions are unfortunate because the captains saw themselves enmeshed in a global struggle. Ireland was among, but only one of, a range of possible tours of duty. Elizabethan military men migrated among theaters of operation seeking opportunities for service, oftentimes at the Queen's direction (see the petitions in the British Library, Lansdowne 1218). Thus this book would benefit from contextualizing Ireland by comparison (as contemporaries and historians do). A literature has been provided for such a task by Canny, Carla Gardina Pestana, Anthony Pagden, William Palmer, Karl S. Bottigheimer, and others. Disappointingly, the author is either unfamiliar or unimpressed with this historiography. An exposition about a handful of disgruntled captains in an operational backwater who disparage government policies, and shape their political thinking to justify mistreatment of the natives, hardly constitutes a revelation. Indeed, Ciaran Brady had already exposed the captains' "games" in a 1996 essay.

Most frustrating is what Rapple missed in his research. The correspondence of the Irish Treasurer-at-War Sir William Wallop illuminates, but one ought also to cull through the treasurer's extensive accounts. Wallop's Exchequer manuscripts (E 351) complement the largely political and personal content of the State Papers. These hefty parchment rolls detail the infrastructure within which the captains operated, sources of crown revenue, and how monies were used. In addition to providing fiscal data, these declared accounts enable historians to reconstruct patron-client relationships, familial affinities, and much more (see, for example, E 351/230, f. 28v). Hundreds of entries for soldiers and civil servants (documenting the establishments of Sir Richard Bingham, Sir Nicholas Malby, and other key actors) reveal the locations of operations, duties assigned, as well as the captains' associates and inferiors. The author devotes a chapter (and the dustcover) to Bingham, making rather puzzling the neglect of Exchequer evidence that yields dozens if not scores of entries on Bingham's fiscal arrangements. Exchequer sources would have helped the author identify and perhaps quantify his data set. Nowhere does he lay out how many captains make up his evidential base, which cannot be a terribly large sample since this book halts analysis in 1593, before the acceleration of violence in Ireland. Upon this slim evidence Rapple challenges David Trim's 2002 London Ph.D. thesis on Elizabethan soldiers (which, unlike the book under review, is a model of international archival research) and generalizes about Elizabethan politics.

This book's topic holds promise if referenced to the contemporaneous exploration of the western hemisphere, colonization, and Tudor war-making. Bolder conceptualization, broader contextualization, and greater engagement with archival evidence and secondary literature might have rescued it from becoming what Jack H. Hexter considered "tunnel history."

MARK CHARLES FISSEL
Augusta State University

STEPHEN WRIGHT. *The Early English Baptists, 1603–1649*. Rochester, N.Y.: Boydell Press. 2006. Pp. x, 278. $105.00.

Stephen Wright has adopted a significant starting date for this closely argued study. Unlike some pioneering Baptist historians who began their story with the tiny group of possibly Anabaptist "Freewillers" of mid-sixteenth-century England, he maintains that the roots of the English Baptist denomination (or perhaps more accurately denominations) lay in the Elizabethan Puritan separatist tradition, which is also the tradition of those who fled to the Netherlands and New England in the early Stuart period. Alienated by the impurities remaining in the established church, Robert Browne was the first in 1581 both to create a covenanted church for the godly and to publish a justification for his actions. After the execution of Henry Barrow, John Penry, and John Greenwood twelve years later for their refusal to recognize the legitimacy of the national church, Francis Johnson assumed the leadership of the exiled English church in Amsterdam. None of these separatists, haunted like Protestant society in general by memories of the social excesses perpetrated by the Munster Anabaptists, looked upon baptism (or re-baptism) as a distinguishing mark of a true church.

The attempt by Archbishop Richard Bancroft to impose a ceremonial uniformity upon the English Church early in the reign of James I precipitated a new outbreak of separatism. John Smyth, a one-time pupil of Francis Johnson at Cambridge, was among the many at this time who were harried for their nonconformity. To avoid persecution Smyth and his supporters migrated from Lincolnshire to Amsterdam in 1607, only to find that Johnson's church fell far below his expectations. Increasingly isolated, in March 1609 Smyth took the momentous step of re-baptizing himself before going on to re-baptize his followers. He soon regretted his action and subsequently made overtures to join the Dutch Anabaptists or Mennonites. This split his congregation, and Thomas Helwys brought the dissenting minority back to England.

Under lay direction this church—which believed that Christ had died for all mankind, rejected the Calvinist doctrines of predestination and election, and allowed that all its members could preach and baptize—survived precariously in London until the Civil War. In the meanwhile the persecution of clergy and laity hostile to Laudian innovations generated more widespread separatism and semi-separatism in the 1630s. One church, founded by Henry Jacob and later led by Henry Jessey, while Calvinist in theology, began questioning the legitimacy of infant baptism. Before the calling of the Long Parliament there were therefore two quite distinct varieties of Baptists, the Particular or Calvinist Baptists and the General Baptists. To add to the complexity some Baptists now resolved that baptism should be administered by total immersion according to biblical precedent and not by "sprinkling," as previously had been the case.

With the breakdown of the old system of ecclesiastical government after 1640, all types of Baptists seized the opportunity to propagate their beliefs. On the setting up of the Westminster Assembly of Divines in 1642 charged with devising a new national church settlement, the Particular Baptists tended to ally with the Independents to gain some degree of religious liberty, helping produce in October 1644 a confession that repudiated universal atonement and envisaged closed congregations of the godly.

The much more theologically and socially radical General Baptists in contrast turned to the army for protection. Some played an active part in the Leveller movement and by 1647 were advocating the abolition of the monarchy and the establishment of a republic. The Agreement of the People of 1649 enabled all Baptists to preach and evangelize freely. While some actively engaged in politics and held office under the Commonwealth and Protectorate, others, disillusioned by the failure of the state to usher in a New Jerusalem, renounced their original loyalties to join the Ranters, Seekers, or Quakers. Lacking effective central direction, the General Baptists failed to create a coherent denomination at this period and the pattern of Baptist allegiance was still incomplete at the time of the Restoration and for some decades afterwards.

In addition to a detailed analysis of some of the key documents for early Baptist history, the book contains in both the text and the appendixes a wealth of biographical information on members of individual congregations. The very different trajectories of the early Baptist churches understandably make for a somewhat discursive monograph in which clarity occasionally falls prey to the complications of the historical circumstances. In anticipation of such criticism, after stressing "the influence of broad political and social factors upon the shifting alignments" of the early Baptist churches, the author warns against "attempts to make denominational loyalties determine politics in any simple sense."

CLAIRE CROSS
University of York

TROY BICKHAM. *Making Headlines: The American Revolution as Seen through the British Press*. DeKalb: Northern Illinois University Press. 2009. Pp. xiii, 303. $38.00.

This useful work connects and extends two relatively recent branches of historical inquiry: first, analyses of the British press that show it to have been an independent, dynamic, and lucrative component of consumer culture, provincial as well as metropolitan, and second, studies that reveal the vitality and complexity of the

British response to the American Revolution, something that was much more than simply an echo of competing parliamentary agendas. Troy Bickham concedes that his study is not exhaustive (that would be an impossible undertaking for a solitary researcher), but he claims that it is comprehensive, based as it is on the systematic sampling of forty-one newspapers, eighteen of them from Scotland and the English provinces.

The press both encouraged and catered to a burgeoning interest in the American colonies across a broad swath of the British population, transcending region, gender, and social status. News and comment about America sold newspapers, which is why profit-minded proprietors filled their pages with them. All those with a stake in the outcome of the colonial crisis—the government of Lord North, opposition parties, the West Indian settler lobby, American loyalists, American revolutionaries and their domestic sympathizers, even military leaders seeking to justify their actions—had resort to the press, but canny publishers, including those with a partisan position on the American crisis, usually ensured that their organs retained independence from the control of vested interests. Newspapers were rarely party bugles as once thought. A notable exception, partially at least, confirms the general rule. In 1776, Reverend Henry Bate, the flamboyant editor of the *Morning Post*, accepted a bribe from the government and overnight his paper became fulsome in its praise for the North ministry and its American policies. Yet because its partisan campaigns were conducted with panache (and perhaps also because the *Post* remained a forum for gossip), the paper became highly profitable, so that even those shareholders with opposition sympathies were content to go along with its unusual sacrifice of editorial independence.

Bickham also shows that even newspapers which cherished their independence could occasionally be manipulated for partisan ends. Perhaps the most striking example was the way in which American revolutionaries and their domestic supporters controlled the flow of information about the first military clashes in the colonies. So successful were they that when General Thomas Gage's reports finally arrived they were greeted with skepticism. But cartels on information could not be sustained indefinitely. A free press meant that news and commentary circulated freely, and from this circumstance Bickham draws the reasonable inference that newspapers reflected public opinion, albeit with the caveat that the press could lead as well as follow popular discourses. His analysis confirms and thickens what we already know about British attitudes to the American Revolution, while adding some original insights. He demonstrates that there were points of unanimity about the course of the conflict that cut across partisan divisions. Newspaper content made it clear that the global conflict that followed France's entry into the war was universally perceived as being of a different order from the colonial rebellion that preceded and accompanied it. At times domestic squabbles over the rebellion itself receded into the background, as the press highlighted the national jubilation—shared alike by habitual government supporters and the pro-Americans in London's Common Council—following naval triumphs like Admiral George Rodney's decisive victory over the Comte de Grasse at the Battle of the Saintes in April 1782. The war thus ended on a triumphal note even as Britons awaited nervously the implications of American independence. Unlike war with the Bourbon powers, that with American rebels was a transatlantic civil war, a family quarrel even. Such characterizations have become something of a cliché in the historical literature, but Bickham's study gives them depth and meaning. He shows, for example, that acute misgivings about the deployment of Indian auxiliaries against colonial rebels extended even to government supporters, in contrast to the Seven Years War when the unleashing of Britain's Indian allies against the French enemy was generally applauded. In the family drama of the American Revolution, George Washington was clearly the favorite son on both sides of the Atlantic. The British press lauded him as a "model of citizenly virtue and the ideal military leader" (p. 185), qualities that were evidently lacking in Britain's army generals.

This is a well-researched, nicely organized book. My one criticism (more of a quibble really) is that having asserted the vitality and autonomy of the provincial press, Bickham might have explored ways in which its take on the revolutionary crisis was distinct from that of the metropolitan press. All he gives us in this regard is the tantalizing hint that it was only London newspapers that called for redoubled military effort after the catastrophe of General John Burgoyne's defeat at Saratoga.

JOHN SAINSBURY
Brock University

LAURIE THRONESS. *A Protestant Purgatory: Theological Origins of the Penitentiary Act, 1779.* Burlington, Vt.: Ashgate Publishing Company. 2008. Pp. vi, 379. £60.00.

This scholarly and primary-source-led monograph offers an intellectual history that explores in depth the importance of theological contexts and belief in the passing of the Penitentiary Act of 1779. Although the penitentiaries envisaged by this statute were not constructed, the legislation provided the foundation for the emergence of a new institutional structure. Underpinning the penitentiary was a distinctive, more powerful, and more deterrent method of punishment in which reform was firmly embedded. As Laurie Throness rightly points out, this legislation has often been given minimal attention by historians working on penal history; in addition, an overtly theological analysis offers something quite radical to the extant historiography. In one sense this is a partial and specific theological study, but it offers insights into the momentous shift in the philosophy and methods of punishment that occurred in England during the late eighteenth and early nineteenth centuries.

The book effectively brings to the fore the seemingly

contradictory responses to penal practice that have been evident for centuries and that continue to exist in the present era. This is most clear in discussion of the motivations and theology underpinning solitary confinement as a punishment intended to strike terror into the heart of evildoers but also to facilitate reflection, penitence, and ultimately reform. Indeed, one of the many strengths of this book is the meticulous and focused consideration of the rationale that drove the use of solitary confinement and debate about the centrality of the redemptive powers of labor. Throness helps to explain what was perceived as original about the penitentiary when many of its ingredients, in particular reform through labor (in the Houses of Correction), had been tried before. There is an excellent exploration of individuals, such as William Blackstone, William Eden, and John Howard, who were important in getting the Penitentiary Act passed and in securing initial efforts to act on its provisions. Throness suggests that the role of evangelicals at this early stage, even of Howard, was not as prominent as has been maintained. The influence of evangelical thought was to be seen primarily in the following century. Similarly, Throness gives a very interesting consideration of how theology met and interrelated with Enlightenment and secular ideas during the eighteenth century: for example, over the appropriate use of man's time on earth and on the issue of proportionality in punishment. Yet, he notes that such well-known legal commentators and reformers as Jeremy Bentham and Samuel Romilly had little or no engagement with the Penitentiary Act prior to its passing.

An original perspective is offered here in a close examination of what the author calls "continuity between heaven and earth"—that the English justice system corresponded to patterns believed by contemporary Christians to have originated in heaven. Much of this is convincing—for example, the comparison of prison as a structure holding inmates prior to trial with an "intermediate state" corresponding to purgatory and as later shifting in purpose to places for punishment, the earthly counterpart of a Protestant conception of Hell. However, some of the assertions seem less concrete: for example, the comparison of earthly justice hierarchies with ranks of "angelic authorities." Surely such hierarchies can be identified from an early date in a range of institutions—i.e., the military—and in non-Western countries.

This book offers a theological understanding of the importance of Christianity to eighteenth-century thinkers and to the origins of the Penitentiary Act of 1779. It is a culturally specific study that leaves the reader thinking about other religious contexts. More directly important is that one is left wondering how theology interrelated with other, more pragmatic factors in the emergence of the penitentiary. Throness acknowledges that all explanations of the penitentiary are partial but also suggests debatably that the explanatory power of theology is broader than other factors.

This meticulous and scholarly publication provides a wealth of primary evidence. Indeed, at times the evidence is so dense that the focus blurs somewhat, although discussion sections in each chapter and in the conclusion provide valuable clarification. The author legitimates the approach, asserting reasonably that his aim is to enable us to hear the voices of contemporaries and to help us understand how lawmakers thought. Throness is right to point out that there is little theological understanding or input in much of the academic writing on this subject, and in that context this book provides an important contribution to comprehending the mental frameworks that led to the development of the penitentiary and the modern prison.

ALYSON BROWN
Edge Hill University

JAMES RAVEN. *The Business of Books: Booksellers and the English Book Trade, 1450-1850*. New Haven: Yale University Press. 2007. Pp. xviii, 493. $65.00.

Booksellers were once pivotally important arbiters and gatekeepers of culture across much of Europe and America. Between the sixteenth century, when bookselling began to be differentiated from the craft of printing, and the early nineteenth century, when the role of the publisher emerged, booksellers were the people who generally decided what got published, how, when, and for which readers. A broad historical understanding of this long period therefore ought to require an account of who the booksellers were, what they did, and how they reached the decisions on which printed culture depended. These are the subjects that James Raven tackles in his new history of bookselling in Britain.

The nearest thing this book has to a predecessor is Marjorie Plant's *The English Book Trade: An Economic History of the Making and Sale of Books*, first published as long ago as 1939. A successor was overdue, and Raven meets the need. Whether read cover-to-cover or consulted on specific topics, his book is now the definitive history of its subject. It provides an even-handed and reliable introduction to a vast body of scholarship that can be dry, technical, and polemical, judiciously weighing arguments and defining sensible compromise positions. Raven's focus ranges very widely across the book trades, balancing fine detail with generalization. As a result, he qualifies prevailing assumptions in ways both small and large.

Raven tends to be skeptical of claims of revolutionary transformation. Two prime examples concern the destruction of perpetual copyright in 1774 and the introduction of steam printing and papermaking in the first decade of the nineteenth century. The first of these has drawn much attention recently, but Raven maintains that it had a less dramatic effect than is often portrayed. In practice, the trade managed to keep its restrictions by maintaining existing "combines" (as opponents called them). Change came, but slowly and cumulatively. Similarly, it took decades for mechanization to affect the mundane practices of publishing, and the changes that did occur, when they came to fruition in the 1840s, were products as much of deep-seated developments in finance and commerce as of technological progress itself.

Yet Raven is not a continuist. He does posit important transitions, simply not the ones that book historians have typically emphasized. Rather than arising within the book trades themselves, Raven's transitions tend to derive from the financial and commercial practices of British businesses in general and from the economy at large. In place of 1774 and 1814 (the year when *The Times* adopted steam printing), we find turning points in the 1740s and the 1840s. The first saw the appearance of dramatically larger printing manufactories and the beginning of a century-long expansion. The latter saw a conjunction of trends—agitation for copyright revision, the abolition of taxes on knowledge, mechanization, and the advent of rail transport—produce the biggest changes in the printing industry since the time of William Caxton. The 1840s are the endpoint of Raven's history, for the reign of booksellers and publishers as culturally powerful individuals would not long survive in the new environment. (Presumably figures like Allen Lane and Victor Gollancz count as exceptions proving the rule.) Although Raven himself does not put it so bluntly, what he is proposing is a different chronological and explanatory framework for the history of the book. In its quiet way his is an ambitiously revisionist work.

The central point for Raven is that bookselling was indeed a business, and that therefore the appropriate way to understand it is in terms of the established approaches of business history. In particular, any bookseller faced two fundamental issues—liquidity and risk—and the history of bookselling is largely the history of strategies to deal with these. Publishing a book meant tying up capital in a product from which no returns could be garnered until the production was complete. This could take months or years. Booksellers were therefore in constant need of inflows of cash to keep them afloat. And they were extraordinarily vulnerable to risk. An impression had to be warehoused while it gradually sold off. Warehouses caught fire, and warehouse-keepers proved lazy or worse. And, of course, there was never a guarantee that an edition would find a market at all. So ways of dealing with risk—the formation of defensive alliances among booksellers, for example, which became the bulwark of literary property—remained fundamental, alongside gambits to bring in ready cash such as the proliferation of serials. Above all, civility required that booksellers extend credit to gentlemen, but customers tended to delay repaying for years. Bookselling remained a face-to-face business: what mattered was deciding whom to trust and how far. It is telling not only that James Lackington, one of the greatest successes of all, refused to offer credit to anyone, but that nobody else dared do likewise. But this was just another sense in which publishing was peculiarly sensitive to shifting norms of financial life.

Raven's business history approach sets this volume apart, but it is not without its drawbacks. How risks were appraised or trade disputes pursued in this face-to-face world remains a little opaque. The culture of labor gets short shrift too. That printers chafed for generations at booksellers who based their status on (literary) property rather than craft skill is an aspect of the history of bookselling relatively downplayed here. And, given that Raven endorses a qualitative distinction between "ideology" and profit-seeking as drivers of practice, the meanings of profit-seeking itself—for example, in the cases of the Scottish and Irish challenges to London, issues of political economy, civility, and nationalism—do not attract his attention. But he is well aware of this selectivity. A concluding "Historiographical Overview" is mainly devoted to listing topics he did not address. The important point is that anyone wanting to address these topics will now have to begin with this book.

ADRIAN JOHNS
University of Chicago

CHRIS OTTER. *The Victorian Eye: A Political History of Light and Vision in Britain, 1800–1910.* Chicago: University of Chicago Press. 2008. Pp. x, 382. Cloth $65.00, paper $25.00.

There is something curiously out of touch about Chris Otter's book tracing the history of light and vision in nineteenth-century Britain: out of touch because it is oddly out of dialogue with the large and influential recent literature that exists on the subject. At the level of content, Otter's book focuses on aspects of technological development such as urban infrastructure, sanitary reform, abattoirs, pavements, mortuaries, lighting the night, electricity, gas, and toilets that are well known to any historian of the nineteenth century in the Western world. Less well known outside the history of technology may be the history of illumination and the history of some of the optical devices to measure light, which Otter chronicles with gusto and which are admirably described and detailed. At the level of argumentation, Otter claims to break new ground in the history of vision and power by arguing that there is a particularly British story to tell bound up with notions of liberalism and freedom. Methodologically, he asserts the superiority of empiricism over what he calls the "limited range of concepts provided by cultural theory" and makes much ado about what he sees as the un-nuanced uses of the panopticon and the flâneur as models of nineteenth-century visuality and for which his book will serve as a corrective.

What is, unfortunately, un-nuanced is Otter's understanding of the literature that has come before him. Scholars long ago abandoned the totalizing quality of Michel Foucault's panopticism. It has been more than twenty years since Tony Bennett wrote about the "exhibitionary complex" and more than fifteen years since Anne Friedberg (not cited) helped recast our ideas about both panopticism and flânerie in terms of freedom and mobility in ways that are consonant with the work of historians such as Judith Walkowitz, Seth D.

Koven, and Erika Diane Rappaport (the last author not even in the bibliography). Reading this study, one wonders who are the historians actually trapped in the Foucauldian straight-jacket, still going on about the instrumentality of the state when it comes to vision and optical culture? Yet, when Otter turns to the culture of inspection of the urban poor or to the inspection of undergrounds, we find no intellectual engagement with Koven's excellent work on slumming or with David L. Pike's two books on the London underground (not cited). When Otter brings us to the mortuary, he invokes the now long outdated work of Philippe Ariès, who argued that death was banished from view, but does not contend with either such phenomena as the spectacle of the morgue in nineteenth-century Paris or the parade of bloody murder in the daily press as documented by scholars such as Dominique Kalifa in *L'encre et le sang: Récits de crimes et société à la Belle Époque* (1995). (Otter cites English-language secondary sources only. Thus, a major book on night, *Les douze heures noires: La nuit à Paris au XIXe siècle* [2000] by Simone Delattre, is regrettably absent as well.) There is little that acknowledges the research contributions of the work on spectacle, which has created an empirical contribution to the history of consumerist technology. If one were to understand the arrival of electricity, it is not merely in its relation as a lighting technology that rivals gas, but as a part of the rich landscape of urban diversions such as department stores, fairgrounds, restaurants, wax museums, and eventually cinemas that constituted a new sociability. Here is a missed opportunity to connect the spectacular and the everyday as Victorian subjects must have done and as Otter might have since he had a historiography on which to build.

Although there is nothing wrong with studying the phenomenon of infrastructure as it relates to vision and optical culture in a single national context, there is nothing singularly British or Victorian about any of the topics and developments investigated here. The trouble begins precisely by presuming a causal correlation between the state and its political investments and phenomena that clearly transcend the boundaries of any one state. In fact, what is so interesting about studying technology and infrastructure is the extent to which states that might share little else (and which may have had divergent ways of hooking up lights or running pipes) did eventually seek electricity and come to refrigerate their meat and their corpses. The question for the historian then becomes can you refrigerate corpses as part of a liberal project in one place and part of an authoritarian project in another? Otter rightly points out that there was nothing inevitable or uniform about the adoption of technologies of illumination and that technological change is a hodgepodge story of transition, but this story of uneven development is already the new standard doxa in the history of technology. From Thomas Edison's international role in developing electricity, to the international community of engineers dredging sewers, to the arc lights on the Nevsky Prospect in 1883 put up by that most authoritarian of regimes, there is nothing essentially "liberal" about the implementation of such infrastructural innovations except for the way the government was organized in England. No one would accuse the French state of resembling the British state of this period given its greater centralization, yet Paris had libraries lit very much on the model Otter describes in his study. So, would this make the French "liberal?"

In his conclusion, Otter mentions photography and film as two kinds of "aesthetic" perception he does not treat in this study. Yet the book contains more than sixty images (engravings and photographs) that are used transparently as mere illustrations. They are, of course, evidence of a Victorian "eye" that has nothing to do with "mere" aesthetics but is very much about the culture of inspection and self-knowledge he is studying. Otter's notes on the history of photography are quite cursory, and scholars will have to go elsewhere for the rich literature on photography and the city and photography and the rise of notions of privacy and the self.

Instead of the notions of panopticism and flânerie, Otter employs the neologism of oligoptic engineering (which denotes a multiplicity of interconnected visual spaces, courtesy of Bruno Latour) designed with human freedom in mind. But he assures us this is not an overarching and totalizing notion; there are, after all, so many examples that do not fit this generalization. He concludes instead with a set of nine patterns too lengthy and qualified to spell out here. Otter has confused empiricism with an unwillingness to make historical generalizations from the actual research he has done into optical technologies on the one hand, while he confirms one of the most tried and true and perhaps even mythological forms of British exceptionalism on the other: that of Liberal England.

VANESSA R. SCHWARTZ
University of Southern California

RYLAND WALLACE. *The Women's Suffrage Movement in Wales, 1866–1928.* (Studies in Welsh History.) Cardiff: University of Wales Press. 2009. Pp. xii, 338. £48.00.

In this survey of the organized campaign for women's parliamentary enfranchisement in Wales between 1866 and 1928, Ryland Wallace makes use of a familiar historiographical recipe for understanding the British women's movement, adding a dash of Welsh seasoning. Eschewing innovations of more recent suffrage historiography that have engaged questions of culture and ideology, the book employs a traditional approach to its subject with narrative chapters on the three main Edwardian women's suffrage organizations: the Women's Social and Political Union (WSPU), the National Union of Women's Suffrage Societies (NUWSS), and the Women's Freedom League (WFL); the organized opposition to women's suffrage; the impact of World War I; and the Campaign for Equal Suffrage, 1918–1928. Wallace's stated goal is to "fill a major lacuna in the historiography of modern Wales . . . and to add substantially to our knowledge and understanding

of the British women's suffrage movement as a whole"
(p. 7). He succeeds admirably at the former but falls
short of accomplishing the latter.

Wallace's narration of the organized campaign for
women's suffrage follows a path well established in the
historiography by the early 1980s and challenged considerably in subsequent years: a relatively small nineteenth-century movement focused on parliamentary reform became a campaign revivified and enlarged by the
introduction of WSPU militancy at the turn of the twentieth century. His emphasis throughout is on militancy's
direct and indirect assistance to the cause as more
women joined the wider campaign, with arguments over
militancy predominating until the outbreak of war in
1914 created a new set of suffragist dynamics. The campaign, and the book, culminates in passage of the Representation of the People Acts of 1918 and 1928: the
first enfranchising British women at the age of thirty
(with property qualification), the second lowering the
age for women's political participation to twenty-one
(to match men's). No part of the story Wallace narrates
rings false, but nothing related here about the Welsh
context casts the broader movement in a new light either. The narrative essentially intertwines the story told
from the center (London) with intriguing details about
individual Welsh women, organizations, and campaigns.

The book's great strength—but ultimately its limitation—is its emphasis on grass-roots activism in Wales.
Wallace notes early in his introduction that "while few
of the records of the many individual local suffrage societies established in Wales have survived, those of the
central bodies which spearheaded and coordinated the
campaign across Britain are comprehensive: these com-
prise minute books, reports, correspondence and other
material," including papers of individual women and
the newspapers of the main suffrage organizations (p.
2). Many of Wallace's sources thus emerge from the
perspective of the national organizations based in London. His best primary sources for Wales turn out to be
local newspapers, which he mines for quotidian details
of suffrage activism but which do not substantively
amend the larger framework within which he works. A
great accomplishment of the book is its recovery of the
contributions of individual suffragists, many of whom
appear only tangentially in accounts told from the center. Here, women like Alix Minnie Clark and Dr. Hel-
ena Jones emerge as significant local players. In the
end, while this narrative is redolent with accounts of the
experiences of women suffragists in Wales in the late
nineteenth and early twentieth centuries, it does little
to transform our understanding of the movement overall.

Wallace's book demonstrates, however, that suffrage
historiography in the British context has reached a critical point in its development. In the introduction, Wallace notes the major shifts that suffrage historiography
has undergone over the past twenty years, especially as
scholars have moved away from an earlier focus on
WSPU militancy and toward investigation of campaigns

at the local level. Scholars undertaking suffrage as a
subject of scrutiny cannot avoid these new approaches.
Yet, Wallace's analysis does not grapple with the central point of that revisionist work: the questioning of the
very dichotomy of militancy versus constitutionalism as
it played out in local contexts. While ostensibly engaging with recent trends in suffrage historiography emphasizing the local over the national, this book does not
accomplish for Wales what either Krista Cowman's
*"Mrs. Brown is a Man and a Brother!" Women in Mer-
seyside's Political Organisations, 1890–1920* (2004) nor
Leah Leneman's *A Guid Cause: The Women's Suffrage
Movement in Scotland* (1991) did for their respective
contexts. Thus, while the book adds a useful dimension
to the historiography on Wales, it fails to demonstrate
how the women's suffrage campaign in Wales transforms our understanding of that movement within Britain overall.

LAURA E. NYM MAYHALL
Catholic University of America

JOHN S. ELLIS. *Investiture: Royal Ceremony and National
Identity in Wales, 1911–1969.* Cardiff: University of
Wales Press. 2008. Pp. x, 344. £55.00.

In recent years, the study of royal ceremonial in the
modern era has been a booming subject, with detailed
monographs on subjects ranging from Meiji Japan to
Romanov Russia, and from Wilhelmine Germany to
early twentieth-century Siam. Building on the insights
of anthropologists (such as Clifford Geertz) and of sociologists (such as Catherine Bell and David I. Kertzer),
and extending (as well as modifying and criticizing) Eric
Hobsbawm's seminal work on what he called the "invention of tradition," a succession of historians have
sought to explore how very different royal regimes, in
very different parts of the world, sought to represent
themselves during the late nineteenth and early twentieth centuries, by elaborating what was not only a more
contrived but also a more popular ceremonial image
appropriate to the new mass societies that were coming
into being in the age of high imperialism. Yet in many
ways, the grandest of all these spectacular monarchies
was Britain, where what had originated as an English
crown had become—by the time of Queen Victoria's
Diamond Jubilee in 1897—a royal cynosure, both of the
United Kingdom of England, Wales, Scotland, and Ireland and also of the far-flung empire on which the sun
never set.

John S. Ellis's important and impressive book not
only broadens this story by considering Wales—which
he does very much in the contexts of the United Kingdom and the British Empire—but also moves it forward
by investigating in depth the two occasions when the
Prince of Wales, as heir to the British throne, was "invested" at Caernarfon Castle in 1911 and 1969. As Ellis
rightly points out, there were earlier precedents for
such pomp and pageantry in the principality, but by the
early eighteenth century they had fallen into desuetude,
and the two most recent extravaganzas were largely—
although not entirely—made up. Here is an ideal cer-

emonial subject for historical inquiry and Ellis makes the most of it.

From one perspective, his book is a case-study in what might be termed the politics and the performance of pageantry: who conceived the idea? Where should the event take place? Who organized it? Who paid for it? Who was invited to it? Who participated in it? What conflicts among those in charge had to be resolved for the ceremonial to take place? The author painstakingly investigates these and related questions, and in so doing sheds new light on the part played by David Lloyd George in the first investiture (when he was Constable of Caernarfon Castle, and also the town's MP and Chancellor of the Exchequer) and on Anthony Armstrong-Jones in the second (when he held the same position, and was also the husband of Princess Margaret and thus the uncle by marriage of Prince Charles).

But at the same time, the book is also a work of "thick description," situating these spectaculars in the broader historical context and teasing out their many, varied, and often contradictory meanings to the general Welsh public who were neither participants nor invitees. Both ceremonials meant different things to people in different parts of Wales: to the aristocracy, to the middle class, and to the working class; and also to those from the largely agricultural north and those from the more heavily industrialized south. The first investiture was an expression of Liberal hegemony that was soon to end with the rise of Labour politics, but the second was an expression of Labour hegemony that was soon to end with the rise of nationalist politics. For some, these ceremonials were an authentic display of Welsh national pride and identity; for others, they were a sham and an insult, which merely confirmed Wales's long and humiliating subordination to British dominance, the British monarchy, and the British class structure. But in the end, Ellis insists, "the controversies over the investitures of 1911 and 1969 were less conflicts between the British state and the Welsh nation than quarrels amongst the people of Wales over who and what constituted Welshness" (p. 322).

Ellis's evidence, which is gathered from a wide range of sources (in both English and Welsh) extending from the press to the papers of major participants, convincingly supports this judicious conclusion. Indeed, from beginning to end his account is admirably paced and well organized as he describes how these two ceremonials came about, evokes what actually happened on the day, and explains how and why their meanings were so contested. As anyone who has tried to write this sort of history knows, these things are not easy to do. But Ellis has written an excellent book, a major contribution to the history of Wales, to the broader history of Britain and its empire, and to the study of royal ceremonial in the modern world.

DAVID CANNADINE
Princeton University

ADRIAN GREGORY. *The Last Great War: British Society and the First World War*. New York: Cambridge University Press. 2008. Pp. viii, 354. Cloth $90.00, paper $34.99.

Vigorous and compelling, without concession to popular or professional received opinion, Adrian Gregory's new book rewrites the social history of Britain between 1914 and 1918. Unlike World War II, the British have come to understand World War I as a "bad" war. While the history of this image is itself of interest, Gregory argues for the recovery of contemporary opinion: for an understanding of the conflict seen as regrettable and uncertain in outcome; as sacrifice of self and community; and as an intensely moral, perhaps even spiritual, battle. To achieve this new understanding he pays careful attention to the particularities of local, quotidian experience, to regional and social variations, and to power relations as they shaped event and expression. He also notes two ways in which historians are sometimes misled: by their overemphasis on discourse and language as deterministic markers of actuality, and by their failure to distinguish between contemporary opinion and subsequent reconstruction of attitudes, especially attitudes after 1945.

Given this framework, the conclusions Gregory reaches are at first sight unsurprising: for example, that there was strong reluctance to engage in the war, or that the British population had a largely realistic view of the catastrophe to come and would genuinely have preferred peace. The conviction that it was necessary to enter the conflict emerged gradually, both before and especially after the Declaration of War in August 1914, as a moral response intended to curb and punish German aggression. The prowar consensus was never absolute, but there was an increasingly widespread view that it was necessary to counter the barbaric German attack on civilized values represented by the sinking of the Lusitania and the attack on Louvain, both in early 1915. Subsequently Britain pursued the war with single-minded ruthlessness; at its end, most people believed they had succeeded.

Yet on almost every point this account challenges accepted opinion. Further, across a range of connected case studies on questions as varied as "war enthusiasm," the manipulation of public opinion, the meaning and function of volunteerism, as well as the connected notions of sacrifice, religious values and popular understanding of the war, social, class and ethnic antagonisms, and post-1918 mythologization of the language of sacrifice, the author questions others and himself unsparingly. "I had always assumed someone would legitimately challenge some of my arguments. It might as well be me" (p. 334).

Good sense, clarity of thought, and careful investigation help Gregory clear away much of the accumulated cultural clutter and mythmaking that surrounds 1914–1918. Considering prewar enthusiasm, mass jingoism, and anti-German feeling, for example, he argues that none of these "caused" the war. Such feelings were not absent, but the onset of the conflict itself massively increased anti-Germanism, and stoked popular patriotism. The view that, to put it crudely, "the masses" were fooled into a patriotic frenzy ignores the gradual evolution of opinion as well as regional, class, and gender differences. Crowd photos show interested spectators; most did not believe the war would be "over by Christmas," as the travails of the Boer War gave a good sense of how elusive military success might be; and dismay, anxiety, and gradual resolve toward engagement followed. Reluctance to join up in haste was a common response that resulted from concern for the financial affairs, perhaps even the survival, of the family members left behind; mass recruitment began following the Battle of Mons on August 25, when the military situation clearly became more serious.

Three connected chapters on the economy, on religious practice, and on labor relations set out Gregory's central argument that the war was interpreted by contemporaries, albeit in varied ways, as "sacrifice." So, for instance, those who were wasteful, who hoarded, or who seemed to profit unduly from the war were condemned for their lack of patriotism. Likewise, while profound suspicion attached itself to religious authority, a tradition dating back not least to the 1640s, the language of religion, especially of Christian self-denial, profoundly colored values and behavior. That sacrifice was conditional became apparent in 1917 with the American entry into the war and the Russian Revolution. The former decreased fears of national bankruptcy, while the latter increased fear of workers' unrest. Strikes followed in Britain because it became possible for the working classes to bargain effectively, to regain some of their lost living standards, and to hold off potential exploitation.

Finally—rethinking some of the themes from his earlier work, *The Silence of Memory: Armistice Day 1919–1946* (1994)—Gregory considers the evolving recollection of 1914–1918, in particular the interwar period: the emergence of a "fictive community" of loss; the redemption of victory, which validated individual and collective sacrifice; the symbolism of Armistice Day cancelled in 1939, which nullified the Great War as victory and as warning.

PETER LEESE
University of Copenhagen

G. C. PEDEN. *Arms, Economics and British Strategy: From Dreadnoughts to Hydrogen Bombs*. (Cambridge Military Histories.) New York: Cambridge University Press. 2007. Pp. xiii, 384. $99.00.

This book is one of a series aimed at producing "vigorous and ground breaking" work. It is certainly vigorous but hardly groundbreaking. Research is almost entirely absent, beyond direct reference to a handful of well-known documents and some minor manipulation of vintage data sets. Instead we have an impressive synthesis of the existing historiography of British strategy in a short twentieth century between 1904 and 1969, which will be indispensible to students and academics.

The text of each chapter is divided between a chronological narrative of events and sections dealing with the experience of each fighting service and the strategic dilemmas facing policy makers. This approach has its strengths and weaknesses, but ultimately it fractures analysis and can leave the separate sections rather limited and lacking in depth, though in sum the narrative is dense and detailed. For example, G. C. Peden's analysis of British aircraft types in World War II utilizes very elderly texts, but his general conclusion that British efforts have been unfairly criticized by polemicists such as Corelli Barnett is valid and requires more extensive consideration.

Peden does not advance any fresh hypotheses or reveal new archival material, but he does have decided views and comments critically on scholarship in the field. Given the ground to be covered and the pace of the narrative, this commentary is rarely extensive; for the most part, scholars whistle past with a few words of admonition or, more rarely, a pat on the back. Aside from the now ritual but necessary condemnation of Barnett, only the work of this reviewer ([Christopher] "Price goes too far") and, to a lesser extent, that of Robert P. Shay concerning the economics of interwar rearmament come in for sharp and sustained criticism. These books contrast most sharply with Peden's earlier published material defending the prewar Treasury, however, so this is only to be expected. Nevertheless, the criticism is speculative and selective and it is also problematical in terms of Peden's wider argument.

Generally, Peden's position is moderate, despite his occasionally acerbic tone, but he ultimately refutes declinist analysis and rejects the case for structural backwardness in the British economy and in Britain's application of technology. Oddly, his criticism of Shay and Price counters this general thesis, and to reconnect with his narrative he is forced to row back from his forthright defence of Neville Chamberlain's government, conceding that "To argue thus is not to say that nothing could have been done." Quite.

Peden's position is nevertheless consistent with his earlier work in that he presents a picture of Britain's retreat from power in terms of insuperable external challenges rather than internal weakness. This is undeniably true of the position after 1945, but the book underplays the extent to which this is a controversial thesis when applied to the position before 1939. The book's rather parochial focus informs this tendency.

Peden's main strength lies in his analysis of the British governmental machine and its labyrinthine functions. The quality of his analysis declines sharply when the wider world or the course of international events are discussed. For example, Peden implies that most of Fighter Command should have been committed to the Battle of France. It would certainly have been a decisive move, though not in a happy sense, and he assumes incorrectly that the French weakness in the air was numerical rather than systemic.

It is also difficult to draw conclusions about British strategy without considering the dynamics of the Anglo-American relationship, and rivalry, in much greater depth throughout the period. This is particularly true in the imperial context. For example, Peden's assumption that the Dominion economies were moving toward the United States before 1939 is simply invalid. Their well-publicized posturing as independent states during the Munich crisis disguised complete dependence on the United Kingdom economy as an export market, which was in itself the result of Britain's status as the pre-eminent global trading power. Peden seems unaware that to primary producers such as Australia, the United States was a feared and bitter trading rival whose domestic market, however large, was effectively closed to their produce. Dominions resisted any weakening of imperial preference and their move into the U.S. orbit during the war was ultimately a side effect of Britain's prior move.

In conclusion, this book is valuable as a scholarly and erudite survey of Britain's decline to the second rank of powers. There are a number of problems with Peden's thesis, however, particularly in the sense that Britain's world role is not fully represented except, in the classic Treasury style, as a liability. The book ultimately performs a service in that the reader is struck by the large volume of research that remains to be done in this field, in a wider range of archives, before final conclusions can be drawn.

CHRISTOPHER PRICE
University of Liverpool

ERIC G. E. ZUELOW. *Making Ireland Irish: Tourism and National Identity since the Irish Civil War.* (Irish Studies.) Syracuse, N.Y.: Syracuse University Press. 2009. Pp. xxxiv, 344. $39.95.

The turbulent political history of Ireland in the twentieth century has traditionally attracted most of the attention of those studying its past. As a consequence other aspects of the history of the new Irish state have long been neglected. In recent decades, however, a new interest in social, cultural, and economic change has produced some stimulating studies. Eric G. E. Zuelow's book on the development of tourism policy between 1923 and 2007 is the first complete overview of this topic to appear and is one of the better examples of the new work. On the basis of a detailed study of government and other primary sources, it does not just trace the interaction among politicians, interest groups, and local activists that shaped tourism policy, but, by analyzing three central aspects of the debate, it tries to illuminate how Irish national identity was formed.

This connection between tourism policy and identity formation is indeed a challenging notion. Tourism policy is potentially an interesting angle to take as it poses questions about how a country presents itself to outsiders and therefore what people think it should constitute. However, to identify what it was that made Ireland Irish from debates on tourism policy is not an easy task. It requires, as Zuelow states, an in-depth analysis of the links among all parties involved and the ability to isolate elements and motivations that were associated with Irishness from those that were not.

Zuelow has a good grasp of the literature on the role of tourism and is well aware of the academic debates on nationalism and identity. He also makes the importance of tourism to Ireland abundantly clear. Apart from its impact on the landscape—for instance, through instigating the "tradition" of painting Irish houses in different colors—tourism's importance can particularly be seen in the economic arena. This also constitutes the most serious problem for the attempt to draw conclusions on national identity. On the few occasions where tourist developments were resisted by various groups, the economic interest always won out. Although language enthusiasts, who were very well represented in the new nationalist elite, were worried about the effects of the influx of mostly English-speaking tourists into Irish-speaking areas, nothing was done to control tourism in these areas—notwithstanding a plan by the minister of finance to isolate tourists and hire local people to speak Irish to them. The fact that economic concerns always won out does, of course, not mean that the Irish language was not important to Irish identity.

An associated problem is that tourism policy was mostly an elite concern. National identity is, as Zuelow argues, created by ordinary people, but this book does not tell the story of ordinary people. Apart from the involvement of some government departments, most of the developments described were engineered by a few interest groups. The most influential was the Irish Tourist Association, a body dominated by hoteliers and other involved parties, whose central role was institutionalized by the government until the 1970s. The fact that its actions brought in regional development and improvement of local amenities, such as rubbish collection, gave the organization popular support in tourist spots, but many areas were entirely untouched and therefore barely involved in the debate on tourist policy.

Decisions with regard to tourism as a result often had less to do with what made Ireland Irish for the Irish than with what visitors imagined made it Irish. The tourist festival An Tóstal, the main government initiative, was based on the Festival of Britain; the large "See Ireland First" campaign was copied from America; and, during the second half of the twentieth century, all tourist brochures were designed by a Dutchman. As a result Zuelow is a bit at a loss to find debates that touch upon Irish identity. In his more analytical chapters he discusses at length the restoration of Kilmainham Jail, which was done in the 1960s by voluntary labor and had no association with tourist policy, and the development of the Guinness brewery as a tourist attraction, which was a purely commercial initiative.

One can only conclude that the scarcity of debate about the content of Irishness and the prominence of economic concerns makes it difficult to draw conclusions about national identity from tourism policy. The book is therefore somewhat descriptive and does not really touch on the debate on Irishness that was engaged in elsewhere. There is nevertheless much to recommend Zuelow's study. It is well researched and written, and provides an excellent insight into how Irish tourism policy was developed and who engineered it. It also shows how Irish politics worked in practice and what elements were emphasized in public debate. The central intention to bring the development of Irish national identity to the fore was, however, probably an overambitious task.

JOOST AUGUSTEIJN
Leiden University

EUNAN O'HALPIN. *Spying on Ireland: British Intelligence and Irish Neutrality during the Second World War.* New York: Oxford University Press. 2008. Pp. xxi, 335. $60.00.

The "Emergency," as World War II came to be known in Ireland, has attracted much interest, a trend visible in recent studies by Brian Girvin and Clair Wills and even a successful stage musical, *Improbable Frequency*, which capitalizes on the comic potential of a wartime Dublin populated by Nazi spies, British agents, and Irish Republican Army (IRA) fifth columnists. Most research has focused on the maintenance of (southern) Irish neutrality within the context of the Anglo-Irish relationship and related issues such as censorship, intelligence, and espionage. Consequently, Eunan O'Halpin's study of British intelligence in Ireland addresses issues that are the subject of a considerable historiography, including British policy on partition, Axis espionage, Anglo-Irish security cooperation, and the propaganda war over neutrality.

However, O'Halpin's sharp focus—his is the first monograph systematically to analyze the role of all British security agencies active in wartime Ireland—and access to declassified sources succeeds in shedding new light on the Emergency. His decision to assess British policy on Ireland within the context of Britain's treatment of other neutral states within its sphere of influence, such as Iraq and Afghanistan, rather than the usual European suspects, coupled with the surprising degree of importance attached to espionage and diplomacy in wartime Ireland by the allies, has resulted in an impressive case study of intelligence and neutrality that transcends its geographical focus.

British intelligence in Ireland was a game of two halves. O'Halpin outlines the remarkable lack of prewar political and security interest in Ireland despite the obvious strategic problems that a neutral Ireland would pose. This was exemplified by the return of the "treaty ports" to Irish control in 1938 without due consideration of the security implications, Britain's lack of intelligence-gathering capabilities in Ireland, and the absence of structures to facilitate bilateral security and political cooperation. Much of this can be attributed to the ambiguous, shifting nature of the interwar Anglo-Irish relationship.

Consequently, when intelligence on Ireland first became an urgent necessity following Germany's occupa-
tion of France in the summer of 1940, British capabilities proved inadequate to the task. The quality of intelligence was poor, there was insufficient cooperation between the intelligence agencies active within Ireland, and little coordination or oversight of their efforts. O'Halpin asserts that the most significant outcome of this "spectacular intelligence failure" (p. 95) was Britain's remarkable offer to support unification in return for Irish support in the war, which he sees as a consequence of a flawed understanding of the relative strengths of Eamon de Valera's government and the pro-German IRA. The threat of invasion receded with Adolf Hitler's invasion of Russia, but Ireland remained a source of concern due to the fear that the presence of Axis legations, working with an IRA fifth column or the German spies periodically parachuted into the country, would compromise the security of the preparations for the invasion of Europe. As a result, the first diplomatic traffic targeted by the Government Code and Cipher School (GC&CS) following the cracking of Germany's diplomatic cipher in 1942 was Berlin-Dublin. It was not until after Operation Overlord that Ireland resumed its former status as a marginal backwater. By then, British intelligence had surmounted its inadequacies in impressive fashion, fashioning an effective security and intelligence capability underpinned both by a strong working relationship between Irish and British security and government officials and effective cooperation between Britain's security agencies.

O'Halpin generally confirms rather than challenges the received wisdom, but he does so in authoritative detail, providing what will surely remain the definitive study of British intelligence in wartime Ireland (despite his lack of access to many Secret Intelligence Service (SIS) records). De Valera's successful defence of neutrality in the face of Axis and Allied intrigue stemmed from a combination of determination, skill, and pragmatic acquiescence to British security interests. Winston Churchill's reputation as a great war leader does not rest on his mastery of the complexities of intelligence and security cooperation. Britain's man in Dublin, John Maffey, played an important role in the successful Anglo-Irish relationship, while the belligerent U.S. representative, David Gray, repeatedly jeopardized its fruits, particularly with his potentially disastrous demand for the expulsion of Axis diplomats prior to Overlord. Irish security forces, north and south, performed effectively, notably Irish military intelligence, G2, which penetrated German and British intelligence-gathering operations without detection.

This case study touches on issues of broader concern. To what extent does intelligence inform political policy and military actions? O'Halpin is candid about the difficulty of demonstrating a direct link, but his study convincingly details the importance attached to intelligence by wartime politicians. Consequently, it raises some salutary points with contemporary resonances. British intelligence failed in 1939–1940 because it had not anticipated the threat posed by Germany due to its preoccupation (for ideological and strategic reasons) with another threat—that of the Soviet Union and communist-nationalist subversion within the British Empire—that did not transpire at that time. Intelligence can also prove a mixed blessing: had Britain cracked German code traffic earlier it may well have resulted in counterproductive decisions in the case of Ireland. This study emphasises how intelligence, rather than occurring within a vacuum, is generated and interpreted for political purposes and how, even when accurate, it can be distorted by the prejudices or requirements of the politicians who must decide how to use it.

FEARGHAL MCGARRY
Queen's University Belfast

DANIEL LEACH. *Fugitive Ireland: European Minority Nationalists and Irish Political Asylum, 1937–2008.* Portland, Oreg.: Four Courts Press. 2009. Pp. 285. $55.00.

After World War II Ireland granted political asylum to a modest number of nationalists from various European ethnic minorities, some wanted by the Allies for war crimes and collaboration with the Axis. An uncritical paradigm has developed portraying Ireland as a sanctuary for pro-Axis fugitives. Daniel Leach challenges this paradigm, arguing that rather than adopting a pro-Axis agenda Dublin followed a more calculating policy intended to safeguard Ireland's national interests.

Leach explains that Ireland had no sentimental attachment toward the new arrivals and Ireland was no place for asylum seekers to nurture their dreams. Independent from Britain since 1922 and neutral during World War II, the primary goal of Dublin's foreign policy was to assert Ireland's autonomy.

One might expect Ireland to look kindly toward others who sought to undermine the British Empire. Not so. Focusing on wartime Scottish nationalists, Leach debunks assumptions that Ireland, because of its independence struggle, offered a welcome to fugitives. Instead the growing security relationship with Britain, established on Irish initiative in 1938, took precedence. Breton nationalists too were unwelcome; there was no pan-Celtic sympathy in Dublin. Their movements were monitored for contacts with the Irish Republican Army or with Axis subversives.

The Allies were interested in the French fascists, Dutch Nazis, Belgian Rexists, and Croatian Ustaše as well as Bretons, Flemings, and Croats who sought postwar refuge in Ireland. They also had their eye on the diplomats from the German mission in Dublin, German prisoners of war, and spies in Irish custody. Dublin's response was simple: Washington and London could seek Irish cooperation in investigating these individuals but could not demand cooperation or expect it to be offered unconditionally.

Countering the interference in Irish affairs of the United States Minister to Ireland David Gray was a major determinant of Dublin's stance. In February 1944 Gray attempted to force Ireland to expel Axis diplomats from Dublin, and in September 1944 he demanded that no Axis war criminal be granted asylum in Ireland. By attacking Irish sovereignty and neutrality Gray brought Irish-American relations to a low point and ensured that Ireland would be slow to offer the Allies assistance. Ireland would follow its own asylum policy based on its own interests. Of course, those interests could often run parallel with those of the Allies.

Formally neutral, Ireland cooperated covertly with the Allies during World War II. Friendly neutrality reaped no rewards postwar. However Leach argues that the presence of Germans and asylum seekers on Irish territory gave Dublin a commodity with which to develop international intelligence contacts at a time when Ireland was isolated internationally.

During the Cold War Ireland was anxious to show its anticommunist credentials and allegiance to the West. Without joining the North Atlantic Treaty Organization, Dublin professed agreement with the terms of the alliance. According to Leach successive Irish governments from the late 1940s were willing to grant asylum to individuals with dubious pasts in the name of combating communism. This was the case with former members of the Breton SS Bezen Perrot unit who had fought the forces of communism in the shape of the French Resistance. Yet to repair relations with the Allies, Irish governments rejected high-profile Breton asylum seekers while allowing a number of discreet Breton entrants.

There was a strong Catholic dimension to Ireland's Cold War asylum policy, as a particularly pro-Vatican stance developed in postwar Irish foreign policy. Leach's assessment of those former members of the Flemish Waffen-SS who entered Ireland places their experience within the context of the "Ratline" and other networks that operated with the complicity of the Catholic Church and Western intelligence services. However, he concludes that Ireland did not play a major role as a staging post in these networks. In this context Leach also suggests that Andrija Artuković, former minister for the interior of the pro-Axis Independent State of Croatia, travelled through Ireland under an assumed name to the United States with the covert assistance of the Irish government and the Irish Catholic Church, a move secretly in accord with the objectives of Western intelligence services.

Leach's diverse subject is held together by a strong argument and wide research, though it is clear in the footnotes to his later chapters that the necessary primary sources were not always available for his sensitive subject. Nonetheless, his account is the first to move Ireland's intelligence relationship with the United States and the United Kingdom into the postwar years, and he has effectively debunked the myth of Ireland offering sympathetic shelter to pro-Axis fugitives. In doing so he has greatly enhanced understanding of the singular stance often adopted by Irish foreign and security policies. He concludes pointedly by quoting Joseph Walshe, the enigmatic head of Ireland's diplomatic service during World War II: "Small nations like Ireland do not and cannot assume the role of defenders of just causes except their own" (p. 221). Critics of Ireland's foreign and security policies through World War II and the Cold War would do well to reflect on these words.

MICHAEL KENNEDY
Royal Irish Academy

GUY ORTOLANO. *The Two Cultures Controversy: Science, Literature and Cultural Politics in Postwar Britain*. New York: Cambridge University Press. 2009. Pp. xi, 295. $99.00.

This book is in part a record of the debate between C. P. Snow and F. R. Leavis on the matter of the "two cultures," but it is also a lot more. In guiding us through the origins, content, and fall-out from this most famous of academic clashes, Guy Ortolano illuminates key aspects of culture and society at a critical moment in British postwar history. He uses the clash between what he terms the "technocratic liberalism" of Snow and the "radical liberalism" of Leavis to take us to the heart of a political disagreement about the trajectory of British politics and economy in the age of Harold Macmillan and Harold Wilson, arguing persuasively that a debate previously understood primarily "as a *disciplinary* dispute about the arts and the sciences was actually an *ideological* conflict between competing views of Britain's past, present and future" (p. 1). Ortolano sees his task here as that of the informed external viewer. He uses the argument between two now largely forgotten figures to "recover the context in which their arguments and reputations thrived" (p. 11), taking as his "objects of study: the 'two cultures' controversy, the postwar British context, and the historical tradition discussing the arts and the sciences" (p. 23). He does so, the better to illuminate "agendas and rivalries that simmered beneath—and occasionally boiled over—a seemingly placid post-war consensus" (p. 24).

The result is a wide-ranging and elegantly written study that brings together a series of integrated stories. The book tells the personal biographies of Snow and Leavis and documents their ongoing, increasingly bitter dispute. It anchors that dispute within a wider post-1956 debate on educational reform in Britain. It explores the minutiae of academic politics in Cambridge University: Snow at Churchill College, Leavis at Downing. It takes us in and out of the Labour Government of 1964–1970, and in and out of debates within both the New Left of the 1960s and the neo-conservatism of the 1970s. It even touches on post-colonial economic development, as well as on the perennial debate on British decline. It explores Snow's vision and contrasts it to that of Leavis; and it takes us to their shared commitment to the creation of a meritocratic Britain: a commitment shared for entirely contradictory purposes, and whose moment largely passed with the advent of Thatcherism.

As someone who lived through this period, knows Labour governments well, and was even at York University as a student when Leavis was there as a visiting professor, I can testify to the success of Ortolano's work in its wider cultural purposes. As I read further and further into this text, I could ever more readily hear and feel, even smell, a Britain now largely gone. Snow the modernizing radical, Ortolano tells us, lost his enthusiasm for radical change as the egalitarianism of the New Left threatened his meritocratic vision. It was a symptomatic change: I knew many Snow equivalents among the intellectuals who first taught me. Leavis imprinted his acerbic vision of how English literature should be studied, and English departments should lead, on a generation of British academics. I remember them well. It is inconceivable today that a petty squabble between two socially mobile elitist Cambridge academics could shape British public debate in the way that Snow and Leavis's dispute did. Ortolano has captured an important *lost* moment—even a *last* moment—in the rise and fall of a Britain dominated by a narrow educational and social ruling stratum. The world in which they debated has fortunately gone.

But its going speaks to a potential weakness in this book that erodes the overall quality of the argument. Ortolano treats the issue of British economic decline—a central concern of Snow's—as "just one possible, and by no means the best, interpretation of postwar British history" (p. 23). He follows the fashion of declining to be a declinist. That is a great pity, for in the half century since Snow's "two cultures" lecture, the British economy has indeed declined, slipping significantly down international league tables on performance and competitiveness, and currently running its largest trade deficit ever. Snow's 1959 analysis of why that decline was likely to occur was woefully inadequate, but it was at least an important wake-up call to a British establishment still preoccupied with empire and ignorant of industry. Imperial powers take their military-industrial capacity seriously—Ortolano is wise here to follow the scholarship of David Edgerton—but great powers do not survive by guns alone. The United States may just be poised to discover that. The United Kingdom was busy discovering it as Snow spoke. Leavis had nothing to say that was even vaguely helpful to that key discussion. Snow at least saw the problem, and deserves honor for the insight.

DAVID COATES
Wake Forest University

ALEXANDRA PARMA COOK and NOBLE DAVID COOK. *The Plague Files: Crisis Management in Sixteenth-Century Seville*. Baton Rouge: Louisiana State University Press. 2009. Pp. x, 296. $40.00.

I began composing this review while waiting to receive an H1N1 vaccination. Over 2,000 people stood in line ahead of me, and the situation had overwhelmed the public health authorities. In addition to chatter about whether the staff had enough injections for everyone (they did not), I overheard conversations about lost jobs, real estate foreclosures, and corrupt bankers. My immediate circumstances provided an appropriate contemporary context for understanding the significance of the stories Alexandra Parma Cook and Noble David Cook tell in their book.

The book focuses on the years Don Fernando de Torres y Portugal, the Count of Villar, served as *asistente* (royal high commissioner or governor) of Seville, 1579–1583. The crown subsequently appointed Villar to the post of viceroy of Peru. The authors deal with their subject by telling stories pulled from the minutes of Seville's municipal council sessions and related documents, including reports from apothecaries and physicians. This approach makes the book a delight to read despite the troubling issues with which Villar and the local authorities dealt. As the title indicates, epidemic disease threatened the city and surrounding towns during these years, but the other three horsemen of the Apocalypse also road through the land. Quarantine disrupted vital commerce with the Americas. Philip II invaded Portugal to assert his claims to the throne, and troops had to be billeted and controlled. *Moriscos*, Christians of Muslim ancestry, organized a rebellion. Locust infestations destroyed grain crops, which forced Seville's leaders to search for supplies as far away as eastern La Mancha and Sicily. Beyond the epidemic, accumulations of garbage and contaminated water supplies on the Guadalquivir River brought endemic disease and death to the overcrowded city. Disease and famine particularly lashed the poor, packed together in their houses and neighborhoods, and overwhelmed social services dedicated to assisting the high percentage of the population living in poverty. A vacant archiepiscopal see and conflicts with inquisitors left ecclesiastical assistance disorganized. Overwhelmed by a conjunction of demands on the municipal treasury, Seville's council resorted to deficit spending and faced bankruptcy.

The narratives reveal that people endured a harsh reality in one of Europe's major cities of the first global age, and by recognizing significant stories and recounting them well, the authors expose aspects of everyday life in the period. Their book possesses particular value for what it shows about the work of those in the health professions. As much as I enjoyed reading the book, however, I think that the authors do not make their readers sufficiently aware of the ways that their sources may distort reality. Notaries used set forms to prepare documents, including municipal council minutes, and their recourse to common patterns of organization and presentation provides us with a greater sense of normalcy than may really have been the case. Medical reports relied on similar standards about what should be included, and individuals' correspondence, reports, and interventions in council meetings were intended in part to demonstrate to others their authors' competency. There is just enough evidence here to indicate that authorities had quite limited control over the movement of goods and people and that orders were frequently ignored. As an anonymous complaint to the crown indicated, municipal officials may not have been as conscientious, vigorous, or honest in their conduct of the commonwealth's business as they sought to project in

their pronouncements to their colleagues and to royal officials.

Human systems are largely nonlinear, in part because of their interactions with nonlinear natural systems, as this book shows well. This nonlinearity means that social networks were disrupted frequently, either by occurrences such as epidemics and wars or by the expansion of opportunities, which was common in the sixteenth century. Social networks served as the loci for creativity and innovation as people responded to these "disruptions" in an effort to establish more robust networks. Although the time period treated in this book is likely too short to illustrate this important process, the authors do provide some examples of strengthening relationships among individuals and groups, and they suggest a number of cases where additional research would likely expose such activity in subsequent years. Also, the overall stability of a nonlinear system, however turbulent such "disruptions" make it appear, depends on a small number of factors which are constantly close to instability. In order to understand the nonlinear system of the first global age better, and to understand why the use of the teleological term "early modern" is so unsatisfactory, research should focus on identifying these factors, and this book supplies some excellent material for those who want to investigate the matter. I hope that the press will issue a paperback version so that it can be assigned for courses dealing with the first global age.

J. B. OWENS
Idaho State University

MERRY WIESNER-HANKS. *The Marvelous Hairy Girls: The Gonzales Sisters and Their Worlds*. New Haven: Yale University Press. 2009. Pp. xiii, 248. $30.00.

This engaging book is about the sixteenth and early seventeenth-century social and political contexts that shaped the ways that people perceived the Gonzales family, many of whom had unusually copious amounts of facial and body hair. The book focuses on the hairy Petrus Gonzales, his non-hairy wife, Catherine, and their seven children, the majority of whom were hairy. Merry Wiesner-Hanks describes the family's trajectory beginning with Petrus's arrival as a boy from the Canary Islands to the court of Henry II and Catherine de Medici in Paris in 1547. Since so much of the book deals with varying members of the Gonzales family, I found the title's focus on the Gonzales sisters puzzling. Far from merely recounting known facts about Petrus and his subsequent family's life, Wiesner-Hanks explores the cultural materials and norms as well as the scientific and religious beliefs that molded the Gonzales's lives and other people's ideas about them.

Wiesner-Hanks devotes the first chapter to ancient and medieval beasts and wonders, and the second to New World myths. The third chapter examines how these concepts influenced people's perceptions of members of the court, such as Protestants' depiction of Catherine de Medici as a monstrous queen. It further investigates the models available to Henry II for how to treat Petrus, including as a dwarf, an exotic savage, and a menial servant, although the king opted to educate him in the humanist style as he did his own children. Chapter four studies the part that early modern courtly customs about marriage, birth, and family life may have played in Petrus and Catherine's union, their children's births, and the latter's own marriages and family life. Chapter five delves into religious tensions that impinged on the Gonzales's artistic portrayals and their meanings, including Catholics' and Protestants' different interpretations of monsters, debates on humans as rational, and disputes about women's status as monstrous and inferior. The book's final chapter situates the Gonzaleses among early modern scientists and collectors who sought to compile complete inventories of the natural world in order to derive universal laws of nature. An intriguing study of seventeenth-century cabinets of curiosities plays an important role in this chapter.

This book is remarkable not only because of its provocative subject, but also on account of Wiesner-Hanks's adept weaving of the Gonzales family history with research on a wide variety of early modern topics. The author draws her analysis of the family from their appearance in "scientific treatises, medical case histories, letters, diplomats' reports, baptismal and death registers, and account books" (p. 7). Yet despite this documentation, many gaps and doubts remain that cause Wiesner-Hanks to speculate about her observations and conclusions. For example, she relies on sixteenth-century marriage norms to submit potential reasons for Catherine's willingness to marry the hairy Petrus, citing his respectable position at Henry II's court and possible pressure from her parents. I was not at all bothered by such theories, since they were always grounded in solid documentation.

Occasionally I wished that Wiesner-Hanks had pushed her analyses a bit further, especially her feminist readings and theoretical issues of identity and the monstrous. With regard to the monstrous, she indicates that Petrus and his family were usually perceived as hybrids or were treated in ambivalent ways, such as when the Flemish painter Joris Hoefnagel seemed to regard the Gonzales children both as miracles to praise and signs to fear. Although this sentiment may have always informed people's perceptions of those deemed different, the social value of monsters changed in the early modern period, a development Wiesner-Hanks does not consider. Whereas the medieval monster was usually integrated into schemes of the mundane and divine orders, as Michael Camille and David Williams suggest, early modern monsters also came to be found in unwanted social groups, such as marginalized or expelled Protestants and Jews. When Wiesner-Hanks states that most people expected to see or meet a marvel or a wonder during their lifetime (p. 46), I wonder if we could say the same about people in previous eras. Just as monsters on the borders of medieval maps and buildings marked the limits of mundane and divine spheres, so do the monstrous things in the cabinets of curiosities in

chapter six constitute efforts at ordering the natural world. Yet the hierarchies implied in some of the early modern collections that Wiesner-Hanks examines contrast with monsters in medieval maps and other sources where they were embraced, suggesting a change in value of the monstrous. Although she says that monsters increasingly became warning signs in the sixteenth century (p. 161), more direct investigation into the relationship among the monstrous's shift in value, the ambivalent attitudes toward the Gonzales family, and their characterization as hybrids may have contributed further depth to this significant book.

JEAN DANGLER
Tulane University

JACOB SOLL. *The Information Master: Jean-Baptiste Colbert's Secret State Intelligence System.* (Cultures of Knowledge in the Early Modern World.) Ann Arbor: University of Michigan Press. 2009. Pp. xi, 277. $65.00.

This original, perceptive commentary on the role of Jean-Baptiste Colbert in the government of Louis XIV sheds new light on a well-known subject. Colbert, the king's finance minister from 1661 to 1683, has enjoyed a variety of historical identities. He has been seen as Cartesian organizer, mercantilist developer, and royal publicist. Textbooks generally treat him as a middle-class upstart who restored the royal finances and promoted mercantilism while struggling to moderate the king's extravagant expenses. Recent scholarship has shown that the Colbert family was more distinguished than had been commonly thought. A devastating recent portrait is Daniel Dessert's view of Colbert as a manipulative mastermind behind the throne. He placed clients in key positions all over France and used his position to enrich his whole family (*Le Royaume de Monsieur Colbert 1661–1683* [2007]).

For Jacob Soll, Colbert was a pioneer of information management. Soll is fascinated by the circulation of political ideas through intellectual channels and their influence on the practice of governance. In his previous book he explored the transmission of Machiavellian governing practices to absolute monarchies (*Publishing "The Prince": History, Reading, and the Birth of Political Criticism* [2005]). Here he approaches the same territory, this time studying government's use of information. Along the way Soll displays a vast knowledge of the broader history of book publishing, libraries, scientific academies, and censorship.

Colbert masterminded the accumulation of useful information about the king's realm. He created the best library in Europe, consisting of books, manuscripts, copies of laws, and excerpts from the deeds and charters of religious houses and municipalities. He hired librarian-scholars to organize and classify these materials, and developed a system of call numbers, indexes, and summaries to facilitate the rapid retrieval of needed information. Unlike the open sharing practiced in the Republic of Letters, the contents of this "data bank" now became classified information reserved for governmental exploitation. His archives gave him the upper hand in disputes between the king and the pope and in treaty negotiations.

Soll sees Colbert's regime as a major step forward in the state's mastery of society. Colbert was ahead of his time in turning an international scholarly accumulation of information into a secret resource designed solely as an organ of state power. Colbert disciplined his son to collect exacting geographic and economic information, write clear reports, and acquire good copies of charters, wills, and deeds. The same hunger for accurate information was transmitted to the *intendants* in the provinces, who similarly had to scramble to fulfill his demands.

This interpretation, based upon intensive research, challenges existing views and raises interesting questions. First, it interrogates our interpretation of absolutism. For the last twenty years the idea of a modernizing Louis XIV, who centralized power and reduced the nobility and the provinces to submission, has been replaced by the revisionist notion that absolutism was a conservative collaboration between king and noble ruling class in defense of a traditional society. By emphasizing Colbert's administrative expertise, Soll breathes new life into the older view.

Second, Colbert's wonderful records can seduce the reader into believing too fervently in the efficacy of royal policies. The papers of royal ministers give a false impression of rational order and measured decision making, downplaying the importance of the king himself. An innocent reader of this book might easily conclude that Louis XIV was a mere figurehead. But the king's well-known personal rule was more than a propagandistic smoke screen. Colbert's ugly manipulation and grasping search for personal gain, as presented by Dessert, is another dimension that would modify Soll's benevolent picture of Colbert the bureaucrat.

Finally, Soll's use of modern terminology to describe an early modern situation is perhaps unwise. He claims that Colbert's system was "a powerful, concrete tool of industrial production and political power" (p. 76) and sees a revolution in "information management technology" (p. 23). He views the *intendants* as "professional informers" (p. 78), and even goes so far as to claim that their activity contained "the germs of modern totalitarian government growing into webs of informants and file-systems" (p. 80). This was a "police state" trying to "micromanage" society (p. 137).

Soll's argument is nuanced and his ideas are productive of new insights. He acknowledges problems. He notes Colbert's disinterest in the Atlantic world and registers the fact that subsequent reigns did not renew his innovations. There are issues to debate, but this important book should be essential reading for anyone interested in seventeenth-century France.

WILLIAM BEIK,
Emeritus
Emory University

MATHIEU MARRAUD. *De la ville à l'état: La bourgeoisie parisienne XVIIe–XVIIIe siècle*. (Bibliothèque Albin Michel Histoire.) Paris: Albin Michel. 2009. Pp. 552. €29.00.

Since at least the eighteenth century, the European bourgeoisie has had to bear more than its share of ideological weight. Variously represented as a rising class, the seat of a developing public sphere, the location for evolving ideas of individualism, the nuclear family, and revolutionary sentiment, in France the bourgeoisie has also been described as so thoroughly enmeshed in a society of orders that its members eagerly abandoned their commercial expertise for the realm of royal office and ennoblement. In his excellent new work, Mathieu Marraud takes a markedly different approach to examining the Parisian bourgeoisie from the mid-seventeenth to the late eighteenth centuries. He sets out to reconstruct the social practices and values that defined the group through a careful examination of their family strategies, alliances, inheritance practices, and business arrangements. A vivid storyteller, Marraud uses extensive genealogies to assemble a picture of the familial practices that together defined this social milieu, and his ability to reconstruct such life histories almost exclusively from notary contracts shows considerable historical expertise. This is not a work that one can read quickly, but it amply repays the attention of readers interested in mercantile elites in early modern Europe, the social and political underpinnings of urban life, the implications of royal office holding in early modern France, and the ways that social history may inform cultural historical interpretations more generally.

Marraud's work is at its strongest in its careful elaboration of the familial practices and assumptions that characterized the Parisian mercantile elite. Starting from an elaborate contemporary investigation into the heirs of a woman who died in 1777, the author successively introduces the numerous family branches related to the deceased whose inheritance decisions, alliance choices, apprenticeships, and business partnerships all serve to delineate bourgeois comportments. For Marraud, the Parisian bourgeoisie adhered to a collective definition of the family and responsibility for its success that assured strictly equal distributions of family property to all children, attempts to marry off as many offspring as possible, and a desire to preserve the monetary and social capital of the family business, although not necessarily in the male line. Such practices, which incidentally assured women an important role in decision making, preserving the family patrimony, and extending alliances, were designed above all to maximize a family's "social surface." Because the Parisian bourgeoisie continued to gauge its own notability through office holding in such important urban institutions as the major guilds, commercial court, parish vestries, and city hall, such visibility through extensive alliance constituted important social capital. In Marraud's view, therefore, Parisian bourgeois families were highly conservative in their social vision and habits: they emphasized collective determinations over individual choices, group destinies over hierarchical authority, and pathways of urban notability in the face of an ever-developing monarchical state. They also tended to adopt strong Jansenist beliefs and were late to experiment in Enlightenment views. As late as the eighteenth century, then, the values of Parisian families drawn to the Catholic League in the sixteenth century, as expounded by historian Robert Descimon, endured in their descendants.

This book also has important points to make in emphasizing the permeability between commerce and royal office holding and between bourgeois and noble status in *ancien régime* France. Although historians have tended to portray office holding and nobility as the ultimate ambitions for French mercantile families and as initiating profound ruptures in social status, Marraud demonstrates that continuities nevertheless endured. Commercial families could view office holding as a way to ensure younger sons a livelihood, while concentrating most capital in trade concerns, or as a means to extend the kinds of financial activities and investments with which they were already familiar. Because certain of these offices were ennobling, bourgeois families could continue to act according to their collective values even as different members officially belonged to different estates. Despite such continuities, however, Marraud's analysis also goes far to suggest that the transition from trade to office holding could be anything but smooth. As members of the Parisian bourgeoisie attempted to enter the realm of high royal office, they could find their financial and social resources unequal to the task, even as they abandoned the kinds of familial customs that had previously assured their success. The result, in Marraud's view, was often financial decline, social isolation, and even genealogical extinction for families desperate to uphold their noble status without sufficient means or background. Thus, for Marraud, the emphases on consumerism and individual choice taking hold in the eighteenth century were the products of failure in navigating social distinctions rather than bourgeois innovation. Whether these conclusions rest on as solid historical evidence as the author's convincing exposition of bourgeois familial customs is uncertain, but they remain interesting hypotheses worthy of further consideration.

HILARY J. BERNSTEIN
*University of California,
Santa Barbara*

JEREMY HAYHOE. *Enlightened Feudalism: Seigneurial Justice and Village Society in Eighteenth-Century Northern Burgundy.* (Changing Perspectives on Early Modern Europe, number 10.) Rochester, N.Y.: University of Rochester Press. 2008. Pp. xii, 309. $80.00.

In yet another sign that the study of French rural history is flourishing, several books have recently examined the important but surprisingly opaque institution of feudal justice. They contribute not only a thorough understanding of the juridical practices of the seigneurial courts but also have begun to use their archives to deepen our understanding of rural society. The new book by Jeremy Hayhoe make an impressive addition to the first of these contributions, with a careful reconstruction of the courts' personnel, docket, and reforms. Yet what makes this book particularly important is his "radical conclusion that court records are essential for understanding social relations not only because they provided evidence of the kinds of social bonds that existed and broke between individuals, but because local courts provided some of the context for the elaboration and construction of social bonds" (p. 98). In arguing his case, Hayhoe has convincingly made the seigneurial court an essential tool for any rural historian.

Historians have generally ignored seigneurial courts for several traditional, if contradictory, reasons. The tradition that portrays the seigneurial regime as a hollow anachronism may conflict with another tradition that paints the resurgence of a predatory system, but both tend to dismiss the principal agency of seigneurial power, its courts, as irrelevant or, at best, burdensome to the French peasant. Peasant communities, we have been told, preferred to deal with their problems informally or through royal courts.

Hayhoe has painstakingly examined the records of fourteen seigneurial courts in northern Burgundy during the second half of the eighteenth century to turn these traditions on their head. He deals quickly but effectively with some of the standard objections to seigneurial courts, pointing out that they adjudicated most issues quickly and cheaply. He has rather more trouble dismissing the inconveniences arising from the fact that few judges lived, or heard cases, in the villages in their jurisdiction, except during the yearly assizes. Since nearly half of the plaintiffs in the other, regular, sessions came from different villages, the need to bring their cases before a judge who generally lived in the seat of the bailliage was probably not too burdensome, but the travel imposed upon the defendants may have dissuaded them from appearing in person. Defendants in other regions of France often failed to appear for minor cases, and I suspect it was similar in Burgundy, though Hayhoe does not give details. He does point out that the distance between the village and its seigneurial court was the single most common complaint made in the region's *cahiers de doléances*.

Yet Hayhoe makes a persuasive case that rural communities turned frequently to seigneurial courts for solving a range of important issues. He calculates that his seigneurial courts were some six times more active, per capita, than the local royal court, which mostly heard cases involving a wealthy, urban population. Instead, peasants clearly thought that the seigneurial court was the appropriate place to settle matters of debt, inheritance, honor, violence, farming, and communal policing. In a beautifully nuanced analysis, Hayhoe argues that peasants felt they could sue when a dispute was not too rancorous or did not involve their own families and that they appreciated the generally nonpunitive nature of court decisions. Even the courts' policing duties reflected communal expectations, as their persistent failure to prosecute taverns for serving locals demonstrates. These and other points allow Hayhoe to claim that "Ordinary people saw seigneurial justice as a form of self-regulation for the community" (p. 131).

At the same time, Hayhoe acknowledges several caveats to his arguments. In the first place, as he carefully demonstrates, the situation in Burgundy was rather different than in other parts of France. For reasons that are not entirely clear, the Burgundian courts appear to have been more accessible and responsive to the needs of rural society than elsewhere; at least the peasants turned to them more frequently and for more issues. In part this was due to reforms that had made the seigneurial courts of Burgundy more responsive. The insistence on yearly assizes, beginning in the 1770s, led to far more cases brought before the seigneurial courts. Thus Hayhoe's argument for the centrality of these courts to the administration and functioning of rural society is somewhat more persuasive at the end of the Old Regime than before. Finally, Hayhoe devotes considerable space to addressing the uses seigneurs made of their courts to reinforce their own power. The seigneurial court allowed seigneurs to defend their rights to forest and fields and to seigneurial dues, and Hayhoe shows that they did so with growing frequency. He argues for a "seigneurial reaction"—a resurgence of feudal exactions through more rigorous enforcement of existing dues. The fact that they were enforced by an institution so central to rural society only added fuel to a revolutionary fire.

THOMAS BRENNAN
U.S. Naval Academy

DARYL M. HAFTER. *Women at Work in Preindustrial France*. University Park: Pennsylvania State University Press. 2007. Pp. ix, 318. $55.00.

Daryl M. Hafter's new book makes an important contribution to our understanding of women's lives in the past. Although its title suggests a general overview, Hafter's book is actually a detailed analysis of women and guilds in the very late eighteenth century. Hafter is not the first to deal with the French guilds in this period of their decline. Steven Kaplan has written extensively on eighteenth-century guilds, and Judith Coffin and Clare Crowston have investigated women's guilds in Paris. Hafter's study differs from these earlier works in that it takes a provincial perspective and utilizes local sources. Hafter selects for investigation two very different cities: Rouen and Lyon. Rouen was a medium-sized commercial center with strong and ancient guilds, including several important all-female guilds. In contrast, Lyon was a populous silk manufacturing center with loosely enforced guild regulations and many women working outside guild structures. In Rouen, guild privilege reigned; in Lyon, labor was relatively free. These differing environments made for differences in women's work experiences. In Rouen, women

in the all-female guilds enjoyed the privileges of mastership and with them independence, self-regulation, and an active role in guild politics. Assaults on the mistresses' privileges did occur. Men's guilds tried to absorb and infiltrate them but the Rouen guildswomen had "a legal universe of privilege" to draw on, and they successfully warded off the attacks (p. 88). Working women's lot in Lyon was much different. There, only two all-female guilds existed, and production of silk involved large numbers of poor, unskilled, and unprotected women.

These differing work environments became particularly important once the French crown undertook the "reform" of the guilds in the late eighteenth century. The effects of the 1777 and 1778 reforms (which followed on Anne-Robert-Jacques Turgot's short-lived suppression of the guilds) constitute the core of Hafter's study. Using the correspondence between the crown and the provinces, Hafter charts the actions of the government. Many guilds were suppressed, others were combined to form new guilds, and guild monopolies on certain kinds of work disappeared. The most striking provision of the reform was the opening of all guilds to women, a means, the royal bureaucrats claimed, to improve women's lot and save them from prostitution. Hafter shows that despite such claims, the intent of the reforms was not wholly charitable. Fees were required of the women who entered male guilds, which along with confiscated guild property went directly to the desperate royal treasury (p. 227).

Whatever the royal reformers' intentions, their policies did little to benefit women workers. Enforcement was slow and uneven. Male guilds, Hafter observes, "used every conceivable dodge to exclude women" (p. 219). Only four percent of Rouen's female workers broke into previously male guilds. Widows—who could become masters long before the reforms—predominated while single and married women seemed unable to pay the steep entry fee. The same was true in Lyon, but the relatively weak position of guilds meant that the reforms had even less impact there.

In March of 1791, the National Assembly abolished corporations altogether, sweeping away the crown reforms and the centuries-old traditions of the guilds. Did the demise of the guilds benefit or hurt women? Hafter provides a qualified answer. On the one hand, women did get the freedom to exercise any trade or perform any kind of work. But on the other, women lost the privileges and political power that female-only guilds bestowed. Political rights in particular were lost. No longer could women as guild mistresses hold guild offices or vote in guild assemblies. To be accurate, the crown's 1778 reform had already barred women from any role in the governance of the newly mixed guilds. The disenfranchisement of women workers preceded the French Revolution. Was this a significant loss for all women? As Hafter points out, the number of female guilds had always been small and the number of politically powerful mistresses smaller still. For the majority of French women, the suppression of the guilds had little impact.

More detrimental to women was the new language of women's work that emerged in the late eighteenth century. Hafter is particularly able at outlining just how thinking about women and work shifted in the eighteenth century. Royal officials began to talk about the preservation of "women's modesty" and the "natural" inferiority of women's minds and bodies. The old language of privilege championed by the guild mistresses gave way to the vocabulary of sex and female subordination. "As the touchstone of privilege waned," remarks Hafter, "sex difference came to stand in its place" (p. 179).

KATHRYN NORBERG
*University of California,
Los Angeles*

MARY TROUILLE. *Wife-Abuse in Eighteenth-Century France.* (SVEC, number 2009:01.) Oxford: Voltaire Foundation. 2009. Pp. xiii, 377. $110.00.

Mary Trouille's new book is a welcome addition to the scholarship on women's grievances in eighteenth-century French law and literature. While several scholars have surveyed this terrain recently (Sarah Maza, Suzanne Desan, and Tracey Rizzo), Trouille telescopes in on a particular issue. At the same time, she telescopes out from legal records to fiction. Textual analyses of four separation suits, two divorces, and three works of fiction constitute the principal chapters of the book. Trouille concludes that "together with novels, these cases helped convince legislators and the public of the need for changes in attitudes, laws, and practices in order to protect abusive wives from husbands" (p. 309). She points to revolutionary legislation regarding the family, especially the liberal divorce law of 1792, to demonstrate the positive influence these texts exerted.

At the same time, Trouille's approach to the subject of wife abuse leaves little room for celebration. Although she states that "notions of violence and abuse are, of course, culturally determined" (p. 2), she concludes her introduction on a sober note with illustrations of husbands' cruelty in contemporary France (a woman is killed by her partner there every three days) and eleventh-century France (pp. 10–12), implying timelessness. Further on, she draws analogies between syphilis and AIDS to illustrate the deliberate use of contagion by men to victimize women, relating an Iowa case of 2005 to a French case of 1771, as though domestic violence is not influenced by location—chronological, geographic, and personal.

Trouille relates the narratives of court cases interestingly and grounds them in a wide range of historical studies published in the last forty years. Unfortunately, one must await the conclusion to see how they relate to each other and her broader argument. Contrasting legal representations of spouse abuse victims with fictional portrayals in the later chapters enables her "to explore the role of genre and discourse" in constructing wom-

en's experience and describe how "separation cases [are] projected into the realm of fiction" (p. 210). Especially strong is her chapter on the murder of the Marquise de Ganges, where she moves easily between four different versions of the case written over a 150-year period, and then offers a close reading of the Marquis de Sade's version. She alleges an evolution of attitudes illustrating that "tolerance of such abuse diminished" over time, evidenced by increasing attention to the marquise's emotional and psychological state and to her suffering in the 1927 version (p. 241). But might it be that increasing attention to the victim's state offers readers a vicarious, even titillating indulgence in the private experience of suffering?

Speaking of titillation, this reviewer finds the chapter on Rétif de la Bretonne's *Ingénue Saxancour* (an autobiographical work about his own daughter, Agnès) to be the most problematic. Although Trouille insists that "most Rétivian scholars agree that the novel reflects strong reformist, even feminist, impulses," the works to which she refers are decades old (p. 305). More recently, Rori Bloom ("Privacy, Publicity, Pornography: Rétif de la Bretonne's *Ingénue Saxancour ou la femme séparée*," *Eighteenth-Century Fiction* 17:2 [2005]) reads Rétif's voyeuristic depictions of his daughter's sexual torture by his son-in-law as a form of prostitution (p. 3). Was he a crusader against spouse abuse or a pornographer working out his own sexual feelings for his daughter by making them public and then making a profit? Trouille considers these questions too but concludes that the work underpins a feminist stance. But Trouille's own victim-blaming precludes this. She suggests that Agnès's "weakness of character," "passive submission," "spinelessness," and disclosure to her father of intimate marital details may have contributed to the development of "full-blown" incest between them (pp. 288, 298). The opposite is more likely: her sexual abuse by her father set Agnès up for victimization by her husband.

Trouille's aim is genealogical, to show that these "literary and legal texts began the arduous process of consciousness-raising in which we are still engaged today" (p. 329). How they did that is unclear; that this constitutes "consciousness-raising," in the sense of creating space for survivors to name their experiences—to be the experts and authorities over it—is arguable. As I found in my own work with legal cases, women's voices are nearly entirely structured by male lawyers, chroniclers, and novelists whose motives are complicated at best. The inclusion of Stéphanie de Genlis (chapter eight) and a handful of other women writers in the conclusion presents some women's perspectives but does not demonstrate that consciousness-raising ensued. Once again, the ahistorical use of a modern term unnecessarily muddles Trouille's larger point; the frequency of such usages detracts from this otherwise solid work. But the book's principal merits, an exhaustive bibliography, well-written case studies, and the bridge from fact to fiction, makes it an appropriate starting place for historians and literary critics interested in women in eighteenth-century French law.

TRACEY RIZZO
University of North Carolina,
Asheville

GUILLAUME MAZEAU. *Le bain de l'histoire: Charlotte Corday et l'attentat contre Marat 1793–2009.* Foreword by JEAN-CLÉMENT MARTIN. (La chose publique.) Seyssel: Champ Vallon. 2009. Pp. 426. €29.00.

This work is a meticulous attempt to unfold what its author calls the "origami" (p. 23) of impressions and interpretations surrounding Charlotte Corday's dramatic intervention in French revolutionary politics on July 13, 1793. To do so, Guillaume Mazeau must navigate a remarkably broad range of fields and forms of source. Beginning with an almost minute-by-minute reconstruction of the attack on Jean-Paul Marat itself and its aftermath, he goes on to explore the political and journalistic contexts in which Corday's deed was taken up and refracted through Girondin and Montagnard lenses, and how Corday's own performance at her trial enhanced, quite deliberately, her emerging legend and foiled official attempts to manage the narrative of what she had done. Beyond these immediate impacts, Mazeau then doubles back to recapture Corday's genteel Norman upbringing, her family's quiet struggles for money and status, and the heritage of religious observance and noble ethos into which she was born and raised.

Each of these sections, which make up in total some two-thirds of the book, keeps the reader engaged, with the sense that there is, somewhere, a true account potentially available. Mazeau complicates this impression in the remaining third of the work, as he undertakes to survey chronologically the diffusion of the idea of Charlotte Corday into French and international cultures, from the end of the Terror far into the twentieth century, and even into present-day appearances on the Internet. These sections have an interest of their own, as we see how the specifics of an historical event and personage become almost infinitely adaptable to the prejudices and goals of a variety of political movements. From pious counterrevolutionaries who collected supposed portraits of Corday that were increasingly indistinguishable from other icons such as the Princesse de Lamballe, to physical anthropologists who vied to discern the signs of criminality in her preserved skull, to crypto-fascist Norman nationalists who turned her blonde and made her an emblem of traditionalist resistance to centralizing power, Marat's assassin has had many students and admirers, but few who seem to have taken her own words on the matter seriously. One of the questions to be raised about this study is whether Mazeau himself sufficiently credits the explanation that came from Corday's own lips, as she studiously prepared to meet a martyr's death.

Corday herself, as the historical record clearly shows, claimed to have been "republican well before the Rev-

olution," and to have killed a man known to be a "hoarder of money" to "save a hundred thousand [men]" (p. 153). Given her also well-defined sympathies for the Girondins who fled to Caen in the summer of 1793, it is not clear quite why Mazeau feels confident in attributing to her the desire to "wash off the dishonor inflicted on her family" (p. 203) through a gesture of noble—specifically noble—self-sacrifice, or to go further and describe the act as based in "religious rationalities" (p. 205). When Corday's own *Adresse aux Français,* which she intended as a post-mortem testament, bathes in a classical language entirely familiar to Jacobins, can it be fair to assert that a "religious dimension" (p. 224) is added by her reference to the value of her self-sacrifice, when for example Maximilien Robespierre had made play of his own prospective demise for *le peuple* countless times by the summer of 1793? The extent to which her expressed motivations are set aside to be supplanted by a focus on familial circumstance does seem to suggest that Mazeau feels Corday is to be faulted for coming from the same kind of gentry background as, for example, Louis Antoine de Saint-Just, or for dwelling as a *pensionnaire* in a convent overseen by a relative—hardly a crime against the revolution, when so many ardent revolutionaries (such as her interrogator François Chabot) had been in holy orders.

As is often the case with French writers on their revolution, one is left by this book with an odd sense that a compulsive playing-out of the very same cultural ruptures occasioned by the original events continues to lie below the surface of the text. Many of the latter sections on the reinventions of Corday work with a language of "antirepublican" imagery, belief, and politics that serves to locate the proponents firmly in the camp of the undesirable—to the author's apparent satisfaction, anyway. To be "antirepublican" is evidently something to be opposed, but not for any reasons that require articulation. In the closing words of his conclusion Mazeau asks if an "engaged history" that "defend[s] a republican concept of history at the heart of democratic debate" while "recogniz[ing] the dignity of all the producers of the past" (p. 354) would be a good thing. It would, of course, but with a little more unpacking of such concepts than is offered here.

DAVID ANDRESS
University of Portsmouth

CHARLES WALTON. *Policing Public Opinion in the French Revolution: The Culture of Calumny and the Problem of Free Speech.* New York: Oxford University Press. 2009. Pp. xiii, 334. $49.95.

More than one-third of cases tried by the Revolutionary Tribunal in 1793–1794 involved crimes of speech and opinion. This fact has prompted Charles Walton to grapple with one of the central questions of the French Revolution: why did men who in 1789 proclaimed freedom of speech turn to killing people for expressing their political opinions? His effort to answer this question sidesteps traditional explanations for the Terror and instead concentrates on struggles to define freedom of expression and appropriate limits on it. This novel approach reveals much about the contested relationship between slander, censorship, and the law from the Enlightenment to Year II. Above all, it makes it clear just how unclear the revolutionaries were about freedom of speech and how dangerous that lack of clarity proved to be.

Slander—or calumny, as Walton prefers—was ambiguous. During the eighteenth century, *ad hominem* criticism did not have to be false to be considered calumny, it simply needed to damage someone's reputation, in which case it became a matter of honor, and possibly a lawsuit or a duel. Men of letters, such as the Marquis de Condorcet, opposed the monarchy's pre-publication censorship while also supporting legal punishment for calumny, especially when directed at private individuals. The *cahiers de doléance* of 1789 also generally insisted on certain limits to freedom of expression. Disagreement arose over protections afforded those in positions of authority, as well as wider moral and religious values. The Declaration of the Rights of Man and Citizen reflected these tensions. This landmark of liberty abolished institutional censorship and proclaimed freedom of religious opinion, while also authorizing punishment for abusive speech. But how would abusive speech be defined? If individuals had a right to protection from defamation, should political figures be treated differently? What if published criticisms of those in power incited popular violence?

Walton tracks the emergence of what he dubs a "quasi-libertarian position" in response to the anti-sedition decrees of 1790 and 1791. Despite this support for the virtues of calumny, the Constitution of 1791 enshrined some serious but ill-defined limits on political speech. One basis for prosecuting political speech became authorial intent, which proved a slippery slope in later years. The National Convention refined limits on political speech by ordering the death penalty for anyone who advocated the restoration of monarchy (December 1792) or anyone who incited pillage and murder (March 1793). The Law of Suspects (September 1793) criminalized a variety of political attitudes, even if not openly expressed, and the Law of Prairial (June 1794) made conviction especially easy by eliminating the need for any proof. Walton's history of the shift from "quasi-libertarian" attitudes to savagely repressive laws suggests that various groups of revolutionaries favored freedom of expression when it enabled them to criticize those in power, but found ways to justify curtailing it when they gained power themselves.

Beginning as early as 1789, revolutionaries used the concept of *lèse-nation* to conjure up various crimes of speech or opinion. Although this crime was never legally defined, the National Assembly gave the judges of the Châtelet exclusive jurisdiction over it and referred a number of cases to them. When that proved unsatisfactory, revolutionaries created the Haute Cour Na-

tionale. Walton's study of cases of *lèse-nation* reveals just how easy it was to exploit this charge. Although there were not many such cases, and even fewer that focused on speech, the trend was unmistakable. Political speech became the subject of exceptional justice well before the Terror. With this context in mind, Walton briefly explores the role of government in shaping civic spirit. Revolutionaries tended to favor spreading propaganda and monitoring public opinion; they just did not trust either the clergy or one another with these tasks. Therefore, despite a lot of talk in 1793 about how best to police and create opinion at the same time, none of the leading proposals for civic censorship was adopted. This may explain why Walton did not develop this important theme more fully; all the same, even a cursory description of the ways in which the Revolutionary Government of 1793–1794 engaged in "policing public opinion," other than simply executing people, would have helped.

Walton's book sheds light on how the revolutionaries' failure to define precise limits on freedom of speech fostered the arbitrariness of the Terror. However, the introduction points the book in a notably different direction. Here, and in a number of later passages, Walton argues that the civil egalitarianism promoted by the French Revolution democratized the "culture of calumny and honor" that existed among the privileged of pre-revolutionary France. The spread of this "culture" to other social groups "unleashed the systemic violence of the Old Regime" (p. 10), because affronts to personal honor such as calumnious speech were now interpreted as insults to larger sources of collective identity, such as the nation, or throne and altar. As a result, the revolutionaries' failure to stem a swelling tide of calumny led to outbursts of popular violence and then to the Terror. This sweeping explanation will prove contentious, not least for implying that it took until 1789 for ordinary French men and women to turn matters of personal honor into lawsuits and violence. In fact, Walton's focus on calumny and honor distorts his analysis of struggles over freedom of speech. Many victims of the Terror died for expressing their political opinions, but very few for slander. Jacobins did not need to stretch the ideas of calumny or honor to cover crimes of counterrevolution; even the transitional concept of *lèse-nation* served the purpose better. Whereas Walton presents this concept as a vestige of the old culture of honor, it was more important as an undefined crime that revolutionaries used to defend their exercise of sovereignty as well as to punish political opponents of various stripes. In other words, as the numerous case histories woven into the book suggest, "the problem of free speech" mentioned in the title was less about regulating calumny or defending honor and more about disputing the legitimacy of a rapidly evolving new order while also seeking to gain a factional advantage. Nonetheless, the book's rich evidence reminds us that the French Revolution was not merely a struggle over abstract principles but a myriad of personal dramas with often tragic outcomes.

HOWARD G. BROWN
Binghamton University, SUNY

JOHN WARNE MONROE. *Laboratories of Faith: Mesmerism, Spiritism, and Occultism in Modern France*. Ithaca: Cornell University Press. 2008. Pp. xi, 293. $35.00.

Across the nineteenth century, French society experienced profound tension around religion, usually imagined as a struggle between Catholic monarchism and freethinking republicanism. Of course these broadly drawn lines left many with complicated allegiances. Some secular republicans rejected the church, yet came to believe that the real world had supernatural components to it. This book is a detailed look at the ideas, behaviors, and organizations of these relatively secular spiritualists.

Mesmerism began in France around the time of the French Revolution. It was never terribly popular and in the mid-nineteenth century, when John Warne Monroe begins his study, it was essentially defunct. Then the American Spiritual movement caught on in France. In New York, in 1848, two girls had claimed they were receiving messages from the dead in the form of "spirit raps." Others soon claimed that they too were spirit-world "intermediaries" or mediums, and by 1852 the craze had caught on in England and, soon after, in France. France had just experienced its second republican revolution, the grand expectations of its Second Republic, and the collapse of all those hopes into the Second Empire of Napoleon III.

From a moment of extraordinary possibility and freedom, left-leaning French men and women found themselves in a world of censorship and authoritarian rule, a reaffirming of social hierarchy, and return of power to the Catholic Church. In this environment, the new movement offered individuality, creativity, and a sensation of power. People held séances, touching hands around a table and witnessing the table jump and spin on its own, a phenomenon called *tables tournantes*. There were famous male and female mediums, and in do-it-yourself home séances the women of the family generally played this role. Mediums transmitted messages in a variety of ways, from listing letters and waiting for a rap of confirmation, to "automatic writing" in which the medium's hand transcribed a note, to a more straightforward channeling of a voice. The séances were associated with families on the political left and perforce outside mainstream religion, and mediums channeled people like Voltaire, and praised revolutionary republicanism.

Séances grew organized under the influence of a math teacher called Allan Kardec, who proposed a mixture of Mesmerism and spiritualism that he called Spiritism. Kardec turned attention toward participants' deceased family members, and while still republican, claimed that progress had a set pace and could not be

accelerated. Thus in matters both personal and political, Kardec offered a doctrine that was primarily consoling.

Monroe's study is a detailed look at the organizations, behaviors, and personnel of Spiritism and related movements, and the response these met with from the Catholic Church, the major newspapers of the time, the courts, and the government. Tracing these various groups is one of the significant contributions made here. Spiritism has been examined in a number of studies, but generally as a component of a larger field of unauthorized religious impulses. Ruth Harris has looked at Lourdes, as has Suzanne Kaufman, and cultural histories of death in the nineteenth century notably those of Philippe Ariès and Thomas Kselman, also show how ordinary people mediated desires outside both church and science.

The climax of Monroe's story comes with the growth of spirit photography, in which ghostly images of long-lost family members appeared in the sitter's portrait. Like the séances, the mood here was of rational inquiry, with the stated hope that scientists would become involved. When skeptics did come in, however, they discovered a second studio where ethereal dolls were fitted with one of many photograph masks, chosen to match whomever the customer was hoping to see. With insight and a nice touch of drama, Monroe recreates the frustration of the magistrate and others as they discovered that no proof of fraud was sufficient to shake the faith of duped customers. Each claimed that in his or her own case, the spirit photograph had been genuine—the likeness was real, they avowed, and brought on feelings too genuine to be doubted. The book's final chapters discuss how these trends grew more heterodox in the years that followed, as "occultists" added esoteric lore to Spiritism, now with the larger purpose of discovering ultimate truth.

French historians were in need of a guide to the workaday realities of Spiritism, and Monroe does an excellent job of providing it. He is most interesting when he reads these details for larger meaning. One early medium Monroe discusses was an uneducated workman who surprised the séance room with an ability to speak as an educated gentleman. Later on, when mediums were mostly women, Kardec effectuated a purge of those who bridled when he dismissed or modified their pronouncements. Throughout this history, Spiritism provided opportunities for self-determination and left records of how that spirit was received.

JENNIFER MICHAEL HECHT
*The New School,
New York City*

KIRRILY FREEMAN. *Bronzes to Bullets: Vichy and the Destruction of French Public Statuary, 1941–1944*. Stanford, Calif.: Stanford University Press. 2009. Pp. xv, 246. $65.00.

Between 1941 and 1944 over 1,500 bronze statues were melted down in France. Was this because of the insatiable German appetite for metal or was it because the Vichy government wanted to get rid of monuments associated with the Third Republic? Kirrily Freeman concludes that the answer is neither. The demands of the German war economy pervaded every decision that was taken in wartime France, but the Germans did not, on the whole, exercise direct control over the destruction of French statuary. Equally, the French government was not directly motivated by the desire to purge public statuary. It simply needed the copper that could be obtained by melting down bronze.

This might sound a rather banal conclusion—the kind of dead end into which much research runs. However, Freeman builds a book on the very absence of a clear political direction behind the removal of statues. She makes absence significant, rather as the empty plinths were sometimes imbued with significance during or after the war. She points out, for one thing, that the absence of political motives does not mean that the policy did not have political overtones. The golden age of French statuary had been in the late nineteenth and early twentieth centuries. Many statues had been erected during the consolidation of the Third Republic; some commemorated republican and anti-clerical heroes. The Vichy regime, clerical and authoritarian, might not have regarded the destruction of such statues as an end in itself, but it certainly saw it as the lesser of the many evils with which it was confronted. In particular, Vichy preferred the destruction of statues to the destruction of church bells. Some Pétainists also suggested that there might be some aesthetically advantageous by-product from the destruction. Abel Bonnard, education minister from 1942 to 1944, was a fastidious *normalien* who believed that many statues were simply too mediocre to deserve preservation. This kind of cultural elitism sometimes brought Vichy into conflict with local cultures—an interesting result given the emphasis that Vichy placed on the virtues of localism. Many statues celebrated local heroes or men (they almost all were men) who had some special association with a town. Their fiercest defenders were often local patriots. To use the language of Charles Maurras, a language that came naturally to some Pétainists, the destruction of statuary often pitted the *pays réel* of locally rooted loyalties against the *pays légal* of the centralized state. Departmental prefects, civil servants appointed by the state, quarreled with mayors who, in small towns, were local notables. Certain statues—such as those of the Provençal poet Frédéric Mistral in Arles—had special local significance of a kind to which Vichy was in theory attached.

The resistance also had its view on statues. Sometimes they became centers of anti-German or anti-Vichy displays. Sometimes statues that were seen to have some particular patriotic or local significance were taken away and hidden to prevent their destruction, though this seems to have been a less common act than postwar stories suggested. In many ways, indeed, the most interesting questions to be asked about the destruction of statuary concern the postwar period. Some-

times statues were replaced or recreated in stone. However, quite large numbers of spaces where statues had formerly stood were simply left empty. There were economic reasons for this, but there also seem to have been political ones. The discrediting of Vichy did not mean a rehabilitation of the Third Republic. The large-bellied, bearded worthies who had presided over town squares in the *belle époque* no longer seemed worth celebrating in post-liberation France. More generally, perhaps, statuary raises questions about the whole culture of commemoration in France after World War II. The heroes and/or victims of the occupation had often been young and relatively obscure. Some of them had died in circumstances that seemed to defy any conventional celebration. Probably the most famous single monument to World War II in France is the ruined village of Oradour-sur-Glane, which was left as it was after soldiers of the SS had burned its buildings and killed most of its inhabitants in 1944. The stark plaques that commemorate resistance fighters usually just give a date of birth (usually some point in the early 1920s), a name, and a date of death (usually in the summer of 1944).

Occasionally, I wondered whether this book might not usefully have given more social context. It would have been interesting to know more about how statues fitted into the lives of communities. Who passed statues in the course of ordinary business, and how much did they notice them? Were statues mainly significant for the bourgeoisie? How frequently were ceremonies organized around them, and what kind of other activities—markets, demonstrations, games of pétanque—took place in their vicinity? These, however, are minor quibbles about a scrupulously researched book.

RICHARD VINEN
King's College London

MYRIAM GREILSAMMER. *La roue de la fortune: Le destin d'une famille d'usuriers lombards dans les Pays-Bas à l'aube des Temps modernes.* Paris: Éditions de l'École des Hautes Études en Sciences Sociales. 2009. Pp. 412. €30.00.

This is three books in one, each a significant contribution to our understanding of the sociocultural history of the mercantile economy in the early modern Low Countries. Myriam Greilsammer's subject is Lowys Porquin, a "Lombard" (an Italian moneylender from the Piedmontese area) who made his fortune as usurer in the sixteenth-century Low Countries. Until Greilsammer's research, he was known principally through a book he published in 1563, which was intended both to inform his children (and his community) about their family and to instruct them on proper living. Porquin's tome, which came in two parts—one a *livre de mémoires* and the other a spiritual testament—was a mini bestseller in the period and until the eighteenth century was regularly reprinted and read in Reformed and Catholic circles alike. Greilsammer published a study of the text in 1989 (*Een pand voor het Paradijs*), but in this book she tells a much larger story.

The first of the three sections of Greilsammer's book, which is based on a prodigious amount of archival research, follows the itinerary Porquin himself sketched (but misrepresented) as he went from town to town, making his career. Here Greilsammer includes information about his two brothers who followed the same profession in the Low Countries, about his family in the Piedmontese town whence they came, and about the official business of usury in this age. And official business it was. Despite the church's condemnation of usury, lay officials authorized the usurers' tables until the late sixteenth century and even beyond, although they alternated their toleration with periodic repression. Officials' double game allowed usurers to amass fortunes with interest charges of about forty percent annually.

It was no accident that Porquin settled in the Low Countries. As the most advanced mercantile economy of the North, the Low Countries were fertile ground for their trade. The French had banned usurers, and the Jews, the Lombards' most likely competitors, had by and large been driven out during the pogroms of the fourteenth century. Usurers' tables were registered throughout the Low Countries; in 1309, there were seventy-seven between the Meuse and the Scheldt rivers alone. The Lombards did more than extend consumption loans as pawnbrokers; confirming recent scholarship, Greilsammer argues that men like Porquin also changed money and financed trade. Nor, again revising older scholarship, were they excluded from proper society. Successful usurers were accepted among the *haute bourgeoisie* of the region and even treated as good Christians (although not without, in the first case, some serious obfuscation of their past and in the second, paying for their spiritual restitution). The story of how Porquin climbed the social ladder, married into a bourgeois Flemish family, obtained a grant of nobility from Charles V, and was incorporated into the Christian community is alone worth the price of Greilsammer's meaty volume.

This happy story was, however, ending during Porquin's time, as lay authorities joined forces with high ecclesiastics more systematically to ban and punish usurers. With the establishment of the Monts-de-Piété in the region in the early seventeenth century, the usurers' tables had real competition, and although they continued to operate in smaller cities well into that century, the tables gradually disappeared.

In his *livre de mémoires* Porquin never mentioned how he had made his fortune. When he published his book, in elegantly bound volumes and written in verse by a local rhetorician, he was an honored member of society in Bergen-op-Zoom, a prosperous city north of Antwerp. Greilsammer carefully distinguishes his *mémoire* from the *ricordanzi* of Italy and similar texts of the genre, showing that it was simply a fiction about his lineage. Greilsammer's point, however, is not to expose his lies but to reveal the cultural values of the day. Social status, although bought with money that had been earned in an ostensibly illicit trade and presumably no

real secret to anyone who wanted to look, was based on lineage and lifestyle. Porquin had established the lifestyle and could fabricate the lineage.

The spiritual testament was as complex a document and it had a particularly complex afterlife. Greilsammer argues that, despite Porquin's supposed loyalty to the Catholic Charles V, his text reeks of reformist ideas. Even the choice of print linked it early Protestantism, for the *style civile* in which it was printed in the original and all but a few subsequent editions was associated with reformist sensibilities. Oddly, however, this did not prevent its popularity in both religious circles. The testament, a conventional recitation of conservative ideas about children's education, wifely obedience, paternal responsibility, civic values, and the like, functioned as a standard schoolbook for generations to come. Thus, Porquin came to be known to posterity not as an ambitious businessman who had made his fortune in the dubious business of usury, but as a devout paterfamilias of good family, who wrote wisely and elegantly about this life and the next.

Greilsammer's book rewards on many levels. She builds on existing scholarship, but adds quantities of original research, especially on the trade of usury and Porquin's career, along with a sensitive intervention in cultural and religious history of the day based on close textual analysis. Although the book is written in a leisurely style that takes the reader into some byways, it amply repays careful reading, perhaps especially for American readers, few of whom have direct access to all the scholarship in Italian, Dutch, French, and German on which the author draws, and fewer of whom can devote the time to the extensive and skilled archival work she has done.

MARTHA C. HOWELL
Columbia University

RANDOLPH C. HEAD. *Jenatsch's Axe: Social Boundaries, Identity, and Myth in the Era of the Thirty Years' War.* (Changing Perspectives on Early Modern Europe, number 9.) Rochester, N.Y.: University of Rochester Press. 2008. Pp. xvi, 177. $70.00.

Randolph C. Head's book is a biography that also confronts wider issues such as the varieties of patriotism in early seventeenth-century Europe and the boundaries between competing confessional groups and political factions. Its hero, Jörg or Georg (sometimes also written Jürg or Giorgio) Jenatsch, was an important political figure in Graubünden during the Thirty Years' War. The small federation of the Grey Leagues, or Grisons, was at that stage a strategically important focus of political interests. Situated between the Swiss Confederation, the Habsburg Tyrol, Venice, and Spanish Milan, the self-governing rural communities of Graubünden controlled the important Valtelline valley. Whenever Spain wanted to send soldiers from northern Italy to the southern Netherlands in the early seventeenth century they had to use the road leading through the Valtellina. Thus both the Spanish and the French but also the Venetian Republic tried to gain a foothold in the Valtellina and Graubünden itself through patronage, military intervention, and downright bribery. Jenatsch, who as a young man became a Calvinist minister, emerged as one of the leaders of the largely Protestant faction allied with Venice. Despite his status as a man of the cloth he exhibited little reluctance to participate in acts of violence, including assassinations and brutal murders. Among the victims of such actions were members of the influential von Planta family, local noblemen closely allied with Spain. Keen on taking revenge, they forced Jenatsch into temporary exile. The former clergyman lived in Venice for some years and in the end became a professional soldier and military entrepreneur. This position provided an important stepping stone for social advancement, and Jenatsch tried to persuade the emperor in Vienna to grant him a noble title and a fief in the 1630s, an objective he was about to achieve when he was killed by an assassin in an inn in the city of Chur in 1639. By this stage Jenatsch had undergone a profound change of religious and political identity by converting to Catholicism. At the same time Jenatsch put an end to his cooperation with France, which had been very close for a couple of years, and sought patronage and protection in Innsbruck and Vienna. But as Head makes clear, Jenatsch's surprising change of sides cannot be explained as a mere act of political expediency; Jenatsch's attitude to the political implications of religious convictions changed considerably over time. As a Protestant he believed that the secular laws had to correspond closely to the commandments of the one true church; as a Catholic, however, he saw religion more as a matter of personal choice important for one's eternal salvation but not necessarily for one's position in the *res publica*. He therefore seems to have accepted the Protestantism of his wife and children and many Grison citizens without much reluctance. Religion was for him, as Head puts it, "one source of identity among many . . . but not a qualification for full personhood in the first place" (p. 52).

Head demonstrates in this fascinating biography that Graubünden was not just a small country divided by the boundaries between a southern Catholic and a northern Protestant culture, as well as by the different language communities of German, Italian, and Romansh, but that these tensions were present in the minds and hearts of each individual man and woman in Graubünden. They were certainly present in the life of Jenatsch, who might appear as a sort of religious and political chameleon but who by this very versatility and capacity to adapt to new challenges may have embodied the real identity of the *Bündner* living within a "cosmopolitan periphery." However, when Jenatsch became a sort of local and national (Swiss) hero in the nineteenth century, in particular after the publication of the famous novel *Jürg Jenatsch* by Conrad Ferdinand Meyer in 1876, these contradictions in his character were often marginalized until he was depicted—in publications of the 1930s—as a charismatic leader who stood for a sort of passionate patriotism that was sometimes nearer to twentieth-century fascism than to the rural democratic traditions of Graubünden. Nevertheless, whatever it was that Jenatsch stood for in his own time, he certainly cared about the liberties and freedom of his country, although this devotion did not prevent him from serving various foreign patrons. Then again, for early seventeenth-century patriots this ambivalence was not necessarily a contradiction.

RONALD G. ASCH
University of Freiburg

H. C. ERIK MIDELFORT. *Exorcism and Enlightenment: Johann Joseph Gassner and the Demons of Eighteenth-Century Germany.* (The Terry Lecture Series.) New Haven: Yale University Press. 2005. Pp. xiii, 219. $35.00.

It is now accepted that the demonology that underlay the witch trials of early modern Europe was not a lingering relic of darker, more superstitious times but a deeply integrated aspect of early modern culture. Belief in demons provided a framework within which many aspects of human experience could be debated and explained. Yet the witch trials had effectively come to an end by the middle of the eighteenth century. It is conceivable that belief in demons would have ended at about the same time. The eighteenth century was, after all, the age of Enlightenment, of Voltaire, David Hume, and Denis Diderot, and also witnessed the triumph of experimental science. In this superb book, H. C. Erik Midelfort argues convincingly that this supposition is false. Belief in and fierce debate about evil spirits active in the world of human beings continued into the final decades of the century. Moreover, the demonological beliefs of the Enlightenment, he contends, were not merely a continuation of earlier ideas but were the product of a religious revival that brought about new ways of thinking about the role of the devil in human life.

The subject of the book is Johann Joseph Gassner, a Catholic priest and exorcist active in the 1770s in southern Germany. For a few years Gassner's exorcisms were extremely popular, drawing large crowds and sparking controversy among Catholics and Protestants alike. His practices, however, did not conform to the traditional image of exorcism. The people he treated did not suffer from frothing at the mouth, speak in foreign tongues, nor tell of distant events. Rather, Gassner treated illnesses that could readily be associated with natural causes: headaches, blindness, epilepsy, and fevers. His alleged cures attracted thousands of supplicants from all walks of life, commoners and nobility. In so doing they polarized debate between those who believed that the Gospels provide firm evidence of spiritual healing and those who saw all instances of apparent possession as cases of misdiagnosed natural illnesses. Midelfort presents Gassner as a figure as much representative of the Enlightenment period as the proponents of reason and skepticism. The nature of the controversy shows that the period was not one of advancing reason casting out the remnants of past superstitions, but one in which the evidence for spiritual influence in human life was as powerful as the reasons for its denial.

The first chapter of the book portrays Gassner as "thinking with demons," whereby the devil is seen as a part of the natural world, providing a tool for understanding human life. Midelfort argues that our conceptual frameworks prefigure what we can experience, so that the responses to Gassner's cures reflected radically divergent ways of experiencing reality. He contends that Gassner's spiritual interpretation of illness shaped the experiences of his patients and gave them a "lived reality" within which their suffering could be understood and possibly controlled. On the other hand, Gassner's critics frequently found possession flatly impossible and saw in his so-called cures merely fraud and deception. In the second chapter Midelfort examines the manner in which the political structure of the Holy Roman Empire provided Gassner with the protection necessary to carry out his experiments in spiritual healing but in the end made it possible for the pope and emperor to shut him down as a threat to the civil order. It is common, Midelfort claims, to see the empire as a fragmented and dysfunctional entity. Yet the Gassner case shows that the empire provided sufficient political autonomy to allow the incubation of new ideas, while at the same time it possessed the ability to squash civil unrest when it was seen to be necessary. The two final chapters investigate aspects of the debate surrounding Gassner's activities. In chapter four Midelfort shows that the debate was not simply one of enlightened rationalism against religious superstition. Debate between detractors and defenders centered on the correct interpretation of the Gospels. Conservative Catholics claimed that a literal interpretation of the New Testament shows clearly that Jesus worked spiritual cures for illnesses in the same manner as Gassner, while critics replied that Jesus's apparent cures simply reflected the common Jewish superstitions of the times. Chapter five looks at the tremendous volume of published literature created by the controversy. While traditional images of the period lead us to expect civil debate guided by reason, Midelfort shows that both supporters and detractors of Gassner resorted to ridicule and mockery, creating two hostile camps unable to listen to or learn from each other.

In sum, Midelfort's book shows that examination of Gassner's career and the controversies it engendered reveals a number of largely unacknowledged realities of the late eighteenth century and teaches some important historiographical lessons about the ways in which we should strive to understand the past.

PETER A. MORTON
Mount Royal University

JON TETSURO SUMIDA. *Decoding Clausewitz: A New Approach to* On War. (Modern War Studies.) Lawrence: University Press of Kansas. 2008. Pp. xix, 234. $29.95.

This book is a well-known naval historian's treatise on *Vom Kriege* (1832), the widely known masterwork of Prussian military theorist Carl von Clausewitz. Although analysts, hostile and sympathetic alike, have lamented *Vom Kriege*'s falling short of the philosophical gravitas that Clausewitz strove to present, Jon Tetsuro Sumida seeks to counter such views by identifying subtexts of profundity and coherence while taking issue with various critics of Clausewitz, most notably B. H. Liddell Hart. While arraying a panoply of relevant excerpts from *Vom Kriege*, the author bolsters his views with selections from Antoine-Henri Jomini, Julian Corbett, Raymond Aron, Peter Paret, and W. B. Gallie. Deeming the aggregate of their efforts "the great bulk of what is known, or what is thought to be known about Clausewitz and his work," Sumida defines as his primary goal the preventing of readers coming to Clausewitz's "work with preconceptions that can be an obstacle to comprehension of his actual text" (p. 6).

That is, of course, a very tall order, considering the wide currency given over the last century and a half to such Clausewitzian tenets as war being an extension of political process by other means, the superiority of defense over attack, "provinces of war," the "fog" of war, "friction," the spectrum of conflict running from all-out war to limited military demonstrations, the significance of *Volk in Waffen* manifested in the Napoleonic Wars, and, last but not least, the "paradoxical trinity"—the metaphysical melding of the spirit of the masses, the capacity of principal leaders, and a nation's political dynamics. As Sumida covers such familiar ground as Clausewitz's likening war to commercial transactions and card games, and the concept of "inner vision," he claims novelty to his approach, for example, in rejecting the widespread view of *Vom Kriege* as an incomplete work and the primacy of "war as an extension of policy by other means" while recasting the significance of the "paradoxical trinity" and "genius." He weighs in on the longstanding interpretive donnybrook over the congruence—or lack thereof—of the terms "absolute" and "real," and "limited" and "unlimited" war, while reappraising Jominian and Clausewitzian perspectives on guerrilla warfare and the impact of various analysts on Clausewitzian theory. As Sumida intertwines Clausewitz's immediate predecessors and contemporaries in the realm of philosophy, like Immanuel Kant and G. W. F. Hegel, with such successors as Charles Sanders Peirce, Ludwig Wittgenstein, and R. G. Collingwood, he also draws on the subsequent evolution of the social sciences and such esoteric domains as chaos theory to demonstrate Clausewitz's exceptional prognosticatory powers.

Like its subject, Sumida's book is heavy slogging and bestrewn with categorizing and the framing of dialectics, although less than wide ranging or exhaustively definitive. Whether due to editorial space limits or selectivity born of not fully defined logic, one finds no mention of the firmament of Russian theorist-practitioners who putatively influenced Clausewitz as an officer in the tsarist army, especially Mikhail Kutuzov and Aleksander Suvorov, or those who were later notably influenced by him, like Vladimir Lenin and Leon

Trotsky. Nor, despite Clausewitz's focus on "genius" and Russian and Soviet interest in Clausewitzian concepts, does Sumida's assemblage of congruent and tangential authorities make reference to such works as psychologist Boris Teplov's "The Mind of the General" or Boris Shaposhnikov's *The Brain of the Army* (1929). Nor are Mao Zedong, T. E. Lawrence, and Martin van Creveld mentioned, and only passing references or none at all are made to such linked Germanic luminaries as Hugo von Freytag-Loringhoven, Moltke the Elder, Hans Delbrück, Friedrich von Cochenhausen, Friedrich von Bernhardi, Hans von Seeckt, or Kurt Dittmar. Also out of focus is Marie von Clausewitz's role in molding the fragments of her husband's work left behind after he died of cholera in 1831 into what became widely seen, whatever its flaws and shortcomings, as the *Meisterwerk* of military theoretics. Nor is there even a passing reference to Ernest Hemingway's *Men at War* (1942), which popularized Clausewitz in the United States during World War II and the early Cold War, and C. S. Forester's having Clausewitz meet Horatio Hornblower during the siege of Riga in his novel, *The Commodore* (1945). Also omitted, with some irony given the appendix on J. S. Bach's *St. Matthew Passion* (1727), is antisemitism, to which Clausewitz, however rational, was not immune in the era of Father Friedrich Jahn and "Deutschland Erwache."

While the above might be seen as nitpicking, a work aimed at blazing a trail to wisdom and devising as well as appraising theory might be expected to be somewhat more exhaustive in charting linkages and effects. In any case, this book does provide a useful bag of tools to those pondering someone whom many have deemed the most critical framer of military philosophy and historical theory.

ROGER BEAUMONT
Texas A&M University

HEIKKI LEMPA. *Beyond the Gymnasium: Educating the Middle-Class Bodies in Classical Germany*. Lanham, Md.: Lexington Books. 2007. Pp. xi, 292. Cloth $80.00, paper $38.95.

This book plunges readers into the social imagination of the body in nineteenth-century Germany. Although Heikki Lempa clearly situates his study in a specific historical era to examine how a multitude of discourses on beauty, health, lifestyle, morality, and propriety emerged to forge a new regime of bodies with concomitant formations of public and private domains, the author's overarching argument remains elusive. In the introductory chapter, Lempa begins with an examination of the contemplations by Daniel G. M. Schreber, who pushed for a new lifestyle science (dietetics) centered on "nutrition," "sleep, regulation of the passions, physical exercise, metabolism, the use and impact of air, and the effects of the environment on all these" (p. 1). After reiterating these discussions "of the relationship between the hygienic and ethical life, between the body and morality," and the significance accorded to "social

practices," Lempa proceeds with the assertion that "in this book," he "will probe why and how these theories arose, practices emerged and how they contributed to the relationship between the body and an ethical life" (p. 2). But this focus is subsequently overtaken by other areas of concern. In the final section of the introduction, Lempa states "that a study of the body and its practices tell an important story about the formation of the German educated middle class and that this story is about anachronistic modernization in which social practices and intellectual vocabularies were accommodated to changing socio-economic and political conditions" and "the willingness to change social conduct and decorum was combined with a reliance on old models and conceptualizations of the body" (p. 6). Without a theoretical frame, only the stylistic format of the book is clearly articulated: the changes in the social history of the body are presented in an inductive and descriptive manner, whereby transformations in discourse and practice are traced and expounded by meticulous attention to detail. But when laboring through 240 pages of descriptive documentation, the question emerges: how are these multiple excursions into the past connected, and what is the theoretical relevance of this informational exposure?

Lempa presents a well-researched treatise, but his body history remains descriptive with little analysis or interpretation to assist readers in conceptually connecting the tangle of details. The material is organized topically, not by conceptual relevance to an overarching theoretical argument. From the beginning, the reader is flooded by a wealth of narrative details, expounded further in footnotes and annotations. The thematic sequence of chapters (dietetics, balance, gymnastics, dance, walking, and cholera) consists of informative excursions into nineteenth-century health concerns and medically directed lifestyle changes. Seeking to incorporate the reimagined "tribal body" (p. 77), rehabilitating "Germanic tribalism" (p. 85), the emergent medical discourse (dietetics) was implanted in health education, schools, and everyday life, legitimated by recourse to images of nature or history. As Lempa suggests, "pre-modern arguments were fully capable of producing modern political strategies" (p. 240). But this assertion as well as related insights about the growing collaboration between medicine and politics in nineteenth-century Germany should have been theorized more carefully in the introduction and throughout the book.

It is troubling that a book on German body history, which is by no means a novel field, ignores or refuses engagement with existing paradigms. (See, for instance, Ute Planert, "Der dreifache Körper des Volkes: Sexualität, Biopolitik und die Wissenschaften vom Leben," *Geschichte und Gesellschaft* 26 [2000]; Dietmar Kamper and Christoph Wulf, eds., *Die Wiederkehr des Körpers* [1982]; Barbara Duden, *Body History* [1990]; Catherine Gallagher and Thomas Laqueur, eds., *The Making of the Modern Body: Sexuality and Society in the Nineteenth Century* [1987]; Michael Feher et al., eds., *Fragments for a History of the Human Body* [1989].) While Norbert Elias is briefly mentioned (p. 5), his pertinent insights about the privatization of bodily practices go unrecognized, although they are relevant to Lempa's discussions about bourgeois strategies of bodily autonomy. Michel Foucault is also invoked in passing (pp. 5, 19), but his conceptual framework regarding technologies of the self, disciplinary practices, and medical technologies and power are not engaged. The problematic concept of modernity is not defined but taken as self-evident. This seems even more troublesome in light of the fact that concepts of the "modern," "premodern," and "tribal" belong to a culturally specific paradigm that is linked to Europe's positivist, capitalist, and imperialistic vision of the world, which likewise produced systems of knowledge, forms of representation, and images of bodies and people that informed national imaginaries in Europe (Stuart Hall et al., eds., *Modernity: An Introduction to Modern Societies* [1996]). Lempa's book offers no such contextualization for the formations of the social body in nineteenth-century Germany. The book, for these reasons, will be most helpful if used as a guide to specific sources and reference works.

ULI LINKE
Rochester Institute of Technology

MATTHEW P. FITZPATRICK. *Liberal Imperialism in Germany: Expansionism and Nationalism, 1848–1884.* (Monographs in German History, number 23.) New York: Berghahn Books. 2008. Pp. 237. $99.95.

Matthew P. Fitzpatrick's elegant account of German liberal imperialism from 1848 until Otto von Bismarck's embrace of a colonial foreign policy in 1884 represents a timely and important contribution to the existing literature: timely, because Fitzpatrick's emphasis on the centrality of imperialist discourse to the liberal nation-state project from its very inception is absolutely in keeping with the postcolonial and transnational turns taken in recent years; important, because this argument represents a fundamental shift in focus. The book builds on the work of historians like Frank Lorenz Müller and Hartmut Pogge von Strandmann, but Fitzpatrick's contribution represents the most sustained attempt to reframe the argument.

The leading treatments of German liberalism in English underplay its imperial yearnings to the point of omission, a trait shared by Thomas Nipperdey's magisterial, multivolume history of nineteenth-century Germany. While the social imperialism thesis posited by Hans-Ulrich Wehler places great emphasis on the domestic origins of German imperialism, it ignores what Fitzpatrick calls the *longue durée* of German imperialism (although whether this phrase should be applied to a mere four decades is open to question). Fitzpatrick overturns the first of these approaches and comprehensively revises the second. He argues that expansionist imperialist visions were central to German national liberalism from the 1840s and that the eco-

nomic and demographic justifications underpinning these visions presented colonialism as a solution to the social question, not a diversion from it.

Here, Fitzpatrick makes a series of interrelated arguments. In the opening chapter, he asserts that support for German colonies and an expansionist naval policy were rare points of unity for the liberal deputies gathered at the Frankfurt parliament of 1848–1849. Thus imperialism was linked inextricably to the struggle for a German act of national unification enacted in accordance with liberal politico-economic priorities, rendering it the "mythopoeic engine" (p. 205 et al.) of a liberal German nation. In chapter two, Fitzpatrick traces the development of key tropes in German imperialist discourse from their origins in the work of Friedrich List. He stresses a belief in the economic utility of colonialism, a concern that mass emigration represented a potentially fatal loss of human capital and economic energy, the hope that colonialism might resolve the social question by providing an outlet for lower class energies, a commitment to the "civilization" of extra-European peoples, and a need to compete with European rivals. Fitzpatrick then shows how German liberal imperialists turned to private sector imperialism and civil society to realize these visions after the failure of the 1848–1849 unification efforts left them without state backing. This analysis provides the context for a nuanced rereading of Bismarck's 1884 decision to embrace colonialism, which Fitzpatrick sees as an attempt to shift the political balance in favor of the National Liberals and preserve the Bismarckian coalition. The last two chapters explore the role of German academics, particularly geographers and anthropologists, in supporting liberal imperialism and the portrayal of extra-European peoples and experiences in German popular culture.

This book is, in many ways, a model historical monograph, well-targeted but with a narrow focus. Despite Fitzpatrick's conceptual sophistication, his horizons are modest. He does not explore the general implications of his findings for our understanding of European liberalism by placing Germany in comparative context. In places, too, he could push the argument further. Rather than seeing Bismarck's colonial turn as the product of a liberal *Zeitgeist*, Fitzpatrick might consider how far the liberal position was itself the product of an imperial and globalizing age. Fitzpatrick asserts that imperialism provided a discursive vehicle for nationalist liberalism as it sought to supplant socialism, conservatism, and Catholicism as rival metanarratives. But liberal Germans were not alone in seeking to learn from the British imperial example, and issues like empire and support for a German fleet also resonated with these rival constituencies. The staunchly conservative George V of Hanover, for instance, believed that the coastline of his little kingdom could form the basis for a maritime nation on the British model. Likewise, it was the Hohenzollern Prince Adalbert of Prussia who authored the plan for a German navy that formed the basis for liberal deliberations in the Frankfurt Parliament (pp. 31–32).

That Adalbert was also the driving force behind Prussian development of a naval base at Wilhelmshaven in Oldenburg during the 1850s suggests a more complex relationship between Prussian state interests and German naval ambitions than Fitzpatrick allows. The same could be said of German imperial ambitions in Eastern Europe. Fitzpatrick stresses the link between *Weltpolitik* and *Lebensraum* in the foundational work of List (pp. 11, 58) but fails to explore either liberal preoccupations with the latter or the way *Lebensraum* drew on Central European traditions of Empire endorsed by the *Grossdeutsch* camp and reaching back to the old Reich. Ultimately, however, the general thrust of Fitzpatrick's argument remains compelling.

ABIGAIL GREEN
Brasenose College,
University of Oxford

MARK A. RUSSELL. *Between Tradition and Modernity: Aby Warburg and the Public Purposes of Art in Hamburg, 1896–1918.* (Monographs in German History, number 19.) New York: Berghahn Books. 2007. Pp. xii, 257. $90.00.

In exchange for the promise that he could use the family fortune to acquire books for the rest of his life, Aby Warburg traded away his inheritance to his younger brother Max at the age of thirteen. In doing so, he relinquished not only his right to control one of the most powerful banking houses in imperial Germany but also the prominent position in local and national politics that fell to the head of this eminent patrician family. While Max went on to a seat on the Hamburg Citizens' Assembly and a role as financial adviser to Kaiser Wilhelm II, Aby immersed himself in the study of art. Exploring the persistence of religion, magic, and astrology in Renaissance Italy, he devised a theory of art as the dialectical interplay of Dionysian and Apollonian impulses that played out over and over in the creative human struggle for control over the chaotic forces of nature and psyche. But above all, Aby bought books. Volumes on art, anthropology, folklore, religion, sociology, and countless other topics were constantly rearranged on Warburg's shelves in classification schemes reflecting his ever-changing theories. Having long outgrown the confines of a private library, in 1926 Warburg's collection opened as a semi-public research facility, the *Kulturwissenschaftliche Bibliothek Warburg*, and eventually (as the Warburg Institute) found its way to London—books and all—after the Nazi seizure of power.

Such bookish inclinations, coupled with his disdain for the world of modern finance, seem to make Warburg an unlikely candidate for inclusion in the progressive-minded milieu of "bourgeois" reformers that has received so much attention in recent scholarship. Yet precisely this unlikelihood is the aim of the present study. Insisting that Warburg was "in no way a hermetic scholar" (p. 222), Mark A. Russell argues that he played an "active role" in the civic politics of Hamburg, striving to use art to ameliorate the social tensions accompanying the rise of industrial capitalism while at the same time preserving the independence of Hamburg's patrician elite in the newly founded German Empire. As have others before him, Russell argues convincingly that Warburg's views on art under the Medici in Renaissance Florence mirrored his views on the cultural role of the commercial elite in nineteenth-century Hamburg. In addition, Russell emphasizes the sociopolitical significance of Warburg's notion of *Denkraum*—the contemplative space he believed art could open up by harnessing the chaos of passion to the rational constraints of form. This coupling, Russell demonstrates, was the true "public purpose of art" in the eyes of Warburg, who saw the production of *Denkraum* as a means to calm the revolutionary ire of the working classes, thus paving the way for their integration into a republican (if not democratic) polis. Having scoured Warburg's papers, Russell focuses on several episodes that provide evidence of such a commitment: Warburg's exhibition and lecture series aimed at the working classes in Hamburg's *Volksheim* in 1905; his support for modern art in opposition to academic tradition; and, most important, his involvement in debates surrounding three projects of monumental art in Hamburg—the Otto von Bismarck memorial designed by Hugo Lederer and Emil Schaudt, Hugo Vogel's murals for Hamburg's new city hall, and Willy von Beckerath's murals for the School of Art and Industry. While praising the monumental works of Lederer, Schaudt, and Beckerath for their successful integration of tradition and modernity, reason and unreason, Warburg rejected Vogel's art as a failure to preserve the balance between Apollonian and Dionysian impulses. In each case, *Denkraum*—along with its sociopolitical ramifications—played a decisive role in Warburg's stance.

How compelling is this reassessment? While Warburg's convictions seem clear at the conceptual level, evidence of practical engagement is scanty at best. He may have collected clippings about the Bismarck memorial but did not actively engage in public debate; his contribution to the controversy over Vogel was limited to a single article; his promotion of Beckerath's murals pales in comparison to his vitriolic response to World War I. As for the *Volksheim* exhibition, Russell admits that it represented a deviation from Warburg's usual disdain for popular art education (as promoted by Alfred Lichtwark). The exhibition was in any case a dismal failure, and the lecture series had to be canceled due to lack of attendance. Furthermore, Warburg's socially conservative views (both he and his brother Max resisted Prussian suffrage reform in 1906) put him at odds with most progressives. The picture that emerges is thus not so much that of an engaged citizen or activist but instead a socially conscious intellectual who talked the talk without walking the walk of more engaged members of the reform milieu. Russell's book is in this sense a valuable scholarly contribution, serving as a useful reminder of the broad spectrum of political views and levels of engagement to be found in the complex confrontations with modernity in late imperial Germany.

KEVIN REPP
Yale University

WILLIAM T. MARKHAM. *Environmental Organizations in Modern Germany: Hardy Survivors in the Twentieth Century and Beyond.* (Monographs in Modern Germany, number 21.) New York: Berghahn Books. 2008. Pp. xiii, 407. $95.00.

William T. Markham's book is a well-researched and highly accessible historical-sociological investigation of German environmental organizations in the twentieth century as well as a critical assessment of the strategic dilemmas and decisions that these groups faced as they entered the twenty-first. A number of recent books have analyzed the ideologies, membership, and political maneuvering of Germany's myriad nature conservation, homeland (*Heimat*) protection, and environmental protection movements, but Markham's is the first to put the emphasis squarely on the organizations themselves. Using insights from sociological theories of organizations and institutions, Markham follows Germany's environmentalist groups as they worked to obtain resources, gain new members, structure themselves effectively, select and implement goals, and, most important, adapt themselves to Germany's radicals shifts in politics and culture. These shifts included rapid industrialization and urbanization, economic depression and hyperinflation, two world wars, the Nazi dictatorship and state socialism, the "economic miracle" and its ecological discontents, confrontations over nuclear power and other environmental issues in the 1970s and 1980s, and reunification and the decline in environmental interest in the 1990s and beyond. The book is particularly strong in examining the fate of early twentieth-century nature conservation groups, which included conservative *Heimat* activists as well as socialist hiking groups, as they struggled to remain relevant amid the grassroots mobilization, anti-nuclear protests, and apocalyptic ecological visions of the 1970s and 1980s.

Markham concentrates his theoretical analysis, particularly the advantages of organizational approaches over competing theories of social movements, interest groups, and civil society, into chapters two and thirteen, which leaves the majority of the text accessible to scholars and advanced undergraduates interested in a general survey of German environmental groups. Markham's commitment to understanding environmental organizations as institutions bound by traditions, normative standards, and culture is evident in the core historical chapters (chapters three through six), which synthesize well recent secondary research, including the often-neglected former German Democratic Republic (GDR). What emerges from Markham's historical account is the remarkable staying power of these organizations and the enormous elasticity of environmental themes, ranging from the conservative critique of modernity characteristic of early twentieth-century nature conservationists to the leftist rejection of capitalist consumerism associated with citizens' initiative associations in the 1970s. As Markham notes, this discursive mutability has produced both right-wing and left-wing variants of German environmentalism; there is no easy association of the German organizations with "progressive" politics, as is often assumed in the U.S. context, nor, we should add, is there any basis for drawing a line of continuity between fascist conservationism and the modern Greens, as Anna Bramwell did in her controversial 1985 book *Blood and Soil: Richard Walther Darre? and Hitler's "Green Party."*

After completing this historical survey, Markham uses chapters seven to twelve to discuss the strategic choices that four key environmental groups faced in the twenty-first century: the German chapters of Greenpeace and the Worldwide Fund for Nature (WWF), the German League for Environment and Nature Protection (BUND), and the German Nature Protection League (formerly League for Bird Protection). This difficult period has witnessed the "graying of the greens" and fading of the environmentalist counterculture, the institutionalization and professionalization of environmentalism in government policy, industrial practice, and public opinion, and declining public support as a result of the enormous costs of reunification and Germany's anemic economic growth. Markham argues that all four have been forced to become more accommodating of the "system" as a result of these trends, and he examines how each found a strategic middle ground amid difficult choices about cooperation versus confrontation with government, industry, and other groups; professionalization versus grass-roots volunteerism; broad-based versus limited goals; and centralization versus democracy.

The focus on creating an effective institutional theory of environmental organizations often leads Markham to overlook some of the more compelling historiographical controversies of interests to specialists in German environmental history, particularly the tensions between regional and national environmental agendas, the legacy of the National Socialist dictatorship, and recent debates over the 1970s as a true watershed in environmental politics. He relies too heavily on a model of early twentieth-century homeland preservationists as conservative reactionaries, whereas recent scholarship has emphasized these groups' reconciliation with industrial society and their vision of an alternative environmental modernity. And though committed to historical analysis, there is far more to be said about how history and culture delimited and shaped environmental groups' strategies, a theme that Jens Ivo Engels's recent book *Naturpolitik in der Bundesrepublik: Ideenwelt und politische Verhaltensstile in Naturschutz und Umweltbewegung 1950–1980* (2006) tackles brilliantly using qualitative sociological models inspired by Martin Dinges and Pierre Bourdieu. Nonetheless, Markham's book is an excellent contribution to a growing historical literature dedicated to the "greening" of German history.

THOMAS LEKAN
University of South Carolina

NINA TREADWELL. *Music and Wonder at the Medici Court: The 1589 Interludes for* La pellegrina. (Musical Meaning and Interpretation; Music and the Early Modern Imagination.) Bloomington: Indiana University Press. 2008. Pp. xviii, 277. $39.95.

With this work, Nina Treadwell becomes the first music historian to explore the significance of the 1589 Florentine court *intermedi*—multimedia extravaganzas performed between the acts of a comedy—as musico-theatrical works in their own right. Previously, music and theater historians have viewed this set of *inter-medi*—staged in the Uffizi theater as the highpoint of a series of celebrations mounted for the wedding of Ferdinando I de' Medici to Christine of Lorraine—as late contributions to a spectacular but waning theatrical genre that deserved attention largely as a forerunner of opera. In this book Treadwell explores the intersection of stagecraft and "statecraft," demonstrating how central the *intermedi* were to the aesthetic and political concepts and concerns of the Medici, particularly as they were manifested in the person of Ferdinando, the newly proclaimed Grand Duke of Florence. In this context, Treadwell's constructs of "the duke as theatrical arbiter" (p. 26) and "the duke as Neoplatonic Magus" (p. 42) are quite revealing and completely convincing. Moreover, her focus on the sixteenth-century audience's reception of these works within a historical and performative context that aimed to inspire wonderment and evoke a sense of mystery is both novel and admirably interdisciplinary in its approach.

The book is in two parts: the first addresses the "aesthetic and political underpinnings" (p. 9) of Medicean court theater, and the second offers readings of each of the six *intermedi*, which combined elaborate stage effects with musical performance. A key element in Treadwell's interpretation is the concept of *meraviglia*, which she approaches not only in the abstract—that is, through the writings of the contemporaneous philosopher Francesco Patrizi—but also by evaluating descriptions written by the official court chronicler as well as by examining eyewitness and unofficial reports. In addition to twenty-nine color illustrations and numerous musical examples, all of which have appeared elsewhere, the volume includes an audio compact disc with twenty-four minutes of music excerpted from the *intermedi*, produced and directed by Treadwell and performed by her along with a dozen colleagues, and an accompanying booklet containing texts and translations. Indeed, some of the author's "readings" of individual *intermedi* in the latter half of the book describe in detail the musical decisions (such as placement and type of ornaments, instrumentation, and so forth) that

went into the recording for the very purpose of attempting to replicate the original elements of technique and style that evoked such a sense of wonder in the listeners. That sonic as well as scenic effects generated *meraviglia* in 1589 is attested in the wealth of commentary about the musical and visual details of the successive interludes, which evidently made a far greater impression on the audience than the comedy (*La Pellegrina* by Girolamo Bargagli) to which the interludes were appended.

One source of wonder—which perhaps receives less attention in Treadwell's discussion than it deserves—was the Uffizi theater itself, the first indoor proscenium stage in Europe. The proscenium arch provided a frame for the three-dimensional scenery, which used machinery engineered by Bernardo Buontalenti to move clouds and water and dispense all manner of fabricated visual effects, thereby creating the illusion of a *tableau vivant*, a painting mysteriously come to life. Another source of astonishment was the solo singing of the young Florentine Jacopo Peri (who composed the first opera a decade later) and the court *virtuosa* Vittoria Archilei, whose extraordinary skill at inventing and executing ornaments struck the listener as superhuman. Particularly interesting is Treadwell's discussion of Peri's success as the legendary Greek poet-musician Arion, who throws himself overboard to escape the murderous intent of mutinous sailors and is brought safely to shore by a dolphin attracted by his singing. She makes a connection between the maritime theme of this Fifth Intermedio, among others, and the new prominence of the Tuscan naval fleet in the Mediterranean. Emphasizing the unusual structure of Arion's song, each verse of which ends with a musical double-echo, she points out the self-referential nature of the echo and its role in calling attention to the source of sound, "like virtuosity itself" (p. 153). She further postulates how the unseen singers might have been positioned in the theater and suggests that one of the two mysterious sources of sound "was produced from a location close to the duke himself" (p. 150), thus enhancing his self-representation as "royal Magus" (p. 153).

One exception to the otherwise well-conceived and well-written argument of the book is the author's effort to refute the influence of humanism on the *intermedi*, which were unquestionably the brainchild of Count Giovanni de' Bardi, notable humanist and founder of the Florentine Camerata. If the "excessively artificial" solo songs do not measure up to the text-based aesthetic set out by the humanist program (and here Treadwell contradicts herself, later demonstrating how at least two of the musical settings partake in that aesthetic, as do some of the others on paper if not in performance), the broader themes of the *intermedi*, based in classical mythologies that celebrate the artistic efficacy of musicians such as Apollo and Arion, not to mention the legendary power of the siren's song, certainly do. The projection of wonder (in Treadwell's felicitous phrase, "singing the marvelous") did not contradict but rather supported humanist ideas about rhetorical virtuosity and the power of music.

BARBARA RUSSANO HANNING
City College of New York, and *The Graduate Center, City University of New York*

MARK I. CHOATE. *Emigrant Nation: The Making of Italy Abroad.* Cambridge: Harvard University Press. 2008. Pp. x, 319. $45.00.

Mark I. Choate very effectively demonstrates that the process of nation building and the fashioning of national identity happened both within and without the geographical borders of Italy. Choate expertly weaves the narratives of diaspora and immigration, imperialism and settlement, culture and politics to illustrate the importance of the diaspora in the making of the Italian nation in the late nineteenth and early twentieth centuries. By examining the crucial period after Unification, Choate shows how discussions of emigration and empire became central to understandings of nation and citizenship. Both inside and outside of Italy, politicians conversed in the languages of nationalism, transnationalism, empire, and diaspora to shape and solidify the image of the motherland and the concept of Italy.

In the seven chapters of the book, Choate relies on an impressive number of archival and published materials to examine the making of Italy abroad. He focuses on such issues as the modification of imperialist discourse to include emigration as part of imperial expansion; ethnography and the concept of irredentism, the "redeeming" of millions of Italians abroad; the importance of remittances in sustaining the connections with the mother country; the importance of teaching standard Italian language abroad to a regionalized people who were to become more homogeneously Italian in the Americas; the role of the church in teaching Italian to first and second-generation emigrants abroad; the shift in nationalist dialogue as emigration became an emotive backdrop for discussing the failures of the Liberals and galvanizing a new national spirit of imperial expansion in Libya; and the poignant response of Italians abroad to the call of duty in times of tragedy and war.

As it became increasingly apparent that Italian efforts to claim colony and empire were unsuccessful, Italian politicians struggled to find new forms of empire that would allow Italy the political voice and international prestige it desired. As Choate elucidates, as early as 1874, Italians were speaking of emigration as a form of imperial expansion, a way to assert international power, and a means, albeit tenuous and volatile, of creating colony and space. Indeed, Italian communities abroad were called *colonie,* the same word used to describe the Italian colonies in Africa. The intertwining of the two discourses, imperialism and emigration, informed the discussions on the creation of a Greater Italy.

"Emigrant colonialism," as Choate terms the policies and programs that dealt specifically with emigrant communities abroad, became an integral part of the national debate on *italianità* and resisting assimilation (p. 2). If emigrants abroad were the new Roman legionnaires settling and defending Italian imperial outposts, the Italian government had to ensure that they knew who Italians were and what Italy represented. Italy needed to assume control of emigration, oversee educational programs, protect remittances home, and defend its colonists abroad. Emigrant colonialism necessitated the redemption of its colonists. Like the irredentist movement in Trent and Trieste, in which both land and people needed to be reclaimed to complete Unification, American emigrants needed to be taught what it meant to be an Italian of Greater Italy. The teaching of a standard Italian language by organizations like the Dante Alighieri Society and the Catholic *Italica Gens* helped not only to ameliorate the regional divisions of illiterate emigrants, but also to facilitate communication between emigrants and officials of the Italian state. Italian language education served as a vehicle for teaching and reinforcing *italianità.* This work became even more vital as politicians feared return migration was only a myth. Despite the best attempts of the Italian Chambers of Commerce abroad, who acted as representatives of the state, to consolidate and protect Italian economic interests, the Italian state continued to lose resources as emigrants chose to remain in their host countries. While Italy paid the "overhead" for raising and training workers, the host countries gained the capital of skilled labor (p. 93). The perceived difficulties and failures of emigration and the inability of the Italian government to protect its citizens abroad informed new nationalist discourse that condemned the Liberals and invoked a renewed spirit of imperial endeavor in Africa. This reinvigorated call to duty ran parallel to the questions of patriotism raised as Italy experienced a series of natural and manmade disasters. The appeal for help after the Messina earthquake of 1908 became politically imbued as Italy asked its citizens abroad to come to the aid of their brothers and sisters. When Italy called on Italians born in the Americas, based on the concept of *jus sanguinis,* to come to the aid of the mother country during World War I, it represented another means of rediscovering "inner patriotism" (p. 200).

This book is a very valuable addition to the literature on diaspora, imperialism, and nationalism. Choate has produced a compelling, impressively researched, and beautifully written book that makes a significant contribution to understanding the ways in which nationalism transcends the boundaries of nation.

ALIZA S. WONG
Texas Tech University

EMILIO GENTILE. *La Grande Italia: The Myth of the Nation in the Twentieth Century.* Translated by SUZANNE DINGEE and JENNIFER PUDNEY. (George L. Mosse Series in Modern European Cultural and Intellectual History.) Madison: University of Wisconsin Press. 2009. Pp. xiv, 406. Cloth $65.00, paper $29.95.

Nationalism is the most ideologically promiscuous of loyalties, willing to cohabit with moderates and radicals, capitalists and communists, devoted believers and militant atheists. As one Italian observer remarked in 1913, nationalism is "a banner hiding the most varied type of goods." In Italy, as in many other parts of the world, the myth of nation may project the image of a united community, but usually turns out to be the source of deep and deadly conflicts. The evolution of these conflicts in twentieth-century Italy is the subject of Emilio Gentile's recently translated book (*La Grande Italia: Ascesa e declino del mito della nazione nel ventesimo secolo* [1997]).

Gentile begins with three events on the eve of World War I: the fifty-year jubilee of Italian unification in 1911 (of which the most aesthetically unfortunate product is the Victor Emmanuel Monument in Rome), the introduction of universal male suffrage, and the Libyan War. These efforts to celebrate, reform, and reinforce the liberal nation created in 1861 could not halt the rising tide of discontent, some of which aspired to the creation of what one young man called "a new fatherland . . . that is alive, that feels, aspires to a renewed soul" (Adolfo Omodeo, quoted on p. 81). Some hoped that Italy's participation in World War I might produce such a revitalized fatherland, but instead the war brought military humiliation, fiscal catastrophe, and diplomatic disappointment. It also opened the way for a fascist regime that would put a radical version of the national myth at the core of its program and policies.

Fascism was a particularly vivid example of what Gentile calls the "ideologizing of the nation," a process in which a political movement demands an exclusive definition of the nation according to its own ideological commitments. These included revolutionary transformations at home, as well as an expansion of Italian power abroad. As Gentile convincingly argues, Benito Mussolini—in contrast to Adolf Hitler—always put the state first. "Without the state," the Duce declared in 1942, "there is no nation. There are only groups of human beings, susceptible to all the disintegrations that history can inflict upon them" (p. 157). Fascism was the national myth's most extreme manifestation and also the cause of its ultimate demise. Mussolini's war was even more disastrous than that of the liberal state he had so passionately attacked. Italy's shattering defeat and occupation, first by the Germans, then by the Allies, left the nation in ruins, its political elite divided and uncertain, its citizens disillusioned. The end of fascism, therefore, marked not only "an end to ambitions for power and greatness but also seemed to destroy the fragile national identity that, despite its many limits, ambitions, and illusions, the Italians had acquired over eighty years as a united nation" (p. 230).

Perhaps the most original chapters in Gentile's book are about Italians' efforts to live amid "the debris of a nation." After a variety of false starts and dead ends, the Christian Democrats and the Communists overcame their original estrangement from the nation and qualified their international commitments to become the postwar custodians of the national idea. But, Gentile concludes, neither party was able "to foster and transmit to the Italians an awareness of their nationality, a national consciousness, love of fatherland and a sense of state, [and] unite these with the principles and values of social democracy, which was the foundation of republican Italy" (p. 335). When this book first appeared in 1997, Gentile believed that the national myth had been hollowed of meaning and emotional force. His brief preface to the English translation, written in October 2005, suggests that there is a "reawakening of the cult of the nation in Italy today" (p. vii). He does not say whether that should be cause for celebration or concern.

A student of the great historian Renzo de Felice, Gentile's best known work is *The Sacralization of Politics in Fascist Italy* (1993; translated in 1996), which clearly reflects the influence of George L. Mosse's views on nationalism as a secular religion. Mosse's influence is less apparent in this book, which is more concerned with ideas and opinions than with cults and rituals. It provides a clear, balanced, and well-informed account of the changing place of national appeals and aspirations in Italian political discourse. We learn much less about how deeply these ideals and aspirations penetrated public life. When, for example, Gentile tells us that "the Italians felt they were citizens of a single fatherland during the First World War" (p. 73), we can't help but wonder about that definite article: did the Italians include everyone, rich and poor, north and south, city dwellers and peasants, men and women? Similarly, when he writes that "fascism" became increasingly "locked into the mythical, visionary element of its political culture" (p. 199), it is not clear who is included in this collective noun. Mussolini was able to create a fascist Italy, but how successful was he in making fascists out of Italians? Such unanswered questions should not diminish our admiration for Gentile's thoughtful analysis of Italian nationalism, but they do suggest that our struggle to understand that most pervasive and elusive of historical phenomena is still far from over.

JAMES J. SHEEHAN
Stanford University

RAY BRANDON and WENDY LOWER, editors. *The Shoah in Ukraine: History, Testimony, Memorialization.* Bloomington: Indiana University Press, with the United States Holocaust Memorial Museum, Washington, D.C. 2008. Pp. ix, 378. $35.00.

This volume addresses an important but neglected topic: the Holocaust in Ukraine. As editors Ray Brandon and Wendy Lower point out in the introduction, focus hitherto has been on the "killing centers" of European Jewry, such as major death camps like Auschwitz. The Soviet Union was unwilling to focus on the plight of Jews specifically, and until 1991 access to its archives was extremely limited. Also, any researcher wishing to study all aspects of the Holocaust was faced with a formidable array of languages to learn and unlikely to have mastery over them all. This collection puts together a group of well-known American and European scholars to uncover various aspects of the Shoah in Ukraine.

Overall the book succeeds admirably. Although the subjects of the various chapters vary widely and perhaps lack a coherent theme, in every case they provide the reader with the results of current and often very exciting research. There are no weak essays in this collection.

Ukraine changed hands several times in the twentieth century. The borders encompassed herein are those at the time of the Soviet annexation of Ukrainian regions of Poland (September 1939) and Romania (June 1940). In turn under German and Romanian rule, its territories were divided into various units, the largest of which were the Reichskommissariat Ukraine (RKU), the Generalgouvernement, and territories under military rule. The book also examines the Romanian-occupied region of Transnistria.

Dieter Pohl's opening essay analyzes the deaths of Ukrainian Jews within the first two occupation zones. The initial invasion sparked a wave of executions, and Jews in Eastern Poland were blamed—with German connivance—for NKVD massacres of prisoners before the Soviet authorities retreated to the east. By mid-September 1941, the SS and police forces embarked on massacres of Jews with willing collaboration from the Army High Command. Pohl maintains that the complete extermination of the Jewish population took place in 1942 starting in Western Ukraine, with about 1.4 million deaths. They died once the new rulers realized that the war would be a long one and lacked means to feed its army.

Timothy Snyder's essay focuses on western Volhynian Jews between 1921 and 1945, initially through the eyes of Henry Jozewski, governor of Volhynia in the interwar period. Snyder notes the role of Ukrainian nationalists as allies of the Germans and the growing complexity of the war in this region as various factors came into play: the Ukrainian Insurgent Army, the Polish Home Army, and Soviet Partisans, in addition to the armies of the USSR and Germany. Frank Golczewski's related essay, "Reflections on Jewish-Ukrainian and German-Ukrainian Relations in Galicia," offers a balanced analysis of collaboration, noting that there was no history of Ukrainian-Jewish animosity before the 1930s and only the emergence of the Organization of Ukrainian Nationalists introduced a systematic program to remove Jews and Poles from this region.

Dennis Deletant's study of Romanian rule in Transnistria highlights some paradoxes. Clearly, Romanian leader Ion Antonescu wished to deport Jews to make his country more homogenous. Ultimately in Transnistria, largely as a result of hunger and disease, some 250,000 Jews and 12,000 Roma died. After the summer of 1942, however, Romanian policy changed as Antonescu refused to take part in the Final Solution and cancelled deportations, partly, the author believes, to assuage the concerns of the Queen Mother. As a result Jews in Transnistria had a better chance of survival than their counterparts elsewhere under Axis rule.

Andrej Angrick looks at the Thoroughfare IV district, an area of 1,360 miles between L'viv and Taganrog. He notes how SS leader Heinrich Himmler took a personal interest in improving the roads to facilitate supply to the army, and how the lack of manpower promoted the occupiers to switch from predominantly POW labor to Jews. He maintains that the role of Reinhard Heydrich and the Reich Main Security Office (RSHA) has been overemphasized and that Himmler's aides controlled this forced labor. The intent was to work the laborers until they died.

Wendy Lower comments on the lower level of the occupying structure; there were 114 county commissars in the RKU charged with the welfare of the Jewish population. Focusing specifically on the Zhytomyr region west of Kiev, with a population of 2.5 million, she notes that 870 Reich Germans ran the twenty-five counties. These commissars, who strutted like "golden pheasants," posted decrees that immediately became law, and they effectively controlled Ukraine. Some took part in killing Jews but later escaped war crimes investigations that targeted primarily the SS policemen under Himmler.

Martin Dean also deals with a lesser-known topic: namely, the role of ethnic Germans in the Holocaust in Ukraine. In 1943 there were 169,000 such Germans in the RKU, over 130,000 in Transnistria, and over 13,000 in the areas under military occupation. Although persecuted under Soviet rule and relatively minor in influence they were nonetheless an integral part of German policy, forming a connection between the new rulers and the subject population. Alexander Kruglov, in an important but inevitably tedious essay, provides numerous charts to support his conclusion that about 1.6 million Jews died in Ukraine and some 100,000 survived the Holocaust. Most deaths occurred in the first year of the war.

Two superb essays round off the book. Karel Berkhoff analyzes meticulously the twelve extant narratives of Dina Pronicheva, one of the few survivors of the Babi Yar massacre in Kiev. While noting some discrepancies—the story of people's hair turning white through fear is a myth, for example—he believes that Pronicheva's testimony remains relevant and more valuable than ideologically driven Soviet texts such as that of Anatolii Kuznetsov. Omer Bartov's travelogue through this territory is a lament for the disappearing memory of Jews in Galicia and is similar to that of his recent book *Erased: Vanishing Traces of Jewish Galicia in Present-Day Ukraine* (2007), but far better documented and thus more persuasive. It is in essence a tilt at the Ukrainian authorities, which not only have failed to preserve the Jewish past but have even erected monuments to some of those who took part in the Holocaust. "We cannot bring back the dead," Bartov writes, "but we can give them a decent burial."

Overall this collection is a worthy enterprise that offers new insights into the Holocaust on the territory of contemporary Ukraine. One could point to minor issues, such as the lack of a glossary listing the endless acronyms and the sometimes hazy numbers—Deletant, for example, lists over 12,000 Roma deaths at the start of his paper, and 10,000–20,000 at the end—but they hardly detract from the quality of these papers and achievements of archival research. The investigation of the Holocaust in Ukraine, as well as in Belarus to the north where some 900,000 Jews died, is finally under way.

DAVID R. MARPLES
University of Alberta

GEORGE E. MUNRO. *The Most Intentional City: St. Petersburg in the Reign of Catherine the Great.* Madison, N.J.: Fairleigh Dickinson University Press. 2008. Pp. 372. $69.50.

Although St. Petersburg is still widely identified with its founder, Peter the Great, few Petrine structures actually remain in the city. During her long reign (1762–1796) Catherine the Great left a far greater impact on the city. According to George E. Munro, St. Petersburg was the model for Catherine's Charter to the Towns, issued on April 21, 1785, which brought about (at least in theory) a coherent system of administration for imperial Russia's towns for nearly a century, until Alexander II enacted the Municipal Reform of 1870. During Catherine's reign some fifty palaces, churches, and government buildings were constructed, while such monuments as the Kazan Cathedral and the public library stem from projects initiated by her.

Munro's book is less concerned with buildings or the imperial court than with governance and the daily life of its residents—what he calls "the living, breathing city that was unplanned and unexpected" (p. 19). In contrast to a long line of Russian historians, including Ivan Ditiatin, Aleksandr Kizevetter, and Paul Miliukov, who found Catherine's governance schemes ineffective, Munro argues that St. Petersburg's administration responded effectively when problems arose: hazardous and polluting industries were moved away from populated areas; free trade was favored but the export of grain was at times controlled or even forbidden to prevent famine and public disorder; numerous regulations were enacted to prevent fires (one example: shop licenses were given in perpetuity only to merchants who built out of brick); paving and street lighting were instituted to make the city safer; public education was adopted in principle; and hospitals and welfare agencies were established. The city's canals, designed to drain bogs, control flooding, and link the city by water transport to the sea and the interior, had become pestilential swamps choked with refuse and alluvial sand. During Catherine's reign, granite embankments were constructed for the canals and the Neva River, and in 1770 Catherine herself issued detailed instructions for the construction of the city's first sewage system. Catherine, in fact, often took an interest in mundane city matters; she required weekly reports on "unusual occurrences" and kept track of wholesale and retail prices for foodstuffs in the local markets. "If one takes respon-

siveness to stated needs as a better instrument for evaluating St. Petersburg's government," Munro concludes, "it must be admitted that administrative bodies responded surprisingly well in attempting to solve problems. Planning was realistic and took into consideration actual grievances by inhabitants" (p. 147).

Poor soil and a very short growing season made reliance on regional foodstuffs impractical except for dairy products, berries, mushrooms, and some vegetables. How then was such a large city provisioned? (In a single year, the imperial court alone consumed many tons of meat and poultry and over a half million fish and eggs.) Aside from fish, which could be purchased locally and cleaned and cooked on the spot or in sheds along boardwalks, much of St. Petersburg's food supply came by boat, barge, and raft from great distances. Delicacies such as pears, oysters, cured meats, cheese, and fine wines came from Europe. Cattle on the hoof came from Ukraine and the lower Volga valley. Perhaps 70,000–80,000 workers came annually on the river and canal boats. "The entire Russian economy benefited from the effort to supply St. Petersburg" (p. 151).

Typically, eighteenth-century shop owners in Europe and Russia lived upstairs from their street-level shops. This residential pattern, though permitted, did not take hold in St. Petersburg, in part because so much trade was concentrated in the great bazaars. St. Petersburg was unusual in that nearly all of its inhabitants were renters. By estimate, only three or four percent owned the homes in which they lived.

Munro's snapshot of St. Petersburg spans only a few decades, but they are important decades, for the city "surpassed Moscow in population, economic importance, and cultural awareness" (p. 285) during these years. Catherine desired to have a grand capital, but her greater goals were to subordinate social and economic activity to state regulation, facilitate effective administration, and raise revenue. Still, for all of the empress's interest in the city, she could not fully mandate its nature nor control its growth. Munro concludes, "On the surface St. Petersburg was a planned city, but the dynamics of its development far exceeded the capacity of planners to plan or the police to control or an empress to foresee" (p. 287).

Munro has been working on this study for many years, and his thoroughly researched and well-written monograph enhances our understanding of the values and objectives of Catherine the Great while providing exceptional detail for those interested in the history of imperial Russia's great capital.

MICHAEL F. HAMM
Centre College

DAVID L. RANSEL. *A Russian Merchant's Tale: The Life and Adventures of Ivan Alekseevich Tolchënov, Based on His Diary.* (Indiana-Michigan Series in Russian and East European Studies.) Bloomington: Indiana University Press. 2009. Pp. xxvi, 320. Cloth $65.00, paper $24.95.

In September 1796, the Russian merchant Ivan Alekseevich Tolchënov began a diary that he kept until December 1804 and titled *A Journal or Notes on the Life and Adventures of I. A. Tolchënov*. Despite its picaresque title, Tolchënov's *Journal* is not a witty romp through the wilds of early modern Russia. It is instead an odd hybrid: part merchant's log, part official protocol, part society diary, part apologetic confession. Precisely because it is so eclectic, it preserves unique details about daily life in early imperial society. Odds and ends that the more ideological writers of the nineteenth century would have cut for narrative clarity or intellectual consistency here get caught in the folds. Such a complex text requires great erudition and insight to unpack, since much of the world it describes is so unfamiliar to us today. Fortunately Tolchënov's *Journal* has found a fluid interpreter in David L. Ransel, whose patient, knowing analysis illuminates the many gems the diary has to offer and thereby lights up many potential paths for future research.

The book reads well as a biography of sorts and can be appreciated simply as a story. It could be assigned to undergraduates: for example, I think it would spark a great discussion when placed side by side with the life of Benjamin Franklin. At the same time, the book has great value for specialists. It represents a meticulous reconstruction of one man's activities in a world that stands outside what Ransel pithily calls the "structure of preserved knowledge" (p. xii). It portrays with unique breadth the middling, provincial world of Russia's widely scattered townsfolk, whose lives only fitfully intersected with state archives and the subsequent traditions built from them.

What is important or unusual about this world? For starters, Tolchënov's *Journal* reminds us that eighteenth-century Russia was a place where people actually lived, not a grand morality play on the relative cultures of "the West" and "the East" or the meaning of autocracy. Tolchënov's most basic aim was to record month by month, and sometimes day by day, what he did as a grain merchant working the watersheds connecting the Volga to St. Petersburg. Whereas imperial Russian archives contain projects for what subjects should do, as well as records of what the government attempted to get them to do, Tolchënov's diary focuses on what he did more or less of his own free will. His simple enumeration of his private acts goes a long way to restoring our sense of the empire as a field for social action, in a manner that our still quite state-bound historical tradition all too often fails to do.

Confronted by this steady record of activity, Ransel faces an important decision: whether to attempt a thematic study, separating out the individual spheres of Tolchënov's life for close analysis, or whether to follow the chronological construction of the diary, presenting events as they unfolded. He chooses the latter approach and organizes his chapters around long excerpts from Tolchënov's journal, which Ransel then proceeds to make comprehensible through supporting narration and commentary. Tolchënov was born into a prosper-

ous family, and the opening stages of his chronicle are consumed by the story of how he learned this craft shuttling back and forth along Russia's great rivers and roads. But Tolchënov's vistas in life suddenly changed in 1779 when his father died unexpectedly, making Ivan the head of household. Over time, as Ransel shows, the diary's focus (and perhaps that of Tolchënov himself) shifts to describe the increasingly cultural pursuits his seniority afforded: his fine house, his gardens, his acquaintances among learned Moscow men, and his occasional brushes with the court. By the late 1790s, financial ruin loomed as Tolchënov's capital collapsed and he found himself unable to maintain the appearance of wealth that sustained his credit. At this point, Tolchënov began to read and write his life through a moral lens, blaming his own idleness for his business failure and searching for the seeds of his fall in his early life. (Tolchënov's chronology is interlaced with reflections on his past inserted later.)

To the extent that it has an overarching story, Ransel's book takes its cue from Tolchënov's anxieties about his self-fashioning. Ransel emphasizes that Tolchënov's actions reveal him to be a man who sought out the new, imperial, and European cultural pastimes then being created in Russia's capitals. This belies the conservative, closed caricature of Russia's merchantry (and its provinces more generally) that is often drawn in literature and history. Whether this taste for luxury actually undid him—as Ransel explains, it was difficult for any family of the time to avoid a sudden turn in luck—is less important than the encyclopedic character this broad range of interests gives his account. Over time, Tolchënov tried his hand at most of what town living in Russia allowed free people to do. While Ransel's chronological presentation does not allow him to linger on any one topic, each moment of Tolchënov's life registers new possibilities for subsequent historians. Students of local politics, religion, science, literature, and (of course) economic life and mobility will find many interesting leads as to how their topics were actually lived. Ransel's close study will bear repeated reading and help historians visualize the world of eighteenth-century Russia across many dimensions.

JOHN RANDOLPH
University of Illinois,
Urbana-Champaign[All reviewers of books by Indiana University faculty are selected with the advice of the Board of Editors.]

MARY W. CAVENDER. *Nests of the Gentry: Family, Estate, and Local Loyalties in Provincial Russia*. Newark: University of Delaware Press. 2007. Pp. 251. $55.00.

Mary W. Cavender's book explores the loyalties and primary concerns of the gentry in the Russian province of Tver' in the first half of the nineteenth century. Cavender explains her decision to focus on the Tver' provincial gentry at the outset. This group of "middling" serfowners shared certain habits and values and, Cavender argues, their influence in the pre-emancipation period was far greater than their numbers might indicate. Tver' province is "typical of the Russian heartland" and, therefore, representative of other provinces in the empire, as well.

Cavender proceeds with a thematic approach, examining the attitudes of the Tver' gentry to family and home life, property and social privilege, service and local politics, and civic duty. Cavender seeks to demonstrate that the provincial nobility of Russia had a rich, complex, and nuanced life away from the capital, one that was not necessarily viewed as inferior to or less fulfilling than life in the big cities. This life went beyond narrow-minded concerns about status, a portrait that has been painted by foreign travelers and even more recent scholars that Cavender wishes to redraw. Instead, letters and other extant documents reveal a gentry rich in emotion, family intimacy, and an interest in domestic happiness. Family members corresponded about health, details about children and family life, and local news, incorporating terms of endearment and other signs of affection. According to Cavender, members of the gentry also felt an emotional tie to their family estate, illustrated especially in death and burial practices, though they simultaneously engaged in many land transactions. In both family and serf relations, paternalism reigned supreme, but this did not preclude efforts at fairness. In agriculture, however, many Tver' landowners had a reformist bent and combined liberal and scientific ideas with traditional practices to create a "paternalist rationalism," a philosophy that sought to implement improved farming techniques while maintaining the notion of serfdom as a morally superior system (p. 116). Citing the case of Aleksandr Vasil'evich Meshcherskii, Cavender argues that Tver' boasted a "community of like-minded proprietors" who visited often, discussing their attempts to implement agricultural reforms (p. 138). Science also played a part in provincial life. Cavender indicates that "the importance of science and scientific method and of the landowner as scientist and progressive educator of gentry and peasantry alike, serving the state through his own private investigations, provided the basis for the movement for rational agriculture in Tver' " (p. 141). These pursuits took on new value and replaced traditional expectations about service to the state. Even the ways in which the gentry supported charitable causes demonstrated a shift from more traditional views to more scientific ones as they began to spend more on schools and hospitals and less on maintaining a community of hangers-on.

Cavender also looks at the question of corporate identity and argues that the Tver' nobility did have a sense of gentry unity but not one defined in opposition to the state. Rather, members of the gentry shared an identity rooted in "historical customs and ideological justifications" about service to the state (p. 191). Moreover, wealthier members of the Tver' gentry used their participation in local bodies to benefit poorer nobles through charity and other aids, such as scholarships for less fortunate boys. Thus, their corporate identity was defined by local needs and relationships rather than by

larger, empire-wide conceptions of noble identity. Cavender makes the bold claim that her findings prove that "older concepts of an active, all-powerful state crushing even its most privileged subjects must be reconsidered in light of the patchwork of gentry activism in the provinces prior to emancipation" (p. 194). Finally, Cavender proposes that while the Tver' gentry may not have had a concept of a civil society, it did support a non-political "civic society" (p. 151).

Cavender's study is based on archival documents from St. Petersburg, Moscow, Tver', and Helsinki, including the local newspaper, land transactions, wills, other legal documents, and family letters. While the majority of her epistolary evidence is drawn from the papers of the Meshcherskii family, Cavender does use documents from a few other families, as well. This book is an informative addition to the literature on the Russian gentry that helps to enrich the portrait of this very important group.

LEE A. FARROW
*Auburn University,
Montgomery*

CLAUDIA VERHOEVEN. *The Odd Man Karakozov: Imperial Russia, Modernity, and the Birth of Terrorism*. Ithaca: Cornell University Press. 2009. Pp. x, 231. $39.95.

In this extraordinary first book, Claudia Verhoeven takes an event usually relegated by historians to the status of a minor aside and convincingly transforms it into a central moment in Russian and even world history. She accomplishes this feat with some of the most brilliant writing this reviewer has ever seen in a book on Russian history. It draws on a large fund of archival and published primary documents, a broad reading of the contemporary periodical press, and many literary texts, all examined slowly and carefully, turned and tilted to gain a truer view, probed freshly and thoroughly, and pieced together with deftness.

On April 4, 1866, an apparently unbalanced former student of aristocratic background named Dmitrii Karakozov fired a shot at Emperor Alexander II. He was captured, tried, and executed. Scholars have noted that the attempt on the life of the tsar precipitated a "White Terror" involving large-scale arrests, the closing of liberal periodicals, the enhancement of arbitrary administrative powers, and institutional changes. Among the latter were the creation within one month of a forty-man security force to protect the emperor, of Russia's first security bureau (Okhrana), and of a bureau for regular criminal investigation. Because the time was not ripe for the emergence of a revolutionary movement in Russia, however, the entire episode was largely dismissed as the isolated act of a febrile-minded loner. The shadowy organization called "Hell," to which the would-be assassin allegedly belonged, never attracted much attention in the historiography either.

Verhoeven, by contrast, sets out to prove Karakozov a bellwether of the Russian revolutionary movement, a harbinger of political terrorism, and a true first expression of social alienation in the modern age. Her method is forensic, psychological, analytic, and literary: in a word, humanistic. In six chapters, which can be read as independent essays, the author considers the act of April 4 from the point of view of the state, educated society, and ordinary people and examines the appearance, the physical person, and the mind of the attempted assassin. A seventh chapter suggests that Fedor Dostoevsky's protagonist Raskolnikov owed much to the case of Karakozov, which unfolded as the novelist was writing *Crime and Punishment* (1866).

The author distinguishes between the French revolutionary Terror, which was legal, legitimate, and part of an ongoing revolutionary process, and terrorism, which "was illegitimate, illegal, and irregular violence that, temporally speaking, meant to short-circuit the historical current and *ignite* historical change" (p. 176). Previous political violence, from Brutus to Felice Orsini, had aimed to remove a specific tyrant, to wreak vengeance for particular acts, or to reestablish the traditional or otherwise proper order of things. By his deed Karakozov sought to put an end to the system of government entirely. Not by his sole tsaricide, of course, but by shattering the people's belief in an unassailable autocracy and provoking popular rebellion—precisely the stated intention of those actors whom historians of Russia have considered the originators of political terrorism, the People's Will.

Having formulated this hypothesis, Verhoeven replows the well-tilled soil of the history of the Russian revolutionary movement, altering the valance of a dozen of its foundational notions. Nihilism before April 4, she notes, had relatively little political content and no connection to violence but seemed inseparable from them afterward. Karakozov inaugurated a new kind of irregular political struggle involving "an invisible enemy—indiscernible precisely since he was in plain view" (p. 106). As such, he was more than a nihilist, whose main attribute was outrageous manners and dress, in order to draw greater attention to the self. Yet the unavoidable mental association of April 4 with nihilism caused the abandonment of those ways for fear of attracting police attention. In other words, Karakozov put an end to nihilism or at least forced it underground and changed its nature. Vera Zasulich, moreover, was not the first political terrorist in the modern sense, because she attacked a specific official for particular reasons and did not attack the system as a whole. Facing the gallows defiantly, "Karakozov stood as the modern era's first public example of a revolutionary death" (p. 156).

Scholars had overlooked these and other implications of the gunshot of April 4 by considering Karakozov and his act odd, untimely, and premature, failing to realize, in the words of Dostoevsky, that the "odd man . . . sometimes . . . bears within himself the heart of the whole" (p. vi).

Aside from a few minor flaws—the first commandment is not "thou shalt not kill"—one laments that Verhoeven, who suggests that "modernity" implies mass media, radical consciousness, and rampant commer-

cialization, fails to explain exactly how modernity developed in Russia.

This book will delight historians in every field.

JONATHAN W. DALY
University of Illinois,
Chicago

JEFFREY VEIDLINGER. *Jewish Public Culture in the Late Russian Empire.* (The Modern Jewish Experience.) Bloomington: Indiana University Press. 2009. Pp. xviii, 382. Cloth $65.00, paper $24.95.

Jeffrey Veidlinger, the author of an outstanding monograph on the Moscow State Yiddish Theater, has cast a wide net in this new book by exploring the evolution of what he calls Jewish public culture in the last few decades before the collapse of tsarism in Russia, and most notably in the years after the Revolution of 1905–1907. Based on research in five languages in a wide range of published sources and on material located in four major archival collections, the book succeeds admirably in depicting the emergence into "modernity" of the largest Jewish community in the world. Veidlinger's aim, as he puts it, is to describe and analyze the "public engagement [of Jews] with culture" and the elevation of "the status of secular culture within the Jewish community" (p. 7).

It is a complicated story, which Veidlinger tells clearly and in great detail by focusing on the involvement of Jews in a series of institutions that made up a sizable sector of what we now call civil society. After an introductory chapter that sets the parameters of his study, Veidlinger examines one institution and cultural activity after another to demonstrate the vast changes that occurred within the span of a few decades. The changes inevitably involved spirited struggles between those who adhered to the "traditional mindset," that is, the fervently religious people who dismissed as misguided and unworthy any activity not related to the study of the Torah and the worship of God, and the "this-worldniks," as they came to be known, the men and women who championed the pursuit of cultural leisure such as the reading of secular literature, attendance at lectures by literary celebrities, theater and musical performances, the enjoyment of art, and the writing of "public history."

Veidlinger pays special attention to the establishment of libraries open to the general public, clearly the first step in facilitating the growth of interest in secular culture. Jews flocked to them in much larger numbers than other ethnic groups: in the municipal library of Bobruisk (Minsk province), for example, eighty-seven percent of the readers were Jews, who made up only about twenty percent of the city's total population. At the same time, Jews were increasingly reading books and journals in Russian rather than in Yiddish or Hebrew, another sign of the drift toward secularism. In a carefully designed chart (p. 91), Veidlinger points out the extent to which Jews were reading such writers as Ivan Turgenev, Alexander Pushkin, Fedor Dostoevsky, and Leo Tolstoy, to mention only a few. In addition, an increasing number of books written in Yiddish dealt with secular subjects.

A central theme in the book is that these new cultural interests of a growing number of East European Jews served not only to transform the community but also to promote a new level of unity within Russian Jewry, because, as Veidlinger notes on the last page of the book, "the task that united the community is the construction of a public cultural object" (p. 291). The enthusiasm of the people for the various cultural activities was remarkable. When the writer S. Y. Abramovich (known generally as Mendele Moykher Sforim) visited Warsaw, he was treated as a celebrity. A large group of admirers met him at the railway station, and a banquet in his honor continued throughout the night and did not end until six o'clock in the morning. When Sholem Aleichem arrived in Lubava (Courland Province) at two a.m., he was "shocked" to notice the large crowds that waited for him. "There were many women there," he noted, "one of whom seemed to be seven months pregnant" (p. 150). In another town, enormous crowds greeted him in the streets even though the weather was miserable. The hunger for secular culture seemed to be insatiable.

Toward the end of his study, Veidlinger devotes two substantial chapters to the new field of secular history, which paid special attention to the legal position and rights of Jews in the Russian Empire. One motive behind the interest in history clearly was political, to buttress the claim that Jews deserved rights of full citizenship, but the interest mushroomed into a scholarly discipline, Jewish history. Several important journals and books were published, some of which are still worth reading today. The most eminent scholar of the period was no doubt Simon Dubnow, to whom Veidlinger devotes several pages, but there were others who were at the forefront of the discipline.

Veidlinger is to be congratulated for having produced a compelling and important study on a cultural development that transformed East European Jewry and that has been crucial in the history of world Jewry over the past century. It is hard to conceive of the various tendencies of present-day Zionism and of other contemporary cultural and political trends—in Israel and among Jewish communities elsewhere—without the emergence of a Jewish public culture in the late Russian Empire.

ABRAHAM ASCHER
Graduate Center,
City University of New York [All reviewers of books by Indiana University faculty are selected with the advice of the Board of Editors.]

ELIZABETH ASTRID PAPAZIAN. *Manufacturing Truth: The Documentary Moment in Early Soviet Culture.* DeKalb: Northern Illinois University Press. 2009. Pp. xiii, 282. $39.00.

Scholars of early Soviet culture have sought to examine the cultural and political implications of what Elizabeth Astrid Papazian terms the "crisis of representation" that the Bolshevik Revolution brought to traditional forms of artistic expression in the 1920s. Artists could not be cultural navel-gazers, nor could they be critical realists of Soviet culture "from outside," but instead they had to be producers of the new communist truth. Ultimately, they were called on directly by Joseph Stalin in 1932 to become "engineer[s] of human souls" (p. 187) for the good of the socialist future. Artists thus had to confront key issues that were existential to their calling: the very role of the artist; the definition of truth or criticism; and the form, content, and purpose of their art. Papazian is interested in the strains placed on the Soviet age of experimentation by the "opposing aspirations . . . [of] objectivity vs. transformation" (p. 53).

Papazian notes the revolutionary authorities' almost obsessive efforts to concretize progress toward socialism by recording its every step. She concentrates on this "documentary aesthetic" (p. 4) as it pertained to four contemporary actors: the polymath writer Sergei Tretiakov, the avant-garde filmmaker Dziga Vertov, the critical realist-turned-socialist realist Maksim Gorky, and the novelist and humorist Mikhail Zoshchenko. She traces this "documentary moment" through its collapse with the adoption of socialist realism at the first Congress of Soviet Writers in 1934.

Papazian problematizes the part played by documentary sources in selected works of each author and the dilemmas presented by such sources in the authors' own roles as manufacturers of truth for the new Soviet reality. Tretiakov, through his publicist journal articles and original plays, questioned the form and purpose of traditional narrative writing, seeking to replace the novelist as "author-creator" (p. 47) with the "*faktovik* [worker in facts], whose material is reality itself" (p. 47). Still, in the late 1920s, Tretiakov moved away from the idea of the author recording the objective facts around him to the idea of the author taking "an *active* role within the observed reality" (p. 48). Vertov, through his newsreels and feature-length films, sought to move away from the fictional form that dominated film-making, regarding it as the product of the oppressive conditions of the prerevolutionary age. He aspired to use the camera lens to "see and know life" (p. 71) and to establish a network of cameras so that the newly evolving Soviet life could be "caught unawares" (p. 71). Gorky, through his travelogues (especially his visit to the Solovki labor camp) and his activities with the History of Factories project, examined the conflict between what he called "two truths" (p. 133): the truth of the past that weighed so heavily on the new truth that should be nurtured for the nascent Soviet society. Gorky was no longer the gadfly critic of past (tsarist) injustices but the producer of the "truth of the future" (p. 134). Zoshchenko, through materials from newspapers, autobiographies, and readers' letters and through participation in group writing projects, cast himself as the "substitute proletarian writer" now doing his part for the Soviet project by engaging mass readers in a literary dialog. His goal was to transform the reader, to reconstruct the reader as an "authentic proletarian" author (p. 168).

Papazian's monograph reveals very well how the individual artists, themselves often unsure of the nature of their experimentation with artistic form and function, sincerely wrestled with their artistic approaches in this new and challenging Soviet context. She also identifies a basic contradiction between their championing of documentary aesthetics (to record or document Soviet reality) and their embrace of their own utopian aspirations to participate in the new Soviet project of modernization (to construct that reality). Given this contradiction, the eventual turn of Tretiakov, Vertov, and Gorky in the direction of socialist realist strictures looks less like an imposition from on high than an outgrowth of their own conflicted aspirations. "The documentary moment," concludes Papazian, "played a major role in the formation of socialist realism precisely because of its twin promises of objectivity and instrumentality" (p. 210). I find Papazian's conclusion less convincing in the case of Zoshchenko, who does not, by her own analysis of his work, appear to have given up his ironic stance even late into the game. Indeed, his efforts in 1944 to argue for the positive effects of his satire on the Soviet project ring particularly hollow in this reader's ears.

Papazian's monograph is a mature, well-argued, and provocative addition to the recent wave of works on in early Soviet culture.

FREDERICK C. CORNEY
The College of William & Mary

MIDDLE EAST AND NORTHERN AFRICA

CHRISTIAN LANGE. *Justice, Punishment, and the Medieval Muslim Imagination.* (Cambridge Studies in Islamic Civilization.) New York: Cambridge University Press. 2008. Pp. viii, 290. $99.00.

Punishment is a grotesque spectacle. When state-based violence is visible, it either looks like a relic of the past (lynching), a glimpse from tribal societies (Taliban tribunals), or a motif in horror movies. The sensationalism associated with punishment often draws our attention to the punishing act and away from what the punishment signaled for the given society. By focusing on the historical significance of punishment employed by the militarized Seljuq state (511/1118–590/1194), Christian Lange remedies the propensity to generalize and sensationalize punishment and offers the reader the first book-length treatment of punishment in Islamic society. He discusses types of punishment (strangling, drawing a needle across the eye, public executions by sword, gibbeting, infliction of severe pain, executions, imprisonment, floggings, ignominious parading, and banishing and exile), those who can punish (ruler, judge, police, and market inspector), and the different realms of punishment (private within the ruling class, penal tribunals before the ruler, and public punishments). He also argues that studying punishment at the hands of the Seljuq military rulers offers a way to understand how legal reasoning and eschatological reflections often were the results of attempts to temper or come to terms with the power of the state.

Lange divides his book into three parts. The first part, "The Politics of Punishment," classifies punishment during the Seljuq era. It uses punishment as a lens into the social and political order of the realm and demonstrates the reach of the state within subjects' lives. One of the most interesting discussions within this part is -the historical significance of punishments that remained within the realm of the court and out of sight from the public. Punishment for the elite- could reprimand and control and still maintain the honor of the punished. By contrast, punishments such as the ignominious parading around town (*tashhir*) were particularly shameful. The second part, "The Eschatology of Punishment," offers a description of punishments in Hell. After discussing the range of punishments in the afterworld, Lange argues the far-reaching influence of punishment was so extensive that it may have also informed the eschatological imagination. He suggests that reflections about punishments in Hell- are less about the fascination with eschatology than they were ways for the subject population to come to terms with punishments in earthly life. While the first two parts of the book deal with the impact of punishment in the political and eschatological realms, the third part, "The Legal Dimensions of Punishment," demonstrates that even though punishments during the Seljuq time were based on political realities, as opposed to *shari'a*, jurists still found ways to influence conceptions of punishment. In a fascinating chapter, Lange discusses the status of analogous reasoning for divinely ordained (*hudud*) punishments and differing Hanafi and Shafi'i interpretations of whether sodomy should be punished in the same way as fornication. He also illuminates the ways jurists attempted to limit the arbitrary power of the state. For example, jurists concurred that only offenses committed in the public realm could be subject to *ta'zir* or discretionary punishment.

Lange makes two interesting methodological choices. First, he situates his consideration of punishment within the period of Seljuq rule. As Lange discusses in his introduction, the Seluqs offer a useful case study not only because they were a Turkish elite who imposed a military administration over society, but also because their aim to centralize the state included the creation of educational institutions (*madrasas*) that reinforced the connections between theology, law, and the power of the state. His analysis- not only offers a generalized vision of punishment in Islamic society but also allows us to contemplate state-based violence against its subjects during the time of what is often considered the revival of Sunni Islam. Second, Lange develops an approach based on "cumulative evidence" (p. 172) in order to recover the cultural imagination surrounding punishment. In this sense, he offers taxonomies of punishment in different realms (political, eschatological, and legal) and asks the reader to make the connections between the three separate parts. The one narrative thread is the punishment of *tashhir*, which involved stripping the accused, often blackening his or her face, and sitting the accused (sometimes backwards) on a donkey, cow, or camel while parading through the town. While Lange demonstrates how the practice of *tashhir* was shameful, he does not consider that the practice was widely used in other societies and time periods. Such a consideration would allow the reader to focus on what makes the parading such an effective shaming device—especially its connections to donkey imagery—and thereby appreciate what made its Seljuq form particularly distinctive. The book offers a useful introduction to the varieties and meanings of punishment in Islamic society. In both content and approach, it makes a valuable contribution to Islamic history.

NERINA RUSTOMJI
St. John's University,
New York

SUB-SAHARAN AFRICA

ARNOLD HUGHES and DAVID PERFECT. *A Political History of the Gambia, 1816–1994.* (Rochester Studies in African History and the Diaspora.) Rochester, N.Y.: University of Rochester Press. 2006. Pp. xviii, 530. $90.00.

Arnold Hughes's and David Perfect's book is the most comprehensive and exhaustively researched political history available on Africa's smallest mainland country, the Gambia. It begins with the British advent in 1816 and concludes with the military termination of democratic rule in 1994. After an introductory chapter that provides readers with a cursory examination of the social, demographic, ethnic, sectarian, and economic settings, the authors launch into an exploration of the constitutional history of the Gambian colony between 1816 and 1894. This era marked the gradual expansion of British rule up the River Gambia amidst a series of territorial disputes with the French, whose imperial excursions and gains would end up leaving the meager British acquisitions encircled and constricted to the narrow stretch of land along the middle and the lower Gambia River basin.

Gambian politics during the nineteenth century and the early part of the twentieth century were dominated by three major groups: the Liberated Africans (Recaptives), mainly from Sierra Leone; resident European merchants; and the coteries of British administrators overseeing the territorial enclave. Over the years, these three groups pursued their commercial and political interests, periodically forming fluid alliances to counter the challenges posed by the unrelenting threat of French imperialism. Initially, European merchants dominated local political affairs. Beginning in the early 1880s, however, an essentially elitist, personalist, limited, and non-elective system of African representation

thrust African power brokers into the center of Gambian affairs.

Until the onset of World War II, constitutional changes in the Gambia followed developments in the other British dependencies of West Africa. While scholars of constitutional reform in West Africa have long debated whether pressure for change came from popular demand or imperial initiatives, the authors argue that in the Gambia the impetus came from above. Similarly, unlike in other parts of West Africa, their successful demobilization and reintegration into society ensured that ex-servicemen played no significant collective role in the development of an anticolonial coalition in postwar Gambian politics. Between 1941 and 1959 politics in the Gambia was essentially an urban and an elitist affair, dominated by a fractious elite whose convergence of personal interests and mutual rivalries enabled them to override ethnic and sectarian differences in pursuit of their political ambitions. The establishment of the People's Progressive Party (PPP) in 1959 and its strategic mobilization of discontent in the protectorate catapulted it to the political dominance which it would retain throughout the postindependence years.

Those with an interest in the political history of modern African nations will do well to peruse this book for its many insights. Its overwhelming electoral majority notwithstanding, the PPP under Dawda Jawara did not follow the path of many of his contemporaries by establishing a presidential dictatorship. He successfully resisted the temptation to exercise tyranny in the name of national unity and social equality, maintaining an independent judiciary, respecting human rights, and permitting freedom of the press and of expression. Coercion rarely took violent forms. Instead of using state terror to maintain power, Jawara relied on patronage. By refusing to play the insidious game of ethnic and sectarian politics, he saved his multi-ethnic nation from the internecine civil strife that has bled and crippled nations like Nigeria, Algeria, Rwanda, and the Sudan. It is an irony that one of the smallest African states provides lessons that have proved perilously elusive to other larger states of the continent.

The authors are effusive in celebrating democracy in the Gambia under Jawara, while paying only scant attention to its weaknesses. However, it was these limitations that eventually led to the demise of democratic order. By concentrating power in his hands, surrounding himself with sycophants and cronies, basking in the glow of personal indispensability, wincing at corruption and electoral abuses, and permitting a semblance of democracy while adroitly emasculating the opposition, Jawara built a state in which his survival came to depend not on the loyalty of his people but on his ability to secure protection from external forces. Those forces restored him to power in 1981; thirteen years later, he had so alienated his allies that his overthrow by dissident soldiers received no more than a whimper of response.

The authors make no serious attempt to place this study within the framework of Gambian or West African studies. While the notes are extensive and valuable, they could have acknowledged the contributions of scholars such as Harry Gailey, David Gamble, Suleyman Nyang, and John Wiseman, without in any way taking away from their own contributions. Apart from the first chapter and the final chapter, this political history of the Gambia was written with almost no reference to the turbulent economic context of pre- and post-independence Gambia. Beyond the politics of prependalism, we are at a loss as to what to make of the economic policies and achievements of the Jawara regime. No doubt the principal player in all this drama was Jawara himself, but he remains an elusive personality. The image we have is that of a smooth operator with no deep-seated convictions devising schemes and manipulating friends and foes to hold on to power. A more penetrating study of his personality and politics could be a salutary lesson in political survival and legitimization. The one map provided in the book is valuable in delineating the boundaries of the country, but entirely unhelpful in situating the Gambia within its semi-landlocked geopolitical situation, especially in relation to Senegal. Similarly, in a study dominated by personalities no pictures or illustrations of any type grace the pages. Such an omission is remarkable. Nevertheless, the publication of this book is a major achievement. Hughes and Perfect deserve our commendation for providing scholars of African history and politics with an exhaustively researched, lucidly written, nuanced and illuminating analysis of the political history of a model modern African state.

FUNSO AFOLAYAN
University of New Hampshire

SEAN HANRETTA. *Islam and Social Change in French West Africa: History of an Emancipatory Community.* (African Studies, number 110.) New York: Cambridge University Press. 2009. Pp. xv, 311. $80.00.

Sean Hanretta's book examines the historical odyssey of a West African branch of the Tijaniyya Sufi order. In August 1929, Yacouba Sylla launched a religious and social reform movement in the town of Kaédi in the French colony of Mauritania. Sylla was a disciple of Shaykh Hamallah, who presided over a dissident branch of the Tijaniyya Sufi order. Hamallah and his followers, many of whom were of low social status, were considered a threat by both the French colonial authorities and the conservative religious establishment. Tensions soon mounted in Kaédi between Sylla's followers and their opponents, and violence broke out by the end of 1929, culminating in the deaths of over twenty of Sylla's disciples and the arrest of over 100 more by the colonial authorities. Yacouba Sylla was deported to the colony of Côte d'Ivoire, where he was jailed until 1938. By that time, Sylla had assuaged the fears of the French and the leaders of the Tijani order, and he reoriented his movement toward the emerging commercial and agricultural opportunities in Côte d'Ivoire. His Sufi community, or *zawiya*, became a leading economic center in

the colony during the next decade, and Sylla remained a notable economic and religious figure within Côte d'Ivoire and the surrounding region until his death in 1988. On the surface, this story easily falls into the now common rubric within the historiography of Islam in West Africa of the mutual accommodation between French colonial rule, with its form of modernization, and an Islamic reform movement, but Hanretta's work pushes the field in new directions.

Drawing from extensive archival research in France, Senegal, Mali, and Côte d'Ivoire, and fieldwork and interviews with the Yacoubist community in West Africa, Hanretta's book is divided into three parts. The first part presents the reader with the historical background of the movement and an account of the birth of Yacouba's revival, its conflicts with French and African authorities, and the transformation of the movement from 1938 to the present. Yacouba's reforms concerning materialism and sexuality are analyzed as critiques of social and religious norms, and Hanretta also traces the changing and multifaceted approach of the colonial authorities. The second part examines the production of knowledge within the range of Hanretta's sources. One chapter is devoted to the French archive and the fractured and heterogeneous production of French knowledge and perceptions of Islam, as seen through the lens of the Yacoubist affair. Notably, Hanretta points out the influence of African authors within the French archive and yet cautions the reader against easily translating that influence as agency. Another chapter concerns the development of a history of the movement by the followers of Yacouba and the ways that Yacoubists have employed that history. The history of the movement plays a central role in the determination of individual and collective identities among Yacouba's followers, and Hanretta invites the reader to consider that the production and transmission of this history is a kind of "faith" for the community. The third part presents Hanretta's interpretations of the role of women within the movement, the emancipatory nature of Yacoubist teachings and practices, the importance of work and gift-giving within the community, and the role played by Yacouba Sylla's followers in the development of modern Côte d'Ivoire.

The book is important from several different perspectives. In a general fashion, Hanretta's analysis is a lesson in the nuances of historiography and a reminder that historical sources themselves have a history. Rather than drawing hard and fast distinctions between his sources—whether they are written or oral, French or African—the author examines the intersections and connections between sources and their mutual development. Within the historiography of Islam in West Africa, the book breaks new ground alongside other recent works that seek to employ local or micro-histories to critique and analyze standard conceptions and to present emerging theories on the larger topic of the development of Islam in Africa. Hanretta's book crosses geographical and chronological boundaries as it traces the history of Sylla's movement from a regional per-

326 Reviews of Books

spective, taking into account the pre-colonial context that served as the roots of both Sylla's reforms and the reaction against his ideas. At its heart, the book is a work of intellectual history, and while scholars and graduate students will find the theoretical issues invigorating, at times the jargon and complex writing style make the book unsuitable for those outside of that audience. There are some minor production issues, such as three missing footnotes for the citations on page 60, and a "Note on References" takes the place of a full bibliography. This in no way detracts from Hanretta's achievements with this work or the importance that his approaches and interpretations will have for the field in years to come.

JOHN GLOVER
University of Redlands

JAMIE MONSON. *Africa's Freedom Railway: How a Chinese Development Project Changed Lives and Livelihoods in Tanzania.* Bloomington: Indiana University Press. 2009. Pp. xii, 199. $39.95.

Jamie Monson's book opens with a breath-taking encounter at Chimala, in southern Tanzania, between a Chinese-Tanzanian group of railway workers and an American-led road construction crew. The chest-thumping that followed this chance encounter was symptomatic of the often confusing mix of ideology and economics in southern Africa's rural infrastructural development throughout the Cold War. The Chinese-built railroad would break Zambia's dependence upon the rail and port facilities of its hostile southern neighbors (Southern Rhodesia, Angola, and South Africa), while the highway would stand for the free movement of people and their goods and services. Accordingly, the Chinese and their Tanzanian and Zambian counterparts dubbed the railway of the Tanzania Zambia Railway Authority (TAZARA) the "Freedom Railway," while the Americans and their allies presented it, rather threateningly, as the "great steel arm of China thrusting its way into the African interior" (p. 2), or worse, a "bamboo railway." In fact the Chinese became involved in the project only after Western donors and the Soviet Union had denied requests from Tanzania and Zambia to fund its construction.

In chapter two of part one, Monson argues that in the histories of railway construction, politics and economics are closely intertwined. For instance, British imperial designs on Africa in the late nineteenth century greatly influenced German colonial advocates who called for the construction of rail lines that would serve as a foundation for a German empire or *Mittelafrika*. At the end of World War I, the British proposed the construction of the "Imperial Link," a network of railroads connecting their southern African colonies. Zambian President Kenneth Kaunda and Tanzanian President Julius Nyerere revived the idea of a rail link that would serve the economic and social needs of their respective countries. China, Tanzania, and Zambia signed the final agreement to construct the railroad in July 1970; the

1,060-mile, $400 million project was completed in 1975. China provided the equipment, materials, and technical expertise while local costs were financed by a commodity credit agreement.

Construction of the "people's railway" revealed some interesting ideological patterns of recruitment as well as contrasting work ethics. In recruiting the labor force, the Chinese and their Tanzanian and Zambian counterparts accorded pride of place to party ideology. However, whereas the Chinese worked hard to complete the project ahead of schedule, their African counterparts balked at the strenuous timetable. Practical and political considerations produced overlapping managerial structures. Nevertheless, a commitment to ideology did nothing to stop the erection of segregated residential and recreational patterns in the camps. In chapter four, "Living along the Railway," the author argues that concentration of the rural population into villages or *ujamaa* between 1973 and 1976 had the opposite effect. Population growth resulted not from forced relocation but from voluntary migration due to new economic opportunities along the railroad.

Part two deals with "The Ordinary Train," which officially began operations in 1976. The author focuses attention on the "passenger belt" of the Kilombero valley in southern Tanzania. Unlike its counterparts, the Express and Goods Trains, the "ordinary train" was the people's lifeline; it carried more passengers and goods across a wide swath of territory. The trains had their fair share of technological malfunctions, management failures, and other related inefficiencies, some of which were offset with the purchase of West German diesel electric engines and infusions of aid from the U.S., Norway, and Sweden. Economic liberalization in the 1990s opened up new markets and opportunities for rural entrepreneurs and wage earners alike. Ironically, in the post-apartheid and postcolonial era, the designers of the "freedom railway" had to rethink their strategy for dealing with their southern neighbors and their competing rail systems.

In chapter six, "Landscape Visions," Monson examines Tanzania's struggle to put into practice lofty visions of a landscape dotted with large-scale, mechanized agricultural projects such as the abandoned North Korean rice project at Mngeta. In their stead were small plots of farmland whose owners often had to find wage employment to supplement their incomes, while new immigrants introduced new crops and farming techniques. The drawback was that migration created tensions between "locals" and "strangers."

The concluding chapter neatly ties up the narrative and highlights the central thesis of the book. Drawing upon life histories, archival material, parcel receipts, and satellite images, the author argues effectively throughout the book that despite its shortcomings, the railroad transformed rural living and work patterns. Inevitably, the future success of TAZARA depends not upon the original socialist model of development but upon the harsh economic realities of the twenty-first century. This insightful account of transnational infrastructure cooperation will no doubt be welcome reading not only for academics and students, but most importantly for African leaders who have to make critical development choices for the benefit of their own people.

PETER A. DUMBUYA
Fort Valley State University

WAYNE DOOLING. *Slavery, Emancipation and Colonial Rule in South Africa*. (Ohio University Research in International Studies, Africa Series, number 87.) Athens, Ohio: Ohio University Press. 2007. Pp. xi, 249. $26.95.

Wayne Dooling's book is a major contribution to the burgeoning corpus of works surrounding the institution of slavery in the early colonial Cape. Yet almost uniquely, neither the enslaved nor the colonial state are at the center of the story it relates, although the author brings both into the story in nuanced and complex ways. Rather, his focus is the cape "gentry," a class that the author goes out of his way to characterize and explore carefully. While the monograph reveals important new information about the actions and perspectives of the enslaved, as well as the colonial and imperial roles in alternately maintaining and attacking the institution of slavery, it tells us even more about this landowning, if often heavily mortgaged, farming class.

At the heart of Dooling's unique definition of the Cape gentry is his argument that they constituted a moral community. This notion requires some processing, and it is to the author's credit that he is able to recover it from the driest of archival records. While he makes clear the often extreme violence associated with both the expansion of the farming frontier in the Cape and the domination of slave-owners over slaves, Dooling is nevertheless able to demonstrate the ways in which tight-knit communities of farmers lent each other money, supported each other's endeavors, and saved each other from ruin in times of crisis such as the emancipation of 1834. Intriguingly, however, Dooling mobilizes this interpretation to challenge rather than support the received view of the Cape gentry as a durable and unchanging class, instead suggesting that they both undertook and were affected by complex pathways and profound adjustments only partly of their own making. In this way, he interpolates their history with that of their slaves and laborers, as well as that of the capital-providing classes of Cape Town and the British Empire as a whole.

As the book's title suggests, a watershed in this story comes at the moment of emancipation. Yet the author is as focused on continuity as he is on transformation, and while he pays due attention to slave liberations and to the immediate crisis of emancipation for slave-owners, he is more concerned with weaving this moment into the longer narrative he constructs. The structure of the book facilitates this approach. Emancipation is contextualized in the first two chapters, the first of which historicizes and defines the Cape gentry and the second of which explores the ambiguous impact of British colonial rule. In the third chapter Dooling turns his attention to investigating the modalities by which workers and former masters attempted to negotiate emancipation's immediate impact. These included desertion, wage demands and the use of courts on the parts of the formerly enslaved, vagrancy laws, and conscious attempts on the part of the gentry to restrict land availability and alternate means of existence for the formerly enslaved. In this and the following chapter, Dooling demonstrates how the gentry managed to survive, partly through the aid of compensation payments from the British government but more consistently through the utilization of their moral community relationships. In the long run, however, the integration of the region into a mechanized and capitalistic global economy forced the gentry to transform and subordinated them to merchants and bankers based in Cape Town and abroad. This is a story told in the final chapter of the book. Yet while the gentry were no longer lords of the land by 1898, they nevertheless began to build the cultural and political organizations that would give them a new role in South Africa in the twentieth century.

If the conclusion of the book does not read as a typical narrative termination, its open-endedness is not unsettling. Dooling is clearly aware that the story he tells is part of many others, and this has affected the way in which it was written. The book is more than the depiction of an important episode in South African history. It is in fact an important contribution to the study of how apartheid society was constructed. Moreover, as a story of liberation, it is a disturbing one to read in this era following the official demise of apartheid. Finally, it is an important addition to the comparative and global histories of emancipation, and one that references experiences elsewhere. Undoubtedly, it will inform both future studies and classroom seminars on these topics.

TREVOR GETZ
San Francisco State University

Collected Essays

These volumes, recently received in the *AHR* office, do not lend themselves readily to unified reviews; the contents are therefore listed.

COMPARATIVE/WORLD

GWYN CAMPBELL, SUZANNE MIERS, and JOSEPH C. MILLER, editors. *Children in Slavery through the Ages*. Athens, Ohio: Ohio University Press. 2009. Pp. vi, 234. Cloth $49.95, paper $19.95.

ANTÓNIO DE ALMEIDA MENDES, Child Slaves in the Early North Atlantic Trade in the Fifteenth and Sixteenth Centuries. RICHARD B. ALLEN, Children and European Slave Trading in the Indian Ocean during the Eighteenth and Early Nineteenth Centuries. FRED MORTON, Small Change: Children in the Nineteenth-Century East African Slave Trade. GEORGE MICHAEL LA RUE, The Brief Life of 'Ali, the Orphan of Kordofan: The Egyptian Slave Trade in the Sudan, 1820–35. SUSAN EVA O'DONOVAN, Traded Babies: Enslaved Children in America's Domestic Migration, 1820–60. KRISTINA RICHARDSON, Singing Slave Girls (*Qiyan*) of the 'Abbasid Court in the Ninth and Tenth Centuries. GULAY YILMAZ, Becoming a *Devşirme*: The Training of Conscripted Children in the Ottoman Empire. BOK-RAE KIM, The Third Gender: Palace Eunuchs. PAULINE PUI-TING POON, The Well-Being of Purchased Female Domestic Servants (*Mui Tsai*) in Hong Kong in the Early Twentieth Century. PIERRE H. BOULLE, Slave and Other Nonwhite Children in Late-Eighteenth-Century France. KENNETH MORGAN, The Struggle for Survival: Slave Infant Mortality in the British Caribbean in the Late Eighteenth and Nineteenth Centuries-.CALVIN SCHERMERHORN, Left Behind but Getting Ahead: Antebellum Slavery's Orphans in the Chesapeake, 1820–60.

JACK P. GREENE, editor. *Exclusionary Empire: English Liberty Overseas, 1600–1900*. New York: Cambridge University Press. 2010. Pp. xiii, 305. Cloth $90.00, paper $26.99.

ELIZABETH MANCKE, The Languages of Liberty in British North America, 1607–1776. JACK P. GREENE, Liberty and Slavery: The Transfer of British Liberty to the West Indies, 1627–1865. JAMES KELLY, "Era of Liberty": The Politics of Civil and Political Rights in Eighteenth-Century Ireland. ELIGA H. GOULD, Liberty and Modernity: The American Revolution and the Making of Parliament's Imperial History. PETER S. ONUF, Federalism, Democracy, and Liberty in the New American Nation. PHILIP GIRARD, Liberty, Order, and Pluralism: The Ca-

nadian Experience. ROBERT TRAVERS, Contested Despotism: Problems of Liberty in British India. RICHARD WATERHOUSE, ." . . a bastard offspring of tyranny under the guise of liberty": Liberty and Representative Government in Australia, 1788–1901. JAMES BELICH, How Much Did Institutions Matter? Cloning Britain in New Zealand. CHRISTOPHER SAUNDERS, The Expansion of British Liberties: The South African Case.

CARIBBEAN AND LATIN AMERICA

BEN VINSON III and MATTHEW RESTALL, editors. *Black Mexico: Race and Society from Colonial to Modern Times*. (Diálogos.) Albuquerque: University of New Mexico Press. 2009. Pp. xiv, 278.

BEN VINSON III, Black Mexico and the Historical Discipline. FRANK "TREY" PROCTOR III, Slave Rebellion and Liberty in Colonial Mexico. ANDREW B. FISHER, Negotiating Two Worlds: The Free-Black Experience in Guerrero's Tierra Caliente. PAT CARROLL, Black Aliens and Black Natives in New Spain's Indigenous Communities. BEN VINSON III, From Dawn 'til Dusk: Black Labor in Late Colonial Mexico. NICOLE VON GERMETEN, Colonial Middle Men? Mulatto Identity in New Spain's Confraternities. JOAN BRISTOL and MATTHEW RESTALL, Potions and Perils: Love-Magic in Seventeenth-Century Afro-Mexico and Afro-Yucatan. LAURA A. LEWIS, "Afro" Mexico in Black, White, and Indian: An Anthropologist Reflects on Fieldwork. BOBBY VAUGHN, My Blackness and Theirs: Viewing Mexican Blackness Up Close. ALVA MOORE STEVENSON, The Thorntons: Saga of an Afro-Mexican Family. JEAN-PHILIBERT MOBWA MOBWA N'DJOLI, The Need to Recognize Afro-Mexicans as an Ethnic Group.

EUROPE: ANCIENT AND MEDIEVAL

JEFF RIDER and ALAN V. MURRAY, editors. *Galbert of Bruges and the Historiography of Medieval Flanders*. Washington, D.C.: Catholic University of America Press. 2009. Pp. xi, 297. $37.95.

JEFF RIDER, "Wonder with Fresh Wonder": Galbert the Writer and the Genesis of the *De multro*. R. C. VAN CAENEGEM, Galbert of Bruges and "Law Is Politics." DIRK HEIRBAUT, Not European Feudalism, but Flemish Feudalism: A New Reading of Galbert of Bruges's Data on Feudalism in the Context of Early Twelfth-Century Flanders. STEVEN ISAAC, Galbert of Bruges and the Urban Experience of Siege. NANCY F. PARTNER, Galbert's Hidden Women: Social Presence and Narrative Concealment. MARTINA HÄCKER, The Language of Misogyny in Galbert of Bruges's Account of the Murder of Charles the Good. BERT DEMYTTENAERE, The Tears of Fromold: The Murder of Charles the Good, Homoeroticism, and the Ruin of the Erembalds. ALAN V. MURRAY, The Devil in Flanders: Galbert of Bruges and the Eschatology of Political Crisis. ROBERT M. STEIN, Death from a Trivial Cause: Events and Their Meanings in Galbert of Bruges's *Chronicle*. LISA H. COOPER and MARY AGNES EDSALL, History as Fabliau and Fabliau as History: The Murder of Charles the Good and *Du provost a l'aumuche*. GODFRIED CROENEN, Chronicles of Revolt: Galbert of Bruges's *De multro* and Jean Froissart's *Chronique de Flandre*.

Documents and Bibliographies

Books listed were recently received in the *AHR* office. Works of these types cannot normally be reviewed by the *AHR*.

COMPARATIVE/WORLD

EUBEN, ROXANNE L., and MUHAMMAD QASIM ZAMAN, editors. *Princeton Readings in Islamist Thought: Texts and Contexts from Al-Banna to Bin Laden*. (Princeton Studies in Muslim Politics.) Princeton: Princeton University Press. 2009. Pp. xv, 516. Cloth $69.50, paper $26.95.

KROSZNER, RANDALL S., and LOUIS PUTTERMAN, editors. *The Economic Nature of the Firm: A Reader*. 3d ed. New York: Cambridge University Press. 2009. Pp. x, 387. Cloth $110.00, paper $39.99.

ASIA

KUMĀRAJĪVA. *Scripture of the Lotus Blossom of the Fine Dharma (The Lotus Sūtra)*. Translated by LEON HURVITZ. (Translations from the Asian Classics.) Rev. ed. New York: Columbia University Press. 2009. Pp. xxviii, 384. Cloth $84.50, paper $29.50.

CANADA AND THE UNITED STATES

BROWNE, G. P., editor. *Documents on the Confederation of British North America*. Introduction by JANET AJZENSTAT. (Carleton Library Series, number 215.) Reprint. Ithaca, N.Y.: McGill-Queen's University Press. 2009. Pp. li, 377. $29.95.

EDMUNDSON, JAMES V. *Letters to Lee: From Pearl Harbor to the War's Final Mission*. Edited by CELIA EDMUNDSON. (World War II: The Global, Human, and Ethical Dimension.) New York: Fordham University Press. 2010. Pp. xi, 222. $35.00.

FENTON, WILLIAM N. *William Fenton: Selected Writings*. Edited and with an introduction by WILLIAM A. STARNA and JACK CAMPISI. (The Iroquoians and Their World.) Lincoln: University of Nebraska Press. 2009. Pp. xxi, 375. $40.00.

HATTENDORF, JOHN B., and PETER M. SWARTZ, editors. *U.S. Naval Strategy in the 1980s: Selected Documents*. (Naval War College, Center for Naval Warfare Studies, Newport Papers, number 33.) Newport, R.I.: Naval War College Press. 2008. Pp. viii, 355.

HUNTLEY, HORACE, and JOHN W. MCKERLEY, editors. *Foot Soldiers for Democracy: The Men, Women, and Children of the Birmingham Civil Rights Movement*. Introductions by ROBIN D. G. KELLEY and ROSE FREEMAN MASSEY. Urbana and Chicago: University of Illinois Press. 2009. Pp. xxxi, 222. Cloth $75.00, paper $25.00.

JOBE, ABRAHAM. *A Mountaineer in Motion: The Memoir of Dr. Abraham Jobe, 1817–1906*. Edited by DAVID C. HSIUNG.

Knoxville: University of Tennessee Press. 2009. Pp. xvi, 206. $37.95.

MANVILL, P. D. *Lucinda; or, The Mountain Mourner: Being Recent Facts, in a Series of Letters, from Mrs. Manvill, in the State of New York, to Her Sister in Pennsylvania*. Edited by MISCHELLE B. ANTHONY. (Writing American Women.) Syracuse, N.Y.: Syracuse University Press. 2009. Pp. lxxxvi, 102. $19.95.

MCCLELLAN, GEORGE BRINTON. *The Mexican War Diary and Correspondence of George B. McClellan*. Edited by THOMAS W. CUTRER. Baton Rouge: Louisiana State University Press. 2009. Pp. vi, 195. $37.50.

ROOSEVELT, ELEANOR, and ISABELLA GREENWAY. *A Volume of Friendship: The Letters of Eleanor Roosevelt and Isabella Greenway, 1904–1953*. Edited by KRISTIE MILLER and ROBERT H. MCGINNIS. Preface by BLANCE WIESEN COOK. Tucson, Ariz.: Arizona Historical Society. 2009. Pp. xvi, 325. $34.95.

SANDOZ, MARI. *"I Do Not Apologize for the Length of This Letter": The Mari Sandoz Letters on Native American Rights, 1940–1965*. Edited by KIMBERLI A. LEE. Foreword by JOHN R. WUNDER. (Plains Histories.) Lubbock: Texas Tech University Press. 2009. Pp. xviii, 197. $45.00.

STACKPOLE, PIERPONT L. *In the Company of Generals: The World War I Diary of Pierpont L. Stackpole*. Edited by ROBERT H. FERRELL. Columbia: University of Missouri Press. 2009. Pp. xi, 209. $34.95.

TAUSSIG, JOSEPH K. *Three Splendid Little Wars: The Diary of Joseph K. Taussig, 1898–1901*. Edited by EVELYN M. CHERPAK. (Naval War College Historical Monograph Series, number 16.) Newport, R.I.: Naval War College Press. 2009. Pp. xxii, 173. $27.00.

THURMAN, HOWARD WASHINGTON. *The Papers of Howard Washington Thurman*. Volume 1: *My People Need Me, June 1918–March 1936*. Edited by WALTER EARL FLUKER et al. Columbia: University of South Carolina Press. 2009. Pp. cv, 377. $59.95.

EUROPE: ANCIENT AND MEDIEVAL

CICERO, MARCUS TULLIUS. *Ten Speeches*. Translated, edited, and foreword by JAMES E. G. ZETZEL. Indianapolis and Cambridge: Hackett Publishing Company, Inc. 2009. Pp. xl, 332. Cloth $44.00, paper $14.95.

EUROPE: EARLY MODERN AND MODERN

BEREND, IVAN T. *History in My Life: A Memoir of Three Eras*. Budapest and New York: Central European University Press. 2009. Pp. 276. $45.00.

BERTHIER, FERDINAND. *Forging Deaf Education in Nineteenth-Century France: Biographical Sketches of Bébian, Sicard, Massieu, and Clerc*. Edited and translated by FREEMAN G.

HENRY. Washington, D.C.: Gallaudet University Press. 2009. Pp. xxxvii, 136. $60.00.

BLACK, JEREMY. *War in European History, 1660–1792.* (Essential Bibliography.) Washington, D.C.: Potomac Books, Inc. 2009. Pp. x, 112. $14.95.

DISRAELI, BENJAMIN. *Benjamin Disraeli Letters.* Volume Eight: *1860–1864.* Edited by M. G. WIEBE et al. (The Disraeli Project.) Buffalo, N.Y.: University of Toronto Press. 2009. Pp. lxiii, 477. £125.00.

HALÉVY, LUDOVIC. *Notes and Remembrances, 1871–1872.* Translated and foreword by ROGER L. WILLIAMS. Newark: University of Delaware Press. 2009. Pp. 141. $42.50.

LUKŠA, JUOZAS. *Forest Brothers: The Account of an Anti-Soviet Lithuanian Freedom Fighter 1944–1948.* Translated and foreword by LAIMA VINCE. Budapest and New York: Central European University Press. 2009. Pp. ix, 411. $45.00.

MACKAY, CHRISTOPHER S. *The Hammer of Witches: A Complete Translation of the* Malleus Maleficarum. New York: Cambridge University Press. 2009. Pp. vii, 657. $29.99.

MACKAY, JOHN, editor and translator. *Four Russian Serf Narratives.* (Wisconsin Studies in Autobiography.) Madison: University of Wisconsin Press. 2009. Pp. xi, 215. $26.95.

SPENDER, LILIAN, and WILFRID SPENDER. *World War I and the Question of Ulster: The Correspondence of Lilian and Wilfrid Spender.* Edited by MARGARET BAGULEY. Dublin: Irish Manuscripts Commission. 2009. Pp. xxxi, 536. €50.00.

Other Books Received

The following books were recently received in the *AHR* office. Books listed here do not include works scheduled for review.

METHODS/THEORY

BASTIAN, JEANNETTE A., and BEN ALEXANDER, editors. *Community Archives: The Shaping of Memory.* (Principles and Practice in Records Management and Archives.) Graested: Facet. 2009. Pp. xxiv, 286. $89.95.

KURKELA, VESA, and LAURI VÄKEVÄ, editors. *De-Canonizing Music History.* Newcastle: Cambridge Scholars Publishing. 2009. Pp. xiii, 199. $59.99.

MACKINLAY, ELIZABETH, BRYDIE-LEIGH BARTLEET, and KATELYN BARNEY, editors. *Musical Islands: Exploring Connections between Music, Place and Research.* Newcastle: Cambridge Scholars Publishing. 2009. Pp. xxv, 459. $74.99.

WATERTON, EMMA, and LAURAJANE SMITH, editors. *Taking Archaeology out of Heritage.* Newcastle: Cambridge Scholars Publishing. 2009. Pp. ix, 238. $59.99.

COMPARATIVE/WORLD

ALLEN, BENJAMIN MARK. *Naked and Alone in a Strange New World: Early Modern Captivity and Its Mythos.* Newcastle: Cambridge Scholars Publishing. 2009. Pp. xxv, 160. £34.99.

BETHENCOURT, FRANCISCO. *The Inquisition: A Global History, 1478–1834.* Translated by JEAN BIRRELL. (Past and Present Publications.) New York: Cambridge University Press. 2009. Pp. xii, 491. Cloth $110.00, paper $39.99.

KARRAS, ALAN L. *Smuggling: Contraband and Corruption in World History.* (Exploring World History.) Lanham, Md.: Rowman and Littlefield. 2010. Pp. xii, 201. $34.95.

LÖTTEL, HOLGER. *Um Ehre und Anerkennung: Englandbilder im Amerikanischen Süden und die Außenpolitik der Konföderation.* (Transatlantische Historische Studien, number 36. Veröffentlichungen des Deutschen Historischen Instituts, Washington, D.C.) Stuttgart: Franz Steiner Verlag. 2009. Pp. 468. €55,00.

MARTIN, RICHARD C., and ABBAS BARZEGAR, editors. *Islamism: Contested Perspectives on Political Islam.* Stanford, Calif.: Stanford University Press. 2010. Pp. xi, 186. Cloth $55.00, paper $19.95.

MARTINI, MANUELA, and PHILIPPE RYGIEL, editors. *Genre et travail migrant: Mondes atlantiques, XIXe–Xxe siècles.* (Actes de l'histoire de l'immigration, number 9.) Paris: éditions Publibook. 2009. €25.00.

PENNA, ANTHONY N. *The Human Footprint: A Global Environmental History.* Malden, Mass.: Wiley-Blackwell. 2010. Pp. xvi, 354. $39.95.

ASIA

BAKER, CHRIS, and PHONGPAICHIT PASUK. *A History of Thailand.* 2d ed. New York: Cambridge University Press. 2009. Pp. xviii, 315. Cloth $90.00, paper $29.99.

BENTON, GREGOR, and LIN CHUN, editors. *Was Mao Really a Monster: The Academic Response to Chang and Halliday's Mao: The Unknown Story.* New York: Routledge. 2010. Pp. viii, 199. $42.95.

BONATZ, DOMINIK, et al. *From Distant Tales: Archaeology and Ethnohistory in the Highlands of Sumatra.* Newcastle: Cambridge Scholars Publishing. 2009. Pp. xiii, 509. $82.99.

BROWN, JUDITH M. *Windows into the Past: Life Histories and the Historian of South Asia.* (Critical Problems in History.) Notre Dame, Ind.: University of Notre Dame Press. 2009. Pp. xii, 118. $20.00.

DREA, EDWARD J. *Japan's Imperial Army: Its Rise and Fall, 1853–1945.* (Modern War Studies.) Lawrence: University Press of Kansas. 2009. Pp. ix, 332. Cloth $34.95.

FARRIS, WILLIAM WAYNE. *Japan to 1600: A Social and Economic History.* Honolulu: University of Hawai'i Press. 2009. Pp. xix, 227. $22.00.

GUSTAFSSON, MAI LAN. *War and Shadows: The Haunting of Vietnam.* Ithaca: Cornell University Press. 2009. Pp. xiv, 206. Cloth $59.95, paper $19.95.

MILLWARD, JAMES. *Eurasian Crossroads: A History of Xinjiang.* Paperback. New York: Columbia University Press. 2007. Pp. xix, 440. Paper $24.50.

PAKULA, HANNAH. *The Last Empress: Madame Chiang Kai-shek and the Birth of Modern China.* New York: Simon and Schuster. 2009. Pp. xix, 787. $30.00.

RAJADHYAKSHA, ASHISH. *Indian Cinema in the Time of Celluloid: From Bollywood to the Emergency.* (South Asian Cinemas.) Bloomington: Indiana University Press. 2009. Pp. x, 441. $27.95.

ROWE, WILLIAM T. *China's Last Emperor: The Great Qing.* Cambridge: Belknap Press of Harvard University Press. 2009. Pp. 360. $35.00.

SCHWENKEL, CHRISTINA L. *The American War in Contemporary Vietnam: Transnational Remembrance and Representation.* (Tracking Globalization.) Bloomington: Indiana University Press. 2009. Pp. xiii, 264. Cloth $65.00, paper $24.95.

SINGH, RANA P. B., editor *Cosmic Order and Cultural Astronomy: Sacred Cities of India.* Foreword by JOHN MCKIM MALVILLE. (Planet Earth & Cultural Understanding, number 4.) Newcastle: Cambridge Scholars Publishing. 2009. Pp. xvi, 248. $59.99.

SLOAN, BILL. *The Darkest Summer: Pusan and Inchon 1950; The Battles that Saved South Korea—and the Marines—from Extinction.* New York: Simon and Schuster. 2009. Pp. 385. $27.00.

TAO, DONGFENG, et al. *Chinese Revolution and Chinese Literature.* Newcastle: Cambridge Scholars Publishing. 2009. Pp. xvi, 303.

TEISER, STEPHEN F., and JACQUELINE I. STONE, editors. *Readings of the Lotus Sūtra.* (Columbia Readings of Buddhist Literature.) New York: Columbia University Press. 2009. Pp. xi, 284. Cloth $79.50, paper $24.50.

WOLPERT, STANLEY. *Shameful Flight: The Last Years of the Brit-*

ish Empire in India. Paperback edition. New York: Oxford University Press. 2009. Pp. xii, 238. $17.95.

OCEANIA AND THE PACIFIC ISLANDS

KENNEDY, JOSEPH. *The Tropical Frontier: America's South Sea Colony.* Mangilao, Guam: Micronesian Area Research Center, University of Guam. 2009. Pp. xix, 245. $35.00.

CANADA AND THE UNITED STATES

ADELEKE, TUNDE. *The Case against Afrocentrism.* Jackson: University Press of Mississippi. 2009. Pp. xiv, 223. $50.00.

AUCHINCLOSS, LOUIS. *Woodrow Wilson: A Life.* (Penguin Lives Series.) Reprint. New York: Penguin. 2009. Pp. 128. $14.00.

BANGS, JEREMY DUPERTUIS. *Strangers and Pilgrims, Travellers and Sojourners: Leiden and the Foundations of Plymouth Plantation.* Plymouth, Mass.: General Society of Mayflower Descendants. 2009. Pp. xxxii, 894. $67.50.

BASS, AMY. *Those about Him Remained Silent: The Battle over W. E. B. Du Bois.* Minneapolis: University of Minnesota Press. 2009. Pp. xxiv, 198. $24.95.

BELLAFAIRE, JUDITH, and MERCEDES HERRERA GRAF. *Women Doctors in War.* (Williams-Ford Texas A&M University Military History Series, number 128.) College Station: Texas A&M University Press. 2009. Pp. xii, 255. $35.00.

BLAIR, WILLIAM A., and KAREN FISHER YOUNGER, editors. *Lincoln's Proclamation: Emancipation Reconsidered.* (The Steven and Janice Brose Lectures in the Civil War Era.) Chapel Hill: University of North Carolina Press. 2009. Pp. xii, 233. $30.00.

BONAN, GORDON B. *The Edge of Mosby's Sword: The Life of Confederate Colonel William Henry Chapman.* Carbondale: Southern Illinois University Press. 2009. Pp. xii, 220. $29.95.

BREAZEALE, J. W. M. *Life as It Is, or, Matters and Things in General, Containing, amongst Other Things, Historical Sketches of the Exploration and First Settlement of the State of Tennessee.* Introduction by JONATHAN M. ATKINS. (Appalachian Echoes Series.) Reprint. Knoxville: University of Tennessee Press. 2009. Pp. xxxvi, 256. $29.95.

BREWER, JOHN. *The American Leonardo: A Tale of Obsession, Art and Money.* New York: Oxford University Press. 2009. Pp. ix, 310. $24.95.

BRIER, JENNIFER. *Infectious Ideas: U.S. Political Responses to the AIDS Crisis.* Chapel Hill: University of North Carolina Press. 2009. Pp. xv, 289. $35.00.

CARLISLE, RODNEY. *Sovereignty at Sea: U.S. Merchant Ships and American Entry into World War I.* Foreword by JAMES C. BRADFORD and GENE ALLEN SMITH. (New Perspectives on Maritime History and Nautical Archaeology.) Gainesville: University Press of Florida. 2009. Pp. xv, 232. $69.95.

CASSITY, MICHAEL, and DANNEY GOBLE. *Divided Hearts: The Presbyterian Journey through Oklahoma History.* Norman: University of Oklahoma Press. 2009. Pp. xix, 340. $24.95.

CHADWICK, BRUCE. *Lincoln for President: An Unlikely Candidate, an Audacious Strategy, and the Victory No One Saw Coming.* Naperville, Ill.: Sourcebooks, Inc.. 2009. Pp. xviii, 396. $24.99.

CONLEY, RICHARD S. *Historical Dictionary of the George W. Bush Era.* (Historical Dictionaries of U.S. Politics and Political Eras, number 15.) Lanham, Md.: Scarecrow Press. 2010. Pp. lvii, 401. $90.00.

COOPER, JOHN MILTON, JR. *Woodrow Wilson: A Biography.* New York: Alfred A. Knopf. 2009. Pp. viii, 702. $35.00.

COOPER, PHILLIP J. *The War against Regulation: From Jimmy Carter to George W. Bush.* (Studies in Government and Public Policy.) Lawrence: University Press of Kansas. 2009. Pp. xvi, 288. $34.95.

COTTRELL, ROBERT C. *Icons of American Popular Culture: From P. T. Barnum to Jennifer Lopez.* Armonk, N.Y.: M. E. Sharpe. 2010. Pp. xxxiv, 243. Cloth $74.95, paper $28.95.

COX, STEPHEN. *The Big House: Image and Reality of the American Prison.* (Icons of America.) New Haven: Yale University Press. 2009. Pp. x, 222. $26.00.

CROWL, THOMAS. *Murder of a Journalist: The True Story of the Death of Donald Ring Mellett.* (True Crime History Series.) Kent, Ohio: Kent State University Press. 2009. Pp. xiii, 210. $26.95.

DALZELL, FREDERICK. *Engineering Invention: Frank J. Sprague and the U.S. Electrical Industry.* Foreword by W. BERNARD CARLSON. Afterword by JOHN SPRAGUE. Cambridge: MIT Press. 2010. Pp. xii, 288. $30.00.

DEL PERO, MARIO. *The Eccentric Realist: Henry Kissinger and the Shaping of American Foreign Policy.* Ithaca: Cornell University Press. 2010. Pp. 193. $24.95.

DENTON, SALLY. *The Pink Lady: The Many Lives of Helen Gahagan Douglas.* New York: Bloomsbury. 2009. Pp. 240. $25.00.

DESJARDIN, THOMAS A. *Stand Firm Ye Boys from Maine: The 20th Maine and the Gettysburg Campaign.* Fifteenth anniversary edition. New York: Oxford University Press. 2009. Pp. xxii, 245. $16.95.

DREISBACH, DANIEL L., MARK DAVID HALL, and JEFFRY H. MORRISON, editors. *The Forgotten Founders on Religion and Public Life.* Foreword by MARK A. NOLL. Notre Dame, Ind.: University of Notre Dame Press. 2009. Pp. xxi, 316. $28.00.

DUGATKIN, LEE ALAN. *Mr. Jefferson and the Giant Moose: Natural History in Early America.* Chicago: University of Chicago Press. 2009. Pp. xii, 166. $26.00.

DUSINBERRE, WILLIAM. *Strategies for Survival: Recollections of Bondage in Antebellum Virginia.* (Carter G. Woodson Institute Series.) Charlottesville: University of Virginia Press. 2009. Pp. x, 251. $40.00.

EARNEST, PETER. *The Real Spy's Guide to Becoming a Spy.* With SUZANNE HARPER. In association with the INTERNATIONAL SPY MUSEUM. New York: Abrams Books for Young Readers. 2009. Pp. 144. $16.95.

ELMORE, A. E. *Lincoln's Gettysburg Address: Echoes of the Bible and Book of Common Prayer.* Carbondale: Southern Illinois University Press. 2009. Pp. xi, 265. $32.95.

ERNEST, JOHN. *Chaotic Justice: Rethinking African American Literary History.* Chapel Hill: University of North Carolina Press. 2009. Pp. xii, 316. Cloth $59.95, paper $22.95.

FABBI, GIOVANNI PAOLO. *Le Trincee Lontane: Il Sud degli Stati Uniti e la Prima Guerra Mondiale: Il Caso del Sud Carolina.* (Nova Americana.) Torino: Otto. 2009. Pp. xi, 234. €20.00.

FATOVIC, CLEMENT. *Outside the Law: Emergency and Executive Power.* (The Johns Hopkins Series in Constitutional Thought.) Baltimore: Johns Hopkins University Press. 2009. Pp. viii, 352. $55.00.

FAWCETT, BILL, editor. *Men at War: A Soldier's-Eye View of the Most Important Battles in History.* New York: Berkley Caliber. 2009. Pp. vi, 329. $15.00.

FELLMAN, MICHAEL. *In the Name of God and Country: Reconsidering Terrorism in American History.* New Haven: Yale University Press. 2010. Pp. 272. $29.95.

FISCHEL, WILLIAM A. *Making the Grade: The Economic Evolution of American School Districts.* Chicago: University of Chicago Press. 2009. Pp. xi, 298. $55.00.

FISET, LOUIS. *Camp Harmony: Seattle's Japanese Americans and the Puyallup Assembly Center.* (The Asian American Experience.) Urbana and Chicago: University of Illinois Press. 2009. Pp. xvi, 210. Cloth $65.00, paper $25.00.

FITZ-ENZ, DAVID G. *Old Ironsides— Eagle of the Sea: The Story of the USS Constitution. Paperback edition. Lanham, Md.: Taylor Trade Publishing. 2009. Pp. xxi, 281. $22.95.

FLEMING, CYNTHIA GRIGGS. *Yes We Did? From King's Dream to Obama's Promise.* Lexington: University Press of Kentucky. 2009. Pp. xxi, 281. $29.95.

FLEMING, THOMAS. *The Intimate Lives of the Founding Fathers.* New York: Smithsonian Books. 2009. Pp. xvi, 456. $27.99.

FRIEDMAN, HAL M. *Arguing over the American Lake: Bureaucracy and Rivalry in the U.S. Pacific, 1945–1947.* (Williams-Ford Texas A&M University Military History Series, number 126.) College Station: Texas A&M University Press. 2009. Pp. xxi, 328. $67.50.

FROMKIN, DAVID. *The King and the Cowboy: Theodore Roosevelt and Edward the Seventh, Secret Partners.* Reprint. New York: Penguin. 2009. Pp. 256. $16.00.

GARDNER, LLOYD C. *Three Kings: The Rise of an American Empire in the Middle East after World War II.* New York: New Press. 2009. Pp. xi, 260. $25.95.

GARDNER, MARK LEE. *To Hell on a Fast Horse: Billy the Kid, Pat Garrett, and the Epic Chase to Justice in the Old West.* New York: William Morrow. 2010. Pp. 314. $26.99.

GARTMAN, DAVID. *From Autos to Architecture: Fordism and Architectural Aesthetics in the Twentieth Century.* New York: Princeton Architectural Press. 2009. Pp. 400. $60.00.

GIANGRECO, D. M. *Hell to Pay: Operation Downfall and the Invasion of Japan, 1945–1947.* Annapolis, Md.: Naval Institute Press. 2009. Pp. xxiii, 362. $36.95.

GOLWAY, TERRY. *Together We Cannot Fail: FDR and the American Presidency in Years of Crisis.* With CD. Naperville, Ill.: Sourcebooks MediaFusion. 2009. Pp. 306. $29.99.

GONZALVES, THEODORE S. *The Day the Dancers Stayed: Performing in the Filipino/American Diaspora.* Philadelphia: Temple University Press. 2010. Pp. xii, 215. Cloth $74.50, paper $27.95.

GOULD, LEWIS L. *The William Howard Taft Presidency.* (American Presidency Series.) Lawrence: University Press of Kansas. 2009. Pp. xv, 269. $34.95.

GRAZIANO, ANTHONY M. *La bell'America: From* La Rivoluzione *to the Great Depression: An Italian Immigrant Family Remembered.* (A LeapSci Book. Leapfrog Science and History.) Teaticket, Mass.: Leapfrog Press. 2009. Pp. xii, 530. $17.95.

GREENSPAN, ANDERS. *Creating Colonial Williamsburg: The Restoration of Virginia's Eighteenth-Century Capital.* 2d ed. Chapel Hill: University of North Carolina Press. 2009. Pp. xii, 226. Cloth $45.00, paper $19.95.

GUSSOW, ADAM. *Mister Satan's Apprentice: A Blues Memoir.* Reprint. Minneapolis: University of Minnesota Press. 2009. Pp. xv, 402. $18.95.

HARRIS, J. WILLIAM. *The Hanging of Thomas Jeremiah: A Free Black Man's Encounter with Liberty.* New Haven: Yale University Press. 2009. Pp. 223. $27.50.

HARRIS, SHARON M. *Dr. Mary Walker: An American Radical, 1832–1919.* New Brunswick: Rutgers University Press. 2009. Pp. ix, 308. $49.95.

HAYES, DEREK. *Historical Atlas of the American West: With Original Maps.* Berkeley and Los Angeles: University of California Press. 2009. Pp. 288. $39.95.

HODES, FREDERICK A. *Rising on the River: St. Louis, 1822 to 1850: Explosive Growth from Town to City.* Tooele, Utah: Patrice Press. 2009. Pp. ix, 914. Cloth $49.95, paper $29.95.

HODGES, ROBERT R., JR. *American Civil War Railroad Tactics.* Illustrated by PETER DENNIS. (Elite, number 171.) Oxford: Osprey. 2009. Pp. 64. $18.95.

HOFFMAN, JON T., et al. *The Panama Canal: An Army's Enterprise.* Washington, D.C.: Center of Military History. 2009. Pp. vi, 97. $12.00.

HOFFMAN, JON T., editor. *Tip of the Spear: U.S. Army Small-Unit Action in Iraq, 2004–2007.* (Global War on Terrorism Series.) Washington, D.C.: Center of Military History, United States Army. 2009. Pp. ix, 201. $22.00.

HOLCOMBE, RANDALL G., and BENJAMIN POWELL, editors. *Housing America: Building out of a Crisis.* New Brunswick, N.J.: Transaction Publishers, in association with the Independent Institute. 2009. Pp. viii, 397. Cloth $59.95, paper $29.95.

HOLTON, WOODY. *Abigail Adams.* New York: Free Press. 2009. Pp. xvii, 483. $30.00.

HOWE, DANIEL WALKER. *Making the American Self: Jonathan Edwards to Abraham Lincoln.* Paperback edition. New York: Oxford University Press. 2009. Pp. 342. $19.95.

HOWE, DANIEL WALKER. *What Hath God Wrought: The Transformation of America, 1815–1848.* (The Oxford History of the United States.) Paperback edition. New York: Oxford University Press. 2009. Pp. xviii, 904. $19.95.

HSIEH, WAYNE WEI-SIANG. *West Pointers and the Civil War: The Old Army in War and Peace.* (Civil War America.) Chapel Hill: University of North Carolina Press. 2009. Pp. xiii, 285. $30.00.

JACK, JORDYNN. *Science on the Home Front: American Women Scientists in World War II.* Urbana and Chicago: University of Illinois Press. 2009. Pp. x, 165. Cloth $60.00, paper $20.00.

JACOBS, JAAP. *The Colony of New Netherland: A Dutch Settlement in Seventeenth-Century America.* Ithaca: Cornell University Press. 2009. Pp. xi, 332. $26.95.

JAMIESON, KATHLEEN HALL, editor. *Electing the President, 2008: The Insiders' View.* With DVD. Philadelphia: University of Pennsylvania Press. 2009. Pp. 224. $24.95.

JOHNSON, ANN. *Hitting the Brakes: Engineering Design and the Production of Knowledge.* Durham, N.C.: Duke University Press. 2009. Pp. xviii, 207. Cloth $79.95, paper $22.95.

JOYNER, CHARLES. *Down by the Riverside: A South Carolina Slave Community.* 25th Anniversary edition. Urbana and Chicago: University of Illinois Press. 2009. Pp. li, 345. $25.00.

KEINER, CHRISTINE. *The Oyster Question: Scientists, Watermen, and the Maryland Chesapeake Bay since 1880.* (Environmental History and the American South.) Athens: University of Georgia Press. 2009. Pp. xvi, 331. $44.95.

KELL, CARL L. *Against the Wind: The Moderate Voice in Baptist Life.* Knoxville: University of Tennessee Press. 2009. Pp. xlviii, 192. $36.95.

KENNEDY, MAXWELL TAYLOR. *Danger's Hour: The Story of the USS* Bunker Hill *and the Kamikaze Pilot Who Crippled Her.* Paperback edition. New York: Simon and Schuster Paperbacks. 2009. Pp. ix, 513. $16.00.

KENNEDY, THOMAS C., and . *A History of Southland College: The Society of Friends and Black Education in Arkansas.* Fayetteville: University of Arkansas Press. 2009. Pp. xii, 349. $39.95.

KIMURA, G. W., editor. *Alaska at 50: The Past, Present, and Next Fifty Years of Statehood.* Fairbanks: University of Alaska Press. 2009. Pp. xvii, 285. $30.00.

KOVAC, JEFFREY. *Refusing War, Affirming Peace: A History of Civilian Public Service Camp #21 at Cascade Locks.* Foreword by PAUL S. BOYER. Corvallis: Oregon State University Press. 2009. Pp. 192. $21.95.

KULIK, GARY. *"War Stories": False Atrocity Tales, Swift Boaters, and Winter Soldiers—What Really Happened in Vietnam.* Washington, D.C.: Potomac Books, Inc. 2009. Pp. xii, 305. $29.95.

KUNHARDT, PHILIP B. III, PETER W. KUNHARDT, and PETER W. KUNHARDT, JR. *Lincoln, Life-Size.* New York: Alfred A. Knopf. 2009. Pp. xiv, 187. $50.00.

LARDAS, MARK. *Ships of the American Revolutionary Navy.* Illustrated by TONY BRYAN. (New Vanguard, number 161.) Oxford: Osprey. 2009. Pp. 48. $17.95.

LARSON, JOHN LAURITZ. *The Market Revolution in America: Liberty, Ambition, and the Eclipse of the Common Good.* (Cambridge Essential Histories.) New York: Cambridge University Press. 2010. Pp. xiii, 208. Cloth $75.00, paper $20.99.

LEIDHOLDT, ALEXANDER S. *Battling Nell: The Life of Southern*

Journalist Cornelia Battle Lewis, 1893–1956. (Southern Biography Series.) Baton Rouge: Louisiana State University Press. 2009. Pp. xi, 331. $47.50.

LEWIS, ANDREW B. *The Shadows of Youth: The Remarkable Journey of the Civil Rights Generation.* New York: Hill and Wang. 2009. Pp. 356. $28.00.

MALONE, PATRICK M. *Waterpower in Lowell: Engineering and Industry in Nineteenth-Century America.* (Johns Hopkins Introductory Studies in the History of Technology.) Baltimore: Johns Hopkins University Press. 2009. Pp. xii, 254. Cloth $50.00, paper $25.00.

MANNINO, EDWARD F. *Shaping America: The Supreme Court and American Society.* Columbia: University of South Carolina Press. 2009. Pp. xxiv, 321. $44.95.

McCONAGHY, LORRAINE. *Warship under Sail: The USS* Decatur *in the Pacific West.* (The Emil and Kathleen Sick Lecture-Book Series in Western History and Biography.) Seattle: Center for the Study of the Pacific Northwest, in association with the University of Washington Press. 2009. Pp. xi, 381. $34.95.

McDONOUGH, JAMES LEE. *The Wars of Myron King: A B-17 Pilot Faces WWII and U.S.-Soviet Intrigue.* Knoxville: University of Tennessee Press. 2009. Pp. xiii, 246. $32.95.

McLACHLAN, SEAN. *American Civil War Guerrilla Tactics.* Illustrated by GERRY EMBLETON and SAMUEL EMBLETON. (Elite, number 174.) Oxford: Osprey. 2009. Pp. 64. $18.95.

McNAB, CHRIS. *Deadly Force: Firearms and American Law Enforcement from the Wild West to the Streets of Today.* Oxford: Osprey. 2009. Pp. 312. $19.95.

McPHERSON, JAMES M. *This Mighty Scourge: Perspectives on the Civil War.* Paperback edition. New York: Oxford University Press. 2009. Pp. xii, 260. $17.95.

MEYERS, DEBRA, and BURKE MILLER, editors. *Inequity in Education: A Historical Perspective.* Lanham, Md.: Lexington Books. 2009. Pp. vi, 276. $75.00.

MIDDLETON, WILLIAM D., and WILLIAM D. MIDDLETON III. *Frank Julian Sprague: Electrical Inventor and Engineer.* Foreword by JOHN L. SPRAGUE. (Railroads Past and Present.) Bloomington: Indiana University Press. 2009. Pp. xviii, 314. $39.95.

MILLER, MARK C. *The View of the Courts from the Hill: Interactions between Congress and the Federal Judiciary.* (Constitutionalism and Democracy.) Charlottesville: University of Virginia Press. 2009. Pp. ix, 248. $45.00.

MINGUS, SCOTT L., SR. *The Louisiana Tigers in the Gettysburg Campaign, June–July 1863.* Foreword by BRENT NOSWORTHY. Baton Rouge: Louisiana State University Press. 2009. Pp. xviii, 315. $34.95.

MORGAN, IWAN. *The Age of Deficits: Presidents and Unbalanced Budgets from Jimmy Carter to George W. Bush.* Lawrence: University Press of Kansas. 2009. Pp. xvi, 375. $34.95.

MYERS, BARTON A. *Executing Daniel Bright: Race, Loyalty, and Guerrilla Violence in a Coastal Carolina Community, 1861–1865.* (Conflicting Worlds: New Dimensions of the American Civil War.) Baton Rouge: Louisiana State University Press. 2009. Pp. xii, 193. $32.50.

MYERS, JOHN L. *Henry Wilson and the Era of Reconstruction.* Lanham, Md.: University Press of America. 2009. Pp. xii, 301. $39.95.

NASH, GEORGE H. *Reappraising the Right: The Past and Future of American Conservatism.* Wilmington: ISI Books. 2009. Pp. xix, 446. $27.95.

NELSON, DANIEL. *A Passion for the Land: John F. Seiberling and the Environmental Movement.* Kent, Ohio: Kent State University Press. 2009. Pp. xiii, 263. $39.95.

NELSON, KEVIN. *Wheels of Change: From Zero to 600 M.P.H.: The Amazing Story of California and the Automobile.* Berkeley, Calif.: Heyday Books, in collaboration with the California Historical Society. 2009. Pp. 405. $24.95.

NICHOLSON, JUNE O., et al. *The Edge of Change: Women in the Twenty-First-Century Press.* Foreword by ELLEN GOODMAN. Urbana and Chicago: University of Illinois Press. 2009. Pp. xxi, 321. Cloth $75.00, paper $25.00.

NOKES, R. GREGORY. *Massacred for Gold: The Chinese in Hells Canyon.* Corvallis: Oregon State University Press. 2009. Pp. 208. $18.95.

NOLL, STEVEN, and DAVID TEGEDER. *Ditch of Dreams: The Cross Florida Barge Canal and the Struggle for Florida's Future.* Foreword by RAYMOND ARSENAULT and GARY R. MORMINO. (Florida History and Culture Series.) Gainesville: University Press of Florida. 2009. Pp. xi, 394. $29.95.

NORD, DAVID PAUL, JOAN SHELLEY RUBIN, and MICHAEL SCHUDSON, editors. *A History of the Book in America, Volume 5: The Enduring Book: Print Culture in Postwar America.* Chapel Hill: University of North Carolina Press, in association with the American Antiquarian Society. 2009. Pp. xvi, 618. $60.00.

O'BRIEN, CONOR CRUISE. *First in Peace: How George Washington Set the Course for America.* Foreword by CHRISTOPHER HITCHENS. Cambridge: Da Capo Press. 2009. Pp. 178. $22.95.

ONDAATJE, MICHAEL L. *Black Conservative Intellectuals in Modern America.* Philadelphia: University of Pennsylvania Press. 2010. Pp. 220. $34.95.

OSSIAN, LISA L. *The Home Fronts of Iowa, 1939–1945.* Columbia: University of Missouri Press. 2009. Pp. xv, 242. $39.95.

PARKS, GORDON. *To Smile in Autumn: A Memoir.* Foreword by ALEX S. D. PATE. Reprint. Minneapolis: University of Minnesota Press. 2009. Pp. 249. $18.95.

PEASE, DONALD E. *The New American Exceptionalism.* (Critical American Studies Series.) Minneapolis: University of Minnesota Press. 2009. Pp. xi, 246. $22.50.

PERMAN, MICHAEL. *Pursuit of Unity: A Political History of the American South.* Chapel Hill: University of North Carolina Press. 2009. Pp. xiv, 390. $35.00.

PODOLSKY, SCOTT H., and CHARLES S. BRYAN, editors. *Oliver Wendell Holmes: Physician and Man of Letters.* Sagamore Beach, Mass.: Science History Publications, for the Boston Medical Library. 2009. Pp. xiv, 274. $35.00.

POLLACK, SHELDON D. *War, Revenue, and State Building: Financing the Development of the American State.* Ithaca: Cornell University Press. 2009. Pp. viii, 328. Cloth $69.95, paper $24.95.

PULIDO, ALBERTO LÓPEZ, BARBARA DRISCOLL DE ALVARADO, and CARMEN SAMORA, editors. *Moving beyond Borders: Julian Samora and the Establishment of Latino Studies.* (Latinos in Chicago and the Midwest.) Urbana and Chicago: University of Illinois Press. 2009. Pp. xxi, 268. Cloth $70.00, paper $30.00.

RAPHAEL, TIMOTHY. *The President Electric: Ronald Reagan and the Politics of Performance.* (Theater: Theory/Text/Performance.) Ann Arbor: University of Michigan Press. 2009. Pp. ix, 271. $26.95.

RATNESAR, ROMESH. *Tear Down This Wall: A City, a President, and the Speech That Ended the Cold War.* New York: Simon and Schuster. 2009. Pp. 229. $27.00.

REED, MERL E. *Educating the Urban New South: Atlanta and the Rise of Georgia State University, 1913–1969.* Macon, Ga.: Mercer University Press. 2009. Pp. xii, 321. $35.00.

REYNOLDS, THOMAS C. *General Sterling Price and the Confederacy.* Edited by ROBERT G. SCHULTZ. St. Louis, Mo.: Missouri History Museum. 2009. Pp. 279. $24.95.

RIFE, JAMES P. and ALAN J. DELLAPENNA, JR. *Caring and Curing: A History of the Indian Health Service.* PHS Commissioner Officers Foundation for the Advancement of Public Health. 2009. Pp. viii, 170. $34.95.

RIFKIN, MARK. *Manifesting America: The Imperial Construction of U.S. National Space.* New York: Oxford University Press. 2009. Pp. vi, 280. $65.00.

RIVERS, LARRY EUGENE, and CANTER BROWN, JR., editors. *The*

Varieties of Women's Experiences: Portraits of Southern Women in the Post–Civil War Century. Gainesville: University Press of Florida. 2009. Pp. xvi, 342. $69.95.

ROSENBAUM, FRED. *Cosmopolitans: A Social and Cultural History of the Jews of the San Francisco Bay Area*. (The S. Mark Taper Foundation Imprint in Jewish Studies.) Berkeley and Los Angeles: University of California Press. 2009. Pp. xviii, 439. $39.95.

ROTTMAN, GORDON L. *World War II US Cavalry Units: Pacific Theater*. Illustrated by PETER DENNIS. (Elite Series, number 175.) Oxford: Osprey. 2009. Pp. 64. $18.95.

ROZNOWSKI, TOM. *An American Hometown: Terre Haute, Indiana, 1927*. Foreword by SCOTT RUSSELL SANDERS. Bloomington, Ind.: Quarry Books. 2009. Pp. xvi, 264. $24.95.

SAMPSELL-WILLMANN, KATE. *Lewis Hine as Social Critic*. Foreword by ALAN TRACHTENBERG. Jackson: University Press of Mississippi. 2009. Pp. xii, 331. $50.00.

SANDINE, AL. *The Taming of the American Crowd: From Stamp Riots to Shopping Sprees*. New York: Monthly Review Press. 2009. Pp. 272. $18.95.

SCHOENBACHLER, MATTHEW G. *Murder and Madness: The Myth of the Kentucky Tragedy*. (Topics in Kentucky History.) Lexington: University Press of Kentucky. 2009. Pp. xii, 371. $35.00.

SCHWARTZ, LOUIS-GEORGES. *Mechanical Witness: A History of Motion Picture Evidence in U.S. Courts*. New York: Oxford University Press. 2009. Pp. 133. $21.95.

SCHWEIKART, LARRY, and LYNNE PIERSON DOTI. *American Entrepreneur: The Fascinating Stories of the People Who Defined Business in the United States*. New York: AMACOM. 2010. Pp. viii, 535. $29.95.

SEE, SARITA ECHAVEZ. *The Decolonized Eye: Filipino American Art and Performance*. Minneapolis: University of Minnesota Press. 2009. Pp. xxxiv, 210. $25.00.

SHALHOPE, ROBERT E. *The Baltimore Bank Riot: Political Upheaval in Antebellum Maryland*. Urbana and Chicago: University of Illinois Press. 2009. Pp. x, 196. $50.00.

SHAW, TODD C. *Now Is the Time! Detroit Black Politics and Grassroots Activism*. Durham, N.C.: Duke University Press. 2009. Pp. xii, 288. Cloth $84.95, paper $23.95.

SHEAR, KENNETH. *Unoriginal Misunderstanding: Press Freedom in Early America and Interpretation of the First Amendment*. Edited by ALICE PORTER. Seattle: Libertary Editions. 2009. Pp. vii, 144. $16.95.

SHIRLEY, CRAIG. *Rendezvous with Destiny: Ronald Reagan and the Campaign That Changed America*. Wilmington: ISI Books. 2009. Pp. xii, 740. $30.00.

SIMON, BRYANT. *Everything but the Coffee: Learning about America from Starbucks*. Berkeley and Los Angeles: University of California Press. 2009. Pp. xi, 304. $25.95.

SINGER, MARGARET FUCHS. *Legacy of a False Promise: A Daughter's Reckoning*. Tuscaloosa: University of Alabama Press. 2009. Pp. xii, 246. $29.95.

SIZER, MONA D. *The Glory Guys: The Story of the U.S. Army Rangers*. Lanham, Md.: Taylor Trade Publishing. 2010. Pp. viii, 293. $24.95.

SMITH, MARK A. *Engineering Security: The Corps of Engineers and Third System Defense Policy, 1815–1861*. Tuscaloosa: University of Alabama Press. 2009. Pp. x, 266. $54.00.

SMITH, RICHARD CÁNDIDA. *The Modern Moves West: California Artists and Democratic Culture in the Twentieth Century*. (The Arts and Intellectual Life in Modern America.) Philadelphia: University of Pennsylvania Press. 2009. Pp. x, 252. $39.95.

SMYTH, J. E. *Edna Ferber's Hollywood: American Fictions of Gender, Race, and History*. Foreword by THOMAS SCHATZ. (Texas Film and Media Studies Series.) Austin: University of Texas Press. 2010. Pp. xiv, 337. $55.00.

SPALDING, MATTHEW. *We Still Hold These Truths: Rediscovering Our Principles, Reclaiming Our Future*. Wilmington: ISI Books. 2009. Pp. xiii, 267. $26.95.

STERNE, JOSEPH R. L. *Combat Correspondents: The Baltimore Sun in World War II*. Baltimore: Maryland Historical Society. 2009. Pp. xviii, 281. $34.00.

SURBRUG, ROBERT, JR. *Beyond Vietnam: The Politics of Protest in Massachusetts, 1974–1990*. (Culture, Politics, and the Cold War.) Amherst: University of Massachusetts Press. 2009. Pp. xi, 323. $29.95.

TAYLOR, PAUL. *Orlando M. Poe: Civil War General and Great Lakes Engineer*. (Civil War in the North.) Kent, Ohio: Kent State University Press. 2009. Pp. xix, 354. $65.00.

TENKOTTE, PAUL A., and JAMES C. CLAYPOOL, editors. *The Encyclopedia of Northern Kentucky*. (A project of the Thomas D. Clark Foundation, Inc.) Lexington: University Press of Kentucky. 2009. Pp. xxii, 1047. $49.95.

TRUETT, JOE C. *Grass: In Search of Human Habitat*. Foreword by HARRY W. GREENE. (Organisms and Environments.) Berkeley and Los Angeles: University of California Press. 2010. Pp. xvii, 217. $34.95.

VAN MINNEN, CORNELIS A., and SYLVIA L. HILTON, editors. *Political Repression in U.S. History*. (European Contributions to American Studies, number 68.) Amsterdam: VU University Press. 2009. Pp. 242. €37,50.

VIZENOR, GERALD. *Native Liberty: Natural Reason and Cultural Survivance*. Lincoln: University of Nebraska Press. 2009. Pp. ix, 321. $30.00.

WALKER, CLARENCE E., and GREGORY D. SMITHERS. *The Preacher and the Politician: Jeremiah Wright, Barack Obama, and Race in America*. Charlottesville: University of Virginia Press. 2009. Pp. 159. $22.95.

WALKER, JULIET E. K. *The History of Black Business in America: Capitalism, Race, Entrepreneurship, Volume I, to 1865*. 2d ed. Chapel Hill: University of North Carolina Press. 2009. Pp. xxiv, 405. Cloth $65.00, paper $24.95.

WAUGH, JOAN. *U. S. Grant: American Hero, American Myth*. (Civil War America.) Chapel Hill: University of North Carolina Press. 2009. Pp. 373. $30.00.

WEINTRAUB, STANLEY. *General Sherman's Christmas: Savannah, 1864*. New York: Smithsonian Books. 2009. Pp. xvi, 238. $24.99.

WINSBORO, IRVIN D. S., editor. *Old South, New South, or Down South? Florida and the Modern Civil Rights Movement*. Morgantown: West Virginia University Press. 2009. Pp. viii, 260. $24.95.

WOLFF, KATHERINE. *Culture Club: The Curious History of the Boston Athenaeum*. Amherst: University of Massachusetts Press. 2009. Pp. xviii, 204. Cloth $80.00, paper $26.95.

CARIBBEAN AND LATIN AMERICA

ACREE, WILLIAM G., JR., and JUAN CARLOS GONZÁLEZ ESPITIA, editors. *Building Nineteenth-Century Latin America: Re-Rooted Cultures, Identities, and Nations*. Nashville, Tenn.: Vanderbilt University Press. 2009. Pp. viii, 285. Cloth $79.95, paper $34.95.

HALLORAN, VIVIAN NUN. *Exhibiting Slavery: The Caribbean Postmodern Novel as Museum*. (New World Studies.) Charlottesville: University of Virginia Press. 2009. Pp. x, 207. Cloth $55.00, paper $21.50.

KLEIN, HERBERT S., and FRANCISCO VIDAL LUNA. *Slavery in Brazil*. New York: Cambridge University Press. 2010. Pp. xi, 364. Cloth $95.00, paper $28.99.

KLINE, HARVEY F. *Showing Teeth to the Dragons: State-Building by Colombian President Álvaro Uribe Vélez, 2002–2006*. Tuscaloosa: University of Alabama Press. 2009. Pp. xiv, 252. Cloth $52.00, paper $32.95.

EUROPE: ANCIENT AND MEDIEVAL

AUFFARTH, CHRISTOPH, editor. *Religion auf dem Lande: Entstehung und Veränderung von Sakrallandschaften unter römischer Herrschaft.* Assisted by TILMAN HANNEMANN and OLIVER ZÜCHNER. (Potsdamer Altertumswissenschaftliche Beiträge, number 28.) Stuttgart: Franz Steiner Verlag. 2009. Pp. 271. €56.00.

BEDUHN, JASON DAVID. *Augustine's Manichaean Dilemma.* Volume 1, *Conversion and Apostasy, 373–388 C.E.* (Divinations: Rereading Late Ancient Religion.) Philadelphia: University of Pennsylvania Press. 2010. Pp. viii, 402. $69.95.

BISKUP, RADOSŁAW. *Das Domkapitel von Samland (1285–1525).* (Prussia Sacra, number 2.) Torun, Poland: Verlag der Nikolaus-Kopernikus Universitat. 2007. Pp. 600. $36.73.

BLEACH, LORNA, et al. *In Search of the Medieval Voice: Expressions of Identity in the Middle Ages.* Newcastle: Cambridge Scholars Publishing. 2009. Pp. xix, 200. $59.99.

CLASTER, JILL N. *Sacred Violence: The European Crusades to the Middle East, 1095–1396.* Buffalo, N.Y.: University of Toronto Press. 2009. Pp. xix, 356. $29.95.

COSS, PETER, and CHRISTOPHER TYERMAN, editors. *Soldiers, Nobles and Gentlemen: Essays in Honour of Maurice Keen.* Rochester, N.Y.: Boydell Press. 2009. Pp. xxii, 371. $115.00.

EHLERS, JOACHIM. *Der Hundertjährige Krieg.* (Wissen, number 2475.) Munich: C. H. Beck. 2009. Pp. 127. €7.90.

IHRIG, STEFAN. *Wer sind die Moldawier? Rumänismus versus Moldowanismus in Historiographie und Schulbüchern der Republik Moldova, 1991–2006.* Foreword by HOLM SUNDHAUSSEN. (Soviet and Post-Soviet Politics and Society, number 76.) Stuttgart: Ibidem. 2008. Pp. 332. €34.90.

JONES, CHRISTOPHER. *New Heroes in Antiquity: From Achilles to Antinoos.* (Revealing Antiquity, number 18.) Cambridge: Harvard University Press. 2010. Pp. 123. $29.95.

LANSING, CAROL, and EDWARD D. ENGLISH, editors. *A Companion to the Medieval World.* (Blackwell Companions to European History.) Malden, Mass.: Wiley-Blackwell. 2009. Pp. xii, 584. $199.95.

MADERO, MARTA. *Tabula Picta: Painting and Writing in Medieval Law.* Translated by MONIQUE DASCHA INCIARTE and ROLAND DAVID VALAYRE. Foreword by ROGER CHARTIER. (Material Texts.) Philadelphia: University of Pennsylvania Press. 2010. Pp. xi, 141. $45.00.

MARTIN, GUNTHER. *Divine Talk: Religious Argumentation in Demosthenes.* (Oxford Classical Monographs.) New York: Oxford University Press. 2009. Pp. ix, 345. $125.00.

MAZEAU, GUILLAUME, editor. *Corday contre Marat: Deux siècles d'images.* Vizille: Musée de la Révolution française, with Éditions Artlys, Versailles. 2009. Pp. 76. €15.00.

PERKINSON, STEPHEN. *The Likeness of the King: A Prehistory of Portraiture in Late Medieval France.* Chicago: University of Chicago Press. 2009. Pp. xiv, 338. $55.00.

POSTEL, VERENA. *Arbeit und Willensfreiheit im Mittelalter.* (Vierteljahrschrift für Sozial- und Wirtschaftsgeschichte, number 207.) Stuttgart: Franz Steiner Verlag. 2009. Pp. 189. €39.00.

RUSSELL, EUGENIA, editor. *Spirituality in Late Byzantium: Essays Presenting New Research by International Scholars.* Newcastle: Cambridge Scholars Publishing. 2009. Pp. xxiv, 161. $52.99.

SPEIDEL, MICHAEL ALEXANDER. *Heer und Herrschaft im Römischen Reich der Hohen Kaiserzeit.* (Mavors, number 16.) Stuttgart: Franz Steiner Verlag. 2009. Pp. 706. €128.00.

STEPHENSON, PAUL. *Constantine: Unconquered Emperor, Christian Victor.* London: Quercus. 2009. Pp. xxv, 358. £30.00.

TANNER, MARCUS. *The Raven King: Matthias Corvinus and the Fate of His Lost Library.* Paperback edition. New Haven: Yale University Press. 2009. Pp. xx, 265. $22.00.

VON HEUSINGER, SABINE. *Die Zunft im Mittelalter: Zur Verflech-* *tung von Politik, Wirtschaft und Gesellschaft in Straßburg.* (Vierteljahrschrift für Sozial- und Wirtschaftsgeschichte, number 206.) Stuttgart: Franz Steiner Verlag. 2009. Pp. 662. €79.00.

WATKIN, DAVID. *The Roman Forum.* (Wonders of the World.) Cambridge: Harvard University Press. 2009. Pp. viii, 279. $19.95.

EUROPE: EARLY MODERN AND MODERN

ANDERSEN, DORTHE SONDRUP. *Kærlighed i Klunketiden: En kavalkade om Danmark 1880–1900 [Love in the Victorian Era: A Cavalcade of Denmark 1880–1900].* Oslo: Gyldendal. 2009. Pp. 247. kr.349.00.

BAJOHR, FRANK, and MICHAEL WILDT, editors. *Volksgemeinschaft: Neue Forschungen zur Gesellschaft des Nationalsozialismus.* (Die Zeit des Nationalsozialismus.) Frankfurt a.M.: Fischer Taschenbuch Verlag. 2009. Pp. 236. €14.95.

BAKER, LEE. *The Second World War on the Eastern Front.* (Seminar Studies in History.) London: Pearson Education Limited. 2009. Pp. xxix, 140. £14.99.

BARTELSON, JENS. *Visions of World Community.* New York: Cambridge University Press. 2009. Pp. x, 215. Cloth $85.00, paper $29.99.

BEALES, DEREK. *Joseph II.* Volume 2, *Against the World 1780–1790.* New York: Cambridge University Press. 2009. Pp. xix, 733. $145.00.

BENNER, ERICA. *Machiavelli's Ethics.* Princeton: Princeton University Press. 2009. Pp. xv, 527. $35.00.

BERG, ANNE, and HANNA ENEFALK, editors. *Det mångsidiga verktyget: Elva utbildningshistoriska uppsatser [The Many-sided Instrument: Eleven Essays on the History of Education].* (Opuscula Historica Upsaliensia, number 39.) Uppsala: Swedish Science Press. 2009. Pp. 211. SEK110.00.

BIZZOCCHI, ROBERTO. *Genealogie incredibili: Scritti di storia nell'Europa moderna.* (Annali dell'Istituto storico italo-germanico in Trento: Monografie, number 52.) Reprint. Bologna: Il Mulino. 2009. Pp. 291. €22.50.

BRIGHTON, TERRY. *Patton, Montgomery, Rommel: Masters of War.* New York: Crown. 2008. Pp. xix, 426. $30.00.

BURNS, JIMMY. *Papa Spy: Love, Faith, and Betrayal in Wartime Spain.* New York: Walker & Company. 2009. Pp. xix, 395. $26.00.

BUSSIÈRE, ÉRIC, MICHEL DUMOULIN, and ÉMILIE WILLAERT, editors. *The Bank of the European Union: The EIB, 1958–2008.* Assisted by CHARLES BARTHEL et al. Luxembourg: Imprimerie Centrale, with the European Investment Bank. 2008. Pp. 384. €25.00.

CALDWELL, MELISSA L., editor. *Food and Everyday Life in the Postsocialist World.* Foreword by MARION NESTLE. Afterword by ELIZABETH CULLEN DUNN. Bloomington: Indiana University Press. 2009. Pp. xiv, 231. Cloth $65.00, paper $24.95.

CARTER, CHRISTOPHER. *Magnetic Fever: Global Imperialism and Empiricism in the Nineteenth Century.* (Transactions of the American Philosophical Society Held at Philadelphia for Promoting Useful Knowledge, number 99:4.) Philadelphia, Penn.: American Philosophical Society. 2009. Pp. xxvi, 168. $35.00.

CAZORLA SÁNCHEZ, ANTONIO. *Fear and Progress: Ordinary Lives in Franco's Spain, 1939–1975.* (Ordinary Lives.) Malden, Mass.: Wiley-Blackwell. 2010. Pp. xi, 279. $34.95.

CEADEL, MARTIN. *Living the Great Illusion: Sir Norman Angell, 1872–1967.* New York: Oxford University Press. 2009. Pp. xiii, 438. $99.00.

CHRISTOFFERSEN, PEDER. *Danmarkshistorien: En krønike fra Oldtiden til nu [Denmark's History: A Chronicle from Antiquity to the Present].* Oslo: Gyldendal. 2009. Pp. 724. kr.299.95.

CIAPPELLI, GIOVANNI, editor. *Memoria, famiglia, identità tra Ita-*

lia ed Europa nell'età moderna. (Annali dell'Istituto storico italo-germanico in Trento: Quaderni, number 77.) Bologna: Il Mulino. 2009. Pp. 282. €22.00.

DE CHAMPS, EMMANUELLE, and JEAN-PIERRE CLÉRO, editors. *Bentham et la France: Fortunes et infortunes de l'utilitarisme.* (SVEC, number 2009:09.) Oxford: Voltaire Foundation. 2009. Pp. xv, 311. $115.00.

EDLING, MAX, and PATRIK WINTON, editors. *Ett nödvändigt ont: Statsskuld och politik I Förenta Staterna och Sverige 1780–1870 [A Necessary Evil: National Debt and Politics in the United States and Sweden 1780–1870].* (Opuscula Historica Upsaliensia, number 38.) Uppsala: Swedish Science Press. 2009. Pp. 259. SEK110.00.

ESDAILE, CHARLES. *Napoleon's Wars: An International History, 1803–1815.* Paperback edition. New York: Penguin. 2009. Pp. xvii, 621. $18.00.

FENLON, IAIN. *Piazza San Marco.* (Wonders of the World.) Cambridge: Harvard University Press. 2009. Pp. xxi, 233. $19.95.

GLANTZ, DAVID M. *Armageddon in Stalingrad: September-November 1942.* Volume 2, *The Stalingrad Trilogy.* Assisted by JONATHAN M. HOUSE. (Modern War Series.) Lawrence: University Press of Kansas. 2009. Pp. xxii, 896. $39.95.

GRIFFITHS, TONY. *Stockholm: A Cultural History.* (Cityscapes.) New York: Oxford University Press. 2009. Pp. xxvii, 228. $16.95.

GRITT, ANDREW. *Family History in Lancashire: Issues and Approaches.* Newcastle: Cambridge Scholars Publishing. 2009. Pp. 143. $34.99.

HALL, RICHARD C. *Consumed by War: European Conflict in the Twentieth Century.* Lexington: University Press of Kentucky. 2010. Pp. 286. $30.00.

HARDY, MATTHEW, editor. *The Venice Charter Revisited: Modernism, Conservation and Tradition in the 21st Century.* Newcastle: Cambridge Scholars Publishing. 2008. Pp. xx, 791. $67.99.

HUNT, LYNN, MARGARET JACOB, and WIJNAND MIJNHARDT, editors. *Bernard Picart and the First Global Vision of Religion.* (Issues & Debates.) Los Angeles: Getty Publications. 2010. Pp. viii, 364. $65.00.

INNES, JOANNA. *Inferior Politics: Social Problems and Social Policies in Eighteenth-Century Britain.* (The *Past & Present* Book Series.) New York: Oxford University Press. 2009. Pp. xviii, 364. $110.00.

KAFKER, FRANK A., and JEFF LOVELAND, editors. *The Early Britannica (1768–1803): The Growth of an Outstanding Encyclopedia.* (SVEC, number 10.) Oxford: Voltaire Foundation. 2009. Pp. xiii, 349. $115.00.

KARONEN, PETRI, editor. *Hopes and Fears for the Future in Early Modern Sweden, 1500–1800.* (Studia Historica, number 79.) Helsinki: Suomalaisen Kirjallisuuden Seura. 2009. Pp. 370. €29.00.

KNAPP, JEFFREY. *Shakespeare Only.* Chicago: University of Chicago Press. 2009. Pp. xvi, 238. $35.00.

KNIGHT, STEPHEN. *Merlin: Knowledge and Power through the Ages.* Ithaca: Cornell University Press. 2009. Pp. xvii, 275. $27.95.

LESTER, TOBY. *The Fourth Part of the World: The Race to the Ends of the Earth, and the Epic Story of the Map that Gave America Its Name.* New York: Free Press. 2009. Pp. xii, 462. $30.00.

MEYER, BEATE, HERMANN SIMON, and CHANA SCHÜTZ, editors. *Jews in Nazi Berlin: From Kristallnacht to Liberation.* (Studies in German-Jewish Cultural History and Literature.) Chicago: University of Chicago Press. 2009. Pp. xix, 392. $40.00.

PETTIFER, JAMES, and MIRANDA VICKERS. *The Albanian Question: Reshaping the Balkans.* Paperback edition. New York: I. B. Tauris. 2009. Pp. xxiii, 312. £12.99.

PICKERING, MARY. *Auguste Comte: An Intellectual Biography.*

Volume 2. New York: Cambridge University Press. 2009. Pp. xiii, 638. $95.00.

PICKERING, MARY. *Auguste Comte: An Intellectual Biography.* Volume 3. New York: Cambridge University Press. 2009. Pp. xiii, 667. $95.00.

POMERANZ, KENNETH. *La force de l'empire: Révolution industrielle et écologie, ou pourquoi l'Angleterre a fait mieux que la Chine.* Foreword by PHILIPPE MINARD. (Chercheurs d'ère: Travaux.) Alfortville, France: Éditions ère, with the Région Île-de-France. 2009. Pp. 157. €15.00.

RITTER, GERHARD A. *Wir sind das Volk! Wir sind ein Volk! Geschichte der deutschen Einigung.* (Beckische Reihe.) Munich: C. H. Beck. 2009. Pp. 190. €12.95.

ROSNER, LISA. *The Anatomy Murders: Being the True and Spectacular History of Edinburgh's Notorious Burke and Hare and of the Man of Science Who Abetted Them in the Commission of Their Most Heinous Crimes.* Philadelphia: University of Pennsylvania Press. 2010. Pp. vi, 328. $29.95.

SCHLÖGL, RUDOLF, editor. *Urban Elections and Decision-Making in Early Modern Europe, 1500–1800.* Assisted by PATRICK OELZE, JAN MARCO SAWILLA, and ALEXANDER SCHLAAK. Newcastle: Cambridge Scholars Publishing. 2009. Pp. vii, 329. $67.99.

SEBIRE, HEATHER, editor. *Pursuits and Joys: Great Victorian Antiquarians and Intellects: The Lukis Family of Guernsey and Their Contemporaries.* Newcastle: Cambridge Scholars Publishing. 2009. Pp. xxi, 213. $39.99.

SHIFRIN, SUSAN, editor. *"The Wandering Life I Led": Essays on Hortense Mancini, Duchess Mazarin and Early Modern Women's Border Crossings.* Newcastle: Cambridge Scholars Publishing. 2009. Pp. xx, 223. €59.99.

SIEGEL, ELIZABETH. *Playing with Pictures: The Art of Victorian Photocollage.* With additional essays by PATRIZIA DI BELLO and MARTA WEISS. Contributions by MIRANDA HOFELT. Chicago: Art Institute of Chicago, in association with Yale University Press. 2009. Pp. 200. $45.00.

SULLIVAN, ROBERT E. *Macaulay: The Tragedy of Power.* Cambridge: Belknap Press of Harvard University Press. 2009. Pp. 614. $39.95.

WASSON, ELLIS. *A History of Modern Britain, 1714 to the Present.* Malden, Mass.: Wiley-Blackwell. 2010. Pp. xviii, 404. $44.95.

WILSON, ANDREW. *The Ukrainians: Unexpected Nation.* 3d ed. New Haven: Yale University Press. 2009. Pp. xviii, 392. $19.00.

YOUNG, ROBERT J. *An American by Degrees: The Extraordinary Lives of French Ambassador Jules Jusserand.* Ithaca, N.Y.: McGill-Queen's University Press. 2009. Pp. xxv, 327. $49.95.

MIDDLE EAST AND NORTHERN AFRICA

CAPLAN, NEIL. *The Israel-Palestine Conflict: Contested Histories.* (Contesting the Past.) Malden, Mass.: Wiley-Blackwell. 2010. Pp. xiv, 317. $34.95.

HASSAN, SALAH M., and CARINA E. RAY, editors. *Darfur and the Crisis of Governance in Sudan: A Critical Reader.* Ithaca: Cornell University Press. Amsterdam: Prince Claus Fund Library. 2009. Pp. 528. $39.95.

HILLIARD, CONSTANCE. *Does Israel Have a Future? The Case for a Post-Zionist State.* Foreword by NORTON MEZVINSKY. Washington, D.C.: Potomac Books, Inc. 2009. Pp. xviii, 183. $27.50.

KATOUZIAN, HOMA. *The Persians: Ancient, Mediaeval and Modern Iran.* New Haven: Yale University Press. 2009. Pp. xi, 452. $50.00.

NEUMANN, RONALD E. *The Other War: Winning and Losing in Afghanistan.* Foreword by BRUCE RIEDEL. (ADST-DACOR Diplomats and Diplomacy Series.) Washington, D.C.: Potomac Books, Inc. 2009. Pp. xxiii, 245. $27.50.

ROGAN, EUGENE. *The Arabs: A History*. New York: Basic Books. 2009. Pp. vii, 553. $35.00.

SUB-SAHARAN AFRICA

FALOLA, TOYIN, and AUGUSTINE AGWUELE, editors. *Africans and the Politics of Popular Culture*. (Rochester Studies in African History and the Diaspora, number 42.) Rochester,

N.Y.: University of Rochester Press. 2009. Pp. viii, 333. $80.00.

OHLS, GARY J. *Somalia . . . From the Sea*. (Newport Papers, number 34.) Newport, R.I.: Naval War College Press. 2009. Pp. vi, 249.

ZVOBGO, CHENGETAI J. M. *A History of Zimbabwe, 1890–2000 and Postscript, Zimbabwe, 2001–2008*. Newcastle: Cambridge Scholars Publishing. 2009. Pp. xiv, 385. $74.99.

Communications

A letter to the editor will be considered only if it relates to an article or review published in this journal; publication is solely at the editors' discretion. The AHA disclaims responsibility for statements, of either fact or opinion, made by the writers. Letters should not exceed one thousand words for articles and seven hundred words for reviews. They can be submitted by e-mail to ahr@indiana.edu, or by the postal service to Editor, American Historical Review, 914 E. Atwater Ave., Bloomington, IN 47401. For detailed information on the policies for this section, see http://www.americanhistoricalreview.org.

ARTICLES

To the Editors:

Rulers have always used historians to spread canards to ensure acceptance of the authorized version of events. The wars in the former Yugoslavia in the 1990s are no exception.

Prof. Charles Ingrao's "Confronting the Yugoslav Controversies: The Scholars' Initiative" (*AHR*, October 2009, 947–962) follows a familiar pattern. Serbs hostile to U.S. and German imperialism, to George Bush's New World Order, and to unrestricted free enterprise are demonized as "inflammatory," "criminal," and "genocidal." He then claims that the Bosnian Serbs massacred 8,000 Muslims in Srebrenica in July 1995 (961).

What Prof. Ingrao did not tell the reader is that Milivoje Ivanišević has punctured this version of human losses in his meticulous *Srebrenica jul 1999: Traganje za istinom* (Belgrade, 2007) and elsewhere. He published the names of a very large number of Muslims on voters' lists in the Bosnian elections in 1996 that figured already in the official Muslim record of Srebrenica July 1999 victims. In addition, he published the names of Muslims who swelled the list of July 1999 victims though they had died or were killed months and years before the tragic event. Last but not least, the heavy losses besieged Muslim troops suffered as they broke out of the Srebrenica pocket in July 1999 cannot be ignored in any assessment of what really happened.

Truth is truly the first victim in war, especially a civil one.

Ivan Avakumović
University of British Columbia

Charles Ingrao responds:

I thank Ivan Avakumović for providing such eloquent testimony to the need for post-conflict societies to confront their past. In dismissing the overwhelming evidence—including the eyewitness testimony of numerous Serbs who directed the massacre—he eschews the courageous path already taken by so many Serbian scholars and government leaders. Instead, he invites the same fate as Holocaust deniers in debasing whatever claim he may have ever had to scholarly integrity. How sad.

Charles Ingrao
Purdue University

REVIEWS

To the Editors:

Although I am very honored by Zsuzsanna Ozsváth's review of my book *Pál Teleki (1879–1941): The Life of a Controversial Hungarian Politician* (*AHR*, December 2009, 1567–1568), some of her statements go far beyond simple scholarly disagreement. I am quite sure that, had she read more carefully, she could have avoided certain misinterpretations, especially with regard to Pál Teleki's antisemitism and his responsibility for the Holocaust, an issue representing approximately two-thirds of her review.

First, Ozsváth seems to be unfamiliar with the recent historiography of the topic when she writes about the "murder of about 6,000 Jews carried out by the Counterrevolutionary Army." Older Hungarian and foreign accounts overestimated the number of victims of the "White Terror," and archival sources thus do not support these. Recent monographs have given an approximate figure of 1,000 victims, including Jews and non-Jews (Ignác Romsics, *Hungary in the Twentieth Century*

[Budapest, 1999], p. 110). To avoid any kind of misinterpretation again: One murder is one murder too many.

Second, Ozsváth writes that "Courting the Germans for the return of Hungary's lost territories, he [Teleki] accepted responsibility for the second anti-Jewish law." Unfortunately, Teleki was a notorious antisemite, and he carried out the preparation of the second and the third anti-Jewish law (1939, 1941) without any serious German pressure or direct relation between territorial revision and antisemitic laws. He assumed full responsibility for those laws, claiming to be their principal initiator. I devoted a whole chapter to this issue (pp. 181–187 and partly 224–225).

Third, contrary to Ozsváth's assertion, I never stated that "Teleki was not an antisemite until he became aware of the threat of 'destruction' the Jews posed to Hungary." She could not have found any such sentence in my book. What I did write was that in his private and public speeches or writings, we cannot find antisemitic positions before the revolutions of 1918–1919. He did not come to antisemitism via the traditional paths in Hungarian politics (such as the Catholic People's Party or the agrarians). Some of his former associates in the eugenics movement became left-wing liberals, socialists, or even communists. Because of that, I did not make a direct link between the two ideas (eugenics and antisemitism), but this does not mean that I seek to minimize or ignore the latter. Over several pages I have tried to describe his "discriminatory" (p. 127), "racial" (p. 76), and "unworthy, cynical" (p. 128) politics.

Generally speaking, Ozsváth appears to take Teleki's statements for my own, ignoring quotation marks and many rhetorical signs conscientiously given ("in Teleki's opinion/view/statement," "according to him," etc.) to distinguish Teleki's position from my own. She seems inclined to give an abridged version of my analysis (for example, in the case of the *numerus clausus* law), omitting the parts which point in the same direction as hers.

My suspicion about Ozsváth's careless reading is reinforced by her assertion that I was unable to face Teleki's figure as "a man being at least partly responsible for the destruction of Hungarian Jewry." On the *exact* same page where she found my objectionable sentence ("Teleki did not know of the Holocaust and had no way of foreseeing it"—it should be recalled that Teleki died in April 1941, before the Russian campaign, before the Holocaust by bullets, before the Wannsee Conference, and, of course, before the deportation of the Hungarian Jews in 1944), after a detailed account about the relation between the second Jewish law and the Holocaust, she could have read about Teleki's responsibility: "He was a convinced anti-Semite who, while torn internally, always represented a radical albeit unacceptable point of view in the Jewish question . . . The coarsening of the political discourse on the Jewish question inevitably brought about the coarsening of the press and the public opinion. It made the social position of the Jews a desirable and attainable quarry and the same was true,

later on, of Jewish property and even Jewish life. In this, Teleki was guilty, his perspective is indefensible. It was a deadend for Hungarian conservatism" (p. 187).

I do not know whether "guilty" or "responsible" should be given greater emphasis, but I think they amount to the same thing.

BALÁZS ABLONCZY
Eotvos Lorand University
Visiting Professor, Indiana University Bloomington

ZSUZSANNA OZSVÁTH RESPONDS:

I would like to reflect on some of the questions Balázs Ablonczy has formulated in his answer to my review of his book. First of all, the exact number of Jews murdered by the members of the Counterrevolutionary Army in Hungary in 1919 is, of course, unknown. All we have are estimates. (See Béla Bodó, "Paramilitary Violence in Hungary after the First World War," *East European Quarterly* 38 [2004]: 132.) Although Romsics estimates the number as low as 1,000, this is at the lowest end of the accepted figures in the literature. For example, the number given by *The Yivo Encyclopedia of Jews in Eastern Europe* (2008) is 3,000 (pp. 782–787). Also, whether the precise number of Jews killed is 1,000, 3,000, or 6,000, the mass murder of such large numbers of Jews cannot be explained by the old adage that finds the Jewish question linked to Bolshevism. This particular atrocity after WWI shook the world to the core, giving a glimpse of the future.

As for my expression of Teleki's "courting the Germans," Ablonczy emphasizes that Teleki did not "court" anybody when pushing for the creation of anti-Jewish laws; rather, he followed his own insight, shaping these laws according to his own volition. In fact, it is true that nobody forced Teleki to bring laws against the Jews. However, since the prime minister wished for "the correction of the territorial arrangements of the manifestly unjust peace treaty," he hoped to achieve this "correction" by *pleasing* the Germans. His approach characterized the Hungarian governments' approach to the anti-Jewish laws from 1938 to 1941. As Raul Hilberg asserts, "The earliest law was drafted in 1938, when Hungary approached the Reich for help in the realization of Hungarian plans against Czechoslovakia. The second law was presented to Ribbentrop in 1939, at a moment when the Budapest government was pleading with the German Foreign Office for its support in the liberation of Hungarian minorities in Romania and Yugoslavia. A third sequence of measures was taken when Hungary joined Germany in the war against Russia" (*The Destruction of the European Jews*, vol. 2, p. 799). Also, see Randolph L. Braham on the topic of Teleki wishing to please the Germans (*The Politics of Genocide*, vol. 1, p. 160). How else could this process be described than "courting the Germans"?

Accusing me of careless reading, Professor Ablonczy insists on his in-depth investigation of Teleki's anti-Semitism. Again, he is partially right. He does mention several times that Teleki was an anti-Semite. But when looking at the nature of the prime minister's hatred for, and actions against, the Jews, Ablonczy looks at him from an "objective distance. " He describes Teleki as a tragic figure who "wanted to produce a Hungarian elite of European standards that was imbued with a distinct sense of national obligation and a Christian spirit." But these attempts cannot be viewed apart from the anti-Jewish actions of Teleki.

The prime minister's intentions and the harm he has done to the Hungarian Jewish community are inseparable. Ablonczy's argument that "Teleki did not know of the Holocaust and had no way of foreseeing it" doesn't hold up to the facts. He did know about the brutality of the anti-Jewish laws in Germany as well as in occupied Europe; he did know about the book-burnings and attacks against the Jews; and he did know about the pre-Auschwitz pogroms and murders in Poland. Whether he could or could not foresee the Shoah, he cannot be absolved of the crimes he committed. In fact, he was one of those personally responsible for making the Holocaust in Hungary possible.

ZSUZSANNA OZSVÁTH
University of Texas at Dallas

ERRATA

Carole Rogel's review of *Confronting the Yugoslav Controversies: A Scholar's Initiative*, edited by Charles Ingrao and Thomas A. Emmert (*AHR*, December 2009, 1569–1570), mistakenly identified Sabrina Ramet as the author of the book's first chapter. The correct authors are Andrew Wachtel and Christopher Bennett. The editors regret the error.

Index to *American Historical Review,* February 2010

The titles of articles in the *AHR* are enclosed in quotation marks, and titles of books reviewed are printed in italics. Books of collected essays are designated by (E). The reviewer of a book or film is designated by (R), the author of a letter for the Communications section by (C).

American Historical Association

Founded in 1884. Chartered by Congress in 1889.
Office: 400 A St. SE, Washington, DC 20003

President: Barbara D. Metcalf, *University of California, Davis emerita*
President-Elect: Anthony T. Grafton, *Princeton University*
Executive Director: Arnita A. Jones
Controller: Randy Norell

MEMBERSHIP: Persons interested in historical studies, whether professionally or otherwise, are invited to membership. The present membership and subscription total is approximately 18,000. Members elect the officers by ballot.

MEETINGS: The Association's next annual meeting will take place January 6 9, 2011, in Boston. Many professional historical groups meet within or jointly with the Association at this time. The Pacific Coast Branch holds separate meetings on the Pacific Coast and publishes the *Pacific Historical Review*.

PUBLICATIONS AND SERVICES: The *American Historical Review* is published five times a year and is sent to all members. It is available by subscription to institutions. The Association also publishes *Perspectives* (a newsmagazine with classified listings) and a variety of pamphlets on historical subjects. To promote history and assist historians, the Association offers other services, including a Department and Organization Services Program. It also maintains close relations with international, specialized, state, and local historical societies through conferences and correspondence.

BOOK PRIZES: The *Herbert Baxter Adams Prize*, awarded annually for a first book in the field of European history. The *George Louis Beer Prize*, awarded annually for a book on any phase of European international history since 1895. The *Albert J. Beveridge Award*, given annually for the best book on the history of the United States, Latin America, or Canada since 1492. The *Paul Birdsall Prize*, awarded biennially for a major work by a U.S. or Canadian historian in European military and strategic history since 1870. The *James Henry Breasted Prize*, awarded annually for the best book in English in any field of history prior to 1000 A.D. The *Albert B. Corey Prize*, awarded biennially for the best book on the history of Canadian-American relations, administered jointly with the Canadian Historical Association. The *John H. Dunning Prize*, awarded biennially for a book on any subject in U.S. history. The *John E. Fagg Prize*, awarded annually for the best publication in the history of Spain, Portugal, or Latin America. The *John K. Fairbank Prize*, awarded annually for East Asian history substantially after the year 1800. The *Morris D. Forkosch Prize*, awarded annually to the best book in British, British imperial, or British Commonwealth history. The *Leo Gershoy Award*, given annually for outstanding work in seventeenth- or eighteenth-century western European history. The *Clarence H. Haring Prize*, awarded every five years for Latin American history by a Latin American. The *J. Franklin Jameson Prize*, awarded every two years for outstanding editorial achievement. The *Joan Kelly Memorial Prize*, awarded annually for the best book in women's history. The *Martin A. Klein Prize in African History*, awarded annually for the most distinguished work of scholarship on continental Africa, including those islands usually treated as countries of Africa. The *Waldo G. Leland Prize*, awarded every five years for the most outstanding reference tool. The *Littleton-Griswold Prize*, awarded annually for the best work on the history of American law and society. The *J. Russell Major Prize*, awarded annually for the best work in English on any aspect of French history. The *Helen and Howard R. Marraro Prize*, awarded annually for Italian or Italian-U.S. history. The *George L. Mosse Prize*, awarded annually for European intellectual and cultural history since the Renaissance. The *Premio del Rey Prize*, awarded biennially for early Spanish history and culture (500–1516 A.D.). The *James A. Rawley Prize in Atlantic History*, awarded annually for an outstanding book in the history of the Atlantic worlds before the twentieth century. The *James Harvey Robinson Prize*, awarded biennially for the teaching aid that has made the most outstanding contribution to the teaching of history. The *Wesley-Logan Prize*, awarded annually in African Diaspora history by the AHA and the Association for the Study of African American Life and History. Book prizes are awarded at each AHA annual meeting.

CORRESPONDENCE: Inquiries for the AHA should be addressed to Executive Director, 400 A St. SE, Washington, DC 20003. Our e-mail address is aha@historians.org. Our web address is http://www.historians.org.

Inquiries for the *AHR* Editorial Office, including correspondence regarding manuscript submissions and books for review, should be addressed to Editor, American Historical Review, 914 E. Atwater Ave., Bloomington, IN 47401. Our e-mail address is ahr@indiana.edu. Please note that no manuscript will be considered for publication if it is concurrently under consideration by another journal or press or if it has been published or is soon to be published elsewhere. Both restrictions apply to the substance as well as to the exact wording of the manuscript. If the manuscript is accepted, the editors expect that its appearance in the *AHR* will precede republication of the essay, or any significant part thereof, in another work. Specific guidelines and policies for the preparation of manuscripts for submission to and publication in the *AHR* can be found at www.americanhistoricalreview.org or will be sent upon request. **Unsolicited book reviews are not accepted.**

Outstanding Scholarship from Cambridge

The Far Enemy
Why Jihad Went Global
2nd Edition
Fawaz A. Gerges
$85.00: Hb: 978-0-521-51935-9: 400 pp.
$24.99: Pb: 978-0-521-73743-2

A History of Islam in America
From the New World to the New World Order
Kambiz GhaneaBassiri
$90.00: Hb: 978-0-521-84964-7: 416 pp.
$27.99: Pb: 978-0-521-61487-0

War Planning 1914
Edited by Richard F. Hamilton and Holger H. Herwig
$85.00: Hb: 978-0-521-11096-9: 280 pp.

Reforming the North
The Kingdoms and Churches of Scandinavia, 1520-1545
James L. Larson
$95.00: Hb: 978-0-521-76514-5: 520 pp.

Strange Parallels
Southeast Asia in Global Context, c. 800-1830
Volume 2: Mainland Mirrors: Europe, Japan, China, South Asia, and the Islands
Victor Lieberman
Studies in Comparative World History
$125.00: Hb: 978-0-521-82352-4: 976 pp.
$39.99: Pb: 978-0-521-53036-1

The Origins of English Financial Markets
Investment and Speculation before the South Sea Bubble
Anne L. Murphy
Cambridge Studies in Economic History - Second Series
$99.00: Hb: 978-0-521-51994-6: 298 pp.

Inventing a Socialist Nation
Heimat and the Politics of Everyday Life in the GDR, 1945-90
Jan Palmowski
New Studies in European History
$99.00: Hb: 978-0-521-11177-5: 360 pp.

The Frankfurt Auschwitz Trial, 1963-1965
Genocide, History and the Limits of the Law
Devin O. Pendas
$29.99: Pb: 978-0-521-12798-1: 360 pp.

Legal Practice and the Written Word in the Early Middle Ages
Frankish Formulae, c. 500-1000
Alice Rio
Cambridge Studies in Medieval Life and Thought: Fourth Series
$99.00: Hb: 978-0-521-51499-6: 312 pp.

Eichmann's Men
Hans Safrian
Translated by Ute Stargardt
$85.00: Hb: 978-0-521-85156-5: 336 pp.
$23.99: Pb: 978-0-521-61726-0

Industrial Violence and the Legal Origins of Child Labor
James D. Schmidt
Cambridge Historical Studies in American Law and Society
$85.00: Hb: 978-0-521-19865-3: 280 pp.
$27.99: Pb: 978-0-521-15505-2

The Strained Alliance
US-European Relations from Nixon to Carter
Edited by Matthias Schulz and Thomas A. Schwartz
Publications of the German Historical Institute
$85.00: Hb: 978-0-521-89999-4: 398 pp.

Post-Zionism, Post-Holocaust
Three Essays on Denial, Forgetting, and the Delegitimation of Israel
Elhanan Yakira
Translated by Michael Swirsky
$85.00: Hb: 978-0-521-11110-2: 356 pp.
$25.99: Pb: 978-0-521-12786-8

Prices subject to change.

 **CAMBRIDGE** UNIVERSITY PRESS

 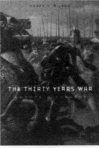   

THE QUOTABLE ABIGAIL ADAMS
ABIGAIL ADAMS
EDITED BY JOHN P. KAMINSKI

The Quotable Abigail Adams invites you to enjoy Abigail Adams's wit and wisdom on a wide range of subjects, drawn from writings throughout her lifetime. Abigail shared her penetrating and often humorous observations with correspondents ranging from friends and neighbors to family members to heads of state, offering lively opinions on human nature, politics, culture, and family life.

Belknap Press / new in cloth / $26.95
Read an excerpt on our web site

THE THIRTY YEARS WAR
Europe's Tragedy
PETER H. WILSON

"Among continental Europeans, the Thirty Years War is etched in memory...A definitive account has been needed, and now Peter Wilson, one of Britain's leading historians of Germany, has provided it. *The Thirty Years War: Europe's Tragedy* is a history of prodigious erudition that manages to corral the byzantine complexity of the Thirty Years War into a coherent narrative."
—Jeffrey Collins, *Wall Street Journal*

Belknap Press / new in cloth / $35.00
Visit the book feature on our web site

AMERICA'S COLD WAR
The Politics of Insecurity
CAMPBELL CRAIG & FREDRIK LOGEVALL

"This is a creative, carefully researched, and incisive analysis of U.S. strategy during the long struggle against the Soviet Union. There are plenty of good books on this topic already, but Craig and Logevall's is one of the best, and their interpretation has important implications for contemporary strategic debates."—Stephen M. Walt, *foreignpolicy.com*

Belknap Press / new in cloth / $26.95
Listen to the authors on our web site

KRISTALLNACHT 1938
ALAN E. STEINWEIS

"Illuminating...To capture the full significance of Kristallnacht, it is necessary to see the pogrom not in hindsight, but through contemporary eyes—and that is the achievement of Steinweis's short but revelatory book. Knowing what came after, we tend to see the pogrom of November 1938 as a prelude to genocide; but to those who lived through it, it was precisely the unprecedented quality of Kristallnacht that made it so momentous."
—Adam Kirsch, *The Tablet*

Belknap Press / new in cloth / $23.95
Read an excerpt on our web site

WE AIN'T WHAT WE OUGHT TO BE
The Black Freedom Struggle from Emancipation to Obama
STEPHEN TUCK

We Ain't What We Ought to Be rejects the traditional narrative that identifies the Southern non-violent civil rights movement as the focal point of the black freedom struggle. Instead, it explores the dynamic relationships between those seeking new freedoms and those looking to preserve racial hierarchies, and between grassroots activists and national leaders. As Stephen Tuck shows, strategies were ultimately contingent on the power of activists to protest amid shifting economic and political circumstances in the U.S. and abroad.

Belknap Press / new in cloth / $29.95

HARVARD UNIVERSITY PRESS
WWW.HUP.HARVARD.EDU
BLOG: HARVARDPRESS.TYPEPAD.COM
TEL: 800.405.1619

   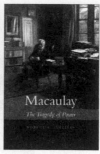 

TROTSKY
A Biography
ROBERT SERVICE

"This is a superb work of scholarship, and above all leaves the reader in no doubt as to the evil of Trotsky, not just in politics but in his personal life... If you seek to know about this crucial figure in the history of Marxism-Leninism, this book will tell you everything."—Simon Heffer, *Daily Telegraph* (UK)

Belknap Press / new in cloth / $35.00

SELECTED WRITINGS
A Tercentenary Celebration
SAMUEL JOHNSON
EDITED BY PETER MARTIN

Writing a century after Johnson, Ruskin wrote of Johnson's essays: He "taught me to measure life, and distrust fortune...he saved me forever from false thoughts and futile speculations." Peter Martin here presents "the heart of Johnson," a selection of some of Johnson's best moral and critical essays. At the center of this collection are the periodical essays from the *Rambler, Adventurer,* and *Idler.*

Belknap Press / new in cloth / $29.95

DOMINION OF GOD
Christendom and Apocalypse in the Middle Ages
BRETT EDWARD WHALEN

Brett Whalen explores the compelling belief that Christendom would spread to every corner of the earth before the end of time. During the High Middle Ages—an era of crusade, mission, and European expansion—the Western followers of Rome imagined the future conversion of Jews, Muslims, pagans, and Eastern Christians into one fold of God's people, assembled under the authority of the Roman Church.

new in cloth / $29.95
Read an excerpt on our web site

MACAULAY
The Tragedy of Power
ROBERT E. SULLIVAN

On the 150th anniversary of the death of the English historian and politician Thomas Babington Macaulay, Robert Sullivan offers a portrait of a Victorian life that probes the cost of power, the practice of empire, and the impact of ideas. Perhaps best known in the West for his classic *History of England,* Macaulay left his most permanent mark on South Asia, where his penal code remains the law.

Belknap Press / new in cloth / $39.95
Read an excerpt on our web site

JEWISH RENAISSANCE IN THE RUSSIAN REVOLUTION
KENNETH B. MOSS

"The brief cultural moment that Kenneth B. Moss resurrects in *Jewish Renaissance in the Russian Revolution* is one of the least known and most fascinating of those aborted futures: a two-year period when writers, artists, and activists in Russia and Ukraine believed they were midwiving the birth of a new Jewish culture...[Moss] is the rare kind of scholar who can both uncover obscure foreign-language sources and also effectively bring ideas to life."—Adam Kirsch, *The Tablet*

new in cloth / $39.95
Read an excerpt on our web site

HARVARD UNIVERSITY PRESS
WWW.HUP.HARVARD.EDU
BLOG: HARVARDPRESS.TYPEPAD.COM
TEL: 800.405.1619

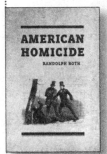

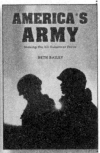

INCEST AND INFLUENCE
The Private Life of Bourgeois England
ADAM KUPER

In a richly detailed narrative, Adam Kuper deploys his expertise as an anthropologist to analyze kin marriages among the Darwins and Wedgwoods, in Quaker and Jewish banking families, and in the Clapham Sect and their descendants over four generations, ending with a revealing account of the Bloomsbury Group, the most eccentric product of English bourgeois endogamy.

New in cloth / $27.95

NATURAL EXPERIMENTS OF HISTORY
EDITED BY JARED DIAMOND AND JAMES A. ROBINSON

Some central questions in the natural and social sciences can't be answered by controlled laboratory experiments, often considered to be the hallmark of the scientific method. This impossibility holds for any science concerned with the past. In the historical disciplines, a fruitful approach has been to use natural experiments or the comparative method.

Belknap Press / New in cloth / $29.95
Read an excerpt on our web site

  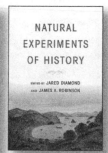  

SETTLER SOVEREIGNTY
Jurisdiction and Indigenous People in America and Australia, 1788–1836
LISA FORD

Lisa Ford argues that modern settler sovereignty emerged not at the moment of settlement or federation, but in the second quarter of the nineteenth century when notions of statehood, sovereignty, empire, and civilization were in rapid, global flux.

New in cloth / $49.95
Read an excerpt on our web site

FREEDOM STRUGGLES
African Americans and World War I
ADRIANE LENTZ-SMITH

For many of the 200,000 black soldiers sent to Europe with the American Expeditionary Forces in World War I, encounters with French civilians and colonial African troops led them to imagine a world beyond Jim Crow. They returned home to join activists working to make that world real.

New in cloth / $35.00
Read an excerpt on our web site

THE TWO HENDRICKS
Unraveling a Mohawk Mystery
ERIC HINDERAKER

"Hinderaker utilizes creative and in-depth research to construct a biography of two Mohawk leaders... Highly recommended as both a historical work and an outstanding example for historiographers in writing ethnohistory."
—John Burch, *Library Journal* (starred review)

New in cloth / $35.00
Read an excerpt on our web site

HARVARD UNIVERSITY PRESS
WWW.HUP.HARVARD.EDU
BLOG: HARVARDPRESS.TYPEPAD.COM
TEL: 800.405.1619

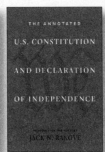
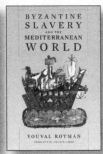

New from Oxford

Japan in World History
JAMES L. HUFFMAN
(New Oxford World History)
2010 Cloth $74.00 Paperback $19.95

Flight from Monticello
Thomas Jefferson at War
MICHAEL KRANISH
2010 Cloth $27.95

After the Fall
German Policy in Occupied France,
1940-1944
THOMAS J. LAUB
2010 Cloth $110.00

Behind the Berlin Wall
East Germany and the Frontiers of Power
PATRICK MAJOR
2010 Cloth $99.00

The Rising
Ireland: Easter 1916
FEARGHAL McGARRY
2010 Cloth $29.95

Freedom Flyers
The Tuskegee Airmen of World War II
J. TODD MOYE
(Oxford Oral History Series)
2010 Cloth $24.95

Defenders of the Motherland
The Tsarist Elite in Revolutionary Russia
MATTHEW RENDLE
2010 Cloth $99.00

Conceiving the Old Regime
Pronatalism and the Politics of
Reproduction in Early Modern France
LESLIE TUTTLE
2010 Cloth $49.95

A New History of Ireland
Volume V: Ireland Under the Union, I:
1801-1870
EDITED BY W. E. VAUGHAN
(New History of Ireland)
2010 Paperback $55.00

Autos and Progress
The Brazilian Search for Modernity
JOEL WOLFE
2010 Cloth $99.00 Paperback $21.95

AFRICA AND THE WEST: A DOCUMENTARY HISTORY

WILLIAM H. WORGER,
NANCY L. CLARK, and
EDWARD A. ALPERS

**Volume 1: From the Slave Trade
to Conquest, 1441-1905**
Second Edition
2010 Paperback $24.95

**Volume 2: From Colonialism to
Independence, 1875 to the Present**
Second Edition
2010 Paperback $24.95

OXFORD
UNIVERSITY PRESS

Visit our website at www.oup.com/us or call 1-800-451-7556
In Canada, call 1-800-387-8020.

Ten Hills Farm

The Forgotten History of Slavery in the North

C. S. Manegold

"C. S. Manegold's admirable clarity, dazzling intelligence, and resourceful reporting well serve the story of the North's participation in U.S. slavery. *Ten Hills Farm* is a feat of historical excavation, and Manegold's contribution to the study of this period of our nation's past is significant."
—Henry Louis Gates, Jr., Harvard University

Cloth $29.95 978-0-691-13152-8

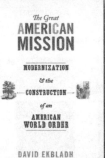

Little Rock

Race and Resistance at Central High School

Karen Anderson

"Telling the fascinating story of the Little Rock crisis in wonderful detail, this book mines newspapers, personal papers, memoirs, interviews, and more, for the background behind the headlines."
—Cheryl Greenberg, Trinity College

Politics and Society in Twentieth-Century America
William Chafe, Gary Gerstle, Linda Gordon, & Julian Zelizer, Series Editors
Cloth $35.00 978-0-691-09293-5

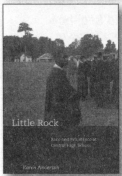

The Great American Mission

Modernization and the Construction of an American World Order

David Ekbladh

"Cogent and compelling. *The Great American Mission* illuminates for the first time how the central characteristics of America's modernization project in the Cold War came together in the prewar period."
—David C. Engerman, Brandeis University

America in the World
Sven Beckert and Jeremi Suri, Series Editors
Cloth $35.00 978-0-691-13330-0

The Last Pharaohs

Egypt Under the Ptolemies, 305–30 BC

J. G. Manning

"This fascinating book has broad views that should appeal to many people who are neither specialists on ancient Egypt nor the ancient Greek world. J. G. Manning has a perfect knowledge of his subject."
—Alain Bresson, University of Chicago

Cloth $39.50 978-0-691-14262-3

PRINCETON UNIVERSITY PRESS

800.777.4726
press.princeton.edu

Trying Leviathan

The Nineteenth-Century New York Court Case That Put the Whale on Trial and Challenged the Order of Nature

D. Graham Burnett

"At once bewitching and bookish, with a Dickensian cast of characters . . . *Trying Leviathan* bristles with insights about the relationships between popular belief, democracy, science and the law that resonate with contemporary controversies over Darwinism and intelligent design."
—Glenn C. Altschuler, *New York Observer*

Paper $21.95 978-0-691-14615-7

The Other Alliance

Student Protest in West Germany and the United States in the Global Sixties

Martin Klimke

"Klimke uncovers all kinds of links between the American and West German student movements; contextualizes these within social movement theory and other models; and teaches readers a great deal about the American and West German New Left and the rebellions of 1968."
—Jeremy Varon, Drew University

America in the World: Sven Beckert & Jeremi Suri, Series Editors
Cloth $39.50 978-0-691-13127-6

Demanding Democracy

American Radicals in Search of a New Politics

Marc Stears

"Writing with a realist's appreciation of the complexities of politics, but with an idealist's care for the lives and fortunes of his subjects, Marc Stears tells the story of those who risked everything to take their place at the democratic table."
—Bonnie Honig, Northwestern University

Cloth $29.95 978-0-691-13340-9

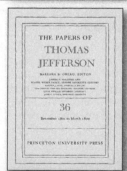

The Papers of Thomas Jefferson

Volume 36: 1 December 1801 to 3 March 1802

Thomas Jefferson

The period covered by this volume brings to a conclusion Thomas Jefferson's first year as president. As he moves into his second year as president, he is optimistic about his legislative program and the Republican majority in Congress.

The Papers of Thomas Jefferson
Barbara B. Oberg, General Editor
Cloth $99.50 978-0-691-13774-2

PRINCETON UNIVERSITY PRESS

800.777.4726
press.princeton.edu

American History
NEW FROM CHICAGO

A Nation of Speechifiers
Making an American Public after the Revolution
Carolyn Eastman

"The peoples of the early American republic were engaged in an epochal struggle over who could claim public citizenship. In a wide-ranging analysis, Carolyn Eastman provides a careful reading of this contest on the boundaries of the public sphere, describing the ways in which traditionally excluded Americans were moving into public space and claiming the title of citizen."—John L. Brooke, the Ohio State University
Cloth $37.50

Schooling Citizens
The Struggle for African American Education in Antebellum America
Hilary J. Moss

"In *Schooling Citizens* Hilary Moss makes a splendid contribution to the history of race relations in the antebellum period. Case studies of episodes in New Haven, Baltimore, and Boston illuminate crucial relationships between schooling, citizenship, and race. The cases require careful analysis because they defy easy generalizations about the legacy of slavery or regional differences. The result is a nuanced view of the attitudes that swirled around white opposition to black education in these years."
—Carl Kaestle, Brown University
Cloth $37.50

New York Undercover
Private Surveillance in the Progressive Era
Jennifer Fronc

"*New York Undercover* is a smart, surprising, and important book. With the keen intelligence and sharp wit of a good investigator, Jennifer Fronc unearths the roots of our culture of surveillance by taking us back to New York at the start of the twentieth century and following the undercover agents who followed gamblers, prostitutes, anarchists, immigrants, children, and men and women just out for a good time."—Ann Fabian, Rutgers, The State University of New Jersey
Cloth $35.00

Whose Fair?
Experience, Memory, and the History of the Great St. Louis Exposition
James Gilbert

"This is an informative, intriguing, wise, and notably well written book by a master historian. *Whose Fair?* is full of important insights and information, lucidly framed and brilliantly analyzed, on what happened at the fair, how it was presented, and how it has been remembered and analyzed."—Carl Smith, Northwestern University
Cloth $35.00

The University of Chicago Press www.press.uchicago.edu

Asian History

From the editor of
The Chicago Manual of Style Q&A

THE SUBVERSIVE COPY EDITOR

Advice from Chicago

(or, How to Negotiate Good Relationships with Your Writers, Your Colleagues, and Yourself)

"Saller's project, in about 100 pages, is to (a) civilize the editing process, and (b) keep copy editors—meticulous and learned and hard-working, but also stubborn and obsessive, sometimes injuriously so—from going insane. . . . There's even a section called 'Dear Writers: A Chapter of Your Own,' which aims to make the editing process—and editors themselves—seem just a tad less exotic."—JENNIFER BALDERAMA, from the *New York Times* Papercuts blog

"If you are a copy editor, an aspirant to copy editing, or a writer dealing with copy editors, a $13 investment will be money well spent on your career." —JOHN E. McINTYRE, *Baltimore Sun*'s You Don't Say blog

"[Saller] wears her experience well, urging flexibility, transparency, and tact—along with, obviously, consistency and reason—in working with authors and their copy." —ALAN MOORES, *Booklist*

Paper $13.00

KANSAS

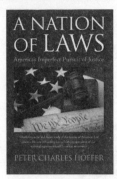   

A Nation of Laws
America's Imperfect Pursuit of Justice
Peter Charles Hoffer

"Hoffer's concise and fluent study of the history of American law packs a lifetime of learning into a fresh and challenging interpretation of the national experience itself."—**Sean Wilentz**, author of *The Rise of American Democracy: Jefferson to Lincoln*

"Beautifully written, this is *the* short book to read on American law—no one else has gotten it so right in so few words. Bravo!"—**Stanley N. Katz**, editor of the *Oxford International Encyclopedia of Legal History*

"Brilliant and eclectic, short and highly readable. . . . A remarkable book."—**Alfred L. Brophy**, author of *Reconstructing the Dreamland: The Tulsa Riot of 1921, Race, Reparations, Reconciliation*

224 pages, Cloth $24.95

The Age of Deficits
Presidents and Unbalanced Budgets from Jimmy Carter to George W. Bush
Iwan Morgan

"In this penetrating study, Morgan reinterprets the nation's post-Watergate political history through the lens of the budgetary process. The result is a strikingly original and illuminating work that should be read by everyone seeking to understand how modern American politics and public policy work. This is history at its most relevant best."
—**Robert M. Collins**, author of *More: The Politics of Economic Growth in Postwar America*

392 pages, Cloth $34.95

Realigning America
McKinley, Bryan, and the Remarkable Election of 1896
R. Hal Williams

"Vintage Williams—an epic story meticulously researched, insightfully argued, and vividly told. This fresh, authoritative account changes our understanding of one of the most momentous elections in the nation's history."—**Michael McGerr**, author of *The Decline of Popular Politics: The American North, 1865–1928*

"Superb, written with his customary grace and skill, well informed about the issues, and balanced in its point of view. In short, a winner."—**Lewis L. Gould**, author of *The Presidency of William McKinley*

American Presidential Elections
272 pages, 20 photographs, Cloth $29.95

Kennedy vs. Carter
The 1980 Battle for the Democratic Party's Soul
Timothy Stanley

"Stanley challenges the conventional wisdom that the 1980 election marked the demise of the New Deal order. By the end of his riveting narrative, readers are likely to conclude that Stanley got it right. More than good history, this book is a serious brief for the enduring relevance of the liberal tradition."—**Allen J. Matusow**, author of *The Unraveling of America: A History of Liberalism in the 1960s*

320 pages, 12 photographs, Cloth $34.95

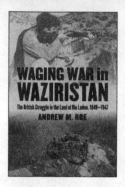

Windows into History

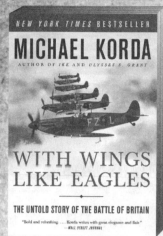

With Wings Like Eagles
The Untold Story of the Battle of Britain
Michael Korda

"Korda's stirring account of the campaign is an absolute masterpiece, written with power, intensity and tremendous fidelity to the historical record." —Donald L. Miller, author of *Masters of the Air*

Harper Perennial: 978-0-06-112536-2 (pb)
$14.99 ($18.99 Can.) • 352 pages

Mrs. Lincoln
A Life
Catherine Clinton

"For a balanced profile of Mary Lincoln one should turn to [*Mrs. Lincoln*].... Clinton provides a fuller, fairer portrait of the Lincolns' marriage than any of the biographies of Abraham." —James M. McPherson, *The New York Review of Books*

Harper Perennial: 978-0-06-076041-0 (pb)
$15.99 ($19.99 Can.) • 432 pages

The Science of Liberty
Democracy, Reason, and the Laws of Nature
Timothy Ferris

Ferris—"the best science writer of his generation" (*The Washington Post*)—makes a passionate case for science as the inspiration behind the rise of liberalism and democracy across the modern world.

Harper: 978-0-06-078150-7 (hc)
$26.99 ($34.99 Can.) • 384 pages

HARPER

HARPER PERENNIAL
Imprints of HarperCollinsPublishers
www.harpercollins.com

Visit www.HarperAcademic.com to sign up for our free e-bulletins.

ISCSC
International Society for the Comparative Study of Civilizations

40th International Conference

International Society for the
Comparative Study of Civilizations

June 15–17, 2010
Brigham Young University, Provo, Utah, USA

Call For Papers

The Future of Civilization

Is a global civilization developing?
Past civilizational crises and the present.
Impact of ecology, culture, economics, politics, religion.
The nature of civilizations.
Civilizations in human history.
Does history repeat itself?
Impact of technology on contemporary civilizations.
The clash of civilizations: necessarily traumatic? Synergistic?
Art, language and culture in past and contemporary civilizations.
War and Peace in the history of civilizations.

Email abstracts/questions to: Michael Andregg at mmandregg@stthomas.edu

Attendees Invited

Last year's meeting had 85 exciting presentations on civilizations. To
attend see the ISCSC website for conference registration information.

www.wmich.edu/iscsc

Encountering Revolution
Haiti and the Making of the
Early Republic
Ashli White

Encountering Revolution looks
afresh at the profound impact of
the Haitian Revolution on the
early United States. It redefines our
understanding of the relationship
between republicanism and slavery
at a foundational moment in
American history.
$55.00 hardcover

Born Southern
Childbirth, Motherhood,
and Social Networks
in the Old South
V. Lynn Kennedy

Kennedy addresses the pivotal roles
of birth and motherhood in slaveholding families and communities
in the Old South.
$65.00 hardcover

New Orleans after
the Civil War
Race, Politics, and a
New Birth of Freedom
Justin A. Nystrom

"Nystrom does an excellent job of
showing Reconstruction, at least in
New Orleans, in a new light."
—Gaines M. Foster, Louisiana
State University
$60.00 hardcover

In the Wake of
Hurricane Katrina
New Paradigms and
Social Visions
edited by Clyde Woods

These essays assess the damage left
by Hurricane Katrina in social,
cultural, and physical terms.
A Special Issue of American Quarterly
$30.00 paperback

Rebellion, reconstruction, revision

For Business and Pleasure
Red-Light Districts and the
Regulation of Vice in the
United States, 1890–1933
Mara L. Keire

A fascinating survey of the business
of pleasure from the 1890s through
the repeal of Prohibition in 1933.
$60.00 hardcover

Washington at Home
An Illustrated History of
Neighborhoods in the Nation's
Capital, *second edition*
edited by
Kathryn Schneider Smith

A fresh look at the social history
of this intriguing city through the
prism of 26 diverse neighborhoods.
$45.00 hardcover

The Estrogen Elixir
A History of Hormone
Replacement Therapy
in America
Elizabeth Siegel Watkins

"A major contribution to the
growing literature on hormonal
therapeutics and research."—*Isis*
$25.00 paperback

Moses of South Carolina
A Jewish Scalawag during
Radical Reconstruction
Benjamin Ginsberg

Revisiting the story of Franklin
Moses Jr., Ginsberg contributes
to a broader understanding of
the essential role southern Jews
played during the Civil War and
Reconstruction.
$50.00 hardcover

Would Trotsky Wear
a Bluetooth?
Technological Utopianism
under Socialism, 1917–1989
Paul R. Josephson

"Josephson has become the fore-
most historian of his generation of
Soviet science and technology."
—Howard Segal, University of
Maine
$65.00 hardcover

Early FM Radio
Incremental Technology in
Twentieth-Century America
Gary L. Frost

A reexamination of one of the
twentieth century's iconic sagas of
invention, heroism, and tragedy.
$60.00 hardcover

Looking for a
Few Good Males
Female Choice in
Evolutionary Biology
Erika Lorraine Milam

Milam presents a broad history of
sexual selection from Darwin to
sociobiology.
$60.00 hardcover

THE JOHNS HOPKINS UNIVERSITY PRESS
1-800-537-5487 • press.jhu.edu

 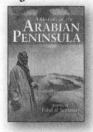   

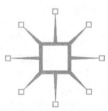

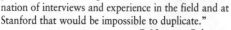

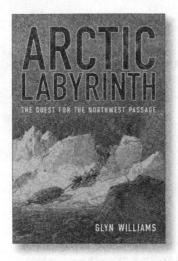
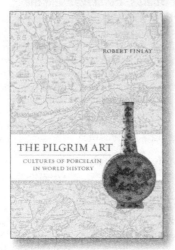

Echoes of Chongqing
Women in Wartime China
DANKE LI

"This insightful study reveals the complex nature of the changes brought by war not only on gender relations, but also on Chinese society, culture, politics, and economics. A major contribution to the study of Chinese history."—Christina Kelley Gilmartin, author of *Engendering the Chinese Revolution: Radical Women, Communist Politics, and Mass Movements in the 1920s*

232 pp. 19 B & W photos, 1 map, 1 table.
*Cloth 978-0-252-03489-3 $70.00;
Paper 978-0-252-07674-9 $25.00

The Selected Papers of Jane Addams
Vol. 2: Venturing into Usefulness, 1881-88
Edited by MARY LYNN MCCREE BRYAN, BARBARA BAIR, and MAREE de ANGURY
with the assistance of Elizabeth Stevens, Stewart Burns, and Ellen Skerrett

"A fascinating collection, illuminating Jane Addams's transition to an independent adult life dedicated to social reform. The book will be indispensable not only for scholars, but also for teachers and students interested in women's education and for young women on the brink of deciding their own futures." —Gwendolyn Mink, author of *Welfare's End*

808 pp. 60 B & W photos, 5 line drawings.
Cloth 978-0-252-03349-0. $75.00

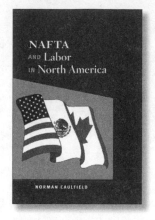

NAFTA and Labor in North America
NORMAN CAULFIELD

"A very important, timely book. This study has monumental and provocative implications that are sure to stir debate among scholars in labor history, industrial relations, and public policy."—Gregg Andrews, author of *Shoulder to Shoulder? The American Federation of Labor, the United States, and the Mexican Revolution, 1910-1924*

264 pp. *Cloth 978-0-252-03492-3 $70.00;
Paper 978-0-252-07670-1 $25.00
The Working Class in American History

Stealing Indian Women
Native Slavery in the Illinois Country
CARL J. EKBERG

256 pp. 6 B & W photos, 8 line drawings, 2 maps, 9 tables. New in Paper 978-0-252-07723-4. $25.00

The Black Hand
Terror by Letter in Chicago
ROBERT M. LOMBARDO

"Stimulating and informative. This book corrects the record of the criminological phenomenon of the Black Hand for the first time, and it presents the truth of its role in the immigrant Italian community in America."—Arthur J. Bilek, author of *The First Vice Lord: Big Jim Colosimo and the Ladies of the Levee*

264 pp. 6 x 9. 16 B & W photos.
*Cloth 978-0-252-03488-6. $65.00.
Paper 978-0-252-07675-6. $25.00

Race and Radicalism in the Union Army
MARK A. LAUSE

"In this study of an obscure but important group of radicals, Lause includes cameos of fascinating figures largely ignored in standard accounts as well as coverage of battles beyond the frame of nearly all Civil War texts. Future work will have to reckon with this marvelous study."—Bruce Laurie, author of *Beyond Garrison: Antislavery and Social Reform*

208 pp. 14 B & W photos, 4 line drawings, 4 maps. Cloth 978-0-252-03446-6 $45.00

The Baltimore Bank Riot
Political Upheaval in Antebellum Maryland
ROBERT E. SHALHOPE

"An exhaustively researched, richly textured account of an important and understudied event of the Jacksonian period. This is a book that all scholars of the period will consult to understand the origins, events, and resolution of that deadly, destructive event."—Thomas Summerhill, author of *Harvest of Dissent: Agrarianism in Nineteenth-Century New York*

208 pp. Cloth 978-0-252-03480-0 $50.00

Remembering *Brown* at Fifty
The University of Illinois Commemorates *Brown v. Board of Education*
Edited by ORVILLE VERNON BURTON and DAVID O'BRIEN

"A valuable book that serves as both a fitting tribute and a careful examination of the *Brown v. Board of Education* decision after a half century. The touching and moving recollections help us understand the human impact the *Brown* case had on the 'ordinary' folks."—William C. Hine, coauthor of *The African-American Odyssey*

456 pp. 6.125 x 9.25. 9 color photos, 21 B & W photos, 9 charts, 1 table. Cloth 978-0-252-03477-0. $75.00. Paper 978-0-252-07665-7. $35.00

*Unjacketed

[[]] **UNIVERSITY OF ILLINOIS PRESS**
Publishing Excellence since 1918   www.press.uillinois.edu

Commemorating

Two
AHA Presidents

&

Two
Public Servants

The *American Historical Association* offers

The Theodore Roosevelt-Woodrow Wilson Public Service Award

Suggestions for nominations are invited

AHA members are invited to suggest names of individuals who can be nominated for the Theodore Roosevelt-Woodrow Wilson Public Service Award. Named for the two former AHA presidents who were also presidents of the United States—Theodore Roosevelt (AHA president in 1912) and Woodrow Wilson (AHA president in 1924)—this honorific award recognizes individuals outside the historical profession who have made a significant contribution to the study, teaching, and public understanding of history.

The suggestions for possible nominees can include (but need not be restricted to), for example, persons who may have made a significant contribution to the support and encouragement of history through their actions. Such noteworthy actions may include philanthropy, supporting or working for the National History Day, helping to protect and preserve a national historical monument or park, or working in the community to develop a regard for history. First presented in 2004, the previous honorees have been Senator Robert C. Byrd (D-W.Va.), Brian Lamb (C-SPAN President and C.E.O.), Steven Spielberg (Founding Chairman, Shoah Visual History Foundation), Representative John Lewis (D-Ga.), Richard Moe (president, National Trust for Historic Preservation), and Adam Hochschild (journalist and author).

The executive director and the AHA president will consider members' suggestions and other names to choose the nominees. The AHA Council will thereupon make the final selection, and the award will be presented at the AHA's Annual Meeting.

Mail your suggestion (along with a one-page note justifying the suggestion) to:
Executive Director, AHA, Attention: The Roosevelt-Wilson Award,
400 A Street, SE, Washington, DC 20003-3889.

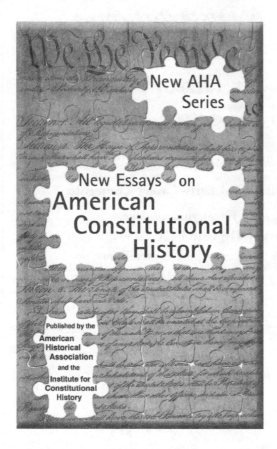

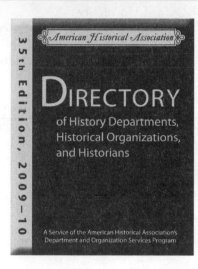

Index of Advertisers